AQA Sociology

Exclusively endorsed by AQA

A2

Julie Cameron
Mark Peace
Tony Flowers
Duncan Watts
Michael Wright
Margaret Hart
Neil Renton

Consultant
Patrick McNeill

Published in 2008 by:
Nelson Thornes Ltd
Delta Place
27 Bath Road
CHELTENHAM
GL53 7TH
United Kingdom

11 12 / 10 9 8 7 6 5 4 3

A catalogue record for this book is available from the British Library

ISBN 978 0 7487 9832 2

Map and illustrations supplied by Redmoor Design

Page make-up by Wearset Ltd, Tyne & Wear

Printed and bound in Egypt by Sahara Printing Company

Contents

Contents

AQA introduction

Nelson Thornes and AQA

Nelson Thornes has worked in partnership with AQA to ensure this book and the accompanying online resources offer you the best support for your A level course.

All resources have been approved by senior AQA examiners so you can feel assured that they closely match the specification for this subject and provide you with everything you need to prepare successfully for your exams.

These print and online resources together **unlock blended learning**; this means that the links between the activities in the book and the activities online blend together to maximise your understanding of a topic and help you achieve your potential.

These online resources are available on **kerboodle!** which can be accessed via the internet at **http://www.kerboodle.com/live**, anytime, anywhere. If your school or college subscribes to this service you will be provided with your own personal login details. Once logged in, access your course and locate the required activity.

For more information and help visit **http://www.kerboodle.com**

Icons in this book indicate where there is material online related to that topic. The following icons are used:

Learning activity

These resources include a variety of interactive and non-interactive activities to support your learning.

Research support

These resources include WebQuests, in which you are assigned a task and provided with a range of weblinks to use as source material for research.

When you see an icon, go to Nelson Thornes learning space at www.nelsonthornes.com/aqagce, enter your access details and select your course. The materials are arranged in the same order as the topics in the book, so you can easily find the resources you need.

Audio stimulus

Each topic has a podcast summarising the important points.

Progress tracking

These resources include a variety of tests that you can use to check your knowledge on particular topics (Test yourself) and a range of resources that enable you to analyse and understand examination questions (On your marks …).

How to use this book

This book covers the specification for your course and is arranged in a sequence approved by AQA.

The book content is divided into seven topics matched to the seven topics of the AQA Sociology A2 specification: Beliefs in society; Global development; Mass media; Power and politics; Crime and deviance; Stratification and differentiation and Theory and methods. Each topic introduction contains a table mapping the topic content to the specification so you can see at a glance where to find the information you need. Topics are then further divided into chapters and sections which are clear and easy to use. Each topic concludes with a summary of the key points that have been covered and examination-style questions.

The features in this book include:

Learning objectives

At the beginning of each section you will find a list of learning objectives that contain targets linked to the requirements of the specification.

Key terms

Terms that you will need to be able to define and understand.

Hint

Hints to aid your understanding of the topics.

Links

This highlights any key areas where topics relate to one another.

Research study

Summaries of important sociological research studies to enhance your knowledge and understanding of a topic.

Take it further

This extends the subject matter further by pointing to an internet resource/further reading or looking at the subject from a different angle, which will stretch and challenge your understanding of the topic.

Summary questions

Short questions that test your understanding of the subject and allow you to apply the skills you develop to different scenarios. Nelson Thornes is responsible for the answers given and they may not constitute the only possible solutions. Answers are supplied free at www.nelsonthornes.com/sociology_answers.

AQA Examiner's tip

Hints from AQA examiners to help you with your study and to prepare for your exam.

Further resources

Suggested reading, films, TV and websites that will add to your understanding of a topic.

AQA Examination-style questions

Questions in the style that you can expect in your exam. Questions are found at the end of each topic.

Example theory and methods questions for the third question of the A2 Unit 4 examination are provided at the end of the Theory and methods topic. However, the main sociological methods questions are tested in the examination-style questions listed at the end of Crime and deviance and Stratification and differentiation.

Topic summary

A bulleted list at the end of each topic summarising the content in an easy-to-follow way.

■ Weblinks in the book

As Nelson Thornes is not responsible for third party content online, there may be some changes to this material that are beyond our control. In order for us to ensure that the links referred to in the book are as up-to-date and stable as possible, the websites are usually homepages with supporting instructions on how to reach the relevant pages if necessary.

Please let us know at **kerboodle@nelsonthornes.com** if you find a link that doesn't work and we will do our best to redirect the link, or to find an alternative site.

AQA examination questions are reproduced by permission of the Assessment and Qualifications Alliance.

Sociology A2 introduction

Introduction for students

Thanks and congratulations for carrying on with your study of sociology to A2 Level. In the introduction to the Nelson Thornes AQA *AS Sociology* textbook, I wrote 'Studying sociology will not change your life but it should change the way you look at life, at people and at society, both in this country and worldwide'. I hope that by now you will have an idea of what I meant. It would be worth spending a few minutes at the beginning of your A2 year thinking about what you have learned in sociology so far and, in particular, about anything you have learned that surprised you or changed how you look at life, people and society.

I also drew your attention to two books, one by Peter Berger, the other by Nick Abercrombie. If you haven't had time to look at them yet, try to do it now. Abercrombie's book should ring more bells for you now than perhaps it did 12 months ago. It is particularly important at A2 because of the way it draws together the different strands of sociology, rather than treating each as a separate area of study. It doesn't have chapters called 'The Family' or 'Research Methods', as a textbook must have. Instead, Abercrombie's chapters have titles such as 'Why don't things fall apart?' and draw on any aspect of sociology that he thinks may help to answer the question. This synoptic approach is the key to getting top marks in the A2 exam and a high grade in your A level.

The book that really began my lifetime fascination with sociology was *The Sociological Imagination* by C. Wright Mills, first published in 1959. I didn't recommend this to you at the start of your AS year because I thought it was possibly too demanding then, but I'm sure you could get a great deal from it now. If any single book can claim credit for the boom in sociology during the 1960s, this is it. But the important point is that almost everything inside is still true today. Its theme is the relationship between history, social structures and the lived experience of individuals. Mills wants to understand 'the larger historical scene in terms of its meanings for the inner life and the external career of a variety of individuals'.

He wants to understand people's everyday feeling that their private lives are a series of traps, that things just seem to happen to them and that, however much they want to break out and do something different, they are prevented by circumstances beyond their control. He emphasises how personal experiences and personal troubles are shaped by public issues, social structures and historical events. Here is an example:

When in a city of 100,000, only one man is unemployed, that is his personal trouble, and for its relief we properly look to the character of the man, his skills, and his immediate opportunities. But when, in a nation of 50 million employees, 15 million men are unemployed, that is an issue, and we may not hope to find its solution within the range of opportunities open to any one individual. The very structure of opportunities has collapsed.

Mills starts from what you may have learned to call a macro perspective – looking at society as a whole – but he links it to individual experience, a micro perspective. Like all the best sociologists, he cannot be slotted into a category such as macro, micro, positivist, interpretivist, Marxist or functionalist, but his writing is inspirational. What does all this have to do with A2 Sociology? The answer is that all the topics at A2 relate to this central question: What is the relationship between the individual and society? Whichever option you take – beliefs in society, global development, mass media, or power and politics in Unit 3, crime and deviance or stratification and differentiation together with theory and methods in Unit 4 – here are three ideas to remember:

- Mills: 'The sociological imagination enables us to grasp history and biography and the relations between the two within society.'
- Berger: 'The sociologist … is a person intensively, endlessly, shamelessly interested in the doings of men.'
- Abercrombie: '[Sociology] tries to identify and solve the puzzles that the everyday world throws up and, in doing so, provides the way of giving a different meaning to the cosy, everyday world around us.'

Sociology at A2

There is a real step up in demand from AS to A2. In the AQA specification, students working towards their A2 exams are required to demonstrate a wider range and greater depth of knowledge and understanding than at AS, and more highly developed skills of application, analysis, interpretation and evaluation than at AS. So, it's about wider range, greater depth and more highly developed skills, as well as some new topics.

There's plenty of work to do this year, and you need to be synoptic. Being synoptic means that in the exams, you should show your overall understanding of sociology and of the connections between its elements – theory, research and evidence. For example, when you are learning about the mass media, try to think about how it links to the topics you've already studied at AS, those you study at A2, and the two core themes: socialisation, culture and identity, and social differentiation, power and stratification.

I hope you enjoy the year and, even if this is your first and last contact with sociology, that you take from it a way of looking at life, at people and society that gives you greater understanding and more control over your lived experience.

■ Introduction for teachers

Having taught the new AQA specification and seen a number of past papers, specimen papers and particularly mark schemes, you should have a fair understanding of how the revised specification and the new examinations aim to emphasise contemporary society, critical and reflective thinking, and the importance of research methods.

These themes were introduced at AS, but they are even more important at A2, together with synopticity, which is briefly explained in the introduction for students. In the past, the requirement for synopticity was effectively confined to just one exam paper, where it was met in a somewhat mechanistic way. In the revised specification, it is more straightforward and is present in both A2 exam papers. At its simplest, being synoptic means 'thinking like a sociologist', which is why the student introduction is all about the sociological perspective and the sociological imagination, not the content of the specification.

The four options in Paper 3 all aim to take account of the specification's emphasis on contemporary society, recent developments in sociology, and a global perspective. Beliefs in society requires the study of non-Christian religions, and secularisation is considered in a global context. In the past, good candidates have put these aspects in exam answers, now all candidates are expected to cover them. The familiar subject of ownership and control of the mass media now needs to consider the shift in control following the growth of digital media and the internet. The theme of globalisation turns up in all the Paper 3 topics, and in crime and deviance on Paper 4, not just in global development.

A2 candidates need a deeper and more sophisticated understanding of sociological methods than at AS and need to consider a range of theoretical issues that are present in many AS topics but are not explicitly examined. Preparing candidates for the 'methods in context' question in Paper 4 cannot ever be a matter of question spotting. The examiner will use the item to introduce an issue from the relevant option and will then ask questions about how various research methods relate to this issue. There are many possible combinations of issues and methods, so a candidate needs a good knowledge and understanding of methods and must be able to apply their knowledge under examination conditions. They will have to think in the exam room, not regurgitate prepared material. That's crucial throughout A2.

Patrick McNeill

We have attempted to contact all copyright holders/controllers. If any items are not credited correctly this will be corrected in future editions.

The authors and publishers wish to thank the following for permission to use copyright material:

Text acknowledgements

Song lyrics by Dire Straits (1982), Industrial Disease;

www.equalities.gov.uk/public_life/parliament.htm extract reprinted under Crown Copyright PSI Licence C2008000256;

The State works. Have faith article by Matthew Paris, www.timesonline.co.uk/tol/comment/columnists/matthew_parris/article3642596. ece reprinted with permission ©NI Syndication, 29 March 2008;

The Sun newspaper p116 and 136, The Daily Star p136, The Daily Express p139

Graphic acknowledgements

p323 Average income per household, 2005/06, United Kingdom graph – information from http://www.statistics.gov.uk/cci/nugget. asp?id=334 reprinted under Crown Copyright PSI Licence C2008000256; Impact of social class on a child's chances of survival beyond the first year of life – original source Childhood, infant and perinatal mortality statistics DH3, Office of National Statistics. http://www.poverty.org.uk/12/index.shtml, reprinted under Crown Copyright PSI Licence C2008000256; Attainment of five or more GCSE grades A* to C 2002 graph –information from http://www.statistics.gov.uk/cci/nugget.asp?id=1003 Office of National Statistics (ONS);

p326 Age-standardised mortality rate by NS-SEC: men aged 25–64, England and Wales 2001-03 graph – information from http://www.statistics.gov.uk/cci/nugget.asp?id=1899 Office of National Statistics (ONS), reprinted under Crown Copyright PSI Licence C2008000256;

p329 Proportion of children living in households below 60 per cent of median income graph – information from http://www.statistics.gov.uk/CCI/nugget.asp?ID=333&Pos=6&ColRank=2&Rank=208, Office of National Statistics (ONS), reprinted under Crown Copyright PSI Licence C2008000256;

p331 Socio-economic classification: by sex, 2005 graph – http://www.esrc.ac.uk/ESRCInfoCentre/facts/UK/index24.aspx?ComponentId=7095&SourcePageId=18130 – information from Social trends 36 (2006) Office of National Statistics (ONS), reprinted under Crown Copyright PSI Licence C2008000256;

p332 Percentage difference in pay between men and women between 1997 – 2006 graph – information from http://www.statistics.gov.uk/CCI/nugget.asp?ID=167&Pos=1&ColRank=1&Rank=208 reprinted under Crown Copyright PSI Licence C2008000256

p332 Division of household chores graph – information from http://www.statistics.gov.uk/cci/nugget.asp?id=440 reprinted under Crown Copyright PSI Licence C2008000256;

p338 Unemployment: by ethnic group and sex, 2004 graph – information from http://www.statistics.gov.uk/cci/nugget.asp?id=462 reprinted under Crown Copyright PSI Licence C2008000256;

p345 Monitoring poverty and social exclusion in the UK 2005 graph – information from http://www.jrf.org.uk/knowledge/findings/socialpolicy/0665.asp. ©New Policy Institute 2005. First published 2005 by the Joseph Rowntree Foundation, reprinted under Crown Copyright PSI Licence C2008000256;

p345 Social exclusion and the onset of disability November 2003 graph – information from http://www.jrf.org.uk/knowledge/findings/socialpolicy/n23.asp. (c) Tania Burchardt, reprinted under Crown Copyright PSI Licence C2008000256

Photo acknowledgements

pvi Getty Images; p6 Corbis/Charles & Josette Lenars; p7 Fotolia; p9 Alamy/David Jones; p11 Flickr/Mamamusings; p13 Alamy/Jake Norton; p16 Getty Images; p17 Corbis/Bettmann; p19 Marie Butler; p20 Getty Images; p21 Corbis/Fabian Cevallos/Sygma; p23 All rights reserved by the Estate of Nan Wood Graham/Licenced by VAGA, New York, NY; p26 Alamy/Israel Images; p29 Corbis/Arvind Garq; p31 Alamy/Country Collection – Homer Sykes; p32 Corbis/Sygma; p35 (top) Alamy/LondonPhotos – Homer Sykes; p35 iStockphotos; p40 Getty Images; p43 Corbis/Warwick Page;

p51 Science Photo Library/W.T. Sullivan III; p56 Hapag Lloyd; p61 iStockphoto; p63 Wikipedia/Taneli Rajala; p75 Fotolia; p81 Corbis/Matthew Cavanaugh/Epa;

p101 (all) Fotolia; p103 John Ditchburn; p109 Corbis/Boris Roessler/epa; p115 (both) John Frost Newspapers; p125 Alamy/Martin Geene/Vario Images; p130 Benetton; p135a Rex Features, b Getty Images, c www.CartoonStock.com;

p 151 Corbis/Karim Chergui/epa; p153 Getty Images; p155 iStockphoto; p163 Getty Images; p172 Corbis/Peter Macdiarmid/epa; p178 Corbis/Richard Olivier; p192 Alamy/Jim West; p199 Getty Images; p203 PA Photos; p214 RSBP Images; p215 Rex Features/Steve Bell; p232 Getty Images;

p243 Rex Features/Roy Rainford/Rohert Harding; p245 PA Photos; p248 Corbis/Steve Starr; p252 Flickr/Mark Hilary; p256 Corbis/Kim Kullish; p258 Getty Images; p270 Rex Features; p274 Alamy/ David R Frazier Photolibrary, Inc; p275 iStockphoto; p280 Corbis/epa; p281 iStockphoto; p286 Alamy/Ace Stock Limited; p289 Topfoto; p293 Corbis/Reuters; p299 Fotolia;

p309 Alamy/David J. Green, David Croucher;

p363 Getty Images; p381 Fotolia; p384 Corbis/Bettmann; p387 iStockphoto; p412 iStockphoto.

TOPIC 1 Beliefs in society

Introduction

The sociological imagination

Many people reading this book will have beliefs. For some, their religious faiths may play a very important part in their daily lives. Religion can influence our behaviour in many ways, such as the type of food we eat or the way we dress. Our attitudes and opinions may also be based on the principles of the religious creed we follow. Our beliefs, therefore, can be an important foundation on which our individual and cultural identities are built.

Some readers will identify themselves as atheists. Their viewpoints cannot, however, be dismissed as an absence of belief and therefore irrelevant to our topic. Although atheism literally means the absence of belief in God, it does not follow that atheists have no beliefs at all. The various forms of atheism are themselves types of belief, and so will be discussed in this section.

When investigating a topic that is important, we must try to exercise our 'sociological imagination'. This is the phrase used by the American sociologist C. Wright Mills to describe our need to stand back from social issues in which we are, as social beings, immersed. In order to examine these issues as objectively as possible, we must put aside our own feelings and views. It is only when we step out of the *personal* that we are able to see the bigger picture, the *social*.

The concerns of the sociologist

When sociologists study beliefs in society, they are not actually concerned with whether they are true or false. What is most interesting for the sociologist is what people believe, why they believe it, and what roles these beliefs play in society. We also look at the various groups that form in which people can practise their beliefs, e.g. churches, sects and new religious movements.

We will explore some topics that are hotly debated:

- The extent to which religion slows down, or indeed stops, social change. The views sociologists take on this topic depends on their attitude to social change. For example, functionalists feel that if social change is too rapid and drastic, then it could lead to a breakdown in social order. Marxists, on the other hand, actually embrace the idea of radical social change to improve the situation of less privileged groups.
- Whether religious beliefs are becoming less important and influential in society. Sociologists who see this taking place are concerned about the effect it is having on the social system. Others argue that people are no less religious than they were in the past. They simply have more freedom of choice. There is a wider range of belief systems available to us nowadays. This means traditional churches today have more competition and consequently smaller congregations.

To begin, it is essential to define the main concepts we are concerned with in this topic, as there is a great deal of ambiguity surrounding them.

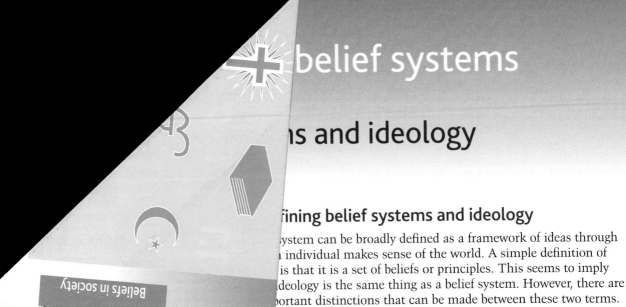

belief systems

...s and ideology

...fining belief systems and ideology

...ystem can be broadly defined as a framework of ideas through
...individual makes sense of the world. A simple definition of
...is that it is a set of beliefs or principles. This seems to imply
...ideology is the same thing as a belief system. However, there are
...portant distinctions that can be made between these two terms.

Firstly, belief systems extend beyond ideologies, to include philosophies
such as phenomenology and existentialism, and religions such as Islam
and Judaism. The phrase 'belief system' can therefore generally be seen as
an umbrella term for any organised set of ideas and principles. Ideologies,
then, are just one type of belief system.

Having said this, belief systems are popularly associated with collections
of ideas that have a **religious** basis, whereas ideology is regarded as a
secular term. So, a more popular definition of belief systems is a set of
principles that underpins a religious conviction.

Religions do not simply claim to explain the world around us, they also
seek to provide us with norms, moral guidelines. This led the philosopher
of science Karl Popper (1945) to describe ideologies as 'secular religions',
for they too contain both descriptive and normative elements. For
example, Marxism is an ideology that sees capitalist society as
characterised by conflict and inequalities. Marxists believe that this is
morally wrong, and that resources should be shared out equally.

However, just as belief systems are commonly associated with religions,
an ideology is usually taken to mean a particular set of political and
economic beliefs. Marx would certainly not have agreed with Popper that
his views were in any way religious. He believed that the 'sacred' is a
social construct, and the only way people can be truly free is to realise
this and so regain power over their own destinies.

Another difference between belief systems and ideologies is to do with
values. The term 'belief system' does not tend to carry any judgements
about the value of the ideas in question, whereas ideology is rarely used
in a neutral way. For example, Popper (1945) thought of ideology as rigid
and inflexible, used to oppress people. This is to do with the way that
ideologies claim a monopoly on truth. Each one proposes a true
explanation of the world and is intolerant of any other view. However,
Popper was a liberal theorist, and liberalism is also an ideology.

Ideology is often used as a negative description of someone else's world
view. For example, feminists would not use the term 'ideology' to describe
their own ideas. Similarly, Marx saw his explanation of society as
scientific fact. He reserved the term 'ideology' for what he saw as the
false, distorted views that were used by the ruling class to mystify the
masses. The elite maintain their powerful position in society by keeping
the working class blind to the reality of their situation. Ideology, in this
sense, involves one social group dominating another.

knowledge.

Key terms

Religious: spiritual, sacred.

Secular: worldly, not sacred.

Social construct: something that
is defined by society and that
changes according to time and
place.

Link

See pages 10–14 for more about
Marx's ideas and sociological
perspectives on religion.

Belief and knowledge

A belief is something we may think is true but that we do not know for certain. Knowledge, on the other hand, is something about which there is no doubt. For example, consider a freshly baked apple pie. We may think it will be delicious. We take a forkful and discover that the cook added salt instead of sugar. We *believed* the pie would be delicious, but were unfortunately wrong. We could not *know* what it would taste like until we tested it, until we had evidence.

Belief therefore involves doubt, whereas knowledge must be true, factual. This means that belief relies upon faith rather than truth. Until evidence is provided to support any theory, we cannot say it is true and claim it as knowledge.

Belief systems, then, are based on what we think but do not actually know. This in turn suggests that philosophies, religions and ideologies have no firm factual basis. They are all attempts to explain the world in the absence of knowledge.

Summary questions

1 Explain the difference between the terms 'ideology' and 'belief systems'.
2 Outline the distinction between belief and knowledge.

Science, religion and spirituality

- Understand the link between religion and belief.

- Understand the link between science and knowledge.

- Examine the characteristics of spirituality.

Fig. 1.1.1 *Trobriand Islanders performing a religious ritual*

Key terms

Animism: an early form of religion that sees humans, animals and plants as all having spirits or souls.

Religion and belief

Religion is a form of belief system. It seeks to explain the origins of the natural world and of human beings. Sociologists and anthropologists have attempted to explain the origins of religion. The chief method is to examine religious beliefs and practices in primitive cultures. According to Weber (1922), every society throughout history has had some form of religious belief. Therefore, by observing primitive cultures today, we may be able to look through a window to our own past.

Research study

In the early 20th century, the functionalist Malinowski (1915) examined the religious beliefs of the Trobriand Islanders in the South Pacific (Figure 1.1.1). He lived with them to observe their culture, an approach which became known as participant observation. This was one of the first ethnographic field studies. Malinowski found that the islanders' religion is based on **animism**. They use magic to try to influence the spirits. For example, the island fishermen undertake rituals and cast spells before going to sea in dangerous waters. This gives them a sense of control over the weather and sea spirits, and reassures them of safety.

According to Tylor (1871), animism is the earliest and most basic type of religion. It still exists today, not only in primitive cultures, but also in the cultic milieu which is examined later.

Early anthropological studies by researchers such as Malinowski suggest that people use religion to plug the gaps in their empirical knowledge of the world. For example, the Trobriand Islanders were highly skilled gardeners who turned to magic when they reached the limits of their practical knowledge. This suggests that we only resort to religious beliefs when we encounter something we cannot factually explain.

If the social origins of religion do stem from the desire to explain the inexplicable, this implies that as we discover more facts about the world through science, the role of religion in society should diminish, as it is not needed. However, religious beliefs have another characteristic, which science does not. Religions have a normative dimension. They provide us with moral guidelines, telling us how God wants us to live. They promise that in return for living moral lives, God will reward us when we die and enter the afterlife.

Is religion an ideology?

Marx (1844) described religion as ideological. He claimed that religion is used by the ruling class to fool the masses into accepting social inequalities. For Marx, ideology is a negative term, describing the means by which one social group subtly imposes its will on another. Religion, he asserted, is the principal mechanism for doing this.

There is one clear similarity between ideologies and religions in that they both claim to have a monopoly on truth. For example, Marxists always start from the assumption that capitalism is an unjust economic system and do not accept any opposing ideology, such as liberalism. Similarly, Christianity asserts that Jesus was the son of God; this is a 'truth' that is not recognised by any other world faith.

Science and knowledge

Before the development of science, people used different ways of gaining knowledge of the world. Every culture throughout history has had its own knowledge system, usually taking the form of a religious belief system. The result was that the knowledge possessed by each society was accepted only within those cultural boundaries. Postmodernists call these bodies of knowledge narratives; there are many narratives in the world, but, in the past, one narrative traditionally dominated each culture. Postmodernists call this a metanarrative, a single comprehensive explanation of the world. Each culture was sure that their knowledge was the truth, founded on tradition and faith.

Since the Enlightenment and the development of scientific rationalism, it has been argued that there is an objective truth that transcends all culture-specific knowledge. It is claimed that the scientific method can provide factual evidence of reality, which religion cannot. What makes the scientific method of gaining knowledge superior is that it is **objective**, whereas all culture-specific methods, meaning religions and traditional wisdom, are **subjective**.

The scientific method involves observation of the natural world, the formulation of a hypothesis based on this observation, and the systematic testing of this hypothesis to try to gain evidence to support it (Figure 1.1.2).

If evidence is gained to support the hypothesis, it may consequently be viewed as a fact. Science is a superior metanarrative that shows all other explanations to be false. **Rationalists** argue that before science there were too many conflicting beliefs for them all to be true. Now, however, we have science to allow us to discover real knowledge about the world. This view asserts that religion has no claim on truth at all. Rationalism puts science and religion in conflict.

Some scientists disagree that science should be given a special status and all other forms of knowledge disregarded. The biologist Gould (1999) proposes that science and religion are two separate realms, or non-overlapping magisteria (NOMA). Science provides certain knowledge about the world, whereas moral guidance is the responsibility of religion. This is the **relativist** view, which sees science as just one of many beliefs, all of which are equally valid. Gellner (1974) disagrees, insisting that the objective nature of science sets it above all other forms of knowledge.

Atheist scientists such as Dawkins (2006) think that relativists such as Gould are only trying to appease powerful religious groups. In American society, atheism is very much frowned upon and atheists can find themselves marginalised and often vilified.

Is science a belief system?

There is a strong debate on whether science is a belief system. Rationalists point out that science is based on fact, whereas beliefs are not: they rely on faith. They claim that arguments for the existence of God are illogical. For example, one explanation proposes that as living things appear to be designed, there must have been a designer, God. But who designed God?

Link

There is more on postmodernism in the section about sociological perspectives on religion. It is covered thoroughly in Topic 7 on theory and methods.

Key terms

Objective: free from bias or subjectivity; based on fact, not emotions.

Subjective: biased; based on personal views or feelings.

Rationalism: the view that knowledge must be based on reason.

Relativism: the idea that all forms of knowledge are of equal status.

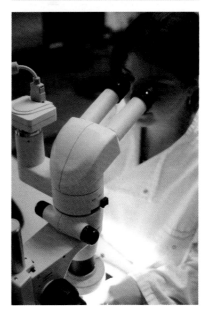

Fig. 1.1.2 *Laboratory science: is it objective knowledge?*

Link

The general American antipathy towards atheism becomes clearer in the context of Bellah's theory of civil religion in the US. See pages 10–14 for more about sociological perspectives on religion.

Take it further

Consider this quotation from Dawkins (2006: 52): 'Creative intelligences, being evolved, necessarily arrive late in the universe, and therefore cannot be responsible for designing it.'

Key terms

Natural selection: Darwin's theory of the survival of those organisms best suited to their environment. The process involves favourable genetic characteristics becoming more common in successive generations, and unfavourable ones becoming less common.

Paradigm: a mode of viewing the world which underlies the theories and methodology of science in a particular period of history.

New Age: a broad movement in Western culture that emphasises the individual's responsibility for their own spiritual development.

Take it further

The rationalist perspective suggests that science is the opposite of ideology, as it produces objective knowledge. It asserts that ideology is subjective as it requires belief. But here is what Heywood proposes: 'Science ... has been linked to the interests of powerful social forces, in particular, those represented by industry and technology. It has therefore contributed to a profound process of social change and become, in a sense, the ruling ideology of industrial society' (Heywood 1992: 295).

Rationalists assert that there is scientific evidence supporting Darwin's theory that human existence is due to evolution rather than divine creation. For example, in 1953 Francis Crick and James Watson described the double-helix structure of DNA, revealing the process through which **natural selection** operates.

Alternatively, the relativist view, which is closely linked to postmodernism, states that there are a multiplicity of beliefs in society and that science is just one of them. Science has no more claim on truth than any other belief.

Moreover, some writers point out that scientists are themselves human and therefore subjective. They have their own personal views and feelings. This makes it impossible for them to be completely objective, which is the main requirement of the scientific method of acquiring knowledge.

The small communities in which science is practised also pose problems of objectivity. Groups of scientists working together have to interpret each other's work. It is suggested that this produces negotiated, subjective knowledge. Kuhn (1972) also points out that scientists work within a set of rules called a **paradigm**. This means that science is a fairly closed system of ideas, which leads to the rejection of evidence that challenges its claims. The way that science overcomes this problem is by eventually creating a new paradigm. However, the existence of paradigms in science again indicates subjectivity.

Atheism and science

There are different shades of atheism. Some atheists may find it difficult to believe in the supernatural phenomena expounded in religious doctrines, and are sceptical. This is generally referred to as agnosticism rather than atheism. Agnostics remain doubtful about the existence of God in the absence of empirical evidence.

Staunch atheists, however, do usually take a rationalist stance. Atheists contest that arguments for the existence of God are illogical. These atheists, such as Dawkins, believe that it is impossible for the God of the world religions to exist. They have often studied religious creeds in some depth. They argue that there is no factual basis for the claims made by world faiths and maintain there is scientific evidence to refute them. An example of this is given above in the discovery made by Crick and Watson.

Atheists reject the relativist view of Gould. They disagree with the idea that religion should be allowed to dominate issues of morality. Many take what could be called a 'human rights' approach, insisting there are universal human values that underpin standards of behaviour. As these norms and values are universal, they are thought to surpass those of different religions and specific cultures.

Spirituality and religion

There has recently been an increase in the number of people who describe themselves as spiritual rather than religious. It is important to define what is meant by spiritual in this context, as Christians often refer to devotion to God as spirituality. However, there is a subtle difference between spirituality in the religious sense, and the spirituality of the **New Age**.

Religious spirituality involves believers submitting to a superior divine being that is external. This contrasts with the New Age form of spirituality, which is focused on the individual discovering the divine within themselves. Whereas religions are belief systems, New Age spirituality is unstructured and includes a diverse range of beliefs. However, many New Age beliefs are based on fundamental sacred principles taken from traditional religions, e.g. Hinduism and Judaism. This questions the extent to which they are actually new.

Heelas and Woodhead (2005) use the term **holistic milieu** to describe the wide variety of beliefs and practices that make up the New Age. It includes everything from tarot and astrology to yoga and complementary therapies such as reflexology (Figure 1.1.3). A large part of the holistic milieu consists of audience and client cults. It also includes paganism and witchcraft, which shows the extent of its diversity.

Despite such variety within the holistic milieu, Bruce (1995) identifies some common themes in line with New Age thinking:

- **Rejection of science** – the New Age favours subjectivity over objectivity. Science, however, denies the validity of personal evidence as a basis for knowledge. New Age believers see lack of scientific evidence for therapies and techniques as revealing the limitations of science.

- **Rejection of organised religion** – New Age followers see organised religion as too authoritarian and traditional. They feel it lacks spiritual intensity.

- **Interest in ecology** – the New Age is very 'green'. Followers respect the earth as a living organism and emphasise the importance of living in harmony with nature.

- **Scepticism of professional expertise** – this is especially evident in what are sometimes called alternative therapies. Practitioners emphasise the importance of treating clients holistically, focusing not only on the body, but also the mind and spirit. They see mainstream professionals such as doctors as narrow-minded for concentrating on the physical body.

So where has New Age spirituality come from? According to Heelas and Woodhead, it is all part of the 'subjective turn'. This refers to a cultural shift 'away from life lived in terms of external or "objective" roles, duties and obligations, and a turn towards life lived by reference to one's own subjective experiences' (Heelas and Woodhead 2005: 2).

Heelas and Woodhead's findings from their study in Kendal suggest that this spiritual revolution is possibly exaggerated. Although they predict a steady growth in the holistic milieu in the future, at present it only involves about 3 per cent of the population.

Key terms

Holistic milieu: the climate of New Age activities.

Link

Audience and client cults are discussed further in Chapter 2 on religious organisations and movements.

Fig. 1.1.3 *New Age shop: selling the sacred?*

Summary questions

3 Explain the term 'knowledge system'?

4 Evaluate the extent to which science can produce objective knowledge.

5 Assess the view that religion and knowledge should be given equal status in society.

6 Explain the link between science and atheism.

7 How does New Age spirituality differ from traditional religion?

Sociological perspectives on religion

Learning objectives:

- Understand the various explanations of religion by different perspectives.

- Evaluate each theory's views.

Link

This links to Topic 7 on theory and methods. Durkheim did not conduct primary research for his study of totemism. His reliance on secondary sources led to criticisms that his findings may lack validity. This is an opportunity for evaluation.

Key terms

Collective conscience: a set of values and moral attitudes shared by everyone in a society.

Totemism: the worship of an object or animal that has a divine significance.

Anomie: a state of normlessness.

Civil religion: a secular religion that unites people in multi-faith societies by instilling a spiritual patriotism.

Structural theories

Functionalism

Durkheim (1912) believed that religion performs an important function for society, binding people together like 'social cement'. Religion provides a set of moral values that form the **collective conscience**, ensuring social stability. Placing these values in the context of the sacred makes it more likely that we will abide by the corresponding social norms. For example, if someone believes it is a sin to steal, they will refrain from stealing to avoid offending God, a supernatural entity much more powerful than themselves. Religion is therefore a key agent of secondary socialisation. From his study of accounts of **totemism** among Australian Aboriginal tribes, Durkheim argued that all societies are divided into sacred and profane:

- **Sacred** – symbols and ceremonies that have a holy meaning.
- **Profane** – everything that makes up our ordinary everyday lives.

The totem could be a plant, bird or animal seen as having holy qualities. The totem was a symbol of the clan and a symbol of the divine spirit that watched over them. When the tribe gathered to worship the spirit, they were also worshipping the clan, their society. Durkheim therefore thought that collective worship plays a crucial part in the continuation of society, as it reinforces social solidarity.

Parsons (1965) identified another important function of religion. He claimed that it helps people to deal with 'life crises', which would otherwise produce **anomie**, threatening social order. For example, when a loved one dies, family and friends attend a religious ceremony, a funeral. Religion gives us comfort by answering difficult questions such as, for example, what happens to us after death? The mourners also offer each other support to help cope with their loss. In this way, religion provides a framework for managing life crises, so people can go back to playing their normal social roles to keep society functioning.

Evaluation of functionalist views

- Marxists point out that religion can actually be dysfunctional for society. One example of this is Northern Ireland, where there has been a history of violent conflict between Catholics and Protestants.

- It is argued that Western societies are becoming secular, with declining church attendance and collective worship. This suggests that religion is no longer influential enough to reinforce the collective conscience.

- Durkheim focused his studies on societies where there was 'one single moral community called a Church' to unite members (Durkheim 1961: 62). How can religion integrate people in modern multi-faith societies?

In answer to this last concern, the neo-functionalist Bellah (1976) argued that in a modern multi-faith society, the bonding function is performed by **civil religion**. He carried out his study in the US and identified the civil religion there as Americanism. It resembles a religion in as much as it uses religious images and phrases to promote and reinforce national identity. Americanism therefore promotes social solidarity, bringing together all the disparate strands of society. The various religious groups, mainly Christians and Jews, are all united under the umbrella of Americanism, where the god being worshipped is one who embraces all Americans.

Evidence of Americanism may be found in everyday life, e.g. coins are inscribed with 'God bless America'. The scriptures of Americanism include the Constitution and the Declaration of Independence. The civil religion also has its saints in the almost mythical national heroes of Jefferson and Lincoln. The Arlington Memorial Cemetery and Mount Rushmore, with its carved images of long-dead presidents, are seen as sacred places (Figure 1.1.4). Moreover, the American flag was deemed sacred when Congress outlawed its 'desecration' – only sacred things can be desecrated.

Marxism

Both Marx (1818–1883) and his colleague Engels (1820–1895) saw religion as a tool of **social control**, used by the ruling class to keep the masses in their place. Engels recognised that in order for the ruling class to maintain the status quo, 'the people must be kept in order by moral means, and the first and foremost of all moral means of action upon the masses is and remains – religion' (quoted in Turner 1991: 75).

Religion acts as a 'social opium', a drug that lessens the pain of hardship experienced by the working class. The church tells them that God will reward their suffering with a place in heaven. It therefore lays the blame for their lowly position in life firmly at the door of God, who is responsible for 'ordering their estate'. This is a phrase from the hymn 'All Things Bright and Beautiful', which is traditionally sung in Anglican churches and schools.

Religion is therefore an example of what Althusser (1971) calls an **ideological apparatus**, used to legitimise ruling-class domination. The working class is brainwashed into accepting social class inequalities as God-given and inevitable. This **false consciousness** prevents them from doing anything to improve their situation, leaving the ruling class free to exploit them for profit and enjoy its privileges.

Neo-Marxism

Gramsci's (1971) views differ from those of Marx, as he did not believe that economic forces alone could maintain the dominance of the ruling class. He argued that in order to keep a strong hold on society, the ruling class has to persuade the masses that the existing system is good and fair for everyone. Gramsci called this **hegemony**. Religious ideas and beliefs are an important part of this control. However, Gramsci did not believe that this was inevitable. He claimed that if the church joined forces with working-class intellectuals, together they could lead the masses to challenge the status quo and free themselves from oppression.

Evaluation of Marxist views

- The Marxist view does not take secularisation into account. How can the ruling class impose its ideology on the masses if the majority of the population does not attend church?
- The church does not always support the ruling class. For example, in the 1980s the Catholic church in Poland opposed the state and actually helped to bring about the downfall of the communist regime.

Fig. 1.1.4 *Mount Rushmore: a shrine to Americanism*

Key terms

Social control: keeping the population in line.

Ideological apparatus: a mechanism for promoting the views and interests of the ruling class.

False consciousness: the illusion instilled into the working class that the capitalist system is fair for everyone in society.

Hegemony: the ideological control that the ruling-class elite have over the masses.

Beliefs in society

- There is no evidence to support the idea of false consciousness. That the working class is blind to its oppression by the ruling class is no more than a biased assumption.

- Phenomenologists criticise the Marxist idea that religion would not be needed in a communist society. They argue that individuals will always want the comfort that religion provides. Similarly, functionalists claim that the social integration function of religion will always be essential.

Feminism

There are several feminist viewpoints. Although they all agree that women are subordinated in society, they disagree about the cause of this subordination. For example, liberal feminists believe that the differences between men and women are not natural, they are due to males and females being socialised differently, which is then reinforced by sexist laws and rules. The solution is the non-gendered socialisation of children and the introduction of laws ensuring sexual equality. This affects how liberal feminists see the role of the church in women's lives. They assert that an important step towards gaining total sexual equality is for women to be allowed to hold office in religious organisations.

On the other hand, radical feminists assert that it is men who are responsible for women's oppression, as they are the ones who directly benefit from women's low social status. According to Daly (1973), religion is infused with **patriarchal ideology**. For instance, it provides specific rules for females to follow, such as Catholic women being traditionally expected to cover their heads in church, whereas men have never been required to do so. Some Muslims place even greater restrictions on how women should appear in public. Feminists have identified an extensive range of ways that religion helps men to maintain their dominance over women in society.

Marxist feminists, however, give more weight to the role of capitalism in reinforcing women's inferior social status. For example, they point out that it is mainly capitalism that benefits from the free domestic labour provided by women, as it allows men to work much longer hours than would otherwise be possible. Marxist feminists emphasise how religion functions as a tool of women's oppression under capitalism. The church reinforces traditional gender roles that serve the interests of the ruling capitalist class. Chapter 4 covers this topic in greater depth.

Evaluation of feminist views

- The situation of women in some religious organisations has improved. For example, since 1992, women have been able to become ordained Anglican ministers. The first female ordination was in Bristol in March 1994.

- Western feminists give **ethnocentric** analyses of the religious practices in other cultures. Some Muslim women claim that wearing the hijab is actually liberating for them. It frees them from being objectified by men.

■ Social action theories

Weber

Weber (1922) believed that religion is actively used by individuals to make sense of day-to-day life. For example, it might be used to explain why someone 'good' dies young and why a 'bad' person continues to prosper.

AQA Examiner's tip

Show that you understand there are two types of structural perspectives. Identify functionalism as a structural consensus theory; identify Marxism, neo-Marxism and feminism as structural conflict views.

■ Key terms

Patriarchal ideology: the universal system of male domination over women.

Ethnocentric: seeing your own culture as superior to others, and using it to judge different norms and values unfavourably.

An element of Weber's analysis seems to echo Marx's view that religion justifies the status quo in society. Weber took a micro view, however, arguing that individuals use religion to explain why some people have wealth, status and power, and others do not. He called this the **theodicy of privilege or non-privilege**. Weber gave the example of the **caste system** in India. Those in the lowest caste use Hinduism to interpret their situation as due to their bad behaviour in a previous life: the only hope of social promotion is through reincarnation (Figure 1.1.5). This leads them to 'cling to caste duties with great tenacity as a prerequisite for their rebirth into a better position' (Weber 1922: 109).

Key terms

Theodicy of privilege or non-privilege: a religious explanation of social inequality.

Caste system: a class structure based on Hinduism, where a person's status is fixed at birth according to the family's social position. Social promotion and demotion is through reincarnation, depending on the person's behaviour in this life.

Beliefs in society

Fig. 1.1.5 *A Hindu 'untouchable': working towards social promotion*

Evaluation of Weber

Weber only provides a partial explanation of the function of religion. By focusing on a bottom-up explanation, he ignored how religion can shape the social reality of individuals. For example, Hinduism justifies the caste system, which then rigidly shapes the lives of believers.

Postmodernism

According to postmodernists such as Lyotard (1992), we are now living in a society which is dynamic and fluid. This is because of the collapse of

Beliefs in society

DIY cocktail: a personalised religion comprised of aspects of different faiths.

Universe of meaning: the collection of shared meanings that make up social reality.

Plausibility structure: the social basis for the continuation of society.

the metanarrative, resulting in a plurality of narratives present in one society. They all coexist and are seen as equally valid. This means that we are now free to choose whichever religion we prefer, rather than having one dominant faith imposed on us, as in the past. We may even take a pick-and-mix approach, selecting those elements of different faiths that appeal to us, ending up with what Madeleine Bunting calls a **DIY cocktail**.

Evaluation of postmodern views

■ A multi-faith society does not necessarily mean that each religion will be seen as having equal status. For example, most people in the British population identify themselves as Christian, suggesting that Christianity is still the dominant religion.

■ It fails to recognise the control that religion continues to exercise over certain groups in society. This is discussed in Chapter 4.

Phenomenology

According to phenomenologists, society is a social construct. The meanings people give to the world are arbitrary, which means they can be changed, so there is no universal standard by which everything can be measured. Berger (1967) describes society as being nothing more than a **universe of meaning**. It is very fragile, as its existence depends on us all sharing the same meanings. This means social reality could be easily shattered. Therefore, society requires constant legitimation in order to survive. We must be told and retold what is real, what is true, what is good and right.

Religion is an important part of this **plausibility structure**. It acts as a sacred canopy, providing answers to all our questions about life. As religion is based on faith, its explanations cannot be questioned. Because of this, religion can be used to legitimate social institutions. For example, laws are often placed in a religious context: 'thou shalt not kill'.

Evaluation of the phenomenological view

■ Like the functionalists, phenomenologists tend to see only the positive, uniting function of religion. They ignore how religion can be divisive.

■ There are societies that have no widespread single religion, which suggests that religion is not required to constantly legitimate society.

■ Summary questions

8 Outline two ways that functionalists see religion uniting people in a society.

9 Describe two ways in which conflict theorists believe religion controls certain social groups.

10 How, according to Weber, do social actors use religion in their daily lives?

11 Explain two criticisms of the postmodern perspective on religion.

12 Phenomenologists think that religion plays a role in maintaining society. Describe that role.

1.2 Religious organisations and movements

Churches and denominations

Learning objectives:

- Identify the key characteristics of churches and denominations.
- Recognise the possible links between church, denomination and sect.

Key terms

Church: a large, formal religious organisation most commonly associated with Christianity. Worldwide examples are the Anglican or Roman Catholic Churches. A national example is the Church of England.

Churches

The classification of religious organisations was first undertaken by Max Weber (1920) and developed by Ernst Troeltsch (1931). They identified a **church** as having the following features which distinguish it from other religious organisations:

- large, formal organisation
- a hierarchy of paid officials
- automatic recruitment
- tries to appeal to all members of society
- may have a close relationship with the state
- accepts wider society
- claims a monopoly on religious truth.

A modern example of a church is the Church of England, which has many of the above characteristics. Its large size means it has to be bureaucratically organised with a hierarchy of professionals, including ministers, bishops and archbishops. This high level of organisation is especially important in those churches which span several societies. The Church of England is part of the worldwide Anglican church. It draws its members from all social classes. However, the upper classes are more likely to join because the Church of England is traditionally conservative and supports the status quo. Consequently, it expects its members to participate fully in social life.

The relationship between church and state, though now weakened in comparison to the Middle Ages, is still evident in England, as the Queen is head of state and head of the church. Automatic recruitment still applies, although the percentage has fallen from 70 per cent of newborns being baptised into the church in the 1930s to less than 30 per cent during the 1990s. The Church of England now tolerates the coexistence of a wide range of other faiths that have contrasting versions of religious truth, such as Islam and Hinduism. Moreover, it participates in the ecumenical movement, which calls on all Christian groups to unite against the threat of secularisation and the growth of non-Christian religions. The Church of England's involvement in this movement still requires it to tolerate other Christian groups' versions of religious truth.

Although Troeltsch's definition of the church was based on Western Christian organisations, it is still applicable to other societies and national faiths. For example, in Iran there is a close relationship between the state and Islam, which also adheres to the other traditional features of a church outlined above. This is also the case with the Catholic church in places such as Spain and the Republic of Ireland.

Troeltsch's classification of religious organisations was mainly limited to churches and sects (page 17) due to his focus on 16th-century Europe. It is clear, therefore, that his study does not include the wide variety of religious groups present in modern societies such as Britain and the US.

■ Denominations

Niebuhr (1929) provided the first analysis of the **denominations** that have steadily increased in number over the past 200 years. They developed from sects that had originated as breakaway groups from the main church. This indicates that these three types of religious organisation (church, denomination and sect) should be viewed as distinct, yet not unrelated, as each may represent a different stage in a group's development. Niebuhr recognised that denominations share some of the characteristics of the church:

- large, formal organisation
- hierarchy of paid officials
- tries to appeal to all members of society.

However, denominations differ from the church in several ways:

- no claim to a monopoly on religious truth
- accept religious diversity
- no close relationship with the state
- may not fully accept wider society.

The fact that a variety of denominations can and do exist within a single society means that it would be difficult for them all to claim possession of religious truth. Brierley (2001) estimated that there were 250 Christian denominations in Britain at the start of the 21st century. This acceptance of other groups' beliefs is, according to Bruce (1995), the most significant difference between the church and denominations. Denominations also tend to be conservative, but advocate the separation of church and state to allow the church to focus on religious matters and avoid political influence. Denominations also tend to place a few minor restrictions on members' participation in social life. For example, Methodists are advised against drinking and gambling. Overall, however, churches and denominations both require a low level of commitment from their members.

Denominations do not have as great an appeal in society as the church. According to Brierley, there were only an estimated 340,500 Methodists in Britain in 2005. This contrasts sharply with the membership of 1,549,940 for Anglican churches (mostly Church of England) in the same year (Figure 1.2.1). However, defining membership is problematic and this will be examined in Chapter 5.

■ Key terms

Denominations: smaller, formal religious groups.

Fig. 1.2.1 *The Queen sets an example in attending church and is head of the Church of England*

■ Summary questions

1 Explain the terms 'church' and 'denomination'.

2 Who first identified denominations as another type of religious organisation?

3 What is the possible relationship between church, sect and denomination?

Sects, cults and new religious movements

Learning objectives:

- Identify the key characteristics of sects and cults.

- Understand the categorisation of new religious movements.

Key terms

Sect: small religious group, often hostile to the outside world.

Charismatic leader: someone who leads a sect because of their powerful personality.

Fig. 1.2.2 *Reverend Jim Jones: charismatic leader of the People's Temple*

AQA Examiner's tip

When you give an example of a religious group, always use it to illustrate characteristics of that type of organisation.

Sects

As denominations have developed over time from churches and sects, they may have features of both. However, Troeltsch's definition of **sects** shows that they are in direct contrast to the church:

- small organisation, with no professional hierarchy
- headed by a charismatic leader
- exclusive membership
- no automatic recruitment
- requires total commitment of members
- opposed to the state and wider society.

Having said this, sects and churches do share one important characteristic: they both claim a monopoly on religious truth.

The main reason for their opposition to the church stems from the origins of sects. Sects are schismatic – most are born of conflict within the church, resulting in a small group breaking away. The source of conflict is usually concern over the church's increasing wealth and ostentation, leading to a lack of focus on religious matters. An example of this is the sect formed by the Wesley brothers, John and Charles, in the 18th century, when they led a small group away from the Church of England. This sect steadily grew and eventually became the Methodist denomination.

Their opposition to the state often results in sects drawing membership from the lower classes, who may feel marginalised by society. Members are required to demonstrate their complete commitment to the sect, which often means withdrawal from society. All of this means that the sect, and in particular the **charismatic leader**, enjoys a great deal of control over members. Charisma, in this context, refers to the possession of unique personal qualities and the power to inspire. For example, Reverend Jim Jones enjoyed considerable power over his sect, the People's Temple, a group largely consisting of poor blacks recruited from the ghettos of California (Figure 1.2.2). He eventually led them to the jungles of Guyana, where they established Jonestown. Jones' control over his members was shown when many of them committed suicide at his command.

Sects are often short-lived, largely due to their reliance on the charismatic leader. As there is no formal organisation, when the leader dies, so does the sect. This is not always the case, however, as is clear with the Emissaries of Divine Light. After the death of Lord Martin Cecil, its leader in Canada, his son took over as leader. This illustrates Weber's claim that heredity is one way in which the leader's charisma can be routinised so the group can continue. This and other examples challenge Neibuhr's claim that sects must evolve into denominations or die out.

Another difference between a sect and a church is that sects require members to join voluntarily as adults, rather than the automatic inclusion of children through baptism. This is to ensure that their commitment is genuine and total, maintaining the strong level of integration within the group.

Hint

The Western mass media refer to some sects as cults. The sects that are often wrongly labelled as cults are usually those that are hostile to the outside world and deemed 'dangerous'. For example, the Branch Davidians, led by David Koresh, lived in a commune in Waco, Texas, and met a violent end in the 1990s; many members died.

Link

One thing that sects and cults have in common is that both are thought of as deviant. Perceptions of deviance are explored further in Topic 5 on crime and deviance.

Key terms

Cults: spiritual associations that emphasise individualism.

Sects vary a great deal in many respects. Most are small, localised groups, such as the Amish in the US. But a few have an international membership, such as the Unification Church, commonly known as the Moonies after its charismatic leader, Reverend Sun Myung Moon. Also, they differ in their level of involvement with the outside world. The Moonies send members out to raise funds for the sect by selling plants, for example, whereas the Family, formerly the Children of God, distribute leaflets to try to recruit new followers. Some leaders, such as Jim Jones, cultivate connections with influential people in the outside world, e.g. politicians, to try to bring about change in society.

Cults

Stark and Bainbridge (1985) explain the difference between sects and cults very clearly. Sects have broken away from another established religious group within a society, whereas cults have no such previous link. However, general confusion over the terms led Wallis (1985) to clearly differentiate **cults** from other types of religious group with his definition:

- minimal organisational structure
- limited formal contact between members
- no control over members' lives
- no claim to a monopoly of religious truth
- affirm life in this world
- tend to be short-lived.

Cults tend not to have a developed theology, or concept of God. They often have a vague mystical element, such as astrology and tarot, which both focus on divination. Such audience cults, as classified by Stark and Bainbridge, are highly individualistic, requiring a very low level of commitment and participation. They tend to attract people who are too interested in a range of new mystical ideas to commit to one single group.

Contact with cult 'members' may be achieved through products such as books and tapes. Stark and Bainbridge call this a 'client cult'. An example is the cult created by American inspirational writer Louise Hay, who offers a range of self-help products aimed at helping the individual to access their 'power within' to achieve their goals in life. A recurring theme in Hay's books is how to increase one's wealth and status, which illustrates the cult's affirmation of the social world. Indeed, cults often take the form of profitable enterprises. In addition to products such as books, some offer short, often expensive, courses that teach healing or meditation techniques. An example is transcendental meditation (TM).

Stark and Bainbridge also identify another type of cult. They describe cult movements as more organised forms of client cult, which also offer members opportunities for regular meetings. An example of a cult movement is Oneness Blessing, which was 'brought into the world' by an Indian husband and wife, Bahgavan and Amma (Figure 1.2.3).

A possible explanation for the short lifespan of some cults is that they fail to fulfil their promise to improve the lives of their customers. This could also explain their estimated high 'membership' turnover, as there is so much choice in this postmodern age that people do not really commit to anything for long, but pick and choose from a series of cultic products.

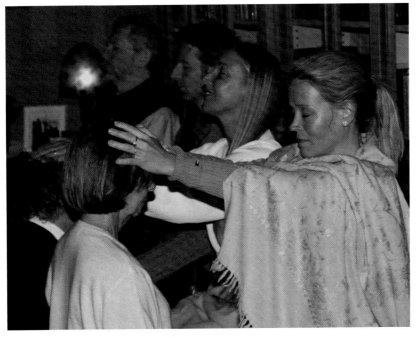

Fig. 1.2.3 *A Oneness Blessing session*

New religious movements

Since the 1960s there has been a huge increase in the number and range of small religious groups throughout Europe and the US. According to Stark and Bainbridge, the difference between sects and cults is that cults do not originate from another group within that society. The terms 'sect' and 'cult' were used interchangeably to describe many of the organisations, especially by the media. Wallis (1985) realised that it was time for a clearer and more up-to-date classification. He categorised these **new religious movements (NRMs)** in accordance with their relationship to the outside world:

- **World-rejecting NRMs** – being highly critical of the outside world, they tend to withdraw from it and adopt a communal lifestyle. They vary in size; most are small, local groups, but a few, such as the Unification Church, are international. Although often politically radical, they tend to be morally conservative. This is similar to Troeltch's definition of sects.

- **World-accommodating NRMs** – they are usually offshoots of existing churches. Subud, for example, has its origins in Islam. Resembling denominations, they are far more politically conservative than world-rejecting NRMs and break away from the church because they believe it has lost its religious purity.

- **World-affirming NRMs** – they have no developed theology or collective worship. They are conservative and offer followers the opportunity to increase their success in terms of the dominant values of society, by attempting to help them discover their spiritual power.

The 1980s and 1990s saw the emergence of a new wave of what Bruce (1995) terms **New Age movements**. They are largely, but not exclusively, audience and client cults, inspired by a wide range of belief systems and tending to have a broadly metaphysical basis. Examples are feng shui and crystal healing. They form part of the holistic milieu explored in Chapters 1 and 5.

Key terms

New religious movements (NRMs): a way of classifying religious groups based on their relationship to the outside world.

New Age movements: an array of hybrid mystical cults that have emerged since the 1980s.

Summary questions

4 Describe the differences between sects and cults.

5 Why do cults tend to have a short lifespan?

6 Explain what is meant by New Age movements?

1.3 Religious belief, social change and stability

Religion and social stability

Learning objective:

- Outline structural perspectives on the relationship between religion and social stability.

The arguments that religion is a **conservative** force in society come from structural theorists:

- **Consensus views** – functionalism and neo-functionalism.
- **Conflict approaches** – Feminism, Marxism and neo-Marxism.

Each of these perspectives takes the view that religion functions to encourage social stability, although they disagree about whether this benefits everyone in society.

Functionalism

Durkheim (1912) said that religion teaches people the moral norms and values they need to stick to the collective conscience, so maintaining social order. Therefore he saw the conservative nature of religion in a positive light, encouraging social harmony. It means that society is safe from rapid social change, such as revolution, which would bring about anomie, leading to a breakdown in social order.

Durkheim was not entirely opposed to social change. He recognised that slow change is necessary to prevent a society becoming stagnant and to allow it to progress. For example, a steady rise in the social status of women in Western societies over the past 100 years has allowed them to play a fuller part in public life, which benefits the whole of society.

Key terms

Conservative: preserving the existing way of life.

Social solidarity: the cohesion needed to make society work effectively.

Neo-functionalism

According to Bellah (1970), civil religion acts as a conservative force in modern multicultural society. It binds together people of different faiths, reinforcing the collective conscience. Civil religion promotes **social solidarity** by blending faith and patriotism. An example of this is the way American schoolchildren traditionally stand with hand on heart every morning and swear allegiance to God and the flag (Figure 1.3.1). Just like Durkheim, Bellah sees this function of religion as necessary and desirable. If these groups were not united by civil religion, conflict between them could result in social disorder.

Fig. 1.3.1 *American schoolchildren swearing allegiance*

Evaluation of functionalist views

Marxists argue that the working class does not benefit from the status quo. This puts them in conflict with the middle class, which means that although religion may be preserving social order, it is not producing social harmony.

Feminism

Many feminists assert that religion socialises women to conform to patriarchal norms. Religious texts proclaim male superiority, placing women in a subordinate position. For example, it is asserted in the Koran that 'men are in charge of women … hence good women are obedient'. Feminists disagree, therefore, with the functionalist view that in maintaining the **status quo**, religion benefits society as a whole. They argue that women do not benefit, as they are oppressed in the male-dominated world advocated by traditional religions. Men use religious texts to legitimate women's subordination and preserve their own social advantage.

Marxism

Marx (1957) thought that religion is a tool employed by the ruling class to prevent mass rebellion that would free the working class from being **wage slaves**. His view is therefore opposite to that of the functionalists. He believed that radical social change would transform society into a communist **utopia**. Religion, then, is a device for staving off this revolution. It is used in this way by the elite because they alone benefit from society staying just as it is. **Classless communism** would mean that economic resources would be shared equally, which clearly threatens the ruling-class monopoly on wealth and power.

Evaluation of the Marxist view

Functionalists argue that the working class *does* benefit from capitalism. Society is meritocratic, so the hard-working and able are rewarded with high status and wealth. Successful business people in turn provide a range of jobs for those with varying levels of ability. This view is criticised by Marxists, who point out that the difference in wealth and income between the middle and working classes continues to increase.

Neo-Marxism

Gramsci (1971) agreed with Marx. He claimed that the ruling class uses religion to maintain hegemonic control over the working class. However, he argued that it is not inevitable that religion must play such a conservative role in society. He was influenced by the Marxist Engels, who recognised that under certain circumstances, religion could become a focal point for the masses to rail against their oppressors.

An example is the strong support in the 1980s given by the Catholic church to the popular Polish trade union Solidarity. Pope John Paul II, formerly the Archbishop of Krakow in Poland, publicly endorsed the union's protest against the communist regime that ruled the country as part of the Soviet Union (Figure 1.3.2). This helped the union to gain significant international attention and support. The struggle resulted in the liberation of Poland from Soviet control in 1989. However, it is also possible to view the cooperation of the Catholic church in this instance as self-interest. It, too, was oppressed under communism. The church's leader in Poland, Cardinal Stefan Wyszynski, had been placed under house arrest for three years in the 1950s for speaking out against the communist leadership. Liberation of the people meant that the church, too, would be free.

Gramsci proposed that the church could work alongside working-class intellectuals to educate the masses about the reality of their plight. This would mean that they would overcome the false consciousness that prevents them realising they are in fact oppressed. In this way, religion *could* be used to empower the working class, spurring them on to improve their social situation. This notion of religion acting as a catalyst for social change is echoed by another neo-Marxist, Maduro, which places him on the opposing side of this debate.

■ Hint

Some religious groups do treat men and women equally. Aldridge (2000) points out that Quakers and Unitarians are committed to gender equality. The status of women in the Anglican church has increased, with female ordination now allowed. This suggests that religion does not inevitably oppress women.

■ Key terms

Status quo: the way things are in a society.

Wage slaves: Marx's term for the working classes, who are forced to sell their labour in order to make a living.

Utopia: a perfect place.

Classless communism: a society in which there is no hierarchical structure and resources are shared out equally.

Fig. 1.3.2 *The Pope showing support for Lech Walesa*

■ Hint

The neo-Marxist view offers a useful evaluation opportunity, as it straddles both sides of the debate.

■ Summary questions

1 Outline the functionalist attitude to social change.

2 Explain how the consensus and conflict perspectives differ in their views of the relationship between religion and social stability.

3 Why did Marx believe that religion would not be necessary in a communist society?

Religion and social change

Key terms

Liberation theology: Christian teachings and beliefs that emphasise the church's duty to help free the people from all types of oppression. It mainly refers to Latin American Catholicism.

Apartheid: the system of racial segregation in South Africa, which led to discrimination against the black population.

Work ethic: dedication to your occupation.

Neo-Marxism

Maduro (1982) focused on the idea, already proposed by fellow conflict theorists such as Engels and Gramsci, that religion could be used to bring about social change. He highlighted cases where this had in fact taken place, such as in Latin America in the 1960s and 1970s, with Catholic priests preaching what Maduro called **liberation theology**. For example, Archbishop Romero of El Salvador was murdered in 1980, allegedly for speaking out against the government concerning the dire social conditions of the country's poor. Some priests even fought alongside the revolutionaries. In Colombia, Father Torres was killed while fighting against the army in 1966, inspiring many other priests to join the struggle against what they saw as a corrupt regime.

Maduro explained that, in these instances, the clergy had played the role of Gramsci's working-class intellectuals. The Catholic church was still very influential in such developing Latin American countries, and the priests were in a strong position to act as a voice for the people.

There are also examples of religion bringing about social change in other parts of the world. For example, Desmond Tutu, the former Anglican Archbishop of Cape Town, played a crucial role in campaigning to end minority rule in South Africa. He was at the forefront of a long struggle to overthrow the **apartheid** regime that oppressed the black majority population. However, despite being arrested and having his passport confiscated, Tutu refused to condone violent opposition to the government. His pacifist approach won him international support and admiration, leading to him being awarded the Nobel Peace Prize. The apartheid regime was finally abolished in February 1990 by President de Klerk.

Weber

Weber (1905) also believed that religion is a force that can bring about social change, but he looked at it more in terms of how religious ideas can influence social change. In his study *The Protestant Ethic and the Spirit of Capitalism*, he described how Calvinism, a type of Protestantism, helped to bring about capitalism.

He explained that in some countries, at various points in history, the material conditions for capitalism were present, but it never actually got off the ground. For example, in places such as India and China there was the technological knowledge, finance and available labour. However, what the entrepreneurs there lacked was the necessary attitude to get capitalism going. They simply did not have the strong **work ethic** that would make them commit all their time, energy and finance to the business. When these businessmen made enough money, they would stop focusing on their ventures and concentrate instead on enjoying their wealth, spending it on fine clothes, food and fun.

According to Weber, to kick-start capitalism, single-minded devotion to the business was required so that profit was ploughed back into the enterprise, enabling it to flourish. It was in 18th-century Europe that this frame of mind finally appeared, due to the influential teachings of Calvinism.

Fig. 1.3.3 *Calvinists tend to lead frugal lifestyles.* American Gothic *(1930) by Grant Wood*

One of the central beliefs in Calvinism is the **doctrine of predestination**. Calvinists had no way of knowing whether they were bound for heaven or hell after death. However, they all wanted to prove to themselves and others that they were part of the elect – God's chosen ones, destined for heaven. This produced a strong work ethic which Weber called the **Protestant ethic**. Calvinists, such as Baptists and Quakers, worked very hard, seeing their careers more like religious callings. They believed that the huge fortunes they made were evidence of God's favour, proving their membership of the elect.

Another important aspect of Calvinism in establishing capitalism is the fact that it is an **ascetic** religion (Figure 1.3.3). The Calvinists therefore had nothing on which to lavish vast amounts of money. This resulted in the **spirit of capitalism**, as unlike the businessmen in China, for example, the Calvinist entrepreneurs repeatedly reinvested their profit back into their companies instead of pursuing material gain.

The reason Weber set out to show that religious ideas resulted in the growth of capitalism was not only that he disagreed with the claim that religion is conservative. He also wanted to challenge Marx's claim that economic forces shape social life. Weber did this here by showing that an aspect of social life, religion, actually shaped the economy.

Key terms

Doctrine of predestination: the belief that when you are born, God has already decided whether you will go to heaven or hell after you die.

Protestant ethic: devotion to work produced by Calvinist beliefs.

Ascetic: denying yourself any luxury.

Spirit of capitalism: the continuous, systematic pursuit of profit.

Evaluation of Weber

■ The Marxist Kautsky (1953) argues that Weber is wrong to claim that Calvinism helped to bring about capitalism. Instead, he asserts that capitalism came first and that Calvinists then used it to indicate their position as the elect.

■ Historians suggest that the spirit of capitalism could not be linked solely with Calvinism. It is just as likely to have sprung from other religions and places, such as the Jews in Central and Eastern Europe.

■ Conclusion

Religion itself is neither conservative nor radical. Its role in society depends on two factors: who has the chance or seizes the chance to use it, and the particular social context in which it is being used. Marxists show how social elites use religion to prevent social change, thereby maintaining their dominant position. However, Weber asserted that religious ideas were opportune in ushering in one of the greatest periods of social change in Western history: the development of capitalism.

This duality is illustrated by the example of the Islamic revolution that took place in Iran in 1979. The Shah of Iran, an authoritarian monarch, was overthrown and replaced by an Islamic regime. The revolutionaries' religious leader, Ayatollah Khomeini, was installed as the new ruler. He was an Islamic fundamentalist who had previously been imprisoned by the shah because of his opposition to the pro-Western government. This is a case of religion bringing about social change.

However, the revolution transformed Iran into an Islamic state. The country is now run in accordance with sharia law, which is based on the Hadith and the principles of the Koran. Hadith are collections of teachings attributed to the prophet Mohammed. Religious leaders have a great deal of political influence. The current government is extremely conservative, exercising strict control over the everyday lives of the people. This means social change is inhibited, ensuring that traditional Islam continues to thrive.

Summary questions

4 What did Maduro mean by the term 'liberation theology'?

5 Outline two examples of religion generating social change.

6 Explain how, according to Weber, the growth of capitalism was assisted by the Protestant ethic.

1.4 Social patterns of belief and participation

Gender, belief and participation

Learning objectives:

Learning objectives:

- Outline gender differences in religious belief and participation.
- Assess the reasons proposed for these gender differences.
- Recognise the relationship between gender, age, social class and religious participation.

Key terms

Polytheistic: having several gods.

Monotheistic: having one god.

Until the middle of the Bronze Age, most religions were **polytheistic**, with male and female gods. According to Armstrong (1993), the goddess had a central role. However, as a consequence of invasions, many of these ancient religions were gradually replaced by the conquerors' own **monotheistic** faiths with masculine gods. This heralded the demise of the goddess and the eventual supremacy of the Hebrew god Yahweh, who is the cornerstone of today's major world faiths: Judaism, Christianity and Islam. Yahweh is a male god and the religions based around him are traditionally patriarchal.

Gender and participation in traditional world faiths

For Holm (1994) the move to the male god of monotheistic religions is the origin of gender inequality in modern religious faiths and their organisations. There are many examples of this male dominance:

- Although males and females can hold religious offices in Buddhism, the male monks have a higher status than the female nuns.
- In Hinduism, only males can become brahmins (priests).
- Catholics do not allow women to hold office.
- In some societies, Muslim women are not permitted to enter mosques for worship.
- Among Orthodox Jews, women are not permitted to participate fully in ceremonies.

Patriarchy in religion is also evident in the Hindu practice of *sati*, where a devout wife is expected to die by throwing herself on her husband's funeral pyre.

Holm claims that the basis for women's subordination is their sexuality. Menstruation, it is thought, makes women unclean, thus polluting holy places. This is why Hindu women are not allowed to go near family shrines if they are menstruating or are pregnant. Muslim females must not come into contact with the Koran, or enter a mosque for any reason, while they are menstruating.

However, not all religions treat women and men unequally. Sikhism allows males and females to hold office, although very few women actually do.

There have also been moves towards gender equality in some religious groups:

- Women have been able to become rabbis since 1972 in Reform Judaism.
- Catholic girls can now become acolytes, assisting the male priests during mass.
- The Presbyterian Church of Scotland has ordained female ministers since 1969.

■ Hint

The Koran sets out guidelines for how men should deal with their wives: 'If you fear high-handedness from your wives, remind them [of the teachings of God], then ignore them when you go to bed, then hit them' (4:34). High-handedness is interpreted as women attempting to be superior to their husbands.

The Koran also defines women largely in terms their sexual behaviour. It stresses the importance of female chastity and modesty. The scriptures tend to support and reinforce traditional gender stereotypes, and in doing so, they legitimate women's subordination.

■ Take it further

Women participate in their religion through activities in the home. This has significance in Judaism, where the mother introduces the children to the rituals of the Sabbath. Thus, the mother is responsible for the religious socialisation of her children. In Hinduism, females are responsible for looking after the family shrine. In Christian churches where women's formal participation is limited, they still have roles such as 'doing the flowers, running the Mothers' Union, working in church offices and running the Sunday school' (Knott 1994: 207). Women's religiosity appears to result from primary socialisation. Children learn that females are the 'religious specialists'.

Fig. 1.4.1 *Jewish women traditionally lead the Sabbath at home*

■ The Church of England first opened the priesthood to women in 1992.

Aldridge (2000) suggests that there was a very practical reason for the Church of England deciding to ordain women. There has been an increasing shortage of men coming forward to join the priesthood.

■ Justifications for women's religious subordination

According to El Sadaawi (1980), religion itself is not oppressive to women. Women's religious subordination stems from their oppression in wider society. For example, the Bible and the Koran were both written against an extremely patriarchal cultural backdrop. Men were dominant in society at the time, and they used the scriptures to justify and reinforce their position. This is illustrated by the patriarchal interpretation of the story of Adam and Eve. Eve tends to be depicted as an evil seductress, corrupting Adam and bringing sin into the world.

Knott (1994) states that the main argument put forward by orthodox Christian churches for the exclusion of women from holding offices is that Jesus and all of his apostles were male. In addition, feminists point out that male and female characters in the Bible are not portrayed equally. The main roles are given to men, who are shown to be strong, aggressive, authoritative and wise. There are fewer prominent women and they are either 'good' mothers and virgins, or 'bad' whores.

In Aldridge's view, this is one reason why women are attracted to New Age movements. They tend to offer a more positive image of femininity than the traditional scriptures.

■ Explaining women's religiosity

Knott points out that women represent over half the active church membership. Females then, it would seem, tend to be more religious than men. There may be practical reasons, such as women having more time to attend services as they work, on average, fewer hours in paid employment than men. Another explanation is that mothers have the responsibility for ensuring that children go to church.

Knott also explains women's religious or spiritual beliefs as linked to their biological role of giving birth. Many women see the creation of new life as a spiritual experience. Davie (1994), too, considers this argument. Interestingly, though, she also points out that the lowest level of religious participation for women is among those of childbearing age.

■ Gender equality in NRMs

Aldridge also points out that Quakers and Unitarians are very committed to gender equality. For example, Unitarians began ordaining women in the 19th century. Now one-third of Unitarian ministers in the UK are female. Brierley (2001) states that the Salvation Army has the highest percentage of female ministers, at nearly 60 per cent in 2000.

In addition, Ruickbie (2004) reveals that there is no empirical evidence of a gender division in witchcraft. This is in spite of popular culture projecting a female identity, e.g. in the hit US television series *Charmed*. However, it may be that women and men join wiccan groups for different reasons. In the sample studied by Ruickbie, the female witches tended to have higher-status jobs or owned their own businesses. They were therefore used to being in positions of power. The largest group of male witches in employment, however, was from skilled or semi-skilled categories. Male witches, then, were drawn from more socially deprived backgrounds.

Aldridge states that New Age movements have reawakened interest in the goddess, giving women a central role. In Aldridge's view, one reason why women are attracted to some New Age movements is that they offer a more positive image of femininity than the traditional scriptures. Stark and Bainbridge agree that New Age groups have a special appeal for women. Unlike many traditional religious organisations, it is easier for women to achieve leadership roles in cults.

Glendinning and Bruce (2006) assert that women are more likely than men to engage in New Age activities such as tarot and astrology. However, there are more men interested in other aspects of New Age pursuits involving personal well-being, e.g. reflexology, yoga and meditation.

Gender, age and social class

There are further social divisions in religious participation in terms of age and social class:

- Men and women interested in New Age therapies are usually middle-class.
- Men involved in New Age movements are more likely to be younger or middle-aged, whereas women are mainly middle-aged.
- Younger, working-class women are more inclined to use divination than well-being therapies, such as aromatherapy and herbalism.
- Middle-class females are more likely to attend traditional churches. They are often users of New Age therapies, but disapprove of divination. So, in line with their religious conservatism, they will accept holistic activities that are available in mainstream culture, but not those with spiritual aspects.

This supports Davie's claim that while the working class is more likely to believe, but not belong, the middle class tends to believe and belong.

Some studies use level of education as a measure of social class, as there is a positive correlation between these two variables. According to Dawkins (2006), there is evidence of an inverse relationship between level of education and religious belief. He highlights a study, reported by Bell in a 2002 issue of *Mensa Magazine*, which set out to investigate the relationship between intelligence and religious belief. The findings indicated that those with higher levels of intelligence and education are less inclined to hold religious beliefs. This would seem to suggest that middle-class churchgoers are in fact belonging without believing.

Link

The link between social class and a higher level of education is made in the AS textbook on page 143.

Summary questions

1 In what ways are women excluded from participating in religious activities?

2 What justifications are given for women's exclusion?

3 Why might women be more religious than men?

4 Why are women especially inclined to join new religious movements?

Ethnicity, belief and participation

■ Link

Chapter 5 examines the decline in Christian Trinitarian membership.

Statistics in *Religious Trends 3* indicate that religion continues to play a central role in the lives of British minority ethnics, whereas there has been an overall decline in membership of the predominantly white Christian groups (Table 1.4.1).

Table 1.4.1 *Membership of religious organisations in the UK (thousands)*

	1995	**2000**	**2005***
Christian Trinitarian	6,284	5,917	5,589
Christian non-Trinitarian	512	533	555
Buddhists	45	50	50
Hindus	155	165	175
Jews	94	383	91
Muslims	580	675	750
Sikhs	350	400	440

*Estimated

Source: Adapted from P. Brierley (ed.) (2001), Religious Trends 3, Christian Research, London

A possible explanation for the increase in Christian non-Trinitarian membership is that groups such as Mormons and Jehovah's Witnesses are extremely active in going out to recruit new followers. There are, however, several contributory factors involved in the sustained growth in non-Christian membership in the UK, which will be considered individually.

■ Reasons for the growth of minority ethnic faiths in the UK

Immigration and cultural identity

Since the 1950s, Britain has become home to an increasing number of immigrants from South Asia and the West Indies. When they settle in this country, they continue to follow the religions of their cultures of origin. Knott states that when elderly Asian women first came to Britain they felt isolated and found comfort in their religions. As Durkheim pointed out, religion helps to maintain social solidarity. Immigrants conscientiously practise their faiths as a way of reinforcing their cultural identity. Collective worship gives them a point of contact with fellow immigrants, thus consolidating the community. Furthermore, immigrants mainly come from deprived areas in their own countries. Weber's notion of the theodicy of privilege and non-privilege explains why they are more likely to be devoutly religious.

The problem facing South Asians newly arrived in Britain was that they had no infrastructure to enable them to practise their religion. They had to build their own mosques and temples, often in the face of much local opposition. However, faith was not a focus for reinforcing the ethnic distinctiveness of all immigrants. Unlike South Asians, who were chiefly Muslim, Sikh or Hindu, West Indian immigrants were mostly Christian, so they had a similar religious culture to that of white Britons. But they, too, experienced racism when they arrived in Britain and did not tend to receive a warm welcome in the churches. West Indians, then, also set about organising their own churches.

Racism

Another factor that explains some ethnic minorities' religious devotion is the hostility they encounter from the host population. Religion positively reinforces their ethnic identity in the face of racism. Ramji found that for the young males in his sample, Islam gives them a degree of status which they feel they cannot achieve in other ways, due to racial discrimination.

However, some ethnic groups' refusal to assimilate into the wider culture can be seen as threatening by the host population, thus fuelling racism. An example of this is the refusal of Sikh men to wear motorcycle helmets because their religion forbids them to remove their turbans (Figure 1.4.2). The police and courts tolerate this breach of the law on the basis of religious freedom. Nevertheless, this is interpreted as a form of discrimination in the eyes of some of the white population, who resent a minority group apparently being allowed to flout the law.

Degree of control

Another factor that may contribute to the higher level of religious participation among minority ethnics in Britain is the amount of control that their faith has over the everyday lives of followers. For example, Muslims must eat specially prepared halal food, Sikh males have to wear turbans. Muslim women may also be expected to wear a veil or hijab. This means that religion is omnipresent in their lives, and of central importance to their identities.

Religion and the second generation

Modood (1994) claims that many second-generation Muslims are not as religious as their parents. For example, many young Muslims flout the 'no alcohol' rule. This is because they have been socialised into the wider culture and their ethnic identity is not so important to them. According to Knott, young Asian women experience difficulties with their parents' demands over how they dress. They often clash with parents over their expectations, e.g. wearing the hijab. Younger Muslim women are able to differentiate between religious and cultural influences in dress. They understand that they can dress in Western clothes and still follow Islam. Butler (1995) explains that this indicates a trend towards **cultural hybridity**, where religion is separated from other aspects of culture. This allows individuals to maintain their identity as Muslim, Sikh, etc., while embracing mainstream British cultural values.

A study carried out by Watson (1994), however, showed that for many Muslim females, dressing in a modest Muslim way is seen as liberating rather than oppressive. For some women, wearing the veil is more of a protest against patriarchy than religious oppression. They see the veil as freeing them from unwanted male attention. Wearing non-Western clothes is also a way of maintaining an Islamic identity for Muslim men. For example, they may refuse to wear ties.

Ramji's (2007) research into gender and religion among young Muslims found that Islam is a way for Muslim men to secure a dominant gender identity. Males in the sample held patriarchal attitudes which they justified with Islam. If a male fails to fulfil the role of breadwinner, he is not a real Muslim man. One male participant said, 'It's *harem* [un-Islamic] to have women in your family working' (page 1176).

Fig. 1.4.2 *Riding out religious intolerance?*

■ Key terms

Cultural hybridity: a blending of cultures.

■ Key terms

Cultural capital: an idea developed by the French sociologist Bourdieu. He argues that the middle classes are able to give their children not just economic advantages but also cultural advantages such as use of language, expression and valued social skills.

■ Link

This links back to the subject of gender and belief. As you will have already discovered, the issues of gender, social class and ethnicity are not discrete topics.

All of the sample felt that Muslim women have a duty to be modest. Some of the sample believed that this involves not only covering up with a veil or hijab, but also staying out of the public sphere. That means they cannot undertake paid employment outside the home. However, not all of the men in the study agreed, and indeed it was suggested that the **cultural capital** a woman acquired through her job could only enhance that of her husband.

Although one female in the sample conceded that women should play a purely domestic role, not all female respondents agreed. One interviewee argued, 'There's nothing un-Islamic about going out to work and getting a degree. That's just what Muslim men have been saying to keep women in their place' (page 1181). Muslim women therefore see education as the way to gain not only cultural capital through employment, but also religious cultural capital: 'Our religion says knowledge is the biggest thing you can have, so the more education you have the better' (page 1181). Thus, Islam is also used by female Muslims to forge an identity.

■ Religious pluralism?

Does the fact that Britain is now a multi-faith society mean that we have religious pluralism? According to Johal (1998), this is far from being the case. Religious pluralism would mean that all religious belief systems are seen to be equally valid. However, the overwhelming majority of the population identify themselves as Christian. Furthermore, the Church of England is still regarded as the main religious organisation. All other religious groups are seen as subordinate minority organisations.

■ Summary questions

5 Briefly explain three reasons for the higher level of religious participation among minority ethnics.

6 Why do second-generation immigrants clash with their parents?

7 What role does religion continue to play in the social identity of the second generation?

Generation, belief and participation

Learning objectives:

- Outline age differences in religious belief and participation in religious activities.

- Identify the reasons proposed for these age differences.

Age and religious participation

According to statistics collated by Brierley (2001), those over age 65 are the most likely to attend church (Figure 1.4.3). There is also a high rate of participation among children under 15, compared with people aged 15–44. This is largely due to parental pressure, as well as their attendance at Sunday schools. The lowest level of participation in religious activities is among people aged 15–19. In the past 30 years there has been an overall decline in church attendance across all age groups, but it has been most marked among the under 15s. Young people's reluctance to attend church is a concern for clergy. In 2000 the Archbishop of Canterbury advised priests to involve musicians and poets in finding ways to appeal to teenagers. He also suggested holding services in non-church locations, such as disused pubs (*Daily Telegraph*, 19 February 2000).

Fig. 1.4.3 *Churches seem to attract elderly congregations*

Research study

The Rural Church Project was an extensive study of religion in a rural community. It revealed that despite low numbers of males attending church, the clergy identified the most under-represented group as teenagers. Age therefore appears to be of greater concern than gender to the churches, perhaps due to the implications this has for the future of religion. The study also identified the stereotypes some people have of the type of person more likely to attend church. Middle-class females aged over 45 were thought of as more inclined towards regular attendance, while young, working-class males were viewed as least likely.

Interestingly, Levitt's (2001) case study of religious practice in a Cornish town also revealed a gender difference in children's participation. This becomes especially marked in teenage years, with a huge fall in church attendance among boys between the ages of 12 and 16. Also, the proportion of each age group attending church declines with each generation. This is thought to be due to society becoming increasingly rational and therefore secular. This topic is dealt with in Chapter 5 on the secularisation debate.

■ Age and belief

Davie states that people aged 15–34 are less likely than those over 54 to believe in God and heaven. She also says that prayer and moral conservatism are more common in the older age group.

This could be due to society becoming more rational and looking to science for explanations concerning human existence. People in Britain born before the Second World War were socialised in an era when the church still exercised a great deal of influence in society. Even if some did not attend church regularly, they had a high level of awareness of Christian principles.

Britain before the Second World War was not multicultural. This means that most of the population were not yet exposed to the variety of other creeds in Britain today. Christianity had no competition. Knowledge of other belief systems is thought by some to weaken religious argument overall. If there are many coexisting versions of the 'truth', whose, if any, is the real one?

■ Age, sects and cults

Young adults are more likely to join sects. This is for two main reasons. Firstly, it is because they have more freedom from social ties than older people. They are free to join groups that withdraw from the world, as they do not yet have dependants. Secondly, as traditional religion has less influence in society, the young may experience anomie. Sects offer them moral guidance and a sense of community.

Middle-aged, middle-class people are more likely to join cults. This group has too much of a stake in society to join a sect, which may require them to withdraw from the world. Also, cults often appeal to those who feel relatively deprived as they promise to make their members more successful in terms of society's goals, as well as making them feel spiritually fulfilled.

Also, despite the youthful image given to witchcraft in popular culture, Ruickbie (2004) states that most of those who actively practise this religion are in their thirties and forties (Figure 1.4.4). This ties in with this age group's interest in cults, as Ruickbie found that women identifying as witches mainly used their religious activities for healing and personal development.

Fig. 1.4.4 'Charmed': *the real face of witchcraft?*

Summary questions

8 Which age groups are more likely to participate in religious activities?

9 Outline two reasons why young people are less inclined to have religious or spiritual beliefs.

10 Explain the relationship between age, sects and cults.

Investigating social patterns

Learning objective:

- Examine the range of research methods used to investigate social patterns of religious belief and participation.

Take it further

The British government's official statistics website (www.statistics. gov.uk) features useful analyses of the statistics.

Also, log on to www.statistics.org and explore the government's official statistics on trends in religious participation.

Then log on to www.cofe.anglican. org, the Church of England's own statistics website. Compare its statistics on church attendance with the government statistics on church attendance.

What factors might affect the validity of these two collections of statistics?

Hint

Another popular source of statistics is *Religious Trends*, edited by Dr Peter Brierley. Again, the problem of bias arises, but this time in regard to selectivity. Published by Christian Research, it does analyse Christian organisations in much greater depth than other groups. However, there are valuable membership statistics on a range of Christian denominations, world religions and over 20 NRMs.

The main drawback of all these statistics is that they do not provide explanations of the patterns in participation. For that, it is necessary to incorporate qualitative data, preferably from a primary source.

Take it further

Go to www.kendalproject.org.uk and read Heelas and Woodhead's complete questionnaires.

Secondary sources: official statistics

Sociologists have access to an enormous amount of official statistics. They can access these statistics quickly and for free. As they are quantitative, they are easy to understand. Therefore it is possible to see trends in religious affiliation and practice over time.

Remember the interpretivists' warning that such reports contain someone else's subjective interpretations and, therefore, bias.

Primary research

When a sociologist undertakes primary research, they have to make choices about which methods to use. In Ramji's study 'Dynamics of religion and gender among young British Muslims', 20 in-depth interviews were conducted. The male and female participants were aged 18–30 and lived in London. They were accessed by snowballing. Interviews lasted 60–90 minutes and were taped for transcription and analysis. This interpretivist approach produced detailed information on these young people's attitudes to gender roles among Muslims. However, because the sample was small, it is impossible to generalise these findings to young British Muslims as a whole.

A more comprehensive research methodology was employed by Heelas and Woodhead (2005) in *The Spiritual Revolution*; their findings are discussed in Chapters 1 and 5. They concentrated their research on Kendal, Cumbria, and their pluralist approach involved:

- detailed study of attendance statistics in the records of four churches, to build up a picture of attendance
- interviews with about 25 holistic practitioners in the same town to gauge the holistic milieu in that area
- study of old brochures and the Yellow Pages going back to 1969 to support the information gained
- case studies that comprised participant observation and interviews, three on holistic organisations and four on particular congregations
- counting membership of church and holistic groups during the study
- a 13-page self-completion questionnaire distributed to church congregations
- a 16-page self-completion questionnaire distributed through holistic practitioners to their clients
- a door-to-door survey using semi-structured interviews in a small area of Kendal.

The study included primary and secondary information. Reliability and validity were maximised by incorporating quantitative and qualitative dimensions. The qualitative aspect allowed the researchers to find out the attitudes and opinions of the samples, enabling them to understand the reasons for religious participation in the various activities.

Summary questions

11 Outline the advantages and disadvantages of using secondary sources to investigate trends in religious participation.

12 Assess the usefulness of Heelas and Woodhead's methodology.

1.5 The secularisation debate

Evidence for secularisation

Learning objectives:

- Be aware of the statistical evidence for a decline in religious participation.

- Understand the survey findings on the decline in religiosity.

- Evaluate the methods used to measure secularisation.

Hint

Secularisation, as defined by Wilson (1966), is a 'process whereby religion loses its influence over the various spheres of social life'.

Sociologists who agree that secularisation is taking place also agree that the main cause is an increasingly rational, scientific outlook in society, which is incompatible with religion. A contributory factor seems to be the move towards a multi-faith society. Turner argues that 'modern society produces numerous contesting gods who have no power. ... There are too many world views for any one to lay claim to "truth"' (Turner 1974: 153). This will be discussed more fully on page 37. Firstly, we must examine the statistical evidence put forward to support the claim that secularisation is indeed occurring.

Statistical evidence for secularisation

Participation in religious activities

According to the British Social Attitudes Survey, the number of people not following a religion has increased from 42.6 per cent of the population in 1996 to 45.6 per cent in 2006. This suggests an increase in atheism and is therefore evidence of secularisation. Table 1.5.1 shows that church attendance has gone down considerably since 1980. At that time the percentage of the population attending church in England was 11.1 per cent. However, in 2005 this had drastically declined to 6.6 per cent.

In addition to this drop in church attendance, there are now fewer churches and ministers (Table 1.5.2) (Figure 1.5.1).

The proportion of each age group attending church declines with each generation. This suggests increasingly smaller congregations in the future.

Table 1.5.1 *Total church attendance in England, 1980–2005*

	1980	1985	1990	1995	2000	2005
Anglican	1,370,400	1,264,600	1,202,800	1,050,400	960,800	879,400
Baptist	286,900	274,000	267,800	275,800	280,000	279,000
Catholic	2,064,000	1,851,500	1,738,500	1,394,100	1,240,200	1,048,900
Independent	239,200	252,900	258,100	198,900	150,200	126,500
Methodist	606,400	560,500	506,400	433,100	372,600	311,100
New churches	75,000	124,700	174,600	213,100	248,400	292,000
Orthodox	10,200	11,300	12,700	20,500	25,600	29,800
Pentecostal	221,100	225,800	235,900	228,600	216,400	209,000
United Reform	188,300	163,000	138,100	128,800	118,700	100,600
Other churches	139,800	116,800	112,100	99,300	89,300	78,800
Total	**5,201,300**	**4,845,100**	**4,647,000**	**4,042,600**	**3,702,200**	**3,355,100**
Fraction of population (%)	11.1	10.2	9.6	8.2	7.4	6.6

Source: from P. Brierley (ed.) (2001), Religious Trends 3, *Christian Research, London*

Furthermore, the number of baptisms and confirmations has fallen. In 2000, the number of births in the Church of England was 161,110, but had fallen to 138,400 in 2006. Similarly, there were 36,387 confirmations in 2000 compared with 29,800 in 2006 (Brierley 2008).

There has also been a downturn in the number of church weddings. Even though the number of civil ceremonies has declined, it has increased as a percentage of all marriages. This suggests a preference for civil weddings over church weddings. Couples may also marry in a church for reasons other than religious belief, for example, to please their families (Figure 1.5.2). The same could be said of baptisms.

Overall, these statistics on participation in religious activities seem to provide overwhelming evidence of secularisation. However, people do not always behave in line with their attitudes, so it is important to examine patterns in belief as well. After all, secularisation is often taken to mean a decline in **religiosity**. To what extent is the decline in religious participation due to a lack of belief?

Statistics on beliefs

A 2004 YouGov poll commissioned by the *Daily Telegraph* also suggests that religious belief is declining (Tables 1.5.3 and 1.5.4).

Table 1.5.3 *Belief in God (%)*

Do you believe in God?	1968 Gallup poll	2004 YouGov poll
Yes, I do	77	44
No, I don't	11	35
Don't know	12	21

Source: Daily Telegraph, *27 December 2004*

Table 1.5.4 *Religious beliefs*

Do you personally believe	1957 Gallup poll			2004 YouGov poll		
	Yes	No	Don't know	Yes	No	Don't know
In life after death?	54	17	29	43	28	29
That there is a devil?	34	42	24	23	51	26
	1968 Gallup poll			2004 YouGov poll		
In heaven?	54	27	19	38	37	25
In hell?	23	58	19	23	51	25

Source: Daily Telegraph, *27 December 2004*

Fig. 1.5.1 *Do empty pews mean a decline in religious participation?*

■ Key terms

Religiosity: the extent to which people hold religious beliefs.

Table 1.5.2 *Total UK churches and ministers*

Year	Churches	Ministers
1995	49,512	35,017
2000	48,949	34,350
2005	47,955	33,558

Source: Adapted from P. Brierley (ed.) (2001), *in* Religious Trends 3, *Christian Research, London*

Fig. 1.5.2 *A church setting may add to the romance of the day*

These statistics not only support the secularisation thesis, but also the associated claim that the population is becoming less religious. However, there is evidence to contradict this. As we saw in Chapter 1, the census question on religious affiliation suggests that the majority of respondents are indeed spiritual; only 15.5 per cent replied that they had no religion. This anomaly leads us to consider the accuracy of the evidence used to support secularisation.

Evaluation of the statistical evidence

There have been many criticisms of using such statistics as a measure of secularisation. Firstly, it is difficult to establish trends in religious participation as the statistics are not always **reliable**. This is due to collection methods varying over time. In addition, the accuracy of the statistics cannot be guaranteed. For example, it has been argued that some religious organisations distort their figures to give a particular impression that benefits them. For instance, Catholic churches may deliberately underestimate the size of their congregations so that they pay lower capitation fees to the central church authority. On the other hand, Anglican churches are more likely to overestimate participation to avoid church closures. Thus, statistics on religious participation may not be **valid**.

The validity of surveys is also questionable. For example, Hadaway *et al.* (1984) investigated levels of attendance at religious services in the US. Where they were unable to access church statistics, they conducted a telephone survey. These findings were then compared with the results of their own attendance count. The data from the survey indicated a much higher attendance than was revealed by the count. Hadaway *et al.* concluded that people will give a socially desirable answer when surveyed, leading to invalid data.

However, the method by which Hadaway *et al.* carried out their attendance count can also be criticised. They estimated church attendance by counting the number of cars in the church car parks. How could they know how many of the congregation had arrived in each car, or how many had walked or used public transport? Therefore their findings may well have lacked validity.

The validity of surveys of people's religious beliefs is doubtful, too. Firstly, there is the issue of social desirability, which may not necessarily be overcome by ensuring anonymity. Secondly, there is the problem of how questions are worded. Many questionnaires focus on Christian beliefs, such as views on heaven and hell. This would not be appropriate for Hindus or Buddhists, as their religions do not include those beliefs. Therefore, if a Hindu replied that they did not believe in heaven or hell, this is not a reflection on their level of religious belief, but it may be taken as such.

What may affect the validity of survey results is how seriously the questionnaire is taken. In the 2001 census, 0.7 per cent of respondents listed their religious persuasion as Jedi Knights. This clearly calls into question the sincerity with which surveys are completed.

The existence of NRMs

The number of new religious movements (NRMs) in Western societies is also seen as evidence of secularisation by some theorists. Wilson (1966) argues that they have many secular aspects, such as individualism and materialism. Cults in particular seldom have a coherent spiritual foundation. He considers sects to be weak, fragile organisations that cannot last.

NRMs are criticised for trivialising religion. They make it easy for people to engage in 'spiritual shopping', rather than providing a constant set of norms and values. Berger (1967) describes sects and cults as a spiritual refuge for the desperate in an increasingly secular society.

Many NRMs actually have few full-time members; the bulk of followers have only loose connections with the groups of their choice. For example, there are less than 500 full-time Hare Krishna members in Britain.

Key terms

Reliable: research is seen as reliable if it produces the same results when repeated using exactly the same methods.

Valid: accurate, giving a true picture of the situation.

Summary questions

1. Identify two ways in which secularisation is measured.

2. What statistical evidence is there for a decline in participation in religious activities?

3. What support exists for the claim that there has been a loss of religious belief in society?

4. Outline two criticisms that can be made of the methods used to measure secularisation.

Explaining secularisation

Learning objective:

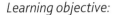 Understand the reasons sociologists propose to explain secularisation.

Key terms

Social fragmentation: loosening of the bonds that tie people together in society.

Desacrilisation: where rational explanations are seen as superior to sacred ones.

Ecumenical movement: where different Christian churches cooperate to offer joint services.

Theoretical explanations

The secularisation thesis is the notion that social change, such as industrialisation and the growth of scientific knowledge, would lead to the weakening or disappearance of religion. Comte (1798–1857), an early functionalist, identifies three stages of human history, each characterised by a different set of intellectual beliefs:

- **Stage 1, theological** – religious beliefs were dominant in society.
- **Stage 2, metaphysical** – an emphasis on the importance of philosophy.
- **Stage 3, positive** – characterised by the dominance of science and rational thought, resulting in the eventual disappearance of religion.

The functionalist Durkheim (1912) believed that industrialisation and urbanisation would result in **social fragmentation**, leading to individualism. Therefore, secularisation reflects the weakening of people's regard for, and belief in, society. However, Durkheim was optimistic about the survival of society and religion. He maintained that as all societies need a sacred element in order to survive, religion would eventually enjoy a resurgence.

On the other hand, Marx believed that the death of religion was inevitable. Industrialisation had produced capitalism, which used religion as previous types of society had used it – to legitimate social class inequality. However, as capitalism would eventually be replaced by classless communism, religion would not be needed in this socialist future society.

Weber also believed that as society became more rational and humans acted less in terms of emotion and tradition, religion would gradually be eroded. Industrialisation introduced capitalism, which is based on rationality, and this undermines religion. He therefore agreed with Marx to an extent, in that he saw secularisation as inevitable. However, he claimed that the reason for this would simply be a more objective, scientific outlook in society, eroding the blind faith necessary to maintain religion. This suggests that rationalism inevitably leads to **desacrilisation**. Weber believed there would be no place for myth and magic in a rational world.

Multi-faith society and individuation

The phenomenologist Berger (1967) stated that people are exposed to a huge array of religions in modern industrialised societies. This is due to urbanisation, geographical and social mobility, and the influence of the mass media. Multi-faith society has meant that shared religious beliefs have become undermined as each creed competes with the rest. How is it possible for each faith to be the sole purveyor of religious truth?

Wilson (1982) states that the **ecumenical movement** is a clear indicator of secularisation. Religious groups only band together when they are individually weak. The proliferation of NRMs is also said by Wilson to be a sign of secularisation. The sheer number of competitors in the religious marketplace weakens the overall spiritual message.

Key terms

Individuation: where individuals follow their own personal spiritual path.

Structural differentiation: a process whereby the functions of one institution become split up between different institutions. Society becomes structurally more complex.

As a further consequence of this, people now regard religious beliefs and practices to be personal matters. Bellah (1976) calls this **individuation**. He does not, however, see it as meaning that people have become less religious. They are just expressing their religiosity differently, in a more individual way.

■ Disengagement

Another suggested reason for secularisation is that the church is no longer closely related to the state. The church used to have many social responsibilities but they have been taken over by the government. An example of this is education provision. Before the 1870 Education Act, a minority of working-class children were able to access a very basic education through the church. Another area of responsibility assumed by the church was providing limited financial help for the poor, if their families were unable to help. It was not until the 1601 Poor Law that the state played a role in social welfare.

In the Middle Ages the church was also politically powerful. Even at a local level, the parish priest had a great deal of authority over the community. Today the political role of the Church of England is limited to 26 bishops having the right to sit in the House of Lords. This reduction in political influence is also said to signify secularisation.

■ Structural differentiation

Not all sociologists agree that disengagement means secularisation. The functionalist Parsons argues that as society develops, each social institution performs fewer functions. For the church, this means it has been stripped of the social functions that it had in the past, but which were not really within its spiritual remit. Because of this process of **structural differentiation**, the church has a reduced scope of influence and power. However, with those extra responsibilities now being carried out by the state, the church is free to concentrate fully on religious matters, providing society with moral guidelines.

■ Summary questions

5 Explain the possible relationship between industrialisation and secularisation.

6 Explain the term 'disengagement'.

7 How can structural differentiation be used as evidence against secularisation?

The continuing importance of belief systems

Learning objectives:

- Be aware of the statistical evidence against the secularisation thesis.

- Understand the arguments against the claim that society is becoming more secular.

Statistical evidence against secularisation

The statistics used to support the secularisation thesis tend to focus on the Christian religion. This has led to the criticism that pro-secularisation theorists are ethnocentric. As a result of their narrow focus, they are thought by some, such as Glock and Bellah (1976), to overestimate the extent of secularisation. If we look at membership figures for non-Christian religions, we see a rather different trend (Table 1.5.5).

Table 1.5.5 *UK religious community, 1975–2005*

Religion	1980	1990	2000	2005
Number (millions)				
Christian Trinitarian	39.8	38.6	37.7	37.2
Non-Trinitarian	0.8	1.1	1.3	1.4
Muslim	0.6	1.0	1.4	1.5
Sikh	0.3	0.5	0.6	0.7
Hindu	0.4	0.4	0.5	0.5
Jew	0.3	0.3	0.3	0.3
Other religions	0.2	0.3	0.4	0.4
Total	42.4	42.2	42.2	42.0
Fraction of population (%)				
Christian Trinitarian	71	67	63	62
Non-Trinitarian	1	2	2	2
Muslim	1	1	3	3
Other non-Christian religions	2	3	3	3
Total	75	73	71	70

Source: Adapted from P. Brierley (ed.) (2001), Religious Trends 3, Christian Research, London

Table 1.5.5 clearly shows a large increase in the Muslim and Sikh communities in the UK, as well as a smaller rise in Hindus and other religions. Part of this increase can be explained by immigration, but some must also be attributed to conversion, often away from Christianity.

Non-Trinitarian religions

Non-Trinitarian religions include groups such as Mormons, Jehovah's Witnesses and Christadelphians. Table 1.5.5 shows that there has been an overall increase in membership of these organisations. For example, according to the Association of Religious Data Archives (www.thearda.com), Mormons had 25.1 per cent growth in membership in the US between 1990 and 2000. Table 1.5.6 shows growth in the membership of Jehovah's Witnesses in the US.

Table 1.5.7 shows there has also been a significant increase in membership in the UK.

Table 1.5.6 *US membership of Jehovah's Witnesses*

Year	Membership
1975	560,897
1985	730,441
1995	966,241
2004	1,029,902

Source: Association of Religious Data Archives (www.thearda.com)

Table 1.5.7 *UK membership of Jehovah's Witnesses*

Year	Membership
1975	80,000
1980	84,000
1985	92,000
1992	130,000

Source: Taylor et al. (1995: 524)

These statistics indicate that there are some Christian organisations which have certainly not experienced a downturn in fortunes.

New religious movements

According to Melton (1993), there were 711 active NRMs in the US in 1990. However, the Association of Religious Data Archives claims that the number is now over 2000. There is also evidence of growth in the membership of sects and cults in Britain. Brierley reports a rise from 14,350 in 1995 to 21,336 in 2000. Table 1.5.8 gives some specific examples.

Table 1.5.8 *Membership of the Unification Church and Scientology*

Year	Unification Church	Scientology
1995	390	1,000
2000	121,800	144,400

Source: Adapted from P. Brierley (ed.) (2001), Religious Trends 3, *Christian Research, London*

This could be interpreted as evidence of a new form of religious activity emerging in society, as opposed to secularisation.

Arguments against secularisation

Although Durkheim asserted that industrialisation would lead to secularisation, he also believed that every society needed a sacred element. He therefore hoped that there would eventually be renewed interest in religion. The proliferation of NRMs could be interpreted as a sign of this **resacrilisation**. However, as we have already seen, some cults and sects have little or no spiritual basis, which calls into question the idea that they are a sign of continuing religiosity.

Furthermore, Stark and Bainbridge (1985) point out that all of the world's major religions started out as sects. For example, Christianity grew out of a small messianic sect that broke away from Judaism. Therefore NRMs should perhaps be taken as evidence for continuing interest in spiritual matters.

Bellah (1976) claims that the decline in church attendance cannot be interpreted as a decline in religiosity. He has a more positive view of Davie's 'believing without belonging'. There has simply been an increase in private worship. Luckmann (1967) says this 'invisible religion' is evidence not of secularisation, but of the emergence of new forms of religious practice. Postmodernists point out that nowadays we have the freedom to choose what we believe and how we engage in religious activities, if at all. We no longer have to follow traditional forms of belief and participation.

One of the new ways in which people participate in religious activities is through the mass media. **Televangelism** was very popular in 1970s America, with a faithful audience among conservative Christians (Figure 1.5.3). The preachers, such as Pat Robinson, became world famous and extremely rich. Thanks to satellite and cable television, the 1990s saw a proliferation of religious channels available worldwide. In 1970s Britain, religious broadcasting was largely limited to the Sunday evening 'God slot' occupied by programmes such as *Songs of Praise*. On Sky TV alone, 15 Christian channels now transmit 24 hours a day.

There are also several radio channels devoted to the Christian religion, such as UCB UK, listed as 'Christian radio for the whole family'. In addition, there are now non-Christian radio stations, such as the multi-faith Asian channel Sukh Sagar, and Amrit Bani for a Sikh audience.

Key terms

Resacrilisation: a resurgence of the sacred in society.

Televangelism: television programmes featuring Christian fundamentalist preachers.

Fig. 1.5.3 *Rev. Robert H. Schuller reaches a global audience with his weekly* Hour of Power *TV show*

Davie argues that the popularity of religious broadcasting is an example of 'believing without belonging par excellence' (Davie 1994: 112). For example, in the 1990s, the BBC had plans to discontinue 'Thought for the Day' in Radio 4's *Today* programme. However, an audience poll indicated an unexpectedly high level of support and it was saved. Yet Davie is ambivalent about the role of religious broadcasting. She explains that although it upholds religious values, it is also a rival for traditional religious participation through the church. Nonetheless, it does show the persistence of religiosity.

■ Explaining the religious revival

Some sociologists, such as Durkheim, remained hopeful that there would be a religious renaissance. The reason usually given is that religion serves a basic human need for reassurance and moral guidance. However, it is possible that there is another explanation. Postmodernists claim that Western societies have moved beyond **modernity**. This suggests that they have transcended the period in history in which rationalism challenged the supremacy of religious knowledge, bringing about secularisation. Science is no longer the metanarrative, which could mean there is room yet again for religious explanations of the world. **Postmodernity**, it is argued, brings new opportunities for religious activity, although this may be very different from traditional participation.

For Giddens (1991), however, we are now in a period of **high modernity**, rather than postmodernity. He makes this distinction because he believes that aspects of modernity persist. For example, people have not given up on the idea of social progress, which is a feature of modernity. In high-modern societies, however, the opportunity for this comes with global technology, which allows us to explore diverse cultural alternatives. We have become more reflexive, constantly looking to improve society. The problem we have is that our ordinary everyday lives have become superficial and separated from the 'existential questions' about who we are and why we are here. This is rather like Durkheim's assertion that every society has profane and sacred elements. This division has reawakened our desire for spiritual fulfilment and has, in Giddens' analysis, led to the rebirth of religion.

On the other hand, Bauman (1992) suggests that now we have abandoned modernist ideals, such as searching for universal truths, we are free to do whatever we wish. Our postmodern world is like a giant supermarket where we shop around for an identity that suits us. The problem with this, though, is that without the rules and regulations that characterised the modern world, we no longer have strict guidelines about how we should behave. The freedom to do what we want has raised the question about moral values. We are now in charge of our own rules of conduct: morality has become a private matter. In response to this uncertainty we turn to the 'moral specialists', religious leaders who can give us the guidance we need, hence the religious revival that is said to be taking place.

Religion in postmodern society, though, is characterised by choice and diversity. There are many faiths to browse, try out and probably discard in favour of a new group that catches our eye. The vast array of NRMs and New Age movements, which some have seen as evidence of secularisation, are simply spiritual products, according to some postmodernists. Lyon (2000) claims that we have become spiritual shoppers, as religion has relocated to the sphere of consumption. He uses the example of a Christian rally held at Disneyland in California to show

■ Key terms

Modernity: a stage in the development of society characterised by a belief in science, complex social structure and a complex division of labour.

Postmodernity: according to postmodernists, this is a new period following modernity. It is distinguished by increased choice and diversity, because of the globalisation made possible by information and communication technology.

High modernity: Giddens' idea that we are now in a new radical phase of modernity.

how there has become a blurring of boundaries between different aspects of social life. Lyon calls this dedifferentiation. In his example, popular culture has merged with religion. This could give religion a new lease of life by allowing people to explore faith in a less traditional and more familiar environment.

Beckford (1996) is extremely critical of the notion of a religious revival. He argues that there never was a religious decline in the first place, and that belief systems have always been of central importance to societies throughout history.

■ Summary questions

8 Outline the statistical evidence against the claim that secularisation is taking place.

9 Assess the role of religious broadcasting in maintaining religiosity in society.

10 Briefly describe two possible explanations for the religious revival that is said to be happening.

The international context: religious fundamentalism

Learning objectives:

- Identify the global trends in religious participation and belief.

- Understand the links between secularisation and religious fundamentalism.

Global trends in religious participation and belief

Despite the criticisms of the statistical evidence for religious affiliation, data for the UK and Europe does seem to indicate that religion has less social influence. Secularisation theorists explain this as being due to Western societies having become more rationalistic, with a strong emphasis on individualism. Having said this, the US is arguably the most rationalistic and individualistic society in the West. However, religious participation appears to have remained stable in the US.

One possible reason for the high level of religiosity in the US is that the main religions of Christianity and Judaism are not followed for strictly religious reasons. According to Bellah (1976), followers are expressing their Americanism rather than their religiosity. It is considered highly un-American to be an atheist, so to be religious is stoutly patriotic.

Herberg (1960), on the other hand, denies that the strong degree of religious participation evident in the US provides a convincing argument against secularisation. He claims that the churches themselves have become secular to keep in step with the rest of society. They now largely ignore spiritual matters, as they are not as important to their congregations as they were in the past. MacIntyre agrees with this view, stating that 'American religion has survived in industrial society only at the cost of itself becoming secular' (Turner 1974: 158).

There are, nonetheless, indications that religion is having an increasing influence within US society, through the rise of Christian fundamentalism. Roof and McKinney (1987) estimated that conservative Protestant groups constituted 15.8 per cent of the US population in 1984; this figure is now thought to be about 25 per cent. Many politicians are conservative Christians, including George W. Bush. This gives Christian fundamentalism considerable political power in the US. Christian fundamentalists oppose premarital sex, abortion and homosexuality. When the California Assembly passed a law to allow same-sex marriages in 2005, there was immediate opposition from right-wing Christians who claimed it threatened the 'sanctity of the family'. They embarked on a political campaign that succeeded in having the law reversed.

Christian fundamentalists in the US also oppose the teaching of evolution in schools. They interpret the Bible literally and insist on children being taught creationism, which is the belief that God made the world as outlined in the book of Genesis.

Fig. 1.5.4 *Religious fundamentalism is on the increase*

Martin (1978) also argues that in Latin America the majority of the population is still very religious. There is an especially strong Catholic following in countries such as Columbia. It seems clear, then, that not all Western societies are experiencing secularisation. Furthermore, not all religious groups in European countries have suffered a decline in membership and participation. The only groups that are affected appear to be traditional Christian churches.

■ Key terms

Religious fundamentalism: a conservative and often reactionary approach to religion. It involves literal interpretations of scriptures and disapproval of liberalisation within society.

■ Religious fundamentalism

The rise in Christian fundamentalism in the US can also be seen as part of a global trend towards general **religious fundamentalism**, such as Jewish fundamentalism in Israel and Islamic fundamentalism throughout the world.

Armstrong (1993) attributes the rise in religious fundamentalism to political and economic factors. The fundamentalist groups all feel that their religions are threatened by liberal values in the secular West. Western societies are now tolerant of abortion and homosexuality, for example, which concerns Christian fundamentalists.

Muslim countries feel let down by Western involvement in their political and economic issues. A prime example of this is the demise of the Shah of Iran. He had come to power as a result of a coup that was largely instigated by the American and British governments. He turned out to be a brutal dictator and was overthrown in a revolution and replaced with an Islamic regime. Another factor in Islamic fundamentalism is the strong support given to Israel in the Middle East by the US. Israel is regarded as an enemy by Muslim countries in the region due to its occupation of Palestine.

Table 1.5.9 *Global membership of world religions (%)*

Religion	1970	2000	2025*
Christians	34	33	33
Muslims	15	20	23
Hindus	13	13	13
Buddhists	6	6	5
Other religions	4	6	7
Non-religious	26	22	19

*Estimate

Source: from P. Brierley (ed.) (2001), Religious Trends 3, *Christian Research, London*

Table 1.5.9 suggests that Islam will continue to thrive and the other world religions will maintain a stable membership in the future. Perhaps the most interesting prediction in relation to the secularisation debate in the West is that Christianity is not expected to decline in the way that statistical evidence for the UK and the rest of Europe suggests.

Yet Giddens expresses concern about the recent development of religious fundamentalism. He emphasises the close proximity in which many different cultures and creeds now exist due to globalisation. This means that religious tolerance has become paramount to maintaining peace, not just within societies, but internationally.

■ Summary questions

11 Describe the trends in religious participation in countries outside Europe.

12 Briefly explain the term 'religious fundamentalism'.

13 Assess the extent to which global trends oppose the secularisation thesis.

Topic summary

Further resources

T. Bilton, K. Bonnett, P. Jones, D. Skinner, M. Stanworth and A. Webster, *Introductory Sociology*, Macmillan, 1996

J. Bird, *Investigating Religion*, Collins, 1999

P. Brierley (ed.), *Religious Trends 3*, Christian Research, 2001

R Dawkins, *The God Delusion*, Bantam, 2006

M. Haralambos and M. Holborn, *Sociology: Themes and Perspectives*, 6th edn, Harper Collins, 2004

P. Selfe and M. Starbuck, *Religion*, Hodder & Stoughton, 1998

- A belief system is a general term for any organised set of beliefs.
- An ideology is a world view.
- Belief involves doubt, whereas knowledge requires factual evidence.
- Religion is based on belief and faith; science is based on rationalism.
- Relativists claim that science is only one of many sources of knowledge.
- Atheism is more than simply an absence of belief in God.
- There has been a recent growth in New Age spirituality.
- Functionalists claim religion provides a set of moral values that form the collective conscience.
- Marxists believe religion is a tool of social control.
- Neo-Marxists believe that religion could be used to liberate the masses.
- Neo-Marxists argue that religion could be a force for social change.
- Feminists see religion as a device for control by men over women.
- Weber said that people use religion to make sense of everyday life.
- Postmodernists claim there is now religious pluralism.
- Phenomenologists assert that religion is a part of the plausibility structure that we use to maintain a fragile society.
- Troeltsch distinguished between two opposing types of religious group: church and sect.
- Niebuhr identified another kind of religious organisation: denominations.
- Niebuhr claimed there is a developmental relationship between churches, sects and denominations.
- Sects and cults are two distinct types of religious organisation.
- Wallis classified the wide range of religious groups that have appeared since the 1960s.
- New Age movements have developed since the 1980s.
- Structural theorists assert that religion acts as a conservative force.
- Functionalists see this as crucial to maintaining social order.
- Conflict theorists point out that only some social groups gain from this religious control.
- Weber maintained that religion can transform society.
- Women tend to be more religious than men, often having responsibility for religious socialisation and practice in the family.
- Women are particularly drawn to new religious movements.
- There are higher levels of religious participation among minority ethnic groups in Britain.
- The elderly are more likely to attend church than any other age group.
- Children have a high level of attendance.
- Teenagers have the lowest rate of religious participation.

Beliefs in society

■ Young people are more likely to join sects; cults appeal more to the middle-aged.

■ There are a range of official statistics on religious participation.

■ Sociologists have been able to provide in-depth qualitative data on reasons behind religious trends.

■ Statistics suggest that secularisation is taking place but they have been criticised for their lack of reliability and validity.

■ Sociologists such as Durkheim argued that secularisation is a consequence of industrialisation.

■ Other explanations for secularisation are disengagement, individuation and structural differentiation.

■ There is data to support the continuing importance of religion in society.

■ Others argue that what some see as secularisation is instead the emergence of new styles of worship.

■ Postmodernists say that people have more freedom to choose how and whether they engage in religious activities.

■ Global trends in religious participation and belief do not support the secularisation thesis.

AQA Examination-style questions

General Certificate of Education

Advanced Level Examination

Section A from Paper 3

SOCIOLOGY Unit 3

For this paper you must have:

a 12-page answer book

Time allowed 1 hour 30 minutes

Instructions

Use black ink or black ball-point pen.

Write the information required on the front of your answer book. The Examining Body for this paper is AQA. The paper reference is SCLY3.

This paper is divided into **four** sections.

Choose **one** section and answer **all** parts of the question from that section.

Do not answer questions from more than one section.

Information

The maximum mark for this paper is 60.

The marks for part questions are shown in brackets.

SAMPLE 1

Section A: Beliefs in Society

If you choose this Section, answer Question 1 and either Question 2 or Question 3.

Total for this section: 60 marks

1   Read Item A below and answer parts (a) and (b) that follow.

> **Item A**
>
> Pro-secularisation thesis sociologists have argued that to assess the level of religious practice and participation in society, it is necessary to examine statistics on such matters as church attendance, marriages in church and member ship of religious institutions. Such sociologists claim that data of this sort is irrefutable evidence for the decline in the importance of religion in Britain in particular, and Western society in general today.
>
> However, sociologists who hold opposing views argue that this approach is too deterministic, and over-simplifies the complex and diverse nature of religious belief and adherence. They say that that, if anything, religious activity in Britain and other advanced societies today is stronger and more widespread than it has been for several decades – far from declining, religion is simply changing.
>
> Source: Written by Hamish Joyce

    (a)   Identify and briefly explain three reasons why statistical data may not present a true reflection of the level of religious activity in Britain today, apart from that referred to in Item A. *(9 marks)*

    (b)   Using material from Item A and elsewhere, assess the view that religion in Britain and other advanced societies today is not declining, but changing. *(18 marks)*

Either

2   'Almost without exception the major world religions claim to promote peace and harmony between people. However, wherever one looks in the world today, religious differences are often the main cause of conflict.' Using recent empirical evidence, examine how far sociological arguments and evidence see religion as a cause of conflict, not harmony. *(33 marks)*

Or

3   Critically assess the contribution of Marxist sociology to our understanding of belief and ideology in contemporary society. *(33 marks)*

SAMPLE 2

Section A: Beliefs in Society

If you choose this Section, answer Question 1 and either Question 2 or Question 3.

Total for this section: 60 marks

1   Read Item A below and answer parts (a) and (b) that follow.

> **Item A**
>
> Functionalist sociologists have painted a largely positive view of the role of religion in society. Along with the family and the education system, religion was seen by traditional functionalists to be crucial for the transmission of social norms and values, and thereby the maintenance of social order. Without this, they claimed, society ran the risk of social breakdown or 'anomie'.
>
> However, many feminist writers argue that the social order upheld by religion is one which systematically and deliberately oppresses women. As evidence for this feminists frequently refer to the low status of women in many religions, and to their virtual exclusion from many religious hierarchies. They also point to practices such as veiling and female circumcision as further evidence of this oppression, and would argue that religion's support for the traditional family structure in Western society merely serves to reinforce gender stereotypes.
>
> Source: Written by Hamish Joyce

    (a)   Identify and briefly explain three ways in which Functionalists believe religion helps maintain social order, other than the 'transmission of social norms and values'. *(9 marks)*

    (b)   Using material from Item A and elsewhere, assess the view that religion oppresses women. *(18 marks)*

Either

2   'Organised religion is a conservative force, which seeks to restrict social change, and which therefore hinders social and economic development in many parts of the world.' How far do sociological arguments and evidence support this view the role of religious institutions in the world today?

(33 marks)

Or

3   Critically assess post-modernist views of the nature and importance of religion in society today.

(33 marks)

END OF THE UNIT 3 SECTION A
SAMPLE QUESTIONS

Introduction

The 20th century was an era of rapid change, bringing technological, economic and political innovation. It produced affluence never before seen – and some now enjoy an existence of unprecedented comfort. However, this experience is that of the minority, as the era is also one of significant inequality, with gaps between rich and poor becoming progressively wider.

Some of the inequalities found in the global context are 'traditional'. They relate, for instance, to wealth. While a throwaway culture emerges in the richest nations, 1.3 billion people live on less than one dollar a day. Life expectancy in the poorest regions is half that in the richest. There is considerable inequality; lack of access to institutions such as education and health care continues to undermine the opportunities of the global majority. Other inequalities are inventions of the contemporary era; environmental inequalities are perhaps the most notable. They exist not only in who treads most heavily on the planet – 80 per cent of the world's resources are consumed by just 20 per cent of its population – but also on the effects of processes such as climate change, which will have the greatest impact on the poor.

In this era and context, sociology is of vital importance. It has always been concerned with the nature and effects of inequality, so it cannot ignore such stark global observations. Sociology can take ideas from a range of areas – history, economics, politics, etc. – and link them to human experience. It demonstrates the links between poverty and inequality together with pressing contemporary concerns such as global insecurity and climate change. The ideas in this chapter are increasingly important to sociology and the global mindset.

As it progresses, this topic revisits earlier ideas and treats them in more sophisticated ways. Chapter 1 explores the building blocks of the topic, including four perspectives which attempt to explain and address development and underdevelopment. It also explores the concept of globalisation, a process which frames the rest of the chapter. Chapter 2 applies these ideas to processes which might help or hinder development. It explores the debates which surround aid, trade and population growth. Chapter 3 examines transnational organisations involved in these processes and some of the effects and experiences produced by development and underdevelopment. They include environmental impacts, war and conflict, health and the experience of women.

Take it further

Throughout this chapter, you can extend your understanding by finding your own empirical examples to illustrate points. Guidance on possible sources can be found on page 97.

Describing and measuring development

Learning objectives:

- Know a range of ways to describe levels of development.

- Describe a range of statistics used to measure development.

- Evaluate classification and measurement approaches.

Hint

The concept of global development is the central theme in this chapter. But this is complicated by the fact that 'development' is a contested concept with no single, universally recognised meaning.

Key terms

First world: rich, capitalist nations such as Britain and Japan.

Second world: communist countries such as China.

Third world: unaligned and often poor countries such as Mexico, Bangladesh and Ghana.

Northern hemisphere: the rich north of the planet.

Southern hemisphere: the poor south of the planet.

Minority world: the richest 20 per cent of the planet's population.

Majority world: the poorest 80 per cent of the planet's population.

Talking about development

The language we use to describe other people and places can have a powerful effect; encapsulating ideologies and values, and constructing realities. Before continuing, it is therefore important that we consider some ways to classify a country's development.

One familiar method divides the world into three: first, second and third. There is a common misconception that this is a simple division into rich, moderate and poor. In reality, the classification is focused on political rather than economic differences. The **first world** and the **second world** are the capitalist and communist blocs, respectively, whereas the **third world** refers to countries which did not align themselves during the Cold War. The approach is useful, as it recognises the importance of non-economic differences; and it is accessible. Critics note that the division of the world into three is a simplification, and that the break-up of the Soviet Union has left the second world somewhat empty. Furthermore, they maintain that the system is based on a value judgement – the first world is better.

Two-world systems simply divide the world into rich and poor. One approach is based on the geographical pattern of affluence, dividing the world into rich **northern hemisphere** and poor **southern hemisphere**. This avoids value judgements and gives useful neutral language through which to talk about development. It is, however, based on an oversimplification, and the presence of countries such as Australia in the south troubles the definition. An alternative two-world model, and the one adopted in this text, is to refer to the rich **minority world** and poor **majority world**. This approach avoids geographical references and overtly politicised language on development; whether this is a strength or criticism depends on one's perspective.

A final approach to classifying development creates more types of country. Here are some conventional types:

- more economically developed countries (MEDCs) such as Britain, Japan and the US
- former communist countries (FCCs) which have moved to capitalism since the end of the Cold War, including much of Eastern Europe
- newly industrialised countries (NICs) such as Brazil and Mexico
- less economically developed countries (LEDCs), the poorest nations, including Bangladesh and Sierra Leone.

This approach is more sensitive to economical and political differences than other alternatives. However, it is based on a hierarchy underpinned by Western values. There are still exceptions and ambiguities in the system, notably where China or Cuba fit in. Ultimately, this problem can only be avoided by adding more and more types, which dilutes the usefulness of the classification.

Measuring development

One clear method of exploring the variety of ways in which development is defined is to explore how it is measured. These measurements suggest a range of outcomes of development, which are underpinned by beliefs about what the process involves.

The most prevalent approach to measuring development focuses on economic growth – how much money a country has. A country's **gross domestic product (GDP)** is the total value of all goods and services it produces. A country's GDP per capita is its GDP divided by its population. A high GDP indicates a productive economy, where wealth will filter down to improve standards of life. The approach is popular because it offers a concrete measure of development. Critics note that it does not account for the distribution of wealth within a country, and the measure can obscure internal inequalities. Wealth could be concentrated in the hands of the elite. Furthermore, the approach is based on a Western capitalist value system that sees wealth as synonymous with well-being, ignoring the potential negative effects of rapid and unfettered accumulation of profit.

Alternative approaches to the measurement of development therefore focus on human experience. In some cases, these statistics relate to how well basic human needs are met, such as access to adequate nutrition and safe water, or outcomes such as life expectancy and infant mortality. More sophisticated measures examine provision of, and access to, social services such as education and health care. Finally, some agencies explore the extent of human freedoms (of speech, sexuality, religious beliefs, etc.). This may involve considering equality within the society, such as between genders. Unlike economic measures, these approaches focus thinking directly on human experiences. However, the dependability and comparability of the statistics can sometimes be challenged. Further, the approach can harbour **ethnocentric** judgements about other cultures, particularly over human rights.

Finally, some development agencies combine different statistics to create **composite indicators**. The most important is the **human development index (HDI)** calculated by the United Nations (Table 2.1.1). It combines indicators on education, wealth and life expectancy to give a score between 0 (least developed) and 1 (most developed). The advantage of this approach is that it does not reduce development to a single factor, so it offers a more rounded insight. Yet even the HDI is not completely comprehensive and, like other statistics, is blind to inequalities within nations.

Table 2.1.1 *HDI considers education, life expectancy and wealth in a country*

Country	HDI	Country	HDI
Norway	0.965	Indonesia	0.711
US	0.948	Guatemala	0.673
UK	0.940	South Africa	0.653
South Korea	0.912	Cambodia	0.583
Brunei	0.871	Bangladesh	0.530
Cuba	0.826	Uganda	0.502
Mexico	0.821	Zimbabwe	0.491
Russia	0.797	Rwanda	0.450
Thailand	0.784	Cote d'Ivoire	0.421
China	0.768	Ethiopia	0.371
Turkey	0.757	Sierra Leone	0.335
Iran	0.746	Niger	0.311

Source: http://hdr.undp.org

■ **Global development**

Key terms

Gross domestic product (GDP): economic statistic calculated by totalling the value of goods and services produced by a country.

Ethnocentrism: making judgements, often negative, about other cultures and places based on one's own cultural experience.

Composite indicator: a measure of development that combines different statistics.

Human development index (HDI): measure of development calculated by the United Nations by combining statistics on life expectancy, education and wealth.

Take it further

The Happy Planet index (www. happyplanetindex.org) offers an alternative method of measuring development. It takes account of self-reports of happiness and environmental impact.

Hint

An alternative way to define development is by exploring the different theoretical models in the process. This is considered in the next section.

Summary questions

1 Identify two systems of describing the development of countries.

2 Describe the three different approaches to the measurement of development.

3 Outline at least two problems with economic approaches to development.

Modernisation theories

Global development

Learning objectives:

- Describe the basic principles of modernisation theories.

- Outline Rostow's stages of development.

- Identify potential barriers and strategies to overcome them.

- Evaluate modernisation theories.

Key terms

Industrialisation: the process through which economies shift to mechanised mass production.

Link

See pages 71–72 for more on industrialisation.

One of the most instinctive definitions of 'development' is the idea that the majority world should become more like the minority world, adopting the life common in Western capitalist industrial nations. This concept is associated with a group of perspectives known as modernisation theories; the most prominent modernisation theorist is the American economist Walt Rostow (1960).

According to Rostow, all societies develop through a series of predictable stages:

- The first stage is traditional society. Here production is largely based on subsistence agriculture; food is grown to feed the growers' families and there is little trade for profit. People are based in small communities, with jobs passed down family lines.

- To move from this stage, technological innovations need to occur, creating the preconditions for take-off. Producers can be more efficient, generating surpluses which can then be sold for profit.

- Take-off occurs when entrepreneurs reinvest cash to expand businesses and generate more profits. To all intents and purposes, this stage is equivalent to **industrialisation** in the West.

- Growing industrialisation generates a range of new social and logistical needs, such as educated workers and roads to transport goods. During the drive to maturity, stable governance and taxation systems evolve and new institutions and infrastructure are created to meet these needs.

- Finally, wealth trickles down to the population as workers' wages rise. At this point, the age of mass consumption, people's lifestyles improve as they begin to afford goods that satisfy more than their basic needs.

Rostow proposed that all societies are at one of these stages. The challenge in development work is to identify why nations are stuck at one stage and to formulate means to overcome these barriers.

Explaining underdevelopment

Modernisation theorists argue that underdevelopment occurs because nations lack key ingredients to move from one stage to the next. Their emphasis lies with a lack of technology or an absence of entrepreneurs, associated with economic and cultural barriers. Theorists such as Rostow argue that majority-world countries are locked into a cycle of poverty. Producers lack the technologies needed to create the surpluses that generate profit. Consequently, they lack the financial resources needed to invest in technology to break the cycle.

Other modernisation theorists, such as Talcott Parsons (1979), think that cultural factors also act as a barrier to development. They argue that majority-world cultures are based on collectivism and ascribed status. Both are counterproductive in creating the kinds of entrepreneurial spirit needed to drive industrial growth. They ensure that people are locked into small, rural communities and deprive industrialists of the concentrated workforces needed to sustain factory-based production. Such cultures tend to be backward-looking and attached to tradition, and this makes them resistant to social change and progress.

Promoting development

Having identified some of the features which might hinder development, modernisation theorists have set out to overcome these problems. The development policies created by modernisation theory are based on the need to provide injections of capital to the majority world. This may be **aid**, in the form of loans and gifts, or it may be investment by **transnational corporations (TNCs)** that set up operations there.

Modernisation theorists hold that investment should focus on technological advancement, creating the industrial infrastructure to achieve economic take-off and the institutions to maintain the drive to maturity. Alternatively, investment should be used to bring about cultural change by creating institutions which permeate modern norms and values, establishing education systems and mass media.

Evaluating modernisation theories

Modernisation theories have been deeply influential; they dominated the period following the Second World War up to the mid 1970s. Crucial to this was the fact that they offer practical solutions to global poverty and inequality. Macroeconomic theories such as modernisation theories can have big impacts – they seem to promise to improve the lives of entire nations. As the approach is based on the histories of developed countries, it draws on firm empirical evidence.

Like any theory, modernisation theories have flaws; most notably, they are ethnocentric. They romanticise Western capitalist industrial society, implying that it has no problems. They underestimate traditional societies, implying that their economies and cultures have no value.

Modernisation theories have a tendency to oversimplify. Most notably, they assume that all societies follow the same basic development path. In doing so, they ignore the diverse resources, histories, cultures and politics present in rich and poor countries. They treat nations as isolated and ignore the connections between them, hence they ignore historical processes such as colonialism. Finally, they tend to locate all barriers to development within majority-world nations, ignoring external barriers such as distortions and unfair policies under which global trade occurs.

Some critics highlight that the industrial model of development is flawed, and inherently unsustainable. These forms of society place pressure on natural resources and produce pollution. Although the model proposes that everybody enjoys the standard of life found in the West, critics question whether the planet has the capacity to maintain this.

Link

See pages 67–68 for more on aid and pages 83–84 for more on TNCs.

Key terms

Aid: the transfer of goods, expertise or capital from nation to nation. It may take the form of gifts or loans.

Transnational corporation (TNC): a large business with operations and outlets in a range of countries.

Link

See pages 75–76 for more on education.

Take it further

The Marshall Plan following the Second World War was one of the earliest examples of modernisation theory in practice, and inspired early World Bank loans. Use the internet to research the Marshall Plan.

Global development

Summary questions

4 According to modernisation theories, what is the central process in development?

5 Name the five stages in Rostow's model of development.

6 Suggest one economic barrier and one cultural barrier to development.

7 Give three ways in which modernisation theorists might focus aid payments.

8 Give one strength and two problems of modernisation theories.

Neoliberalism

Learning objectives:

- Outline the basic principles of the neoliberal perspective on development.

- Identify factors which neoliberals emphasise in explaining underdevelopment.

- Describe the characteristics of structural adjustment plans.

- Evaluate the neoliberal perspective.

Key terms

New Right: a political perspective dominant from the 1980s, deeply influenced by functionalist thought and by a belief in the free market.

Free market: an economic system in which government interference is minimised and all activity is governed only by laws of supply and demand.

Hint

A supporter of neoliberalism is called a neoliberal, not a neoliberalist.

Link

See pages 69–70 for more on trade.

Since the 1970s, international development has shifted away from modernisation theories towards neoliberalism, a perspective associated with economists such as Milton Friedman (1962) and Peter Bauer (1971) and with the **New Right** governments of the 1980s. It has remained dominant and now underpins the principles of many major development organisations, such as the World Bank and the International Monetary Fund (IMF), and the priorities of many Western governments.

Like modernisation theory, neoliberalism's central idea is that the majority world should follow the rich world's path to development, but it disagrees on the nature of the path (Figure 2.1.1). Most notably, it rejects aid as a central process and questions how countries such as Britain were able to develop without a rich nation to provide cash.

Fig. 2.1.1 *Neoliberals think that countries develop by maximising their exports and sales on the global market*

Instead, neoliberalism sees trade as the crucial process in development. Its advocates hold that growth can only occur in an environment where trade is encouraged by limiting barriers and increasing incentives for corporate growth and individual entrepreneurialism. In practice, neoliberals argue that this should be achieved by creating a **free market**, in which governments minimise their interference in the economy and reduce red tape and taxation wherever possible. All economic activity should be governed only by what the classical theorist Adam Smith (1776) calls the 'invisible hand' of supply and demand. Once this occurs, growth will be self-sustaining and quality of life will rise.

Explaining underdevelopment

Neoliberals therefore highlight trade restrictions in explaining underdevelopment. They focus on factors which might discourage investment by corporations or entrepreneurialism in populations.

A great deal of focus is with the governments of majority-world nations. Neoliberals argue that outright corruption blights all levels in the governance of many countries. Valuable economic capital is diverted from development to the coffers of officials, or to fund frivolous vanity projects.

In addition, neoliberals argue that economic mismanagement has hindered development. They are critical, for instance, of governments overstretching themselves in providing public services such as education, health care and water. They argue that state provision is costly and creates a tax burden which discourages investment and business creation. The private sector is seen as far more effective, because it creates competition between providers, which benefits consumers. Finally, neoliberals argue that many countries have focused on centralised planning, stringent legal restrictions on business, and on protectionist policies such as **import tariffs** and **subsidies**. These, they argue, distort the free market, keeping industries artificially buoyant and preventing them from becoming more efficient and competitive.

Neoliberal theorists also argue that conventional aid-centred policies have actually hindered growth. Theorists such as Bauer argue that these approaches make countries stagnate by preventing painful but necessary changes. Aid is seen, for instance, as propping up corrupt governments, which are relieved of the need to care for their populations. Furthermore, aid is seen as breeding a culture of reliance on handouts. Finally, it acts as a subsidy, and thus stops local industries from evolving.

Promoting development

In order for development to occur, neoliberals see a need for better governance and management in the majority world, and their development strategies reflect these priorities, most notably **structural adjustment planning**. This involves attaching terms and conditions to the loans provided by development agencies such as the World Bank and IMF. The conditions usually focus on these core ideas:

- an agreement not to subsidise producers, and to reduce import tariffs
- turning over provision of public services to the private sector
- focusing production on exports
- deregulation, or cutting red tape, to reduce labour and environmental laws and business taxes.

The aim is to create conditions which attract outside investment from TNCs that will nurture new businesses inside the country and export in the global market.

Evaluation

The neoliberal perspective has been very influential and is easily the most dominant perspective in modern development theory. Its most important strength is that it is based on firm economic principles on how to prompt, sustain and manage growth. Furthermore, it places emphasis on the responsibility of the majority world in addressing corruption and inadequate governance. Finally, the focus on minimising government control over the economy can also have secondary benefits, increasing social and cultural freedoms such as individual rights to religious beliefs.

One of the most pressing criticisms of neoliberalism is that it has misguided ideas about the free market. Some detractors argue that allowing free rein for businesses allows them to pursue their one instinct

Key terms

Import tariffs: taxes levied on goods brought into a country, to make them more expensive than domestically produced goods.

Subsidies: payments given by governments to their producers to make them more competitive in the global market.

Structural adjustment planning: a policy of economic planning drawn up by the IMF and attached to World Bank loans. It requires recipient nations to move towards free trade.

Link

See pages 67–68 for more on aid.

Link

See pages 81–82 for more on intergovernmental organisations (IGOs).

Take it further

The World Trade Organisation (WTO) was set up in an attempt to liberalise trade. For more information, visit www.wto.org.

Global development

– to accumulate profit – without restriction and at huge costs to people and the environment. Furthermore, sceptics highlight that businesses from the rich world have a head start in the efficiency of their techniques and their ability to benefit from economies of scale. This gives them an advantage over the majority world in the global 'free market'. Finally, some question whether neoliberals are, in fact, bringing about a free market. They highlight that rich countries continue to subsidise their producers and that this creates unfairness in the terms of trade.

A second branch of criticism attacks structural adjustment directly. Critics argue that although the policies may make economic sense, they can be deeply harmful to people in recipient countries. For instance, local producers are thrown into the turbulent global market without protection. At the same time, employees find themselves without the protections of health and safety laws and minimum wages. Finally, the privatisation of public services often leads the very poorest locked out of provision of education, health care and even water supplies.

Summary questions

9. What do neoliberals consider to be the key process in development?

10. Identify three factors which neoliberals think may hinder development.

11. Describe the key characteristics of structural adjustment plans.

12. Give one strength and two weaknesses of the neoliberal perspective.

Dependency theory

Global development

- Outline the basic principles of dependency theory.
- Describe the three stages in Frank's model of exploitation.
- Evaluate dependency theory.

Hint

Because dependency theory emerged first in South America, its proponents are often called dependistas, but you could simply call them dependency theorists.

Take it further

One example of an informal trade network is what is known as the triangular trade. In this network, slaves were taken from Africa to the Caribbean, where they were sold on and replaced with sugar, cotton and tobacco. This was then taken back to the European homelands, where it was sold and exchanged for manufactured goods to be taken back to Africa and sold or used as bribes, beginning the process again.

Take it further

Use http://hdr.undp.org and http://en.wikipedia.org/wiki/List_of_former_European_colonies to research the association between colonialism and key development statistics.

Link

See pages 69–70 for the long-term impact of colonialism on global trade, pages 72–74 for its effects on global stability, and pages 75–76 and 88–89 for its impact on education and health.

So far, we have focused on mainstream approaches. Here we shift to examine more radical approaches. Dependency theory, the first of these approaches, evolved in the late 1960s from the work of Marxist academics in the minority and majority worlds, particularly South America.

This approach disagrees with the assumption that poverty is a natural, causeless state. Instead, dependistas maintain that global poverty and affluence are intimately connected, that both have been created by the systematic and total exploitation of the majority world by the minority world.

One of the most significant contributors to dependency theory was Andre Gunder Frank (1967). Frank conducted a historical analysis, concluding that exploitative relationships had evolved through three distinct phases.

Mercantile capitalism

Frank argues that exploitative relationships began to evolve some 700 years ago, when European merchant explorers, such as Columbus, set out to discover trade routes and encountered civilisations with sophisticated economies and cultures. The incoming merchants ensured that trade occurred on terms which favoured them. In some cases, this was because local value systems did not emphasise ownership of property. Elsewhere local leaders were bribed. Finally, exploitation was facilitated with outright threats of violence, using more advanced European military technologies.

During this time a number of informal trade networks were established, through which European capitalists generated massive profits, which later funded industrial revolutions.

Colonialism

The informal exploitative relationships were formalised when, under colonialism, the European powers took direct control over the regions of the majority world. This happened in gradual phases: Spain and Portugal's conquests began in the 15th century, and other European powers began acquiring colonies in the 17th and 18th centuries. There was a great scramble as major powers tried to acquire territory before their competitors.

According to dependency theory, this era wrought devastation on the majority world, with a number of distinct themes.

- **Economies** were reshaped, with a shift from diverse agriculture to the production of raw materials and cash crops needed by the empires. At the same time, indigenous industries collapsed, unable to compete with the empires' industrial mass production.
- **Geopolitics** was distorted as the colonial powers created nation states in the territories they had claimed, often breaking apart families or forcing together groups with nothing in common or with existing hostilities. Governance systems were established which were corrupt at all levels.

■ **Cultures** were undermined and existing knowledge systems destroyed. The European powers saw them as primitive and inferior, so they tried to impose more 'civilised' ways of life.

Dependistas argue that this phase of history had long-term and devastating effects, which would leave the majority world on an uneven footing. These distortions, they argue, are responsible for the inequalities present in modern society.

■ Neocolonialism

The 19th and 20th centuries saw a rapid process of decolonisation as Europe pulled out of its colonies. Dependency theorists argue that this only created the illusion that exploitation had been removed. In reality, all the mechanisms of exploitation remained, and nation states were replaced by corporations as the exploitative powers.

Dependency theorists therefore describe the contemporary era as neocolonial rather than post-colonial, to emphasise the continuity of exploitative relations. They argue that historical forces have created a world capitalist system in which **satellite nations**, the former colonies, remain dependent and subservient to their former colonial administrators, or **metropolis nations**. Further, they note that a number of modern processes maintain this inequality, such as the ways in which global trade regulations benefit the already rich.

■ Evaluation

Dependency theory makes crucial contributions to development discourse. Most notably, it does not locate barriers to development within countries and it avoids blaming the victims of poverty for their situation. Indeed, the approach blames the rich world. The theory treats the world as an interconnected system in which nations are not sealed units but are linked through historical and contemporary processes.

But there are significant problems with dependency theory. It does not make many suggestions to address global inequalities, beyond vague yearnings for isolation or global communism. It implies that no development is possible within the majority world, and struggles to deal with progress in regions such as India and South America.

There are also significant ambiguities in the theory and evidence which refutes it. Some poor countries, such as Ethiopia, have never been colonies, whereas some rich nations, such as Norway, have never held colonies. Furthermore, some former colonies, such as Canada and Australia, enjoy considerable wealth. Dependency theory struggles to incorporate any of these points.

Finally, it could be argued that dependency theory focuses only on the negative aspects of the relationship between rich and poor worlds. Some commentators argue that colonialism gave democracy to the modern world plus governance and the nascent industries on which to base their later growth. These commentators emphasise the potentially positive aspects of many contemporary processes and actors, such as aid or corporate investment.

■ **Link**

See pages 67–68, 69–71 and 83–84 for neocolonial interpretations of aid, trade and TNCs.

■ **Key terms**

Satellite nations: used by dependency theorists to describe former colonies.

Metropolis nations: used by dependency theorists to describe former colonial powers.

Summary questions

13 According to dependency theory, what is the process that has created poverty and affluence?

14 Identify Frank's three stages of exploitation.

15 Give one strength and two problems with dependency theory.

Counter-industrial movements

Learning objectives:

- Outline environmental and social problems with industrialisation.

- Describe key features of people-centred development strategies.

- Evaluate counter-industrial movements.

Link

See pages 90–91 for more on the associations between development and the environment.

Fig. 2.1.2 *Some theorists argue that the industrial model of development can have damaging effects*

Key terms

Swadeshi: Gandhi's ideal of small, self-reliant communities.

Hint

Although we commonly speak of Mahatma Ghandi, 'Mahatma' is actually Sanskrit for 'Great Soul', a term of respect. Ghandi's first name was Mohandas.

Take it further

Learn more about people-centred development at www.livelihoods.org/info/pcdl/index.html.

All of the perspectives agree that the Western model of industrial development is ultimately desirable. They diverge only on whether it is possible for the majority world to follow this path. A second group of critical perspectives disagree, arguing that the Western model of development is flawed.

Environmentalism

One critique of this model maintains that industrialisation inevitably results in vast ecological damage with three distinct themes:

- degradation of the biosphere as toxins are emitted into the atmosphere, land and water
- overuse of resources as industrial production is energy-hungry and requires large amounts of raw materials, much of them wasted
- loss of biodiversity as habitats are eroded to make way for industrial infrastructure and the space to obtain raw produce.

Thus, the perspective argues that any benefits yielded by industrialisation can only ever be short-lived, as they stretch the planet's carrying capacity to its limits (Figure 2.1.2).

Neopopulism

An alternative criticism focuses on the social costs of industrialisation. This approach is associated with neopopulism, whose most vocal proponent was Ernst Schumacher (1973). The perspective highlights a range of human costs of the process:

- **Loss of existing artisans** – existing artisans are unable to compete with more cost-effective techniques.
- **Loss of employment** – mechanisation requires fewer people to perform the same amount of labour.
- **Destruction of communities** – industrialisation drives urbanisation. This creates alienation and problems with crime, substance abuse and mental illness.
- **Dependency** – there is dependency on rich nations for the expertise and materials to maintain industrial technology.

The approach therefore argues that, when examined closely, the outcomes of industrialisation are displacing and dehumanising, seemingly the opposite of development.

Schumacher argues that the Western model of development is flawed as it is based on the assumption that consumption is the key to human happiness. This, he argues, creates conditions where people consume more and more in a futile attempt to gain fulfilment, when it is creativity that is important to welfare.

People-centred approaches

The approaches explored here reject the Western model of development. Their alternative model has its roots with Mohandas Gandhi (1924), who proposed the idea of **swadeshi**, self-sufficient community-based

■ Key terms

Sustainable development: development which meets the needs of the present without compromising the ability of future generations to meet their needs.

Intermediate technology: technology which improves on the techniques currently employed rather than replacing them with Western alternatives; sometimes called appropriate technology.

Microcredit: initiatives which make small loans available to people who would otherwise be unable to access credit to invest in businesses.

■ Take it further

Learn more about the Grameen Bank at www.grameen-info.org.

■ Take it further

Some commentators argue that the perspectives explored in this section are too focused on the short-term impacts of industrialisation. Although the process may produce damage in the short term, this fades over time. For instance, neoliberals argue that market forces will eventually produce more ecologically neutral technologies as these less wasteful approaches are also more profitable.

microeconomics. Contemporary people-centred development approaches focus on individuals and communities, attempting to develop and improve, not replace, local industries and lifestyles.

Gandhi also proposed the notion of 'moral economics', in which individuals take only what they need. In a contemporary context, this is similar to **sustainable development**, as popularised in the Brundtland Report of 1987. There are several types of sustainability:

■ **Environmental sustainability**, perhaps the most familiar, is the use of natural resources no faster than they can be replenished.
■ **Economic sustainability** is sustainability that does not rely on outside funds, such as aid payments, for its continuity.
■ **Social sustainability** is sustainability that includes all the community and does not marginalise any group, such as women.

People-centred projects have also developed practical initiatives to realise their aims. One of the most important is Ernst Schumacher's concept of **intermediate technology**. The aim is to empower producers to be more profitable and efficient, and expand their workforces. So, for instance, coffee producers may be given generators or roasting machines so that they can cut out 'middle men' who erode their profits.

A second important initiative derived from people-centred approaches is the provision of small loans, or **microcredit**. The schemes often work as cooperatives where interest is used to make further loans available. The first and most famous example is the Grameen Bank in Bangladesh, based on principles developed by Muhammad Yunus (1983).

■ Evaluation

The approaches covered in this section emphasise that development can never be measured in purely economic terms; we must be sensitive to the social and environmental costs. Furthermore, the approaches encourage a more long-term focus, and the concept of sustainability has been deeply influential. Finally, the actual development initiatives are significant because they empower the people they help, ensuring that development is something done with people, not to people.

Critics note that the approaches can only have limited impact. The focus on communities, rather than governments, means that the number of people affected is reduced. People-centred approaches do not set out to transform entire regions of the world. They try to realise development within limits, so they might be seen as preventing the majority world from attaining the living standards of the minority world.

There is also a tendency for the dependency approach to place too much emphasis on the poor world as a source of environmental damage. Thus, commentators may express alarm at the growing industrialisation of nations such as China and India and understate that developed countries have caused most of the ecological damage to the world.

■ Summary questions

16 Give at least two environmental and two social problems with industrialisation.

17 Outline four key features of people-centred development strategies.

18 Identify one strength and two problems with counter-industrial movements.

Globalisation

Learning objectives:

- Define globalisation.

- Outline a range of causes and effects of globalisation.

- Consider positive and negative stances on globalisation.

- Describe debates over the status of globalisation as a new era of history.

Key terms

Globalisation: increased world interconnectedness through the flow of nations, people, ideas, technology and culture in general.

Trade liberalisation: the neoliberal process of removing barriers to free trade.

Globalisation is a concept at the heart of contemporary development debate, so it frames and underpins all the topics in this chapter (Figure 2.1.3). In brief, it refers to the process by which previously isolated nations have become interconnected. Thus, regions of the world – and the people who live there – now influence one another to an extent without historical precedent. Although this definition will serve for this chapter, it is important to recognise that **globalisation** is multifaceted. At the very least, be sensitive to its distinct economic, political and cultural aspects; this is the framework adopted here.

Fig. 2.1.3 *Globalisation in a city environment*

Causes of globalisation

Globalisation is a complex phenomenon driven by many innovations and changes. Economic developments have been central to the process of globalisation. New transport technologies have, for instance, made movement of goods more cost-effective. At the same time, the dominance of neoliberalism as a political stance has led to increased **trade liberalisation**, and many barriers to international trade have been diminished. Finally, the 20th century has seen the rise of large TNCs, able to take advantage of this.

Political factors have hastened globalisation. These include a range of crises that necessitate global cooperation: acid rain, ozone depletion and global warming. At the same time, several IGOs have evolved into discussion forums, such as the United Nations and the European Union. Finally, the end of the Cold War in the early 1990s united the capitalist bloc and the communist bloc.

Sociocultural factors have also contributed to globalisation. One of the most cited causes is the development of the internet, which has transformed interaction and access to knowledge. According to Marshall

McLuhan (1962), improvements to media technologies have created a global village, where communication with distant people is as easy as talking over the garden fence. Other developments in mass media have also been important, most notably the increase in satellite communications. This allows us to see instantly what is happening elsewhere in the world in a way that was impossible just 20 years ago. It could also be argued that cheaper transport technology has facilitated tourism and greater immigration, so people are experiencing other cultures directly.

Effects of globalisation

Globalisation has a wide variety of causes and can produce wide-ranging effects. Three core themes run through this discussion. Globalisation has had economic impacts, transforming how goods are produced and sold. Supply chains have become more diffuse. Thus, components of a given product may be manufactured and assembled in several countries. The growing size of corporations, and their relative autonomy and independence, has meant they have become dislocated from the nation state and now exist almost as separate entities. National economies have been integrated into a global system. Consequently, turbulence in one region of the world can affect the markets and financial stability of faraway places.

Globalisation has had political effects – it has reshaped decision-making. This partly involves the elevation of power from the hands of nation states to transnational organisations (TNOs), corporate or governmental. Equally, power has been devolved from governments to individuals, who now exercise direct influence on the world by their choices of what to buy or boycott.

The sociocultural effects of globalisation can be found in the increasing diversity and pluralism across global cultures. For instance, it is common to encounter entertainment, food, clothing and religious beliefs from across the world. At the same time, there is an increasing sense of homogeneity as the same cultural artefacts are found from one country to the next; think about the shops in most high streets. Globalisation has also affected interpersonal networks, which can be increasingly diffuse and extended, such as MySpace or Facebook networks. The effects of globalisation are often somewhat contradictory: diffusion and integration, elevation and devolution of power, diversity and homogeneity.

Positive stances on globalisation

Although there is general agreement on potential causes and effects of globalisation, there is more contention over whether its outcomes are positive or negative. For some, globalisation heralds a new golden age of civil society, where each dimension confers distinct advantages for people and nations.

On an economic level, neoliberal theorists note that the emergence of a global economy is creating vast opportunities for trade plus the potential to generate wealth for rich and poor alike. At the same time, TNCs have evolved that can most efficiently tap into these new markets and spread employment and wealth. Finally, economic co-dependence leads to increased political stability. Thomas Friedman (1999) notes, for instance, that if nations have economic interests in one another, governments are more likely to persist in attempting to resolve disagreements through diplomacy.

Take it further

Thomas Friedman's book *The Lexus and the Olive Tree* gives an introduction to the pro-globalisation perspective.

Link

See pages 83–84 for more on TNCs, and pages 69–70 for more on trade.

Globalisation is seen as increasing the political forums through which international agreement can be built, which makes the world a more stable and safe environment. The rise of consumer power concentrates power directly in the hands of the individual, and is therefore seen as essentially more democratic.

Finally, the cultural effects of globalisation are seen as positive as they increase freedom of choice, in the context of a more diverse and pluralistic world. Cultural globalisation also ensures that people are more aware of their connections to one another. Thus, they are oriented to global affairs, pressuring their governments to address and avert crises.

Negative stances on globalisation

Other theorists are more critical of the impacts of globalisation. This is not to say that they are anti globalisation, but that they are critical of how the process has been hijacked by the agenda of the rich world, what John Williamson (1990) calls the 'Washington Consensus'.

On an economic level, therefore, critics argue that the current wave of neoliberal-dominated globalisation has aggressively imposed free-market politics on the majority world, regardless of its capacity to work within these principles. At the same time, the minority world's control over institutions of global trade regulation, such as the WTO, has enabled it to maintain **protectionist policies**. Consequently, there is an imbalance in the terms of trade that benefits the already rich.

Critics such as the philanthropist George Soros (1998) argue that neoliberal globalisation has created an environment of uncontrolled capitalism. Large corporations are free to pursue their only instinct – to return profits – without thought for the human or environmental costs. Governments are unable to restrain businesses.

On a political level, critics such as Noam Chomsky argue that globalisation has seen an increasing polarisation of power in favour of the rich, and a move away from democratic organisations. The minority world has more say, for instance, in the new institutions aimed at global governance. In some cases, such as the **Bretton Woods institutions**, this is because they are run on a dollar per vote basis. Elsewhere the developed world has the power to veto decisions, as in the United Nations. Critical theorists note that the increased consumer power generated through globalisation disproportionately benefits the rich, as their wealth offers them increased choice over their consumption patterns.

Finally, theorists with a negative stance on cultural globalisation argue that the process has not been one of exchange or dialogue. Rather, it has been a process of cultural imperialism, the imposition of one way of life and one set of norms and values on the rest of the world. In this respect, some critical theorists might even argue that globalisation is, in reality, a process of Americanisation.

Is globalisation new?

Before leaving this topic, it is worth noting that debates over globalisation are not confined to whether it is good or bad. Some commentators have also questioned whether, in fact, the process represents a new and distinct era of human history. In exploring this debate, David Held (1999) proposes that there are three main perspectives on the nature of globalisation.

Global development

Take it further

Susan George's book *Another World Is Possible If …* provides a good introduction to these critical stances and the rest of this chapter.

Link

See pages 81–82 for more on IGOs.

Take it further

Consider this quotation from Noam Chomsky (2001): 'Globalisation just means international integration. That is a fine thing. So everyone is in favour of globalisation. But the term is used in a special way … to refer to a specific form of … integration that has been imposed … by a small sector of wealthy and powerful nations.'

Key terms

Protectionist policies: initiatives such as subsidies and import tariffs through which a nation tries to protect its producers in the global economy.

Bretton Woods institutions: collective name for the World Bank, International Monetary Fund and sometimes the World Trade Organisation. They were formed at the Bretton Woods Conference following the Second World War.

Key terms

Hyperglobalisers: theorists who see globalisation as a new era of human history.

Sceptics: theorists who see globalisation as simply the continuation of a historical process of global interconnection.

Transformationalists: theorists who see globalisation as new, but think that old power relations and inequalities will continue alongside new ones.

Some theorists think that globalisation heralds a new era of history; Held calls them **hyperglobalisers**. According to hyperglobalisers, never before have goods, services, cultures, technologies and ideas flowed across local borders to the current extent. They maintain this is creating a global world system, for good or ill, in which all forms of relationship – personal, political, economic, etc. – are unconstrained by geography. Ultimately, this increasing connectivity will lead to the demise of the nation state. This is the perspective from which the positive and negative theorists usually originate.

By contrast, **sceptics** are dubious that globalisation exists as a distinct and new phase. They highlight that, for millennia, societies have sought out connections with one another. For evidence, one only needs to look at ancient trade routes such as the Silk Road, which ran from China to the Mediterranean from the 3rd century BC, or the spread of religions. The approach does recognise that there has been an intensification of global connections over the past century. However, it argues that these connections reflect well-established patterns of power and inequality. Theorists who take this perspective prefer the term 'internationalisation' to 'globalisation'; they maintain that the nation state will remain the primary unit of global existence for a long time to come.

Theorists called **transformationalists** occupy the middle ground between the hyperglobalisers and the sceptics. Like hyperglobalisers, they argue that contemporary levels of global integration and exchange are without historical precedent. And, like the sceptics, they reject the idea that the nation state will inevitably decline. They see the current era as a moment of flux when the world adapts to new tensions between national sovereignty and transnational governance. They argue that this will ultimately result in the restructuring of government, social institutions and ways of thinking – a transformation of the nation state but not a decline. Within this transformation, new inequalities and power relations will arise alongside existing global relationships.

The three perspectives disagree on a number of central questions: whether globalisation is new, whether it signals the decline of the nation state, whether old inequalities and power relations will disappear, and whether new ones will evolve.

Summary questions

19 Explain what is meant by globalisation.

20 Identify at least three causes of globalisation.

21 Suggest three positive results of globalisation.

22 Give three negative outcomes of globalisation.

23 Briefly define each of Held's three perspectives on globalisation.

Aid

Learning objectives:

- Distinguish between different types of aid.

- Compare and contrast two models of development aid.

- Outline criticisms of aid as a development strategy.

- Discuss controversies relating to loans and debt.

Take it further

Find out who gives what using http://hdrstats.undp.org/indicators. Scroll down to the data sets on official development assistance.

Key terms

Non-governmental organisation (NGO): a non-profit group largely funded by private contributions, e.g. charities, generally with social, political and environmental agendas.

Bilateral aid: aid given directly by one nation to another.

Multilateral aid: aid paid by various countries into a central pot then redistributed; the World Bank operates like this.

Relief aid: short-term aid following a natural or man-made disaster which aims to prevent the situation from deteriorating.

Development aid: long-term aid which attempts to build infrastructure and expertise at national or local levels in an attempt to bring about improvements.

Link

See page 87 for more on people-centred approaches.

Chapter 1 placed the idea of development in a theoretical context. Here we focus more specifically on the actual processes which might help or hinder development. We begin by considering aid.

Types of aid

Aid can be described in several ways (Figure 2.2.1). It is possible to describe aid by what is sent – food, cash, medicine, building materials, technology, expertise, weapons, etc. – and by how it is offered –- as a gift or as a loan. Aid can also be described by who sends it; **non-governmental organisations (NGOs)** may deliver aid and commercial banks may make loans. The main origin of aid is governments, which give **bilaterally** or **multilaterally**. It is also possible to describe aid by its purpose; there is a difference between **relief aid** and **development aid**.

Models of development aid

There is no homogeneous model for development aid. Different perspectives, informed by different theoretical principles, formulate aid packages that contain different resources and have different purposes.

Modernisation theory

For modernisation theorists, aid should aim at large-scale reforms that enable countries to rapidly emulate the development path of rich nations. The aid packages should try to overcome key barriers.

Most directly, aid can overcome economic barriers by breaking cycles of poverty. Modernisation theorists say that aid should comprise industrial technologies and expertise. Aid can develop the infrastructure needed to support industrialisation by helping to build road networks, docks and the infrastructure utilities such as electricity and water. Aid may also overcome cultural barriers, through investment in education, to pass on values such as individualism, achievement, competition and entrepreneurial spirit.

People-centred perspectives

For people-centred theorists, aid should be focused on small communities rather than national economies. Projects should be sensitive and appropriate to local needs, and allow local producers to grow and expand. In practice, this might be achieved through investment in intermediate technologies or microcredit schemes, or investment to support and augment local educators or health practitioners.

Critical perspectives on aid

One of the most fundamental misconceptions about aid is that it is intrinsically positive. Some theorists have noted that it can cause harm.

■ Links

See pages 54–55 for more on modernisation theory.

See pages 71–72 for more on industrialisation and pages 75–76 for more on education.

See pages 61–62 for more on counter-industrial and people-centred perspectives.

See pages 56–58 for an overview of the neoliberal perspective.

See pages 59–60 for more detail on dependency theory.

■ Take it further

Go to www.alertnet.org/thefacts/reliefresources/108418153847.htm and read how the War on Terror has had an impact on aid.

■ Key terms

Tied aid: aid given on the condition that it is spent on particular goods from specific producers.

Debt boomerang: Susan George's term to describe how the ill effects of majority-world debt can affect the rich world.

■ Summary questions

1 Distinguish between development aid and relief aid.

2 Identify two perspectives that are positive about development aid.

3 Explain how these perspectives differ in their models of development aid.

4 Give Bauer's three problems with development aid.

5 According to dependency theory, what are the two ways in which aid is used to benefit the rich?

Neoliberalism

Neoliberal theorists are among the vocal critics of aid. Peter Bauer (1971), for instance, argues that aid is ultimately counterproductive. Although it may bring about short-term relief, it actively prevents changes needed for true development to occur, across three dimensions:

■ **Political** – aid props up corrupt governments.

■ **Cultural** – aid makes people reliant on handouts, removing the incentive to be entrepreneurial.

■ **Economic** – aid keeps industry artificially buoyant, preventing it from becoming more efficient and competitive.

Thus, neoliberals argue that not only is aid ineffective, but it can also be actively harmful.

Dependency theory

Dependency theory's criticism is that aid is used to manipulate. This critique relates to how aid is used as a political tool to buy allegiances. Historically, this agenda was framed by the Cold War, and payments were given as a means of holding back communism. Thus, aid was given to a number of oppressive right-wing governments, such as the Pinochet government in Chile, and to groups such as the mujahideen in Afghanistan during the Soviet occupation. Osama Bin Laden was a member of the mujahideen. When the Cold War ended in 1989, aid declined. The aid that remains has continued to be politically framed, notably by the US War on Terror.

Another critique relates to the economic agenda of aid. In part, this focuses on how aid is used to push through structural adjustment plans, creating conditions where exploitation is easier. Dependency theorists also note the prevalence of **tied aid**. This benefits the rich world in three ways:

■ Subsidies are hidden under the guise of aid. Thus, rich nations are able to indirectly support and protect their producers without contravening trade agreements.

■ New markets are created for big corporations; in the longer term the receivers of aid will need support and spare parts.

■ Local industries are undermined, which ensures that competition with rich corporations is kept to a minimum.

Dependency theorists consider 'aid' a misleading term as these forms of transfer benefit the donors far more than the recipients.

■ Loans and debt

The use of loans as a form of aid has been a target of considerable debate. Some theorists think loans are a more efficient form of aid, as once they have been repaid, the money can be used again, plus the need for repayment deters corruption. People-centred approaches also see a place for loans in the form of microcredit. These schemes are much smaller and run on a not-for-profit basis by community cooperatives.

Other perspectives, particularly dependency theory, are far more critical. They note a common situation in which nations spend large amounts servicing the interest on loans, sometimes taking out further loans, without reducing the amount they have borrowed. Capital which could be used for development is redirected to repayment. Susan George (1992) also notes that loans can have broader negative effects. She argues that a **debt boomerang** has been created, rebounding on the donor nations. These ill effects include environmental overexploitation, increased migration, war and conflict, and loss of exports and employment.

Trade

Learning objectives:

- Outline the neoliberal perspective on the ideals of free trade.

- Explain how the terms of trade have been distorted.

- Describe how fair trade aims to address the unfair terms of trade.

- Understand criticisms of the fair-trade model.

Links

See pages 54–55 for more on modernisation theory and pages 56–58 for more on neoliberalism.

See page 82 for more on the World Bank and the WTO.

See pages 59–60 for more on dependency theory.

Key terms

Cash crops: high-demand products such as sugar, coffee, cocoa, rubber and tea.

Primary resources: unprocessed goods such as grain, raw minerals, ores and unrefined oil.

Crop monocultures: reliance on a single agricultural product, common in majority-world economies.

Aid is most popularly associated with development, but trade may have the biggest effect on development.

Ideals

Most perspectives agree that trade is an important process relating to development, and this is borne out by statistics on its potential impact. Cecil Nartey (2006), for instance, estimates that a 5 per cent increase in the majority world's market share would generate $350 billion – seven times the amount received in aid. In Africa, income from debt relief and aid would be dwarfed by a mere 1 per cent increase.

Perspectives differ on how to tap into these potential benefits. Modernisation theorists see industrialisation as central, because it allows greater returns to be made. Neoliberal theorists emphasise the creation of a free market in which goods and services can be bought and sold without any restriction. Factors which distort this market – high taxation, subsidies, import tariffs, etc. – should be eliminated.

In practice, neoliberals use two key means to create this free market. The first is negotiation within agencies such as the World Trade Organisation (WTO). Here agreements are forged between nation states to cut back on protectionist policies and to open markets to global competition. The second is structural adjustment plans to accompany World Bank loans. These plans compel recipient nations to reform their economies using free-market principles.

Distortions

Other theorists, notably dependency theorists, say the ideals outlined above are currently unattainable, because trade has been distorted by historical and contemporary processes. As a result, the terms of trade operate to benefit the minority world.

This distortion of trade has its roots in the colonial era. When imperial powers took control of countries, they shifted their economies away from diverse agriculture and made them produce resources for the imperial powers, usually a narrow range of **cash crops** and **primary resources**. These patterns of production persisted after the decline of colonialism. As a result, the majority world is overly dependent on **crop monocultures** and this creates two problems:

- Countries have no industries to fall back on if crops fail. This can lead to disaster, especially when a country relies on food imports.
- Oversupply of cash crops leads to overcompetition, driving down the price on the global market.

As a result, the price paid for majority-world produce has been in a steady decline. Teresa Hayter (1990) notes that, faced with falling incomes, the only possible response is for majority-world producers to sell more of their goods. But this yields only false riches, as the glut it creates will further depress prices.

Dependency theorists also note some contemporary processes that distort the terms of trade in favour of the rich. Structural adjustment plans,

Key terms

Dumping: the corporate practice of selling surplus goods at cost in the majority world.

Fair trade: people-centred trade initiatives that attempt to address some of the unfair terms of global trade.

Cooperatives: networks of producers who group together as one organisation for mutual benefit.

Link

See pages 75–76 for more on people-centred approaches.

Take it further

Find out more about fair trade at www.fairtrade.org.uk.

Link

See pages 83–84 for more information on TNCs.

for example, compel the poor world to cease protectionist policies which the rich world continues to practise; for instance, the European Union subsidises farmers. As a result, producers in the rich world can afford to charge less and be more competitive on the global market. This problem has been compounded by rich companies through the practice of **dumping**. Majority-world producers are already unable to compete in the global market, and dumping makes them unable to compete in their domestic market.

Fair trade

Some activists have tried to offer practical solutions to unfairness in global trade. **Fair trade** initiatives originate from a people-centred perspective and aim to equip small producers with the technologies, expertise and social networks to get a fairer deal.

One of the most important aspects of fair-trade initiatives is the formation of **cooperatives**. Cooperatives offer several advantages. Competition is lessened and producers have improved bargaining power, which tempers the declining price of their produce. Cooperatives can offer more produce and can deal directly with large outlets, cutting out middlemen who might erode profits. Fair-trade projects also help their members to invest in intermediate technologies through which cooperatives might process their own raw materials, further removing the need for middlemen. Finally, the initiatives set minimum prices for goods, and establish rules for environmental and social responsibility; prices often contain a premium that is spent on community projects such as schools and medical centres.

Fair trade has had a big impact but it is not a panacea and it has also been criticised. Neoliberals, for instance, say it creates intentional distortions in the market and is counterproductive in the long term. Other critics point out that the small range of fair-trade products effectively encourages producers to specialise in cocoa, coffee or bananas, exacerbating problems with overcompetition. Finally, the fair-trade kitemark has been used somewhat cynically by some large corporations to create a facade of social responsibility. There has been unease over Nestlé releasing a fair-trade brand of coffee, when some of its other production practices have run contrary to the aims of fair trade.

Summary questions

6 Identify two tools used by neoliberal theorists to engineer a free market.

7 Give one historical and one contemporary process through which the terms of trade may be distorted.

8 Identify three features of fair-trade initiatives.

9 Give at least two criticisms of fair trade.

Industrialisation

Learning objectives:

■ Outline the historical context of industrialisation.

■ Examine methods of managing.

■ Understand criticisms of industrialisation as a development process.

The process of industrialisation is often considered central to development; some perspectives see industrialisation and development as one and the same. Industrialisation is an economic process, involving mechanisation and the rise of mass production (Figure 2.2.2). However, its impacts on employment and on lifestyles are accompanied by social, cultural and political shifts. Sociologists are therefore interested in the process and these wider shifts.

Fig. 2.2.2 *Some theorists think that mechanisation and mass production are crucial to economic development*

The Industrial Revolutions began in Great Britain then Western Europe and the US during the 18th and 19th centuries, prompted by a combination of technological innovation, an entrepreneurial artisan class and colonial riches. In other nations, such as Japan and Russia, industrialisation was less organic, and the state attempted to orchestrate the shift to mass production, with varying success.

In the 1960s, a different form of industrialisation occurred in the **tiger economies**, a set of East Asian countries including Taiwan, Singapore and South Korea. Industrialists focused exclusively on a small number of components, such as transistors and microchips, in high demand among larger economies; each item yielded a small profit but the sales volumes were huge. This model has been imitated by other developing countries.

■ Promoting and managing industrialisation

Some theorists see three reasons why industrialisation is crucial to development. Firstly, industrialisation entails more efficient and profitable production techniques, driving economic growth and increasing wealth. Secondly, it creates more affordable products, so everyday people can buy a wider range of goods and services to improve their lifestyles. Finally, industrialisation is associated with a series of cultural and political changes; advocates argue that it leads to freer and more democratic societies.

Modernisation theory emphasises the use of aid to promote development, invested in technologies, expertise and institutions that will promote cultural change. Beyond this broad strategy, some specific economic policies have been developed to manage industrialisation most effectively.

■ Key terms

Tiger economies: a group of nations in East Asia, including Taiwan, Singapore and South Korea, which have experienced dramatic economic success following a process of export-focused industrialisation.

■ Take it further

Go to www.pupilvision.com/uppersixth/tiger.htm for more on tiger economies.

■ Links

See pages 75 and 85 for more on modernisation theory.

See pages 69–70 for more on trade.

Global development

■ Key terms

Import substitution industrialisation (ISI): economic policy which focuses production on replacing imports with domestic produce and strong protectionist policies.

Export-oriented industrialisation (EOI): economic policy in which all production is focused on a small number of high-demand products, with other needs met by imports.

■ Links

See pages 56–58 for more on neoliberalism.

See pages 81–82 for more on IGOs such as the World Bank.

■ Link

See pages 61–62 for more on counter-industrial movements.

See pages 75 and 85–86 for more on dependency theory.

■ Summary questions

10 Identify three different historical forms of industrialisation.

11 Give three advantages of industrialisation.

12 Explain the difference between ISI and EOI.

13 Identify and briefly illustrate three critical arguments associated with industrialisation.

One policy that dominated early development strategy is **import substitution industrialisation (ISI)**. Here goods which a nation usually imports from other countries are gradually replaced by domestic mass production, with local industries protected by subsidies to make their goods cheaper and import tariffs to raise the prices of imported goods. The idea behind this approach, advocated by modernisation and dependency theorists, is that infant industries can begin to grow and strengthen, protected from outside competition. In areas of South America heavily influenced by dependency theory, this approach was used to help them become more independent of the global capitalist system. Elsewhere, notably South Korea, it was used to develop economic strength to focus on global exports.

ISI can be extremely successful; for instance, it produced massive economic growth in Mexico between 1930 and 1970. But ISI strategies are fundamentally based on protectionist policy, and this has led to criticism. Neoliberal theorists argue that it distorts the free market and keeps industries artificially buoyant. This means that they do not become efficient and competitive, so they depend on wasteful subsidies to stay in business. Neoliberals contend that an overreliance on the approach led to a lost decade of development in South America during the 1980s.

Neoliberals advocate **export-oriented industrialisation (EOI)**. Here the economy is focused almost exclusively on the production and export of goods that compete in the world market; other products are imported. Protectionist policies are removed. Firstly, this allows the nation to negotiate with intergovernmental organisations (IGOs) such as the WTO on its access to world markets. Secondly, it ensures that the goods the nation imports are as cheap as possible.

Advocates of EOI strategies contend that they are the most efficient method of development, based on rational economic theory. Advocates highlight the successes of the approach in the Asian tiger economies. Critics say the approach can be brutal in its effects. This is because small producers tend to be destroyed as they cannot compete with larger organisations. Detractors also note that the Asian tigers have been highly susceptible to market fluctuation, such as in 1998; success has partly been linked to a nation's willingness to subsidise when necessary.

■ Critical perspectives

Not all commentators see industrialisation as a positive aspect of global development. They note that the process can have devastating environmental consequences, destroying habitats and using up natural resources. They question the sustainability of global industrialisation, arguing that the planet is only capable of supporting the process in the short term.

Critics note that industrialisation can have social costs. The process can lead to a loss of jobs, as fewer people are needed to complete the same amount of work, and the destruction of small producers. This is accompanied by many more general social problems such as community breakdown and associated problems of crime and substance abuse.

Some dependency theorists have also noted that industrialisation in the majority world often serves the needs of the rich. They argue that the output of newly industrialised countries (NICs) is merely providing a plentiful and cheap source of manufactured resources for affluent nations, in the same way that colonies provided raw materials to empires.

Urbanisation

Global development

Learning objectives:

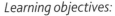

- Explore patterns and trends in global urbanisation.

- Identify reasons for the expansion of cities.

- Outline positive effects of urbanisation for development.

- Examine negative effects of urbanisation in the majority world.

Key terms

Urbanisation: the process of migration from rural areas to cities.

Megacities: cities that have a population of over 10 million and a population density of over 2,000 per square kilometre.

Agribusiness: the production, distribution, etc., of farming produce and agricultural equipment and supplies; any of the group of industries engaged in this; agriculture as a business using advanced technology.

Link

See pages 75 and 85 for more on modernisation theory.

Cities feature heavily in the imagery of modern society, and **urbanisation** is an important theme. The scale of urban growth in the 20th century makes it even more important to study urbanisation. In 1900 about 14 per cent of the global population occupied cities, by 2000 it had grown to 50 per cent. At the end of the 19th century, most of the largest cities were in the rich world. By the onset of the 20th century, seven of the ten largest urban areas were located in the majority world. They are, in order of population size (largest to smallest): Tokyo, Seoul, Mexico City, New York City, Mumbai, Jakarta, Sao Paulo, Delhi, Kyoto, Shanghai. These cities continue to expand, and many are known as **megacities**.

Reasons for urban growth

Many factors underpin the migration of people from rural to city living. Related pressures push people away from rural areas and pull them to the city. One of the prime reasons for urban migration is a lack of job opportunities in rural areas; there are a limited range of career positions and generally lower wages. Rural poverty can be further intensified by development elsewhere, as the introduction of large mechanised **agribusiness** can leave small farmers uncompetitive. The formalisation of ownership law can lead to loss of land. Finally, the infrastructure in rural areas is less advanced, so there is a lack of power and sewerage and a scarcity of public services such as health care. As a result, rural areas can experience the extremes of underdevelopment and of natural and man-made disasters. In contrast, cities offer improved infrastructure and opportunities. The glamorous and modern associations with urban areas – the bright lights of the city – also appeal to young people who want to break away from traditional lifestyles.

Positive aspects

Some theorists, such as modernisation theorists, think the growth of cities in the majority world is a positive phenomenon. They are enthusiastic about the growth of cities for their own sake, as this mirrors the development of the minority world. They note the potential for urbanisation to overcome barriers to development, to support and prompt industrial growth.

Cities perform economic functions, notably in providing the large numbers of densely concentrated workers needed for mass production. In this respect, the associated growth of urban areas such as Manchester were vital in allowing industrialisation to take hold in Britain and other Western capitalist nations. Modernisation theorists also maintain that cities can perform important functions in overcoming cultural barriers, acting as beacons which signal the modern norms and values conducive to development, and environments in which new ideas spread quickly. Cities are seen as progressive and open-minded environments, hence more future-oriented and accepting of change. Cities break down the reliance on community and extended family, thus promoting values of achievement and individualism. Cities are seen as crucial in breeding entrepreneurs to push forward development.

■ Take it further

Extend your understanding of this topic by researching life in urban slums such as Kibera or the favelas of Brazil.

■ Key terms

Urban sprawl: the steady and haphazard expansion of cities into surrounding areas, often in unplanned ways.

Dual-sector economy: situation in which legal and regulated jobs are limited, leading to an overspill into unregulated or illegal employment.

Primate city: a city which forms the political and economic centre of a country and at least twice the size of any non-primate city. The existence of primate cities often indicates uneven development.

■ Urban sprawl

Although modernisation theorists are positive about the growth of cities in the majority world, other commentators are more cautious. They note that urbanisation in the southern hemisphere has been far more rapid than urbanisation in the northern hemisphere, and this has generated a set of distinct problems associated with **urban sprawl**. The infrastructure of newly expanding cities struggles to accommodate rapidly growing numbers of people. Electricity, water provision and sewerage can be unpredictable or non-existent. Housing is often of poor quality, and slums and tenements are common in the majority world. The mismatch of people and infrastructure can produce sizeable shanty towns, favelas and barridos. Kibera is a slum on the outskirts of Kenya's capital, Nairobi; it has a population of between 600,000 and 1.2 million people.

Rapidly expanding cities commonly evolve a **dual-sector economy**. The lucky few can find employment within a tiny formal sector with legitimate, unionised and regulated employment. But most people are forced to seek work in a bloated informal sector, where work is at best unregulated and without union protection, and at worst illegal. These are conditions in which organised crime and gang cultures can thrive, and this breeds social problems, from violence to drug abuse and addiction.

■ Colonial legacies

A final critique of majority-world urbanisation, posited by dependency theorists, notes that cities have been intimately entangled with the structures and processes of colonialism and neocolonialism. These structures and processes have shaped the evolution and function of urban areas in ways that maintain exploitative and dependent relationships. Under the colonial era, cities were used as 'staging posts' from which administrators would coordinate the export of raw materials and exploit the surrounding country. According to dependency theorists, this has persisted and executives of large TNCs have taken the place of colonial authorities. In this respect, cities can offer a more comfortable and modern lifestyle, but to a very specific and select elite, consisting of the corporate powers and the local dignitaries which they need to buy off. They can also become large and bloated **primate cities**, sucking and exporting the resources and labour of the surrounding country, and maintaining underdevelopment.

■ Summary questions

14 Give two trends in global urbanisation.

15 Outline three reasons for urban migration.

16 Suggest three problems associated with rapid urbanisation.

17 Give two ways in which colonialism distorted the functioning of majority-world cities.

Education

Learning objectives:

- Examine different models of education as an aspect of development strategy.

- Explore critical perspectives on education.

Fig. 2.2.3 *Many Westerners believe that education is central to personal improvement, and therefore to social development*

Link

See pages 85 and 88 for more on modernisation theory.

Western cultures put great faith in education as a transformative institution through which a person can grow and realise their potential, and through which to ensure a strong and healthy economy supplied with well-qualified workers (Figure 2.2.3). This belief has influenced development policy, and education is central to debates over global inequalities.

Education as a development strategy

Some theorists agree that education has a crucial role to play in international development, but they disagree on the design and purposes of the education systems.

Modernisation theory

Modernisation theorists maintain that education is crucial in overcoming barriers to promoting economic growth. They argue that an education system should be universal and informed by the core principle that the poor world should imitate the rich; they argue that the structure and curriculum of schools should follow the model of Western meritocratic systems. The intent is twofold.

Education is seen to play a vocational role, helping to overcome economic barriers. In this respect, the perspective is informed by the earlier work of functionalist sociologists such as Emile Durkheim and Talcott Parsons, which emphasised the importance of education to Western capitalist societies. The institution is vital, in that it ensures workers are skilled and sorts them by ability into appropriate jobs, an increasingly important function as economies develop and jobs become more specialised. This idea has been developed further by Theodore Schultz (1971) and Gary Becker (1975) in the form of human capital theory. They argue that investment in industrial technologies and infrastructure must be accompanied by investment in human expertise. According to them, this is an efficient use of resources, because equipment loses value over time, but education gains value as parents can pass benefits on to children.

For modernisation theorists, education also performs important functions in overcoming cultural barriers to development. The imposition of Western curriculums shifts knowledge systems away from superstition and folklore to more rational, scientific thought. Bert Hoselitz (1965) also adds that education in the Western model is based on meritocracy, so it transmits values of individualism, competition and achievement. Thus, education can be crucial in breaking down traditional values of collectivism and ascription which, according to modernisation theorists, hinder entrepreneurialism.

People-centred approaches

Like modernisation theorists, people-centred approaches see education as crucial to development. Beyond this, however, they disagree completely. People-centred theorists argue that education should serve the needs of people, rather than the economy. They highlight that without basic skills of literacy and numeracy, individuals are left at risk of being exploited. This is particularly the case where evolving legal systems may lead to land ownership being formalised in written contracts.

Link

See page 87 for more on people-centred approaches.

People-centred theorists also disagree with modernisation theory over the design and structure of education. They argue that haphazardly imposing a Western system may not be appropriate to local contexts and will destroy indigenous cultures and knowledge systems. These theorists remain faithful to their mantra of 'improving not replacing' and seek to build on any existing education provision. They also think that the curriculum should be rooted in existing knowledge systems and maintain sensitivity to the local context.

■ Critical perspectives

Other perspectives are more critical of the blithe assumption that education is intrinsically positive as a development strategy. Different perspectives have different rationales for their critiques.

Neoliberalism

Neoliberalism is most overtly critical of placing state education at the centre of development policy. Neoliberals recognise that education offers benefits but they are critical of any state provision of public services, as this raises taxation and undermines development in two ways:

- It discourages entrepreneurialism by reducing the rewards earned through investment in private enterprise.
- It creates conditions which are less attractive to TNCs.

Instead of focusing on state education, neoliberals advocate opening public services to the private sector, which can provide services more efficiently and without creating a tax burden. This will lead to more entrepreneurialism and higher investment from corporations, raising the general level of wealth. People will then be able to pay for private education and choose their education supplier.

Dependency theory

Like neoliberalism, dependency theory has a critical stance on education. It argues that colonialism left education systems of the majority world stunted, twisted and inappropriate. The imperial powers undermined local knowledge systems, creating a sense of intellectual inferiority, which left the majority world dependent on the minority as a source of truth. Where education systems were allowed to exist, they existed to manipulate local populations by buying off elites with free education and creating the illusion that social mobility was possible. Neocolonial processes have ensured that education systems remain stunted. Debt, for instance, has hindered the majority world's ability to invest in education systems, whereas the imposition of structural adjustment plans has forced governments to cut back spending on public services.

■ Links

See pages 85–86 for more on dependency theory.

■ Take it further

Theorists operating from this perspective are not entirely negative about education. Paulo Freire (1972) argued that education has the potential to be a radical, liberating force, helping people to better understand and change the nature of their lives. For this to happen, there needs to be a shift away from what he calls the **banking model**. Instead, education systems should be collaborative and based on an exchange of expertise between teacher and student. Learn more about Paulo Freire at www.infed. org/thinkers/et-freir.htm.

■ Key terms

Banking model: Paulo Freire's term for education which attempts to fill students with official knowledge, reinscribing power inequalities and discouraging free thought.

■ Summary questions

18 Give two ways in which education might meet the purposes of modernisation theorists.

19 Outline two ways in which people-centred approaches differ from modernisation theorists in their model of education.

20 Explain why neoliberals criticise state-funded education.

21 Give three basic arguments made by dependency theorists on education.

Population and demography

Global development

Learning objectives:

- Explore trends in global population.

- Examine the Malthusian perspective on population growth.

- Evaluate and contrast the Malthusian perspective with alternatives.

Take it further

Explore trends in population at www.xist.org/charts.

The United Nations declared that 12 October 1999 was the symbolic point at which the world's population had reached 6 billion. This was the product of a period of growth, beginning slowly in the late 17th century then rapidly increasing from the turn of the 20th century, when it quadrupled in just 80 years (Figure 2.2.4). This growth was initially driven by the minority world, but growth rates have now largely stabilised or are in decline. It is the majority world that now accounts for global population growth, containing nearly 95 per cent of the world's newborns. The nature, causes and potential effects of population growth are vitally important and could raise challenges for everybody, not just the developing world.

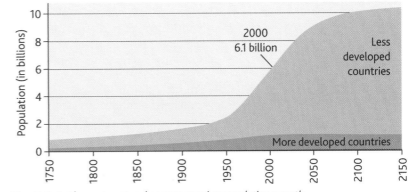

Fig. 2.2.4 *The past century has seen massive population growth*

Malthusianism

For many people, population growth has negative, even apocalyptic connotations. The assumption is that a growth in the number of people is intrinsically harmful as it may produce too many mouths to feed, with calamitous consequences. Although it may seem to be a contemporary concern, it was first articulated at the end of the 18th century by **demographer** Thomas Malthus (Malthus 1798). His ideas have been so dominant, they are often the only ones expressed in debates over population growth.

Key terms

Demography: the statistical study of trends and patterns in population size and structure.

Malthusian checks: man-made or natural disasters which bring down population size.

Malthus' basic argument, the principle of population, was that populations almost inevitably tend to outgrow available food. This is because people can reproduce at a geometric rate – 2, 4, 8, 16, 32, etc. – but agricultural production can only progress arithmetically – 1, 2, 3, 4, 5, etc. Inevitably, there will be a moment of crisis at which the number of people outweighs available food. Nature, according to Malthus, has its own mechanisms to prevent overpopulation in any species. High population leads to famine, disease, perhaps even riots and wars as people fight over scarce resources. In this context, they are known as **Malthusian checks**. According to Malthus, the only way to prevent such 'natural' checks is to encourage people to exercise moral restraint by marrying later and producing fewer children. Indeed, relief efforts such as the welfare state could be counterproductive, as they tackle symptoms not causes, helping to alleviate starvation and allowing the population to grow without limits.

Links

See pages 90–91 for more on the relationships between development and the environment.

See pages 94–95 for more about the impact of development on war and conflict.

See pages 75 and 85 for more on modernisation theory and page 76 for more on neoliberalism.

Key terms

Fertility period: the segment of her life through which a woman is actively producing children.

Agricultural intensification: the process by which food production becomes more industrialised and mechanised, with high use of fertilisers and pesticides to make up for loss of soil fertility.

Neo-Malthusianism

Malthus' arguments were focused mainly on the context of Western Europe during the 19th century. New waves of neo-Malthusian theorists have taken up his legacy and applied the ideas to the global context. The most famous is Paul Ehrlich (1972), who set out the main thrust of the argument in *The Population Bomb*: 'The birth-rate must be brought into balance, or mankind will breed itself into oblivion.'

In a position typical of Malthusian theorists, Ehrlich argues that many of the world's problems stem from a growing population and our difficulty in sustaining it. However, the industrial era and the global context raise more complicated processes than faced Malthus. Contemporary theorists highlight that problems stem not just from demand for food, but also from demand for other resources such as water, oil, metals and minerals, even physical space. The scramble to accumulate and process these goods has generated a new set of disastrous effects, such as pollution, desertification and loss of biodiversity.

A second wave of neo-Malthusian theory has linked overpopulation to political violence. Barbara Harff and Ted Gurr (2002), for instance, conducted an empirical study of the causes of genocides and other civil tensions, such as in Congo and Palestine; they found that competition and environmental scarcity were key variables. Similarly, Catherine Andre and Jean-Phillipe Platteau (1996) apply the Malthusian model to explain the conditions leading up to the Rwandan genocide of 1994.

Neo-Malthusian thought has inspired some development policy. For neoliberals, it provides further evidence that 'aid for aid's sake' can be counterproductive. Modernisation theorists note that high birth rates may be a product of traditional patriarchal cultures, which see masculinity as defined by a man's fertility, and which are attached to religious values that eschew contraception. But for both perspectives, it is important to grasp the central message of Malthusianism and provide interventions which lower birth rates. This might be direct intervention through the provision of contraception or it could be indirect intervention through education, which creates an opportunity to give family planning advice and helps women into employment, which lowers their **fertility period**.

Counter-Malthusian perspectives

Malthusianism is by far the dominant perspective on population, but it is not the only perspective. Other models have challenged the approach, noting that it is based on several flawed assumptions.

Ester Boserup

Danish economist Ester Boserup (1965) challenged the idea that food supply determined population. She argued that agricultural technologies respond to population pressures. When population is low, land is used in an intermittent, unsystematic way and soil fertility is maintained through slash-and-burn techniques and allowing fields to remain fallow. As populations grow, there is a movement towards annual cultivation, with fields used for the whole year. This is far less efficient as soil fertility is lower. Consequently, efforts tend to be focused on **agricultural intensification**, with the development of fertilisers, field preparation and irrigation, pesticides and weed control, accompanied by skilled labour and technology. Boserup's ideas call into question the received wisdom that population growth will inevitably create too many mouths to feed.

Indeed, her arguments seem to have held true in the contemporary world, and global food production has kept pace with increasing population size. Current agricultural output runs at 110 per cent of that necessary to give everybody an adequate diet.

The demographic transition model

A second important challenge to Malthusianism was first proposed by the American demographer Warren Thompson (1929) and later developed by Frank Notestein (1945). The demographic transition model challenges the causal direction at the heart of Malthusianism. It argues that population size does not determine development, but that levels of development lead to changes in population structures. The model is based on observations of the population of minority-world countries as they have industrialised, noting a fairly predictable pattern of four stages, each triggered by social changes linked to development:

Link

The demographic transition model is linked to the epidemiologic transition model on page 88.

- **Stage 1** – birth and death rates are high and subject to significant fluctuation due to outside variables such as natural disasters. The result is a fairly stable and young population.
- **Stage 2** – the death rate begins to fall, linked to improvements in medical science, food production, food distribution and social infrastructure such as sewerage. This creates an imbalance between births and deaths, so a population explosion occurs.
- **Stage 3** – the birth rate also begins to fall. This is, triggered by social changes such as the availability of contraception, secularisation, lower infant mortality (so fewer children are required) and more access to careers for women.
- **Stage 4** – the birth and death rates reach equilibrium, and the population stabilises again.

According to some theorists, many rich nations have now entered a fifth stage associated with deindustrialisation and a shift from manufacturing to service jobs. Birth rates have continued to fall and are below the level needed to replenish the population. This has led to social problems such as a pensions crisis as the population becomes increasingly elderly, and the need for increased immigration.

Hint

The conclusions of the demographic transition model have strong links with modernisation theory's idea that the majority world should follow the path of the minority.

The demographic transition model offers an important challenge to Malthusianism's apocalyptic tendencies. It sees population change as a positive symptom of development and highlights that social checks, not natural checks, will tend to control growth. But it has been criticised on several fronts; for instance, the population changes in the majority world have occurred much more rapidly and without the constantly expanding resources provided by empire.

Overconsumption

A final critique of the Malthusian perspective maintains that population size is a red herring to explain current tensions and challenges. In reality, the planet has the carrying capacity to sustain every person – food production has kept pace with population – and the difficulties arise from patterns of consumption.

In this analysis, the unavoidable conclusion is that the rich world consumes far more than its fair share. In fact, the richest 20 per cent of people consume about 80 per cent of the world's resources, leaving only 20 per cent for the vast majority. In practice, Vittachi (1992) argues that the average inhabitant of the world's richest nations consumes about 20 times as much as their counterpart in the poor world. Obesity is now a major challenge in the minority world. The problem is linked to what is consumed, not just how much.

Westerners have recently developed a habit of eating meat every day, but meat is an incredibly wasteful means of nourishment. The land used to produce 200 kg of cow protein could grow 2,500 kg of crop protein. Similarly, 1 calorie of meat-based energy requires 20 calories of feed; 1 kg of beef requires 15 m³ of water, whereas 1 kg of grain requires just 3 m³ of water. It is estimated that world hunger could be eradicated if 10 per cent of the cereals given to animals were given to people.

Food is not the only resource that is overconsumed by the rich world. It also makes huge demands on raw materials, driving extractive industries such as mining for ores and minerals. Rich-world lifestyles are incredibly oil-thirsty to generate power and to produce plastics for goods and packaging. As a result, Western overconsumption accounts for 80 per cent of global pollution and intensifies conflicts elsewhere in the world.

Theorists have devised the concept of **ecological footprints** to measure the extent of overconsumption. Ecological footprints demonstrate how much land and sea is required, on average, to sustain a particular lifestyle (Table 2.2.1). They can be used to show which nations tend to consume more than their fair share of 2 ha (hectares). The average North American has a footprint of 10 ha and the average European has a footprint of 5 ha (Table 2.2.1). The average Indian has a footprint of 2 ha, a fair share.

Table 2.2.1 *Three lifestyles: number of planets needed to sustain each lifestyle for all the world's population*

Lifestyle	Number of planets
North American	5
European	2.5
Indian	1

Key terms

Ecological footprint: a measure of consumption that uses information on lifestyle to calculate the amount of land and sea needed to sustain a person.

Take it further

Calculate your ecological footprint at http://footprint.wwf.org.uk.

Summary questions

22 How have trends in population changed in recent years?

23 Outline the basic points of the Malthusian perspective on population.

24 Give the criticisms levelled at Malthusianism by three alternative perspectives.

Actors and outcomes

Transnational organisations

Learning objectives:

- Examine different types of TNO.

- Explore controversies over TNOs and the Bretton Woods institutions.

This chapter shifts the focus to some of the actors and institutions that govern and contribute to the processes explored so far. It explores the activities and controversies surrounding a range of transnational organisations (TNOs), agencies which transcend the borders of nation states (Figure 2.3.1).

Fig. 2.3.1 *The Bretton Woods institutions were set up after the Second World War to manage development*

Intergovernmental organisations

Many TNOs are governmental in nature, representing and coordinating the interests of nation states across various aspects of international relations. It is possible to classify them by function:

- **Legal-political institutions** have the broadest remit and represent countries on a range of issues. They include the United Nations, the European Union and the African Union.

- **Economic organisations** focus on monetary policy and trade agreements. They include the Bretton Woods institutions (see below) and other agencies such as the Organisation of Petroleum Exporting Countries (OPEC).

- **Special-remit organisations** have a specific purpose, such as the global policing network, Interpol, the World Health Organisation (WHO) and the International Organisation for Standardisation (ISO).

Intergovernmental organisations (IGOs) can be classified by membership criteria. Some operate on a global or regional basis, such as the United Nations and the European Union, respectively. Others have more specific membership criteria, such as shared history for the Commonwealth and economic ties for OPEC. The three Bretton Woods institutions are perhaps the most powerful and controversial IGOs involved in international development. They are named after the venue of a conference following the Second World War.

■ **World Bank Group** – five different agencies tasked with providing loans and advice on economic development and poverty reduction.

■ **International Monetary Fund (IMF)** – it oversees the management of the global economy and tries to ensure that turbulence in one country does not disturb others.

■ **World Trade Organisation (WTO)** – it negotiates trade agreements to remove barriers and engineer a free market. The WTO was technically not established until 1995 but its foundations were laid at the Bretton Woods conference in the form of the General Agreement on Tariffs and Trade (Gatt).

The Bretton Woods institutions aimed to provide a centralised method of carefully planning and delivering development in an efficient way. Advocates say the institutions can draw on a vast array of academic expertise and significant resources, potentially invaluable for majority-world governments.

The Bretton Woods institutions have been the target of considerable criticism. This is because they represent a notably neoliberal agenda with a strong commitment to the principles of the free market and the process of trade liberalisation. They attract the attentions of those who oppose the perspective, as figureheads of its potentially malign effects on the world's poorest people. Critics have also noted that the organisations are run in an undemocratic fashion; decision-making is weighted towards the world's richest nations. This is because the institutions are run on a dollar per vote basis; those who contribute the most dollars have the most say over what they do. The richest industrialised countries can ensure that any decisions do not harm their economic interests, and this may be at the expense of less affluent and less influential nations.

■ Non-governmental organisations

Non-governmental organisations (NGOs) are independent of national governments and may operate internationally; a good example is the charity Oxfam. Anheier *et al.* (2001) estimate that 40,000 NGOs operate in the global community. It is possible to classify NGOs by their activities, and the World Bank distinguishes two broad types:

■ **Operational NGOs** focus on implementing development-related initiatives and projects. They include organisations such as Oxfam, WaterAid, Christian Aid and Islamic aid. They can be subdivided according to whether they focus on development or relief, whether they are religious or secular, and by the stakeholder groups they work with.

■ **Advocacy NGOs** focus on lobbying to defend or promote a cause. They concentrate on environmental concerns, such as Greenpeace, or human and social rights issues, such as Amnesty International, or a combination of the two.

NGOs are normally subject to the laws and regulations of their countries of origin and operation, except for the International Committee of the Red Cross. This agency is a sovereign entity with all the legal rights and protections of a nation state; it is answerable only to itself and the international community, not to any single country. The Red Cross needs this independence and protection as it was created to monitor whether nations comply with humanitarian law outlined in the Geneva Convention.

Transnational corporations

Perhaps the most controversial form of international organisation is the transnational corporation (TNC). The earliest example is probably the Dutch East India Company, which was granted charter by the Netherlands in 1602 to administer colonial business. The past century has seen a massive explosion in the number and size of TNCs, and this has generated significant debate.

Positive perspectives

For some commentators, TNCs are a vital engine for economic growth. Neoliberals note, for instance, that **foreign direct investment** provides a means of bringing capital, expertise and technology to the majority world without the risks of aid. Furthermore, corporations create employment and an opportunity for local people to earn a higher income, which might then be reinvested. Critics argue that TNCs pay low wages, but neoliberals say that TNC wages are still higher than the pre-TNC wages and that the local cost of living must be considered.

Modernisation theorists add that TNCs can be important in promoting cultural change. They are likely to have modern employment practices, transmitting values such as competition, achievement and individualism, and may be more likely to employ women. Finally, Eskeland and Harrison (1997) analysed TNC activities and found that their tendency to use newer technology not only modernises the economy, but is also far better for the environment than the practices of local companies.

In order to attract TNCs, countries are advised to follow structural adjustment plans, cutting back on red tape and taxation, and removing barriers to the global market. Countries increasingly create **free trade zones**.

Negative perspectives

Other theorists echo dependency theory in highlighting that TNC activity often has exploitative undertones. There is significant evidence that large companies abuse labour, environment and markets in the majority world.

According to George Soros (1998, 2000), the growing size and power of corporations is partly linked to the collapse of communism, which left capitalism as an unchallenged ideology. The resulting rise of extreme neoliberal policy, which he calls **market fundamentalism**, has created an environment of uncontrolled capitalism. TNCs grow until their power outstrips democratic processes, and they are able to pursue their only instinct – to return profits – without limit. Theorists such as Elmar Altvater (1998) think the result of these processes is a growing 'disconnect' in which it is difficult to 'embed' TNCs in the moral, legal and political frameworks of civil society. In other words, the global economic environment is one where no agency can bring large corporations to order.

There are several aspects to this context. One dimension is that TNCs are so large that majority-world economies become dependent on their activities. This gives corporations the power to influence lawmaking and enforcement, and they can demand preferential treatment by threatening to move operations elsewhere. Nike, for instance, has a common practice of pulling production away from countries when workers' wages begin to rise. More dramatically, Nigeria is heavily reliant on the oil producer

Global development

Key terms

Foreign direct investment: technical term for the corporate investment in facilities or outlets within a nation.

Free trade zones: regions in the majority world where legislation and taxation are reduced to a minimum, in the hope of attracting corporate investment.

Market fundamentalism: coined by George Soros to describe the strong neoliberal belief that the free market should govern all human affairs and the resultant compulsion to remove barriers to this free market.

Take it further

Find out more about unethical corporate activity at www. corpwatch.org but remember this is an anti-corporation website.

Royal Dutch–Shell, which has used its position to ensure its operations continue unhindered by the protests of local communities such as the Ogoni. These conflicts came to the fore in 1995, when the Nigerian government hanged eight local protesters, prompting international outrage.

A further problem arises from the fact that corporations operate in different countries, with different legal systems. They can pick and mix the laws that govern them and use loopholes to ensure maximum profitability. Nestlé and various corporations have missold powdered baby formula to mothers in the majority world. This has included misleading advertising, such as images of nurses, and giving away free samples until parents become dependent on the powdered product. WHO estimates that, where this activity has occurred, it has increased infant mortality by about 25 times as parents are forced to dilute the formula with unsafe water. Although the corporations have broken laws in their country of origin, this patent malpractice continues, largely because many poor countries have no legal framework for advertising.

Corporations can use their subsidiaries to avoid prosecution. In 1984 lack of safety precautions at the Union Carbide chemical plant in Bhopal, India, led to a gas leak which engulfed the town. More than 3,000 were killed, and many more have died or suffered long-term illness. Union Carbide has distanced itself from the disaster and blames the local factory administration for the breach. Similar strategies are adopted by clothing manufacturers. Gap and Nike subcontract clothing production to local factories and say that any sweatshop conditions are due to the local management.

A final challenge is how to punish TNCs which act in questionable ways. This relates to a lack of global laws and the institutions to enforce them. Corporations are subject to a collection of inconsistent and sometimes contradictory rules. The manner of punishment can also be problematic; fines are often insignificant compared to massive TNC turnovers, so TNCs have a high rate of recidivism.

Summary questions

1. Give three types of IGO.
2. Identify one strength and one controversy associated with the Bretton Woods institutions.
3. Give two types of NGO.
4. Outline two positive effects of TNCs.
5. Identify three reasons why corporations are able to act in unethical ways.

Gender

Learning objectives:

- Examine how women experience inequality.

- Explore different explanations of gender inequality.

- Evaluate and contrast different approaches to address gender inequalities.

Key terms

Horizontal segregation: where men and women in the same class do different jobs; for example, women do care work and men do computer work.

Vertical segregation: segregation according to pay and status. High-status and high-paid occupations are more likely to go to men.

People within nations can have different experiences. According to Amartya Sen (1992), ignoring these specific experiences has created 100 million women 'lost' to the effects of development (Figure 2.3.2). He argues that gender inequalities tend to surface in seven ways:

- **Nationality** – the patriarchal culture of some countries leads to child gender preference. As a result, baby girls have been victims of abandonment, infanticide and sex-selective abortion.
- **Mortality** – women generally outlive men, but there are areas of the world where this does not hold true, notably North Africa, China and South Asia.
- **Basic facilities** – across the developing world, women lack access to institutions, particularly education, which could enable them to profit from their abilities.
- **Special opportunities** – beyond basic provision, women encounter even greater barriers. They are particularly restricted in the context of higher education and training.
- **Professional** – **horizontal segregation** and **vertical segregation** in the workplace restrict women's opportunities, so they are under-represented in professions.
- **Ownership** – assets such as property are shared unevenly in many societies. This can restrict women's social influence, and their ability to engage in business and commerce.
- **Household** – power within families may favour men and may skew decision-making. The expectation that women do housework can further limit their access to employment.

Many of Sen's observations are not confined to the majority world, and hold true in many developed nations.

Explaining gender inequality

According to Susan Tiano (1994), there are three broad perspectives in explaining gender inequalities; they can be characterised using two of our core theoretical perspectives, modernisation theory and dependency theory.

Modernisation theory

Link

See pages 75 and 88 for more on modernisation theory.

Modernisation theorists tend to subscribe to what Tiano calls the integration thesis. They maintain that traditional cultures are patriarchal and emphasise ascribed statuses. As a result, women are locked into subordinate lives from birth. It is only with modernisation that women are integrated into mainstream society. These theorists also see gender inequalities as a barrier to development, because it prevents 50 per cent of the population from engaging in economic activity.

Dependency theory

Link

See page 68 for more on dependency theory.

Modernisation theory sees gender inequality as an inherent feature of traditional society, whereas dependency theories hold that patriarchy has been imposed on the majority world. They argue that colonial powers

Global development

brought with them a patriarchal culture, which replaced the existing cultures which were gradually discouraged. But there is some internal debate about whether this was an active or passive process.

According to what Tiano calls the marginalisation thesis, the creation of gender inequalities was a passive process, born of the systematic failure to include women in the public sphere, and relegating them to the private, domestic arena. The colonial powers introduced cash economies based on paid employment, which absorbed male members of the population but left women in the home and reliant on their husbands. Patriarchal bias in aid has further contributed to the contemporary marginalisation of women, with projects disproportionately targeting men.

Tiano's exploitation thesis implies that gender inequalities have been actively created, as capitalism needs a patriarchal system to exist. In part, this is because women in the domestic sphere perform unpaid labour for the capitalist system, such as housework and raising the next generation of workers. In addition, they provide a cheap and easily exploited source of formal labour for large corporations. For instance, Daisy Francis (1995) found that over 85 per cent of workers on low wages and in poor conditions in free trade zones were female.

Fig. 2.3.2 *Women who spend time fetching water may be socially and economically isolated*

Addressing inequalities

Modernisation theory

According to modernisation theorists such as Ronald Inglehart (1997), diminishing gender inequality is an inevitable outcome of industrialisation. Based on data from 43 societies, he argues that economic development, cultural change and political change go hand in hand. He notes, however, that there can often be a generational lag in the impact of economic change on world views. To promote cultural change, modernisation theorists advocate a familiar combination of education and mass media, funded by aid. They also see a place for TNCs, which will have more modern employment practices and allow women to access jobs.

People-centred approaches

Initiatives derived from a people-centred approach have been crucial in trying to tackle gender inequality. Their potency lies in their focus on communities and individuals, allowing them to work directly with women on the ground. The perspective generally expresses commitment to social sustainability, which implies development that incorporates all members of society, allowing everybody to benefit in the long term. People-centred theorists evaluate their strategies not on their overall effect, but on whether any benefits are shared throughout the community. Their education, health care and trade projects set out to ensure the inclusion of women, and many specifically target them. Some further people-centred strategies have been used to provide practical solutions to gender inequities. Microcredit, though now more widely available, has always had a core aim of targeting women, allowing them access to the resources needed to improve their lives through investment and enterprise.

Link

See page 67 for more on people-centred perspectives.

Take it further

Find out more about strategies to address gender inequality in two different settings at www.womenstrust.org and https://promujer.org.

Summary questions

6 Identify at least three of Sen's dimensions of gender inequality.

7 Briefly explain Tiano's three explanations of gender inequality.

8 Explain the key differences between the solutions to gender inequality suggested by modernisation theory and people-centred approaches.

Health

Global development

Learning objectives:

- Explore global patterns of health and illness.

- Examine competing explanations of majority-world health.

- Outline different approaches to addressing health inequalities.

Key terms

Mortality rate: the death rate per 1,000 of the population in a given country.

Morbidity rate: prevalence of disease; the extent or degree of prevalence of disease in a district or country.

Communicable disease: a disease that can be caught, such as malaria, typhoid and diphtheria.

Diseases of consumption: illnesses associated with particular behaviours and lifestyle choices, such as cancers and heart disease.

Take it further

Got to www.who.int and find out more about global health.

Link

See pages 75 and 85 for more on modernisation theory. See page 79 for more on the demographic transition model, which is linked to the epidemiologic transition model.

Link

See pages 68 and 76 for more on dependency theory.

Causes of illness vary across the world and throughout history; patterns in health are crucially influenced by development. Thomas McKeown (1988) argues that, historically, **mortality rates** and **morbidity rates** in the minority world were driven by **communicable diseases** and those linked to poor living standards and nutrition, such as measles and tuberculosis. But as these nations have developed, illness has shifted and **diseases of consumption** are now far more prevalent.

Health in the majority world remains hindered by traditional diseases. In addition, diseases associated with the rich world, such as heart disease, are a small but growing problem, creating a dual burden of traditional and modern illnesses. The HIV/AIDS pandemic has had a big effect on the majority world. Sub-Saharan Africa has 70 per cent of cases and 36 per cent of adults in Botswana are infected. HIV/AIDS affects what should be the most productive demographic, so it severely undermines development.

Explaining health inequalities

Why do different patterns of health and illness occur? That is the most fundamental question in this chapter. Theoretical perspectives on development offer different explanations.

Modernisation theory

Modernisation theorists see changes in health as linked to the progression towards a point of social maturity, and the shift from traditional medical practices to modern technologies and interventions. Some theorists therefore argue that development brings a series of predictable stages in health. Abdel Omran (1971) proposed a model of health called the epidemiologic transition model, three stages through which he says all societies will pass as they develop:

- **Pestilence and famine** – infectious and parasitic diseases are widespread. Death rates and infant mortality are therefore high and life expectancy is low.

- **Receding pandemics** – this follows improvements to sanitation, hygiene and nutrition. The prevalence of communicable illness begins to fall, consolidated by improvements in education, technologies and sewerage.

- **Degenerative and man-made diseases** – communicable illness falls to negligible levels and people die from longer-term diseases linked to lifestyle.

Although this basic framework remains dominant, other theorists have added to it. Most notably, Rogers and Hackenberg (1987) add a fourth stage, the hybristic stage. In the hybristic stage, overconfidence in the medical profession results in self-destructive behaviours such as smoking, hence a massive and alarming rise in degenerative and man-made diseases.

Dependency theory

Modernisation theory sees ill health in the majority world as rooted with internal processes, whereas dependency theorists emphasise the role of external pressures in creating and maintaining patterns of ill health. In part, the perspective emphasises the long-term effects of colonialism.

The imperial powers undermined indigenous knowledge systems, ensuring that the majority world had few health-care structures on which to build. They inadvertently introduced new diseases which devastated populations and further undermined existing health care.

Dependency theorists point to a range of contemporary, neocolonial processes which maintain and extend poor health in the majority world. This is linked to the continued stunting of health-care systems by the imposition of structural adjustment plans that compel governments to cut back spending on public services. This perspective implicates corporate activity. Pharmaceutical companies have prevented poor countries from producing cheap generic drugs such as antiretrovirals for HIV. More broadly implicated are the dumping of unhealthy sugar-based food and the unethical selling of products such as powdered baby milk, together with the poor environmental practices of corporations.

Addressing health inequalities

Improving majority-world health is bound up with a range of other factors, such as access to nutrition, safe water and good education. Different theoretical perspectives have divergent ideas on the nature and scale of health-care provision.

Modernisation theory

For modernisation theorists, the transition away from communicable disease can only be realised by replacing traditional health-care practices and technologies, based on superstition and ritual, with more modern ones rooted in scientific inquiry. To this end, the perspective emphasises the need to establish centralised primary health care in the Western model – hospitals and GP practices in areas of major population – and the provision of mass inoculation campaigns. Directed financial aid is needed to realise this aim, plus expertise and technology from Western countries and corporations.

The approach advocated by modernisation theorists has been popular, and can be effective in reaching large numbers of people. But critics argue that it marginalises the majority of people who live in rural areas and who cannot access centralised provision. It can lead to an emphasis on treatment rather than prevention, and to neglect of more fundamental priorities.

People-centred approaches

In contrast to modernisation theory, people-centred approaches aim to improve and build on existing provision, providing training and resources to health-care workers already active in the majority world. This approach is less centralised and far more community-focused. The advantage is that it can reach people spread across rural areas, and it uses the trust already invested in local healers. Critics have noted that, like many people-centred initiatives, it is inefficient at producing large-scale changes.

Link

See pages 75 and 85 for more on modernisation theory.

Link

See pages 75–76 and 87 for more on people-centred approaches.

Global development

Summary questions

9 Identify how patterns in minority-world health have changed.

10 Give three types of illness in the majority world.

11 Outline the three stages of the epidemiologic transition.

12 Give three factors which, according to dependency theory, have affected majority-world health.

13 Contrast the two models of majority-world health care.

Environment

Learning objectives:

- Examine the relationship between development and the environment.

- Explore contrasting methods of managing the environmental impact of development.

Take it further

Find out about environmental issues using NGO websites such as www.greenpeace.org.uk and www.foe.co.uk and by reading the Guardian's environment pages at www.guardian.co.uk/environment.

Key terms

Externalities: costs or benefits arising from production of goods and services which are not reflected in market prices, but which may well have an effect on the well-being of people or environments.

Link

See pages 83–84 for more on TNCs.

The relationship between development and environment sparks many crucial debates. The process of development seems to lead inevitably to environmental harm. At the same time, some question whether the rich world, already benefiting from the spoils of development, has any right to deny development to the poor. This raises important questions of responsibilities and entitlements plus practical challenges in finding workable and equitable ways forward.

The origins of environmental damage

Some theorists think environmental damage is an inevitable consequence of development, at least of the Western capitalist industrial model of development. Some think this is because the Western lifestyle is driven by ever greater consumption, which must be met by mass production on an industrial scale and corresponding demands on resources and pollution.

Other critics emphasise the dominance of corporations as an element of the Western example of development. TNCs, they argue, are inherently environmentally toxic, as their sole objective is to pursue ever greater profits for their shareholders. A key way of doing this is by creating **externalities**, and environmental problems become a way of pushing costs of production onto other social actors. Essentially, these two positions disagree on whether capitalist environmental damage is a product of demand, implicating lifestyle, or supply, focusing on corporate activity, or a combination of the two.

It is simplistic to assume a one-way correlation in which increasing development leads to increasing environmental damage. It may be that poverty forces individuals to exploit their environment to ensure their own survival. People in Central Africa commonly rely on bush meats, wild meats often from threatened species such as the gorilla. This is partly linked to tradition, hence cultural factors, but the overwhelming cause is poverty, which leaves families with no alternative sustenance.

Environmental management

Many organisations have turned their attention to developing strategies aimed at addressing some of the environmental challenges associated with development. These strategies can be put into two broad categories:

- **Top-down strategies** work as the transnational level, creating legislation to limit environmental damage.
- **Bottom-up strategies** focus on communities, enabling them to manage and protect local environments more effectively.

The rest of this section will briefly consider examples from each category.

Top-down approaches

Perhaps the most straightforward approach to environmental protection is through international treaties to curb pollution and resource use and to protect habitats. It has the potential to enact wide-ranging impacts, but critics argue that it crudely blocks economic growth for rich and poor alike. Furthermore, the international community have struggled to obtain universal agreements, and lack the power to enforce the agreements they get.

A more subtle top-down environmental initiative is emissions trading. Here a fair share of pollution is allocated to each nation, its corporations and individuals. If a business or country needs to use more than this share, they have to purchase the rights allocated to another. This has two aims. Firstly, it aims to reduce externalities and create incentives to adopt more sustainable practices. Secondly, it aims to create a means of redistributing wealth as the rich, who make more environmental demands, must purchase emission rights from the poor.

The approach has been criticised. Some neoliberal critics say that intentional distortion of the market is misplaced. It limits economic growth, and with it the ability of corporations to invest in development of more efficient technology. Other critics are uneasy that emissions trading takes privatisation to an extreme conclusion. The air that we breathe becomes commodified – capable of being owned, bought and sold – opening up new forms of inequality and exploitation.

Bottom-up approaches

Some theorists think that a more effective and less bureaucratic approach to environmental protection is to empower local people to become custodians of their own local habitats. This is common to people-centred initiatives. For instance, fair-trade cooperatives are often accredited based on preservation of biodiversity on farmland. In contrast to large agribusiness, small farmers are well equipped to do this, as they do not need to clear vast areas of land to make space for crop monocultures.

An alternative approach is through sustainable tourism, in which resorts or attractions are created with the dual purpose of preserving biodiversity and promoting economic growth for local communities. For example, the Komodo National Park in Indonesia uses income from tourism to fund wildlife preservation, while creating employment and other economic opportunities for local people.

The key advantage of this form of approach is that it preserves habitats and allows local people to pursue better standards of life. In the regions where they operate, the approaches can also be extremely effective at preserving biodiversity and ensuring sustainability. However, the strategies are inevitably small-scale, and do not offer a means to address global warming and other challenges that require international cooperation.

Link

See page 68 for more on neoliberalism.

Global development

Link

See pages 75–76 and 87 for more on people-centred approaches; see page 70 for more on fair trade.

Summary questions

14 Give two reasons why development might lead to environmental damage.

15 Outline one way in which underdevelopment might threaten environments.

16 Explain the difference between top-down and bottom-up approaches to environmental management.

17 Outline two strengths and two limitations of emissions trading.

18 Give two examples of bottom-up strategies for environmental management.

19 Outline one strength and one limitation of bottom-up strategies for environmental management.

Employment

Global development

Learning objectives:

- Examine the historical context of changes to employment.
- Explore the impacts of globalisation on employment markets.
- Outline some of the responses to this impact.

Link

See pages 75 and 85 for more on modernisation theory.

Key terms

Cottage industries: small, home-based enterprises focused on the production of a particular product, such as low-yield textiles.

Taylorism: a European movement which tried to improve the efficiency of production by adopting scientific principles and the standardisation of job functions and routines.

Fordism: a North American strategy to improve profits by giving workers increasingly specialised and simple functions in the production chain.

Conjugal roles: a term used to describe the division of labour (who does what) within the family.

The process of development is intimately connected with economic change, and for most people these changes are most directly experienced through shifts in the nature of work and employment.

Modernisation theory

Some sociologists have argued that development is a predictable process, based fundamentally on economic principles. This implies that employment, too, will evolve in a predictable way. They observe a set of distinct stages through which the nature of work changes as a society progresses, stages that mirror the theoretical basis of modernisation theory.

In early social organisation, home and work are indistinguishable; the economy is entirely informal and there is no concept of employment. Small groups hunt and gather sustenance. As these groups develop into more formal social structures, agriculture or nomadic herding may begin to emerge, but there is no real distinction between home and work. Most families do subsistence farming, rather than profit-making activities. At the point of colonialism, work in many African regions took this form, and it continues to be dominant in many parts of sub-Saharan Africa.

Some basic exchange between individuals eventually begins to develop together with some limited specialisation. This leads to the emergence of small **cottage industries**. The division between home and work remains blurred, as employment is essentially within the family and often occurs inside the home. This mode of employment was dominant across much of India at the onset of British imperialism, focused particularly on textile production.

It is only really with industrialisation that the employment sphere became separate from the domestic sphere. Mechanisation caused most of the population to become employed in the true sense, and in buildings separate from their place of residence. The process also sees increasing specialisation among workers, each performing a specific task in the production process. This model of employment was further refined in Western Europe by **Taylorism**, which attempted to organise workplaces through scientific principles and standardisation of jobs and routines. Taylorism was shortly followed in the US by **Fordism**, after the car manufacturer Ford, which simplified tasks to make greater profits using unskilled workers.

These changes in employment also bring broader social, political and cultural changes. Increased specialisation, for instance, creates a demand for more universal education, as the family cannot transfer all necessary skills. Furthermore, shifts in employment towards industrial ends drive urban migration and even affect **conjugal roles** in the family.

Employment and globalisation

Modernisation theorists see industrialisation and its impact on employment as the endpoint of development. Other commentators have increasingly noted that employment has once again changed over the past 40 years, in a complicated response to processes related to globalisation. These shifts have affected the majority world and minority world in reciprocal ways.

The most fundamental of these changes has been a shift in unskilled manual work away from the minority world to poorer regions and countries. The key to this shift is the abundant cheap labour in the majority world, which allows TNCs to cut costs and extract higher profits. Consequently, poor countries such as Bangladesh have seen an explosion of employment opportunities for outsourced manufacturing, fuelling a shift away from rural lifestyles and traditional jobs. Rich nations have seen significant deindustrialisation, with a decline in traditionally working-class manufacturing jobs. This has been accompanied by a rise in service sector employment, facilitated by new information and communication technologies.

Such is the magnitude of these changes that some theorists argue the minority world has entered a new post-Fordist phase. The idea of a job for life has disappeared, and employers need people with broad skills, initiative and the ability to acquire new competencies independently, not the ability to follow orders for monotonous, simple tasks, as under Fordism. Since 2001 there has been a further wave of shifts. Advances in telecoms technologies have allowed newer working-class jobs, e.g. call-centre work, to be outsourced to rapidly developing countries such as India, where they are coveted by an aspiring middle class.

There is disagreement about the nature of the employment changes created by globalisation. For some theorists, particularly neoliberal theorists, the shifts represent a success of the free market, with employment markets able to offer the skill set they can provide most competitively. Others have been more critical. The loss of traditional working-class employment has produced an outcry in the minority world and has even been implicated in broader social problems, such as the educational underachievement of working-class boys. Furthermore, critics note that the inequalities created by Fordism have been polarised across the world; manual work is outsourced to poor people with extremely low pay and dismal working conditions.

 Link

See page 68 for more on neoliberalism.

Summary questions

20 Identify five stages of development in employment markets identified by modernisation theorists.

21 Identify two effects of globalisation on the structure of employment.

22 Give two criticisms associated with the impact of globalisation on employment.

War and conflict

Learning objectives:

- Describe how global development may lead to crime, conflict and insecurity.

- Examine case studies on processes that lead to crime, conflict and insecurity.

Links

Dependency theorists focus on the long-term legacies of colonialism; see pages 68 and 76 for more on dependency theorists.

A slump in coffee prices precipitated the Rwandan genocide. The slump was linked to the collapse of the International Coffee Agreement (ICA), which set a minimum price for coffee. The ICA faltered in the face of a neoliberal agenda that saw it as distorting the free market.

Take it further

Go to http://news.bbc.co.uk/hi/english/static/in_depth/south_asia/2002/india_pakistan/timeline/default.stm and read about the conflict between Pakistan and India.

Link

See pages 77–80 and pages 90–91 for more about perspectives on population and environment.

In recent years there has been a growing awareness that global conflicts and insecurities are inseparable from inequalities in power and wealth. Some sociologists have argued that tackling global poverty and creating a more equitable world not only satisfies a moral imperative but might also make the planet safer. This section examines three dimensions through which development might be linked to conflict and insecurity.

Colonial legacies

Some conflicts have origins in colonialism. The imperial powers reshaped the geography and politics of their dominions, and some argue that this created a 'time bomb' which would inevitably result in civil conflicts and even genocides.

The Rwandan genocide of 1994, in which over 1 million people died, was partly precipitated by the actions of colonial powers, first German then Belgian, in giving preference to the Tutsi people over their Hutu neighbours. The result was an undercurrent of resentment in Rwanda, which boiled into a violent backlash, fuelled by economic problems brought on by a slump in coffee prices. A similarly destructive process occurred with the religious partition of India at the end of British rule in 1947, creating Pakistan and Bangladesh (Figure 2.3.3). The immediate mass migration caused conflict over local land, followed by long-lived hostility between the two nuclear powers and focused on the border region of Kashmir.

Current tensions in Iraq could be partly linked to colonial processes. Iraq was 'invented' by the League of Nations, forerunner to the UN, following the collapse of the Ottoman Empire. It grouped together diverse ethnicities, Arab and Kurd, and religions, notably Sunni and Shi'ite Muslims. In this context, dictatorial leaders such as Saddam Hussein provided the only means of unification. Without this artificial source of order, it is feared that traditional hostilities might surface again.

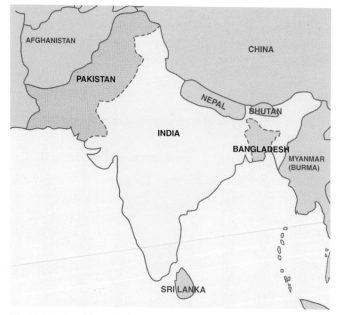

Fig. 2.3.3 *Partition of India has led to long-term conflicts and instabilities*

Environment

Conflict can also originate from the way environments are used. At the most basic level, this can relate to growing demand for land and water to produce food, or for declining natural resources such as oil. From a neo-Malthusian perspective, these problems are a product of overpopulation; conflicts act as a form of Malthusian check. Other perspectives argue that they are a problem linked to overconsumption by the rich world, which exports crises to sustain its own lifestyle.

The process of climate change is likely to intensify local and international conflicts. Its effects will probably be more acute in the minority world; they are already being felt among some of the world's most vulnerable communities. The conflict in Darfur is partly fuelled by desertification of arable land, which creates competition between herding and agricultural communities.

Local environments can also be a site of conflict and insecurity, particularly where stakeholders have different perspectives on how land and resources should be used. Shell extracts and processes oil in the Niger Delta. The local Ogoni people complain that oil leakages pollute their land and that gas flares pollute the air. Frustrated by a lack of success, protest groups have become increasingly militant; some Shell employees have been kidnapped and equipment has been sabotaged. The Nigerian government has taken draconian action to prevent Ogoni protests; 80 protesters have been killed and in 1995 the government executed the protest leader Ken Saro-Wiwa and eight other people.

Link

See pages 83–84 for more on the nature and impact of TNCs on the environment.

Globalisation

The broad process of globalisation can also be seen as a source of insecurity. Increased migration has produced local conflicts, with tensions emerging between existing communities and new immigrants, and a rise in far right politics. International terrorism can be linked to globalisation; growing interconnections between nations act as a catalyst and facilitator for conflict. Groups such as Al-Qaeda are motivated by resistance to perceived American cultural imperialism, particularly in sacred places. Its transnational and decentralised operations are made possible by the same communication technologies that help globalisation.

Some theorists think that the neoliberal agenda at the heart of the current wave of globalisation has been a source of local conflict, particularly where neoliberal policies have allowed large TNCs to take private ownership of public services. In the late 1990s, the water supply of the Bolivian city of Cochabamba was privatised by Bechtel at the behest of the World Bank. Within weeks, connection fees had risen beyond the reach of most people, so they organised mass protests. When the government responded with armed police, 175 people were injured and there were 6 deaths.

Links

See pages 63–66 for more on globalisation.

See pages 83–84 for more on the nature and impact of TNCs on globalisation. See page 68 for more on neoliberal policy.

The impact of war and conflict

War and conflict also create substantial barriers to development. On the broadest level, internal divisions caused by civil conflicts can prevent effective governance, as in Somalia, and can divert national revenue to arms instead of development. The overspill from conflict can also destroy infrastructure and leave land dangerous, strewn with mines and unexploded ordnance. This reduces resources for development and makes countries unattractive to outside investment. Finally, war and conflict devastate working populations, lead to migration and dislocation, interrupt education and create orphans and the war-injured, which diverts development spending to care.

Summary questions

23 Give two examples of how colonialism may have created conditions for future conflict.

24 Give three ways in which the environment might be a source of conflict and insecurity.

25 Identify three examples of globalisation as a catalyst for local and global insecurities.

26 Identify at least four ways in which conflict may act as a barrier to development.

Topic summary

- Development is a contested concept; there are several ways to define and measure the process – economic and human.

- Modernisation theorists see development as a process of becoming like the rich world, arguing that industrialisation will bring with it economic growth and cultural maturity.

- Neoliberals argue that development is built through trade, and is predicated on a free market. They therefore set out to reduce barriers which might distort this market.

- Dependency theorists highlight that poverty and underdevelopment are not natural and have been created through exploitation under colonialism and neocolonialism.

- Counter-industrial movements highlight that the Western development path brings with it environmental and social costs. They advocate more people-centred development approaches.

- The process of globalisation frames the topic, with economic, cultural and political themes. Debates on the process focus on whether it is positive or negative.

- Aid is seen as crucial by modernisation theorists and people-centred approaches, although they disagree over its focus and purpose.

- Trade is central to the neoliberal stance. Dependency theory is critical, arguing that trade occurs on unfair grounds. People-centred approaches have created fair-trade projects which attempt to even these odds.

- Industrialisation has also been an emphasis of modernisation theory, and there are competing methods of managing the process. Other perspectives are dubious that it is a desirable development path.

- Push and pull factors have led to urban growth. Modernisation theorists see this as positive. Critics highlight the problems associated with urban sprawl and the impact of colonialism on majority-world cities.

- Education has often been a central development strategy for modernisation theorists and people-centred approaches. Neoliberals are critical of public services as they create a tax burden. Dependency theorists highlight that education can perform ideological functions but it has the potential to be liberating.

- Malthusian perspectives see population growth as damaging. Others see it as a symptom of development that will self-regulate. And some argue that patterns of consumption are more important than population sizes.

- Transnational organisations (TNOs) are large organisations that operate on an international scale; they can be governmental or non-governmental. Some theorists think transnational corporations (TNCs) drive economic growth and others see them as exploitative.

- Women in developing countries experience extreme inequality. Some explanations emphasise internal factors and others emphasise external factors.

- Health patterns change over time and between countries. There is debate over whether ill health in the majority world is caused by internal or external factors.

- The impact of development on the environment has become an increasingly important topic of debate. Two competing approaches attempt to protect the biosphere.

- Employment shifts as countries develop, and there is some evidence that globalisation is affecting job markets in the rich and poor worlds.

- War and insecurity can be caused by underdevelopment; conflicts can have a detrimental effect on a country's ability to develop.

Further resources

To develop your understanding and boost your exam score, one of the best things you can do is to find contemporary examples and illustrations of the ideas in this chapter.

Websites

- www.newint.org
  New Internationalist is a monthly magazine on global issues. All articles from the past decade are stored online; the Mega Index is particularly useful

- www.guardian.co.uk
  The *Guardian* is a British newspaper. Its environment section and the comment blogs are especially useful, but the rest of the website is also worth reading

Television

- *Unreported World*
  This is a long-running documentary on Channel 4 television; it gives in-depth coverage of issues facing the majority world

Films

A recent spate of documentary and Hollywood films explore issues of global development. Here are four that are especially worth watching:

- *The Corporation* (2006)

- *Blood Diamond* (2006)

- *Hotel Rwanda* (2005)

- *The Last King of Scotland* (2006)

Books

You could explore these books to extend your theoretical understanding:

- Joel Bakan, *The Corporation*, Robinson, 2005

- Noam Chomsky, *Understanding Power*, Vintage, 2003

- Paul Collier, *The Bottom Billion*, Oxford University Press, 2007

- Susan George, *Another World is Possible If …*, Verso, 2004

- Jeffrey Sachs, *The End of Poverty*, Penguin, 2005

- Joseph Stiglitz, *Globalisation and its Discontents*, Penguin, 2003

AQA Examination-style questions

General Certificate of Education
Advanced Level Examination
Section B from Paper 3

SOCIOLOGY Unit 3
For this paper you must have:
a 12-page answer book
Time allowed 1 hour 30 minutes

SAMPLE 1

Section B: Global Development

If you choose this Section, answer Question 4 and either Question 5 or Question 6.

Total for this section: 60 marks

4   Read Item B below and answer parts (a) and (b) that follow.

> **Item B**
>
> Over the last fifty years there has been a rapid growth in more affluent
> countries of charities seeking to address global poverty and its impact
> on the inhabitants of Third World societies. Many of these charities are
> now highly professional in their organisation, and therefore increasingly
> indistinguishable from more established international agencies run by
> bodies such as the United Nations. A particular feature has been the huge
> growth in celebrity-led organisations such as Live Aid, Live 8 and so on.
>
> Supporters of such organisations argue that because they are less likely
> to be seen as politically-motivated and have huge media appeal, they are
> more effective at getting aid quickly to those who are in the greatest need.
> However, critics argue that organisations such as Live Aid are simply
> vehicles for calming the guilty consciences of the wealthy and for giving
> free publicity to the celebrities involved. As a consequence, they argue, any
> aid coming from such groups has little long-term impact.
>
> Source: Written by Hamish Joyce

(a)   Identify and briefly explain three reasons why there has been 'a rapid growth
        in more affluent countries of charities seeking to address global poverty.'   *(9 marks)*

(b)   Using material from Item B and elsewhere, assess the view that aid can only
        ever have short-term impact on poverty.   *(18 marks)*

Either

5   'Under-development is primarily a consequence of cultural, rather than economic
        factors.' To what extent do sociological evidence and arguments support this view of
        under-development in the world today?   *(33 marks)*

Or

6   How far do arguments and evidence support the view that the impact of globalisation
        is increasingly blurring traditional sociological assumptions about distinctions between
        the developed and under-developed world?   *(33 marks)*

General Certificate of Education
Advanced Level Examination
Section B from Paper 3

SOCIOLOGY Unit 3
For this paper you must have:
a 12-page answer book
Time allowed 1 hour 30 minutes

SAMPLE 2

Section B: Global Development

If you choose this Section, answer Question 4 and either Question 5 or Question 6.

Total for this section: 60 marks

4   Read Item B below and answer parts (a) and (b) that follow.

> **Item B**
>
> Until fairly recently it was felt that the negative effects of rapid industrial development on the environment of third world countries was a short-term issue, and one that was outweighed by the long-term economic and social benefits. Where there were environmental disasters such as Bhopal these were seen as a consequence of poor regulation of the activities of foreign companies, rather than of development per se. The view that development was innately beneficial was one that was particularly fostered by the USA, in part because it was unwilling to regulate its own economy to reduce impact on the environment.
>
> However, the rapid growth in the last decade of the economies of the two most populous countries in the world (India and China) has led to a growing awareness of the world-wide environmental impact of rapid industrialisation. Similarly, rapid industrialisation has a very significant impact on the day to day lives of the citizens of the developing country.

    (a)   Identify and briefly explain three ways in which rapid industrialisation can impact on the 'day to day lives of the citizens of a developing country'.   *(9 marks)*

    (b)   Using material from Item B and elsewhere, assess the view that rapid development will always bring more negative than positive consequences for the environment.   *(18 marks)*

Either

5   'The growth of Transnational Corporations, the increasing impact of instantaneous global communication, the global financial system and other aspects of a global economy have rendered traditional theories of development largely redundant in thecontemporary world.' To what extent do sociological arguments and evidence support this view?   *(33 marks)*

Or

6   Critically examine the view that over-population is a consequence rather than a cause of under-development.   *(33 marks)*

END OF THE UNIT 3 SECTION B
SAMPLE QUESTIONS

Mass media

Introduction

It used to be relatively easy to define the mass media. Here is a basic definition: 'The mass media are means of communication from a small number of producers to a very large number of consumers. Such communications may be written, oral and/or visual.' Television, cinema, radio, newspapers and magazines all fit these criteria; for example, the BBC produces television programmes transmitted to millions of people.

Over the past 30 years there have been significant changes. New media have been developed which are not directly controlled by single institutions. These newer forms are often described as the digital media and include CDs, DVDs, PCs and the internet. There are more interpersonal and interactive forms of communication, for example mobile phones, where communication is between individuals, and the internet, which allows response and reaction from those using it. The innovation that has allowed the development of this new media has also transformed the old media, through technologies such as digital television and image manipulation software.

These developments have led to a dramatic increase in the types of mass media available to people and the effects of this are still unclear. Do satellite broadcasting, mobile phones and the internet mean a new age of personal media and consumer choice, or will media conglomerates come to dominate these media forms too?

It is hard to imagine a world where lives are not dominated by the media, yet this is a relatively modern phenomenon which, until very recently, was largely confined to industrial societies. Popular newspapers, cinema and radio were developed during the latter part of the 19th century. Television did not become available to the masses until the 1950s. There is no doubt, however, that the mass media have changed the way we see and think about the world. Images, ideas and products can be communicated to millions of people in an instant. The world has shrunk. To quote Marshall McLuhan (1962), we all inhabit a 'global village'. The mass media enables us to know a lot more about the world we live in, but the nature of this knowledge has changed significantly. Most of what we know is second-hand and filtered by the media; we only know what we are told. In the past, people may have known less, but most of their knowledge was first-hand, the result of direct experience and observation.

When postmodernists like Strinati (1993) claim that 'the media is reality', this is what they are alluding to. We harbour a healthy suspicion of the accuracy of the mass media but cannot check most information we receive; there are no non-media sources to compare it with. This is not a problem if we take a pluralist view. Pluralists argue that the diversity of the media means a wide range of opinions and perspectives. Marxists, however, argue that because huge capitalist companies control the mass media, its content is determined by their interests and this creates a one-sided view.

Mass media

Key media developments

Learning objectives:

- Understand the impact of technological developments on media ownership and control.

- Recognise how structural and organisational changes affect media ownership and control.

- Evaluate the future impact of changes on patterns of media ownership and control.

Key terms

Transnational corporation (TNC): a large business with operations and outlets in a range of countries.

Cross-media ownership: when a company owns a range of media forms, such as TV and newspapers.

Media conglomerate: an organisation that owns large numbers of companies in various mass media such as television, radio, publishing and film.

Vertical integration: when a media company controls every stage of media production, e.g. it makes and broadcasts TV programmes.

Hint

When addressing the issue of ownership and control, be sure to assess the impact of recent media developments.

To better understand the nature and importance of media ownership and control, it is helpful to look at contemporary developments in this context. There has been an increased concentration of ownership into a few giant media corporations.

Media companies have become more and more transnational, i.e. they operate in countries all over the world. They have also become more diverse, having many media interests: TV, publishing, music, software, etc. They have become conglomerates and branched into other areas of economic activity. There is a danger that they may use their media power to promote their other interests.

Marxists argue that these giant corporations put across their capitalist interests and ideology all over the world, often destroying other cultures. Western consumer culture increasingly dominates the world. Technological developments such as satellite TV, which can broadcast to whole continents, are also important in this context; you can watch MTV in India and CNN virtually anywhere in the world. Digital broadcasting has dramatically increased the choice of channels and programmes.

Governments can no longer fully control what their people can see or listen to. In fact, some sociologists, such as Anthony Giddens (1999), argue that the communist bloc in Eastern Europe was seriously undermined by access to Western media. The internet and mobile phones could produce the greatest changes of all. They are not subject to the same degree of vertical control, i.e. control by owners and institutions, that characterises the old media.

Mass media ownership and control

Ownership of the mass media has increasingly been concentrated into fewer and fewer **transnational corporations (TNCs)**. Nine out of 10 of the biggest companies are American-owned and there is considerable concern that as these giant corporations buy up more and more smaller companies all over the world, they will undermine indigenous cultures (Figure 3.1.1). The growth of these media mega-corporations involves a number of other important changes and developments.

Media companies like Rupert Murdoch's News Corp. have a wide range of media interests, including broadcasting, cinema, newspapers and publishing. This **cross-media ownership** produces **media conglomerates**. Media companies may also diversify by investing in other non-media products. Disney is an obvious example, with its theme parks and hotels, but other media giants have invested in a wide range of leisure and other businesses.

These media conglomerates have also increased the pace of **vertical integration**. This is when media companies attempt to control every stage in the production of media content. A film production company, for example, may also own transport and distribution companies and

FUTURE TELEVISION REMOTE.

FUTURE MEDIA OWNERSHIP REMOTE.

Fig. 3.1.1 *Media ownership: cartoon by John Ditchburn*

cinemas, and thus controls every stage of the film industry from shooting the picture to showing the film, even selling the popcorn and ice cream.

Digital technology has enabled the convergence of separate communications technology, allowing companies to diversify into a much wider range of products and markets. The merger of Time Warner and AOL (see page 145) is a classic example of this. By merging with AOL, Time Warner gained the crucial internet link to help it become and remain one of the most powerful media corporations in the world. Already the first integrated home entertainment packages have gone on sale, providing TV, DVD, PC, radio and telephone functions. BT and Virgin are offering TV and film on demand, and mobile phones have also become cameras with internet, film and TV access. The move towards media integration is called **synergy**. Synergy refers to two complementary processes:

- The way in which media products that were once separate can be packaged, so when the latest *X-Men* movie comes out we will also be able to buy the computer game, the CD, the action figures and the graphic novel.
- The ownership of the different companies responsible for all these products is increasingly in the hands of one giant corporation. Disney, for example, can use its DVDs to promote its films, toys and books through intracorporate cross-promotion.

Mass media

Key terms

Synergy: integration of different media forms.

Take it further

Several websites examine the impact of current media developments; try www.opendemocracy.net.

Summary questions

1 With reference to the text, explain the point made in Figure 3.1.1.

2 Why are many sociologists concerned about the development of transnational media conglomerates?

Ownership and control

- Understand the key arguments of pluralists on ownership and control.

- Understand the pluralist view of how new media affect ownership and control.

Hint

Get a clear general understanding of functionalist and pluralist theory, so you have a clear context for understanding the specific theoretical arguments about the media.

Key terms

Market mechanism: of the media, a pluralist argument that media content is determined by audiences through supply and demand.

Do those who own the mass media also control its content? If those who own the media do control its content, can they effectively use it to put forward their own interests and control the masses, as in the Marxist hegemonic model, or does the media have to be diverse, reflecting the many interests and attitudes of its consumers, as in the pluralist or market model?

Functionalist and pluralist theories

Functionalists think the mass media is an agency of socialisation and helps to integrate people by communicating the common values, norms and aspirations of society; in this sense it performs complementary functions to the family and education. The mass media thus reflects and reinforces value consensus: individualism, competition and financial success are all emphasised and encouraged.

By the 1970s this view of the mass media was seen as too simplistic. Functionalists see individuals as essentially passive recipients of socialisation. By this time, sociologists were beginning to see the relationship between audiences and mass media as far more complex. In addition, the changing nature of society made the functionalist view seem outdated. Pluralist views now began to dominate media analysis. Although many pluralists agree that the mass media reflects common values to some extent, they also argue that as society has become more diverse, with a more complex system of stratification and increasing ethnic diversity, the media has changed to reflect these developments and differences. There are now radio and TV channels and programmes aimed at young people and numerous minority groups. Pluralists such as Jean Blondel (1969) argue that no single group in society has a monopoly of power and control. Similarly, the mass media is competitive and diverse and therefore no single group controls it.

Supporting arguments

There is a free media

Everyone has the right to set up newspapers, magazines, etc., in a free capitalist society. A wide range of views will be expressed. New technology – digital broadcasting, video cameras, desktop publishing, the internet, etc. – means that even small groups or people with limited funds can express their opinions.

Audience demand and the market mechanism

The size and diversity of modern mass media corporations means that owners cannot control what is produced. Day-to-day decisions about media content are made by editors and journalists. These decisions are primarily based on the demands of their consumers. The **market mechanism** ensures that audiences control content. They will not watch or buy if their needs are not catered for. Media companies must compete to satisfy these needs. Thus we have a wide variety of media catering for a wide variety of audiences and their demands.

An excellent illustration of this argument comes from John Whale's study of the *Sun* newspaper. In the early 1960s the *Sun* was a socialist newspaper that sought to 'educate and inform' working-class people. Its circulation was falling and it was in considerable financial trouble. An Australian media tycoon, Rupert Murdoch, bought the *Sun* and transformed it into an entertaining tabloid newspaper, complete with topless page three girls. He was so successful that eventually the Sun overtook the *Daily Mirror* as the most popular newspaper in Britain. The key to this success was that Murdoch 'gave the consumers what they wanted'.

Access and interactivity

Even the **old media** gave audiences the opportunity to reply and comment. Newspapers have always featured readers' letters and TV and radio stations have featured programmes like *Points of View* and, more recently, phone-ins. The **new media** have greatly increased this facility. The internet and emails have enabled audiences to respond instantly to media output. News and current affairs programmes have increasingly made audience reactions an integral part of their broadcasts.

People can express their opinions via the internet

People and small groups can produce webpages and blogs on any subject they wish. Desktop publishing and cheap video and DVD cameras have also enhanced individual media production.

Laws require broadcasting media to be balanced and fair

Laws require broadcasting media to be balanced and fair. This means that a wide variety of opinions are heard. So if a government minister speaks on an environmental issue, there is likely to be a contribution from Greenpeace or a similar group. This allows the voices of pressure groups and minority interests to be heard. Pressure groups, i.e. non-party-political organisations that put forward the interests of a wide range of different groups, have a crucial role in maintaining diversity and balance in society in general and the media in particular.

The sheer diversity of the media is another safeguard

There are so many sources of information – local, national and international – that no one group can dominate. There is also public broadcasting. The BBC is not owned by big business and does not rely on advertising money. It is controlled by representatives of the community through a selection process, chaired by a senior civil servant and confirmed by the democratically elected government of the day. The charter of this BBC Trust, established in 2007, specifically requires that the interests of the public are its main priority.

Key terms

Old media: analogue media such as cinema, TV and print.

New media: digital media such as internet, PCs and digital TV.

Mass media

Summary questions

3 Why is the market mechanism so important in a pluralist analysis of media ownership and control?

4 How does the nature of the new media support pluralist arguments?

5 What is the pluralist view of the distribution of power in democratic societies? How does this argument support the idea of a free and diverse media?

Marxist theory and the media

Learning objectives:

- Understand Marxist and neo-Marxist theories of media ownership and control.

- Analyse relevant evidence and studies by Marxist and neo-Marxist theorists.

Link

The question of media ownership and control is linked to issues of class and stratification, and power and politics.

Hint

When addressing the issue of media ownership and control, consider how media developments and changes have affected the debate. Do these changes add support to pluralist or Marxist views?

Key terms

Ideological state apparatus (ISA): a collection of institutions that transmit ideology that supports the existing social arrangements.

Legitimation: making the system seem just and fair.

Hegemony: the ideological control that the ruling-class elite have over the masses.

Traditional Marxists argue that the owners of the media control its content. They may not have day-to-day control of every media item but they employ managers and editors who support their views and policies. Rupert Murdoch said, when he first came to Britain, 'I did not come all this way not to interfere.' A few immensely powerful corporations and individuals that have made their money in the capitalist system own the media. It would be surprising if they were critical of the system. These media magnates have influence with politicians because of their media control. Before their election victory in 1997, leading members of the Labour Party spent a great deal of time seeking Murdoch's political support. Murdoch has also been accused of censoring news coverage of the Chinese suppression of dissidents in order to promote the business interests of his satellite TV company Star TV.

Political influence is usually indirect but the media magnate Silvio Berlusconi used his dominance of the Italian media to form Forza Italia, a right-wing political party which defeated the left in the general elections of 1992, 2001 and 2007 even though Berlusconi has faced corruption charges.

Critics of this analysis say it ignores the many rules and regulations that restrict the power of the media, such as the UK Official Secrets Act and UK libel laws. In addition, the size and complexity of media organisations mean direct control is impossible. Nevertheless, there is substantial evidence of media manipulation, and the assertion by Rupert Murdoch (2007) that he does control the political line taken by the *Sun* and the *News of the World* but not the *Times* and *Sunday Times* is interesting in this context. Marxists say this shows that he feels it necessary to control the politics of the tabloid newspapers aimed at a working-class readership, but not those read by higher social classes.

You may think the traditional Marxist approach sounds like a conspiracy theory. Many neo-Marxists – Marxist thinkers who have developed and adapted Marxist theory – would agree with you. Neo-Marxists, like traditional Marxists, think that the media help to put across an ideology, that is values, beliefs and information that support capitalism, but they do not see this as primarily the result of actions taken by media owners. Louis Althusser, for example, argues that the mass media are part of the **ideological state apparatus (ISA)**. Along with education, the family and religion, the media puts across an overwhelmingly pro-capitalist message that eventually comes to be seen as common sense. Most people therefore accept this ideology, or at least can see no alternatives.

Neo-Marxists use the term **legitimation** to describe the process by which the ideology of the ruling class is made to seem fair and legitimate. They also accept that there are other views expressed in capitalist societies and that there is even resistance to this ideology, but through their overwhelming dominance of the ISA and control of the repressive state apparatus (RSA) – police, army, etc. – the ruling class is able to dominate and control the rest of society. Neo-Marxists call this process of dominance **hegemony**. These are some of the ways in which this ideological domination works.

Ralph Miliband argues that although a variety of views are expressed through the media, the vast majority come from a limited moderate spectrum that supports the system. The media labels radical, critical views and the people who express them as extremist and abnormal; 'loony left' is a common term of abuse. In the 1980s, the *Sun* ran a series of these stories; for example a London council was accused of banning 'Baa Baa Black Sheep' because the nursery rhyme was racist. Views outside this normal spectrum are labelled as extreme, even dangerous.

Herbert Marcuse, a member of the Frankfurt School of philosophers, argues that the masses are given **false consciousness** by the media. Consumerism becomes the meaning of life. Just as Roman emperors kept the masses happy with bread and circuses, we are controlled by media entertainment and consumerism. Soaps and bland comedies provide unthinking escapism. Lifestyle programmes encourage us to buy the latest fashions and household appliances. Quizzes encourage greed, as do the adverts that bombard us in almost all forms of mass media. Pluralists point to the choice of media material, much of which is intellectually demanding, educational and informative, but Marxist critics, like Bourdieu, argue that most people lack the education to appreciate or even understand them.

The Glasgow University Media Group (GUMG) used content analysis to investigate political bias in the news media. The controllers of the media set the agenda, in other words determine what topics should be published. Vital in this context are gatekeepers, editors and managers who decide what is published. Their decisions will be informed by the policies and principles (ideology) laid down by owners and, as neo-Marxists point out, these news professionals come from similar backgrounds and viewpoints, so major conflicts between owners and professionals are unlikely. Even in public broadcasting, the position is not substantially different. The government appoints establishment figures to the BBC Trust, people who support the system and are from higher classes. The BBC is also increasingly subject to commercial pressures and is indirectly influenced by advertising because it must compete with the commercial media, which relies on advertising.

Key terms

False consciousness: the illusion instilled into the working class that the capitalist system is fair for everyone in society.

Mass media

Research study

The GUMG study of the 'Glasgow rubbish strike' (Bad News 1976) argues that news coverage focused on the health hazards rather than the strikers' grievances. Managers and 'experts' were regularly interviewed, but strikers were not. He says that media coverage was pro-establishment and anti-union.

AQA Examiner's tip

Questions on ownership and control tend to focus on an evaluation or comparison of pluralist and Marxist theory. To achieve the highest marks, introduce other relevant arguments and evidence from other relevant areas, such as globalisation and the impact of new media.

Summary questions

6 Outline the basic differences between traditional and neo-Marxist analyses of media ownership and control.

7 Using the GUMG source, explain why Marxists regard news coverage as ideologically biased.

8 How would Marxist theorists interpret the effects of new media on the issue of ownership and control?

Mass media and mass culture

Mass media

There is considerable debate in sociology about whether the development of a mass media along with mass consumerism has led to the development of a **mass culture**, characterised by low standards and consumed by a passive, uncritical audience.

Mass culture theory

In the past, so the argument goes, there were distinct cultures based on the different life experiences of different social groups. Sociologists often use the term 'high culture' to refer to the culture of the elite and 'folk culture' to describe the culture of ordinary people. These cultural differences include differences in values, norms and beliefs as well as in music, literature and art. Throughout history, the elite have sponsored artists and musicians. Cultural forms like opera, literature and the fine arts have always tended to be the preserve of the rich. In contrast, many forms of craft, folk tales and folk music have been associated with the lower social classes. Folk culture was produced by and for the people and grew out of their everyday experiences.

Nowadays, both elite and folk culture have been largely encompassed by a mass culture produced by big business and distributed and promoted by the mass media. Great paintings become posters and T-shirts; classical music is made into jingles to advertise consumer goods; blues, country and folk music are transformed into pop music performed by manufactured bands. Those who argue that a mass culture has been developed, and are highly critical of it, come from both sides of the political spectrum.

Right-wing critics, often called Elite theorists, such as Elliott and Leavis see mass culture as threatening high culture, which not only encompasses the finest forms of artistic endeavour but also superior values and morality, thus providing a positive example to the lower social orders. Mass culture represents a dumbing down of culture. Critics like Hoggart combine fierce criticisms of the Americanisation and massification of popular culture with a nostalgic, idealised view of traditional working-class culture.

Left-wing critics of mass culture share some of these sentiments. The neo-Marxist Frankfurt School developed critical theory, which argued that capitalism imposes culture on the masses and creates an illusion of choice. In reality, standardisation and banal mass culture conceal a manipulative ideology in which consumerism and conformity replace consciousness. Marcuse sees mass culture as reducing people to uncritical, passive consumers. The media is the new opiate of the masses, drugging its victims with a mixture of consumerism and crass entertainment.

Advertising encourages consumerism, greed and selfishness. Traditional working-class values – loyalty, solidarity and cooperation – are undermined. Pro-capitalist values – competition and selfishness – are encouraged. People become one-dimensional and consumerism becomes the meaning of life (Figure 3.2.1). Moreover, as people become more isolated and atomised, they are easier to control, making it easier for the

Fig. 3.2.1 *Is this our identity in a postmodern society?*

ruling class to maintain their ideological domination or hegemony. The Frankfurt School were essentially pessimistic about the future. They believed that US capitalism and mass culture presented as great a threat to the working classes as had Nazism, that the possibility of radical social change 'had been smashed between the concentration camps and TV for the masses' (Srinati 1995).

Pluralist and postmodernist viewpoints

Pluralists argue that the media, like society, has become more diverse; it offers greater variety and choice than ever. Folk culture, high culture and different ethnic cultures, from all over the world, are available to everyone. Through the media we can all experience music that ranges from classical to country, reggae to rap. Gans emphasises the unprecedented cultural choices available to people today, thanks to the mass media. In the past, fine art and classical music were only available to the elite, now thanks to mass production, they are available to all. Postmodernists argue that the media provides us with cultural artefacts from many times and places, allowing us to forge our own identities through our consumer choices. We are no longer bound by our social backgrounds; according to Lyotard, class, gender, age and ethnicity are no longer the main determinants of identity.

The value and quality of **popular culture** remains a source of heated debate but the argument that it is bland and uncritical is difficult to sustain. The pop music of the Beatles, Bob Dylan and Radiohead, among many others, can hardly be described in this way. TV has also produced a range of inspiring and educational dramas and factual programmes. Good examples are David Attenborough's many documentaries about the natural world and Bruce Parry's anthropological studies of tribes.

Key terms

Popular culture: the view that contemporary culture is the product of interaction between mass culture and other cultural forms such as high culture and folk culture.

Research study

Michael Batkhin argues that many media forms subvert authority, like the carnival of medieval times. Films like *Fight Club*, *Borat* and the *Carry On* movies, comedies and cartoons like *Benny Hill*, the *Simpsons* and *South Park* are 'politically incorrect' and ridicule our 'social betters'.

Mass media

The internet and related technologies have enabled people to produce their own culture in the form of blogs, websites and films. These developments demonstrate the desire of people to be active participants in the creation of popular culture, their culture.

Perhaps the crucial point to make about this debate is that the opposing theories see contemporary culture in very different ways. Mass culture theorists see today's culture as very much the product of big business and the media. It is consumed by the masses in a passive and uncritical manner. Their opponents use the term 'popular culture' and, although they would agree that business and the media are responsible for the production of much cultural material, they argue that consumers take a far more active role in interpreting and adapting this material for their own uses.

Birmingham CCCS

The neo-Marxist Birmingham Centre for Contemporary Cultural Studies has made a major contribution to the study of contemporary popular culture. It was influenced by the philosopher Raymond Williams, who defined culture as 'not just a body of intellectual and imaginative work but a whole way of life'. Williams argued that popular culture is not only valuable but that it is vital to culture as it is lived. Stuart Hall is probably the most influential thinker associated with the CCCS. He rejected the idea of passive audiences and emphasised that there were basically three ways of interpreting, or decoding, the ideological messages of the mass media:

- **Dominant** – members of the audience uncritically accept the ideological message.
- **Negotiated** – members of the audience only partially accept the message; they may enjoy an advert but not be persuaded to buy the product.
- **Oppositional** – the message is totally rejected.

Other writers such as Paul Willis and Phil Cohen have developed and illustrated Hall's ideas. Cohen's classic work, *Resistance through Ritual*, linked class, leisure and cultural opposition and showed how skinheads adopted exaggerated working-class dress – denim and bovver boots – and values – machismo and racism – as they sought to defend their territory in response to increasing immigration.

Willis has demonstrated the complex and dynamic nature of popular culture. Big business often exploits youth culture – music, fashion, etc. – in pursuit of profit. Thus rap music, originally highly antagonistic to the system, is transformed into a multimillion-dollar business. But even as big business incorporates aspects of youth culture, new forms of subculture develop. Moreover, young people adapt and customise mass-produced goods for their own purposes, e.g. Mods in the 1960s transformed unfashionable scooters and parkas into cool, trendy objects of desire. The key point is the interaction between the producers of mass culture and its consumers. The consumers can reject and adapt the products provided for them, but big business has considerably more power in this interaction.

Mass media

Hint

Be clear about the differences between mass culture and popular culture. Look for other examples of popular culture; many can be found among youth subcultures.

Take it further

The CCCS website (www.sociology. bham.ac.uk/cccs.shtml) has a wealth of material relevant to this topic including excellent examples and studies.

Summary questions

1. Clearly explain, with examples, the differences between folk culture, high culture and mass culture.

2. Outline the basic criticisms of mass culture made by
   a left-wing critics and
   b right-wing critics.

3. Explain, with examples, the difference between the concepts of mass culture and popular culture.

Globalisation, culture and the mass media

Mass media

Learning objectives:

- Understand cultural and media imperialism theories of globalisation.

- Know cultural flows and network and reception theories of globalisation.

- Examine studies and evidence of competing models of globalisation.

Link

Globalisation has strong links to culture and identity, politics and power, and development.

Key terms

Globalisation: increased world interconnectedness through the flow of nations, people, ideas, technology and culture in general.

Cultural imperialism: when the cultural output of one region dominates the cultural output of other regions, especially the aggressive promotion of Western culture, specifically American culture, as superior to non-Western cultures.

The debate over the nature of contemporary culture and the role of the media in its formation has increasingly taken an international perspective. **Globalisation**, according to authorities such as Anthony Giddens, is the crucial issue of our times.

The media plays a central role in the process of globalisation, but sociologists are divided about its effects. Marxists see the transfer of ideas and culture from the developed world to the underdeveloped world as an essentially one-way process that produces a homogenisation of culture based on capitalist, consumerist values. The process of globalisation therefore threatens the indigenous cultures of the underdeveloped world. Liberals and pluralists suggest that the flow of ideas occurs in multiple directions, producing a more multicultural world and increasing diversity in ideas and lifestyles.

Cultural and media imperialism theory

The theory of **cultural imperialism** argues that the global economic system is dominated by transnational companies that are based in the rich capitalist countries of the world. These companies control the production and distribution of goods. Sawen estimates that the richest 200 capitalist corporations control half of all world economic activity. Coca-Cola-isation or McDonaldisation are sometimes used to describe this process. Coca-Cola and McDonald's compete with indigenous producers, and McDonald's is responsible for fundamental changes in behaviour – it has changed the way people eat.

Mass media corporations play a major role in this dominance. Not only are they among the richest and most powerful of these organisations, they are also the dominant force in distribution of information and advertising. Nine of the top 10 media companies are based in the US. In Marxist terms, capitalist corporations control the means of production and the mental means of production throughout the world (i.e. they control the content and distribution of knowledge and ideas). Some sociologists regard this process of cultural dominance as purposeful and intentional; others see it as an inevitable consequence of capitalist corporations seeking new markets and higher profits. In either case the mass media is a driving force in the process of cultural imperialism.

Cultural flows, network model, reception theory

Critics such as Tomlinson (1999) reject this analysis. They adopt the cultural flows model, arguing that cultural and media influences do not originate solely from the capitalist West. A complex network of communications, media messages and influences flows in many different directions. Globalisation, therefore, does not produce a homogeneous world culture based on Western capitalist values. Instead it encourages the mixing of a variety of cultural influences to create hybrid cultures for an increasingly multicultural world.

Reception theory focuses on how audiences use the media. It rejects the media imperialism idea that audiences passively accept the mass-mediated news, information and entertainment provided for them by transnational media companies. Audiences respond actively, rather than passively. The way they interpret media messages will depend on a number of social factors, particularly ethnicity, gender and social class. Different societies and different individuals deal with the impact of media and cultural globalisation in different ways.

■ Mass media and globalisation in Asia

To help evaluate the different theories, consider how media globalisation has affected developing countries. Asia, with its huge population and diverse cultural heritage, provides interesting examples:

■ A number of Asian countries have successfully pursued policies aimed at limiting Western media influence. Some authoritarian regimes (e.g. China, Singapore and Malaysia) have censored or even banned satellite TV.

■ Many countries in the region also operate state-owned television channels, which broadcast government-controlled news to counter the influence of Western news channels such as CNN and the BBC.

■ A less censorial approach has been the adopting and modifying of Western television formats to fit the indigenous cultures, such as the Chinese version of *Sesame Street*.

■ Television programmes and films based on national folklore, history and myth remain highly popular with viewers throughout Asia.

■ India has a huge population, much of it very poor by Western standards, yet TV is crowded with adverts aimed at the growing consumer power of the Indian middle classes. Star TV, owned by News Corp., is a dominant player in the Indian television market.

■ Indian soaps share some features with their Western counterparts but they are distinctly Indian in their characterisation and acting style. Bollywood films go from strength to strength without losing their distinctive cultural style. *Bride and Prejudice* had huge international success.

■ The film industries in countries such as Korea and Hong Kong have also had considerable success in the West. Furthermore, they have influenced Hollywood film-makers; for example, Chinese martial arts movies and thrillers have been remade or reworked by Quentin Tarantino and other US directors. There have also been successful remakes of Asian horror films, such as *The Ring* and *The Grudge*.

In a 2001 article entitled 'Globalization and Tradition', Josefina Santos argues that in her native Philippines, Western values such as individual achievement do not fit with the prevailing cultural norms. Philippine values are more family- and class-based and are strongly influenced by their colonial Spanish past. The most popular TV programmes in the Philippines are Mexican-made romantic soap operas dubbed into Filipino. Many Filipinos can readily identify with the characters in these soaps, particularly the poor peasant women who often obtain high status. These stories reflect their own dreams and fantasies. Santos argues that this shows how a globalised media may reinforce existing values and beliefs rather than change them.

■ The internet and globalisation

Transnationalisation, particularly the growth of the web, has led optimistic observers to picture a new world in which the free exchange of ideas and information will produce worldwide democracy and participation. Giddens argues that the fall of the communist bloc in Eastern Europe was partly the result of its citizens gaining access to information about living standards and lifestyles in the West.

The internet is particularly important in this context. It is not controlled by media conglomerates, it is controlled by the individuals and groups who use it – there is horizontal rather than vertical control. This seems to correspond to Habermas's concept of the **public sphere**, which he defines as the area of social life that is not controlled by governments or the market.

There are problems with this analysis. The poor of the world have little internet access. Its users are predominantly from the rich Western nations. In addition, the internet is increasingly dominated by transnational businesses, such as the Google search engine. The internet is not immune to political interference. In 2007 the Burmese government closed down the internet to prevent users publicising its suppression of protestors.

Research study

Steve Buckley argues that 'old-fashioned' radio is still the most important communication medium in the developing world. In Latin America, for example, trade unions, farming cooperatives, etc., own and operate their own radio stations for educational and political purposes. Poor people have much more access to radio than the internet.

Evaluation

Any assessment of media globalisation theories must recognise that the trends and developments are complex and contradictory. Media globalisation is not simply a one-way process involving the cultural dominance of the capitalist West, but the worldwide media is dominated by transnational media conglomerates based in Western capitalist societies. The global media market has grown as a result of new technologies and deregulation of national media industries. The costs of media production and distribution and the required capital investment means that only the mega-rich can possibly compete.

Summary questions

4 Outline the basic arguments about globalisation put forward by cultural imperialism theorists.

5 What key criticisms do reception theorists and cultural flows theorists make of cultural imperialism theories?

6 Why is the concept of the public sphere so important in this context?

Key terms

Public sphere: a real or virtual place where people come together as equal participants in democratic discussions.

Take it further

The openDemocracy website (www. opendemocracy.net) has a lot of largely critical material relevant to this issue.

Mass media

AQA Examiner's tip

Questions and essays on this topic will probably ask you to contest theories about the relationship between globalisation and the media. Make sure you can interpret and apply evidence to support and criticise the different theories.

Theoretical perspectives and the influence of news values

Learning objectives:

■ Evaluate perspectives on selection and production of news and current affairs.

■ Know the nature and influence of news values.

■ Understand interpretation and application of evidence and studies on the influence of news values.

The mass media plays a crucial role in what Habermas calls the public sphere. Most of the news and information we receive about the world comes via the mass media. This raises two critical questions:

■ Who or what decides what news and information we receive?

■ Do we receive a balanced view of the world, or is the news we receive systematically biased?

What is incontestable is that the mass media is selective in its coverage of news and current affairs. It is impossible to report everything. The key issue is to examine why some events are reported and not others. Let us look at some theoretical approaches to this question.

If we were to ask journalists and editors, they would probably argue that the news media provide a window on the world, an accurate reflection of what is happening. Few would deny that there is bias in news coverage but they would add that there are a wide variety of sources for us to check the authenticity of news reports. They would probably also draw a distinction between news and comment. News reportage involves journalists reporting an honest and accurate account of an event; comment involves interpretation and evaluation of that event. These views closely coincide with those of pluralist theorists. The media gives people what they want; this applies to news and current affairs, just as it applies to other media information. Pluralists emphasise the wide variety of options available to news consumers.

The development of 24-hour news channels and the internet has hugely increased such choice. Again, the market argument is crucial; the media must reflect the values and interests of its consumers otherwise they will not buy the product. Pluralists also point to the safeguards to ensure that a balanced and honest picture is presented. The law of libel, for example, allows people to seek legal redress and compensation if they think they have been defamed. Bodies like the Press Complaints Commission and the Advertising Standards Authority also help to ensure that standards are maintained. Moreover, the broadcasting media (TV and radio) have to be fair and balanced by law.

According to Marxists, the media is part of the ISA and puts across the values and interests of the ruling class. The form and content of the news, etc., is presented so it supports and transmits ruling-class ideology. The roles played by agenda setters and gatekeepers are important here (see ownership and control). The news media decide what is important and how issues are treated. Gatekeepers (editors, for example) ensure that news fits in with the style of their newspaper or news programme. They will make sure that news reportage also corresponds to the policies laid down by owners and managers.

Research study

The GUMG showed that the media's representations of industrial conflicts are ideological. The language demonstrates a fundamental bias. Trades unions make threats and demands whereas bosses and managers make offers and pleas.

News values

One of the key factors that determine the selection of news is to what extent stories are newsworthy. When journalists and editors consider whether to include a story, they apply criteria, or **news values**. If a story scores highly on these news values, it is more likely to be included in a newspaper or programme. These values vary between different newspapers and broadcasters. What the *Sun* considers newsworthy may not be covered in the *Daily Telegraph* (Figure 3.3.1).

Key terms

News values: the criteria used by journalists and editors to decide if a story is newsworthy.

Fig. 3.3.1 *Two classic front pages reflect the* Sun's *news values*

General news values

Drama

Disasters such as earthquakes, plane crashes and wars are all 'good' news stories. The GUMG puts it like this: 'Bad news is good news.'

Human interest

Human-interest stories are increasingly popular. They may be stories of personal tragedy, survival against the odds and human relationships.

Personalities

Important people and celebrities make good news stories. This is often combined with human-interest dimensions. The sex, drugs and violence stories of celebrities such as Amy Winehouse, Kate Moss and Britney Spears make excellent news copy. There is nothing new in this; the Beatles, the Rolling Stones and many other pop artists have received similar coverage.

Sensationalism

Sensationalism is also important. Extraordinary stories attract the attention of the public and encourage them to buy or watch. A classic *Sun* headline is 'Freddie Starr ate my hamster'.

Proximity

News stories focus on Britain, followed by places with which we have close ties, such as Europe, the US and Australia. Stories about the developing world are rare and are usually concerned with major disasters and wars. Cohen and Young (1973) argue that by emphasising bad news about these countries, people are made to feel that the Western capitalist world is superior. In Marxist terms, this helps to prevent dissension among the lower social orders. Similarly negative reporting of ethnic minorities divides the working class on racial grounds. The white working class blame immigrants for lack of jobs and crime, diverting attention away from those really responsible – capitalist companies and the state that represents their interests.

Visual impact

Dramatic film or photographs makes a story far more reportable. A story about a pensioner who has been mugged, for example, is much more newsworthy if the newspaper can produce a graphic picture of her injuries.

■ Research study

Uttley (1999) showed that in the 1990s, despite globalisation, news broadcasting of world events in the US decreased by 50 per cent. Golding and McLachlan demonstrated that, in Britain, the *Guardian's* coverage of foreign affairs dropped from 2 stories per page in 1962 to 0.6 stories per page in 1999; in the *Times* it fell from 3.7 to 0.4.

Complex changes

The reasons for these changes in news coverage are complex but major factors are more commercialisation and fiercer competition. The view that the media is **dumbing down** is supported by the increase in exciting and sensational news articles that concentrate on human-interest stories and celebrities. When foreign news is reported, the emphasis is on the immediate and the dramatic, not on the causes and long-term consequences, so the audience obtains a limited and superficial understanding.

Narrative is an important concept for how news is selected and structured. Narratives are stories, and good stories have a beginning, a middle and an end. Unfortunately, in real life, this is not always the case; stories are often messy and unresolved. Nevertheless, the media tries to fit news stories into this conventional form. If we apply this concept to the tsunami of December 2004, the beginning is the catastrophic event, the middle is the destruction of property and lives, and the end is the relief effort and the solving of the problem. Though this is not the real story of the tsunami – there has been no solution – it is possible to present the tsunami story in traditional **narrative** terms. Compare this to the media treatment (or lack of it) of the civil wars and destruction in Sudan or the Congo. These stories do not fit our narrative structure, for here there is no foreseeable end.

■ Key terms

Dumbing down: the idea that news has become more populist and more sensational, less intelligent and less informative.

Narrative: the idea that news stories should have a beginning, middle and end. Journalists and editors try to fit stories into this structure.

In theoretical terms, pluralists and liberals regard news values as reflecting public interests, values and demands. They emphasise the diversity of news values and content in different media forms. Marxists stress the overall homogeneity of news values and their role in maintaining ideological control by reinforcing capitalist and consumerist values.

News values and the Asian tsunami

The tsunami of December 2004 was rightly portrayed as one of the greatest natural disasters to have occurred in the past 100 years. Some 200,000 people died in the tsunami, and media and public reaction was immediate and intense. However, the tsunami did not kill nearly as many people as the recent war in the Congo (3 million deaths) or in Sudan (2 million deaths). How then do we explain the urgent and immediate response to the tsunami? Why did the tsunami create more news coverage in a day than the Congo War received in a year? We can answer this question by applying the concept of news values.

Firstly, the tsunami was an extraordinary, bad news story. The fact that it occurred on Boxing Day made it even more poignant. There were amazing pictures and dozens of human-interest stories. It was also easy news, requiring a lot of sympathy but little analysis. One ITN reporter was frequently shown handing out food and other relief items to victims. This helped personalise the story.

The tsunami affected many people in the Western world. There were thousands of tourists in the affected regions, and many more of us have holidayed in these countries. There were many touching stories of tourists who had lost their families and others' tales of miraculous escapes. The *Daily Mail* had front-page headlines of British casualties for several days, but they were a tiny proportion of those who died. Media coverage undoubtedly encouraged charitable giving; however, the reaction was short-lived. We may be happy to give in an emergency but the media does not help us understand underlying causes and consequences.

After the tsunami, the cameras and reporters moved on, but the people affected will have to deal with the consequences of the disaster for years to come. Dealing with the consequences is not news and receives little attention. The cynicism and parochialism of the Western media can be illustrated by a debate on CNN on the Sunday after the tsunami. The main focus of the discussion was that the tsunami would be good news for President Bush because it would keep the war in Iraq off the front pages. Peter Phillips makes a related point. In the period before the tsunami an estimated 100,000 civilians had died in the Iraqi conflict, yet media coverage of these deaths was negligible.

Link

News values links to theory and methods and politics and power.

Mass media

Take it further

Analyse the front pages of a range of newspapers on the same day. Compare the news values that have influenced them.

Summary questions

1. Outline the news values apparent in the *Sun* front pages shown in Figure 3.3.1.

2. Compare pluralist and Marxist explanations of news content. Which do you find most convincing? Why?

Influences on news content

Learning objective:

- Understand the various influences behind the selection of media news content.

Advertising

Most mass media depend on advertising to make a profit (Figure 3.3.2). Capitalist companies are hardly likely to advertise in media that are antagonistic to business or the capitalist system in general, a problem for radical, left-wing media as this source of funding is unavailable to them. This does not mean there are no alternative voices in the media. Michael Moore has produced a series of highly critical films and *Supersize Me* was a humorous but effective attack on fast food, McDonald's in particular. There are also radical magazines and other media forms, often with small circulations. Nor does it mean that the mass media is always uncritical. Investigative journalism, such as Mark Thomas's documentary on Coca-Cola, shown on Channel 4 in 2007, is far from unique. Nevertheless, such examples tend to be the exceptions that prove the rule. One could argue that the media allows criticism to help it portray itself as free and fair. Advertisers' demands present no problems for mainstream media. Advertisers and mainstream media are part of the same capitalist community and share the same values and interests.

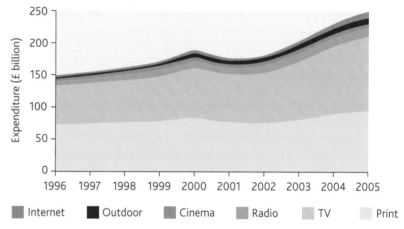

Fig. 3.3.2 *There has been huge growth in spending on internet advertising*
Source: Ofcom Report 2007

Breaking stories

We have already seen how deregulation and other changes have increased media commercialisation and competition. This has increased the importance of exclusives and of being the first with the news. Consequently, there is a tendency to produce speculative and unsubstantiated stories. It can also increase dependency on 'official sources' that are quick and easy to obtain. In a Sri Lankan study, Thilak Jayarathe analysed 913 news articles and broadcasts on the aftermath of the tsunami. He found that all were based on the information and opinions given by those in power in Sri Lanka, the experts. The voices of ordinary people did not feature.

Financial considerations

Financial considerations, especially in relation to foreign news, are also an influence. It is prohibitively expensive to maintain a team of reporters in a faraway country, plus cameramen, technicians and equipment, so news media often rely on second-hand reports from news agencies like Reuters. They may even find themselves unable to report events in depth or at all. News media are subject to budgetary constraints. If they spend too much on one story, they have to scrimp on another story. One example of this was when the BBC spent a huge sum covering the pro-democracy protests in Tiananmen Square in 1989 and their ruthless suppression by the Chinese government. So when the Berlin Wall fell, later that year, the BBC did not have enough money to give it full coverage.

Political influence

Bob Franklin argues that governments increasingly try to control media news output through **news management** techniques, often called spin, which influences the media to give the government's preferred interpretation of events. There are links between politicians and journalists. Journalists rely on politicians to give them insider information and exclusives. In return, politicians expect a sympathetic portrayal and a media rubbishing of their opponents. This does not mean that politicians don't face criticism. But the system is rarely questioned. The agenda is about how capitalism should be run. Marxists argue that the focus on personalities and individuals actually detracts from political debate.

Time and space

The news has to be fitted into a fairly fixed time or space. Despite their many sections and supplements, newspapers have a limited number of pages, and news broadcasts have very limited time. The huge amount of raw news out there has to be selected and structured so it fits these formats. Newspapers also fit news into fairly rigid sections such as home and foreign news, entertainment and sport. The sports journalists wouldn't be happy if foreign affairs took their space for a day. News broadcasts also have their own narratives: a serious item to begin and a funny story to cheer people up at the end. This constrains what is reported and how it is presented.

News diary

Reporters do not simply go out and look for news. They plan their news-gathering, using a **news diary** of upcoming events (Schleissenger 1978). It is reasonable for journalists to plan in this way: a political correspondent, for example, is bound to pencil in major speeches by the prime minister or leader of the Opposition. Party conferences, demonstrations and a range of other political events will be included in the diary. Interviews with important people have to be booked in advance. This means that what is news today was partly decided days ago, and this involves journalists and editors making value judgements about what or who is important.

In conclusion, it is easy to see why interactionists and neo-Marxists describe news as **socially constructed**. The material that we eventually see on screen or in our newspapers is the result of a whole series of interactions and decisions. The people included in this process are those involved in the events, journalists and gatekeepers. The gatekeepers have the ultimate power to decide what to select as news. Whether these decisions reflect public demand or ideological considerations is a long-running debate.

Key terms

News management: spin; the way that governments and others try to manipulate the presentation of news to show themselves in a favourable light.

News diary: a journalist's planner of future newsworthy events.

Social construct: something that is defined by society and that changes according to time and place.

Mass media

Link

There is a clear link to power and politics plus theory and methods.

AQA Examiner's tip

Exam questions tend to focus on the relative importance of different factors in deciding news content. Prepare a mind map of the different factors involved. If you are asked to assess the importance of a particular factor, such as news values, remember to examine other factors so you can give a balanced evaluation.

Summary questions

3 What do interactionists mean when they say the news is socially constructed?

4 Outline how practical factors influence news content.

Mass media effects: models and theories

Learning objectives:

- Understand different models of media effects.

- Understand studies and application of evidence in relation to media effects.

- Evaluate explanations of media effects, contrasting effects and reception models.

Mass media

How and how much the media affects its audiences are crucial questions. The media effects approach focuses on precisely this issue, that is the impact of media texts on audience understandings, opinions and behaviours. A number of models have been developed to try to explain these effects.

Hypodermic syringe model

The earliest studies of media effects took a simple positivist approach. The media injects messages into a passive and homogeneous audience; the audience reacts. The process is a simple one of cause and effect, and the media can have an immediate and direct effect on people's attitudes and behaviour. Copycat crimes and violence are one example. A more positive example is the increased use of condoms after a media campaign to raise AIDS awareness.

The classic illustration of this model is the radio dramatisation of H. G. Wells' *War of the Worlds* by Orson Welles in 1938. The broadcast was transmitted in the form of news bulletins, and many listeners were convinced that the Martians had landed. Accounts of audience reactions reveal the panic caused by the programme: schoolgirls huddled in dormitories, waiting to phone their parents, for what they thought might be the last time.

Much of the media effects research at this time was done by psychologists and focused on how people reacted to things like media violence; they did not attempt to examine the effects on society as a whole. Sociological influence improved this situation but the assumption of the passive **homogeneous audience** was the guiding principle for a considerable time. Functionalists saw the media as reinforcing value consensus, Marxists as transmitting ruling-class ideology. Little attention was given to how audiences experienced and interpreted media texts. Even during the *War of the Worlds* broadcast, different sections of the audience reacted in different ways. Schoolgirls separated from their families may well have panicked, but other people deduced that the programme was fictional. The obvious inadequacies of the hypodermic syringe model led to the development of new approaches in the 1950s that focused not so much on what the media does to people as what people do with the media.

Key terms

Homogeneous audience: an assumption that audiences have common social characteristics and react in similar ways to media texts.

Active audience models

There are several active audience approaches but all share the view that audiences are neither homogeneous nor passive. In addition, all argue that media messages are mediated, or influenced, by other factors in people's lives and culture: their class, ethnicity, gender, etc. In other words, the interpretation and effect of a media text will be affected by the context in which it is consumed: for example, an advertisement that celebrates women in the housewife role is likely to receive a very different response in a traditional family than a feminist family.

Katz and Lazarsfield (1955) developed the concept of two-step flow, arguing that media and non-media communications are interrelated. People discuss media texts within the **social networks** – friends, families, work, etc. – that they belong to and these networks will influence their interpretations. **Opinion leaders**, dominant individuals within these social networks, often have a considerable effect on the views of other members. Think about how you discuss TV programmes with your friends and family, and how your opinions are affected by these discussions. Theoretically, active audience approaches are mostly associated with interactionist sociologists.

Research study

Morley (1980) studied viewers' interpretations of *Nationwide*, a popular TV news and current affairs programme. His conclusions echoed Hall's model of media reception in that people responded in three basic ways:

- **Dominant** – people accept the views expressed.
- **Negotiated** – people partly accept the views expressed.
- **Oppositional** – people reject the views expressed.

Postmodernists go further and argue that individuals create their own meanings from texts. Postmodernists reject the idea that it is possible to generalise about media effects on audiences.

Uses and gratifications model

McQuail (1968) was concerned with what people do with the media. He argued that different individuals and groups of people use the media to satisfy their specific needs. Viewers make conscious choices in deciding when and what to watch, in the case of television. For example, older people may keep the TV or radio on all day, for company, and men are more likely to watch sport than women. This model relates to pluralist theory in its emphasis on consumer choice. Media companies have to provide a **heterogeneous audience** with its many and varied demands, otherwise they will go out of business.

Cultural effects model

The cultural effects model combines elements of the hypodermic syringe and active audience approaches, arguing that the media does have important effects but not in such immediate and direct ways as the hypodermic syringe model suggests. Effects tend to be gradual and long-term, more like a drip feed than a hypodermic syringe: for example, if the media continually presents a stereotypical image of the perfect female form, this is likely to filter into audiences' consciousness and may cause eating disorders in the long term.

Research study

In the 1970s the *Sun* shifted its political support from Labour to the Conservatives. Ivor Crewe found no immediate change in readers' voting affiliations, but over a longer period of time some readers' values and voting behaviour did change. The *Sun* shifted its support back to Labour in the 1990s.

Key terms

Social networks: groups of people such as friends and family, who influence our uses and interpretations of media texts.

Opinion leaders: influential individuals in social networks.

Heterogeneous audience: a view that audiences have very different social characteristics and react differently to media texts.

AQA Examiner's tip

Questions and essays will often ask you to assess different models. You should do this by comparing the model in question with other models; use a range of examples such as crime, violence and stereotypes (see below). The Philo study is particularly useful in answering this kind of question.

Mass media

Neo-Marxists tend to adopt this model of media effects. They argue that the media constantly communicates ruling-class ideology to the lower classes, and that most people come to accept this pro-capitalist viewpoint, the 'dominant reading' as Morley describes it. This model is also influenced by interactionism.

Greg Philo (1990) and the miners' strike

Greg Philo of the GUMG provides a classic application of media effects theory in his study of the 1984/85 miners' strike. Philo used a very interesting methodology. Groups of people, including miners and police who were involved in the strike, and a number of others who were not, were asked to produce news stories and headlines about the strike. They were given a small number of photographs to act as a stimulus.

The groups were all very clear about the intended message of the news reporting: that the picketing was violent and that the miners were to blame. It was not the case that conservative groups saw the miners as the 'baddies' and that the miners and those who were sympathetic to them saw the police as the villains. The differences came over whether the groups believed the media message. People used a range of criteria to decide this. Some used logic. One man noted, 'If it had really been that violent, the police couldn't have coped. It would have to have been the army.' A politically conservative couple from Kent rejected media accounts because of personal experience. They had met miners' families while on holiday in the north of England and couldn't believe they were violent types.

The majority of the participants, however, believed the media accounts. Some of those who had been sympathetic to the miners changed their views because of media reporting. This was especially true of those with no direct experience of the dispute. It was also interesting that people's memories of the media coverage were so clear that they could actually repeat specific headlines and phrases used by the media.

Philo does not reject active audience theories altogether. He demonstrates that personal experiences and a number of other factors can affect whether audiences accept media messages. But he does reject more extreme versions of this model. People do not simply create the meanings they attach to texts; they are very clear about intended meanings. He also demonstrates that the media has significant effects. Most people believed the media reporting – this supports the cultural effects model and even the hypodermic syringe model – especially when the media was the sole or main source of information.

■ Hint

Relate the models of media effects to wider theory: the hypodermic syringe model to positivist theories, active audience approaches to interactionist theories, and so on.

■ Summary questions

1 What evidence is there to support the view that the mass media can have an immediate effect on audience attitudes and behaviour?

2 Examine the Philo study. What does this study tell us about the influence of the media on audiences' behaviour and attitudes?

Mass media

Mass media effects: crime and violence

Mass media

Learning objectives:

- Understand the relationship between crime and violence in the media and in real life.

- Understand the application of evidence and studies of crime and violence in the media and in real life.

- Evaluate theories on the relationship between crime and violence in the media and in real life.

Mass media effects studies have tended to focus on the issues of crime and violence. This probably reflects public and political concern and the consequent availability of funds to carry out the research. The media's portrayal of crime and violence has a number of consequences.

Consequences of media reporting

Fear of crime and violence

The media concentrates on sensational or newsworthy crimes such as rape, murder and other forms of violence. This can cause fear among some social groups; many surveys have shown that women and elderly people are afraid to go out alone after dark. The media gives people a false impression about the amount of crime in society and the nature of crimes committed. Opinion polls show that people overestimate the amount of violent crime in society and that a majority of people believe that crime is increasing, whereas police figures and the British Crime Survey (BCS) show a consistent fall in crime during the past decade.

Scapegoating and labelling

As well as focusing on specific types of crime, the media focuses on specific kinds of criminals. Young males and minority ethnics, for example, are stereotyped as deviant and criminal. Lurid tales of drug abuse, joyriding and gang violence make good news copy. Ironically, these groups are more likely to be the victims of violent crime. Marxists argue that the crimes of the powerful are all but ignored – fraud, corporate crime, etc. – showing the media's ideological support for the interests of the ruling class.

Folk devils and moral panics

In the 1960s and 1970s some influential studies examined the role of the media in producing **moral panics** in society. These studies were influenced by interactionist theory and were particularly concerned with the way the mass media portrayed youth subcultures. Stan Cohen's study (1972) of Mods and Rockers shows how a few minor scuffles and drunken episodes in Brighton and Margate one bank holiday weekend were exaggerated out of all proportion by the media. This resulted in public alarm, or moral panic, police crackdown and increased **secondary deviance**, as during the next bank holiday more Mods and Rockers turned up and reacted to police pressure by becoming more aggressive. This illustrates another effect of media publicity on crime. The media makes a problem seem worse than it is, and although this draws condemnation from the general public, it may encourage others to join in. Those who take an oppositional interpretation of the text, see such deviance as good fun. This increase in deviance because of media publicity is defined as **deviancy amplification**.

Cohen argues that the media, and the public at large see these deviant groups as a threat to order and stability, as folk devils. He explains that moral panics are the result of tensions and insecurities in society as a whole. The media and the public look for someone to blame, a **scapegoat**. Such groups are often powerless and young, but the effect of a moral

Key terms

Moral panic: when society reacts against perceived deviance, because of media representations.

Secondary deviance: when crackdowns on deviance produce further deviance in response to action by police and others.

Deviancy amplification: when the actions of the media or police cause more crime to be detected or committed.

Scapegoat: a group blamed for the problems of society.

panic is to draw the rest of society together against the threat, thus consensus and stability are restored.

Research study

Stuart Hall (1978) argues that the 1970s saw a 'crisis of capitalism'. There were deep social and economic problems, such as unemployment, inflation and riots. The moral panic that the media whipped up against 'black muggers' served the dual purpose of dividing the working class along racial lines and encouraging public support for repressive laws.

In recent years, moral panics have become an almost continuous feature of increasingly sensationalised news coverage: paedophilia, asylum seekers, hoodies, computer games and binge drinking are just a few examples. This has, ironically, led to criticisms of the concept. Some pluralists and postmodernists argue that the sheer volume of moral panics means that the media is less able to produce the same depth of reaction; audiences have become more cynical and distrustful of media accounts.

One of the recurring moral panics of the past 30 years or more has been the concern over the relationship between media and social violence. Early studies of media violence tended to take a simplistic hypodermic syringe and direct effects approach. The psychological experiments to test the impact of media violence were crude and open to substantial criticism, and although techniques have become more sophisticated, there are still major shortcomings.

What is in no doubt is the amount of violence and aggression in the media, however it is measured. George Gerber's longitudinal study of TV violence reveals that in the US there are an average of six violent episodes per hour and 18 in cartoons, and cartoons are mostly watched by children. He estimates that by age 12 the average child has watched 100,000 acts of violence and that by age 18 a person will have seen 20,000 killings.

Sociologists have several problems when studying the effects of violence:

- Should they include only actual, physical violence or should other forms of aggressive behaviour be counted, such as verbal violence or threats? Is smacking a child violent?
- Not all violence is necessarily bad. Examples are sport, self-defence, protecting others.
- Is society really more violent today? In the days before the mass media, we had major wars and other violence of all kinds, often far worse than today. In Victorian times, even young children were hanged for minor crimes and it was socially acceptable to give beatings to women and children.

Violence and the media

Bandura's famous Bobo doll experiment of 1963 is a classic experiment on the effects of media violence on children. A Bobo doll is a large rubber doll that has a rounded base. When it is knocked down it automatically stands up again. Bandura exposed three groups of children to a film and cartoon showing a Bobo doll being attacked by a mallet. A fourth group, the control group, were not shown the violence. The children were then taken to a room full of toys, only to be told that they could not play with them. They were then taken to another room with a Bobo doll in it, and observed through a one-way mirror. The children who had seen the violence behaved far more aggressively than those who had not. Bandura concluded that media violence caused an increase in aggressiveness in children.

This experiment illustrates some of the major problems with the experimental or effects approach. The Bobo doll experiment lacked ecological validity because the children were placed in an artificial situation, so we cannot say if their reaction was natural. Secondly, a Bobo doll is designed to be hit. It is not a real person. Perhaps the children who had watched the films had merely learned how to play with the toy. It is difficult to conclude that they would be more likely to behave aggressively in real life. As Aronson (1996) says, 'Who cares what a kid does to a rubber doll?'

Bandura's experiment was obviously based on a hypodermic syringe model of media effects. This model is simple to understand and appears to be a common-sense view of media violence, that it inspires others to act out what they have seen: copycat violence. A number of other studies and incidents have supported this approach. When the infant Jamie Bulger was kidnapped, tortured and killed by two 10-year-old boys in 1993, the judge suggested that the two killers may have been influenced by *Child's Play 3*, a violent video. But there was no proof that Jamie's assailants had seen the film.

Research study

Anderson and Bushman (2001) compared the effects of playing violent and non-violent video games. They found that playing violent games produced a greater degree of physiological arousal. However, arousal is not the same as aggression. Perhaps the violent video games were just more exciting.

In more recent years the focus of effects research has increasingly moved to new technologies such as the internet and video games (Figure 3.4.1). James Friedman (2002) makes a number of important points in his

Fig. 3.4.1 *Video game violence*

review of video game experiments. He argues that although there may be a correlation between violent video games and social violence, there is no evidence of a causal link. It may be that violent video games attract violent people. He also demonstrates that increases in arousal and aggression after playing such games are temporary and there is no evidence to support the view that they have long-term effects.

The realism and interactivity of video game violence, and the fact that video games are mostly played by young people, have become a major source of concern for media analysts. Anderson and Dill (2000) argue that the youths responsible for the Columbine School massacre were influenced by the video game *Manhunt*. Cumberbatch (2004) says that they should be 'ashamed of themselves' because they have no real evidence and their assertions are based on 'second-hand and hearsay evidence'.

There is also some disagreement about the nature of the effect produced by media violence. It is possible that the effect may be cathartic, in other words that media violence may enable audiences to get their aggression out of their systems and prevent real-life violence, but there is only limited evidence to support this view.

Research study

Fesbach and Sanger (1971) conducted an experiment on two groups of people from diverse backgrounds. Each group watched either violent or non-violent TV programmes for a period of six weeks. The group who had watched non-violent programmes were more aggressive at the end of the experiment.

A more plausible argument is that the steady diet of violence the media feeds us may cause desensitisation, i.e. we come to accept a higher level of violence as normal. This drip-feed idea is central to the cultural effects model. However, it can be argued that media violence may have the reverse effect, causing sensitisation. We may be so appalled by the violence we observe that we are less likely to be aggressive. Freedman (2002) makes the point succinctly when he asks, 'How many people would be encouraged to be warlike or violent after seeing the film *Schindler's List*?'

Other criticisms

Countries such as Japan and Canada have just as much media violence as the US and Britain, yet they have far lower levels of social violence. Rates of violent crime in the US have dropped dramatically during the past decade, yet no one would suggest that the American media has become less violent. There is also the rather obvious question of why some members of an audience may copy violence whereas the vast majority do not. The answer to this must be that there are other factors in some people's lives that cause them to be aggressive. This points to another failing of effects theorists. They tend to regard audiences as a homogeneous mass, instead of diverse groupings and individuals who interpret and act on the meanings of media texts in different ways.

Effects studies tend to ignore the context and nature of the media violence. Morrison (1999) showed a series of violent incidents to a range of people taken from different groups, including women, war veterans and young men. All of the participants found the most realistic violence, a

Take it further

GUMG has an excellent website (www.gla.ac.uk/centres/mediagroup) that summarises many of its research studies. Its interviews with Greg Philo and others can be used to supplement your knowledge of media effects.

man beating his wife in the film *Ladybird, Ladybird*, to be the most upsetting. They regarded the far more graphic violence of *Pulp Fiction* as amusing and unreal, demonstrating that people make distinctions between real and fantasy violence.

Effects studies cannot isolate other variables. How do we know that it is violent TV or videos that are the causal factor in producing aggression? There are dozens of other possible factors. In recent years, such concerns have led to a change of approach to the study of media violence: the focus has moved towards reception theory and active audience approaches. The crucial point is that people do not experience the media in a vacuum. How we react will depend on our own cultural history and the influence of family, peers and others. People who have violent backgrounds may be more susceptible to media violence than others, but it would be very surprising if an ordinary person committed an act of violence just because they had watched a TV programme. Himmelweit (1958) argues that it is 'not so much what children see on TV that matters, but what they bring with them'; in other words, the influence of family, peers, school, etc., is far more important than the media content itself. According to this argument, studies of media effects are fatally flawed if they do not analyse the social contexts.

Link

There is a strong link to crime and deviance, especially interactionist theories, and to theory and methods.

Summary questions

3 In what ways does the concept of moral panics help us to understand the public's view of crime and criminality?

4 Outline the problems involved in using laboratory-style experiments to examine the relationship between media violence and real-life violence.

5 Why has video game violence become an increasing cause for concern?

Mass media

127

Media stereotypes, advertising and consumerism

Mass media

Learning objectives:

- Understand the nature of stereotypes.
- Understand the relationship between advertising, consumerism and media representations.

Key terms

Stereotype: a preconceived, standardised and oversimplified impression of the characteristics which typify a person, situation, etc., often shared by all members of a society or certain social groups; an attitude based on such a preconception.

Summary questions

1 Why do we all stereotype people?

2 What does Williams mean when he argues that media advertising creates a 'magic world'?

Media representations of social groups have been a source of sociological concern for years. The media often presents simplified and stereotypical representations of women and other social groups.

A **stereotype** is closely linked with the idea of labelling and can have negative consequences for the people stereotyped: for example, it has been demonstrated that black children who are stereotyped or labelled as disruptive are far more likely to be excluded from school. We all stereotype people to categorise them and make sense of the world. It is not simply a question of the media being responsible for stereotyping; family, peers, schools, etc., all help to create and sustain stereotypes. One of the questions we should ask ourselves is, 'To what extent does the media create stereotypes and to what extent does the media reflect stereotypes in society?'

The content of the mass media is greatly affected by advertising. Increased competition has deepened this dependency. Most media rely on advertising to be profitable. Advertisers are concerned with making profits, so they must present images that appeal to people and encourage them to buy products. Stereotypes often help here.

One of the stereotypes that is constantly portrayed in advertisements is the nuclear family. This is presented as the norm and the ideal; in fact, it is so pervasive that the two-parent, two-child family is often called the cereal packet family. Media advertising creates a 'magic world' (Williams 1980) where the meaning of life, for the individual and family, is consumption. The family can achieve happiness and contentment through the goods they buy. Critical theorists such as Williams have long been concerned with the effects of this 'obsessive consumerism', arguing that our preoccupation with consumer goods means that we, as a society, do not concern ourselves with trying to improve the structures of our society.

Why do the media and advertising focus on the nuclear, privatised family? To sell more products. This family type consumes more than people living a communal lifestyle would. They are isolated and atomised and are easy to manipulate. The media and advertisers are not just trying to sell a number of different goods and services; they are trying to sell a whole way of life. The increasing number of lifestyle TV programmes and channels is another reflection of this; fashion and decorating programmes teach us that we can buy happiness. Makeover programmes such as *What Not to Wear*, originally with Trinny and Susannah, suggest that improved fashion sense and beauty trips will not only enhance our quality of life but can be the remedy for psychological and relationship problems. Consumerism is God in our secular world and the home its temple.

Media representations of gender

Learning objectives:

- Evaluate ideas and evidence on media representations of gender.

- Understand and explain changes in media representations of gender.

Link

Gender stereotypes links to culture and identity, and stratification.

Key terms

Patriarchal: male dominance of society, and the means by which this is transmitted from generation to generation, e.g. the media.

Take it further

The Mediaknowall website (www.mediaknowall.com) has a lot of useful articles and information on this topic.

Representations of women

In the 1970s and 1980s feminist analyses of the mass media were very much based on the effects approach. Many studies using content analysis presented a remarkably consistent picture of the **patriarchal** nature of the media, particularly television.

Gaye Tuchman's 1978 book *Hearth and Home: Images of Women in the Mass Media* is a classic example of this kind of study. Here are three of its findings:

- Women were overwhelmingly presented in two roles, domestic (housewife and mother) and sexual (including romantic). Men were portrayed as authority figures, workers, breadwinners and sportsmen.

- Men outnumbered women by three to one on television. Women suffered 'symbolic annihilation' by the media 'through absence, condemnation or trivialisation'.

- Game shows, quizzes and discussion programmes were invariably presented by men (authority figures).

Butler and Paisley (1980) in their analysis of TV advertisements very much support Tuchman's analysis:

- 90 per cent of voiceovers in adverts were male, again showing male authority.

- 70 per cent of women, compared with 10 per cent of men, were shown doing domestic chores. Men were presented as the recipients of women's labours: eating the food, wearing the freshly laundered clothes, etc. When women were not doing housework, they were obsessed with their looks: make-up, fashion, dieting, etc.

- 60 per cent of women were shown in family roles, compared with only 16 per cent of men.

Changes

Brundsman *et al.* argue that, since the 1980s, US and UK television have changed significantly in their representations of women. TV now features numerous 'strong women' and single mothers as well as 'other female types who are integral to the feminist critique' of the media. Abercrombie (1999) even says that soap storylines are actually driven by strong female figures, such as Peggy Mitchell in *EastEnders*. Women also feature in TV genres where once they were peripheral, such as police dramas. In the 1970s, programmes such as *The Sweeney* were male centred; women played bit parts as wives and prostitutes. Now, in programmes like *The Bill* and *Prime Suspect*, they are centre stage and hold positions of authority.

Situation comedies show similar developments. In the 1970s many sitcoms, like *Dad's Army* and *Steptoe and Son* had virtually no female characters at all. Anderson (1998) argues that women now play major roles in such comedies. Indeed sitcoms like *Roseanne* and *2 Point 4 Children* are housewife comedies whose main characters actually challenge male power and deconstruct the myths of idealised family life and the role of women in the family.

Mass media

Some sociologists have interpreted these changes as reflecting societal developments – increased gender equality and greater confidence among young women. Many feminists are more circumspect, pointing to the fact that the new women celebrities and presenters that dominate our screen are young, glamorous and sexy – sex still sells. There are many websites dedicated to sexy female news presenters and weather girls. Moreover, the overwhelming message of women-oriented media is still that women need to look good for their man, a point underlined by the predominance of cosmetics, fashion and plastic surgery advertisements in women's magazines. An unattainable ideal of size zero feminine beauty is presented, which may be linked to anorexia and other eating disorders.

The methods and forms of studies have also changed since the 1980s, reflecting the influence of active audience theories and **reception analysis**. Radway (1984) did a pioneering study on women readers of romantic fiction in the US. An effects approach would see such women as conforming to stereotypical women's interests and roles. But Radway found that the position was far more complex. From the viewpoint of these women, reading romances gave them 'space' from the demands of housework in patriarchal households. In a sense, reading romantic fiction was a kind of rebellion. Active audience studies have shown that women are not a homogeneous audience. They will choose and interpret media texts and representations in different ways. This point is emphasised by postmodernists who point to the choices available to today's women in the construction of their identities (Figure 3.5.1).

■ **Key terms**

Reception analysis: an analysis of how people interpret and use media texts in different ways.

Fig. 3.5.1 *Women in adverts – progress or change?*

In the 1970s the content of women's magazines was dominated by traditional, stereotypical female roles and concerns. Magazines such as *Woman* and *Good Housekeeping* focused on cooking, childcare and romance. But in 1999 a Policy Studies Institute (PSI) report analysed the significant changes in the new women's magazines that had been trailblazed by *Cosmopolitan*. It found an emphasis on having a good time, sex, relationships and looks. According to these magazines, the new woman is consumerist, sexually and socially assertive, vain and pleasure-loving. This phenomenon is not confined to magazines; a new generation of feisty, female, celebrity presenters have emerged on TV and radio, such as Denise Van Outen, Penny Smith and Anthea Turner. Winship (1987), however, argues that women's magazines provide images of femininity that emphasise independence and confidence, present women with far more choices for their identity, and tackle real concerns that were once taboo, such as domestic violence and sexual abuse.

Women, the media and power

There is no doubt that women are still greatly under-represented in positions of power in the media, especially at the top. The glass ceiling remains unbroken. A study of the advertising industry by Amber found that all the managing directors of the top 20 firms were men. A similar picture emerges when one examines the owners and controllers of all media enterprises. Though women have progressed – there are far more female directors, journalists and even editors – the top jobs still elude them. Furthermore, van Zomen (1994) argues that to succeed in the media, women have to adapt to the patriarchal ideology that dominates media companies.

Men

Many studies have shown that the mass media still tends to reinforce a dominant ideal of masculinity. Kibly argues that popular shows in the 1980s such as *The A-Team* and *Magnum* represented masculinity as being related to 'power, authority, aggression and technology'. Content analyses, such as Butler and Paisley's study (see above) showed that men were as stereotyped as women (as workers, authority figures, etc.). As with women, such depictions have changed over the years. Police dramas such as *Cracker* and *NYPD Blue* have blurred gender differences, presenting a feminised representation of men frequently uncertain of their roles and in touch with their feelings. Such characters are more emotional and less authoritative.

Sport, however, provides refuge for men from the increasingly confused concepts of masculinity they encounter. Sport is about aggression, strength and action, and the media's coverage of sport reflects this. Media sport also focuses on success. A series of surveys by Crechen showed that a large majority of people regarded women's sport as inferior to men's and thought that some sports were unsuitable for women. Various analyses have shown that 80 to 90 per cent of media coverage is dedicated to men's sport.

Absolutely Fabulous *and* Men Behaving Badly

A comparison of the two sitcoms *Absolutely Fabulous* and *Men Behaving Badly* gives insight into the current state of play in media representations of gender. In *Absolutely Fabulous*, Eddy and Patsy are independent, selfish, consumerist and aggressive. Patsy is a sexual predator who uses young men for her own sexual gratification and makes excessive use of alcohol and drugs. Eddy takes little maternal responsibility for her daughter, Saffy, and she ignores and verbally abuses her mother. She does no housework. Traditional female roles are rejected and mocked.

Lewisham argues that *Men Behaving Badly* has leading male characters who say 'bollocks to the sensitive caring, new man'. To be a new lad means being self-centred, rude and boorish, 'getting pissed on beer, swearing, bragging, belching, farting, fantasising, spewing and publicly rearranging [your] genitals'. Such behaviour is constantly being ridiculed by the two female characters, who are more sophisticated and intelligent. The emergence of the new lad is also supported by the incredible success of men's lifestyle magazines since the 1980s. Publications such as *Maxim*

AQA Examiner's tip

Questions and essays on gender representations should include women and men, unless you are specifically instructed to focus on one or the other.

Mass media

and *Loaded* can be seen as the male equivalent of magazines like *Cosmopolitan*. They concentrate on traditional male interests: booze, birds, gadgets and sport. Gauntlet (2002), however, argues that commentators have taken the new laddism of such magazines too seriously. He argues that much of the sexism expressed is, in fact, light-hearted and ironic; a reaction to the hypocritical political correctness of wider society.

Theoretical perspectives

In theoretical terms, Marxists and Marxist feminists see the media as essentially sexist in its presentation as it wishes to maximise profits for itself and its advertisers. Changes in presentation reflect new business opportunities. Radical feminists see media representations as a way of reinforcing patriarchy, restricting women's roles and maintaining their subservience. Liberal feminists accept that media representations of women are still stereotypical in many ways, but point to improvements and argue that as the number of women working in the media continues to increase, media depictions will become more realistic. Pluralists, particularly postmodernists, emphasise the diversity and choices for gender identities offered by today's media. The heterogeneous audiences of today select and use the media texts that appeal to them and interpret them in their own ways.

■ **Hint**

In analysing gender representations and all the other stereotypes we will examine, bear in mind the models and theories of media effects. In particular, remember that the media is not solely responsible for stereotypes. Ask yourself to what extent the media creates stereotypes or merely reflects and reinforces them.

■ **Summary questions**

3 How have media representations of women changed in recent years?

4 How have media representations of men changed in recent years?

5 How do reception theorists criticise effects studies on media representation of gender?

Ethnicity, racism and stereotypes

Mass media

Learning objectives:

- ▪ Understand analysis of how minority ethnics are represented in the media.

- ▪ Understand analysis of changes in media representations of minority ethnics.

The media is often accused of being racist and presenting stereotypical images of minority ethnics, such as the thick Irishman, the black mugger and the Asian shopkeeper. Minority ethnics are greatly under-represented in the media. There are few people of colour in top media positions and few programmes are aimed at minority ethnics.

Research study

Angela Barry in 'Black Mythologies: Representation of Black People on British Television' reports that when black people are portrayed they are depicted as troublemakers, dependants or sports figures. There is a big emphasis on cultural differences, criminality and racial conflict. Stuart Hall's showed how the media presented mugging as a black crime.

Key terms

Tokenism: the inclusion of a figure who may be black, female, gay, and so on, into a media text to show that the text is not racist, sexist, etc.

The GUMG, among others, has shown how news and current affairs programmes are essentially nationalistic. Developing countries are presented as problems; disasters, wars, famines, etc., are the newsworthy stories we associate with them. From a Marxist viewpoint, such portrayals reinforce the capitalist system by showing the superiority of white Western culture. Until recent years, blacks have been portrayed as servants, figures of fun, slaves. This has been replaced by **tokenism**, where members of minority ethnics are included to show that the media product is not racist. The TV series *South Park* pokes fun at this phenomena; the forename of its only black character is 'Token'.

Hartman and Husband argue that the media operates within a culture that sees foreigners, especially blacks, as inferior. The media emphasises racial conflict and problems and presents negative images of minority ethnics. This is likely to increase problems in mixed-race areas and in all-white communities. If this is people's only source of information, it is likely to increase prejudices.

Van Djilks (1991) studied the inner-city riots of the 1980s and showed how the tabloid press focused on a racial and criminal explanation of the riots, even though many young white people were involved. The *Sun* dismissed sociological explanations of the riots as 'making excuses for criminals'. Using a form of content analysis called discourse analysis, Van Djilks analysed the meanings and ideology behind these portrayals. He argued that the British media constantly flatters its readers with statements like 'the British are a kind and tolerant people' always followed by the racist 'but'; then minority ethnics are accused of abusing our hospitality, being social security scroungers, bogus asylum seekers, criminals and terrorist sympathisers.

▪ Changes in media portrayals of minority ethnics

Hall (1989) argues that, in the past, the three basic representations of blacks in the cinema and on TV were as natives, entertainers and slaves. Ethnicity is viewed 'through the white eye' and interpreted through the 'grammar of race'. The media's view of minority ethnics is coloured by colonialism and the dominance of the white Western world. This goes beyond blacks; think of the depiction of Native Americans in cowboy films – the noble warrior, the scalping savage, etc. Minority ethnics are presented as inferior or subordinate, whites as dominant or superior.

■ Research study

Jones and Jones argue that the use of minority ethnic actors to play aliens in TV series and films demonstrates the 'otherness' of minority ethnics.

Appreciation of black culture has grown. There are now major figures in music, the arts and the media in general, plus far more programmes and TV channels specifically for minority ethnics, partly as a result of digital technologies, which make small audience channels economically viable. More important is the crossover of minority ethnic culture into the mainstream. Programmes like *Goodness Gracious Me* and *The Kumars at No. 42* and films such as *Bend It Like Beckham* and *Bride and Prejudice*, a Bollywood adaptation of Jane Austen's novel *Pride and Prejudice*, are extremely popular with white audiences, which demonstrates a more multicultural media in the 21st century.

■ Research study

Abercrombie (1996) argues that nowhere are these positive changes more apparent than in soaps, where minority ethnics are treated in a far less stereotypical way than in the past, as ordinary people rather than exotic and dangerous others.

In news and current affairs programmes, however, black criminality remains a major concern. Hall argues that blacks, especially young males, are still presented as dangerous and a social problem – blacks as criminals, gangstas and drug addicts. Hall also points out that blacks are only allowed to excel in certain areas, such as sport and music, which require physical, not intellectual skills – a new variation on blacks as entertainers.

'Fair Play', a 2001 study by Children Now illustrates the continuation of gender and ethnic stereotypes in video games. It covered all the main game systems and found that 86 per cent of heroes were white. Eight out of 10 black characters were portrayed as competitors in sports games. Latinos only appeared in sports games and 86 per cent of black female characters were portrayed as victims of violence. It seems from this evidence that the new media aimed at younger people is more stereotypical than traditional media.

The War on Terror has also produced a new stereotype: the Muslim terrorist or suicide bomber. Media representations have, in this instance, helped to provoke anxiety in Muslim and non-Muslim communities. Dr Haideh Moghissi is professor of sociology at York University. She argues that Muslims are 'huddled together' by the media, which ignores the huge range of differences between Muslims in class, beliefs and culture. Since 9/11 and 7/7 there has been a moral panic about Islam and coverage of Muslim culture has been overwhelmingly negative. The veil has been presented as a symbol of the subjugation of Muslim women. The media has reported a number of horrific so-called honour killings by Asians, and young Muslim men have been labelled as potential terrorists.

There has been far less reception analysis on ethnicity than on gender. However, similar arguments are applicable. There are numerous minority ethnics in every society, and there are major variations between and within minority ethnics on how they interpret and use media texts. A 1992 study by Jhaaly and Lewis found that black women, white women and black men had very different perceptions of *The Cosby Show*.

Research study

Reid found that black women were heavily critical of *The Cosby Show* because its depiction of blacks was idealised and unrealistic. Black women were equally critical of documentaries that reinforced negative stereotypes of blacks.

The media and ethnicity

Functionalists argue that media presentations of minority ethnics reflect their position in society. These depictions change to reflect the integration of minority ethnics into mainstream culture; one example is the positive portrayal of successful Asian businessmen. Pluralists would also argue that the poor representation of some minority ethnics reflects their current social standing. The media is reflecting mainstream (white) opinions and values in its portrayal of minority ethnics. News values – the emphasis on conflict, crime and the sensational – also play a major role (Figure 3.5.2).

Marxists and neo-Marxists see things very differently. In broad terms, they emphasise how the media uses racism to promote the interests of the powerful. Moral panics about immigrants and asylum seekers help to divide the working class on racial grounds and produce false consciousness. The blame for economic and social problems, like unemployment and crime, is focused on minority ethnics rather than the real causes – capitalism and the injustices that are part of its nature.

Take it further

The media pages of the *Guardian* website (www.guardian.co.uk/media) have a range of useful articles on this and other issues relating to stereotypes.

Link

Media representations of minority ethnics links to culture and identity, crime and deviance, and stratification.

Summary questions

6 Outline how media depictions of minority ethnics have become more positive in recent years.

7 Negative portrayals of minority ethnics by the media are still remarkably persistent. What evidence is there to support this view?

a

b

"... And what makes you think you'd be a good candidate for the next series of 'Big Brother'?"

c

Fig. 3.5.2 a and b *In the reality TV show* Celebrity Big Brother *(CBB), Jade Goody and others were accused of racially abusing Indian contestant Shilpa Shetty. Many commentators felt that Channel 4 had exploited the situation to boost flagging audience numbers.*
c *CBB meets KKK*

Representations of sexuality and disability

Learning objectives:

- Understand how sexuality and disability are represented in the mass media.

- Evaluate changes in representations of sexuality and disability.

Key terms

Camp: depiction of gay people as effeminate, mincing men with high voices.

Heterosexual gaze: the idea that homosexual issues are presented by the media from a heterosexual viewpoint.

Sexuality: a gay-friendly media?

According to Dyer (2002), representations of male homosexuality in the media have tended to be dominated by **camp** characters – effeminate, mincing men with high voices – who make fun of the serious and respectable. Although such characters may have a slightly subversive role, they are also a safe form of sexual stereotype, unchallenging to traditional masculinity.

They may also be seen as an example of carnival (page 109). The roles played by comic actors such as Kenneth Williams and Charles Hawtrey in the bawdy *Carry On* films are excellent examples of this. Such representations are still extremely popular; the success of Graham Norton and Julian Clary show the continuing popularity of camp. Other media depictions of homosexuals have, however, been far more negative and hostile. In the 1980s most of the media's attention to gay issues was directed at AIDS. The *Sun* newspaper headlined it 'the gay plague'. Homosexuality as a threat is another common stereotype. During the debate over gays in the military, the *Daily Star* ran the headline 'Poofters on parade'. In 2000 the *Sun* claimed that a 'gay mafia' controlled the Labour government.

In more recent years, TV drama and comedy have been somewhat kinder to homosexuals and lesbians. *Brookside* and *Friends* featured lesbian relationships in a reasonably sympathetic way. *EastEnders* and other soaps have featured major homosexual characters. However, their plots still tend to focus on homosexuality as a problem and on gays coming to terms with their sexuality. In other words, homosexual storylines are constructed for a heterosexual audience and viewed through a **heterosexual gaze**. Male homosexual characters are overwhelmingly white and middle class. Gross (1993) observes that there are no 'just plain gay folks' in the media.

The 1999 TV series *Queer as Folk* was ground-breaking in its treatment of homosexuality. The main characters were young, stylish and gay. The sex was explicit and the gay characters far from nice. Russell Davies, the gay creator of the series, received acclaim and criticism from homosexuals and heterosexuals. Davies argued that the series showed that gay representations in the media had grown up – gays could be selfish and bad now, not just respectable representatives of the gay community.

Lesbians and lesbianism have received less attention from the media than gay men. There are stock characters – dungaree-wearing, man-hating, hairy-legged 'dykes' – but lesbian relationships are usually implicit. *Xena: Warrior Princess* became a cult series among some lesbians in the late 1990s. There is no explicit lesbian activity but the show revolves around Xena's relationship with her young female companion, Gabrielle. The series demonstrates the variety of interpretations (reception theory) that audiences place on media texts. Some saw subliminal lesbianism, others saw an adventure story.

Perhaps the limited portrayal of lesbianism in the past reflects the threat it poses to traditional concepts of masculinity. Interestingly, a distinct and popular genre of pornography presents lesbian sex for the gratification of men. In more mainstream media the invisibility of lesbianism is also less apparent. Lesbian films such as *Bound* and *Kissing Jessica Stein* achieved box office success, though as Whelehan argues, they feature images 'that have nothing to do with the way lesbians might perceive each other and a great deal to do with male, heterosexual fantasies'.

Series such as *Oranges Are Not the Only Fruit* and *Tipping the Velvet* show that explicit lesbian sex and lesbian issues can now be sold to heterosexuals. Naomi Klein (2000) argues that this is a result of the diversification of society and recognition by the media and advertisers that there is money to be made from homosexuality – the pink pound. Homosexuality and lesbianism have become commodities from which big business can profit.

Disability: victims and miracles?

The past 20 years have seen considerable changes in societal attitudes towards disability. Equal opportunities legislation has attempted to outlaw discrimination on the grounds of disability. Institutions and commercial premises are required by law to provide access for disabled people. Has the media changed to reflect these developments in society? Or are the disabled still ignored or patronised by mainstream media organisations?

Anne Karpf (1988) argued that the media has two main approaches to disability: an obsession with miracle cures, and with disabled people as victims, especially children. These 'victims' appear on telethons so we pity them and treat them as charity cases. Medicine is seen as a cure and charity is seen as offering help. We are encouraged to pity the disabled and praise them for courage in dealing with their problems. Disabled people very rarely appear in ordinary programmes, leading ordinary lives.

Cumberbatch and Negrine (1992) found that there were no disabled people on any of the current affairs programmes or TV quizzes. They also made up only 0.5 per cent of characters in fictional programmes. Although telethons may raise valuable funds, they also maintain negative stereotypes. They may humiliate disabled people and are often patronising. Their main benefit, Karpf argues, is to give cheap advertising and a positive image to the big corporations that donate money.

Disabled people are rarely asked to contribute to discussions on issues like abortion and genetic engineering, where they may have an obvious input. Advances in medicine may contribute to cures for disability but they also enable women to identify genetic defects in their unborn babies and offer the opportunity to abort. Surely disabled people, who are likely to be most affected by such developments, should be among the first to discuss them. Yet the media almost always seeks the views of doctors, churchmen and other experts.

There have been improvements in some areas. O'Sullivan and Jewkes (1997) argue that there are now far more disabled people on TV. Disabled people are presented in a far more rounded way in films such as *My Left Foot*, *Rain Man* and *The Piano*.

Take it further

PinkNews (www.pinknews.co.uk) has some very interesting material from a gay viewpoint.

Summary questions

8 How have media depictions of gay characters and issues changed in recent years?

9 To what extent have media depictions of disability and media attitudes towards disability changed in the past 10 years?

Mass media

Representations of class and age

Mass media

Learning objectives:

- Understand how social classes and age groups are represented by the media.

- Examine evidence and theories on representation of social classes and age groups.

- Evaluate changes in representations of social classes, the old and the young.

Link

There is a direct link to stratification, culture and identity, politics and power and theory and methods. The effectiveness of content analysis is an important idea.

Representations of class

Marxists argue that the media is controlled by upper-class and professional people. It is ideological and this is reflected in its portrayal of the working class. Neo-Marxist thinkers, such as the GUMG, focus on the media's anti-union attitudes. In the miners' strike of 1984, pickets were depicted as violent and a threat to public order. Trade unions, in general, are presented as making threats and being militant and unreasonable. This anti-union bias strengthens employers' hands in negotiations. Managers are also given time to explain their viewpoint and are interviewed in their offices in a calm atmosphere, whereas workers are often briefly interviewed on the picket lines, which adds to the impression of militancy. Strikes are depicted as bad, whatever the causes, and media reports often say things like this: 'The union is holding the country to ransom.'

Other working-class stereotypes are sympathetic but often mocking: a good example is Del Boy, the cheerful cockney conman in *Only Fools and Horses*. Richard Butsch (2002) in his study of US TV programmes 'Ralph, Fred, Archie and Homer' argues that TV recreates the stereotype of white working-class men as buffoons who are immature, irresponsible and require the supervision of their betters. In terms of gender, middle-class wives are more prevalent in US and British TV. They are also presented in a positive way, as career women. Working-class wives tend to be invisible and are mostly featured in soaps.

In 'The Silenced Majority' Barbara Ehrenreich (1989) argues that TV rarely represents the interests of working-class people. News and current affairs programmes feature 'white, professional, experts' to discuss issues of relevance to the working class. When working-class men are portrayed, they are 'dumb, inarticulate and old-fashioned'. The British sitcom *The Royle Family* captures another set of stereotypes: idle father and long-suffering mother in a family of couch potatoes that endlessly watch TV and wait for their lottery numbers to come up. Since the 1960s there have been attempts to adopt a more realistic and sympathetic approach to working-class life. Alan Bleasdale's classic *Blackstuff* dramas dealt with the problems of working-class life in Thatcher's Britain. This has continued in Paul Abbot's *Shameless* and Jimmy McGovern's *The Street*.

Soaps are the most popular of all British TV programmes. Their common feature is that they are mostly based in working-class communities. It seems that as real working-class communities have declined, these fictional ones have multiplied. Geraghty (1991) argues that people feel they can interact with these fictional communities, so soaps help compensate for loss of community. People often become attached to the characters in soaps; Marxists see this as another form of alienation and a source of false consciousness. The characters in soaps tend to be stereotypical – tart, bastard, gossip, etc. – and much of the action takes place in the pub or the local shop, the traditional focuses of working-class community, so the mainly working-class viewers can temporarily inhabit a virtual community.

Representations of age

Old age

Both the old and the young have suffered from negative media stereotyping, primarily because working adults have had the most disposable income. Youth, beauty and success go hand in hand, and consumers are encouraged to buy a vast range of products to stay that way.

Old age has tended to be presented as a social and economic problem, with emphasis on poverty, ill health and loss of independence. The old are 'out of touch' with modern technology and lifestyles. Christopher Lasch (1979) argues, from a Marxist viewpoint, that this is because the old are economically useless to capitalism. They do not work or produce and most have little to spend. Old age is to be feared and delayed. Fortunately, advertising and business can provide us with a vast array of products to postpone this awful fate: cosmetics, fitness aids and the fastest-growing market of all, cosmetic surgery.

Ageism is liberally mixed with sexism. A US survey in 2001 found that only 3 per cent of prime-time TV characters were over 70, compared to 10 per cent in the population as a whole; 33 per cent of prime-time male characters were over 40, compared to 19 per cent of prime-time female characters. Hollywood is even more guilty of double standards in this context; male stars are regularly given leading ladies less than half their age.

But like the other representations we have examined, things are changing. Over the past 20 years or so, the number of middle-class, affluent retired people has grown significantly. This so-called 'third age' has been identified as a potentially lucrative source of revenue by the media and business. The 'grey pound' has produced a range of media material aimed at the affluent elderly, from TV programmes to magazines such as *Saga* and *Choice*. The demand for holidays and leisure activities from this social group has become big business.

In his 1998 book *Ageing and Popular Culture*, Blaikie also points to changes in attitudes towards old age. The old cliché of 'mutton dressed as lamb' is no longer applied to celebrities like Mick Jagger and Cher – the over 50s now have a far more positive image.

Youth

Like old age, youth is a socially constructed concept and it tends to be defined by adults. We have already examined the negative stereotyping of youths in the context of media crime and moral panics (page 123). On 15 February 2007 the *Daily Express* ran the headline 'Clockwork Orange Britain', a reference to a notorious film that featured gangs of drug-crazed youths with bizarre clothing and make-up attacking and killing ordinary people. Other newspapers featured similar headlines. The reports referred to a spate of brutal murders committed by youths 'high on cheap alcohol and drugs'. This was the latest of a series of moral panics concerning young people since 2000 – knife crime, gangsta rap, binge drinking, hoodies, teenage pregnancies and gun crimes. Some sociologists argue that it has become pointless to talk about moral panics, because they are so frequent as to be almost continuous.

The representations of youth in today's media focus on dramatic, sensational bad news, but there is also an emphasis on consumerism. The youth market has become increasingly lucrative since the 1950s and

Mass media

AQA Examiner's tip

In exam questions, do not restrict yourself to ideas from this section. Use material from other sections, such as Greg Philo's research (page 122). The section on media crime and violence contains a lot of relevant material for representations of youth.

a whole range of youth-oriented goods are advertised in the media, such as alcopops, music, fashion and console games. There has been a dramatic increase in the number of magazines, TV channels and other media formats aimed at the young. Consequently, the media has an ambivalent attitude towards youth and this is clearly apparent in its coverage. There is almost always a brief mention that the vast majority of young people are well-behaved and sensible, then an overwhelming focus on the negative side. Well-behaved young people are hardly newsworthy.

Issues of class, ethnicity and gender are inevitably linked to media representations of youth – the 'black mugger' highlighted in Stuart Hall's study is a classic example of this. In the past, girls have received less media attention than boys, who were seen as the main perpetrators of crime and antisocial behaviour. This has changed somewhat as stories of girl gangs and laddette binge drinking have made the headlines. Another major feature in the media treatment of teenage girls is a concern over girls' low self-esteem and their obsession with body image, which may lead to eating disorders. Mazzarella and Pecara (2001) studied newspaper stories about teenage girls in the US. They found that over half the articles they studied were concerned with intervention and prevention of problems like these, along with teenage pregnancy, sexual diseases, etc. Furthermore, in only 20 per cent of these stories were there any quotes or other input from teenage girls; instead the media called on an expert to give their views and offer solutions.

Take it further

Media Awareness Network (www.media-awareness.ca) and Mediaknowall (www.mediaknowall.com) contain relevant and up-to-date material on representations of class and age and on all media stereotypes. Newspaper websites such as www.timesonline.co.uk, www.independent.co.uk and www.guardian.co.uk have in-depth coverage of many contemporary studies; they can also be used for the other sections of the topic.

Summary questions

10 What evidence is there to suggest the working class is portrayed as dumb, inarticulate and old-fashioned?

11 To what extent does the media depict old age as a social problem?

12 To what extent does the media portray youth as bad news?

3.6 New media

Old and new media

Learning objectives:

- Understand the nature of and relationships between old and new media.
- Evaluate the impact of the new media, including theoretical perspectives.
- Analyse the implications of the interactive nature of the new media.

Travelling by plane is a very different experience than it was 20 years ago. Back-of-seat screens can show many films, TV channels and video games. You can listen to your iPod or work on your laptop. Twenty years ago, there would have been a newspaper or magazine at best. What has created this revolution in airborne entertainment? The new digital media that lets us connect wherever we are. However, most airlines still forbid in-flight use of mobile phones. Twenty years ago, passengers would light up the second they left a smoke-free flight, now they reach desperately for their mobiles.

The old media primarily relied on print and analogue communication, such as newspapers and magazines, TV and radio. The past 25 years have seen a revolution in media based on digital computers, such as the internet, digital TV and digital radio; they are new media. Even print media have adopted digital technologies, producing internet editions and employing image manipulation through desktop publishing.

Research study

Shapiro (1999) argues that the development of digital technologies presents 'a potentially radical shift in who controls information, experience and resources'. Old media content was under vertical control by media corporations, whereas new media content is under horizontal control of its participants and audience.

Neuman (2003) argues that the new media will:

- produce a huge increase in the volume of communication
- change the meaning of geographical distance (virtual, internet, worldwide, communities with instant personal communication)
- provide the opportunity for interactive communication
- allow previously separate forms of communication to interconnect and overlap
- blur the distinction between personal and mass communication and between public and private communication.

The effects of these changes are debatable. Kellner (1995) argues for the 'democratising' potential of the new media and the internet, because this new 'public sphere' encourages non-hierarchical interaction and debate. However, critics such as McChesney (2000) are less optimistic, pointing to increasing control of the new media by transnational corporations.

Early studies of the new media tended to be **technologically determinist**, seeing the technology itself as the cause of change. More recent studies have tended to focus on the complex social and economic factors that influence the nature and effects of the new media. People use the internet not only for personal communication but also to bank, shop, entertain

Key terms

Technological determinism: the concept that a society's technology determines its cultural values, social structure or history.

Link

Habermas's concept of the public sphere also links to the topic on power and politics.

Key terms

Interactivity: when audiences and participants play an active role in creating and responding to media content.

Virtual community: a community that is formed through digital interaction and that has no physical existence.

Hint

The development of the new media is very important in considering all other media topics. For example, how does the development of the new media affect issues of ownership and control, the production of news, etc?

AQA Examiner's tip

Use the development of the new media to add a dimension to questions on all subtopics (see the hint above). In particular, remember the importance of the new media in issues of control and power.

and educate themselves. Consumerism has been a driving force in the development of the new media, as shown by the success of eBay and the proliferation of internet advertising, a far cry from Habermas's concept of a public sphere independent of big business.

The new media: an interactive revolution?

A key claim made by proponents of the new media is the potential for **interactivity**. The vertical, one-to-many nature of the old media is replaced by a horizontal, many-to-many form of communication. Anyone who has access to a computer and the internet can produce and transmit their own text and images to other members of the **virtual community** that is the web. Most poor people are still excluded from this process, but the growth of internet cafes throughout the developing world, even in small villages, is enabling more and more people to have internet access. There is the obvious potential to create a democratic public sphere. A wide range of views can be expressed, including minority and alternative opinions. However there are several concerns about the nature and development of the internet:

- Many of the most successful websites are being acquired by media corporations.
- Terrorist tracts and other extremist material can be communicated via the internet.
- It is often difficult to work out where messages come from and who is sending them. Businesses often present what are essentially advertisements for diets, cosmetics, etc., as public information. Similarly, religious and political groups often present their views and opinions as objective factual material.
- The very freedom of the web has allowed access to controversial material such as pornography and violence.
- The internet has facilitated identity theft, financial fraud and other criminal behaviour. One of my students put their details on Facebook. Someone stole their identity and used it to start an online romance with another Facebook member.

The difficulties of the interactive public sphere have raised many other moral issues: paedophiles use chatlines to groom children for sexual abuse; others use the internet to distribute pictures of child abuse; violent pornography has been implicated in copycat crimes; terrorist groups and religious sects use websites to recruit members; people become addicted to online gambling; suicide sites may encourage young people to take their own lives. At the start of 2008, police investigated the role of websites in a cluster of suicides by young people centred on Bridgend, Wales.

To some extent, these concerns are similar to concerns about the old media – the effects of media violence, etc. – but interactivity introduces an extra dimension. The very freedom of expression offered by the new media increases the possibility of abuse. An internet user can adopt a completely different persona, effectively become a different virtual person. This leads to questions about the reality and nature of identity. The postmodernist view that identity is a matter of choice is given its ultimate, disturbing realisation.

Interactive games are another important element. Flew (2005) argues that people can live their lives through games such as *Sims*. This phenomenon can be interpreted in a more negative way. The isolated computer nerd is a stereotype, but it has a grain of truth. Computer games can be socially isolating and provide an unhealthy escapism. For Marxists, such developments reflect the alienation that many people suffer in capitalist societies. If a person takes on a false identity or depends on a virtual life to achieve fulfilment, what does this say about the nature of real life in consumerist societies?

Research study

Terry Flew (2005) argues that the interactive games industry is responsible for some of the most significant innovations in the new media. Although Flew is largely referring to technical developments, he also makes the point that interactive games allow players to establish relationships 'across the boundaries of time and space'.

An interesting example is *World of Warcraft* (WOW), a fantasy, role-playing game in which players adopt characters and try to work their way from level 1 to level 80 by fighting with other players and acquiring weapons and magical artefacts. Some adept players work characters up to high levels then sell them with magic weapons, etc., for hundreds of real dollars. Dr Maressa Orzack, a clinical psychologist who studies games addiction, argues that up to 40 per cent of the 6 million US WOWers are addicted to the game, but she presents little evidence to support this claim. The Chinese government is bringing in legislation to prevent the 20 million Chinese 'WOWers' from playing the game for too long because of the 'social and economic damage' caused by such addiction. The stereotypical depictions of gender, ethnic groups, etc., in such games is another cause for concern.

Take it further

There are a huge range of websites dedicated to the new media and its developments. NMA (www.nma.co.uk) is a useful source, as are the BBC website (www.bbc.co.uk) and newspaper websites.

Fig. 3.6.1 *Hundreds attended a virtual funeral for a young gamer who died in the real world*

No analysis of the new media would be complete without a reference to the ubiquitous mobile phone. The growth in the number of mobile phone users over the past decade has been phenomenal; even people in developing countries use mobile phones for business and personal calls. The mobile phone is a personal portable device that can now provide

Link

There are direct links to culture and identity, politics and power.

AQA Examiner's tip

Use the development of the new media to add a dimension to all questions on mass media. In particular, remember the importance of the new media for issues of control and power.

radio, TV, films and the internet plus a means of personal contact through phone calls and texts. The mobile phone is not just a means of communication, it is a status symbol, fashion accessory and badge of identity that must be regularly updated.

Summary questions

1 Give two key differences between old media and new media.

2 Outline the possible effects of the new media on individual and social behaviour.

3 Examine the importance of new media in media ownership and control.

Mass media

New media and globalisation

Mass media

Learning objectives:

- Understand the impact of the new media on globalisation.

- Understand studies of the relationship between the new media and globalisation.

AQA Examiner's tip

Globalisation and the new media adds an extra dimension to essays and questions on ownership and control and culture.

Take it further

The openDemocracy website (www.opendemocracy.net) provides a range of useful studies and comment on new media and globalisation.

Summary questions

4 What is the significance of the merger between AOL and Time Warner?

5 How can the development of the new media be seen as an aid to democracy in the process of globalisation?

The global impact of the new media has been an integral part of the analysis in this section, as well as a major element in the section on globalisation. Although the new media have had an impact in poorer countries, there is still a big divide between the information rich and the information poor. Some commentators have seen this as yet another fundamental form of inequality between the rich world and the poor world that is likely to further increase economic and social inequalities in general.

The new media will have a considerable impact but it is hard to predict exactly what will happen. The crucial question is whether the new media will help to facilitate a more democratic world, where people and groups can exercise influence and interact in the public sphere, or will transnational media corporations, plus other forms of big business and indeed governments, exercise control over the new media and its messages? The following points illustrate the contradictory developments that may characterise the global impact of the new media in the years to come.

The merger of AOL and Time Warner in January 2000 was perhaps an appropriate way to herald a new media century. Time Warner was an old media company producing print, film, music, TV, etc. AOL was new media. They brought together internet, broadband, cable and content sources to become the biggest media conglomerate in the world, and demonstrated that the future lies in integrated media controlled by mega-media TNCs. In September 2003 the board of AOL Time Warner Inc. voted to drop AOL from its name and AOL is now a division of Time Warner. In 2008 News Corp. and Microsoft considered separate takeovers of the Yahoo! search engine. There will doubtless be many more mergers.

Croteau and Hoynes (2003) found that people were spending more and more time online but they were visiting fewer websites. The big websites, run by big business, receive far more hits because their names are more familiar and they frequently pay to come top of the search rankings. The millions of smaller sites are unknown and seldom visited. This trend must be disappointing for those who see the internet as a potential source of democratic debate and varied viewpoints.

Governments also control and censor the internet to preserve their authority. The Burmese government closed down the net during the anti-government protests of 2007. Google has been accused of bowing to political pressure from the Chinese government. In 2008 Pakistan's government closed down Facebook because it found some of its material offensive; this made the service unavailable worldwide for a short period.

There are more optimistic developments. The internet has been used to plan and coordinate global protest movements. It is ironic that the 1999 meeting of the World Trade Organisation (WTO) in Seattle was overshadowed by anti-globalisation street protests that were largely organised online by Independent Media Centre, a radical media website. Images and news of the protests were transmitted to the whole world by old and new media.

One might also argue that attempts by business and governments to control the internet are an indication of their concern about its potential power. We are likely to see a continued conflict between those who seek to control the new media and maintain the status quo, and those who seek to use it to undermine the existing political, economic and social order.

Topic summary

- Few sociologists argue with the contention that the mass media has transformed how people communicate, interact, shop and are informed and entertained.

- Marxists, and in a more sophisticated way neo-Marxists, argue that the media is owned and controlled by big business and is ideological, i.e. transmits the values and interests of the ruling class. Pluralists argue that the media presents a diverse range of materials and views, and its content is determined by audiences through the market mechanism.

- Neo-Marxists argue that mass production and the mass media have produced a culture based on consumerism. Elite theorists argue that mass culture destroys the aesthetically superior high culture. Critics of mass culture theory emphasise the complex nature of contemporary culture. Postmodernists argue that the mass media and mass culture provide far more identity choices. Marxists argue that globalisation is characterised by cultural and media imperialism that destroys indigenous cultures. Supporters of globalisation argue that cultural exchange is by no means a one-way process.

- Pluralists argue that a wide range of materials and views are produced in response to the varied demands of audiences in a diverse, multicultural society. Marxists claim that the selection and presentation of news is ideological and reflects the interests of owners and managers, and ultimately the ruling class.

- Some models and theories claim that the media has a direct impact on audiences (hypodermic syringe), others argue that effects are mediated by social networks (audience interaction). Cultural effects theory combines elements of both these approaches. Much research has focused on the impact of the media on societal crime and violence. Although many studies have claimed to prove a causal relationship, the methods used to analyse media violence (experiments, etc.) have been criticised as lacking validity. There are also problems in defining and measuring media violence.

- The media has been accused of presenting negative representations of various social groups. There is a debate over the extent to which the media creates stereotypes or merely reflects existing stereotypes. Media representations are continually changing. This may reflect increased social tolerance or the needs of the media and advertising to exploit new markets.

- The new media has had an enormous effect on how people communicate and interact. There is an ongoing debate among sociologists about whether the internet will help create a new public sphere where people can communicate without interference from governments or business, or whether mergers between old and new media and the increasing control of transnational corporations will maintain the status quo. Concerns are also expressed about the possible negative social effects of the new media.

Further resources

Books

- A. Briggs and P. Cobley, *The Media: An Introduction*, 2nd edn, Longman, 2002
  Aimed at media students but useful for sociology students; readings that are mostly short and to the point

- J. Curran and M. Gurevitch, *Mass Media and Society*, Hodder Arnold, 2005
  A very impressive range of articles, including analysis of the internet and globalisation

- M. Jones and E. Jones, *Mass Media*, Palgrave Macmillan, 1999
  Part of the series 'Skills-based Sociology', it has excellent summaries of theories and concepts. Directly related to the A2 Sociology syllabus

- T. Sullivan and Y. Jewkes, *The Media Studies Reader*, 1996
  A wide range of useful readings

- P. Trowler, *Investigating the Media*, Collins, 1988
  Strong on media representations, models, concepts and theories; an accessible and very good basic media text

- Paul Willis, *Moving Culture*, Calouste Gulbenkian Foundation, 1990
  Short but very useful book about popular culture; lots of good ethnographic examples

Websites

- www.guardian.co.uk/media
  Media Guardian

- www.mediaawareness.com
  Media Awareness Network

- www.mediawatchuk.org.uk
  Media Watch

- www.mediaknowall.com
  Mediaknowall A-level media studies page

- www.studymedia.org
  Studymedia

Mass media

General Certificate of Education
Advanced Level Examination
Section C from Paper 3

SOCIOLOGY Unit 3

For this paper you must have:

a 12-page answer book

Time allowed 1 hour 30 minutes

SAMPLE 1

Section C: Mass Media

If you choose this Section, answer Question 7 and either Question 8 or Question 9.

Total for this section: 60 marks

7   Read Item C below and answer parts (a) and (b) that follow.

> **Item C**
>
> Traditional Marxist approaches to the mass media placed an emphasis
> on its role as an ideological weapon in the hands of the ruling class,
> and assumed that the media was able to 'inject' its message into an
> uncomprehending subject class, who remained largely ignorant of what was
> being done to them. This approach is known as the hypodermic syringe
> model.
>
> More recent Marxian analysis recognises the ability of the audience to
> make apparently rational choices, and refers to the need for the ruling
> class to secure some measure of subject class agreement to their position
> in the social hierarchy. Typically this approach is encapsulated in Gramsci's
> concept of hegemony.

Source: Written by Hamish Joyce

    (a)   Identify and briefly explain three criticisms of the hypodermic syringe model
(other than 'rational choice').   *(9 marks)*

    (b)   Using material from Item C and elsewhere, assess the view that the mass
media reinforce ruling class ideology.   *(18 marks)*

Either

8   'There is a profound and sustained difference between men and women's use and
interpretation of the mass media.' How far do sociological evidence and arguments
support this view of the media in Britain today?   *(33 marks)*

Or

9   'Existing theoretical approaches to ownership and control of the mass media have
increasingly little relevance in an era of globalised media. Today people in all parts
of the world can freely access cultural and political information and viewpoints.'
How far do sociological arguments and evidence support this view?   *(33 marks)*

General Certificate of Education

Advanced Level Examination

Section C from Paper 3

SOCIOLOGY Unit 3

For this paper you must have:

a 12-page answer book

Time allowed 1 hour 30 minutes

SAMPLE 2

Section C: Mass Media

If you choose this Section, answer Question 7 and either Question 8 or Question 9.

Total for this section: 60 marks

7   Read Item C below and answer parts (a) and (b) that follow.

Item C

In the 1980s sociological commentary on media depiction of ethnic minorities tended to focus on the roles in which such groups appeared. In particular it was claimed by sociologists such as Stuart Hall that the mass media negatively stereotyped black people for ideological reasons.

More recent research would seem to indicate that some of these negative stereotypes are breaking down. For example, many current affairs and news programmes feature ethnic minority reporters and presenters, and sports programmes feature black sports people as positive role models. We even have the slightly bizarre spectacle of a middle-class Jewish actor (Sasha Baron Cohen) playing a black 'gangsta' character for laughs. However, radical commentators still point to the under-representation of ethnic minorities in mainstream visual media, and to serial misrepresentation of ethnic minorities (particularly young Asian men) in the print media.

Source: Written by Hamish Joyce

(a)   Identify and briefly explain three ways in which the mass media negatively stereotype ethnic minorities (other than those referred to in the extract).   *(9 marks)*

(b)   Using material from Item C and elsewhere, assess the view that ethnic and other minority groups are negatively represented in contemporary British media for ideological reasons.   *(18 marks)*

Either

8   The popular view assumes that there is a direct correlation between media depiction of deviant behaviour and subsequent social action. How far do sociological evidence, argument and theory support this in contemporary society?   *(33 marks)*

Or

9   'Contrary to the views of some sociologists, media consumption is a complex and diverse affair, and one in which individual social actors make rational choices as to their use of media sources.' Critically discuss this approach to the relationship between the mass media and its audience in contemporary society.   *(33 marks)*

END OF THE UNIT 3 SECTION C
SAMPLE QUESTIONS

Introduction

Key terms

Politics: the struggle for power and influence between competing individuals and groups in society.

Government: the exercise of political authority over the actions and affairs of a political unit. The government is the policymaking branch of the state, enforcing its rulings and acting under its authority.

Democracy: people power; in Abraham Lincoln's phrase, 'government of the people, by the people and for the people'.

Equality: the belief that people should be treated equally and given equal opportunities.

Tyranny: oppressive and unjust government by a tyrant or despot.

Political sociology: the study of politics in a social context, particularly the relationship between politics, personalities and the social structure.

Political parties: organisations of broadly like-minded men and women that seek to win elections and implement their policies.

Pressure group: a body that does not stand for election but seeks to influence people in public office.

Liberal democracies: democracies that emphasise liberal values.

State: a political association that establishes sovereign jurisdiction within defined territorial borders.

Politics is about how we are governed. It concerns the ways in which decisions are made about **government**, state and public affairs: where power lies, how governments and states work, and different theories and practices such as **democracy**, **equality**, **tyranny** and violence.

In society, people have different values and different ideas about what goals should be pursued and about the best means of achieving those goals. Whenever they are engaged in making decisions, conflict is inevitable. It may be mild verbal disagreement or it may be more dramatic physical confrontation. The process of resolving conflicts about the way we organise our society and the priorities we establish is a political process. Those charged with making decisions exercise power and authority over us. They have the ability to influence the way our community is run and the way we live our lives. The concept of power is central to any study of politics, which is why some people define politics as 'the struggle for power and influence' or as 'the authority to govern'.

Power is also a key concept in **political sociology**, which is concerned with viewing politics in a social context and examining the relationship between the social structure and political behaviour. Primarily we are concerned with power in the state and the directly political behaviour of **political parties**, **pressure groups** and voters, although the theories examined in this topic apply more generally to the exercise of power in other elements of social life. As Foucault (1977) suggests, politics can be present in all social relationships, hence Worsley's (1970) observation that 'we can be said to act politically when we exercise constraint on others to behave as we want them to … the exercise of constraint in any relationship is political'.

It has long been a widely held belief in Western democracies that the political system that has been created is the best means of providing for the legitimate exercise of power. Many journalists, politicians and writers adopt a liberal, pluralist perspective which portrays politics as the quest for power in order to achieve desirable public policies. They argue that these policies result from a process of conflict, negotiation and, ultimately, compromise between relevant parties which caters for a wide variety of interests. This is how change comes about. In **liberal democracies**, conflict and change can be accommodated because the system is fundamentally legitimate and commands general approval and respect. Western democracy works.

Some social analysts challenge this view as being far too complacent. They point to the existence of a ruling class which has such power and resources that it can thwart any radical change involving a redistribution of income, wealth and opportunity. Marxists have always maintained that there is a fusion of economic and political power in the hands of the bourgeoisie and that the bourgeoisie uses its position to exploit and oppress the proletariat. For them, the modern **state** 'is not a neutral instrument of administration, but a tool of class dominance'.

Power and politics

What is politics all about?

Learning objectives:

- Understand that politics can be understood in different ways.
- Recognise the difference between power and authority.
- Know other relevant concepts such as democracy, equality and influence.
- Understand the difference between democratic and authoritarian regimes.
- Appreciate that there are situations where power is exercised.
- Recognise the importance of power as a concept in political sociology.

Key terms

Direct democracy: a form of democracy in which citizens assemble to debate and decide issues of public importance.

Referendum: a vote of the people on a single issue of public policy, such as a proposed law or policy, perhaps to amend the constitution.

Initiative: a means through which an individual or group may seek to propose legislation by securing the signatures of a required number of qualified voters. If this is achieved, then a popular vote may be held on the issue.

Representative democracy: democracy where the people elect representatives who make decisions on their behalf; also called indirect democracy.

Wherever people exercise power, be it a football team, a school or a government, there will be questions like these:

- Who gave you the right to order us about?
- Are you going to make me do it?
- What authority do you have for saying that?

They help us explain what we mean when we speak of power and authority. Power is the ability to demand that people do something and to say how it should be done or organised. Dictators and unpopular governments can maintain themselves in power by the use of force, if required, but in democracies the power of governments is justified by consent, which means that people have given their agreement to what is being done. Where power is granted by consent, the term 'authority' is used.

A note on democracy and its forms

According to Abraham Lincoln, democracy is 'government of the people, by the people and for the people'. The ancient Greeks were the first people to develop democratic ideas; democracy in Athens was practised in a small city-state (Figure 4.1.1). In ancient Athens, every qualified citizen – this did not include women, slaves and non-Athenians – had the opportunity to gather together and vote directly on issues of current interest and concern. This was **direct democracy** in action. The use of **referendums** and **initiatives** helps to keep the flame of direct popular involvement in decision-making alive.

Representative democracy

In today's large and more industrialised societies, people cannot all get together to discuss and vote on issues. They elect representatives to act on their behalf. This is **representative democracy**. Some key elements of a modern representative democracy are popular control of policymakers, the existence of opposition, political equality (one person, one vote), political freedoms and majority rule.

Elections are central to representative democracy; the people are consigned to the role of 'deciding who will decide'. In a democracy, a few govern and the mass follows. The electors cast votes every few years at election time, but in between they have little say. This is obviously a

Take it further

Use the internet to find examples of referendums and initiatives that have been held in the UK and other parts of the world. Using knowledge derived from family experience, foreign travel or the internet, consider which of these countries meet the listed criteria for democracy: Albania, Belgium, China, Cuba, France, Germany, Greece, India, Iran, Iraq, Italy, Pakistan, Russia, Spain, the US.

form of people power, but a limited one, for the voters are giving away the right of decision-making to a small number of elected representatives who make decisions on their behalf.

Liberal democracy

Britain and other Western democracies are often described as liberal democracies. Besides the features of representative democracy already mentioned, liberal democracies are noted for their commitment to the ideas of pluralism, limited government, civil liberties and civil rights, open government, an independent judiciary, and a free and open media.

The difference between the two concepts can be seen in various examples. A medieval king had the power to increase the tax on beer. After an election victory, a prime minister has the authority to ask for an increase in taxation. What justifies their authority is **legitimacy**. The freely elected government of a **country** is often known as the legitimate government, for it is rightfully in office. A police officer has power and authority, whereas a blackmailer has power but no authority.

Power can depend on naked force or coercion. It is used in many **authoritarian regimes** to maintain leaders in office; often the rule of dictators ultimately relies on intimidation and physical threat. Zimbabwe, under Robert Mugabe, and China, under its **communist** leadership, are obvious modern examples. In 1989 China's ruling regime ruthlessly crushed the expressions of dissent in Tiananmen Square, when many thousands of people gathered to show their support for greater democracy.

In a democracy, those who govern have the authority to govern. They derive their legitimate authority from the consent of those they govern, as determined in periodic, free and meaningful elections in which there is a genuine choice of candidates with a range of viewpoints. In a democracy there is free competition between parties and **participation** by the mass of voters in elections. Power enables the collective decisions of government ministers to be made and enforced. Hague and Harrop (2004) put it like this: 'Without power, a government would be as useless as a car without an engine. Power is the tool that enables rulers both to serve and to exploit their subjects.' Hay (2002) has described politics as concerned with 'the distribution, exercise and consequences of power'.

Power affects many relationships in everyday life. In UK politics, it is often used for the formal political battle at Westminster, but it affects many other political interactions that happen in government departments and localities. It also features in prisons, schools, working environments or families, whether it may concern the relationship of parent and child or of husband and wife. People often use the phrase 'office politics' to describe a workplace struggle for power and recognition. Michel Foucault (1977) went further, stressing that power mechanisms operate everywhere, in all aspects of our social and political life.

The exercise of power takes different forms. Hague and Harrop make the useful distinction between 'power over' and 'power to'. The former is concerned with overcoming opposition from and exercising control over other individuals, governments or countries. The latter is about the ability of an individual, government or country to achieve its goals. Both ideas are represented in the theories that follow. The distribution of power can be difficult to locate. Its expression is sometimes brutally evident in authoritarian countries, but less obvious in democracies where there is no single focus of decision-making.

Fig. 4.1.1 *The Pnyx was the original site of direct democracy in ancient Athens*

Key terms

Legitimacy: implies some justification for the exercise of ruling power. A legitimate system of government is one where the authority of the government is widely accepted by those who are subject to it.

Country: usually refers to a state's territory and population, rather than its government.

Authoritarian regime: a non-democratic regime in which there is very strong central direction and control. There may be elections, but the range of candidates is usually limited or the campaigning is made very difficult for those who take an alternative view to those in power.

Communist: someone who believes in a classless society in which private business and property are abolished and the means of production belong to the whole community, leading to complete equality between everyone. Communist thinking is heavily based on the writing of Karl Marx, who viewed history in terms of class conflict and revolutionary struggle.

Participation: the engagement of the population in forms of political action.

Hint

Read the section carefully and get a clear idea about the nature of power. It is a basic concept in politics and sociology. Understanding it will help you appreciate the context of British political and social life.

Power and politics

■ The importance of power in sociology

Power is a concept that was hotly debated and contested by sociologists throughout the 20th century. The classic writing on the topic was produced by the German sociologist Max Weber (1864–1920). He distinguished power from authority. He thought that power ultimately depends on force to achieve its ends, and he distinguished three main forms of authority: traditional (custom, the established way of doing things), charismatic (the intense commitment to the leader and their message) and legal-rational (which depends on rules and procedures, rather than the person in office).

Sociologists have debated the Weberian view, which concentrated on the exercise of power in the decision-making process. Among other very influential theorists, Stephen Lukes (1974) distinguished between three 'faces' of power: the focus on decision-making power (the Weber approach), non-decision-making power (where issues are prevented from reaching the point of decision) and ideological power (where people are persuaded to accept the exercise of power even when this is not in their interests). The next section considers these and other theories.

■ Summary questions

1. What do you understand by the word 'politics'?

2. What is the difference between power and authority?

3. How do direct democracies differ from indirect democracies?

4. What are the distinguishing features of a representative democracy and a liberal democracy?

Theories on power in the modern state

Learning objectives:

- Examine the main sociological theories on the exercise and distribution of power.

- Evaluate some of their strengths and weaknesses.

Take it further

Think of any two recent or present-day figures whose authority was at least partly based on their perceived charisma. Research their qualities and assess how and why they inspired people to follow them.

Key terms

Patriarchy: a system of society or government in which men hold the power and women are largely excluded from it.

Fig. 4.1.2 *Karl Marx was an influential figure*

Three types of authority

The traditional distinction made between power and authority owes much to the pioneering approach of Max Weber (1922). He portrayed power as 'the chance of a man or a number of men to realise their own will in a communal action, even against the resistance of others'. In effect, this is coercive power – it depends on force or repression – as opposed to authority. When it was legitimately exercised, power became authority, which Weber saw as more effective precisely because it was based on legitimacy. He distinguished three means by which political power was legitimised, although they are not necessarily exclusive; the same person may carry authority because of any combination of them.

Traditional authority

Traditional authority is based on custom, 'piety for what actually, allegedly or presumably has always existed'. Traditional rulers such as British and other European monarchs in a pre-democratic age had no need to justify their authority: it was accepted as rightful and part of the natural order that they ruled, because their ruling houses had always done so. Traditional authority was usually based on **patriarchy**, the right to rule of the father or eldest male. In some non-democratic countries, for instance in the Middle East, the entire political system functions on the basis of formidable patriarchal authority. In modern Britain, any remaining power exercised by today's constitutional monarchy is based on the legitimacy acquired through long continuity.

Charismatic authority

Charismatic authority rests on the obedience ruling figures inspire because of the intense commitment of their followers to the message they convey and the personality they offer. They are obeyed because it seems that they are endowed with exceptional qualities that hold out the prospect of a better life ahead. Some revolutionary leaders such as Jesus, Gandhi, Che Guevara and Martin Luther King Jr were perceived to have charismatic authority. Charismatic leaders tend to emerge in times of crisis, when people feel the need to be led towards some 'promised land'. In time, representatives of a younger generation challenge their authority and their authority recedes. Weber described this as 'the development of permanent institutional structures' and it is sometimes known as the routinisation of charisma.

Legal-rational authority

Legal-rational authority is based more on a legal framework of principles and procedures, rather a traditional leader or charismatic figure. The framework places clear limits on the power of an office-holder. Weber believed this was the source of authority that would eventually become dominant, especially in liberal democracies that set out to limit authority and provide for the rights of the citizen. An example is the right of an officer in the armed forces to giver orders to those in a subordinate position, because this authority is laid down in military regulations.

Weber's views emphasised the importance of the office-holders who made decisions and the process of decision-making. Critics have pointed out that sometimes a kind of power is exercised in more subtle ways. Those in power may decide not to make decisions or take action, perhaps because they do not feel the need to do so; it may not be in their interests to take an initiative. Moreover, with the skilful use of propaganda, rulers can exercise significant power by shaping the desires of those they rule. Modern advertising campaigns exert power by influencing the attitudes and habits of consumers. Party political broadcasts and party election broadcasts are used to market political personalities and ideas.

The Marxist approach

Marxist theories are based on the ideas of Karl Marx (1818–1883), a German philosopher and revolutionary (Figure 4.1.2). He co-wrote *The Communist Manifesto* with Friedrich Engels in 1848 and is most famous for his 1867 book *Das Kapital*, a detailed study of the economic mechanisms of society. Unlike Weber, who later advanced his views in response to Marxian thinking, Marx was less interested in the characteristics and whims of individuals and more interested in the structural relationships within society.

Marxists have traditionally portrayed the state as the instrument of the ruling capitalist class. Marx and Engels (1848) describe the state as 'a committee for managing the affairs of the whole bourgeoisie'. They see it as an entity designed to further the interests of those who own the means of production, distribution and exchange, maintaining and preserving their position. This leads them to believe that elections are without real meaning, for although they convey the impression that everyone can express a preference at the polling station, the contest will ultimately change nothing. The choice will be between people committed to preserving the existing form of society.

Marx argued that for much of human history, power has been concentrated in the hands of a few people in the ruling class, who control the economic system by virtue of their ownership of land, equipment and wealth. He used the terms 'class conflict' and 'class struggle' to refer to the antagonism that arose between social classes over the distribution of wealth and power in society.

In the developing world of the Industrial Revolution, Marx believed that the power of masters over slaves in the ancient world and nobles over **serfs** in **feudal systems** had by then come to reside with the **capitalists**, often known as the **bourgeoisie**, who were the people who owned the means of production, distribution and exchange. They dominated and exploited the labour of those who worked for them, the **proletariat**. Marx claimed that the time would come when the proletariat would seize power from the owners of production. They would then assume control of the state to secure their defeat of the capitalist class. When this was achieved, there would be a **withering of the state**.

Marx argued that 'the ideas of the ruling class are in every epoch the ruling ideas'. Members of that class – wishing to perpetuate their survival as the dominant order – would endeavour to persuade the rest of society that a continuation of the status quo was in their interest as well. They could do this by numbing any radical instincts, so that their own values could prevail.

Since his original writings, many adherents of his broad approach have made their own contributions to Marxist thinking. Four who provided some reinterpretation of Marx's ideas are Miliband, Althusser, Gramsci and Poulantzas.

Key terms

Serfs: members of the lowest class under the manorial economic system of the Middle Ages. They were attached to the land owned by the lord of the manor and required to perform work in return for legal or customary rights.

Feudal system: the social and economic system that developed in the 8th century and characterised most European societies in the Middle Ages. Vassals served a lord in war and in other ways, and in return the lord protected his vassals. Also called feudalism.

Capitalists: the owners of capital and wealth, such as those who own factories and other productive enterprises. They control the means of production, distribution and exchange.

Bourgeoisie: a loose term for the groupings in society who wish to cling on to its existing structure; the ruling class of urban society. Derived from the French for 'of the town'.

Proletariat: those who provide the labour necessary to operate factories and other productive enterprises; the working class.

Withering of the state: the last stage in Marx's hypothetical historical sequence. The proletariat seize power from the bourgeoisie and establish a 'dictatorship of the proletariat'; as socialism is established, the state withers away because there is no class oppression in a classless society.

The British Marxist, Ralph Miliband (1969), claimed that the state would always operate to the advantage of the ruling economic class, the owners of capital. Although it comprises many differing elements – parliaments, local councils, courts and a wide range of pressure groups – all of which provide checks and balances, governments usually ensure there is no threat to the interests of those who own capital. The Labour Party, traditionally regarded as a **socialist** party, has not challenged big business, according to critics on the political left. Often, it seems to be in the business of showing that it can operate a capitalist system more efficiently and effectively, because it does so in a more humane and socially conscious way.

Miliband noted the social background of those who occupied senior positions in British life. Bishops, civil servants, judges, police officers or politicians tended to come from a privileged background that predisposed them to accept the interests of the owners of wealth and the state of society as it was rather than as it might be. The result was that all key personnel had a vested interest in ensuring that the existing form and power structure of society was preserved.

Louis Althusser (1969), a French Marxist, was less interested in the background and behaviour of state functionaries. He drew attention to the way the operation of the state supports the capitalist mode of production. He distinguished the state as narrowly conceived, with its repressive state apparatus – the army, the police and the judiciary – and the wider view of an ideological apparatus – the church, education, the family and the media – which helps to maintain the dominance of the ruling class by **legitimation**.

Antonio Gramsci (1971) was an Italian Marxist and early exponent of the notion of **hegemony** in society. Hegemony is the idea that the ruling class achieved dominance because their values (e.g. support of private ownership, free enterprise and the search for profit) were accepted as the norm. Unlike Marx, he did not accept that the domination of the capitalist class could be explained by economic forces only, and was wary of reliance on material or economic factors as a determinant of historical change. It required political force, essentially a matter of state power, and some means of ensuring the consent of the classes who were subordinate.

Like Althusser, Gramsci claimed that the ideological apparatus through which this acquiescence or support could be achieved included institutions of **civil society** such as churches, the family, the educational system and trade unions. In particular, he saw the mass media as having a key role. He believed that the media was a powerful means of retaining class dominance, because media proprietors could convey their message across the nation and into every home. They denied access to those who would peddle challenging ideas and kept the rest of the population in a state of bemused satisfaction, partly as a result of the diet of entertainment and gossip they presented.

Nicos Poulantzas (1975), a Greek sociologist, was also concerned with the repressive apparatus of the state – the armed forces, the police and the security services – as well as its 'manipulative' ideological apparatus, such as churches, schools and the media. He recognised that some state agencies could be relatively free to operate as they wished, rather than as capitalists wished them to do. Yet ultimately the needs of those who owned capital would prevail. He was less interested in the people who achieve the 'top' positions in society, for he argued that the state operates in the same way whoever holds the key offices and whether or not they possess a similar background.

Link

See page 11 for Marxist views on religion.

Key terms

Socialist: someone who believes that unrestrained capitalism or free enterprise is responsible for a variety of social evils, such as the exploitation of working people and the pursuit of greed and selfishness. Socialists favour cooperative values, which emphasise the values of community, equality and justice, and state action to promote these values.

Legitimation: making the system seem just and fair.

Hegemony: the ideological control that the ruling-class elite have over the masses.

Civil society: the arena of social life above the personal realm of the family but beneath the state. It comprises mainly voluntary organisations and civil associations that allow people to work together in groups, freely and independently of state regulation.

Take it further

Go on the internet and find further information about the nature of socialism. How might you attempt to distinguish it from communism?

AQA Examiner's tip

As you examine the three main theoretical perspectives on power – Marxist, pluralist and elitist – consider for each one how its principal thinkers proposed that power was exercised and distributed. You need to understand their reasoning. Remember a few of them, so you can mention them in your essays.

Power and politics

Like Miliband, he drew attention to the failure of Labour governments to achieve the social change and wealth redistribution they espoused. This happened because their leading figures were unable or unwilling to take on the businessmen and financiers who benefited from the prevailing social and economic system. For Poulantzas, those who owned industry and controlled the production of goods would always ensure that their interests prevailed, irrespective of the wishes of other classes and groups.

■ The pluralist approach

American sociologists conceived and developed the idea of pluralism in the 1950s and 1960s. Unlike Marxists, pluralists do not accept that power generally resides in one class. They believe that it is dispersed among many competing groups, such as cultural, economic, educational, professional and religious groups. Wealth is a factor, but so are prestige, organisational clout and personal charisma. The result is that some power is available to almost everyone. No person can expect to achieve all the outcomes they want, but by a process of negotiation most can realise some of their goals and prevent the introduction of policies they regard as detrimental. In the world of industry, pluralists believe that power is distributed between owners, the management and workers. In more recent decades, consumers may be added to the mix.

Pluralist theorists portray the state as a neutral party that represents the interests of every group within society. In their view, the state behaves as a kind of 'honest broker' that 'holds the ring', acting neutrally to ensure there is an opportunity for all viewpoints to be expressed and so the voice of the disadvantaged does not go unnoticed. Over time there will be a balancing out of group influence.

Robert Dahl (1961) was the pre-eminent pluralist writer. He was responsible for a famous definition of power, namely that it was a matter of getting people to behave in a way that does not come naturally to them: 'A has power over B to the extent that s/he can get B to do something s/he wouldn't have otherwise done.' Dahl asserted that in American society, influential people did not always get their way and that there were mechanisms that allowed the political interests of all sections of the community – including the disadvantaged – to be addressed. *Who Governs?* is his study of New Haven, Connecticut. His study points out that key decisions were made by a range of different groups and that over time power became increasingly diffuse. He concluded that 'no one, and certainly no group of more than a few individuals, is entirely lacking in [power]'.

Dahl accepted that in modern representative democracies, there are few direct opportunities for the mass of people to become actively involved in making decisions. But he felt that those who were responsible for decision-making derived their support from the wishes of the electorate as expressed through the ballot box. In between elections, they may choose to join political parties or be active in pressure groups and through these outlets express their viewpoints.

Supporters see pluralism as the way in which modern democracies operate and point to the evidence of local research such as the work of Polsby (1963) and Dahl. Critics claim that it is an inadequate or inaccurate description of the exercise of political power in most democracies, including the US and Britain. Far from being model democracies in which power is dispersed, they concentrate power in the hands of a relatively small number of people or groups. Some pressure groups dominate others. For instance, as a broad trend in most Western countries, proprietors and management have acquired more power than labour in matters of industrial relations.

In response, some **elite pluralists** have accepted that: in most democratic countries there is an unequal distribution of income and wealth; that within the media there is a concentration of ownership which limits the diversity of opinions available; that pressure groups possess unequal resources and influence; and that some groups in society have significantly less clout than others. Accordingly, they have modified the classical pluralist position. Writing 28 years after his original publication, Dahl conceded there was no equality of influence in the US. However, pluralists continue to assert that there are opportunities for disadvantaged groups to get their voice heard, not least because they constitute a significant portion of the electorate. Any parliamentary candidate in many of Britain's most sizeable towns and cities would be unwise to forget that constituencies contain voters from diverse ethnic backgrounds.

Power elite theory

According to power elite theory, in almost all societies, be they communist or liberal democratic, it seems inevitable that politics is conducted by a small minority of individuals. They may be the super-rich or perhaps people endowed with particular personal gifts that equip them for leadership. Given the narrowness of this elite, there is no real choice for the voters at election time. Moreover, there exists an inequality of group influence, so it is impossible to have meaningful competition in the market for ideas and influence. The opinions and demands of some groups remain unnoticed and the views of the elite go unchallenged.

Gaetano Mosca was a leading member of the Italian school of elite theorists, along with Pareto (see below) and Michels. He is often credited with developing the theory of elitism and the idea of a political class. Mosca's (1939) key observation was to point out that all but the most primitive societies are ruled in fact, if not in theory, by a numerical minority, the political class. He defined modern elites in term of their superior organisational skills, which were especially useful in gaining political power in modern societies. In his view, these elites were not hereditary, so in theory, people from all walks of life could become the elite. Over time, given the constant competition between elites, one elite group would come to replace another, as part of a 'circulation of elites'.

Another Italian theorist of the same school was Vilfredo Pareto. He was critical of Marxist theory and did not view society as an unending struggle between the owners of wealth and capital and the dispossessed. Pareto (1963) placed more emphasis on the personalities of those in leadership positions, distinguishing between the lions and the foxes. The lions were people who were at ease with the exercise of force to gain and maintain power (e.g. military dictators), whereas the foxes in Western democracies had an ability to use their low cunning to get what they wanted. The bulk of the population fell into neither category, so that Pareto was sceptical about their ability to play a useful role in choosing or serving in governments.

Exponents of elite theory sometimes targeted the political left, sometimes the political right. Mosca and Pareto targeted the political left and were seeking to develop a universal theory of political society. Later sociologists of the elite school took a different view. Rejecting pluralist assertions, American elite theorists pointed to research that highlighted the

Key terms

Elite pluralist: a pluralist who accepts that some disadvantaged groups such as minority ethnics are under-represented in key positions in society and that they are also denied the access to policymakers given to more influential sections of society.

Power and politics

■ Hint

As you think about the three main theories, try to apply Lukes' view of the three faces of power. To what extent do the various thinkers deal with power in each of Lukes' three faces?

■ Key terms

Functionalist: someone who believes in functionalism, which provides a framework in which society is seen as a complex system whose individual parts and the interrelationships between them work together to promote solidity and stability. In other words, there is more to society than the sum of its parts. Functionalism was the dominant theoretical perspective in sociology of the early to middle 20th century, especially reflected in the work of Emile Durkheim.

■ Hint

Now that you are familiar with the main theories concerning power, consider their possible merits or demerits. Use Table 4.1.1 to help you. Perhaps make a note of key words or phrases you associate with each theory.

dominance of leading families in some American states. In Atlanta, Floyd Hunter (1963) found no single family that monopolised power, but found that no more than 40 people controlled the top positions in city business and politics. His observations echoed the better-known findings of Charles Wright Mills (1956), who also strongly criticised the pluralist theory of the state.

In his study of the US in the 1950s, Mills commented on the importance of three sectors in American public life: the government, the military and the business corporations. Sometimes the same people make their mark in all three worlds. For instance, in America, the army general Alexander Haig went on to hold influential positions in private business before becoming a Secretary of State under President Ronald Reagan. In the Clinton and particularly the Bush administrations, many Secretaries emerged from business corporations, where some were millionaires. Mills also noted how business dealings, intermarriage and movement between groups can perpetuate power within the three groups. Some families, endowed with income, prestige, wealth and power, and sometimes interlinked by marriage, dominated the world of business, in the same way as the Murdochs dominate mass communications. They had a large and sometimes decisive influence over the national agenda. They occupied what Mills called the 'command posts'.

■ Some other perspectives

Talcott Parsons (1967) was a **functionalist**. He did not view power as necessarily involving conflict and coercion. An exponent of the 'power to' approach, he defined power as 'a positive social capacity for achieving communal ends'. In particular, he believed that power was a collective resource for promoting the general good rather than a possession of individuals. In his view, if A and B cooperate, not only will they increase their own power, but they will also contribute to the general good. He viewed the power of governments as the capacity to achieve beneficial purposes such as maintaining law and order and protecting the environment. He was not afraid of power or its exercise. On the contrary, in his view the greater the power, the better life could be.

The German political theorist Hannah Arendt (1951) echoed Parson's thinking in her emphasis on power as the ability to act and 'to act in concert'. She recognised that by uniting and cooperating, people can achieve more than by acting alone. She rejected the notion of power as coercion, and she saw power and violence as antagonistic: 'Where the one rules, the other is absent. Violence can destroy power; it is utterly incapable of creating it.'

More recently, Stephen Lukes wrote about the 'three faces of power'. He concluded that A exerts power over B when A affects B in a manner contrary to B's interests, even if B is unaware of the damage caused. He claimed that governments have three ways of controlling people: decision-making power, non-decision-making power and ideological power.

Decision-making power is the most well-known of the three faces and is the one by which governments like to be judged. Non-decision-making power is the power that governments have to control the agenda in debates. Political and social intercourse is limited to topics on which there is a broad consensus, with the result that those likely to provoke difficulty for the people in power do not get an airing. For instance, the possible merits of communism in the US are rarely debated, as they are

Table 4.1.1 *Theories of power*

In favour	Doubts
Marxist: Marx, Althusser, Gramsci, Miliband In history, power has tended to reside with an elite of wealth owners. Marxists see the importance of economic factors. They recognise that the media and other bodies exercise formidable influence in controlling the agenda for debate and persuading people to accept their position and be content, via hegemony, etc. Marxists understand that there are limits to the value of Western democracies, with their low participation in elections. This may be because democracy is a sham, giving an illusion of choice when in reality elections can change very little. Marxists have faith in the masses, who are seen as capable of casting off their oppressors and ultimately establishing a better society	Wealth based on economic power is not the only form of control. Elites in non-communist countries are not always united in support of the capitalist viewpoint. Power is not necessarily finite as the **zero-sum model** assumes, nor is it necessarily held by a single group. There has been a separation of ownership and control in many modern industries, so that not all involved in determining a company's fortunes share the same capitalist stance; pension funds often have significant shareholdings. No withering away of the state has yet occurred in any communist country. Marxism is a theory of how society has evolved; its assumptions are not easily demonstrated
Pluralist: Weber, Dahl, Polsby Pluralism appears to be based on life in the US and Britain, as revealed in various local and national studies. Political power is not based on one powerful economic class. Economic and political power do not necessarily overlap. Power is dispersed and fluid; many democracies with strong governments run into obstacles over difficult and contentious issues. The theory is more widely based than Marxism, recognising other social divisions such as those based on ethnicity, gender or location. In the UK there is no pattern of continuous domination by one pressure group. All groups can influence decision-making. Whatever their faults, liberal democracies offer the best opportunities for all groups to express themselves and have their voice heard. Governments consult widely with a range of interests on most issues of policy. Some, but not most, pluralists recognise that there is no fixed amount of power, the **variable-sum model**. For all their faults, democracies grant some powers to everyone, offering substantial benefits and rights for citizens who can ultimately remove governments they dislike	It ignores Lukes' second face of power, only concentrating on decision-making. Some issues are deliberately kept off the political agenda. Bachrach and Baratz (1963) quote the example of the discontent in Northern Ireland; it remained beneath the surface until it finally erupted in the late 1960s. Governments had been content to remain silent about what was happening in the province, acquiescing in injustices. Pluralism makes no allowance for the third face of power, by which voters are persuaded to accept what is not in their best interests. Some studies show that specific groups have greater influence than others; business has greater influence that other groups under Labour and Conservative governments. Different groups have very different resources, leading to unequal opportunities; there is not a free market for ideas. Some of the claims for liberal democracies are overstated; elections do not offer a real choice, as Marxists often point out. The right to vote conceals huge inequalities in society. Democracy has not achieved significant redistribution of wealth
Elite: Mosca, Pareto, Mills Elite theories are based on how societies actually work, be they democratic or authoritarian. Elites flourish and take decisions that are in their own interests. Many agree with Mills that voters in the US are offered little genuine choice at election time, simply more of the same. Advocates are not unhappy that such domination exists. For instance, according to Pareto, the mass of people are not up to the task of making decisions. The top jobs in societies tend to be filled by people with appropriate understanding	Members of elites may be of similar background, but that does not mean they all share a similar perception of their own interests. People of the same class may have very different outlooks and champion their own policies. Although there are faults with democracy on both sides of the Atlantic, sometimes governments have produced real change that benefits the majority, such as Labour's introduction of the welfare state. In 1945 voters were presented with a clear choice, contrary to what Mills says

▨ Key terms

Zero-sum model: a model of power that assumes there is a fixed amount of power to be shared by all groups and interests. If someone gains power, another person must lose power.

Variable-sum model: a model of power that assumes the total amount of power can fluctuate according to how effectively it is used and the situation involved.

considered unacceptable for discussion in moderate public forums. The third and most important face of power is ideological power, which is the power to influence or manipulate people's wishes and thoughts and make them want things other than what would benefit them. An example is the persuasion of women into supporting a patriarchal society. A man and his wife might discuss how they will arrange their family life, but the man will direct the discussion so that his wife recognises it is obviously desirable that she stays at home and rears their child while he is the breadwinner.

Summary questions

5 What were Weber's three means by which coercive power could be transformed into legitimate authority?

6 What are the key differences between Marxist and pluralist theories of power and between pluralist and elite theories of power?

7 What is the Marxist view of the state?

The distribution of power in modern Britain

Learning objectives:

- Understand the diverse focuses of power in Britain today.

- Know that the locations of power can fluctuate over time.

- Understand that post-1945 some power has moved beyond the UK.

- Recognise that the very powerful tend to have a similar social background.

Key terms

Executive: the branch of government responsible for directing the nation's affairs and the initiation and execution of laws and policies; an example is the UK government.

Cabinet: the 20–24 senior members of the government. Once it was the key formal decision-making body in the executive. It directed the work of government and coordinated the activities of government departments. Its role as a decision-making body has diminished.

Civil Service: all the non-military branches of state administration.

Whitehall departments: the main departments of state, such as the Foreign Office and the Home Office. They used to have their headquarters in and around the former royal palace of Whitehall.

Whitehall: often used to refer to the central core of the Civil Service.

Executive agency: a semi-autonomous agency that carries out some of the administrative functions of government that used to be done by Civil Service departments. An executive agency operates at arm's length from the sponsoring department.

Political power is greatly concerned with the ability to make decisions that affect the way society is organised and the goals it chooses to pursue – Lukes' first face of power. Yet it is no longer possible to speak of political power in isolation from other types of power. Economic power, military power and media power all influence the political system and the effectiveness of political leaders, and so do changing circumstances. Power can be influenced by problems that suddenly erupt onto the political scene and cause huge headaches for government ministers. A crisis abroad, an outbreak of foot and mouth disease, a run on a bank in difficulty can appear to arise out of nowhere. They can throw a government off course and make ministers look ineffectual – in office but not in power.

It is possible to make a case that Britain's political power rests with the **executive**, in particular the political executive, better known as the elected government (Figure 4.1.3). Members of the government, especially the prime minister and the **Cabinet**, develop policies and bring bills to Parliament. Most bills become laws that govern the whole population. A government with a reasonable majority in the House of Commons can normally get its bills passed into law. Governments therefore have the power to change the way we live, such as where we can use mobile phones, when we can drink in pubs and whether a pregnant woman can have an abortion.

Fig. 4.1.3 *The prime minister's residence is 10 Downing Street*

Some say that the official executive, the **Civil Service**, is the seat of power. It is responsible for administering the laws that Parliament has passed. The 750–800 senior officials, based in the large **Whitehall departments** and a range of **executive agencies**, carry key functions such as advising ministers, preparing and drafting discussion documents and legislation, and implementing government decisions. Over recent decades

Power and politics

163

■ Key terms

Mandarin power: the power and influence of civil servants in the top administrative grades (often known as the higher civil service).

Legislature: a type of representative assembly with the power to make or adopt laws.

European Union (EU): an organisation of 27 states with economic and political aims. Previously known as the European Community, it was established in 1957 by the Treaty of Rome.

■ Take it further

Think about these locations of power in the UK: elected politicians, the European Union (EU), the devolved bodies, the City and especially the Bank of England, the media, multinational companies (MNCs), UK businesses and employers, trade unions, the European Court of Human Rights. Perhaps with help from the internet, consider whether each is a key focus of power. Some of the groups such as the mass media, MNCs and the City are rarely accountable to anyone. Does this matter? Using the main sociological theories, judge how power is distributed in the UK political system. Which explanation seems most appropriate?

these higher civil servants have not only given advice to ministers, but have also taken some of the decisions. Because of their abilities, experience, expertise and permanence, they can exert a powerful influence over what happens in a department, hence the phrase **mandarin power**.

Some argue that power resides with the **legislature**, or Parliament. Parliament comprises the more powerful House of Commons and the less powerful House of Lords. The doctrine of parliamentary sovereignty gives Parliament supreme and unique legislative authority, with the power to make, amend or unmake laws. In reality, Parliament debates and votes on bills. Most bills are introduced by the government but a few are introduced by individual members, MPs in the House of Commons and peers in the House of Lords. Parliament tends to pass laws rather than make laws. But Parliament can exert influence, particularly when the government has a small majority or is in political difficulties.

Most academics and commentators on British politics say that, over many decades, power has passed from Parliament to the executive, which dominates the House of Commons by controlling its timetable and agenda. Many go much further and say that in recent years there has been a centralisation of power in 10 Downing Street, with strong prime ministers able to dominate their administrations and even to hide their plans from some Cabinet members.

It could also be said that power resides with the judiciary. The political role of unelected judges has increased throughout the Western world over recent decades. They have been far more willing to rule on political matters. In Britain, judicial intervention in public policy has become apparent in several ways. They are much more willing to perform judicial reviews – to review the legality of government action. Judges have been involved in many issues brought under the European Convention on Human Rights or, more recently, the Human Rights Act. They are more willing to publicly air their disapproval of government policies.

Others argue that in a democracy, power must ultimately reside with the people, hence the phrase 'people power'. But most people are only called on to make a decision at a general election, once every four or five years. The UK has had very few national or local referendums, so UK voters have had few opportunities to decide specific issues, particularly issues that arise during a government's lifetime and are not explained in election manifestos. In normal circumstances, therefore, it is difficult to argue that the individual is armed with much actual power. Indeed, some commentators see the individual voter as largely powerless, unable to influence the course of events.

In 1973 Britain joined the European Economic Community, now called the **European Union (EU)**. Membership means that many important decisions, including several that relate to economic policy, agriculture and the environment, are no longer made in London but in Brussels. As part of its package of constitutional changes, the Labour government after 1997 introduced a policy of devolution. This involved establishing a parliament in Scotland, an assembly in Wales and an assembly in Northern Ireland. Key powers have been transferred: for example, decisions on Scottish education, health and welfare are now primarily taken by the Scottish Parliament in Edinburgh.

Modern government has become highly complex. The age of centralised decision-making in London has passed, and there are new focuses in Edinburgh, Belfast and Cardiff. Political power is divided among many

The state, its role and how it functions

Learning objectives:

- Understand the distinction between the state and the government.

- Recognise the characteristics of nations and the nation state.

- Recognise the instruments of state power and how states maintain internal order.

- Identify the difficulties of states in maintaining security.

Take it further

Find out more about the EU and multinational companies. Both of them have implications for the power of nation states.

Key terms

Sovereign power: sovereignty, complete power.

Consensus: agreement; a political consensus is where a large proportion of the population and the political community broadly agree on specific values, even if there is some disagreement on emphasis or detail.

Mandate: the authority of the government to carry out its programme according to the promises in its manifesto.

Supranationalism: a system of government where an organisation such as the EU can impose its will on member states, which agree to pool their sovereignty in specified areas. By joining the EU, Britain agreed to transfer powers to the EU for joint decision-making in several policy sectors.

It is important to distinguish between 'state' and 'government'. A state exercises **sovereign power** and authority over all individuals and groups within a defined territory. It is an abstract and permanent body that does not change when a new government is elected or when political leaders are replaced. It has the power to use **consensus** or, if necessary, coercion to effect its policies. The state is more than its government. A government is the body that has the authority to run the state. It enforces the rulings of the state and acts under its authority. Unlike the state, the government is transient. In Britain it is elected for a maximum of five years. It has a **mandate** to administer or change the laws, according to what it promised in its manifesto.

The rise of the nation state

A nation refers to the population within a state. A nation state is therefore a sovereign entity dominated by a single nation (Table 4.2.1). Nation states are the primary unit when discussing international relations. The 19th century was noted for the interest in and attempts at nation building, although in the 20th century many colonial peoples fought for their independence in liberationist struggles against their rulers. Today the term 'nation state' remains appropriate for discussion of the many countries where there is one dominant nationality, such as France, Germany and Israel.

Arguably, as other bodies have acquired importance in international affairs (e.g. the EU and MNCs), there has been a decline in the importance of nation states. The EU reflects the rise of **supranationalism**, which has made the model of single-level sovereignty less relevant than it was in the first half of the 20th century. Moreover, even in nation states such as France, Germany and Israel, there are still significant minorities as the increased migration of recent decades has changed the pattern of the population. For instance, France now has a significant number of Algerian and Moroccan inhabitants.

Table 4.2.1 *Nations and states*

Category	Label	Definition	Examples
Nation state	State	A state with its own nation	France, Iceland
Multinational state	State	A state with more than one nation	Scotland and Wales in the UK
Stateless nation	Nation	A nation that lacks its own state and whose people form a part of several countries	Palestinians, Kurds
Diaspora	Nation	A dispersed nation that has no homeland or is dispersed in many countries plus a home state	Jews

Source: Hague and Harrop (2004)

Power and politics

Hint

As you read through this section, think carefully about the nation state and the pressures on it. Ask yourself what role it fulfils and why it is necessary.

Take it further

Besides the police, most countries have national organisations to deal with special criminal activities and intelligence. The US has the Federal Bureau of Investigation (FBI). The UK has the Security Service, also known as MI5, and the Secret Intelligence Service (SIS), also known as MI6. Look up the duties of these three services.

Take it further

Use the internet to find out more about Basque nationalists, Palestinian bombers and Al-Qaeda.

The mechanisms of state power

In a democracy, the state has a monopoly on the use of authorised force. It claims the capacity and the right to use it. As Weber (1922) noted, the exclusive feature of the state is its integration of force with authority. He defined a state as 'a human community that (successfully) claims the monopoly of the legitimate use of physical force within a given territory'. When the state is threatened, it must resort to its right to wield force, perhaps military force, to defend itself.

Law enforcement and punishment of offenders are among the widely acknowledged tasks of the state. Protecting the state and its citizens from internal threats and external aggression is the most traditional role of any government. Most citizens expect their life and liberty to be safeguarded and that those who transgress and threaten their safety and property will be punished and brought to justice. Many disputes between countries can be resolved without resorting to actual military hostilities. Diplomatic pressure, economic sanctions and the threat of using violence may be sufficient to settle disputes, but the threat of military action may sometimes be backed by the use of armed force.

Maintaining internal order

Within any state, it is expected that people will abide by its rules. Transgression of the rules is likely to lead to some sanction or punishment. Defending law and order has long been the traditional priority of any government. Government ministers are responsible for maintaining internal security from those who threaten the fabric of the state. The Government is ultimately responsible for ensuring that suitable procedures and funding exist so the police can maintain civil order in the community. The Government also develops policies to punish those who break the law; there are four motivations for punishment:

- **Retribution** – to pay someone back for wrongdoing.
- **Deterrence** – to discourage others from committing similar acts.
- **Prevention** – to stop a repeat offence.
- **Reformation** – to improve the offender's future behaviour.

The armed forces in any country possess enormous physical power; they have the weapons plus other technology and expertise to intervene in political life and ultimately to seize control of the state. In some parts of the world, the army has intervened to bring down civilian regimes. Some countries are ruled by the military. In other countries, the military have been asked to restore law and order.

Over the past decade or so, military regimes have become less common. Having ruled unsuccessfully for a period of years, some militaries are now less inclined to become involved in political disputes. Those who might consider leading them are aware that they lack international legitimacy and respect, and would be under pressure from other countries to hold elections. Finally, with the fall of the Berlin Wall and the ending of the Cold War, the old justification for military rule as a bastion against communism has lost much of its impact. Consequently, rule by the military has gone out of fashion and only exists in countries such as Burma, Fiji and Libya.

Direct military involvement in political life is rare in Western democracies. Military power gives way to political authority, and leaders of the armed forces recognise that they must take instructions from their elected political masters who expect to rule without military pressure or interference.

In Britain the recognition by the military of its subservience to the government limits its power to act independently. It acts when authorised by the government, which is answerable to Parliament. Apart from its involvement in waging war overseas, the armed services have taken action in the name of the state. In 1969 British troops were sent into Northern Ireland to prevent escalation of bitter sectarian strife between the majority Protestants and the minority Catholics. At other times, when there have been civil emergencies such as flooding or social disturbance in parts of the country, the troops have been called to assist. When fire brigade workers took industrial action in 1997 and 2002, ministers used their emergency powers to call in basic firefighting from the army.

The limitations of state security

Governments devote much time and money to protecting the state and those who live in it (Figure 4.2.1). But their powers are limited. No government can guarantee a risk-free society, just as no government can eliminate crime. Developments in the modern world make the problem of maintaining order more difficult than ever. The growing interdependence and interconnectedness of peoples across the world means that national borders are now less effective at preserving a state's control over what happens in its own territory. Two particular challenges to security are international crime and **terrorism**.

Key terms

Terrorism: the use of forms of violence such as bombing, hijacking, kidnapping, murder and torture to spread fear and horror in a population for the pursuit of political goals.

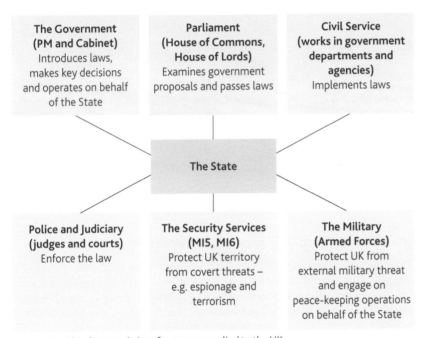

Fig. 4.2.1 *The characteristics of a state as applied to the UK*

Crime has become internationalised. Its most profitable forms can be extremely lucrative for those who organise them and the chances of being caught are not high, partly because it is difficult to coordinate national and international police operations to control them. The arms trade, drug trafficking and the trade in women for prostitution do not stop at national borders. They tend to export people or goods from poorer parts of the world to more affluent places in Western Europe and the US.

Link

See Topic 5 on crime and deviance.

Terrorism may be domestic or global. It has existed for a very long time, but recent events have made it more obvious. Most terrorist groups act against states or governments they disapprove of, although innocent third parties can get caught up. Some groups that have used terrorism are the Irish Republican Army (IRA), Palestinian bombers, Al-Qaeda and ETA, which is a group of Basque nationalists.

From the late 1960s to the mid 1990s, during the worst period of the troubles in Northern Ireland, bombings, kidnappings, money laundering and other crimes were committed in Northern Ireland and sometimes on the mainland. But the nature of terrorism has changed in recent years. Irish republicans used terrorist methods as part of their bid to achieve a political or strategic goal, yet today's Islamic terrorism appears to make no demands about grievances that can readily be addressed. From a Western perspective, the London bombings of 7 July 2005 and a fortnight later, and earlier attacks in Madrid, Bali and New York, seemed to be arbitrary and totally destructive brutality. The London bombings were the first example of suicide bombing on British soil (Figure 4.2.2). Suicide bombers are a potent threat as they do not fear capture or death.

Fig. 4.2.2 *The London bombings took place on 7 July 2005*

The state's control of ideas and information

In democracies, freedom of expression is legally protected, with politics being a battleground over which governments, parties and pressure groups seek to influence public opinion. However, if democracies flourish on the free flow of ideas and information, authoritarian regimes survive by imposing constraints on freedom of expression, so that many journalists find it easier and prudent to defer to political power rather than to expose its abuses.

◼ Key elements of the state: a summary

◼ **Territory** – the state covers a clearly defined geographical area and possesses recognised boundaries.

◼ **Sovereignty** – the state has ultimate legal power over the citizens and groups within its territory.

Take it further

Contemporary China, with its tight control over the means of mass communication, offers an interesting example to those studying state power. Access to information has long been available only on a need-to-know basis, as part of a bid to discourage dissent. In 2000 its government introduced new regulations for internet providers, by which – among other things – website providers were required to:

◼ record the content of their sites (and website visitors for 60 days)

◼ avoid any content that undermines state power or harms the country's reputation.

- **Legitimacy** – decisions of the state are binding on all citizens, as the state represents the interests of society as expressed in free elections.
- **Nation** – the body of people identified by common background, culture, language or traditions, who make up the state. Citizens of a state are born there or have acquired citizenship there.
- **Institutions** – state power is delegated to institutions such as Parliament, the police and the armed forces.
- **Constitution** – every state has a written or unwritten **constitution** that sets out the powers and composition of state institutions, their relationship to one another and to the **citizens**.
- **Civil society** – the arena of social life between the state and the family (e.g. voluntary organisations) that operates under the authority of the state.

Key terms

Constitution: the set of fundamental principles according to which a state is constituted and governed.

Citizen: someone who has rights in the state in which he or she resides.

Summary questions

1. What is the distinction between the state and the government?
2. In recent years, why has it become more difficult for states to maintain internal security?
3. Why and how is the nation state under threat in the modern age?

Power and politics

Theories of the state

Learning objectives:

- Understand Marxist, pluralist and elite theories of the state.

- Recognise different thinking about the state in recent years.

- Understand the impact of globalisation on the state.

Hint

As you read through the various theories of the state, including recent thinking, try to reach a judgement about how convincingly they correspond with reality as you see it. See if you can detect any flaws in the approaches.

Sociologists have advanced several models of the state, how it functions and in whose interests it functions. Refer back to the theories of political power (pages 155–162). They are summarised in Table 4.2.2.

Table 4.2.2 *Theories of political power*

Marxist theory: key points
Under capitalism, states are run in the interests of the owners of wealth, whose wishes will always ultimately prevail as they seek to maintain their position
Miliband (1969) thought they are the instruments of the ruling class, which comprises people of similar backgrounds
The domination of the state extends to all institutions that seek to perpetuate capitalist values
Elections do not provide a meaningful choice of viewpoints, because people who contest elections are committed to maintaining the existing form of society
Marx believed that the state would eventually wither away. States are needed because societies are divided in a class struggle; once that struggle has ended, the state is unnecessary

Pluralist theory: key points
Power is diffuse and fragmented. In a democracy, power is legitimately exercised, because elections provide an opportunity for all groups and interests to have their views represented and the voters make the final choice
Politics is about the competition between rival interests in a market for ideas and influence; many groups seek influence, but none achieve dominance
Groups act as a counterweight to the excessive concentration of power in a few hands
The state is a neutral broker, not siding with one interest against another but acting in the interests of all

Elite theory: key points
For classical elitists, such as Mosca and Pareto, elites exist in all societies. For Mills they are not inevitable nor are they always based on class distinctions, as Marxists suggest
Several studies (e.g. Stanworth and Giddens (1974)) draw attention to the fact that the institutions of states (army officers, top civil servants, judges, military and religious leaders), and politicians under any government are run by people who have similar backgrounds
The views of the elite go largely unchallenged. Groups have unequal resources, enabling some to dominate the political process. Elections do not provide a meaningful choice

Recent thinking on the role of the state and government

The New Right

New Right thinkers saw the free market as the cornerstone of economic and political freedom. The most notable articulations are by Friedrich

Hayek (1944, 1964) and the American economist Milton Friedman (1962), but New Right theory can be traced back to the political economist, Adam Smith, in the late 18th century and his supporters in the 19th century.

In the 1970s, the **neoliberals** of the New Right began to argue for a reduction or rolling back of state power. They disliked the degree of state intervention that had characterised Britain in the post-1945 era, as the role of government had been expanded in areas such as education, health and welfare. They felt that the state had assumed too much responsibility over social and economic life, and that it was damaging the economy and threatening individual freedom. They wished to see a **market economy** with as little state intervention as possible.

Critics of the New Right felt that the growth of state interventionism had protected the position of the most disadvantaged sections of the community. If the **welfare state** was seriously pruned or even dismantled as proposed by some New Right thinkers, this would leave the powerless unprotected. Critics argued that market forces might favour the creators of wealth and encourage competition and efficiency, but they were unlikely to promote social justice.

The Third Way and the future of nation states

Events in the post-1945 world and the drive towards increasing globalisation have had a significant impact on the role of the state (pages 227–235). On one hand, there is the tendency towards states cooperating and pooling some of their sovereignty in transnational bodies such as the EU. On the other hand, there is the tendency towards fragmentation – former Yugoslavia became engulfed in territorial warfare and ethnic cleansing – and break-up – Czechoslovakia separated into the Czech Republic and Slovakia – and pressure from nationalist elements that seek to govern themselves. **Unitary states** such as the UK and Spain have been under pressure to devolve power from nationalist groups, which has resulted in the creation of subnational tiers of government. In the UK, devolution has involved the granting of decision-making powers to devolved assemblies in Scotland and Wales.

In some respects, power over events in the UK has passed outside Britain to suprastate bodies such as the European Court of Human Rights. MNCs exercise power over the UK economy, and the run on Northern Rock showed that developments outside the UK can seriously affect governments in the UK. An economic slowdown or actual recession in one part of the world, particularly in the US, can undermine the economies of other countries, especially if their economies are closely connected with the American market. Pages 230–235 considers how globalisation and the internet have further eroded the power of the state.

Anthony Giddens has written extensively on the role of the nation state in an age of globalisation (especially 1990 and 1999). He notes the apparently opposite tendencies of integration and fragmentation, centralisation and decentralisation. Daniel Bell and other writers are pessimistic about the role of the nation state. Bell (1987) thinks the state is 'too small for the big problems of life, and too big for the small problems of life'. Giddens is more optimistic, and says there are now more nation states than ever, given the break-up of colonial empires. He sees the need for increasing global government to tackle some of the problems that are too large for individual countries to handle, such as AIDS, financial instability and environmental issues.

Key terms

Neoliberal: someone who follows an economic philosophy developed in the late 1970s and associated with Margaret Thatcher and the Conservative right. Neoliberals reject state control and positive government intervention in the economy and focus on free-market methods, fewer restrictions on business enterprise and the importance of property rights.

Market economy: an economy that has almost total private control of capital, labour and land. The state has a generally passive role in the economy and leaves decisions to be made by open competition between companies that operate in a free market without state interference.

Welfare state: a system in which the government has the main responsibility for providing social and economic security of the population via free health care, pensions and a range of other social security benefits.

Unitary state: a country in which sovereignty lies exclusively with central government.

Power and politics

Key terms

Social democracy: a moderate, reformist strand of socialism that favours a balance between the market and the state, rather than the wholesale abolition of capitalism.

Giddens' Third Way (1998) seeks to transcend the old ideological division of capitalism and socialism and create a middle way that blends economic efficiency and social justice. Giddens rejects the New Right vision of the minimal state but finds the traditional left model of state intervention bureaucratic and ineffective. The Third Way tries to find a middle course between right and left, unrestrained free markets and socialist interventionism. It appeals to centre-left progressives and moderate social democrats.

The Third Way was the theoretical basis of the Blair governments from 1997 to 2007 and Blair's vision for reshaping British politics and society. It is also a strategy about creating a new left-of-centre progressive consensus in Britain and elsewhere. Its exponents share a commitment to practical **social democracy**. Shunning an excess of ideology, they proclaim that 'what matters is what works'.

Transnational capitalism

Globalisation has created a situation in which multinational corporations and the capitalists who control them have become extremely powerful. They have the capacity to take decisions that can have a significant impact on government policy, not least through the threat of market withdrawal (pages 231–232). Sklair (1995, 2003) sees the nation state as under threat. He says the transnational capitalist class has acquired power at the expense of the nation state and argues that 'those who own and control the institutions that drive globalisation presently wield most of the power in the global system'. He divides the class into four main 'fractions': the owners and controllers of transnational companies (TNCs) and their local affiliates; globalising bureaucrats and politicians; globalising professionals; and consumerist elites (merchants and the media).

Sklair notes that 'to some extent the exact disposition of these four fractions and the people and institutions from which they derive their power can differ over time and locality'. But whatever the different interests that might divide them, taken together the leading personnel in these groups constitute a global power elite, dominant class or inner circle in the sense that these terms have been used to characterise the dominant class structures of specific countries. This transnational capitalist class is opposed by anti-capitalists, who reject capitalism as a way of life or an economic system, and by capitalists who reject globalisation.

Summary questions

4 Compare the Marxist and pluralist theories of the state.

5 What is Giddens' Third Way?

6 What does Sklair see as the main challenge to the nation state in the 21st century?

Government and its role today

Learning objectives:

- Know the main forms of government.

- Understand the role of government.

- Recognise how government intervention developed in the 20th century.

- Know the reasons why governments legislate.

- Evaluate whether we have too much government.

Take it further

Use the internet to find out about life in two authoritarian or totalitarian regimes. Think about how it differs from life in a Western liberal democracy.

Key terms

Junta: a group of military officers holding the reins of power in a country, especially after a sudden violent or illegal seizure of power.

Totalitarian regime: a non-democratic regime in which there is very strong central direction and control of political, social and economic life.

Theocracy: a government led by religious leaders, such as the regime in Iran that followed the overthrow of the shah in 1979.

The government is the executive agent of the state (page 169). It enforces the laws of the state and acts under its authority. In other words, it runs the country. The state is a permanent, abstract entity, but its institutions can change and evolve and the people who run them may come and go. In a narrow sense, the government is just the highest tier of political appointments; in Britain that means the prime minister and the Cabinet. In a wider sense, the government is all bodies concerned with making and implementing decisions on behalf of the community. By this definition, civil servants, judges and the police all form part of the government, although they are not elected. In this wider sense, the government provides the landscape of institutions in which we experience public authority.

Governments make decisions on the running of public affairs. They resolve outstanding doubts and problems about what is to be done. They also work out how to implement those decisions. Wars must be fought, taxes raised and a whole range of other policies have to be implemented by turning them into laws. The people have to abide by these laws. If you break the laws, you may end up in prison; the government can lay down punishments for those who transgress. The core functions of the government are therefore to make law (legislation), to implement law (execution) and to interpret law (adjudication). There is no escape from government. Even if you leave the country and go elsewhere, you will live under another government. Life without government is not an option, but the nature of the governing regime varies across the world.

Types of government

There are various types of government. Democracy became an increasingly popular form of government in the closing decades of the 20th century. Until then, most of the global population lived in authoritarian states of one type or another. This has been the norm throughout human history. Within the past 80 years, there have been several brutal dictatorships, including Mussolini's Italy, Hitler's Germany, Stalin's Russia, Mao's China, Pol Pot's Cambodia, Saddam's Iraq and Mugabe's Zimbabwe.

Authoritarian regimes are non-democratic regimes in which those who rule wield great power and enforce their will on those they have power over. They include forms of military rule where a head of the armed forces rules on their own or a military clique rule as a **junta**. Many authoritarian regimes are also **totalitarian regimes**. Several of the 20th century dictatorships were totalitarian. Communist and fascist rulers believed in an ideology that they sought to impose upon their country. They wished to transform society and were brutal to anyone who opposed their vision. In totalitarian regimes, the state influences every aspect of everyday life, national and local. **Theocracies** are a much less common form of authoritarian rule. In Iran the religious leaders, ayatollahs and mullahs, play a leading role.

Power and politics

■ Key terms

Laissez-faire: the principle of minimum government interference or no government interference in economic matters, which are left to the economic forces of the market. From the French for 'allow to do'.

Nationalisation: the transfer of industries and utilities from private ownership to public ownership.

Beveridge Report: a 1942 report which formed the basis for Labour's post-1945 welfare state, especially the National Health Service.

AQA Examiner's tip

Examiners like to see up-to-date examples of laws. Find three or four recent UK examples and details about them. You might consider finding out why the Human Rights Act and the Scotland Act (both passed in 1998) were introduced.

Fig. 4.2.3 *Margaret Thatcher wanted less government intervention in national life*

Government in the UK

In the middle of the 19th century, the role of government in national life was straightforward and limited. Its main priorities were the defence of the community against external attack and the maintenance of law and order. Governments were not expected to solve society's economic and social problems. This was an era of **laissez-faire**, of minimal government intervention and regulation. There was only very basic provision of welfare for the destitute. But as the 20th century got under way, the idea developed that the state needed to play a more positive role in promoting the economic and social well-being of its citizens.

Governments during the 1920s and 1930s gradually began to play a more interventionist role in the economic and social life of the nation. After 1945 there was a new emphasis on collectivism, where we all have a responsibility for each other. This involved higher social spending to support those in various forms of need. State welfare was to be a new priority. In a programme of **nationalisation**, the state took over the running of key industries and utilities, such as coal, electricity, gas and the railways.

The phrase 'welfare state' was first used in the 1930s, but it only came into common use when the Labour government of 1945–51 introduced measures to maintain high levels of employment, provide security and a better life for all. Decent living standards began to be thought of as an entitlement, rather than as a cause of gratitude. Today most of us have come to assume that the state has a responsibility for our welfare and we have come to expect comprehensive protection against sickness, poverty, unemployment, ignorance and squalor, the five 'giant evils' recognised in the **Beveridge Report**.

Beveridge spoke of care 'from cradle to grave', others use the phrase 'from womb to tomb'. Most of us experience state provision at various points throughout our lives. We may be born in a National Health Service (NHS) hospital or with help from an NHS midwife. We may attend state-funded nursery facilities. We go through compulsory state education from age 5 to 16. Then we are subsidised to go to university, go to work and pay taxes to the government, or receive benefits if we are unemployed or incapacitated. We receive a retirement pension from the state. We are buried in a local authority cemetery or incinerated in a crematorium. If we fall ill, we receive NHS care. We are entitled to benefits such as maternity grants for pregnant women, and welfare benefits for people on low incomes. Victims of crime may receive victim support compensation. Litigants may receive legal aid. People sold inferior goods can use the consumer protection laws. Government matters to us all.

Too much or too little government?

In recent decades it has been fashionable for all politicians to seek a reduced role for government. The New Right of the Thatcher era favoured a reduction in government intervention in national life. Thatcherite thinking influenced the other two main parties, and all three parties propose greater decentralisation and localism (Figure 4.2.3). Labour has traditionally been the party most willing to use the power of government to achieve change in society, but New Labour is less identified with interventionism. In a 2008 column for *The Times* (www.timesonline.co.uk/tol/comment/columnists/matthew_parris/article3642596.ece), Matthew Parris says there is still a key role for government:

All sides have suffered a slow but disabling collapse of confidence in the ability of central government to do things, to mend things, to start things or to run things properly. Nobody seems to believe in the State any more.

I do. My message to the Left is keep the faith, baby. My message to the Right is beware the siren calls of laissez faire and localism. People need governing. People need governments, strong governments. People need certainty. People need consistency. People need constraining, inspiring, harnessing and directing, and they need it done with the clarity and command that central government alone can offer. In a thousand places, from the strategic heights to the nooks and crannies of everyday life, there arise necessities to which the answer must be that only government can do this.

Only government could have put Canary Wharf itself on to the map. ...

Only government now can get Crossrail built to link Canary Wharf properly into an east-west route across the metropolis. ... Private industry may do the actual construction of mass-transit public transport links, but government alone can knock heads together to initiate. The same is true of roads.

Only government can get decent healthcare for those who are poor and chronically sick. ...

Only government can protect us abroad, and police us at home. Only governments can force the pace on climate change. Only government can frame, amend and administer the law. Only government, and its legislation, can defend the interests of the generality against the appetites of individuals.

Summary questions

7 Why do we need laws?

8 In the 20th century, why did British governments move from a laissez-faire approach to a more interventionist approach?

How people participate

Learning objectives:

- Recognise the opportunities for individual participation in UK political life.

- Understand the types of person most likely and least likely to become involved.

- Know the arguments for and against the importance of participation in political life.

Take it further

For each of the following types of election in the UK, find out how often they are held and when they were last held: general elections, local elections, European elections, by-elections, and elections to the Scottish Parliament, Welsh Assembly and Northern Ireland Assembly.

Key terms

Electorate: all qualified voters.

Direct action: political action outside the constitutional and legal framework, such as obstructing access to a building or holding up road construction. Terrorism is an extreme and violent form.

Citizen participation is basic to the democratic system. In a representative democracy, people may not be able to make decisions directly, but those who do make them are accountable to the **electorate** at election time. Other than voting in elections, people may go to the polls to take part in referendums. In Britain, the only form of direct democracy is the use of referendums at the national and local levels. The turnout varies, but in Britain's national referendums it has averaged an impressive 62.1 per cent. Yet referendums are at best an irregular and infrequent means of popular involvement in political life.

Participation by other means than voting

Besides voting, there are many possibilities for individual involvement in the political system. Here are some examples: a pensioner who contacts their local authority to claim a reduction in council tax; a canvasser at election time who wears a party rosette; a green activist who lies in the path of construction workers trying to build a new highway; and the terrorists who planned the London bombings of July 2005. And here are the main means of participation besides voting:

- Become a member of a political party; more active membership might involve serving on a committee.

- Wear a party badge at election time or put up a campaign poster.

- Seek election to the Westminster Parliament, the devolved bodies in Scotland, Wales and Northern Ireland, or a local council.

- Join a pressure group; more active membership might involve holding office, perhaps as a trade union representative.

- Attend a meeting, distribute leaflets, canvas people on the doorstep, write to elected representatives or a newspaper, take part in a television show or radio phone-in, respond to an opinion poll, attend a focus group, or even set up a website.

- Participate in **direct action** such as a protest march, a demonstration or a sit-down protest, scribble political graffiti on a wall, go on strike, chain yourself to a public building, damage property or riot against the government.

- Kidnap a person, hijack a plane or commit some other form of political violence.

More orthodox forms of participation have declined in recent years. Figures for electoral turnout, party membership and doorstep canvassing are all much lower than a few decades ago. These are signs of public disengagement from the traditional democratic process.

Who participates and to what extent?

In most established democracies, such as Britain and the US, the level of popular participation falls well below the ideal. Beyond voting, other major forms of participation are sporadic, confined to a small minority, even among the more educated and well-off.

Many voters are ill-informed about political issues or any other issues affecting public affairs. In Britain, surveys have shown that many voters lack knowledge and understanding. Large numbers are unable to name their MP, MEP and local councillors, and are not very interested in what goes on at Westminster or in the European Parliament. Crewe *et al.*'s (1996) survey of young people in Britain and the US found that 80 per cent of British pupils engaged in very little or no discussion of public affairs at home, including local issues important to their own communities.

Two studies have expanded our knowledge about levels of political participation. In the US, Milbrath and Goel (1977) used the language of Roman gladiatorial contests to label the population according to their levels of involvement (Figure 4.3.1):

- **Gladiators** are the relatively small percentage of activists who are keen participants.
- **Spectators** are those who observe the contest but who limit their participation to voting; most people are spectators.
- **Apathetics** are the non-participants; they do not even watch the contest and are indifferent to its outcome.

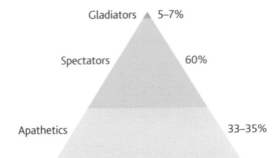

Fig. 4.3.1 *Milbrath and Goel (1977) labelled the population by level of involvement*

In Britain, Parry *et al.* (1992) surveyed more than 1,500 respondents and gave them a list of 23 different political actions, ranging from attending meetings to contacting an MP. They concluded that not everyone participates, and of those that do, they do not participate at the same rate or in the same way. Only a quarter of the population was involved in any significant activity. Three out of four interviewed were active to some degree: many were voters only – considerably fewer people voted in 2001 and 2005 – and the rest were inactive.

The fieldwork in Parry's survey was conducted more than 20 years ago. He dealt more with old-style participation rather than some of the newer forms such as purchase of a product for ethical reasons (e.g. fair-trade coffee), mass blockades, trespasses, **anti-globalisation** and anti-war demonstrations, and various forms of political violence.

In Britain and the US, a significant element of the population forms an underclass, uninformed about the political system, uninterested in it and alienated from it. There is widespread scepticism about politicians and what they promise and deliver. Those who are alienated feel that politics

Key terms

Anti-globalisation: a political outlook that protests against global trade agreements and their impact on the poorest people, the environment and the prospects for international peace. Global Justice is an anti-globalisation movement.

Power and politics

Take it further

Study the figures in Table 4.3.1 and think about any reasons why, on balance, women participate less than men in political activity. Consider the sort of political activities in which young people most commonly engage. Why do you think that they are generally reluctant to get involved? The information in Table 4.3.2 may assist you.

Table 4.3.1 *Political activism in the UK: participation by men and women (%)*

	Women	Men
Voting		
Voted in 2001 election	68	66
Campaign-oriented		
Contacted a politician	17	20
Donated money to a party	6	9
Worked for a party	2	4
Had been a party member	2	4
Had worn a campaign badge	10	11
Cause-oriented		
Signed a petition	42	36
Bought a product for a political reason	36	29
Boycotted a product	27	25
Demonstrated illegally	5	4
Protested illegally	1	1
Civic: member of		
Church group	18	10
Environmental group	6	6
Humanitarian group	3	4
Educational group	6	7
Trade union	15	16
Hobby group	14	19
Social club	13	19
Consumer group	28	35
Professional group	9	17
Sports club	20	33

Source: Adapted from Campbell et al. (2004)

Key terms

40:30:30 society: a society in which 40 per cent of the population have secure employment and are well off or comfortably off, 30 per cent have insecure employment and the remaining 30 per cent are economically and socially marginalised, jobless or working for poverty wages and barely able to subsist.

has nothing to offer them. It seems irrelevant to their lives. This group is concentrated among the least well off who feel marginalised from the rest of society. Large numbers live below the poverty line, and the minority populations are heavily concentrated in this category. They are at the wrong end of what Will Hutton (1996) has called a **40:30:30 society**. Among members of this least-educated and lower-income group, it is easy to feel discouraged and disillusioned. At election time, they may feel that they have no effective political outlet as the two main parties have little to say that is relevant to their predicament.

Disenchantment with the political system

Trust in government has declined, and fewer people think that politicians are truthful, reliable and willing to act in the public interest. Parry's study in 1992 found that in comparison with other advanced industrial countries, Britain came in the middle on a scale of trust in government

Table 4.3.2 *Some factors affecting levels of participation in political activity*

Factor	Impact on participation
Age	People under 35 are less likely to vote and less interested in traditional political outlets (such as joining youth wings of main parties), than their elders. They are more interested in direct action to promote animal rights, etc. Middle-aged and older people are more likely to vote and are more interested in supporting parties and established pressure groups such as unions
Ethnic origin	On polling day there is a high turnout of Jewish people, moderate to high turnout of Asians but low turnout of Afro-Caribbeans
Gender	Men have been traditionally more likely to vote and join organisations, but in recent years women have become more active in voting and joining or supporting causes. Some argue that, in the past, male political scientists did not see what was to them 'invisible' female participation via groups such as the Women's Institute
Location of residence	Participation is more likely in urban areas than in rural areas; difficulties of transport may play a part. In inner cities, turnout is often very low
Socialisation and personality	People brought up in families that were politically active and involved children in discussions and decisions are more likely to participate, as are more outgoing personalities. Family background is an important determinant
Social class	Professionals and business people, with a better education and higher income, are much more likely to participate in various ways, especially on polling day. Education is a strong determinant, as much activity involves organising, talking and writing, skills often associated with higher levels of attainment

Source: Adapted from findings of Parry et al. (1992) and Evans (1997)

and politicians: less trusting and more cynical than West Germany, Austria and Switzerland, but more trusting and less cynical than the US and Italy.

Putnam (2000) has echoed some of Parry's concerns. He detects a really profound change of feeling that is more serious than a sense of apathy and alienation. In his view, there is a decline in civil participation and public trust that together constitute 'a worrying decline' in America's **social capital**. A degree of scepticism about those who govern may be healthy and desirable, but democracy is based on the consent of the governed. If they lack confidence in their political leaders, this may be a sign that the system is not serving the people well.

Putnam uses the term 'social capital' in reference to social networks, the connections among individuals and the feelings of mutuality and trustworthiness that arise from them. In other words, interaction enables people to build communities, to commit themselves to each other and to knit the social fabric. It is argued that a sense of belonging, and the relationships of trust and tolerance they involve, can bring great benefits to people. In his words, it is the ability of a community to 'develop the "I" into the "we"'.

The beneficial effects of participation

For most political theorists, popular involvement is the essence of democracy. The more people debate issues, the more likely it is that the

Key terms

Socialisation: the instilling of political attitudes and values by agencies such as family upbringing, education and the media.

Social capital: the connections between individuals and the social networks and trustworthiness that arise from them. A strong fund of social capital may enable a community to develop political institutions and processes that can solve society's problems.

truth will emerge. Political discussion makes people more informed and better able to get those who govern to account for their actions. Decision-making will be improved if those who make decisions know that their actions are being scrutinised by an informed populace.

The 1998 Report of the Advisory Group on Citizenship, known as the Crick Report, paved the way for the introduction of compulsory citizenship lessons in schools. It observed: 'In the political tradition stemming from the Greek city states and the Roman Republic, citizenship has meant involvement in public affairs by those who uphold the rights of citizens to take part in public debate and, directly or indirectly, shape the laws and decisions of a state.' For Crick and his team, such participation was a right and a duty, the foundation of a democratic society and a safeguard for its preservation and protection.

Summary questions

1. Do low levels of participation reflect a general distrust of political life and politicians in Britain?

2. Are there any steps that can or should be taken to encourage greater participation in British political life?

3. Are you in favour of greater participation? If so, why?

4. Can you think of any arguments against greater participation?

Voting behaviour

Key terms

Voting behaviour: how people vote and why they vote the way they do.

Socialisation: the instilling of political attitudes and values by agencies such as family upbringing, education and the media.

Partisan alignment: the long-term allegiance of voters to a political party.

Partisan dealignment: the breakdown, since the 1970s, of long-term voter allegiance to a particular party.

Social class: the hierarchical distinctions between individuals or groups in society. The division of people with similar characteristics into strata or layers. Class is usually assessed on characteristics such as background, education and occupation.

Class alignment: the strong association of membership of a social class with support for a political party.

Class dealignment: the breakdown, since the 1970s, of the long-term association of a social class with support for a particular political party.

People study voting behaviour to see how people vote and why they vote the way they do. Four main theories have been advanced to explain **voting behaviour** in the post-war era.

Four theories of voting behaviour

Party identification theory

Supporters of the party identification theory placed much emphasis on political **socialisation**, which explained how people learned their political attitudes and behaviour via the process of growing up, in settings like their family and schools. Children discovered which party their parents favoured and were influenced by their parents' leanings, many of them staying with the party of their parents. In this way, political loyalties were developed. These loyalties tended to be confirmed by membership of particular groups and other social experiences. People developed an attachment to their parties, a sense of identity often called **partisan alignment**. The way they voted reflected this identification, so voting was a long-term manifestation of strongly held beliefs and loyalties. In recent decades, **partisan dealignment** has been much noted. In Britain and elsewhere, the level of party identification is now markedly less than in the past. Clarke *et al.* (2001) pointed out that the 'very strong' identification levels with Labour or the Conservatives sampled in 1964 (45 per cent) had fallen to 21 per cent by 1979 and 13 per cent by 2001.

Sociological theory

Sociological theorists pointed to the way people's social characteristics influenced their participation in politics. In particular, social class was seen as important in shaping political attitudes, especially in Britain. This view was so widely held that in 1967 Pulzer wrote: 'Class is the basis of British politics; all else is embellishment and detail.' To a large extent, the party system was regarded as mirroring the class system. Middle-class people were expected to vote Conservative and the working classes were seen as strongly pro-Labour. There were always many people who deviated from this pattern of voting, and much study was devoted to working-class Conservatives. Other characteristics such as ethnicity, gender, region and religion were also long-term factors often linked to voting behaviour. However, the link between **social class** and voting, or **class alignment**, was by far the most important connection. Similar to partisan dealignment, **class dealignment** has occurred in many Western countries, so the class analysis of politics is less convincing today. Class mobility has increased. The old concept of class solidarity – that everyone in a particular social class behaves in the same way – has been undermined.

Rational choice theory

In the 1980s, the emphasis shifted from the psychological and sociological approaches to the role of the individual in making a rational judgement and consequently acting in a calculated and deliberate way. According to Himmelweit *et al.* (1981), this may be a judgement based on the past performance of a particular administration, or it may be more related to the prospects for the individual and their family under any alternative. Either way, their assessments of parties were based on self-interest – the voters' perception of the likely effect on their life and well-being in the present and near future. In effect, voters were behaving as consumers in the marketplace, selecting a package that best suited their preferences. They compared products and made their decisions according to cost, quality and usefulness. One version of this consumerist approach was the idea advanced by Sanders (1995) that the state of the economy and the voters' view of how it was affecting their lives was very important in helping people decide on how to exercise their vote.

More people were opting for **instrumental voting**, using it as a means to achieve their goals. If that was so, it was necessary for parties to adjust what they offered the electorate in line with what they believed voters wanted. To win support, they also needed to place heavy emphasis on selling their potential and achievements to the electorate. Party managers were well aware of the need for careful management and manipulation of the media. In particular, they understood the importance of giving the leader a high profile in the campaign and exploiting the leader's assets. Some studies in the 1980s and 1990s have cast doubt on the rationality of the choice which voters make. If they are exposed to slanted news and current affairs in the media, their judgement may be affected by any misleading impression they receive.

Dominant ideology theory

Dunleavy and Husbands (1985) have argued that individual choices are influenced by media misrepresentation. In their view, the newspapers and television distort the process of political communication, help to determine the agenda for debate and consciously or unconsciously provide a partial coverage of the news. This is even more important in an age of dealignment, for in the absence of traditional factors such as class and party loyalties, voters are more likely to be swayed by what they hear, see and read.

In this theory, the media is seen as reflecting a dominant prevailing **ideology**. If that view is harsh about welfare claimants or the rights of various minorities in society, voters will be influenced to vote for parties that advance policies that conform to the current thinking of the opinion formers. The credibility of the dominant ideology theory is open to question. Whether or not you think that voters will succumb to a barrage of media manipulation is a matter of opinion. But the other theories are also incomplete or inadequate explanations of voting behaviour. None of them provides a totally convincing explanation of how and why people vote as they do. They all need to be borne in mind when considering the subject and each has its merits. They are not necessarily mutually exclusive.

■ Determinants of voting behaviour

Two long-term influences are party identification and loyalty, and social class. Electors identify with a particular party and loyalties are forged, so there is a strong long-term alignment (partisanship). Whereas in the US, the deep-seated association with a party is often stressed, in Britain more attention is paid to membership of some social grouping. Other factors that have a long-term influence relate to the social structure, such as age, gender, region, occupation, membership of an **ethnic group** or **minority ethnic group**, and religion.

Key terms

Instrumental voting: a one-off assessment of the parties' policies and reputations, based on their past performances as well as a judgement about their abilities to deliver their promises.

Ideology: a system of ideas or way of thinking pertaining to a class or individual, especially as a basis of some economic or political theory or system, regarded as justifying actions and especially to be maintained irrespective of events.

Ethnic group: people who share a common sense of identity as a result of kinship, culture, religion or, often, skin colour.

Minority ethnic group: normally used for non-white ethnic groups that are mainly the product of past immigration.

Take it further

Use the internet to find out how a person's social class is usually assessed.

Power and politics

Other factors have short-term influences. The economy covers levels of inflation, unemployment and disposable income, and whether voters feel good about their future prospects. Governments like to go to the country, or hold elections, when people feel good about money, jobs and their future prospects. The personal qualities and appeal of the party leaders have become more important because the media has become infatuated with personalities. The media may or may not have a direct influence on how voters vote, but it helps to determine what the election is about and the issues that are important. It provides information and dramatic headlines that can damage the standing of leaders. The style and effectiveness of party campaigning have changed considerably over recent decades.

The **Winter of Discontent** wrecked Labour's electoral chances in 1979. Britain's humiliating withdrawal from the **ERM** in 1992 and the **Major government's** reputation for **sleaze** had seriously undermined faith in the Conservatives by the 1997 election. More recently, the handling of the war in Iraq seriously damaged the reputation of the Labour government, and made many voters questioned the truthfulness of Tony Blair. Parties need to inspire trust in their own policies and competence, and to cast doubt on their opponents. Voters shop around for a set of policies that best suit their own priorities. They tend to have generalised images of the parties. Labour is the party of the working class and in favour of higher social spending. The Conservatives are the party of the middle and upper classes, more committed to lower taxation than public spending on health and welfare. The image is based on what the parties have done in the past, and a vague impression of policy positions and the qualities projected by the party leadership.

Broadly, long-term influences have become less important in British politics and short-term influences have become more significant. The breakdown of traditional associations is very important for the parties as they can no longer count on the support they once took for granted.

Post-war trends

The academic literature of the early post-war era pointed to a positive relationship between membership of a social class and the way people cast their vote. However, from the 1970s onwards, the process of class dealignment was reflected in a reduction in Conservative support from the professional and managerial classes and a reduction in Labour support from the working classes. In 1997 Labour increased its support across all social classes and for some years it continued to broaden its appeal in **Middle England**.

Here are some of the features most noted from after the war to the 1970s:

- There were stable voting patterns, as people stayed loyal to the party they had always supported. Punnett (1971) put it like this: 'For most people, voting behaviour is habitual and ingrained.'
- Elections were determined by a body of floating voters in key marginal constituencies, whose votes needed to be targeted by the parties if they were to have a chance of success.
- The uniform **electoral swing** across the UK showed that voters in one area tended to behave in much the same way as voters elsewhere.
- Between them, the two main parties could count on the support of the majority of the electorate. This reached a high point in 1951 when the Conservatives and Labour gained 96.8 per cent of the vote; in 1966 they still got 89.8 per cent.

Key terms

Winter of Discontent: widespread industrial unrest during the winter of 1978/79 that seriously disrupted everyday life and damaged the prospects of the Labour government at the time.

ERM: Exchange Rate Mechanism; a mechanism for regulating the exchange rates of currencies used by the member states of the European Community and later the EU in the period before the introduction of a single currency.

Major government: the Conservative government led by John Major from 1990 to 1997.

Sleaze: a collective noun for financial and sexual scandals under recent governments.

Middle England: the political middle ground, often seen as occupied by the aspirational middle, lower middle and working classes of England, those who want to better themselves and whose views are often equated to those of the Daily Mail.

Electoral swing: the figure used to indicate the scale of voter change between two political parties from one election to another.

Power and politics

Power and politics

Key terms

Third parties: parties that can gather a sizeable percentage of popular support and regularly gain seats in the legislature, but which have no meaningful chance of being the majority party and forming a government after an election. A UK example is the Liberal Democrat Party.

Demographic change: a change that relates to the size and distribution of the population.

Embourgeoisement: the tendency of better-off working people with aspirations to become more like the middle classes in their social outlook and voting behaviour.

Hint

The social class groupings in **Table 4.3.4** are commonly used by polling companies.

In the decades since the 1970s, many assumptions have ceased to be valid. The two major parties can no longer expect the degree of support they once enjoyed. **Third parties** have made inroads into the vote share of the two main parties (Table 4.3.3).

Table 4.3.3 *Post-war elections: average share of the vote for each party (%)*

	Conservative	Labour	Liberal or Liberal Democrat
1945–1970	45.3	46.0	7.1
1974–2005	37.9	36.3	19.4

Source: Calculated from figures in Kavanagh and Butler (2005)

The weakening link between class and voting

Sarlvik and Crewe's *Decade of Dealignment*, published in 1983, used data from Essex University's British Election Study. It analysed elections in the 1970s, culminating in the Conservative victory of 1979. It showed how far the two parties had steadily lost their reliable supporters, the people who voted for the same party at each election.

Table 4.3.4 *Social class groupings*

Category	Fraction of population (%)	Groups included
AB	28	Higher managerial, lower managerial, professional and administrative
C1	29	White-collar, skilled, supervisory or lower non-manual
C2	19	Skilled manual
D/E	23	Semi-skilled and unskilled, casual workers, long term unemployed and very poor

In particular, Sarlvik and Crewe discovered that **demographic changes** were taking their toll on Labour, because the old working-class communities were being destroyed by redevelopment schemes, and inner cities were emptying. Workers moving to new towns and expanding small towns around London were less likely to vote Labour. Areas of population decline (like the north of England and South Wales) were traditionally Labour, while growth areas (mainly in the south-east) were strongly Conservative, emphasised by changes to the constituency boundaries. Labour's electoral base was being eroded, which led Kellner (1983) to write that the 'sense of class solidarity which propelled Labour to power in 1945 has all but evaporated'.

The Sarlvik and Crewe (1983) study was particularly famous for its distinction between the old and the new working class. They wrote about 'the traditional working class of the council estates, the public sector, industrial Scotland and the north, and the old industrial unions ... the affluent and expanding working class of the new estates and new service economy of the South'. The new working class are often known as the C2s. By the 1980s, it seemed that **embourgeoisement** was a significant factor favouring the Conservatives, for in 1979 members of the skilled 'new' working class were won over by Thatcherite support for tax cuts and shared Conservative attitudes on race, unions, nationalisation and crime.

Initially, Sarlvik and Crewe's views were widely accepted and seemed set to become the new orthodoxy. However, they were contested by some academics, most notably Heath *et al.* (1985), who were unconvinced by the idea that class voting had been diminishing. They used a more sophisticated five-point classification to redefine class, rather than the simple but 'wholly inadequate' division of working class and middle class. Basing their studies on a review of the results of the 1983 election, they claimed that there had been no progressive class dealignment, but a 'trendless fluctuation'.

Heath *et al.* thought that Labour's decline reflected changes in the relative sizes of the different classes rather than any change in the level of class voting. Between 1964 and 1983, the working class contracted whereas the salariat and routine non-manual classes expanded. This accounted for nearly half of Labour's decline. Much of the remaining loss of support reflected a widespread perception that Labour had become too left-wing. Its ideological stance was out of touch with the bulk of the electorate.

Class and voting in British elections since 1997

Labour's claim to be the party of the working class took a strong blow in the Thatcher years. It may be true that the Labour vote remained largely working-class, but the working class was no longer largely Labour. To be successful again, Labour had to attract more skilled workers. Under the Blair leadership, the position improved dramatically. In 1997 and 2001, New Labour did well in all social categories and only among the AB voters did the Conservatives retain a lead (Table 4.3.5).

Table 4.3.5 *Labour support by social class in the 1997 and 2001 elections (%)*

Social class	1997	2001
AB	31	30
C1	39	38
C2	50	49
DE	59	55

Source: Based on Butler and Kavanagh (2005)

In 2005 the social class divide was arguably weaker than ever. The Conservative lead in the share of the AB vote was down to 9 per cent from 32 per cent in 1992, but the ABs and C1s remained the most significant element in Conservative support. Even in a year when it did badly compared with the two previous elections, New Labour was still able to capture 28 per cent of the AB vote. Although it lagged behind the Conservatives among the C1s, it was well ahead among the C2s and the DEs.

Regional variations are related to class variations. The outcome in 2005 varied across the country, and only the south-east became evidently more Conservative. Labour had a clear lead over its rivals in Greater London, the north-east, north-west, Yorkshire and Humberside, Scotland and Wales, and a narrower lead in the West Midlands and East Midlands. It was behind in the east, the south-east and the south-west.

Take it further

Look at Table 4.3.6. Consider whether the result of the 2005 election confirms or undermines the view that the middle classes lean to the Conservatives and the poorest section of the working classes lean to Labour.

Power and politics

Table 4.3.6 *Party support in the 2005 election by social class (%)*

Class	Labour	Conservative	Lib Dem	Other
AB	28	37	29	6
C1	32	36	23	9
C2	40	33	19	8
DE	48	25	18	9

Source: Based on figures from the Observer, 8 May 2005

Key terms

Volatility: significant changes in voting habits that have made voting less consistent and more unpredictable. It involves a shift of voter support between parties or between voting and abstention, a process sometimes known as churning.

As a broad trend, social changes have occurred in all developed countries and voters have become less committed to their long-term allegiances. Stability rather than change was once the established pattern in voting behaviour, with many voters being reluctant or unwilling to deviate from their regular habits. In recent years, as a result of partisan dealignment, there has been a weakening of the old loyalties. A new **volatility** exists in the electorate. However, parties retain their core voters, those who remain loyal under almost any circumstances.

Age, gender and ethnicity

Age

Most early voting surveys suggested that young people, especially people aged 18–24, were more inclined to vote Labour, whereas older people, especially the over 55s, were more likely to vote Conservative. In a major analysis conducted in the 1960s, Butler and Stokes (1969) wrote of 'senescent Conservatism', the idea that the more senile you become, the more likely you are to be a Conservative.

The usual explanation given was that young people tend to be more idealistic in their thinking, wanting a better and more peaceful world with more social justice and a genuine attempt to tackle world poverty. They favoured policies involving more public spending on domestic and international policies, not least because the burden of the necessary taxation would not fall upon them. As they become older, people have a more realistic and perhaps more cynical view of what can be achieved by social change at home and abroad. They have mortgages to pay plus other costs associated with family responsibilities, and would be alarmed by high taxation to finance public spending. Once their finances are more sound, in their fifties and sixties, they are particularly likely to be affronted by having to pay more to finance the education of young students and other groups who rely on government handouts.

Another influence was the era in which a person was brought up; each generation is influenced by the issues and circumstances of the day. Any person who was 80 in 1960 would have been brought up in an era when there was no national Labour Party, so their formative influences would have been Conservative or Liberal.

In Labour's 1997 landslide, it did better than the Conservatives among all age groups except the over 65s. In 2005 the progressive parties, Labour and the Liberal Democrats, again fared better among young people. Labour scored well among people aged 35–44, the age group most involved with family responsibilities. The Liberal Democrats did especially well with those under 34. Labour's policy on tuition fees was widely believed to have troubled many voters in constituencies that had a university. The more students in a constituency, the greater the fall in the Labour vote and the rise in the Liberal Democrat vote.

Gender

Early surveys usually found that women were more strongly pro-Conservative than men across all the social classes. According to Pulzer (1967), women were 'overwhelmingly' more pro-Conservative. Here are the explanations they gave:

- Women often stayed at home and were protected from bad working conditions and from the pull of trade union membership.

- When women did go out to work, they tended to be in cleaner and more pleasant environments such as offices.
- Women had a greater commitment to the traditional values of family and religion.
- Women were naturally more cautious in their attitude to social change.

In the 1980s there was evidence that this gender gap was being reversed and women were becoming more inclined to vote Labour, perhaps attracted by its less harsh outlook on issues such as immigration and by its commitment to family matters such as education and health. In 1997 the swing to Labour was greater among women than men, although in both groups there was a strong pro-Labour lead. In 2005, as in 2001, women were more likely than men to vote Labour, although the party had lost some female support. Childs (2005) found that Labour's general appeal to women was largely based on policy considerations, notably the introduction of family tax credits, Sure Start, child trust funds, the expansion of childcare provision and a reduction in child poverty.

Ethnicity

Minority ethnics have traditionally been more likely to vote Labour than Conservative (Figure 4.3.2). The tendency has been most marked among Afro-Caribbeans, slightly less marked among Asians. Voter turnout is relatively low for all minority ethnics. Saggar's (2000) findings, based on data derived from the 1997 election, suggested that of those who voted, 89 per cent of black and 81 per cent of Asians opted for Labour. As several within these categories would have been working-class people living in poorer areas of large cities, their association with Labour was perhaps unsurprising. Traditionally tough, more restrictive Conservative attitudes on immigration and race relations made the trend even more understandable. Successful middle-class professionals and businessmen, many of them Asian, may also have viewed Labour as the party that was more committed to social justice.

Fig. 4.3.2 *Minority ethnics go to the polls: more likely to vote Labour?*

Table 4.3.7 *Impact of the Muslim vote on the main parties in the 2005 general election*

Muslim voters as a fraction of all voters in the constituency (%)	Change in vote share (%)		
	Conservative	Labour	Lib Dem
< 1	0.4	−4.8	3.1
1–5	0.4	−6.4	4.1
5–10	−0.1	−8.1	6.1
> 10	−1.8	−10.6	8.8

Source: Adapted from Kavanagh and Butler (2005)

Non-voting and turnouts in British elections

Voter turnout refers to the percentage of the qualified voting-age population that actually turns out on polling day. A good turnout of voters is often considered to be a healthy sign in any democracy as it appears to indicate vitality and interest. Many advanced countries have turnouts consistently above 75 per cent, some over 90 per cent, but those with exceptionally high figures (e.g. Australia, Belgium and Italy) have compulsory voting laws.

Britain has usually had lower turnout figures than those recorded in other established European democracies over the past few decades. Turnout in

Take it further

Table 4.3.7 gives figures for the 2005 general election and shows what happened to vote share in constituencies where Muslims were a big fraction of the electorate. Suggest reasons for the strong performance of the Liberal Democrats. To what extent did the Conservative Party benefit from Labour's difficulties in the seats where Muslims were a big fraction of the electorate? Can you explain your findings?

Power and politics

general elections has varied considerably from one general election to the next. The variation from constituency to constituency is also very large, from over 90 per cent to just over 40 per cent. The turnout in the 2001 general election was 59.4 per cent and the turnout in the 2005 general election was 61.3 per cent. Turnouts in elections for local councils, devolved assemblies and the European Parliament have usually been very low at about 30–45 per cent.

The turnout in the 2005 general election was slightly better than in 2001, perhaps because the contest looked closer. Although the Conservatives lacked popular appeal, there was the opportunity to pass a verdict on Prime Minister Blair and give him a bloody nose. The result of the 2001 election seemed to be a foregone conclusion. At the 2005 election, turnout was higher in constituencies where political change was a genuine prospect.

A general decline in turnout in Europe and the US

Turnouts have declined for most democracies in the past few elections (Table 4.3.8), and this has led to alarm about voter apathy, or even voter **alienation** from the political system. Many voters across Europe and America seem increasingly disillusioned with the performance of parties in office and with the politicians who represent them. Media analysis has sometimes encouraged the view that promise has not always been matched by outcome, so many voters perceive all parties and politicians to be as bad as each other. Moreover, party differences have narrowed as some of the big Cold War issues such as capitalism versus communism, peace versus war become less relevant. Nowadays, the distinctions between party programmes are seldom fundamental.

> ### Key terms
>
> **Alienation:** a feeling of separateness, of being alone and apart from others; where a worker is denied their essential human nature.

Table 4.3.8 *UK: turnout in general elections and European elections, 1979–2005 (%)*

General elections		European elections	
Year	Turnout (%)	Year	Turnout (%)
1979	76.0	1979	31.6
1983	72.7	1984	32.6
1987	75.3	1989	36.2
1992	77.7	1994	36.5
1997	71.4	1999	23.6
2001	59.4	2004	38.8
2005	61.3		

Source: Adapted from figures provided in Kavanagh and Butler (2005) and Nugent (2006)

It may be that the descendants of yesterday's committed voters are today's pressure-group campaigners. Perhaps in a post-materialist age when most people live a much better life than previous generations, they care more about quality-of-life issues such as ecology and minority rights. Pressure groups arguably represent these causes more effectively than the parties which contest elections.

Finally, some writers suggest that lower turnouts are not a sign of apathy and resentment, but may reflect broad contentment. Abstention or non-voting may amount to general satisfaction with the conduct of affairs, and voters do not feel stirred to express their feelings at the ballot box. The motives of voters may vary: some may not feel the need to vote because everything seems satisfactory, whereas others – often the young, the poor and minority ethnics – may feel that no party or candidate on the ballot paper is relevant to them.

Summary questions

5   How has the behaviour of voters changed over recent decades?

6   Why has class voting broken down in recent decades?

7   What was the relationship between social class and voting in the 2005 election?

8   Labour is the party of the industrial urban and inner-city areas of the north of England, Scotland and Wales, whereas the Conservatives are the party of rural areas and the suburbs in the south. Is this statement still true?

9   Do you think that voting in Britain is based on class?

10 Why might female voters still prefer Labour?

11 What do you think are the main influences on why people vote as they do? Are sociological theories adequate to explain voting behaviour?

12 Why has the turnout of voters broadly declined in most democracies in recent years?

Power and politics

Party and pressure group membership

Power and politics

Learning objectives:

- Explore the state of party membership in the UK.

- Understand the opportunities for people to be active in political parties.

- Understand why people join groups.

- Identify that group activity has rapidly increased.

- Identify that most people have some involvement in pressure groups.

- Know the advantages of pressure groups as vehicles for popular involvement.

Take it further

Using party websites to help you, try to find out the benefits of joining the Conservative Party and the Labour Party. Full membership of the Conservative Party costs £25 per year. Membership of the Labour Party costs £36 per year.

Parties and pressure groups offer opportunities for popular participation. This may be more passive participation such as being a member, or it may be more active participation, such as becoming an elected representative, spokesperson or campaigner.

Involvement in political parties

Party membership has been declining in most of Europe over the past few decades, but party membership is particularly low in the UK (Tables 4.3.9 to 4.3.11). Commentators often portray declining membership as an indication of lessening enthusiasm for political parties and falling interest in them. They point to the loss of members by established parties and compare it to the growth in pressure-group activity. The low figures quoted may also reflect the fact that parties today spend less time recruiting than in the past, for they once needed activists to do voluntary work and rally the local voters to turn out in support of their candidate. Now much campaigning is done by television, so there is more emphasis on the party leaders and their senior colleagues. Finally, there may be too many other things that people can do with their time. Politics has a very low priority in many people's lives. Others give it a lower priority than they used to, perhaps because many of the big issues of world peace and hunger have lost much of their impact in Europe.

Table 4.3.9 *Party membership as a fraction of the electorate in 1990–2000*

	Fraction of the electorate who belong to a political party (%)
Austria	18
Finland	10
Norway	7
Germany	3
UK	2

Source: Based on P. Mair and I. van Biezen (2001)

Table 4.3.10 *Party membership in Britain, December 2006*

	Membership
Conservative	250,000
Labour	200,000
Lib Dem	73,000
SNP	12,000
Plaid Cymru	8,000

Source: Based on contacts with party headquarters

Table 4.3.11 *Membership of the British Labour and Conservative Parties, 1955–2005*

	1955	2005
Conservative	2,600,000	251,000
Labour	1,000,000	205,000

Source: Based on McKenzie (1963) and contacts with parties

The opportunities of members to influence party policy

Those who belong to parties join their local **constituency** associations, many of which were created when the right to vote was extended to many working-class male voters in the late 19th century. At that time, decisions were taken from the centre in London and handed down to the local branches. The active members performed a useful role in canvassing the electorate, trying to persuade voters to choose their party on polling day.

The pattern of policymaking described was noted almost 100 years ago by Michels (1911), who developed an **iron law of oligarchy**. He argued that parties that claimed to be democratic were usually run by a ruling clique of leaders and officials who possessed well-developed organisational skills and an understanding of what was necessary to keep the party and themselves in power. Ordinary members were usually prepared to accept this, as they were keen to see the party prosper in and between elections.

Over the past two decades, there has been more emphasis on giving members a greater say in how their party functions, while at the same time ensuring that the leadership retains key powers, such as to keep out dissidents who might discredit the organisation and undermine its electoral chances. The Green Party has been particularly interested in democratic consultation with its membership.

Membership of pressure groups

Human beings are social animals and have a natural inclination to form groups, but there is another sound motivation. On their own, a person is rarely able to influence policy and decisions that affect their lives, but by acting with others in a group, they have a say over issues they care about.

Since the 1960s there has been an astonishing rate of growth in the formation of issue and cause groups, be they national or grass-roots. So dense is the modern group system that most people belong to at least one voluntary association, such as a church, a social club, a sports club, or an organisation that promotes civil liberties or rights. Minorities and women have organised themselves to demand access to the social and political benefits long denied to them. Women have campaigned to have their rights recognised in law and have spoken out on central issues of procreation and reproduction.

Besides the large interest groups in business, finance, labour and the professions, there are many registered charities, development **NGOs**, community groups, women's organisations, faith-based organisations, professional associations, trade unions, self-help groups and social movements. Some are long-lasting, others are transient; some are national, others local; some are giants firmly rooted in the public mind, others are little known.

Key terms

Constituency: the area that elects an MP to Parliament. The UK has 646 constituencies.

Iron law of oligarchy: states that mass organisations cannot by nature be democratic. They are and always will be controlled by a ruling elite. Leaders of political parties, who have expert knowledge, specialist skills and a desire to enhance their prospects of retaining power, dominate the organisations they lead.

NGO: non-governmental organisation; a non-profit group largely funded by private contributions, e.g. charities, generally with social, political and environmental agendas.

Power and politics

■ Key terms

Movement: a large body of people who are interested in a common theme that is of continuing significance. The women's movement consists of individuals and groups that seek to advance the position of women in society.

NSM: new social movement; any social movement that emerged since the 1960s. NSMs deal with a new range of issues and do not wish to be absorbed into the established political system. Members often provide a radical critique of society and institutions. They are interested in finding different ways of organising political activity.

Participation in green groups

British environmental groups and **movements**, especially **NSMs**, have experienced an impressive rate of growth over the past generation (Table 4.3.12). Many groups experienced a substantial increase in membership in the 1980s and 1990s. Whereas Lowe and Goyder (1983) identified nearly 100 national environmental groups and several thousand local ones, with a combined membership approaching 3 million in 1980, more recent estimates place the figure at 4.5 million, probably rather more. The Green Party has failed to make significant electoral headway in the UK. Group activity and direct action seem to be more productive. Several new and more radical organisations have flourished, often loosely affiliated to some larger body but operating at a local level.

Table 4.3.12 *Growth in membership of the largest environmental groups, 1981–2005*

	1981	2005
National Trust	1,050,000	3,400,000
RSPB	440,000	1,049,000
Wildlife Trust	140,000	600,000
WWF	60,000	430,000
Greenpeace	30,000	221,000
Friends of the Earth	18,000	102,000
Ramblers' Association	37,000	140,000
Woodland Trust	20,000	130,000
CPRE	29,000	60,000

Source: Garner (2000) plus websites and direct contact

Other forms of pressure group activity

Some populist movements, including some NSMs, have gained widespread support in the UK and the rest of Europe. They bring together people who would not normally take an active part in political life and who are willing to attend mass demonstrations. The Countryside Alliance and Make Poverty History are examples, as were the fuel tax protesters in 2005. All have benefited from careful use of the media and the trends in communications technology – email and fax, mobile phones and the internet – that have made it easier for protesters to contact each other. Here are some other factors they have in common:

■ Often they emerge abruptly, perhaps ignited by a spark which makes a sudden impact; the 1996 Dunblane massacre inspired the Snowdrop campaign.

■ They tend to be based on issues that arouse an emotional response, perhaps fuelled by a tabloid campaign and accompanying television coverage.

■ They use direct action to draw attention to the demands being made.

■ They get a swift and well-managed government response to head off the escalating discontent.

The advantages of groups as vehicles for participation

Many people only directly participate in political life at election time, but elections are held only every four or five years and do not allow voters to express a preference on individual issues. In contrast, people can play a more regular part in the workings of democracy by joining groups that can influence the decisions of public bodies. This is considered a significant virtue by those who favour a more participatory form of democracy. Far more people belong to a pressure group – sometimes they join two or three – than belong to a political party. Members can hone their political skills and make new contacts through networking, plus they enjoy the fellowship of people who share their vision and goals for society.

Groups provide an outlet for people with little interest in party politics but who become galvanised by an issue that relates to them much more directly. In particular, many environmentalists believe that traditional party politics is incapable of resolving ecological problems. They portray party politicians as essentially self-interested power-seekers, whose main preoccupation is to remain in power for as long as possible. To do this, they need to advance a party platform that offends as few voters as possible, especially the very powerful. That is why the major parties resemble each other.

Groups also provide an outlet for political recruitment. There is an overlap between politicians of the centre-left and active involvement in campaigning activity, particularly on civil rights and social policy. Many politicians began their careers as group activists. For instance, Harriet Harman championed individual rights at Liberty. It is easy to overstate popular involvement in groups. Many people choose not to get involved and some prefer not vote. Many people who join groups have no desire to play an active role and often join for just a short time; some groups have a high membership turnover. Many group members limit their involvement to signing a few petitions, joining a march or paying their subscription.

Summary questions

13 What are the advantages of
   a party membership and
   b pressure group membership?

14 Can British parties build larger mass memberships? If they can, should they try?

15 Why do you think that many young people find involvement in new social movements more appealing than belonging to political parties?

Power and politics

New social movements

Learning objectives:

■ Understand the nature and characteristics of NSMs.

■ Recognise sociologists' theories on why NSMs arise.

Take it further

Make a list of the main similarities and differences between old and new social movements. Think of one area of interest to you, such as animal welfare, the environment, global justice or anti-globalisation protests. Find out the names of any relevant pressure groups or NSMs.

AQA Examiner's tip

Examiners like to see evidence of your own research. Choose any two NSMs and find out more about them, so you can give good examples in exam answers.

Take it further

Make a list of the main writers on NSMs mentioned in the text and then add a brief summary of their ideas.

Social movements were defined by Tarrow (1998) as 'collective challenges by people with common purposes and solidarity in sustained interaction with elites, opponents and authorities'. Whereas the old social movements (OSMs) of the 19th century were concerned with issues such as labour conditions and the struggle for factory reform, new social movements (NSMs) are concerned with causes such as environmental and women's issues. Old and new movements have set out to challenge dominant ideas and a given constellation of power. They want to place different priorities on the political agenda.

NSMs have a radical edge and have a vision of a world transformed by their demands. They have what Hague and Harrop (2004) label 'a coating of anti-politics' about them, because they comprise people from beyond the political mainstream who mount an unconventional challenge to the existing political order. They do not seek power, but indirectly to influence government decisions. They clearly focus on a single issue, such as feminism, nuclear power or the environment. Their methods range from demonstrations and sit-ins to boycotts and political strikes. Their structure is loose, as they lack the leadership, membership and subscriptions that characterise political parties and pressure groups. They are national and international in scope; the trends towards global interconnectedness require them to operate across national boundaries. They have supporters across the world.

The environmental movements are among the most radical, because they think that saving the planet requires a reversal of existing use and distribution of economic resources. They want to reverse a way of life built around consumption and the pursuit of material well-being. Because they have post-materialist values, Giddens (2001) says that NSMs represent 'the new politics of lifestyles'.

Categories and theories for NSMs

Hallsworth (1994) distinguished two categories of NSM, defensive and offensive. In the defensive category he placed animal rights, environmentalists and peace campaigners, all of which try to preserve some feature of the existing natural and social environment. Some subdivide defensive NSMs into the traditional nature conservation groups, and the political ecology and anti-nuclear movements, often characterised as part of the New Left. Offensive NSMs are more concerned with equal rights for marginalised groups that often suffer discrimination. In this group, he placed civil rights movements and groups concerned with disability, feminist and gay issues. Feminist movements around the world have tried to place civil and political rights on the political agenda, and have added issues from abortion to contraception, from childcare to domestic violence.

Why social movements happen

Princen and Finger (1994) note that the collective action of movements can be triggered 'as a result of relative deprivation, as a strategy to articulate common interests, or as a response to economic and political conflicts … the purpose is social change'. This is true of NSMs and was equally true of OSMs. Melucci (1989) echoes Princen and Finger when he says that people join NSMs to acquire a sense of collective identity.

Explanations of NSMs focus on three broad reasons: post-materialist values, the experiences of a post-industrial world and postmodernism. Ingelhart (1977, 1990) and others stress the 'value shift' in society, as offered by post-materialist theorists: 'A shift from Materialist to Postmaterialist value priorities has brought new political issues to the center of the state and provided much of the impetus for new political movements … from giving top priority to physical sustenance and safety toward heavier emphasis on belonging, self-expression, and the quality of life.'

In poorer parts of the world, the post-materialist thesis fits the situation less well than in the West. Movements may be based on the fight for survival and security needs in situations made worse by environmental degradation, as with the struggles of the Ogoni people in Nigeria against pollution caused by oil companies (Figure 4.3.3).

Post-industrialist theorists argue that advanced capitalism, be it in Western markets or in state-centred regimes such as the former Soviet Union, push the earth, its habitats and its species to extinction by their pursuit of growth at all costs. Initially, the environmental costs were not recognised or were portrayed as a necessary by-product of creating more wealth and prosperity. Boggs (1986) says the 'radicalism of new social movements tends to flow from the deep crisis of industrial society'. He continues: 'The eclipse of the industrial growth model, the threat of nuclear catastrophe, bureaucratisation, destruction of natural habitat, social anomie … cannot be expected to disappear simply through the good intentions of political leaders.' Boggs thinks the post-industrial setting provides the climate in which the formation of NSMs is promoted.

Postmodern theorists argue that conventional politics have becoming increasingly detached from ideology and more preoccupied with superficialities such as presentation. Baudrillard (1983) and Lyotard (1984) claimed that in many Western democracies there is no longer any choice between the parties, for they do not represent clear ideological standpoints. Politics is no longer about principles and the battle for 'big ideas', but about achieving more limited things on a pragmatic basis. Fraser (1995) notes how politics has moved from the state-centred public sphere to the private sphere. Politics was previously conducted in the public sphere, but in today's politics many previously personal or private issues such as domestic violence have now become political. A range of new issues, such as ethnicity and gender, have become more important, providing greater opportunities for involvement by those who previously lacked power, such as black people and women.

Crook *et al.* (1992), among others, wrote about the shift from the conventional 'old politics' to the new. They note the decline of class and how class decomposition means that people who seem to be in the same class may no longer share similar characteristics. In their view, the emergence of a volatile electorate and the penetration of the media have helped to create new interests and concerns in a postmodernising society, and these interests are met by NSMs. The media highlights global problems, encouraging some people to think they can and must do something about them.

Giddens (2001) does not accept that we now live in a postmodern age. He portrays NSMs as a response to the risks in modern society, many of

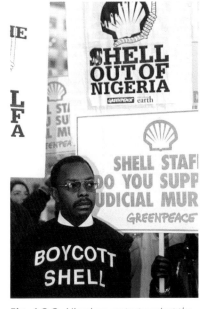

Fig. 4.3.3 *Nigerians protest against the oil company Shell*

■ Take it further

Go to www.globaljusticemovement. org and read about the Global Justice Movement (GJM). Find out what it does and the people and groups that support it.

Power and politics

which transcend national boundaries. Examples of these many risks are challenges to the environment, such as accidental oil spills, leakages from power plants, climate change, depletion of species and disappearing rainforests. Many people have lost faith in the ability of conventional politics to tackle these risks effectively. They see NSMs as a possible vehicle for action, an outlet for their desire to see something done. Unlike some writers who suggest that people are unwilling to participate in political life, Giddens sees NSMs as evidence that they are willing to get involved. He regards them as a means of 'highlighting complex moral issues and putting them at the centre of social life'.

Callinicos (1989), a Marxist, does not accept the ideas of post-industrialism or post-materialism as distinctive explanations for the rise of NSMs. He thinks politics is still about the class struggle and, given today's global problems, this means that exploited workers worldwide engage in a struggle to overthrow capitalism, which he regards as responsible for most of the global problems that NSMs aim to tackle: for instance, he blames capitalism for the hazards created by pollution. The one movement to which he is committed is the anti-capitalist movement, which campaigns against globalisation and for radical politics and social justice.

Summary questions

16 How do NSMs differ from OSMs?

17 Can anti-globalisation protests such as those associated with the Global Justice Movement protests be classified as NSMs?

18 What sort of people are attracted to NSMs? Why might many working-class people be unenthusiastic about joining NSMs?

19 People join NSMs because they no longer have faith in traditional politics. Is this true?

20 Are NSMs an indication of postmodernism?

Women and minority ethnics

Learning objectives:

- Recognise that women and minority ethnics are under-represented on political bodies.

- Understand the reasons for the under-representation of women.

- Know the reaction of male MPs to women in the House of Commons.

Key terms

Career politician: people committed to politics, which they regard as their vocation. Career politicians know little beyond the world of politics, policymaking and elections.

Proportional representation: the collective term for electoral systems that award seats in the legislature in proportion to the number of votes cast for each party. Such systems are often said to be fairer than the British system of FPTP. They use multi-member constituencies for which each party puts up a number of candidates. This may encourage them to adopt more women and members of ethnic minorities.

FPTP (First Past the Post): the system used in the UK to elect MPs to the House of Commons. It is based on single-member constituencies for which each party puts up one candidate. The candidate with the most votes (even if he or she lacks an overall majority) wins.

Elected assemblies in most countries are often criticised as being unrepresentative of society. Often they are categorised as being white, male, middle-class and middle-aged. This is true of all Europe's elected legislatures. So legislatures are not a microcosm or mirror image of the population on whose behalf they act. And as politics becomes more professionalised, many politicians go into politics as a career; these **career politicians** arrive in Parliament without having done another job.

British MPs are overwhelmingly white and male, but the 2005 election returned a record number of minority ethnic MPs. All minority ethnic MPs had been Labour up to 2005, but the 2005 election produced two for the Conservatives. Four MPs in the current House are Muslims, an increase on the previous Parliament. There are two non-white women MPs, Diane Abbot and Dawn Butler, both Labour. Overall, there is a low number of women MPs.

How much does under-representation matter? If 5 per cent of a population is Muslim, does the legislature have to be 5 per cent Muslim? Should the proportion of gay people in Parliament reflect the proportion of gay people in the population? Could it be achieved?

Take it further

Minority ethnics may serve as councillors in local government or in devolved legislatures such as the Scottish Parliament. They may be active in pressure groups, especially self-help groups and community action groups. Find out (a) how many minority ethnics serve as councillors in England and Wales and (b) the names of any groups that represent minority ethnic interests or in which members of ethnic communities are well represented. To begin, go to www.mcb.org.uk/affiliates.php, the affiliates section on the website of the Muslim Council of Britain.

Women in legislatures

Women are still under-represented in most of the world's legislatures, partly through insufficient educational opportunities in some parts of the world, but also because of their responsibilities in childbearing and, traditionally, homemaking. Males are often portrayed as especially suited to political discussion and political leadership. This portrayal deters women, which reinforces the idea and perpetuates women's low participation. Europe has huge variations in representation by women: over 33 per cent in Sweden, about 33 per cent in the European Parliament, about 20 per cent in the House of Commons, and about 10 per cent in France and Italy. Women do better under **proportional representation** than under **FPTP** systems. Scandinavia's legislatures have the highest percentages of women among all European legislatures, and women generally do better in Protestant countries than in Catholic or Orthodox countries, such as France, Greece and Italy.

British MPs are overwhelmingly male. Progress on women's representation in the House of Commons was slow in the 20th century and did not increase to beyond 5 per cent of the membership until 1987. In 1997 the number of women elected to the Commons doubled to 120, then rose to 128 in 2005. This still leaves Britain with a lower proportion

Power and politics

of female representation than many countries not known for their democratic credentials, from Mozambique to Rwanda and Argentina to Cuba. Other than in 1970 and 1983, the bulk of female MPs have been on the Labour side. Today, Labour is well ahead of the other parties in moving towards gender equality. There is a long way to go, but there are 98 women MPs on the Labour side, 27.5 per cent of all Labour MPs.

■ Women in British politics: service in Parliament and other bodies

Representation of women in the House of Commons has significantly increased in recent years, averaging about 3 per cent in the 1950s and fractionally under 20 per cent since the 2005 election (Table 4.3.13). Much of the increase in recent years has been due to Labour's determination to boost women's representation by use of all-women shortlists. The Conservative Party has traditionally relied on voluntaryism, hoping that persuasion of local Conservative associations would encourage them to adopt more women candidates to stand for Westminster elections.

Table 4.3.13 *UK: women in political office*

	Number of members	Number of women	Fraction of women (%)
European Parliament: British MEPs	78	20	25.6
Westminster: House of Commons*	646	128	19.6
Westminster: House of Lords	748	143	19.1
Cabinet: first one led by Gordon Brown	22	5	22.7
Scottish Parliament	129	43	33.3
Welsh Assembly	60	28	46.7
Northern Ireland Assembly	108	18	16.7
London Assembly	25	9	36.0
Local authorities: England, 2004 data	19,689	577	29.3
Local authorities: Wales, 2004 data	1,257	274	21.8

*The UK is ranked 14th in the EU by fraction of women in the lower chamber of the legislature

Source: Government Equalities Office

Proportional voting has helped women in Scotland and Wales. There are 43 women MSPs in the Scottish Parliament and 28 women AMs in the Welsh Assembly. For a brief period up to May 2007, there were 31 women AMs out of a total of 60, and the Welsh Assembly was the only legislature in the world to have a majority of female members. Women participate in politics in other ways: for example, they work in local government, serve as judges and magistrates, and join pressure groups and political protests. Women remain outnumbered by men in these areas too.

■ Why are women under-represented in Parliament?

Childbearing and homemaking responsibilities have traditionally prevented many women from seeking a parliamentary career until their children have become teenagers, particularly given the long and often

■ Take it further

Find out how the scheme of all-women shortlists operated in the Labour Party in the 1990s. What effects did it have? What happened in the Jepson case? What is the position today? Go to the website of the Fawcett Society (www.fawcettsociety.org.uk) and read more about its findings on attitudes and barriers to women in politics.

unsociable hours that MPs work. Selection committees, particularly Conservative selection committees, have often questioned women about existing or future children. Proportional representation encourages the adoption of gender-balanced candidate lists. Women candidates are less likely in single-member constituencies. Parliamentary life tends to be masculine and aggressive. Would-be female politicians may find themselves out of sympathy with the atmosphere of the House of Commons, where some members have a macho attitude and are obsessed with scoring points and slinging abuse.

The Fawcett Society claims there is active discrimination against women across the political parties, particularly in candidate selection. It cites examples of direct and indirect discrimination in candidate selection plus instances of sexual harassment. According to the Fawcett Society, four Cs prevent women from standing for Parliament:

- **Culture** – women think Westminster has a yob culture and male public school attitudes.
- **Childcare** – women find it difficult to arrange childcare during candidate selection and hard to combine family responsibilities with the duties of an MP.
- **Cash** – women earn less than men in most employment sectors, and this affects their ability to afford accommodation and childcare.
- **Confidence** – based on their perceptions of what most MPs are like, women think it is difficult to compete at candidate selection.

Reactions to women in the House of Commons

Women MPs: what they say

> The whole place is organised for men working in the city and popping into the club for dinner and a vote. (Tess Kingham, when she was MP for Gloucester)

> What worries me about my own party is the rampant 'laddism'. It's New Labour, new sexism, as far as I can see. You get it in the younger male MPs and the constituency parties. (Jenny Jones, when she was MP for Wolverhampton)

> This is … a terrible place to work. Women aren't as good at tub-thumping, dispatch box speeches and it's childish. I don't want to be like that. (Julia Drown, when she was MP for Swindon South)

> I thought people in Parliament would be progressive. It is still a shock that they are not. … Over the past 400-plus years, the only black people – and black women in particular – in Parliament have been there to cook and clean. For some politicians, it's still a shock to come face to face with a black woman with any real power. Racism and sexism is Parliament's dirty little secret. (Dawn Butler MP, quoted in the *Observer*, 13 April 2008)

Sexism and racism

Joni Lovenduski's 2005 survey of 83 current and recent women MPs found male MPs asking to 'roger' colleagues, juggling imaginary breasts and crying 'melons' as women tried to speak in the chamber.

Dawn Butler is the third black woman to become an MP (Figure 4.3.4). She told the *Observer* (www.guardian.co.uk/world/2008/apr/13/race. houseofcommons) that she faced frequent racism from politicians of all parties and that an official complaint she made was 'stonewalled'. One of

Take it further

Think about these quotations. How far do they illustrate the explanations given in the text for the under-representation of women? Do you think that women can succeed at Westminster? If so, what qualities do they need? Tess Kingham and Jenny Jones decided to leave the House in 2001, after four years. What is your impression of the way men in the House of Commons react to women in the House of Commons?

Fig. 4.3.4 *Dawn Butler is MP for Brent South*

Power and politics

the Conservative MPs whose attitude she complained about, David Heathcote-Amory, noted that part of the difficulty was that too few black and minority MPs were elected: 'The trouble is that feminism has trumped everything. We are a bit obsessed with getting more women in and I think genuinely broad-based politics is one that takes people from every social and religious group. But we are exaggeratedly courteous to anyone with a different skin colour, so the idea that anything I have said is racist is absurd.'

The impact of women on the House

The Government Equalities Office (GEO) was recently established to put equality at the heart of government. It says there are clear benefits in having greater female participation. Consider this extract from its website (www.equalities.gov.uk/public_life/parliament.htm):

> An increase in the number of women elected would lead to a higher quality of decision-making, reflecting the greater diversity of experience of those making the decisions.

> There is evidence in the newly devolved institutions in Scotland and Wales that the relatively high number of women have had a discernable impact on shaping their policy agendas. In both bodies, women parliamentarians have championed issues such as childcare, the social economy and equal pay.

> In addition, the UK faces a serious problem of lack of interest in the political system from the electorate. If politics looks old, white and male, it can seem irrelevant and dull to many people, and lead to lower participation rates and a reduction in democracy. Research published by the Electoral Commission suggests that having more women elected representatives actually encourages greater participation rates amongst women more generally.

> Representation also plays a symbolic role. It is important for decision-makers to be effective role models and to be truly representative of their electors.

Summary questions

21 What sociological explanations can be given for the under-representation of women and minority ethnics at Westminster?

22 In what respects can and do women have a beneficial impact on the House of Commons?

23 Would you like to see more women elected?

24 Read the Dawn Butler quotation from the *Observer* on page 203. How do you explain the survival of the attitudes she describes?

Political parties and the UK party system

Learning objectives:

■ Understand the role of political parties in a democracy.

■ Explore the nature of the party system in the UK.

■ Analyse whether political parties are in long-term decline.

Western liberal democracy is unthinkable without competition between political parties. They bring together a variety of interests in society. Via the electoral process, they determine the shape of governments. Democracies in Europe, the US and elsewhere are party democracies. The UK has a system of party government. The party that wins the majority of seats in the House of Commons in a general election assumes office and its leader becomes prime minister. Parties have played a significant role in British politics for more than 200 years. They influence all aspects of government and politics. Their primary purpose is to win elections. This is the main feature that distinguishes them from pressure groups, which may try to influence elections but do not usually put up candidates for office. Parties are central to British democracy. They fulfil several functions.

■ The functions of political parties

■ Parties sift ideas and organise opinion. They take on board the ideas of individuals and groups then put them together and simplify them into a package of policies. Voters can choose the party that best satisfies their own policy preferences.

■ Parties are a source of political knowledge. Even for voters who lack any strong party ties, their ideas and outlook are likely to be influenced by the information that parties offer and by their perception of what the parties support.

■ Parties act as a link between the individual and the political system. Most people rely on various political interests to represent their concerns and demands. Parties formulate, aggregate and communicate a package to meet voters' concerns and demands. If a party wins power, it tries to implement its package. So parties act as mediators between the conflicting interests of government and the electorate.

■ Parties mobilise and recruit activists. Parties offer a structure into which people can channel their interests. They provide contact with other people and groups and an opportunity to become political foot soldiers or local or national politicians. A key task in many democracies, including Britain, is the recruitment, selection and training of parliamentary candidates. Parties offer candidates support during election campaigns and are responsible for local and national campaigning.

■ Parties provide an organisational structure to coordinate government action; they encourage party members to work towards shared objectives. Leaders and their colleagues, including **party whips**, try to persuade members of the legislature to vote for their policies. Where necessary they do coalition deals to secure a majority for particular programmes.

■ Parties are a source of opposition. The parties not in government provide explicit, organised opposition. Britain has Her Majesty's Loyal Opposition, a fully institutionalised party with a shadow ministerial team.

■ Key terms

Party whip: a member of a party in Parliament appointed to control its parliamentary discipline and tactics, and especially to ensure attendance and voting in debates.

Power and politics

Key terms

Two-party system: a party system in which two parties compete for political power with a reasonable prospect of success. Third and minor parties may exist, but they do not have a meaningful chance of winning.

Take it further

Use the internet to help you compile a list of all of the political parties represented in the present House of Commons. How many MPs does each party have?

The party system in Britain

Britain has a **two-party system** in which each of the two main parties has a strong chance of obtaining a majority of seats in the legislature and winning political power. Some of the other parties are sizeable but they had no realistic hope of winning recent elections (Table 4.4.1).

Table 4.4.1 *The outcome of the 2005 general election*

	Vote share (%)	Number of seats won	Fraction of seats won (%)
Labour	35.2	356	55.1
Conservative	32.3	197	30.5
Lib Dem	22.0	62	9.6
Others	12.5	30	4.8

Source: Kavanagh and Butler (2005)

The British two-party system in recent years

Britain has had a two-party system for most of the past 200 years, Labour and the Conservatives have been the dominant parties since the 1930s. Only once since 1945 has one of the major parties failed to win an outright majority in the House of Commons. The peak of the two-party system was in 1951, when Labour and the Conservatives won 98.6 per cent of the votes and 96.8 per cent of the seats. Since then, the two-party system has generally been resilient, although the rise in third-party support since the mid 1970s has made the picture more confused. The two main parties have lost electoral support and their overwhelming dominance in parliamentary seats.

The 2005 general election provided confusing evidence on whether we still have a two-party system. The two main parties won just over two-thirds of the popular vote, yet between them gained 554 of the 646 seats at Westminster. Their joint share of the parliamentary seats was the lowest in any post-war election (85.6 per cent), and the Liberal Democrats won 62 seats, the strongest performance by a third party since 1923. In view of the strength of this third party, some commentators say that the UK has a two-and-a-half party system, or a two-party system and three-party politics.

In fact, the situation is more complex than this. In 2005 no fewer than six parties and two independents won seats in Great Britain and another four parties won seats in Northern Ireland. Moreover, in recent elections, there have been national and regional variations that make the two-party system primarily an English phenomenon. Leaving aside Northern Ireland, which has its own political system, Scotland and Wales both have a strong nationalist party. In general elections, Labour is the largest of the four parties in both countries, so that in effect there is one-party dominance but four-party politics.

Third and minor UK parties

By a third party, we usually mean a party that can gather a sizeable percentage of popular support and regularly gains seats in the legislature: an example is the Liberal Democrats. Sometimes the party may win, or threaten to win, sufficient support to influence the outcome of an election. A minor party is a party that gains only a tiny percentage of popular support and almost never gains representation in the legislature, although it may win representation on local councils: examples are the Green Party and the British National Party (BNP).

The Green Party is one of the most well known and electorally successful of the UK's minor parties. It has no MPs in Parliament but it has members in the European Parliament, the London Assembly and in local government. Elections to the European Parliament and the London Assembly use proportional voting. The Green Party has had MSPs in the Scottish Parliament and AMs in the Welsh Assembly.

Third parties and minor parties have some useful roles:

- They take up particular causes neglected by the other parties; the ProLife Alliance took up the issue of abortion in the British general elections of 1997 and 2001. Similarly, the Greens in many countries give special emphasis to environmental policies.
- They air grievances not taken up by traditional parties. The Scottish National Party (SNP) and Plaid Cymru long argued for more attention to the needs of Scotland and Wales, respectively.
- They can act as a haven for protest voters. The Liberal Democrats and their predecessors have often fulfilled this role in British politics. Such protest can spur traditional parties into action, saving them from apathy and indifference.
- At times, they may affect the outcome of elections. In the British system, where the government depends on majority support in the legislature, there may be times when a third party can maintain a government in power; this is the present situation in the Scottish Parliament.

Parties in the devolved bodies in Scotland and Wales

As a result of the hybrid electoral system to elect members in Scotland and Wales, partly proportional and partly FPTP, no one party usually gains an overall majority of seats. The largest party requires the backing of another party to remain in power. **Coalition government** or **minority government** has been the norm. In 2007 the SNP emerged as the largest party in the Scottish Parliament. It governs as a minority administration, with support from two members of the Scottish Green Party. Similarly, no party holds a majority of seats in the Welsh Assembly. After the 2007 election, there was talk of a nationalist-led rainbow coalition with the Conservatives and Liberal Democrats, but what actually happened was a red-green coalition between the Welsh Labour Party and Plaid Cymru. Between them, they have 41 seats out of 60 and Labour is the larger party in the coalition.

Do parties matter any more?

Some writers suggest that parties are in long-term decline. They often point to the disappearance of ideological differences between political parties. According to US sociologist Daniel Bell (1960), 'the end of ideology' came about soon after the end of the Second World War, with the collapse of fascism in Italy and of Nazism in Germany. Francis Fukuyama's (1989) more recent work *The End of History and the Last Man* was written against the background of the collapse of communism in Eastern Europe, which he portrayed as the decline of Marxism as a doctrine of world-historical significance.

The suggestion is that ideological questions have become increasingly irrelevant in the post-1945 era. There is no longer the major clash of democracy versus dictatorship that characterised much of the 20th century, as many parts of the globe now broadly accept democratic values. In Western societies of the past few decades, party competition has been

Take it further

Look up details of the Green Party programme. Can you think of any reasons why people might be more tempted to join a green pressure group or an NSM rather than the Green Party?

Key terms

Coalition government: when no single party has an overall majority in the legislature, two or more parties may reach a compromise to form a government.

Minority government: when a government does not have a majority of seats in the legislature, it may continue to govern by reaching an agreement with another party.

Power and politics

Take it further

Look up the ideas and thinking of the two main parties in the UK. Do you detect any fundamental differences between them, or are elections more a contest to decide which party can manage broadly the same policies better? Jot down any major policy differences between the Republican and Democratic candidates in the 2008 presidential election in the USA.

Key terms

Mixed economy: an economy in which there is a significant role for private and public ownership.

Oligarchy: government or dominance by a few.

less about the traditional struggle between socialism and capitalism, and more about how parties can best deliver economic growth and material well-being. What Bell was suggesting back in 1960 was that there was a broad ideological consensus among major parties in support of 'welfare capitalism'. In Britain, commentators have labelled the post-war years as years of consensus politics, in which there was widespread commitment to the **mixed economy**, full employment, the development of the welfare state and the importance of national defence.

Critics of parties also note the decline in party membership, increasing partisan dealignment and the rise of extremist parties. Parties such as far right parties in many parts of Europe are sometimes called anti-party parties, because they aim to subvert traditional party politics, rejecting parliamentary compromise and emphasising popular mobilisation. Established parties in several countries are finding their task more difficult. They have been the victims of public disillusion as voters compare the promise and performance of parties in government. They have also lost support because many young people feel that they do not talk about issues that matter to young people. Their ideas seem less relevant to a post-materialist society. On topics such as animal rights, gender, nuclear power and the environment, pressure groups express popular feeling more successfully than parties.

Why have traditional parties lost some of their support?

Single-issue protest politics seems more relevant and exciting, particularly to the young. They seem to prefer more loosely organised, less authoritarian and centralised parties, compared with the **oligarchical** established parties whose membership is often inactive or engaged in dull, routine tasks. Pressure groups, especially NSMs (pages 198–200), are seen as better at expressing the direct material or identity needs of those who support them.

Parties and their politicians may become tainted by power and lose their freshness and appeal. They are seen as sleazy, jaded failures, sometimes prone to lapses of financial probity. Often they have failed to keep their promises and have lost respect. Perhaps countries are more difficult to govern today. Politicians find it hard to satisfy people's high expectations, because they have limited influence in an age of globalisation.

The media has helped to undermine trust in politicians, by spreading cynicism about how they operate. In an age of 24-hour news, media scrutiny of politicians can make it difficult for them to function and maintain a positive image over the long term. Yet despite signs of weakness and fatigue, parties are unlikely to become extinct. If the bonds are tenuous, they remain the main mechanism that links the voters and those who rule them. Parties continue to perform useful tasks:

- Parties recruit representatives for national legislatures, so they influence and, in Britain, determine the choice of people who serve in government.
- Parties are the best way to ensure competitive elections that offer a meaningful choice of candidates.
- Parties educate the electorate by developing, elaborating and promoting policies, thereby offering a reasonably predictable set of responses to new and traditional problems.
- Parties offer an opportunity for popular participation in the political process, even if it is shunned by most voters.

In recent years there have been challenges to the dominance of the UK's two main parties, but politicians and voters still think in party terms. Parties matter.

Summary questions

1. List three pieces of evidence to support the idea that parties have become less significant than a few decades ago, and three pieces of evidence to support the idea that they retain their significance.

2. Antipathy towards traditional parties and electoral apathy suggest that parties have had their day; they are in long-term decline. Can you counter this assertion?

3. Are parties beneficial to British democracy?

4. Is ideology still useful in establishing the identity and direction of the main parties?

Pressure groups: their role and characteristics

Power and politics

Learning objectives:

- Understand the main perspectives by which group activity can be assessed.

- Know the different ways to classify groups.

- Recognise different approaches to lobbying, including direct action.

- Explore whether groups are beneficial for democracy.

Key terms

Peak or umbrella organisation: an organisation that coordinates and represents the broad activities and interests of business or labour, such as the Confederation of British Industry (CBI) and the Trades Union Congress (TUC). Their members are not individual citizens, but bodies such as firms, trade associations and labour unions.

Bruges Group: an independent all-party think tank set up in 1989 to promote the idea of a less centralised EU, as laid out by Margaret Thatcher in a speech she gave in Bruges when she was prime minister.

Fabian Society: a centre-left think tank that aims to advance the principles of social democracy by evolutionary rather than revolutionary means. Gradualist and reformist in approach, it has been influential in the Labour movement.

Think tank: a group formed to research and develop policy proposals. Some think tanks have considerable influence on political parties. The think tank Demos has influenced the ideas of the Labour Party.

Theoretical perspectives on group power

Sociological theories help explain the operations and importance of pressure groups in political life. In particular, they help to explain how **peak or umbrella organisations** such as those representing employers and employees perform a role in government alongside the role of the state. Apart from New Right thinking, all the theories in Table 4.4.2 see groups as having a significant role. However, they differ considerably in how they view group involvement in the political system, their perceptions of the balance of power between groups, and on whether such associations enhance or undermine democratic life. The perspectives are relevant to Britain and to other democracies too. Within each theory, different writers sometimes have significant differences over the details.

The nature of groups and the growth of group activity

Pressure groups are organised bodies that seek to influence government and the development of public policy by defending their common interest or promoting a cause. There is some overlap between political parties and pressure groups. Both are vehicles through which opinions can be expressed and serve as outlets for popular participation. Both have a role in the workings of government: in the case of parties by forming or opposing an administration, in the case of groups by providing information and assisting in government inquiries. In other respects too, there is an overlap between pressure groups and parties:

- There may be a close relationship between pressure groups and particular political parties; 15 trade unions are affiliated to the Labour Party.

- Within the parties there are groups that seek to influence party thinking, in effect pressure groups within the party; examples are the **Bruges Group** in the Conservative Party and the **Fabian Society** in the Labour Party.

- Some **think tanks** act alongside the political parties, sharing their broad outlook but acting independently and seeking to have an impact on the general thrust of public policy. The Institute for Public Policy Research (IPPR) operates on the moderate left.

- Some groups actually put up candidates in an election, as did the ProLife Alliance in 1997 and 2001.

However, pressure groups differ from political parties. They do not seek to win elections to gain political office, but they do wish to influence those in office. They rarely contest elections, and if they do, it is mainly to highlight a matter of national concern or to gain publicity. Their goals are narrower and they do not offer a whole range of public policy. Some of their aspirations may be non-political. Pressure group activity has a long history, although recent decades have seen a dramatic increase in the number and range of organisations. The reasons for this are listed on page 212.

Table 4.4.2 *Models of group influence*

Characteristics	General observations
Pluralism Pluralism sees groups as essential to democracy, providing additional opportunities for participation and representation. Decision-making results from interaction between government and a wide range of groups. Access to government is generally open, so lobbyists and campaigners can get their views across. Groups can act as a useful check on the power of government. There is nothing to stop any section of society forming a group. No group is predominant in society, because the influence of one group is offset by the influence of another group. For example, anti-abortionists vie with pro-abortionists to influence decision-makers. This is the Galbraithian idea of counterbalance	Most writers on pressure groups have adopted the pluralist perspective, and much of the literature is based on US experience. Critics doubt the ease of access that all groups in society have to the political system. Neo-pluralists have reinterpreted the traditional case. They accept that producer groups have an advantage and that businesses are better-resourced than other groups. They also note how governments try to persuade groups to support their proposals. The proliferation of cause groups suggests that it is relatively easy to form new groups, as pluralists suggest. Because many people belong to more than one group, this helps prevent the dominance of just a few groups
Marxism Marxism sees the fundamental problem in society as the unequal distribution of wealth and power associated with capitalism. It sees pressure groups as relatively ineffective, because they cannot bring about major change. It recognises that inevitably the interests of big business and manufacturing will predominate. They will act to their own advantage in an exploitative way which entrenches and perpetuates economic and social inequality. Labour organisations will be in a weaker position, unable to challenge the problems caused by the capitalist system. They can exert only modest influence, but Miliband sees unions as 'groups which governments have to reckon with'	Marxists say capitalism has survived because rulers have bought off the working classes with concessions. Critics question the marginal role of unions in the past and suggest that workers won benefits because trade unions promoted the welfare state, full employment, better wage deals, workers' rights, etc. Miliband (1992) and others suggest that, contrary to usual Marxist thinking, other organisations can be influential. They note that women's movements, peace movements and environmental movements have had an impact, and so have pro-immigrant bodies. All can modify the impact of capitalism and all can become agencies for transformation of capitalist society
New Right thinking Influenced by **Olson's critique of groups**, New Right thinking is critical of group activity which throttles democratic politics and imperils economic growth. New Right thinkers dislike the **corporatist approach** associated with national decline in Britain during the 1960s and 1970s. They accused corporatism's advocates of wrecking the economy. In particular, New Right thinkers are hostile to excessive power of major sectional economic interests that do deals with government away from the public gaze. They say this undermines Parliament and democratic accountability. They want no involvement of consumers and taxpayers.	New Right thinking inspired a backlash against **tripartism** and hastened its decline in the 1980s. Not confined to Britain, its ideas are relevant on parts of the Continent and in the US. Under the Conservatives and subsequently New Labour, governments have kept the CBI and TUC at a distance and given them no special favours. New Right thinkers are not sympathetic to groups in general. They see professional groups such as doctors and teachers as wielding too much influence over welfare policy. But New Right thinkers exist in their own groups: think tanks and right-wing business organisations such as the Freedom Association

■ Key terms

Olson's critique of groups: the views of Mancur Olson (1968), an American who was wary of coercion or self-interest as reasons for joining groups. He thought that interest group pressure, especially from powerful unions, was a major barrier to the prosperity of some states such as the UK.

Corporatist approach: an approach favoured by supporters of corporatism, a system of policymaking in which major economic interests work closely together with government to devise and carry out public policies on economic matters, especially wage and price restraint.

Tripartism: a loose, less centralised form of corporatism than in some parts of Europe. In the UK it was operated by Labour and Conservative governments during the 1960s and 1970s.

Power and politics

■ The extent and scope of government activity grew in the second half of the 20th century, especially in national economic management and social services. Many people want to see more and better facilities plus improvements in education, health and housing.

■ Modern life is becoming more complex and specialised. People belong to many subgroups besides occupational subgroups. For instance, ambulance drivers and paramedics may belong to specialised associations as well as the more general union for health service workers.

■ There has been a surge of interest in single-issue campaigning on subjects from gay rights to animal transportation, from gun control to motorway building.

■ A multi-ethnic and multicultural society has developed since the middle of the 20th century. Groups have been formed to represent ethic and cultural interests.

■ Post-materialism and other new issues have emerged. Many younger, better-educated voters want to express their views about a better environment, the future of nuclear energy and the need for social and political empowerment.

■ Communication tools, such as email and text messages, have helped to stimulate associations, organisations and groups; they make it easier to protest against globalisation.

■ Classifying groups

Early studies of pressure groups sometimes distinguished between groups involved in different areas of activity, such as the labour lobby, civic groups and educational, recreational and cultural groups. However, there are two more usual ways of classifying them. The first describes them by what and whom they represent, the second by their relationship with government and how they operate. Stewart (1958) divided groups into protective groups and promotional groups, and many authors since Stewart have used this division.

Protective groups

Protective, defensive, interest or sectional groups are primarily self-interested bodies that seek to cater for the needs and defend the rights of persons or categories of persons in society. Business interests, such as motor manufacturers and shipbuilders, are among the most powerful and well known. Many of them are represented in peak or umbrella organisations, which bring together within one organisation a whole range of other bodies and coordinate their activity and speak on their behalf: for example, the British Retail Consortium (BRC) represents the interests of 11,000 stores. Trade unions defend the interests of working people. Other highly significant protective groups look after the interests of professionals. Here are some examples: British Association of Hospitality Accountants (BAHA), Association of Specialist Providers to Dentists (ASPD), British Medical Association (BMA), Law Society and Voice, the union for education professionals.

Promotional groups

Promotional, propaganda, cause or ideas groups seek to advance particular causes and ideas not of immediate benefit to themselves, except in a very general sense. They are also open to people from all sections of the community who share the same values, whereas members

■ **Hint**

Beware of words like 'protect' or 'save' in the title of pressure groups. The Campaign to Protect Rural England (CPRE), one of the longest-established and most respected environmental groups, campaigns for a sustainable future for the English countryside. Although it is concerned to 'protect' the countryside, it is a promotional group. It promotes the idea of protecting the countryside. Members of a protective group belong for the sake of defending their own interests, not to advance a cause of general benefit.

Power and politics

of interest groups have a shared experience. Unlike the many interest groups that have existed for several decades, many promotional groups have a short lifespan; they are wound up after they have achieved their objectives. Promotional groups are defined by the cause or idea they represent. The Royal Society for the Prevention of Cruelty to Animals (RSPCA) is concerned with the welfare of animals, Friends of the Earth (FoE) urges greater environmental awareness and Amnesty International campaigns on behalf of political prisoners. Many cause groups are **single-issue groups**.

Insider groups and outsider groups

Wyn Grant (2000) found the protective versus promotional distinction unsatisfactory as it tends to assume that protective groups are more influential than promotional groups, because protective groups represent powerful interests. And it is easy to assume that promotional groups are of greater benefit to society than protective groups because they are more concerned with the general good rather than personal advantage. So in the 1980s Grant proposed an alternative classification.

Grant's preferred approach is based on the relationship of groups with the central decision-makers in government, whether a particular group wants acceptance by government, and if so, whether it gets that acceptance. Here is what he said: 'The principle on which such a typology is based is that in order to understand pressure groups, one needs to look not just at the behaviour of the groups but also at the behaviour of government.'

Grant divides groups into insider groups and outsider groups. Insider groups are regularly consulted by government and have good access to the corridors of power. Outsider groups do not want such access or they want it but cannot get it. Many but not all protective groups are insider groups and have consultative status in Whitehall. Similarly, most promotional groups are outsider groups. However, there are significant exceptions, such as the Howard League for Penal Reform and the Royal Society for the Protection of Birds (RSPB).

The Grant typology has been criticised. The distinction is not clear-cut, as some groups pursue insider and outsider strategies at the same time. Friends of the Earth has dialogue with government and business, and takes direct action that attracts money and popular support. More groups have insider status than Grant originally suggested. About 200 bodies are on the consultation list for issues relating to motorcycles, so consultation is hardly a special privilege for insiders. The influence of some groups may be marginal.

The distinction is less valid today because new forms of politics have arisen since the 1990s. Pressure-group politics has changed, with more middle-class involvement in issues such as animal welfare and anti-roads protests. There are more arenas today, most obviously the EU. Some groups concentrate much of their time on Brussels, where key decisions are made. Some promotional groups that do not gain much attention in Whitehall may be listened to by EU machinery.

How groups operate

A free society has many **access points**, formal parts of the government structure that are accessible to group influence. The most obvious ones are the executive – ministers and civil servants – and the legislature – the House of Commons and the House of Lords – although some groups have recently used the courts to further their cause.

Key terms

Single-issue group: a group that concentrates on a single objective, such as to outlaw abortion.

Access points: parts of the government structure that are accessible to pressure group influence.

AQA Examiner's tip

Now that you have read about the different types of pressure group, learn some useful examples to put in your exam answers.

Take it further

List two examples of protective groups, promotional groups, insider groups and outsider groups. Look up some well-known pressure groups, the issues they tackle, and how many members they have.

Take it further

A pressure group's effectiveness depends on three factors: resources, access to people in power, and the political climate and circumstances. Think about these three factors and how they relate to the section on the RSPB. Why is the BMA normally considered a powerful group?

Power and politics

213

Key terms

Lobby: seek to influence policy decisions, especially in the executive and legislative branches of government. A lobby is a body of people who represent a particular interest or cause to ministers, officials and legislators.

Nimby group: a local action group whose members want to protect their lifestyle. Nimby groups often campaign against developments they think will harm the view from their windows or reduce the value of their property. Nimby originally came from the slogan 'not in my backyard'.

RSPB: a case study

The Royal Society for the Protection of Birds (RSPB) is an insider promotional group, (Figure 4.4.1). It has developed into Europe's largest wildlife conservation charity, with more than 1 million members, 10 times more than 30 years ago, and 175 local groups. Membership is open to anyone willing to pay the annual subscription. It began to **lobby** Whitehall when it took a stance against the trade in wild plumage. Today it tackles many issues, including big issues such as climate change, agricultural intensification, the expansion of urban areas and transport infrastructure, and overexploitation of the seas. It is currently trying to persuade individual MPs to support climate change legislation.

Apart from working with government and Parliament on policy issues in its sector, the RSPB has been an effective campaigning organisation. It has marketed its cause with great skill and success, using methods such as direct mailing and catalogue trading, and taking opportunities to convey its views via press advertising and other media. It cooperated with the RSPCA to tackle the international trade in rare birds. It lobbies the EU and worked with the European Commission to formulate the directive on conservation of wild birds. The RSPB enjoys high public sympathy, along with other animal welfare and environmental organisations. It deals with an issue that people really care about. It is effective because it is big, well resourced and well organised and has expert staff.

Fig. 4.4.1 *The RSPB lobbies on behalf of birds. This was an early protest against the plume trade*

■ Protest politics: the use of direct action

Direct action is not new. People have protested for centuries. But in the past few decades there has been a remarkable upsurge in the variety of direct action by individuals and groups. Some examples are demonstrations, sit-ins, squatting, striking, interrupting televised events, non-payment of taxes, and invasion of buildings. Opponents of hunting or mistreatment of animals have often taken direct action. Some promotional groups have tried to persuade governments by taking direct action. Mass protests or demonstrations often receive television coverage, which helps promote the cause and may boost the group's subscriptions. **Nimby groups** have often used direct action to block new housing estates on greenbelt land, or to stop the felling of ancient trees. Dramatic protests by local action groups make headlines in local papers.

Plane Stupid is part of the new wave of radical green activism in today's Britain, inspired by networks like Earth First! and the anti-roads protests of the mid 1990s. Plane Stupid has no hierarchy or central leadership; it is a network of small 'affinity groups' that organise themselves. It originally came together in 2005, when a group of activists decided to disrupt an international aviation conference at a London hotel. Its Camp for Climate Action at Heathrow Airport in September 2007 was a week of action and education, with workshops on a wide range of environmental and social issues, such as how people can reduce their carbon footprint (Figure 4.4.2).

Pressure groups: for and against

Do groups enhance or diminish the quality of our democratic political system? This is not an easy question, because we are dealing with thousands of organisations whose aims, composition and methods vary significantly. Some may serve the public good for much of the time, others have only a marginal benefit. The following general points may not apply to individual cases. In recent years, the tendency of many politicians has been to criticise pressure-group activity as damaging to the democratic process. Groups are seen as essentially self-interested and lacking in concern for the needs of the wider public. Yet this is only part of the picture, for they also raise issues of popular concern and provide a useful channel through which preferences may be expressed. They are at the heart of the policymaking process and democracy would be unable to function without them. They need to be monitored to ensure they are efficient, open and representative, but their contributions cannot be ignored or removed. Here are some arguments for and against groups.

For

In a pluralist society, pressure groups are considered to be at the heart of the democratic process. In particular, they perform a valuable function within the political system, as they allow ordinary people to participate in decision-making. Many people participate in political life only at election time, but they can join groups that influence the decisions of public bodies. Groups can give special knowledge and expertise to government departments. Sometimes they cooperate with a government to administer a particular policy and monitor its effectiveness. Regular, sometimes frequent, consultation with groups is an essential part of government decision-making. Most farmers are in the National Farmers' Union (NFU), so its voice is representative. The same goes for other groups.

Groups act as a defence for minority interests, especially interests connected with parties not in government. They counter the monopoly of the political process by political parties and sometimes they raise matters which fall outside the realm of party ideas and policy, and which tend not to appear in manifestos. They made the running on green issues before political parties became interested. Groups are inevitable in a democracy such as Britain. Freedom to voice a viewpoint is basic to a democratic system. The group system has mushroomed and is unlikely to diminish.

Plane Stupid: a network of groups that take action against airport expansion and aviation's climate impact.

Fig. 4.4.2 *Plane Stupid camp at Heathrow Airport*

Hint

As you consider the views for and against group activity, think about how they relate to the theories of pressure groups. Do they support the pluralist, Marxist or New Right models?

Against

Everyone is free to join a group, but some groups are more influential than others. Ideas groups, in particular, are much less likely to be acknowledged. The Child Poverty Action Group and other welfare groups failed to prevent Labour from cutting benefits to one-parent families and the disabled. Consumers are difficult to organise, except at the ballot box, whereas producers, the unions and industrialists, have easier access to Whitehall.

The leadership of some groups is unrepresentative. The government passed legislation to make unions hold elections for the post of general secretary, but unrepresentative leaderships remain in other groups. A government needs to know that the leaders it consults genuinely reflect their members' wishes, and that deals made with leaders will be backed by the group members. Some people worry about secret bargains between interest groups and Whitehall departments, hence Finer's (1967) plea of 'Light, more light.' And people fear that too many MPs are beholden to outside groups and business commitments.

A pressure group, by definition, represents broadly like-minded citizens. In other words, it is a sectional interest, in the way that the NFU represents farmers and the NUM represents miners. Governments have to govern in the national interest, and consider the views and needs of all sections of the community, not just the voice of the powerful. The TUC still represents a substantial proportion of working people, but by no means all workers: the miners' voice on pay may be strong, but consumers may have to finance miners' pay by paying more for their coal and electricity.

Group consultation slows down the process of government and can be a barrier to action. The civil liberties lobby has been an annoyance to Home Secretaries who have tried to introduce legislation on asylum seekers, identity cards and prevention of terrorism. Home Secretaries have tended to regard many opponents as out of touch with public concerns over asylum seeking and the dangers of terrorism. Groups tend to oppose developments such as new roads, industrial installations and power plants, even though they may be in the broader public interest. This is what Tony Blair said when pressure groups were campaigning against genetically modified (GM) food: 'We should resist the tyranny of pressure groups.'

Summary questions

5 How do pluralists and New Right thinkers differ in their approaches to pressure groups?

6 Why have pressure groups proliferated in the modern age?

7 How do pressure groups seek to influence the British government?

8 What are the main differences between NSMs and mainstream protective and cause groups?

9 Why are some groups more successful than others?

10 Do pressure groups make government and society more democratic?

The mass media: theories and perspectives

Learning objectives:

- Understand the main theories of sociologists on the media.

- Evaluate the merits of the perspectives they adopt.

- Understand the role of the mass media in the political process.

 Link

See Topic 3 for a more detailed treatment of this material.

Studies of the media usually consider ownership, control and output of television and newspapers, and their possible effects on the audience. Sociologists use theories that help them put issues in a broader social context. Much European writing on the media has adopted the Marxist (manipulative) model. In the US, pluralist thinking has been common. More recently, postmodernist theory has been in the ascendancy.

Marxist theory

Marxists suggest that manipulation in the media occurs in two ways. Proprietors of the main broadcasting and newspaper organisations control content and seek to influence the thinking of their audience. In other words, the rich and powerful media owners use their organisations to spread propaganda.

What supporters say

- Ownership is concentrated in a few companies, often across a variety of forms such as newspapers, publishing and television.

- These owners tend to stifle competition. Rival organisations tried to kill off the *Independent* when it began.

- Proprietors try to exercise control of their programmes and papers. Rupert Murdoch has often blatantly intervened in the running of his papers, not least by dismissing editors who have disagreed with him.

- A few leading capitalist news agencies such as Agence France Press, Reuters and United Press International monopolise the supply of news.

- The distribution and production of many media is controlled by the owners of wealth. Newspaper distribution is mainly in the hands of a few retail outlets; poster sites are monopolised by a few main contractors.

- A state of contentment is induced in readers and viewers by the use of the media for entertainment. Soap operas, game shows and the rest of the vapid assortment give consumers the impression of satisfaction and divert attention from the inequalities in society.

Miliband, Gramsci, Habermas

Miliband (1969) argued that the media 'in all capitalist societies have been consistently and predominantly agencies of conservative indoctrination', replacing religion as the new 'opium of the people'. Within the British press, he found a 'strong … passionate hostility to anything further to the left than the milder forms of social democracy'.

Gramsci (1971) stressed the importance of ideas in helping to preserve the status quo. If the ruling class received popular approval and consent, then it acquired hegemony. He felt that the media had a significant role in shaping approval and consent. In his view, the ruling elites who run commercial organisations convey their message across the nation and deny access to challenging ideas. They keep the rest in a state of bemused satisfaction by feeding them a menu largely composed of entertainment. Films and broadcasting ensure the beliefs and tenets of these elites are so widely held that they are seldom seriously discussed.

Hint

As you read through each perspective on media ownership and effects, make a list of the key theorists and briefly summarise their ideas.

Power and politics

217

Habermas (1986) was a neo-Marxist who disagreed with Marx's view that the fall of capitalism was ultimately inevitable. He argued that the collapse could be indefinitely delayed. Whereas Marx believed that there was potential for class conflict to go on increasing, Habermas felt that the possibilities of 'class compromise' might make this unlikely – the workers could be won over and bought off. One way this might happen is through the media.

Like Habermas, Adorno (1991) and others have also claimed that a media diet of undemanding entertainment blunts the critical senses of the audience. The Dire Straits song 'Industrial Disease' encapsulates these ideas:

> They're pointing out the enemy to keep you deaf and blind
> They wanna sap your energy, incarcerate your mind
> They give you Rule Britannia, gassy beer, Page Three
> Two weeks in Espana and Sunday striptease.

Media effects

Members of the ruling class wish to perpetuate their dominance and maintain the status quo. They try to foist their outlook on readers and listeners. They are consciously seeking to influence the public mood by ensuring their media outlets serve their purposes. They try to suppress any radical notions, so their conservative values can prevail.

Doubts

Manipulative theory is sometimes called the hypodermic syringe, as a passive audience is indoctrinated with a single viewpoint like a hospital patient is inoculated with a hypodermic needle. Marxists argued that 'the ideas of the ruling class are in every epoch the ruling ideas'. Critics say there may be plenty of evidence for media concentration and biased content, but this is not the same as evidence for audience indoctrination. Pluralists such as Katz and Lazarsfeld (1955) reject the notion that readers and viewers are passive and uncritical recipients of the media, with no control over its content and influence.

■ Hegemonic theory: the qualified left critique

Hegemonic theory, advanced by the Glasgow University Media Group (GUMG), is sometimes called the qualified left critique because it is similar to traditional Marxist theory. It says the media is dominated by the comfortable elements of society drawn from a narrow and often privileged sector of the community; editors and journalists tend to be white, male and middle-aged. They are likely to take a safe 'consensus' view on many issues, reflecting broadly conservative values and are uncomfortable with ideas that radically challenge the status quo.

Hegemonic theory differs from Marxist theory in several ways:

- Marxists concentrate on the division between capitalists and the proletariat, whereas hegemonists are more interested in the groups whose views are sometimes ridiculed or shunned, such as blacks, gays and women.

- Marxists concentrate on the proprietors who seek to influence media content, whereas hegemonists suggest that content is more a result of the background and outlook of those who work in the media, notably editors and journalists.

Take it further

Go to the GUMG website (www.gla.ac.uk/centres/mediagroup) and read the theories advanced by some of its sociologists.

■ Marxists see bias in the media as deriving from the deliberate attempt of owners to influence their product, whereas hegemonists argue that it reflects the unconscious preferences of those who inhabit the media world.

Effects

The GUMG's research (1976, 1985) stressed the importance of **agenda setting** by television and newspapers. This suggests that the media influences the electorate in more subtle ways, by determining what is seen and heard. The media may not determine what people think, but it does determine what they think about. GUMG went further and argued that hidden bias, resulting from the background and outlook of those who work as television journalists, tends to make us more favourable to moderate, consensual views and critical of people who challenge society's prevailing ideas, people such as strikers, protesters and others portrayed as extremists, militants or members of the 'loony left'.

What critics say

■ Some journalists do not share the dominant ideology and are prepared to expose the unacceptable face of capitalism.

■ Investigative journalists have exposed many scandals such as Watergate in the US and the misdeeds of politicians during the Major and Blair governments.

■ If they try to peddle a particular line, editors have to be careful not to alienate their audience.

■ Journalists have to keep news values in mind. News values are paramount in determining content.

■ Pluralist theory

Pluralists argue that the audience is supreme in a market economy, because the proprietors, editors and journalists are in the business of pleasing their consumers. They cannot afford to ignore market demand, as they need public approval to sell their products and make a profit.

Pluralists accept that there is bias in the media; many newspapers in the UK are pro-Conservative and some television programmes reflect the safe consensus views of the programme makers. But pluralists are largely unworried by these tendencies, because they think that owners and producers seek to provide what the public wants. If the public does not like what it gets, it can shop around for something else.

Pluralists stress that the consumer is king and that because there is a diversity of ownership and a range of materials reflecting a wide span of opinions, it is not difficult to obtain a wide variety of political or social thinking. *Spare Rib* catered for radical feminists – it ceased publication in 1993 – the *Morning Star* caters for far left readers, and there are radio and television programmes for minority ethnics.

John Whale (1977) is an exponent of the pluralist approach. Here are some ideas he stresses:

■ Proprietorial control by powerful capitalists is no serious threat to the freedom of the media. Britain has a diverse, free press and free broadcasting institutions. We must look to the totalitarian countries for examples of a threat to the freedom of the media.

■ Key terms

Agenda setting: the theory that the mass media may not exercise much influence over what we think, but can significantly influence what we think about. By focusing on some issues and not others, the media can highlight the importance of those issues in the public mind.

Power and politics

219

- There are a plurality of media outlets, and many of them adopt different types of bias according to their different audiences.
- The nature of any bias is determined by audience preference.
- People get what they want from the media.
- There is little evidence that the media converts people. Rather than changing popular attitudes, the media tends to reinforce views that already exist.

Effects

Far from viewers or readers being passive recipients of views injected into them, they are a heterogeneous group of consumers who use the media to suit their needs. They take from it what they wish, which is why pluralist theory is sometimes called the uses and gratifications model. Pluralists such as Lazarsfeld in the US developed the idea that television and newspapers reinforce existing ideas. His 'minimum effects' theory says that voters already have their own preconceptions and ideas, and they act as a barrier to any message received from the media.

The media may increase the sum of knowledge and 'firm up' existing views, but it does not create or mould them, hence Lazarsfeld's ideas are sometimes known as reinforcement theory. Birch (1964) later adopted a similar approach, suggesting that 'people expose themselves mainly to communications with which they are predisposed to agree, and tend to remember the content only of those items with which they are in agreement'. The basis for the Lazarsfeld (1968) approach lay in the theory of **cognitive dissonance**, advanced by the American psychologist Leon **Festinger** (1957).

Doubts

Marxists criticise the pluralist perspective. They suggest that the various media act as agencies of social control by reproducing and reinforcing the inequalities in society. They worry about the monopolistic tendencies of ownership, so that even if the actual number of titles, channels and stations is ever increasing, the number of companies owning and controlling them is in decline; there may be more channels of opinion, but their is no real choice of content. In spite of the range of programmes and journals, it is not easy to find sources that express dissident or unpopular views or retailers that stock them.

■ Postmodernist theory

In the past decade or so, postmodern thinking has emphasised the key role of the media in an age when we are saturated with television coverage and many other forms of mass communication which have transformed our lives. We have all become consumers of the messages conveyed by media products. Politics has become media-driven to the extent that we no longer understand what is real and what is illusion. It is all about simulation and a multiplicity of images. Often the information from one source conflicts with information from other sources, so we have multiple realities and are unsure how to interpret them and what to believe. People become confused about what the truth is. They are liable to become increasingly disenchanted and disbelieving about what they hear or see.

Baudrillard (1991) argued that whatever is really happening in the world is no longer as significant as the images and information we receive in the media-mediated world of signs and simulacra. Giddens (1997) puts it

---

■ Take it further

Find out more about Festinger's explanation of how people filter out unwanted information. This will help you understand reinforcement theory.

■ Key terms

Cognitive dissonance: the state of having inconsistent thoughts, beliefs or attitudes, especially as relating to behavioural decisions and attitude change.

Festinger: argued that when they are confronted with challenging new information, most people seek to preserve their current understanding of the world by rejecting, explaining away, or avoiding the new information or by convincing themselves that no conflict really exists.

like this: '[According to Baudrillard,] TV does not just "represent" the world to us, it increasingly defines what the world in which we live actually is.'

Using the example of the Gulf War in 1990–91, Baudrillard claimed that viewers received a hyperreal representation of what was happening – the planning, the bombings and the atrocities – in the comfort of their homes, detached from what was happening, hence his book *The Gulf War Did Not Take Place*. A conflict of the media age, the Gulf War was a television spectacle for political leaders on either side. The media has become its own reality, and we are awash with its products.

Doubts

Critics point out that postmodernist theory has nothing to say about those who own the media and their backgrounds. They are unconvinced about people's inability to distinguish reality. They recognise that the media – newspapers and sometimes television – can present a slanted picture of what actually happens. Greg Philo finds the postmodernist approach unproven, overstated and lacking in evidence (2002).

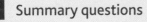 **Final thoughts**

There are elements of truth in all these media models. Ownership is concentrated in ever fewer hands, as manipulation theorists suggest, and views at the margin are often shunned in favour of a consensual image. But this does not prove that concentration and one prevailing set of values have an effect on the audience. That remains to be demonstrated. Yet the trend to monopoly ownership threatens the diversity of views on offer, and pluralists would be unwise to ignore it. It is difficult to air views beyond the political mainstream when the media is controlled by the rich and the powerful or run by people with broadly similar backgrounds and attitudes. As the postmodernists say, we are saturated by the media. Television has the greatest impact, and for some people, its images are reality, its soap characters real people.

Summary questions

11 Do the media manipulate public attitudes?

12 Does reinforcement theory underestimate the influence of the mass media on British politics?

The mass media: development, trends, ownership and effects

Learning objectives:

- Know media forms, including more recent means of mass communication.
- Understand the impact of commercialisation, fragmentation and globalisation.
- Know the empires that own some newspapers and broadcasting in the UK.
- Consider press bias and impartiality in television coverage.
- Explore how the media influences public opinion.

Key terms

Blog: a personal website on which an individual or group of users record opinions, links to other sites, etc., on a regular basis.

YouTube: a website where users can upload, view and share video clips. Unregistered users can view most of the videos and registered users can upload any number of videos.

Tabloid: a newspaper, usually popular in style with easily assimilable news and features, bold headlines, large photographs, and pages half the size of those in the average broadsheet. Two examples are the *Sun* and the *Daily Mirror*.

Red-top: colloquial term for a tabloid newspaper that derives from the red background on which the titles of some British tabloids are printed.

Broadsheet: a newspaper with a large format. In the past, most quality papers were broadsheet. Two examples are the *Financial Times* and the *Daily Telegraph*.

Compact: a quality newspaper printed in a tabloid format. Two examples are the *Times* and the *Independent*.

The catch-all phrase 'mass media' includes all popular means of communication such as newspapers, periodicals, magazines, posters, the cinema, radio, television and video, as well as more recent innovations such as email and the internet. All are concerned with the transmission of ideas and information in some way. For much of the past few decades, the press and broadcasting have been the dominant forms. But the media continually changes to take in new developments, such as **blogging** and **YouTube**.

Many people take a newspaper or have access to one. On an average day, nearly 60 per cent of people over age 15 read a morning paper. Depending on the newspaper, there is usually coverage of news and political events, rather less in the **tabloids**, especially the **red-tops**, rather more in the **broadsheets** and quality **compacts**, but even they carry a declining amount. Over 97 per cent of homes have a television, and some have two or three. Many programmes are for entertainment, but current affairs, documentaries and news bulletins regularly cover political stories.

Internet access in UK homes has grown at an astonishing rate. Some 50 per cent of UK homes now have internet access; this is strongly linked to income and education. There are more than 77 million mobile phone subscribers in the UK, equivalent to 127.6 per cent of the population. Mobiles have evolved from being a voice communicator to a hub for services such as text messaging, email and multimedia messaging. Mobile phones are an important way to connect with people.

Commercialisation, fragmentation and globalisation

Over the past few decades, there have been three main themes in the development of the media: commercialisation, fragmentation and globalisation. Commercialisation means TV for profit instead of public service broadcasting by, for example, the BBC. Fragmentation means more channels by cable and satellite, on top of the five terrestrial channels, and globalisation means better access to overseas events and media. The duopoly of the BBC and ITV has been broken down by cable and satellite players from both the UK and overseas. New commercial channels have been created to widen choice still further; there are even unlicensed pirate channels. This has splintered the audience, so ITV now struggles to retain a big market share. Viewers can see immediate coverage from around the world. British and American viewers saw the invasion of Iraq as it happened. Just a few years earlier, there would have been a time lag as film was flown back for broadcasting. Pictures can be broadcast by satellite from parts of the world once beyond the reach of television.

The overall effects of the three themes are to reduce national political control over broadcasting; to allow listeners and viewers greater choice and more ways to escape from news and current affairs if they wish; and to encourage the growth of open and informed societies. Governments can no longer easily isolate their populations from stories and developments they would prefer them not to know.

Press ownership and leanings

In most Western countries, ownership of newspapers tends to be concentrated among a few rich and right-wing proprietors. In the UK, several national dailies and Sundays, as well as much of the regional and evening press, are owned by a few large commercial organisations. Newspapers are free to print what they like as long as they do not break the law. The main constraint is not to offend their readership and jeopardise sales.

Newspapers, especially the tabloids, tend to be biased and partisan. Each paper has its own identity, but for many years the bulk of the British press was pro-Conservative. An anti-Labour, anti-union bias was evident in tabloids such as the *Sun*. In the 1980s and 1990s, editors often gave Labour a hard time, especially Neil Kinnock when he was party leader. Here is the *Sun's* election-day headline in 1992: 'If Kinnock wins today, will the last person to leave Britain please turn out the lights.'

In 1997, after very careful wooing by Tony Blair, the *Sun* supported Labour, which also had a remarkably favourable treatment from several other papers. Even the pro-Conservative *Daily Mail* ran several damaging stories about divisions in the Conservative Party over Europe. In 1997, 2001 and 2005 most newspapers supported Labour (Table 4.4.3). However, the support was more grudging; the *Sun's* final headline read, 'One last chance'. As the political climate became increasingly difficult for Labour towards the end of the Blair era, it lost press support. The process was accelerated in late 2007/early 2008 as problems beset the Brown government.

Table 4.4.3 *UK national dailies: who owns them and who they supported in the 2005 general election*

Newspapers	Owned by	Party supported in 2005
Popular		
Daily Mirror	Trinity Mirror	Labour
Daily Star	Northern and Shell	No preference declared
Sun	News International	Labour
Mid-market		
Daily Mail	Daily Mail and General Trust	Not a Labour victory
Daily Express	Northern and Shell	Conservative
Qualities		
Financial Times	Pearson	Labour
Daily Telegraph	Telegraph Group	Conservative
Guardian	Guardian Media Group	Labour
Independent	Independent Newspapers	More Liberal Democrats wanted
Times	News International	Labour

Television ownership

The British Broadcasting Corporation (BBC) was established as a **public corporation** in 1927. Its charter made it responsible for **public service broadcasting** in the UK and it had to provide high-quality programmes of broad appeal. The BBC is financed by the **television licence** fee levied on all who own at least one television. Pearson is a private company with television interests (Table 4.4.4).

Power and politics

■ Take it further

On a single evening, listen to three or four main news bulletins, such as BBC, ITV, Channel 4, Five or Sky. Make a list of the five main stories in each bulletin and compare their treatment and priority. Record your findings. Is there evidence of overt or indirect bias? On a single day, take a tabloid and a broadsheet paper. Compare the front-page news stories, the headlines and the style of coverage. Record any similarities and differences.

Table 4.4.4 *Some of Pearson's wide-ranging media interests*

Newspapers, journals and magazines	Television	Books
Financial Times	Thames TV	Addison Wesley Longman
Economist	Grundy in Australia	Penguin
Westminster Press	Sky	Simon & Schuster
More than 100 local titles		Future Publishing

Commercial television was established by the Television Act 1954. Ownership of the regional television companies was to be in private hands, but subject to public regulation and strict guidelines. Although there were significant differences in its ethos and funding, ITV was largely fashioned in the BBC's image. It was expected to follow a commitment to public service broadcasting.

As Wedell (1968) has observed, ITV and the BBC shared a belief in the importance of news and current affairs programming, and the importance of informing the nation. They became two halves of the same system 'derived from a single root' and 'instead of diverging over the years … stabilised their concentration more or less in parallel. There was a circumscribed form of competition as BBC and ITV producers vied for their reputations, critical renown and audience approval.'

These features underpinned the duopoly of British broadcasting. The dominance of the BBC and ITV remained unchallenged until the 1980s, when Channel 4 was launched and direct satellite broadcasting began. Satellite broadcasting soon fell into the hands of BSkyB, owned by Rupert Murdoch, Margaret Thatcher's favourite media mogul.

Cross-media ownership

As the potential profitability of television became apparent, news and radio proprietors were keen to buy into television and this created a pattern of cross-media ownership. Critics say this can have very detrimental effects. Cross-media companies can determine entry into the media market, promoting their own interests by eliminating rivalry. They can reduce diversity, so the public receives less varied information and more homogeneous presentation of issues.

Cross-media companies reduce the availability of power centres that can challenge government policy. If the powerful proprietors are sympathetic to those in office, there is less likely to be any serious dissent or critical analysis, and there may be no-go areas for investigative reporting. It is alleged that Rupert Murdoch is reluctant to criticise the Chinese government in case it jeopardises the prospects of his company Star TV. Cross-media proprietors may use their outlets as a megaphone for their social and political ambitions.

Is television biased?

The charters of the BBC and ITV require them to be impartial in their political coverage and to be fair and objective. The commitment to impartiality means that neither channel is supposed to support one particular party or standpoint. It also means that they are supposed to report events in a neutral fashion, presenting a balanced picture that covers all sides of an argument.

Overt bias in television coverage of news and current affairs on the main terrestrial channels is rare, but the GUMG has detected and researched 'hidden bias'. It claims that the intonation or emphasis of the newsreader, interviewer or commentator can be important. The GUMG has documented reports on industrial disputes. Managers were interviewed calmly at their desks, whereas union leaders were filmed addressing their members about strike action. Some critics claim that television bias does not result from any deliberate manipulation of the news. It arises from the background of those who work in the media. Many journalists, especially those at or near the top, are white, male and middle-class. They have moderate, broadly safe and conservative views; it is said this inclines them to prefer middle-of-the-road politics and makes them suspicious of minority groups such as minority ethnics, gays and republicans.

How the media influences public opinion

There is much controversy about the extent of media influence on individuals and society. People's opinions are shaped by many things. Their social class, race, religion, locality and working environment may all play a part, but it is impossible to disentangle all the factors. Media, especially television, are the main sources of information for most voters.

Neither pluralists, Marxists or hegemonists offer a totally convincing explanation of how media influences public opinion. Pluralist theories of reinforcement were for years the standard orthodoxy, but today they are more open to question. Television has become more pervasive since pluralist theories were first proposed and it is hard to believe that the effects are as minimal as Lazarsfeld and others implied. Marxist manipulative theory may exaggerate the scale of media influence, as many people do not simply absorb all they see or hear. There is merit in the more modern versions which stress the importance of agenda setting and the broadly conservative values of people who work in the media.

Many writers now support the independent effects theory. Television is watched for so long and by so many people that common sense suggests it must influence us. Saturation coverage of politics at election time means that we cannot escape the barrage of news and views. This must have some effect, even if we cannot be sure what it is. Media, especially television, expands our knowledge; we should know more than our parents and grandparents could ever find out. Over a long period, it probably has some, imprecise influence over our thinking. The effects may be different on different people. Some may be passive spectators who take little notice of what they see, others may be much more involved and open to persuasion. Above all, voting behaviour is now more volatile; many voters' long-held party allegiances have broken down. Their vote is up for grabs, so what they see or hear may matter more.

If the effects of media influence are not immediately apparent in the short term, longer-term exposure may make a more lasting impression. There has been no major study on the long-term impact of broadcasting or newspapers on **public opinion** and voting. It would be very difficult and costly to organise, but it might reveal slow and subtle changes over a period of years.

The parties' professional advisers clearly think that television has a significant impact. They place considerable emphasis on carefully packaging their campaigns for television and showing their candidates in their best light. New Labour cultivated the press in opposition. New owners and editors of national tabloids often found a warm welcome from the party leadership, particularly if they were seen as susceptible to

■ **Take it further**

Election campaigns today are made for television. It dictates the form and style of electioneering and, in addition, it has a significant influence over the agenda for discussion. Agenda-setting has an important effect on what people learn about the politicians and their beliefs. TV producers have the power to draw attention to issues that they believe to be interesting and/or contentious. By stressing some areas and ignoring others, they can assist in shaping the impression the public sphere acquire of particular parties, leaders and policies.

Producers like a good story, particularly one with pictures, and party media advisers seek to ensure that they are given a plentiful supply of both.

■ Key terms

Public opinion: defined as the prevalent view or views held by the majority of the community. In fact, it is a vague term for a collection of individual opinions that vary in detail, intensity and permanence.

Power and politics

Take it further

Using the internet and any other coverage to assist you, look up details of election campaigning in the US presidential election of November 2008. Note the role of the new media in the election and find out examples of blogging and the use of video clips on YouTube. Try to come to some judgement about the impact they make on the campaign.

influence. New Labour also developed an increasingly systematic and professional approach to media management. Its spin doctors were convinced that the media matters in shaping the opinions of the electorate. That is why they worked to get fair coverage for their party and often complained loudly about stories they considered unfavourable.

■ Summary questions

13 Does the concentration of media ownership really matter?

14 Does the present state of media ownership in the UK support Marxist or pluralist theory?

15 Is television coverage on the BBC and ITV biased in any way?

16 Which theory of media influence do you find most convincing?

Global power and politics: today's political landscape

The rise of international governance: international cooperation

Learning objectives:

- Understand why many states have joined regional and worldwide groupings.

- Know about changes in Europe after the fall of the Soviet Empire.

- Identify the strengths and weaknesses of nation states today.

We live in a world where more and more states are joining groups, and the groups make policies that benefit their members (Figure 4.5.1). That does not mean new superstates are being created, but that we are living in a world where layers of **governance** overlap in many ways. For the past few centuries, government has primarily been conducted by the nation state. Most people continue to think in these terms. They relate to countries, rather than international bodies. We think of India or the US, Norway or Slovenia, and so on. Each country has its own political machinery to govern its own political territory and the citizens within it. Yet if much of the world's political life remains firmly divided into nation states, this has not been true of its economics. The massive expansion of international commerce in the second half of the 20th century forced even the most affluent nations to pay more heed to international competition. Produces and financiers were increasingly freed from national restraints.

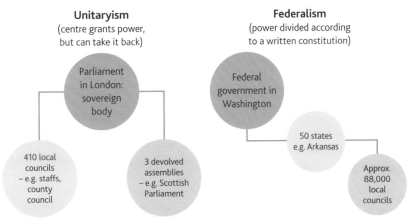

Fig. 4.5.1 *The UK is a unitary state and the US is a federal state*

Key terms

Governance: the action, manner or fact of governing. A wider term than government, it emphasises the importance of the processes of government rather than its institutions. It also embraces the relations between the public, private and voluntary organisations that provide services to the public.

Intergovernmental union: a union in which decisions are reached by cooperation between national governments, by bargaining and often by consensus. It may be contrasted with supranationalism.

Federal union: a union that divides power between a central (federal) government and a number of state or provincial governments, according to a written constitution. An example is the US.

In today's global economy, finance and trade routinely cross national boundaries. MNCs may extend into many countries. As the Cold War came to an end, most countries formed regular trade arrangements with their neighbours. The oldest among them formed the EU, a unique body that combined the characteristics of an **intergovernmental union** and a **federal union**. Moreover, the rapid spread of information technology has brought peoples from a range of countries into contact with each other. Communications technologies such as fibre-optic cables transmit information around the world. International machinery to promote international harmony and cooperation existed before the Second World War; a good example is the League of Nations. However, since 1945 the political world has experienced a shift towards a new era of international governance. That trend has accelerated in recent years.

The most obvious expression of the new tier of global government was the creation of the United Nations (UN) in 1945. This spawned many

Key terms

UNHCR: United Nations High Commission for Refugees; a humanitarian organisation mandated by the UN to coordinate international action for the worldwide protection of refugees and the resolution of refugee problems.

UNICEF: United Nations Children's Fund; it provides long-term humanitarian and developmental assistance to mothers and children in 191 countries. It was created by the UN in 1946.

World Bank: an internationally supported bank that provides loans to developing countries to finance programmes that have the stated goal of reducing poverty.

Treaty of Rome: the agreement signed by six Western European countries in 1957 to establish the European Economic Community, which later became the EU.

USSR: Union of Soviet Socialist Republics.

New world order: the period following the end of the Cold War in which it was hoped that a spirit of cooperation would prevail between the great powers, making international tension less likely.

NATO: North Atlantic Treaty Organisation; an alliance of 26 countries from North America and Europe committed to the goals of the North Atlantic Treaty of 4 April 1949. Its member states agree to mutual defence in response to an attack by any external party.

International law: the principles and rules that constrain states and other international political actors in their mutual relations. Idealists admire international law and see it as a way of resolving conflicts by reference to moral code.

Take it further

Find out how the EU blends intergovernmental and supranational principles.

other organisations, ranging from **UNHCR** to **UNICEF**, from the **World Bank** to the IMF. Within a few years, regional bodies had been created. As Hague and Harrop (2004) explain, countries that had 'once sheltered under the skirts of a superpower have turned to their neighbours to find a response to international economic pressures'. Most are straightforward free-trade areas, designed to secure trade advantages without compromising their ability to control their own affairs. However, the EU has political as well as economic goals, which is why some politicians see it as a threat to traditional ideas of national sovereignty. In 1957 the **Treaty of Rome** set out its purpose – to create 'an ever closer union' between European peoples.

The end of the Cold War and a new world order

Palmer (1992) was an early writer on the seismic changes that transformed Europe following the removal of the Berlin Wall, which triggered the abandonment of the Soviet Empire then the downfall of the **USSR** itself. The shift from state socialism within the country was dramatic, involving the downfall of the political elites that controlled the country. It might have led to the creation of some new political system midway between the old order and Western capitalism. This did not happen and the regimes that came to power in Central and Eastern Europe were keen to adopt models of government that resembled the more liberal democratic regimes of the West, partly because they wished to be viewed as eligible for EU membership.

Outside of the USSR, the changes for Europe and the world were of enormous consequence. The Cold War was over and the US was left as the surviving superpower. It was easy to be optimistic about the **new world order**, as envisaged by President George H. W. Bush, the president before Bill Clinton. Hopes of a new era of peace and prosperity soon received a setback. The Gulf War of 1990–91 illustrated the dangers from 'rogue states' in the Middle East. Thereafter, other threats to international harmony soon arose, such as civil war and ethnic cleansing in former Yugoslavia, genocide in Rwanda and clan wars and banditry in Somalia. The new world order was looking rather tarnished by the end of the decade. There was no clear view of the circumstances under which outside states should intervene in the internal affairs of other countries and the limitations of the EU and UN as peacekeepers were seriously exposed. Much depended on the lead by the US or **NATO**, operating under US leadership.

However, it was the 9/11 attacks on New York that exposed one of the greatest menaces to peace and security. Their aftermath revealed the weakness of global institutions. The response by the US and its allies, primarily the UK government led by Tony Blair, was to wage 'war on terrorism' in Afghanistan then Iraq. **International law** provided no restraint. In situations that appeared to demand international agreement and cooperation, it was clear that the US felt unwilling to commit itself to collective measures.

Bilton *et al.* (2002) quote McGrew's (1992) five proposed ways forward for the world community:

- **A transformed world** – there is a new emphasis on global machinery to meet the challenges of globalisation.

- **The primacy of continuity** – today's competitive and conflict-ridden world will continue.

- **The world in crisis** – economic, environmental and population problems will lead to international chaos.

- **A bifurcated world** – the world will consist of nation states and transnational agencies.
- **Global politics in transition** – global change will create a new situation with an uncertain outcome.

The future of nation states

It may be argued that several factors have reduced the role of the nation state in recent decades. The development of international agencies and regional groupings, the globalisation of capitalism and the power of transnational companies, and the subnational pressure for greater self-government all pose a problem for nation states. They indicate that few nation states can retain their national sovereignty in the modern world and that most are willing to trade some of their control over their own affairs in return for greater influence through some larger body.

Eric Hobsbawm (2000) has considered the idea of the nation state that is sovereign, independent and with which no one interferes. He says this no longer corresponds to the reality of the world today: 'There is one such state – the US – and perhaps Japan and China qualify. But in the rest of the world we are subject to the influence of the international markets, global corporations and bodies like the World Trade Organisation, which … affect all our lives.'

Yet although the nation state in many European countries may seem to be under threat, it continues to exercise considerable cultural sway over many Europeans, perhaps even most Europeans. People still tend to see themselves as Danish, French or Swedish, or even to a lesser extent as Belgian, British or Spanish. This sense of identity is daily reinforced by what Billig (1995) calls the 'banal nationalism' of popular culture, be it sport or prime-time television. Bale (2005) sums up the challenge for European countries as 'to reconcile its population's persistent attachment to nation states with its movement toward a "multilevel governance" that, institutionally anyway, can override and undermine them'.

Those who see the process of **integration** within the EU as a threat to national sovereignty point to some of the outward symbols we traditionally associate with a state – a flag, a passport, an anthem and, if the **Lisbon treaty** were to be ratified in some form, probably a mini constitution. But the EU has no real European army or foreign policy; it has a limited budget, much less in percentage terms than any of its member states; and it fails to command the primary loyalty of what, under the terms of the Maastricht treaty, it likes to call its citizens. It has failed to inspire affection among many of those living within its borders.

Hint

Re-read pages 169–173 and 175–176 on the nation state. Try to reach a clear conclusion on how much you think the nation state is under threat. Be able to name writers who think the nation state is in decline and writers who think it retains an important role.

Key terms

Integration: the process by which independent states relinquish or pool national sovereignty to maximise their collective power and interests.

Lisbon treaty: an EU amending treaty to enable EU institutions to function better. It was drafted after the people of France and the Netherlands voted no in referendums on a proposed EU constitution. The Lisbon treaty requires ratification by all 27 member states, but the Irish government cannot ratify it, following a referendum in June 2008 in which the Irish people rejected ratification.

Summary questions

1. To what extent does the nation state retain significant power in spite of globalisation?
2. How has globalisation changed the role of the state?
3. What impact does globalisation have on democracy?

Power and politics

The impact of globalisation and reactions to it

Learning objectives:

- Understand the meaning of globalisation and the forms it can take.

- Recognise how economic globalisation affects politics.

- Know about opposition to MNCs and globalisation and the reasons for it.

- Examine different perspectives on globalisation.

Link

See Topic 2 for a deeper treatment of this material.

Key terms

Consumerism: a culture that emphasises the production, marketing, sale and purchase of consumer goods.

Cultural imperialism: when the cultural output of one region dominates the cultural output of other regions, especially the aggressive promotion of Western culture, specifically American culture, as being superior to non-Western cultures.

Post-Fordist production techniques: an increasingly computer-controlled economic system based on flexibility and the production of specialised and tailor-made goods to meet the demands of a competitive global economy.

Waters (2000) defines globalisation as 'a process in which the constraints of geography on social and cultural arrangements recede and in which people become increasingly aware that they are receding'. It concerns the ways in which the international and global context affects what happens in particular states and societies. It suggests that state boundaries are losing much of their former importance. Globalisation takes several forms.

Three forms of globalisation

Cultural globalisation

We are in an era of mass communications where people can easily contact each other and have similar experiences. They can watch the same television programmes or videos on YouTube, buy and sell on eBay, or visit McDonald's. **Consumerism** and its culture have a powerful grip across the world. Coca-Cola, Gap, Lara Croft and Microsoft have global recognition and universal consumer appeal created by advertising in transnational media. Neo-Marxist sociologists such as Becker *et al.* (1987) and Tunstall (1977) argue that the ability to sell and export goods and ideas sustains our levels of consumption and secures the strength of world capitalism.

Media, especially television, have had a massive impact on cultural values. On the one hand, there is the worldwide availability of media products to transmit and receive information. On the other, the media plays a role in promoting product familiarity. Many people spend much of their leisure time in media-related activities that help to establish a broad range of social norms and values. Large and powerful companies prevent the establishment of local media forms, soon crushing them out of existence. Local cultures are undermined and people frequently receive information and programmes in English, now a world language; this is a form of **cultural imperialism**.

Economic globalisation

Economic globalisation involves the growth of giant international corporations such as Sony and Wal-Mart and the dealings in currency, shares and other financial transactions on a worldwide scale. Central to the globalisation of industrial production has been the growth of multinational companies; many originally had headquarters in Europe, Japan or the US but they are now effectively placeless.

Sklair (1991) wrote about the transnational capitalist class and its priorities to keep production costs low, target production at changing markets and keep pace with new scientific and technological developments. The idea is to establish lean production – to keep costs down by using low-cost labour in less developed countries, free from union involvement. **Post-Fordist techniques of production** from the 1970s onwards often rely on computer-controlled machinery; they have enabled companies to fine-tune their manufacturing, shed much of their blue-collar labour and design products for the global market.

Political globalisation

Political globalisation has happened as more nation states have become part of the regional and international organisations described earlier.

Economic globalisation and its impact

The interdependent global economy has had a variety of impacts on economically developed Western states and the less developed, often post-colonial states. In the days of state-owned industries and national control over markets, the economic weaknesses in the developed world were often concealed. However, as **economic deregulation** developed in the 1980s and after, there was more emphasis on the economic competitiveness of national economies. Governments tended to pursue policies that added to the inequalities within states. Unskilled workers often felt that they lost out, facing downward pressures on their incomes as companies increasingly produced goods in low-wage countries such as China. Meanwhile competent managers, whatever their background, are in big demand and command very high salaries plus bonuses and share options.

Less developed nations face much greater challenges, because they find themselves in an exposed position. They depend on exporting basic foodstuffs or minerals, which often involves a single product or a single market. Nigeria depends on oil, the West Indies depends on bananas and Mexico depends on its exports to the US. Poor countries become locked into dependence and have their economies shaped by developed countries. David Held (1993), a leading writer on globalisation, notes how globalisation has caused uneven development, greater inequality and new divisions. He cites the example of workers in the same multinational firm. In one sense they are interconnected by their common employment, but they are actually weaker and less able to act collectively to defend their interests, as the employer can easily move production to another location:

> The impact of global and regional processes is likely to vary under different international and national conditions – for instance, a nation's location in the international economy, its space in particular power blocs, its position with respect to awareness of political difference as much as an awareness of common identity; enhanced international communications can highlight conflicts of interest and ideology, and not merely remove obstacles to mutual understanding.

The impact of multinational corporations

The development of multinational corporations (MNCs) or transnational corporations (TNCs) has affected the power of nation states. Very large MNCs have budgets that exceed those of many small countries, so politics is dissolving into business as corporations gain strength. Such is their economic power and so great are their resources that MNCs can have a powerful influence on national economies and international relations. Brecher *et al.* (2000) illustrated this most vividly in his finding that of the 100 largest economies in the world, 51 were corporations rather than countries.

Because of their size, MNCs can have a significant impact on government policy, not least through the threat of withdrawal. If Ford decides to close its works in a town or city, the impact of unemployment on the local

Key terms

Economic deregulation: reduction or elimination of measures such as worker protection legislation in a particular industry, usually to create more competition and more employment opportunities. The aim is to create a business environment controlled more by market forces than by government regulation.

Hint

Develop a clear view on the importance of MNCs. Know some examples of economic globalisation and cultural imperialism. Find out the top five MNCs in the world today.

Power and politics

community can be very serious. People lose their jobs in the Ford works and perhaps in companies that did business with the Ford works. The government loses tax revenue and may have to pay social benefits to the people who lost their jobs. Powerful MNCs arouse much opposition and their headquarters are sometimes targeted by anti-globalisation demonstrations.

Anti-globalisation protests

A widespread anti-globalisation movement emerged in the 1990s. It is hard to characterise, but here are three points. Firstly, the anti-globalisation movement is diffuse. There are self-appointed spokespersons such as Ralph Nader, Naomi Klein and Anita Roddick rather than accredited leaders and there is little formal organisation. Anti-globalisation is best thought of as an umbrella term covering a wide range of groups with a wide range of ideas: environmentalists, debt-relief campaigners, human rights activists, etc.

Secondly, the greatest opposition is towards economic globalisation, not technological or cultural globalisation. Opponents see American-style capitalism as the root cause of world poverty, the debt crisis and environmental pollution. Anti-globalisation largely equates with anti-capitalism. Anti-globalisation activists have targeted high-level conferences (Figure 4.5.2 and Table 4.5.1). Some demonstrations have ended violently but it is not true that most anti-globalisation activists support violent protest.

Thirdly, there is a strong thread of anti-Americanism in the anti-globalisation movement. The US is seen as the architect of the international economic order, the world's worst polluter and home to the most powerful MNCs. Otherwise disparate groups can unite against the US, particularly when its administration has close links with leading MNCs.

Fig. 4.5.2 *Protesters campaign against globalisation, blocking the line at Heiligendamm (the venue of the 2007 G8 summit)*

Table 4.5.1 *Some of the major anti-globalisation demonstrations*

Year	Location	What happened
1999	London	A May Day demonstration in the City, London's financial district, caused extensive damage to property
1999	Seattle	The Battle of Seattle happened when 50,000 demonstrators protested at a WTO conference; there were 600 arrests
2000	Davos	Dozens were injured and hundreds arrested during demonstrations at the annual meeting of the World Economic Forum
2001	Quebec	Police clashed with 30,000 street protestors at the Summit of the Americas; over 400 people were arrested
2001	Genoa	One protestor was shot dead and dozens injured when 100,000 protested at the G8 summit for leaders of the world's eight most powerful economies

Summary questions

4 What do we mean by globalisation?

5 What are the dangers of MNCs? Are they exaggerated?

6 Why has an anti-globalisation movement developed?

Different perspectives on globalisation

Several sociologists have tackled the issues raised by globalisation. Although it has long been recognised that different states and societies are interconnected, it is widely agreed that in the past 20 years or so we have entered a new phase where interconnections have happened more rapidly.

Hindle (2003) provides a historical perspective on globalisation. He believes that we are currently in its third age. He explains that the first age took place mostly in the post-war years when large companies sold products abroad that had been made in their home-country factories – UK products made in the UK. The second age, from the 1960s onwards, saw these companies transfer the production facilities abroad, while maintaining their head offices in their home countries. In this sense, global business decisions were still taken on home soil. In the third age, now emerging, companies start to transfer the location of their head offices to different countries to include more 'local' considerations in the decision-making process. In Hindle's view, most companies are somewhere between the second and third ages.

In the past, sociologists were primarily concerned with examining and theorising about the distribution of power in individual states, but in recent years they have adopted a wider view. They recognise that states operate in a global context and that national boundaries have lost at least some of their former relevance. Sociologists have adopted various approaches to globalisation. Some portray it as the overriding theme in the modern world, noting how it affects all countries irrespective of their economic development and the inability of national governments to control it. The internationalisation of business and trade has created a vast interlinked economy dominated by massive MNCs. The ease of modern communications enables these MNCs to sell goods to consumers across the world.

According to Ohmae (1990, 2005), national boundaries have lost much of their relevance in the face of globalisation. He identifies communications, capital, corporations and consumers as the four key business factors, and on these four factors the world is already effectively integrated. He looks at thriving regions such as Ireland, Finland and Dalian in China, and explains how they have capitalised on emerging trends. By showing the transformation of regions from traditional economies into global powerhouses, Ohmae foresees a world run by dynamic regions rather than nations.

Ohmae thinks the flexible region state has become the most effective form of government in the global economy. The key function of governments is not to create growth, but to allow the conditions for growth to exist. Most importantly, governments must promote education, especially in business and the sciences: 'If, as I believe, the global economy is powered by technology, then knowledge is its precious metal.'

Although much of Ohmae's focus was on the positive effects of globalisation on societies and business, he recognised that power rests not with national governments, but increasingly with the financiers, MNCs and consumers. He ignores the control that countries have over trading access to their own national markets. He also ignores the fact there is more than one form of power. Military power is still based on the nation state.

Sklair (page 230) recognises that states have some power, but that much of it has passed to the multinationals and the multinational capitalist class that monopolises economic power. He also points to the inequalities that globalisation has created and the depletion of the environment that arises as business interests exploit reserves without thinking about **sustainable development**. All this, he claims, derives from the pursuit of profit by capitalists whose activities and goals are beyond national control.

Ulrich Beck (1992) argues that we now live in a global order that poses risks to our security, including environmental risks never previously experienced or acknowledged. He claims that individual states are no longer capable of tackling the problems that confront them, and he calls this a **global risk society**. Many contemporary issues are not susceptible to national solutions, most obviously environmental hazards such as pollution and climate change, but also diseases, drug trafficking and international terrorism. They require international responses.

David Held (1993) is aware of the threats from globalisation, particularly MNCs. He notes that many states have little control over their national economies and says the answer lies in a system of global democracy. Ideally, the UN might try to find solutions to international problems but the UN is weak, so Held proposes a system of regional parliaments, where each regional parliament covers a group of national parliaments. Like Monbiot (2004) he also envisages a world parliament as 'an authoritative international centre for the consideration and examination of pressing global issues'.

Others are less convinced by the notion of globalisation. Paul Hirst and Grahame Thompson (1996) are sceptical about much work from its more radical advocates. They believe that globalisation has become 'a fashionable concept in the social sciences, a core dictum in the prescriptions of management gurus, and a catch-phrase for journalists'. They say the advocates of globalisation 'portray current developments as unique and without historical precedent'. Here are some points they make in response:

■ The present highly internationalised economy is not unique.
■ Genuine TNCs are rare.
■ Capital mobility is not producing a massive shift in investment and employment from advanced countries to developing countries.
■ The world economy is far from global, as investment and trade tend to be concentrated in Europe, Japan and North America.

Hirst and Thompson emphasise that much business activity is still based within national boundaries; companies produce and sell their goods primarily in local markets. Moreover, nation states continue to exercise control over their geographic territories and their populations, which still retain their national allegiances. People still feel that they belong to them.

Anthony Giddens (1990) adopts a midway approach. He accepts the impact of globalisation, noting that its impact in business and finance has led to some diminution in the role of nation states. Yet like Hirst and Thompson, he does not see this as the end of the nation state. Maybe nation states can cooperate to do more to control the activities of MNCs and ensure that they operate to the public benefit. But they have not

Key terms

Sustainable development: development which meets the needs of the present without compromising the ability of future generations to meet their needs.

Global risk society: an industrial society in which risks have a different magnitude than in the past, because of globalisation and advances in technology.

Power and politics

surrendered all economic power. Moreover, they continue to arouse affection and loyalty from their inhabitants and exert considerable influence on them.

Giddens sees some benefits in globalisation, most obviously in wealth generation and the spread of democracy in many parts of the world. He acknowledges the problems it poses by perpetuating and accentuating economic inequalities, creating high levels of personal anxiety and weakening the power of states to shape their own destiny. He recognises that nation states are attacked from above and below, given the opposite tendencies towards integration and fragmentation in modern political systems. But overall he is not gloomy about their prospects in the future.

Giddens also sees value in global governance and argues that the search for improved mechanisms will be a major challenge in the 21st century. He thinks the EU is one response to globalisation; an attempt to create a supranational association of European countries to compensate for the diminishing power of nation states.

Anti-globalisation: Callinicos

The Marxist Alex Callinicos (2003) is one of the leading thinkers in the anti-capitalist or anti-globalisation movement. He recognises that capitalism operates on a worldwide scale and makes these observations:

- The breakdown of communism in Central and Eastern Europe has left free-market ideas in the ascendancy among national politicians.
- MNCs have considerable power.
- There is opposition to US practices in Mexico and other developing countries.
- There are strikes in developed countries against worker exploitation: French public sector workers went on strike in 1995.
- Jubilee 2000 and other campaigns have sought debt relief for developing countries.

Callinocos sees anti-globalisation protests as part of the global class struggle. He dismisses bodies such as the World Trade Organisation (WTO) for their attempts to shore up a failing capitalist system. He argues that anarchists, environmentalists, socialists and all who campaign for social justice should join together to fight international capitalism:

> Ultimate success will depend upon what happened briefly in Seattle – the coming together of organised workers and anti-globalisation activists – becoming a sustained movement. And that in turn will require anti-capitalism, currently defined primarily by what it is against – neo-liberal policies and multinational corporations – developing into a much more coherent socialist consciousness. All this is ABC for revolutionary Marxists. The fact remains that this is the greatest opening for the Left since the 1960s.

Summary questions

7 Why does Ohmae believe that national boundaries have lost much of their relevance?

8 In what ways are Hirst and Thompson sceptical about the notion of globalisation?

9 What are Giddens' views on the issue?

10 Why does Callinicos believe that globalisation presents an opportunity for the Marxist left?

Power and politics

Topic summary

- Power is central to any study of politics or political sociology.

- Weber distinguished between power, based on coercion, and authority, based on consent.

- Marx believed that a ruling class controlled the economic system and was determined to cling to its privileged position.

- Pluralists claim that in liberal democracies power is dispersed among competing groups.

- Power elite theorists maintain that in democratic and authoritarian countries power is exercised by a small minority of individuals, an elite.

- Lukes has distinguished different types of power: decision-making, non-decision-making and ideological.

- The state exercises sovereign power over the individuals of a defined territory. The government has the authority to run the state and enforce its rulings.

- Nation states are sovereign entities dominated by a single nation.

- Marx claimed that states were run in the interests of the wealthy, whereas pluralists see power as fragmented. Elite theorists argue that the institutions of any state are run by people of similar backgrounds.

- The New Right dislikes the all-powerful state and the degree of government interventionism in post-1945 Britain.

- Advocates of a third way seek a middle path between the unrestrained operation of the free market and excessive state planning.

- The nation state has been undermined in recent years.

- Citizen participation is mainly exercised by voting in elections.

- Few participate in other ways. The least educated and lower-income groups lack effective political outlets.

- Young people often shun traditional democratic forms; some prefer to engage in protest politics.

- Family background and social class were traditionally seen as determinants of voting behaviour, but today short-term influences are significant.

- Turnout in elections has declined since the years immediately after the Second World War.

- Party membership has declined, membership of environmental groups has increased. NSMs have increasing appeal.

- Parties have a central role in Western liberal democracies.

- Britain has a two-party system, but three- or four-party politics.

- Traditional parties are in decline, victims of public disillusion.

- Pressure group activity has mushroomed in recent decades.

- Some see groups as damaging to the democratic process, yet they are basic to modern government.

- Ownership of the media is concentrated in a few powerful conglomerates.

- The media determines the form of electioneering and influences popular opinion.

- There is a trend in international politics towards forms of international cooperation and governance.

- In today's global economy, finance and trade cross national boundaries, especially via MNCs.

- Nation states are under attack from above (e.g. the supranational EU) and below (e.g. the devolved machinery in the UK).

- Despite the ending of the Cold War, the world is beset by other threats: civil war, global poverty and international terrorism.

- Globalisation takes several forms: cultural, economic and political.

- The anti-globalisation movement holds demonstrations to articulate anxiety about globalisation.

■ Further resources

General

- www.atss.org.uk
  Excellent list of useful sociology websites and assorted resources

- www.sociology.org.uk
  Sociology Central: good resources (worksheets, revision cards, etc.) on a range of themes, including politics

- www.politicaleducationforum.com
  Political Education Forum: good range of politics resources, including an online journal, E-Pol

- www.hansardsociety.org.uk
  Hansard Society: seeks to promote parliamentary democracy; has some free resources and resources for purchase

- www.politicalcompass.org
  Covers ideology and political awareness; its test enables you to think about your own political ideas and location on the political spectrum

British

- www.statistics.gov.uk
  Government online statistics; a snapshot of the UK covering a range of areas such as population and health

- www.explore.parliament.uk
  Parliament: information and free written resources, plus videos, etc.; see the information offices of the House of Commons and the House of Lords

- www.scottish.parliament.uk
  Scottish Parliament

- www.assemblywales.org
  Welsh Assembly

- www.niassembly.gov.uk
  Northern Ireland Assembly

- www.lga.gov.uk
  Local Government Association

- www.europarl.europa.eu
  European Parliament

- www.ukelect.co.uk
  UK Elect: useful data on past elections

www.idea.int
Institute for Democracy and Electoral Assistance: information and resources on international politics

www.ipu.org
Inter-Parliamentary Union: information on national parliaments and up-to-date database on women in national legislatures around the world

www.conservatives.com
Conservative Party

www.labour.org.uk
Labour Party

www.libdems.org.uk
Liberal Democrat Party

www.plaidcymru.org
Plaid Cymru

www.snp.org
Scottish National Party

www.feminist.com
Site challenging sexism in society and promoting feminist beliefs

www.globaljusticemovement.org
Global Justice: urges global justice, respect for the earth, etc. Google 'anti-globalisation' for many sites on this topic

www.bbc.co.uk
BBC: news and current affairs; information on political issues and events, current campaigns, etc.

www.channel4.com
Channel 4: information on political issues and events, current campaigns, etc.

For information on various pressure groups, their campaigns and how they operate consult individual organisations such as:

www.bma.org.uk
British Medical Association

www.cbi.org.uk
Confederation of British Industry

www.countryside-alliance.org
Countryside Alliance

www.fathers-4-justice.org
Fathers4Justice

www.foe.co.uk
Friends of the Earth

www.greenpeace.org.uk
Greenpeace

www.tuc.org.uk
Trades Union Congress

AQA Examination-style questions

General Certificate of Education

Advanced Level Examination

Section D from Paper 3

SOCIOLOGY Unit 3

For this paper you must have:

a 12-page answer book

Time allowed 1 hour 30 minutes

Instructions

Use black ink or black ball-point pen.

Write the information required on the front of your answer book. The Examining Body for this paper is AQA. The paper reference is SCLY3.

This paper is divided into **four** sections.

Choose **one** section and answer **all** parts of the question from that section.

Do not answer questions from more than one section.

Information

The maximum mark for this paper is 60.

The marks for part questions are shown in brackets.

SAMPLE 1

Section D: Power and Politics

If you choose this Section, answer Question 10 and either Question 11 or Question 12.

Total for this section: 60 marks

10   Read Item D below and answer parts (a) and (b) that follow.

> **Item D**
>
> Young peoples' participation in traditional party political activity has been in decline for some time now. Recent research in a northern industrial town indicated that fewer than one in two 14-18 year olds questioned knew who the Prime Minister was, and fewer than in one in four knew the name of the Leader of the Opposition. Fewer than one in three felt they were likely to vote once they achieved the age of majority.
>
> However, at the same time as they appear to show little interest in party politics, most young people express strong views on issues such as global warming, poverty, homosexuality and so forth. It seems increasingly likely that, far from being politically apathetic, young people are simply not interested in traditional party politics.

Source: Written by Hamish Joyce

(a)   Identify and briefly explain three reasons why young people are apparently uninterested in traditional party politics *(9 marks)*

(b)   Using material from Item D and elsewhere, assess the view that social class remains the main variable in party political affiliation and involvement. *(18 marks)*

Either

11   'The growth of the globalised economy makes the pluralist model of decision-making, with its emphasis on the role of the state as honest broker between interest groups increasingly unrealistic.' Using sociological evidence and arguments, critically assess this view of the nature and distribution of power in the world today. *(33 marks)*

Or

12   Making appropriate reference to contemporary sociological evidence, critically assess the contribution of elite theorists to our understanding of the nature and distribution of power in Britain today. *(33 marks)*

SAMPLE 2

Section D: Power and Politics

If you choose this Section, answer Question 10 and either Question 11 or Question 12.

Total for this section: 60 marks

10   Read Item D below and answer parts (a) and (b) that follow.

Item D

Direct political action as a means of trying to secure social and economic change for the otherwise powerless has a long and some would argue proud heritage, both in Britain and in Europe. Marxist historians frequently cited events such as the French Revolution and Chartism in Britain as examples of this. More recently, commentators might point to the miners' strikes in the last quarter of the twentieth century as another instance when less powerful social groups attempted to secure change by direct action against the state.

Studies of the media's role in the miners' strikes by Glasgow University Media Group and others suggested that the mass media deliberately misrepresented the views of the strikers and presented them in an unfavourable light. GUMG carried out detailed content analysis and study to reach these conclusions. Some commentators have suggested that the British print and visual media only portray direct action and New Social Movements in a favourable light if it suits their political purposes. However, post-modernists argue that in a time of instantaneous news coverage and open access to the internet, the media can no longer shape opinion in this way.

Source: Written by Hamish Joyce

(a)   Identify and briefly explain three of the reasons why people use direct political action to secure social or economic change. *(9 marks)*

(b)   Using material from Item D and elsewhere, assess post-modernist views on the formation of political opinion in contemporary society. *(18 marks)*

Either

11 'Politics in Britain and other European countries is more and more a contest as to which political party can occupy the centre ground and please an increasingly indifferent electorate. The old battlegrounds of social class and ideology are no longer relevant.' Using sociological evidence from the last thirty years, explore this view of political participation and non-participation. *(33 marks)*

Or

12 'Despite all the social and economic change there has been since the early days of Marxist political thought, Marxism in its various modern forms remains the most complete and convincing theoretical account of the nature and distribution of power in contemporary society.' Using relevant sociological argument and evidence, critically examine this statement. *(33 marks)*

END OF THE UNIT 3 SECTION D
SAMPLE QUESTIONS

Introduction

Crime and deviance is a key topic within sociology, one that has generated much detailed study and research. The media is full of graphic stories of crime and its victims. Politicians are constantly developing policies on how best to deal with crime Many people will have crimes committed against them. There is a general fear that crime is getting worse. This chapter will show that crime is far more complex and multidimensional than the media or politicians would have us believe.

Crime is normally seen as behaviour that breaks the formal, written laws of a society. This can range from a relatively minor crime such as dropping litter, through to theft, rape and murder. Deviance is a broader term; it refers to any kind of behaviour that goes against the norms in a society. All crime is deviant but not all deviant behaviour is criminal. Deviant behaviour that isn't criminal could include farting in public or wearing bizarre clothing. It is a very elastic term. Two serious examples of deviant behaviour are examined, mental illness and suicide. They are not criminal in the UK, but they are considered deviant by most people.

Crime and deviance as social constructs

Crime and deviance are both **social constructs**; what is considered criminal and deviant behaviour has changed considerably over the years. Suicide is a good example; until 1961 it was criminal in the UK to kill yourself. Another example is homosexuality, which was decriminalised in England in 1967 for men over age 21. In the UK, smoking in an enclosed public place used to be legal but it was recently made illegal.

Who are the criminals?

Who are the criminals? It depends on the theoretical viewpoint held by the sociologist. Some criminologists, particularly the earlier ones, accept the official crime statistics compiled from court and police records, which show that most criminals are young, working-class men. If you were to visit a typical prison in the UK or the US, they would be the typical prisoners. There would also be a disproportionate number of Afro-Caribbeans. It is possible to develop theories that explain why they are the most criminal, perhaps focusing on family background, education and peer pressure.

On the other hand, many criminologists do not accept the official crime statistics as social facts, but see them as social constructs. The prisons are full of working-class men because they are the ones targeted and labelled by an unfair and biased system. The 'real criminals' are just as likely to be those wearing suits and running companies, or older people, or women, depending on the sociologist's theoretical viewpoint. If you accept this, and don't trust the official statistics, you can develop alternative theories about why and how some groups avoid getting caught and going to prison, and why other groups don't.

Key terms

Social construct: something that is defined by society and that changes according to time and place.

Take it further

The internet is a rich source for cross-cultural and historical examples of deviance as a social construct. It may also be useful to explore contrasting religious views of deviance and punishment.

AQA Examiner's tip

It is very important to recognise how different sociological perspectives hold different views of official statistics on crime and the variables of social class, gender, ethnicity and age.

Crime and deviance

Functionalist theory

Learning objectives:

- Understand the functionalist perspective on crime.
- Evaluate the functionalist perspective on crime.

Take it further

This is clearly as much a philosophical debate as a sociological debate. You may wish to consider characters throughout history who were considered deviant in a positive or negative way. See if the positives outweigh the negatives.

Emile Durkheim

One of the earliest sociologists to look at crime and deviance was Emile Durkheim (1938). He argued that crime has four key characteristics; it is inevitable, universal, relative and functional:

- **Inevitable** means that crime will always exist. It can be reduced but never eliminated.
- **Universal** means that crime exists in every society.
- **Relative** means that what is seen as criminal behaviour varies from society to society and over time; in other words, crime is a social construct.
- **Functional** means that a limited amount of crime and deviance can actually benefit a society, because the experience of crime strengthens bonds between people.

When someone is punished for a crime it reinforces norms and values, reminding people of the boundaries of acceptable behaviour. Furthermore, some deviant behaviour is necessary to stop society stagnating. Crime could be reduced if individuals were constantly controlled, but this would prevent the development of positive deviants who go against society's norms and values, yet move society forward. Philosophers, writers and inventors need freedom to create, and the price we pay for their freedoms are the negative deviants such as criminals, terrorists and drug addicts.

Durkheim didn't give a detailed description of the causes of crime. This was left to an American functionalist writer, R. K Merton.

Merton

R. K. Merton (1949) argued that many types of crime exist because society shares the same American dream – to be rich, successful and fulfilled – but not everyone can achieve these things lawfully. A strain exists between the goals and ambitions of people and their ability to achieve them. This is why Merton's ideas are sometimes called strain theory. Merton argued that there were five different ways to respond to the American dream:

- **Conformity** – this is the response of the majority. It means going to school, gaining qualifications and trying to achieve the American dream by working your way up the career ladder.
- **Innovation** – Merton argued that innovation can take legal and illegal forms. In its illegal form it is the most important criminal response. It means trying to achieve the American dream illegally. This could be any crime that involves making a financial profit such as burglary or bank robbery.
- **Ritualism** – this is a deviant response but not a criminal response. It is when you give up on the American dream. An example of this would be when someone no longer seeks a pay rise.

- **Retreatism** – this is when you give up on the America dream and turn to drink or drugs. This is a deviant and sometimes criminal response.

- **Rebellion** – this is when you want to replace the American dream (Figure 5.1.1). Terrorist organisations like Al-Qaeda fit into this category. This is also a criminal response.

Fig. 5.1.1 *Rebellion is one way to describe this response to the American dream*

Take it further

You may find it useful to consider alternatives to the American dream. Would they be dreams to some but nightmares to others?

Hint

Some students find that it helps to summarise information on postcards they can refer to. For Durkheim you could list the four characteristics of crime, for Merton the five responses to the American dream.

Criticisms of Merton

Merton has successfully linked strains in the structure of society to criminal behaviour. His ideas work well in explaining crimes that make a financial profit. He has also shown that if a society values financial success above all else, then those who don't achieve success by a legitimate way will choose an illegitimate way. These ideas have been taken up by Messner and Rosenheld (1994), who argue that the crime rate is so high in America because of the value American society places on material wealth. If a country promotes other values such as civic responsibility, crime is lower. In Japan, for example, children learn from an early age to respect their schools and each other. In many schools the children clean their own classrooms and serve each other at mealtimes. This could explain why crimes such as vandalism and antisocial behaviour are lower in Japan than in other countries.

Link

Merton's ideas link to education, particularly the ideas of the functionalist Durkheim, who argues that citizenship should be reinforced in schools. If children learned to value and respect society, then less antisocial behaviour would be committed.

Take it further

One problem with Merton's ideas is that they can only explain crimes that involve making a profit. Stealing a car then selling it makes you an innovator but what about stealing a car then setting fire to it? Merton assumes that everyone wants to achieve the American dream, but is this always true? Why do some conform and others innovate? There are many people in society who haven't achieved much financially but who don't turn to crime. Much crime is committed collectively, not individually as Merton seems to imply.

AQA Examiner's tip

It is common to dismiss functionalist views as outdated. Don't make this mistake. Merton's ideas, in particular, are still very relevant for explaining many crimes today.

Crime and deviance

Official statistics and theories on crime

Many of the early theories on crime and deviance, including functionalism, subcultural theory and environmental theory, and even some later theories such as perspectives from the right, tend to take official statistics on crime at face value. In other words, they trust the official statistics that say young working-class men, for example, are the most criminal group then devise theories to explain this pattern. Other theories, such as social action theory and Marxism, do not accept official statistics as the truth, and do not agree that young working-class men are the most criminal. This view leads them to develop alternative theories looking at the middle and upper classes or ethnicity, for example. Nearly all the theories pay little attention to crime by women.

As you read each of the theories, ask yourself these two questions:

- Does the theory see official statistics on crime and deviance as social facts or social constructs?
- What does the theory say about crime and how it links to social class, ethnicity, age and gender?

Link

See pages 272–275 for more on women.

Summary questions

1. According to Durkheim, what are the four characteristics of crime?
2. In what ways can crime be functional?
3. How does Merton explain crime?

Subcultural theory

Learning objectives:

■ Understand subcultural views on crime.

■ Evaluate subcultural views on crime.

Key terms

Subculture: a group within a society whose members share common values and have similar behaviour patterns.

Delinquent behaviour: antisocial and criminal behaviour committed by children and teenagers.

Status frustration: the anger and resentment felt when individuals have their aspirations blocked.

Link

There is a clear link here to education. Working-class boys do less well at school compared to middle-class boys. Research has focused on factors at school and at home to explain this difference.

Hint

Try to link each person with just a few words to describe their key ideas. Here are some examples: Cohen, status frustration; Cloward and Ohlin, criminal, conflict, retreatist; Miller, focal concerns.

Merton's ideas are very good at explaining crimes for profit, but many crimes do not produce financial gain. Antisocial crimes such as vandalism, graffiti, joyriding and violent behaviour need to be considered using different concepts, and the key idea is the gang or **subculture**.

■ Early studies and gangs

US studies

Albert Cohen (1955) was one of the earliest subcultural theorists. He argued that **delinquent behaviour** was most likely to develop among working-class boys doing badly at school. He argued that they suffered from **status frustration**. They recognised that achieving status through academic success would be very difficult for them. Instead they could gain status from their peers by being good at delinquent behaviour such as stealing, fighting and vandalism.

Cloward and Ohlin (1961) developed Cohen's ideas. They argued that working-class boys can belong to three subcultures. The criminal subculture is most likely to be found in stable working-class areas. Status is gained through gang membership and promotion is possible within the gang. Most crimes involve making a financial gain. If there is no established criminal subculture, a conflict subculture might develop. This is more concerned with antisocial, violent and aggressive behaviour than making money. The retreatist subculture puts the main focus on alcohol or drugs.

Miller (1962) argued that many working-class American boys get into trouble with the police simply because they have a different set of norms and values to the rest of the population. He calls them focal concerns. Three of the key focal concerns are trouble (accepting that life involves violence), toughness ('real men' fight, drink and womanise) and excitement (always on the lookout for fun and 'having a laff'). These focal concerns mean that working-class men will often end up breaking the law, often after a night out with the lads and after drinking to excess. Miller isn't arguing that working-class men intend to break the law, but that the focal concerns they hold make it inevitable that crimes will be committed.

US gangs

Gangs are a key feature of many American cities and are usually ethnically divided. Territory, or turf, is very important as each gang seeks to monopolise part of the city. Gangs often establish distinctive ways of identifying themselves with specific colours, styles of clothing and hair, hand signals and graffiti tags. Two of the most infamous gangs are the mainly African-American Crips and Bloods of Los Angeles, involved in robbery, drug dealing and murder. Although originally two single gangs, because of the large number of members, they have split into many different groups or sets and often fight among themselves or with rival gangs. They are found in many other cities in the US. The Crips identify themselves using the colour blue, and the Bloods use red, although this has declined as it makes identification very easy for the police and other gangs (Figure 5.1.2). There are a growing number of Hispanic

Fig. 5.1.2 *The Crips, a street gang demanding full commitment and with a particular dress code*

(Latin American) gangs, and the two main rivals are Mexican Americans born in the US and recent immigrants from Mexico or other Spanish-speaking countries.

Nightingale (1993) has studied young black gangs in an inner-city area of Philadelphia, US. He shows that the gang members want to achieve the American dream of having the latest consumer goods, as reinforced by American TV programmes and Hollywood films. However, as they are excluded educationally, economically and politically from mainstream US culture, they are forced to gain them through crime.

UK studies

Most early British subcultural studies differed from the American studies in that they found little evidence of serious gang activity. David Downes (1966) found that many working-class boys 'hung around' together but were not in any sense an organised gang. He found little evidence of the American ideas of status frustration (Cohen), different types of gangs (Cloward and Ohlin) or focal concerns (Miller). Even in large cities like London and Birmingham there seemed to be little evidence of the equivalents of the Bloods or the Crips – serious and organised gangs that demanded total commitment to the gang's values.

UK gangs

If media reports are to be believed, UK gangs now exist in the same way as American gangs. The difficulty is that little serious sociological research has been done on today's UK gangs and most information is provided by newspapers, TV programmes and crime writers. What certainly seems to be the case is that gun crime and stabbings have increased, and this is often linked to some kind of gang activity. Some preliminary research into UK gangs has been carried out by Bennett and Holloway (2004) at Glamorgan University. They studied data from interviews with almost 5,000 arrestees across England and Wales and found that 15 per cent had current or past experience as gang members. From this research it has been estimated that there could be 20,000 active gang members in the UK aged 18 or over. But this is speculation; a major study into UK gangs has yet to be carried out.

Middle-class gangs

Most subcultural studies focus on working-class gang activity. Korem (1994) is unusual in that he examines the middle-class gang. He conducted research over seven years in the UK, the US and other countries. He argues that affluent middle-class boys are forming gangs in ever increasing numbers. The key factor that pushes someone into a gang seems to be family problems. This could be because of divorce, or simply because parents are too busy working to spend quality time with their children. In a sense the gang becomes a substitute family. Korem argues that family problems are a better predictor than low incomes in explaining why someone joins a gang.

Female gangs

Very little research has been carried out on female gang activity compared to male gang activity. One of the reasons has been the assumption that women do not join gangs. When Thrasher researched 1,313 gangs in the US in the 1920s, he found only 6 female gangs and argued, as other sociologists have since, that female gang activity is 'auxiliary in nature'. This means that women have a very limited role in gangs, and exist only to serve the male gang members in a social or sexual sense. Since then a number of other studies have been carried out, including Anne Campbell's 1984 study of New York girl gangs, which focuses on the experiences of just three gang members and the limited choices available to working-class inner-city American girls. In a more recent study, Laidler and Hunt (2001) interviewed 141 female gang members from the San Francisco Bay area of the US. Although the 'homegirls' committed crimes, within the gang they conformed to traditional gender roles and had to ensure that they didn't have sex with too many male gang members in case they were labelled negatively.

■ Marxist subcultural theory

An alternative subcultural approach is taken by some Marxist sociologists who argue that working-class boys may join gangs as a form of resistance to capitalism. Working-class boys are disadvantaged under capitalism and often do badly at school. With fewer unskilled jobs available, they often have difficulty in finding work or are made unemployed. Joining a gang offers some sort of 'solution' to these problems, where they can join other equally disadvantaged lads. Given these circumstances, it is almost inevitable, according to this perspective, that some crime will occur. The solution is to provide better educational and job opportunities for working-class boys, so they won't be forced into crime.

Marxist subcultural theorists have also examined the youth subcultures that developed in the post-war years, such as the Teddy boys, Mods and Rockers, skinheads and punks, and have linked them to capitalism. The uniform and look of the skinheads, for example, who were a working-class subculture from the late 1960s onwards, consisted of cropped hair, jeans held up by braces, and boots. According to Marxist subcultural theorists, this uniform is similar to factory clothing worn at the turn of the century, and the skinheads were symbolically embracing a working-class culture that no longer existed. Even the football hooliganism of some skinheads was seen as an attempt to reclaim territory and reinforce a sense of community. The clear problem with these ideas is that the Marxist subcultural theorists may be reading too much into the uniform of the skinheads. The short hair may simply be harder to grab in a fight, and the bovver boots may be to inflict more pain, not for any symbolism.

■ Criticisms of subcultural theory

One of the biggest problems with subcultural research is that it is based on accepting the validity of the official crime statistics. Subcultural theorists start from the belief that most crime is committed by young working-class men, often in gangs, and that theories need to be developed to explain why this is the case. Other sociologists have challenged this assumption (see later).

David Matza (1964) argues that much research into gangs is too deterministic. This means that the studies imply that once you join a gang, you cannot escape and that you commit yourself to a deviant lifestyle. He argues that this isn't the case, that many young men simply drift in and out of criminal activity, and that they are just looking for excitement and fun, although often at the wrong place and time. He calls this the search for 'subterranean values'. When caught they use 'techniques of neutralisation', which are simply excuses for their behaviour such as 'everyone does it', 'I couldn't let my mates down' or 'they deserved it'.

Social action theorists argue that young men are targeted and picked by the police. They call this process labelling. Middle-class boys simply get away with more and are treated more leniently by the police. Marxists argue that the real criminals in society are not working-class gang members but corporate criminals. Like social action theorists, they argue that the criminal justice system is biased.

AQA Examiner's tip

Subcultural theory is a very broad area, so include as many aspects as possible in your essays. There is no point writing two sides on just one theorist then ignoring the broader picture.

■ Link

See pages 254–256 for more on social action theory and pages 260–262 for more on Marxist theory.

■ Summary questions

4 According to Cohen, why do young men join gangs?

5 Who looked at middle-class gangs?

6 How is the Marxist subcultural approach different to the other subcultural approaches?

Environmental theory

Learning objectives:

- Understand environmental views on crime.

- Evaluate environmental views on crime.

Key terms

Concentric zones: a series of circles within one big circle; each circle represents one zone of a city.

Link

See page 266 for more on Charles Murray.

Environmental theory, sometimes called urban criminology, looks at the relationship between patterns of crime and where people live, work and spend their leisure. It moves beyond the subcultural focus on gangs to a wider focus on whole urban areas.

Shaw and McKay

In the 1930s Shaw and McKay, two American sociologists at Chicago University, began plotting the addresses of people who had committed crimes in the city. Their results showed that if you divided the city into **concentric zones**, each of the five zones they identified had different levels of crime. Zone 2 was nearest the city centre and this had the most crime; the levels of crime decreased as you went further away from the city centre to the suburbs. The reason crime was higher in zone 2 was because it was a zone of transition – an area with a high rate of population turnover. In Chicago, recent immigrants to the city would move into zone 2 as it was the cheapest area to live. Over time some would be successful and move out to the better areas, then newer immigrants would move in. This high rate of population turnover caused social disorganisation. It meant that zone 2 wasn't as stable as the other areas and had less sense of community. People did not know each other and did not care about their neighbours; the result was a higher crime rate.

In later writings, Shaw and McKay developed cultural transmission theory. They argued that in the poorest and most socially disorganised parts of a city, crime becomes seen as the norm and as culturally acceptable for some members of the working class. In some families, crime becomes a way of life, and these deviant values are passed from one generation to the next. This is very similar to the views of the New Right sociologist Charles Murray.

Sutherland and Cressey

Sutherland (1974) introduced the concept of differential association. This simply means that everyone in society associates with, or comes into contact with, different people. Some of these people will be law-abiding and some won't. Sutherland argues that the more time you spend with people who aren't law-abiding, the more likely you are to turn to crime yourself. The status of the people you associate with also makes a difference – family members influence you more than strangers. Other relevant factors include how much time you spend with them, and the stage in your life when you have these associations – younger people are more likely to be influenced. The implication is that there is more crime in the inner city because there are more people with criminal attitudes who influence each other. One of the problems with this idea is that it suggests people are very easily influenced by those around them, and that they cannot exercise free will.

Crime and deviance

■ British studies

Most early British studies failed to find such a clear pattern as Shaw and McKay in Chicago. They also failed to find evidence of differential association. Morris (1957) studied Croydon and argued that it was the local council's policy of housing 'problem' families together that created high-crime areas. These ideas were reinforced in a later study by Baldwin and Bottoms (1976), who examined the process of tipping. Tipping occurs when an area is seen as going downhill. This may be because of council policies of putting problem families all in one place, or it may be because of a real or imagined increase in antisocial behaviour or graffiti, for example. Law-abiding and respectable families leave as soon as they can, and those who wish to enter the estate tend to be the friends or relatives of the problem families, so tipping speeds up. If the antisocial families in an area outweigh the respectable families, the area has tipped and becomes seen as a problem estate. The solution is clearly to stop the process of tipping as soon as it occurs, and to ensure that antisocial families are not all placed together. The process of tipping is very similar to the broken windows theory of Wilson and Kelling (1982). This argues that if a single broken window in an abandoned house is left unmended, other windows will get broken and the area will soon go downhill (Figure 5.1.3).

Fig. 5.1.3 *One unmended window can soon lead to others*

Privatisation of public space

Privatisation of public space is the argument that in recent years public spaces such as shopping and leisure centres have become privately policed. This means that private security guards and closed-circuit television (CCTV) are used to control how people access and use them. 'Undesirables' are kept out or kicked out. Some shopping centres even have dress codes such as no hoodies. The police have become increasingly confined to other parts of towns and cities, particularly the poorer estates. The exclusion of groups of teenagers from privatised public spaces forces them to the estates, where they are more likely to become deviant and encounter the police.

Nocturnal economy

Sociologists need to focus not just on the link between place and crime, but also between time and crime. Hobbs and Lister (2000) focus on the rise of the nocturnal economy. This refers to the growth in the UK of pubs and clubs in cities such as Nottingham, Birmingham and Manchester. Thousands of drunken teenagers in the early hours of Friday and Saturday will lead to increased crime. It has been estimated that about three-quarters of all violent incidents in urban areas occur between 9 pm and 3 am during the weekend. Most of this violence is between drunk or drugged males, but young women are increasingly involved.

■ Criticisms of environmental theory

One of the main problems with environmental theory, like subcultural theory, is that the research is based on accepting official statistics as the truth. An alternative social action approach has been taken by Owen Gill (1977), who examined the Luke Street area of Liverpool. This area of council housing was used as a dumping ground for problem families, but that doesn't explain why it developed into a delinquent area. Gill argues that over time Luke Street developed a bad reputation, so if you had a Luke Street address it was hard to find a job. The men also felt the need to act tough to defend the street's reputation, which often got them into trouble. Most importantly, the police targeted the area whenever a crime had been committed; this led to further resentment and more fighting with the police, hence more arrests. The mass media had a role to play; the *Crosley News*, the local newspaper, frequently carried negative stories about Luke Street. The police were influenced by these newspaper reports and Luke Street's poor reputation was continually reinforced. Gill argues that Luke Street developed into a delinquent area not simply because the people were bad, but because of the way other people interacted with them and labelled them. These ideas will be examined in more detail in the next section.

Summary questions

7 What is meant by 'differential association'?

8 What is meant by 'tipping'?

9 How does Owen Gill differ from other environmental criminologists?

Social action theory and crime

Learning objectives:

- Understand social action views on crime.
- Evaluate social action views on crime.

Key terms

Labelling: the process by which agents of social control such as the police and courts attach negative stereotypes to less powerful groups.

Cultural capital: an idea developed by the French sociologist Bourdieu. He argues that the middle classes are able to give their children not just economic advantages but also cultural advantages such as use of language, expression and valued social skills.

Self-fulfilling prophecy: when a label is accepted and becomes fulfilled.

Link

Cultural capital is an important idea in the sociology of education, and is one reason for the greater success of middle-class students.

Social action theory is very different from the other theories discussed so far. Firstly, functionalist, subcultural and environmental theories, and perspectives from the right (see later) all start with the assumption that crime and deviance are limited to a relatively small fraction of the population. Social action theorists argue that the vast majority of the population have broken the law and could be seen as criminal. Secondly, the previous theories tend to trust the official statistics on who are the criminals. Social action theorists challenge these official statistics and argue that they are no more than social constructs. Thirdly, the previous theories consider why people break the law and become criminals. Social action theorists are more concerned with how some groups, particularly the poor, working class, minority ethnics and men, become **labelled** as criminal by those with more power in society.

Howard Becker

Howard Becker is one of the most important and influential writers within this perspective. In his 1963 book *Outsiders* he famously wrote that 'the deviant is one to whom the label has successfully been applied; deviant behaviour is behaviour that people so label'. By this he means that deviance is a relative concept and that deviance only exists because those with power in society have decided that something is deviant. Whether or not the label 'deviant' will be applied to an act also depends on who commits the act, when and where they commit it, and who sees it. It also depends on the negotiations that take place between those committing the act and the police. Some people may be better at negotiating with the police than others, especially the middle class, who may be able to use their **cultural capital** to talk their way out of trouble.

Becker also introduced the idea of the 'master label' and the 'deviant career'. The 'master label' refers to a label that takes precedence over all other labels. Examples of negative master labels could be criminal, prostitute, junkie and paedophile. Master labels override all other labels such as friend, parent or neighbour. Those with a master label will be treated negatively, and this may lead to the development of a negative self-image. In other words, a **self-fulfilling prophecy** occurs and the master label becomes internalised or accepted. A deviant career could also develop. This is when a person is given and accepts the master label. Suppose someone is labelled a criminal, this leads to further rejection by society as that person can't find work because of the label. This leads to further crime and eventually to a deviant subculture where others with the same label can support each other. These ideas are explored in more detail by Jock Young.

Jock Young

Jock Young put the theoretical ideas of Becker into practice with his 1971 study of 'hippie' marijuana users in Notting Hill, London. Young argued that smoking marijuana was initially only a minor and relatively insignificant event for the majority of the hippies. But over time, because of the negative way the police labelled and treated them, the hippies 'closed ranks' as a form of self-defence. They were increasingly rejected and treated as different by mainstream society, so they acted out the role of hippie in a more exaggerated form. In Becker's terms, they had accepted the master label of 'hippie drug user'. A deviant career of buying and selling drugs developed as it became increasingly difficult for the hippies to enter 'normal' society. In other words, the actions of the police had actually caused more crime. This process is known as **deviancy amplification**, examined in the next section.

W. J. Chambliss

More recent research from this perspective is provided by W. J. Chambliss, an American professor of sociology whose ideas are relevant to social action theory and traditional Marxism.

Saints and Roughnecks

Chambliss's 1973 study entitled 'The Saints and the Roughnecks' focuses on two groups of boys who went to the same American high school. One group, the Saints, were eight middle-class delinquent boys. The other group, the Roughnecks, were six working-class delinquent boys. Despite committing pretty much the same amount of antisocial behaviour, the Saints were not seen as delinquent and rarely came into contact with the police, partly because most of their criminal behaviour took place out of town. The Roughnecks, on the other hand, were labelled as delinquent by the local community and the police, partly because most of their behaviour took place in the local area. When the Saints did occasionally come into contact with the police, they were able to use their cultural capital to negotiate their way out of trouble. Over time a self-fulfilling prophecy took place as the Roughnecks accepted the negative label they had been given. Two of the Roughnecks were able to escape their label and become teachers, two became serious criminal offenders and two are frequently in trouble with the police. All of the Saints graduated from college and gained middle-class jobs. In other words, both groups lived up to their labels.

The RDU

Chambliss's 1994 study of the Rapid Deployment Unit (RDU) demonstrates the racist policing strategies of some Washington DC police officers, and how they policed the 'black' areas of the city with more aggression and suspicion than they policed the 'white' areas. They effectively labelled black men as criminals and would stop more cars being driven by blacks than whites, especially newer expensive cars, in the belief that the driver must be a drug dealer. When they questioned a black man suspected of drug dealing, one officer said, 'I should kick your little black ass right here for dealing that shit. You are a worthless little scumbag, do you realise that?' Another officer asked, 'What is your mother's name, son? My mistake … she is probably a whore and you are just a ghetto bastard. Am I right?' Chambliss is not arguing that that all officers were as racist as this, but clearly some officers were racist and were treating people differently based on their ethnicity. These ideas will be explored in more detail later on.

Braithwaite: labelling and shaming

Braithwaite (1989) has examined the labelling theorists' claim that the process of labelling leads to further crime because of the development of the master label and the deviant career. Braithwaite says that shaming is

Crime and deviance

an important issue to consider, where disapproval of offenders is expressed to cause them to feel remorse and guilt. Disintegrative shaming has the effect discussed by labelling theorists such as Becker. The offender is made to feel an outsider and not worthy of reintroduction into normal society (Figure 5.1.4). This exclusion makes it more likely they will rejoin a criminal subculture and continue to break the law. Reintegrative shaming has the opposite effect. The offender experiences the disapproval of the community but is not cast out; the offender is reabsorbed and given another chance. In countries such as the UK and the US, disintegrative shaming is the norm. In Japan, where there is a strong sense of community and people are more interdependent, shaming tends to be reintegrative and crime rates low.

Fig. 5.1.4 *Offenders are made to feel excluded*

■ Criticisms of social action theory

■ Social action theorists have been accused of having too much sympathy for the criminals and not enough for the victims.

■ They focus too much on the labelling process and not enough on why someone breaks the law in the first place.

■ They are too deterministic and imply that once you have been labelled, a deviant career is inevitable. Ironically, perhaps, this is the same as the accusation often thrown at subcultural theorists.

■ Marxists accuse them of focusing too much on the working class and not on corporate criminals.

Summary questions

10 What is a master label?

11 What two groups did Chambliss study?

12 How does social action theory differ from the other theories examined so far?

Social action theory and deviance: mental illness

Learning objectives:

 Understand social action views on mental illness.

■ Evaluate social action views on mental illness.

■ **Key terms**

Stigmatised: when a group is given a negative label and treated with suspicion or hostility.

■ **Link**

Mental illness links to the sociology of health and illness, where the medical model and labelling models are explored in more detail.

In the UK it is not criminal to be mentally ill but it is often regarded as deviant. A mental illness such as depression or stress is not seen in the same way as a physical illness such as a disease or a broken leg. The mentally ill are often treated with suspicion and are **stigmatised** by society. They are generally given less sympathy and may be blamed for their condition.

■ The medical/psychiatric model

In the Western world, the dominant and most powerful approach to mental illness has been the medical/psychiatric model. This takes the approach that people who exhibit signs of bizarre behaviour are suffering from a real condition and need to be treated by a qualified medical practitioner. According to this perspective, mental illness is caused by two main factors: disturbing experiences and chemical or hormonal imbalances. Disturbing experiences have normally occurred in childhood and need to be treated by a psychoanalytic approach. This seeks to liberate patients from negative unconscious thoughts. A chemical or hormonal imbalance in the brain can be treated by antidepressants.

■ The labelling model of mental illness

The labelling model of mental illness takes a very different approach to the medical/psychiatric model. In this context, labelling theory is about the power of some groups in society to label other less powerful groups in a negative way, and treat them differently because of the label. Labelling theory and mental illness is all about the power of doctors and psychiatrists to label some people as mentally ill, then treat them with medication, therapy or even long-term residential care. This is worrying for labelling theorists as, according to them, mental illness doesn't even exist – it is just a convenient label to explain away strange and 'bizarre' behaviour.

The concept of mental illness

Two of the most important writers in this area are Thomas Szasz and Thomas Scheff, who argue that there is no such thing as mental illness. They argue that people go through stages in their lives when they feel unhappy, lonely and miserable, but to label this as 'clinical depression' and then treat it as an illness is simply wrong. In the UK, doctors are prescribing antidepressant drugs to an increasing number of people, but Szasz, Scheff and similar writers say they are treating a condition that doesn't even exist.

The effects of labelling

Once a person is labelled as mentally ill, other people will treat them differently. All that they say and do will be seen as a symptom of mental illness. If they protest that they are not mentally ill, they will be seen as aggressive. If they don't respond, they are too passive. It is difficult to convince someone that you are not mentally ill when the experts say you are.

Admittance to an institution

In the past, but less so today, patients labelled as mentally ill could be admitted to a mental hospital or an asylum. Once the labelling process has reached this stage, it is increasingly difficult to convince people that you are not ill. Rosenhan's famous experiment illustrates even specialists' inability to distinguish between the sane and the insane once admitted to an institution.

Rosenhan (1973) asked eight perfectly normal researchers to admit themselves to various American psychiatric hospitals by pretending that they were hearing voices. Once admitted, they behaved perfectly normally but were all treated as if they were mentally ill and diagnosed as schizophrenics. Whatever they did in the institution, even simple things like writing notes, were seen as a sign that they were mentally ill. Each of

Fig. 5.1.5 *Admission to an asylum used to guarantee treatment of a kind*

these pseudo (pretend) patients remained in hospital for 7–52 days. Although they were not detected by the staff, many of the genuine patients suspected that they weren't ill at all (Figure 5.1.5). In a separate experiment, staff at another hospital and who knew about the Rosenhan study were informed that during the next three months one or more pseudo patients would attempt to be admitted. Out of 193 patients, 41 were considered by staff to be impostors. The trick was that no pseudo patients were used at all; all patients suspected as impostors were genuine patients.

Criticisms of the labelling model

The obvious and very important criticism of this perspective is that mental illness is not just a social construct but a very real condition that affects an increasing number of people. Mental illness may be more difficult to diagnose and treat than a physical condition but it is no less serious or real. Psychiatrists are quick to defend their profession and see the labelling approach as naive or even dangerous. Some sociologists also disagree with labelling theory and argue that mental illness is real and caused by social processes such as poverty, unemployment and racism. Mental illness affects women more than men and minority ethnics more than whites. In addition, the work of people like Rosenhan is seen as dated as institutional care for the mentally ill has become increasingly replaced by a focus on care in the community. This means patients are treated at home or in day centres. Rosenhan can also be criticised on ethical grounds and for the small sample used.

Summary questions

13 How does the traditional medical model explain mental illness?

14 How is the social action approach different?

15 How can the social action approach be criticised?

Examiner's tip

Mental illness is very important in any question about deviant behaviour, but it is not relevant in questions about criminal behaviour.

Link

See page 301 for more on criticisms of the Rosenhan study.

Take it further

If you are studying sociology and psychology, ask your psychology teachers about the views of the labelling theorist. See how they respond.

Crime and deviance

Traditional Marxist views on crime

Learning objectives:

- Understand traditional Marxist views on crime.

- Evaluate traditional Marxist views on crime.

Key terms

Bourgeoisie: a loose term for the groupings in society who wish to cling on to its existing structure; the ruling class of urban society. Derived from the French for 'of the town'.

Proletariat: those who provide the labour necessary to operate factories and other productive enterprises; the working class.

Capitalist society: a society like the UK or US characterised by private ownership of business and property.

Communism: an economic system without private business and property. Everything in society is owned by every member of society, with complete equality between everyone.

Link

See page 276 for more on white-collar crime and page 283 for more on state crime.

Marx himself wrote very little about crime, but that hasn't stopped other Marxists from developing a traditional Marxist perspective on crime. It is called traditional because the ideas are linked to the original ideas of Marx on the relationship between the **bourgeoisie** and the **proletariat**, and the nature of **capitalist society**. More recent or contemporary Marxists have taken different approaches, explored in the next chapter.

Crime in a capitalist society

Traditional Marxists argue that capitalism is itself a crime and that capitalism causes crime. The idea that it is a crime is clearly a very different definition of crime compared to the normal sociological definition of crime as a breach in the law. According to Marxists, capitalism should be seen as a crime because it is an economic system based on the exploitation of the many by the few. The proletariat work for the bourgeoisie and make a profit for them. It is not an equal relationship but a criminal relationship. The only reason it isn't seen as a crime is because all laws are made by and on behalf of the bourgeoisie. The fact that society is so unequal is a crime. The fact that the rich can afford luxury cars and yachts while the world's poor starve is a crime.

Capitalism causes crime because it is an economic system based on competition, selfishness and greed. It encourages a dog eat dog, survival of the fittest approach to life. We are socialised from an early age into these values, so it is no surprise that crime is so high in capitalist countries like the UK and the US. In a way, these views are similar to those of the functionalist Merton explored earlier. The difference is that Merton believes capitalism is ultimately the best economic system, but that it can be made fairer. For traditional Marxists, the problem is capitalism, and capitalism needs to be replaced with **communism**, where they believe crime would cease to exist.

Corporate, white-collar and state crime

Slapper and Tombs (1999) have argued that corporate crime should be defined as law-breaking committed by or for corporations which furthers the interests of the corporation. Most research in this area has been carried out using a traditional Marxist perspective, and will therefore be examined in this chapter. The two main types of corporate crime are financial crimes and negligence.

Slapper and Tombs argue that the term 'white-collar crime' should be applied to 'crimes by the individually rich or powerful which are committed in the furtherance of their own interests, often against corporations within which they are working'. White-collar crime can also be defined as crimes committed not just by the rich and powerful but by anyone in a middle-class occupation such as doctors, lawyers and accountants.

State crime can be defined as crimes committed by the government such as terrorism, torture, war crimes, genocide and corruption. Traditional Marxists are obviously interested in white-collar and state crimes, but other theorists consider them too, so they will be explored in later chapters.

Financial crimes

In 1998 it was revealed that an investment fund called Long Term Capital Management (LTCM), whose founders included two winners of the Nobel Prize in economics, had lost billions of dollars by borrowing $900 billion, more than 250 times their capital. The losses were so big that major Western governments had to put together a $3.5 billion rescue package to prevent their economies being affected.

Slapper and Tombs (1999) have examined the misselling of pensions in the UK. Leading pension providers have provided illegal and misleading advice to people investing in personal pensions, leading them to invest in inappropriate personal pensions that result in a financial loss. Endowment mortgages were offered to home buyers with misleading promises of financial rewards; a huge number of people made successful compensation claims against the mortgage providers for misselling.

More recently, some companies in America have produced fictitious accounts to mislead investors (Figure 5.1.6). In 2001 it was revealed that Enron of the US had tried to conceal huge debts; it was forced into bankruptcy, owing about $50 billion.

Fig. 5.1.6 *Boardroom baddies count their cash*

Negligence

From a traditional Marxist perspective, businesses will try to maximise profit by minimising health and safety, often putting workers at risk. One strategy is to locate in the developing world, where health and safety regulations are less rigorously enforced. One notorious example is the escape of poisonous gas from a chemical plant at Bhopal, India,

AQA Examiner's tip

Remember that there are three Marxist approaches to the topic of crime and deviance. These three approaches are similar but they are distinguished by some key differences.

in 1984. More than 3,000 people were killed and many more were injured. The accident was caused by inadequate safety measures. No criminal charges were brought against the owners of the company, Union Carbide of the US, but it agreed to pay $470 million in compensation. Although industrial accidents in the UK are not as deadly, every year hundreds die and thousands are injured because of inadequate safety precautions. On the rare occasions when an accident is investigated and the company owners found guilty, the punishment is a fine.

Sociological views on corporate crime

Traditional Marxists such as Box (1981) have highlighted the success of capitalist organisations in convincing the general public, politicians and the media that corporate crime is less serious and less harmful than other types of crime. Box calls this 'mystification' and says it explains why so few prosecutions are ever filed against capitalists. It is probably fair to say that official statistics underestimate the extent of corporate and white-collar crime more than crime in general, and this creates the false view that most crime is committed by the working class.

Criticisms of traditional Marxism

■ If, as Marxists assume, crime is caused by capitalism, why does crime exist in communist countries such as China, Russia and Cuba? Perhaps, as Durkheim claimed, crime is simply inevitable, regardless of the economic system.

■ It has been argued that communist countries such as China and the former Soviet Union have had a poor record on negligence, working conditions and pollution, whereas Western capitalist counties have the strictest health and safety laws to protect workers and the strictest laws to protect the environment.

■ Despite the cost of financial crimes such as tax evasion and fraud, most people are more concerned with more mundane crimes such as mugging, car theft and burglary.

■ Many victims of crime are working-class.

■ If capitalism causes crime, shouldn't the greatest amount of crime be committed by the poorest people in society, such as the elderly?

Summary questions

16 What is the difference between white-collar, corporate and state crime?

17 What do Marxists mean by negligence?

18 How can Marxist theory be challenged?

The new criminology and New Left realism

Learning objectives:

- Understand contemporary Marxist views on crime.

- Evaluate contemporary Marxist views on crime.

Key terms

Moral panic: when society reacts against perceived deviance, because of media representations.

The new criminology

A new or contemporary Marxist approach to crime and deviance was developed in *The New Criminology* (Taylor *et al.* 1973). Most of the book is a critique of existing theories, and the last chapter is the most important and significant. This puts forward what the authors call a 'fully social theory of crime and deviance'. It has seven quite complex and abstract elements, but it means that criminologists need to look in detail at every aspect of a crime, including the reasons behind each criminal act, the role played by the police, courts and mass media, and finally at politics and capitalism itself. All of this is very theoretical, but it inspired *Policing the Crisis* (Hall *et al.* 1978), which attempted to use its theoretical ideas to examine a real crime: mugging.

Policing the Crisis

Policing the Crisis examines the **moral panic** that developed over the crime of mugging in the 1970s. Despite sensationalist newspaper reports that claimed there was an increase in mugging – violent street crime – particularly by young Afro-Caribbean men, Hall's own research showed that it was actually growing more slowly than in the previous decade. Hall wanted to show that mugging could be explained using the fully social theory of Taylor *et al.* and part of this involved looking beyond the crime of mugging to see what was going on in British capitalism and politics at the time. Hall argues that the moral panic developed because capitalism was in crisis. There was an economic crisis linked to unemployment and strikes, and a hegemonic crisis, which means a crisis over authority.

The British public was losing faith in the government and authorities. The moral panic over mugging came at the right time for the authorities, who could scapegoat the black muggers to distract attention from their real problems. It also divided the working class on ethnic lines, and the media maintained the deception as it helped sell more newspapers. The police increasingly labelled young black men as muggers and arrests for this group increased. The media reported it and the cycle continued. This is another example of deviancy amplification. Hall and others see crime statistics as no more than social constructs. Those Afro-Caribbeans who turned to crime did so because of unemployment or out of frustration with having to do low-paid and low-status jobs, or 'white man's shit work'.

The myth of black criminality

Paul Gilroy (1982) explores what he calls the 'myth of black criminality'. Like Hall, he writes as a new criminologist. He argues that Afro-Caribbean men are no more criminal than whites, but they are labelled by the police and courts and treated unfairly. Even when young black men do break the law, it is best seen as a political act. In effect, they are fighting back against a racist white society and are continuing the battle against white society that started with the slave trade, the British Empire and colonialism. Gilroy argues that the high unemployment rates of the 1980s led to a 'surplus population' and that it was convenient for the authorities to focus on the myth of black crime, rather than their failure to ensure full employment.

Criticisms of the new criminology

Both Hall and Gilroy contradict themselves. On the one hand, they claim that Afro-Caribbean men are no more criminal than white men, but are victims of labelling by a racist society. On the other hand, they say that the black crime rate was bound to rise because of unemployment. If the black crime rate did rise, then clearly it wasn't a moral panic but a real event. The claim that some types of crime are more common among minority ethnics than whites has been developed by Lea and Young, who formulated New Left realism.

New Left realism

New Left realism was developed by Jock Young and John Lea in their 1984 book *What is to be Done about Law and Order?* They are critical of other theories, including traditional Marxism and the new criminology, which they accuse of having idealistic views of criminals as 'political revolutionaries' somehow fighting back against capitalism or racism. They take what they see as a realistic approach to crime:

- Crime is a serious problem and is getting worse. The victims of crime are often ignored, and they are often the very working class that Marxists are supposed to be concerned for.
- Crime, especially street crime, is growing and it is not all down to labelling or racist policing.
- Some urban areas have become increasingly dangerous, especially for women.
- The official statistics on crime are broadly correct. They are not just social constructs, as claimed by the traditional Marxists and new criminologists.
- There is an ethnic dimension to crime.
- Afro-Caribbean men are more likely to be involved in street crimes such as mugging than whites, and white men are more likely to be involved in crimes such as burglary.

The ideas of Hall and Gilroy are particularly called into question. Lea and Young challenge the claim that the police simply label all Afro-Caribbean men as criminals. They point out that 92 per cent of crimes are brought to the attention of the police by the public, and it isn't as if the police are 'out there' in society looking for black men to arrest. They argue that the recorded crime rates among first-generation immigrants were lower than among whites.

They do accept that policing polices may exaggerate the minority ethnic crime rate, but nevertheless believe there has been a real increase in the number of street crimes committed by Afro-Caribbeans. They also argue that most of the victims of crimes committed by Afro-Caribbeans are Afro-Caribbean themselves, so to talk as Gilroy does about black men fighting back against racism or slavery clearly makes no sense. Lea and Young put forward three reasons to explain the increase in black street crime:

- **Relative deprivation** – some people will commit crime when they feel deprived in comparison to others, although they may not be deprived in real terms. The media today stresses the importance of economic goods, and some minority ethnic groups, especially young black men, will turn to crime to gain these goods.
- **Subculture** – if a group of individuals share a sense of relative deprivation, they may respond by forming subcultures, or gangs.

Marginalisation – young black men are on the margin (edge) of society and have no group such as a trade union or pressure group to stand up for them. The frustration, resentment and anger this causes may lead to street crime.

Evaluation of New Left realism

Gordon Hughes (1991) has pointed out many strengths of the New Left realist approach to crime. He argues that it focuses more on the victims of crime; it is a balanced theory that neither demonises nor glorifies the police or the state; it has promoted debate about the very real problems of street crime; it has revived useful sociological concepts such as relative deprivation.

However, new Left realism has been criticised in a number of ways. Firstly, there is very little new about New Left realism. The ideas can be seen as a mixture of Merton's strain theory and subcultural studies, reapplied to ethnicity. Secondly, from a traditional Marxist perspective, there is too much of an emphasis on street crime, and not enough on white-collar or corporate crime. Thirdly, there is no reference to women and crime.

AQA Examiner's tip

The arguments of the new criminologists and New Left realists are very relevant in any question on ethnicity and crime, as they have very different views and provide a useful contrast.

Summary questions

19 Who suggested the need for a fully social theory of crime and deviance?

20 Why does Gilroy talk of the 'myth' of black criminality?

21 How does New Left realism differ from the new criminology?

Perspectives from the right

Learning objectives:

- Understand perspectives from the right on crime.

- Analyse perspectives from the right on crime.

Key terms

Left-wing: a political view that tends to support the rights of the working class and is often critical of capitalism.

Right-wing: a political view that tends to support elites in society and is supportive of capitalism.

Zero tolerance: a policing policy in which all criminal offences are acted on, no matter how trivial. The policy was claimed to have been a great success in cleaning up New York.

Link

See page 252 for more on tipping and broken windows.

Link

The ideas of Charles Murray are relevant in the sociology of the family. He has written about the rise of the 'underclass', a group of welfare dependants, including single parents, who he sees as responsible for the moral and economic decline of countries such as the US and the UK.

Take it further

Find out more about the New York experience of zero tolerance. How successful was it in eliminating crime? Did it merely move the crime somewhere else?

In the same way that there are different **left-wing** or Marxist views on crime and deviance, there are different **right-wing** or conservative views. Two of the most important are right realism and rational choice or administrative criminology.

Although right-wing views have distinctive features, they all tend to share some common ground. Firstly, they argue that criminals have made a rational choice to break the law. They weren't forced to become criminals but have weighed up the pros and cons of their intended actions. Secondly, the role of government is not to eliminate the mythical 'root causes' of crime, such as poverty or educational underachievement, but to punish the criminal. Thirdly, humans are naturally selfish and greedy, and if they receive poor socialisation, crime will be the inevitable result. Crime can never be eliminated, merely reduced.

Right realism

One of the most influential of the conservative views, particularly in the US, has been right realism, and one of the key right realists is James Q. Wilson, an adviser to President Reagan in the 1980s. It can be argued that these views have also influenced British governments throughout the 1980s and 1990s, and possibly even today. Right realists argue that it is futile to try to eliminate crime by focusing on improving social conditions. The US tried this in the 1960s and it didn't work. And it is no good left-wing sociologists blaming crime on such things as poverty, as many old people are poor and do not turn to crime. Right realists tend to focus instead on community breakdown, the underclass and family breakdown, and inappropriate policing styles. Community breakdown can lead to tipping or broken windows.

Right realists such as the US sociologist Charles Murray have focused on the development of an underclass of single-parent families dependent on state welfare. He blames children and teenagers from these single-parent families for much delinquent behaviour (Figure 5.1.7). Children need two parents and role models, and a single parent cannot provide adequate socialisation. This view has been challenged by Jane Mooney (1998), who claims 'there is not a single substantial scrap of evidence' that there is a link between single parenthood and criminal behaviour. According to her own research on single mothers in London, they are more likely to be victims of crime than causes. One in five of the single mothers in her research had suffered violent attacks in the previous year, twice the average rate for the other women in her study.

Right realists also argue that the police need to be far tougher and adopt a **zero tolerance** approach to crime. Minor crimes such as littering and graffiti need stamping on hard, and the police need to move groups on if they look as if they might cause trouble.

Rational choice and administrative criminology

Rational choice theorists argue that we all make a rational choice when it comes to committing a criminal act. We see whether the benefits outweigh the costs. The benefit of a crime is normally financial reward,

Crime and deviance

Fig. 5.1.7 *Right realists focus on single-parent families*

but it could also be excitement or peer group approval. The costs are clearly getting caught and being punished. The simple way to reduce crime is to ensure that the costs always outweigh the benefits through harsher penalties and by making crime harder to commit. These ideas have been influential in the UK; known as administrative criminology, they have influenced the Home Office, particularly on the introduction of **neighbourhood watch schemes**, increased use of **CCTV** and **target hardening**.

Summary questions

22 What is meant by the idea that we make 'rational' choices?

23 What causes crime according to right realists?

24 How can the increased use of CCTV be criticised?

Key terms

Neighbourhood watch scheme: a scheme where neighbours look out for each other and act as a deterrent to burglars and other criminals.

CCTV: closed-circuit television; used to monitor behaviour and deter crime.

Target hardening: an approach to reducing crime that emphasises making it more difficult for criminals to commit crimes. This could be by better street lighting, tougher doors and windows, alarms or even redesigning housing estates.

Crime and deviance

Postmodernity

Learning objectives:

- Understand postmodern views on crime.
- Evaluate postmodern views on crime.

Link

See page 289 for more on Michael Foucault's ideas about prisons and the surveillance society.

Postmodernism is the belief that we are now living in a postmodern age, as different to the modern as the modern was to the pre-modern. Most postmodernists are French philosophers, and they generally argue that the Western world became postmodern in the 1970s and 1980s. The postmodern world is characterised by individuality, choice and flexibility. Concepts such as social class, age and ethnicity are no longer seen as important. Postmodernists tend to reject all grand narratives or metanarratives (big stories) such as sociological theories, science or religion. They haven't written a great deal about crime and deviance, although Michael Foucault's ideas about prisons and the surveillance society can be seen as postmodern in some respects. More generally, postmodernists would be expected to find theories on crime and deviance an easy target, as they are very much part of the modernist grand narrative of welfare reform and social engineering that postmodernists reject.

Postmodernist approaches to crime

Postmodernists argue that there is no point trying to explain crime using grand narratives such as functionalism, Marxism or feminism. All you can do is treat each criminal act as a unique one-off event and describe it in detail. This doesn't seem a very useful approach and ignores the wealth of sociological evidence that suggests some groups are more likely to commit specific crimes than others. Concepts such as social class, ethnicity, gender and age are clearly very important when attempting to explain and categorise crime, and to dismiss them seems foolish.

Some postmodernists would also see crime as part of an individual's lifestyle choice, self-expression and creativity, available to all of us in a postmodern age. You may choose an identity as a drug addict, bank robber or prostitute. Again, this doesn't seem a very useful approach; it almost celebrates criminality and ignores the many social factors which have led to you becoming a criminal. Most prostitutes or drug addicts would have very little to celebrate with their supposedly freely chosen postmodern identity.

Policing styles is another area postmodernism could address. Some postmodernists argue that to fully recognise and support diversity and choice, different policing styles are needed for different areas. Ghettos and suburbs need to be treated differently to allow the criminal justice system to take account of people's diverse lifestyles. There are many problems with this approach, and many sociologists such as social action theorists and Marxists claim that the police already treat groups differently, normally at the expense of the young, the poor and minority ethnics.

Summary questions

25 What is meant by the term 'postmodern'?

26 What is a grand narrative?

27 What is the postmodern view on crime?

Crime and deviance

Ethnicity

Learning objective:

- Understand the relationship between ethnicity and crime.

About 91 per cent of people in the UK are white and 9 per cent are non-white. Of this 9 per cent, approximately 5 per cent are Asian, 2 per cent Afro-Caribbean, and 2 per cent mixed and other. When looking at crime and deviance, these statistics are important as they show that some groups are over-represented among the prison population. Although these figures vary each year, of the 80,000 or so men in prison, approximately 74 per cent are white, 15 per cent are Afro-Caribbean, 7 per cent are Asian, 3 per cent are mixed, and 1 per cent are Chinese and other. Criminologists are obviously interested in the large number of black men in prison, out of all proportion to their numbers in the population.

Of the 7,000 or so women in prison, about 8 per cent of the total prison population, approximately 70 per cent are white, 21 per cent are Afro-Caribbean, 5 per cent are mixed, 2 per cent are Asian, and 2 per cent are Chinese and other. Again, it is the disproportionate number of black women in prison that interests criminologists.

The situation in the US is very similar. Black Americans make up about 13 per cent of the general population, but approximately 50 per cent of the prison population. Over 5 per cent of all black males in the US are in prison (0.5 per cent for whites), and for black males aged 25–29 the figure rises to 13 per cent. There are more black men in prison in the US than there are black men imprisoned in the rest of the world combined. Research also shows black people are more likely to be prosecuted when caught than whites, more likely to be remanded in custody, and less likely to be released on bail.

Broadly speaking, sociologists have taken two approaches to these statistics. Firstly, the legal system isn't fair and Afro-Caribbeans are simply victims of racism and discrimination. Secondly, the legal system is generally fair but Afro-Caribbeans are simply more criminal than whites in some areas, and reasons for their criminality need to be explored.

The legal system is biased

Hall and Gilroy, writing in the late 1970s and early 1980s, argued that young black men were no more criminal than whites, and that the legal system was biased. In his 1994 study of the RDU (page 255) Chambliss shows the negative labelling of black men in the US. Since this research, a number of more recent studies have been written which argue the same thing. Philips and Bowling (2002) argue that the UK criminal justice system is racist. They point to the higher number of stop and searches of black men (5–8 times higher than for whites), higher number of arrests, overpolicing in inner-city areas, use of racially abusive language and the higher imprisonment rate for black men arrested compared to whites. After the racist murder of the black youth Stephen Lawrence (pictured on page 271) in 1993, the Macpherson Inquiry was set up to examine the circumstances of his death. It concluded by saying that the police were institutionally racist. This means 'procedures, practices and a culture

Fig. 5.2.1 *Stephen Lawrence, racially murdered in 1993. His killers have never been convicted*

that tend to exclude or to disadvantage non-white people'. The Macpherson Inquiry effectively confirmed what many sociologists had been arguing for years.

■ Stop and search and ethnicity

Waddington *et al.* (2004), published in the *British Journal of Criminology*, agree that the police do stop a proportionately higher number of minority ethnics compared to whites, but do not agree that this is due to racism. They argue that there are simply more young minority ethnic men out at night in city centres compared to whites. In other words, the police will target anyone in high-crime areas, and if these people are disproportionately black or Asian, they are targeted not because of their ethnicity but simply because of their presence in an area.

■ Reasons for the high criminality of Afro-Caribbeans

Lea and Young, writing as New Left realists, were among the first sociologists to claim, controversially, that young black men were not simply victims of police racism, but that for street crimes especially, they were more criminal than whites or other ethnic groups. They put this down to relative deprivation, subcultures and marginalisation. The new criminologists Hall and Gilroy also argued that when young black men did turn to crime it was down to structural factors such as poverty, unemployment and poor housing. They therefore contradicted themselves when they claimed the high black crime rate was just a moral panic. Here are some other arguments put forward to explain the higher street crime rates for blacks.

Lack of educational success

Afro-Caribbean boys leave school with the lowest qualifications of any ethnic group. In 2006 only 23 per cent of black boys gained five or more good GCSEs compared to the national average of 44 per cent. This clearly has an effect on self-confidence, the ability to go on to further and higher education, and employment opportunities. With some avenues for success blocked, street crime is going to be one possible route to financial gain and peer group status. Clearly the early sociological theories of Merton and the subcultural theorists are relevant here.

Family structure

Sixty per cent of young black children live with just one parent, normally the mother, compared to 20 per cent of white children. This lack of a positive male role model may be a factor in the higher level of black street crime. On the other hand, single-parent families, regardless of ethnicity, are poorer than two-parent families, so the lack of money may be the more relevant factor in pushing some adolescents into crime.

Influence of the mass media

A possibly more controversial argument is the influence of the mass media, particularly predominately black rap artists. According to conservative politicians, social commentators and even some sociologists, particularly from the New Right, rap music's emphasis on bling, violence, guns, sex and drugs, and its generally sexist attitude to women, may not provide positive role models for young black men. But this view has been

■ Link

See page 264 for more on Lea and Young's ideas on young black criminals.

■ Link

There has been a great deal of research into the exam results of different ethnic groups in the UK. Explanations for the underachievement of black boys have focused on home-based factors such as family structure and parental support, and school-based factors such as prejudice and discrimination.

Crime and deviance

challenged, as there are plenty of examples of rap about equality, harmony and respect, and it is questionable to ascribe so much influence to just one form of entertainment. Listening to 50 Cent or watching a Tarantino film will not automatically turn you to crime.

Crime among other minority ethnics

The recorded crime rate for Asian people is broadly in proportion to numbers in the population but has risen over the past 10 years. Early studies of ethnicity and crime tended to focus on the influence of religion and culture to explain the relatively low crime rate. More recent studies have explained the rise by looking at the declining influence of religion among some young Asian boys, and how increased integration into British culture has weakened the controls previously provided by a tight-knit family structure and sense of community in Asian areas.

Summary questions

1. What aspect of the UK prison population most interests sociologists?
2. What is bias in the UK criminal justice system?
3. Why were the ideas of Young and Lea considered controversial?

Gender

Learning objectives:

- Understand the relationship between gender and crime.

Link

See pages 263–264 for more on the new criminology.

A notable feature of the theories discussed so far is how little they refer to gender. This is not because the writers ignored gender on purpose but because they considered crime to be relevant to the male gender only. Women may be the victims of crime, but the assumption has always been that men are the criminals, and most theories have concentrated on why some men turn to crime. The feminists Abbott and Wallace (1990) have argued that most sociology has traditionally been research on men and theories to explain male behaviour. Within crime and deviance, women become invisible or are included as an afterthought. Even more recent theories like the new criminology make no reference to women.

Official crime statistics and gender

According to the official statistics, women commit relatively few crimes compared to men and are far less likely to be arrested and sent to prison; 8 per cent of the total UK prison population is female. This could mean that women are very good at crime and are less likely to be caught or that they commit less detectable crimes, but most sociologists accept that women are simply less criminal than men. Some sociologists have also argued that the police and courts treat women more favourably than men, the so-called chivalry argument. This takes the view that women are able to get away with more than men. When stopped by the police they are able to use their femininity and cultural capital to talk their way out of minor offences. In court they may be seen as having been led astray by a more dominant male partner and may receive more favourable treatment. Yet the evidence for such claims is inconclusive and other studies have argued that in rape cases, for example, the woman is often seen as partly responsible for the attack because she was drinking or dressed provocatively.

Can traditional theories be applied to women?

To try to bring women into the sociology of crime, some feminists started by looking at the existing theories to see if they could be applied to women. This reveals how biased the existing theories are in their lack of reference to women.

Merton and strain theory

If not being able to achieve the American dream causes some men to innovate, why don't more women innovate? Eileen Leonard (1982) argued that women's goals are more about successful relationships than making money, so the need to steal isn't an issue. As Leonard argues, 'Women have low aspirations and their goals are extremely accessible.'

Subcultural theory and environmental theory

Women aren't considered in any of the early subcultural studies. It was simply taken for granted that only men joined gangs and that women had other areas and interests to occupy and concern them. The environmental studies tend to focus on social class, and again women are invisible. In Shaw and McKay's work, for example, it is taken for granted that the higher levels of crime in the zones closest to the city centre are the result of male, not female, criminal activity.

Labelling theory

Labelling theory is concerned with social class and not gender. All the studies mentioned, such as Chambliss's research on the Saints and the Roughnecks, look at male, not female criminal activity. Yet feminists have argued that labelling is a very important concept which can be used to explain why the police and courts treat men and women differently.

Marxist theories

Traditional Marxist theories focus on social class and ignore gender. If working-class men may be forced into crime by the nature of capitalism, then why not working-class women? The new criminology, which claimed to propose a 'fully social theory of crime', was not fully social enough for feminists as it ignored over half the population. Likewise, New Left realism, while bringing ethnicity into the picture, left women out of it.

Feminist views on why some women turn to crime

Freda Adler

One of the first attempts to explain crime from a feminist perspective was *Sisters in Crime* (Adler 1975). Adler argued that the female crime rate was increasing and that this increase was due to women's liberation. In the Western world, since the 1960s, women had been entering the labour market in increasing numbers, and a range of laws were introduced to help and protect them from discrimination. Women were starting to compete with men for jobs and were becoming more like men in other ways too, such as increased smoking, drinking and sexual activity. Adler argues that one other way women were copying men was an increase in criminal activity. Women were no longer afraid to be deviant. Women also now had more opportunity to commit crimes as they were in the public domain. In the past, when women had the housewife role, opportunities for crime were more limited.

Evaluation of Adler

Adler is certainly correct when she argues that women's behaviour has changed since the 1960s, especially in sexual activity and drinking, but her argument that women's liberation has caused more women to become criminal is less convincing. Most female criminals, at least according to the official statistics, are working-class and not middle-class, but this is the group least affected by women's liberation. If Adler's analysis were correct, we would see an increase in crime by liberated middle-class women, yet this hasn't happened. The increase in working-class female crime can be explained more effectively by taking a different approach, as the next section illustrates.

Pat Carlen

Pat Carlen (1988) conducted research on 39 women aged 15–46 who had been convicted of one or more crimes. These crimes included theft, fraud, burglary, drug offences and prostitution. Most of the women were working-class and from the London area. Carlen rejected Adler's arguments as these women had been largely untouched by women's

■ Link

See pages 266–267 for more on
Carlen's rational choice theory.

Fig. 5.2.2 *Carlen says women turn to crime after broken deals on class and gender*

■ Link

Gender can be linked to the sociology of the family, particularly the feminist idea of the triple shift of paid work, housework and emotional work, which leaves women little time for crime.

liberation. Instead Carlen focused on a version of rational choice theory which argues that all of us have the potential to be criminal and will turn to crime if the advantages seem to outweigh the disadvantages. Carlen argues that working-class women have traditionally been controlled by what she calls the 'class deal' and the 'gender deal', and that crime arises when these deals break down (Figure 5.2.2).

The class deal and the gender deal

The class deal refers to working-class women being controlled by the possibility of a reasonably paid job and the ability to buy consumer goods and enjoy a decent quality of life. The gender deal refers to working-class women being controlled by the possibility of decent relationships with men and having children. For the majority of working-class women, these deals ensure they don't turn to crime. For the women Carlen studied, the deals had broken down. The women's limited educational success and lack of qualifications meant that they had found it difficult to find decent regular paid work, and most were unemployed. The class deal wasn't working for them, and crime offered them the possibility of the money and consumer goods that most working-class women worked for. The gender deal had broken down because many of the women had not been raised in warm and loving families, but had been brought up in care and many had been sexually or physically abused. Without the support of a decent family or partner, it was almost inevitable that many of them turned to criminal behaviour. They had very little to lose and everything to gain.

Evaluation of Carlen

The main problem with Carlen's work is her small research sample of just 39 mainly working-class women. It is dangerous to generalise from her findings, however convincing her argument appears. Another problem is that many women suffer from a breakdown in class and/or gender deals at some point in their lives, but they don't turn to crime.

■ Feminist views on why most women don't turn to crime

Feminists have also considered the reasons why most women don't become criminal. Here are the four main arguments.

Differential socialisation

Boys and girls are socialised differently. Boys are brought up to be masculine, tough, aggressive and competitive, which can lead them into criminal behaviour later on. Girls are socialised to be more passive, nurturing and caring, qualities which lead them away from criminal behaviour.

Opportunities

Women are more likely to have childcare responsibilities, which prevents them from being criminal. Women are more likely to be responsible for the majority of housework, which gives them fewer opportunities to be criminal compared to men (Figure 5.2.3). In the past, women were less likely to work, which reduced their chances of white-collar crime.

Fig. 5.2.3 *Housework and childcare leave little time for crime*

Risk-taking

Women take fewer risks in life compared to men. Men play more dangerous sports, drive fast and have more dangerous hobbies. Crime is a high-risk activity, which makes it more appealing to men. Women prefer low-risk, high-gain activities such as nurturing children, religion and shopping. Crime is simply too high-risk for most women. This argument may be considered sexist and dated.

Knowledge

Women haven't the technical skills needed to steal a car, rob a bank or commit cybercrime. Women would like to be criminal but aren't skilled enough. This is clearly a sexist and dated argument.

Summary questions

4 What percentage of the UK prison population is female?

5 What research method did Carlen use?

6 What reasons have been suggested for why women don't turn to crime?

> **AQA Examiner's tip**
>
> In any question on gender and crime, look at men and women, not just at one group. Most research has been on men and crime, which is why a separate gender section is needed to redress the balance and focus on women separately. A good exam answer will take a balanced approach.

Crime and deviance

Social class and age

Learning objective:

- Understand the relationship between social class and age and crime.

Linking theory to social class and age

According to the official statistics, young people are more criminal than older people, and the working class are more criminal than the middle or upper classes. They are far more likely to break the law in the first place and to encounter the police, courts and prisons. A typical prisoner in the UK will be under 30 and working-class. Many early sociological theories took this for granted then developed theories to explain why the working class, especially young men, broke the law. Later sociological theories have challenged this.

- **Functionalists** such as Merton argue that young people from the working class are more criminal because they have more need to innovate, possibly because of educational failure.

- **Early subcultural theorists** also assume that only teenagers from the working class will join gangs, possibly due to status frustration because of educational failure. Later theorists such as Korem did look at middle-class gang membership, focusing on family breakdown.

- **Environmental theorists** tend to look at why working-class areas have higher rates of crime than middle-class areas, and focus on explanations such as zones of transition and differential association. Owen Gill suggested that police labelling and deviancy amplification may feature.

- **Right theorists**, although writing later than these early sociological theorists, tend to agree that the typical criminal is a working-class (male) teenager.

- **Social action theorists** were the first sociologists to challenge these assumptions. They argue that young working-class people, especially boys, are more likely to be labelled by the police and courts as criminal. Chambliss illustrates this in his work on the Saints and the Roughnecks.

- **Traditional Marxists** agree that the working class are no more criminal than the other social classes. Their work on corporate crime, for example, shows that the real criminals in society are older businessmen.

- **New criminologists** focus more on ethnicity than the other theorists, and argue in a similar way to social action theorists that the police label young working-class black men as criminal, and ignore other groups that are equally criminal if not more criminal.

- **New Left realists** argue that all social classes and ages commit crimes, but that violent street crimes are more likely to be committed by young working-class black men.

One area that involves both class and age is **white-collar crime**. Edwin Sutherland (1960) was the first sociologist to study this area. David Nelken (2002) points out that Sutherland's definition of white-collar crime is open to criticism, as the phrase 'persons of high social status' is ambiguous, and also that crimes may be committed by people outside of their occupations.

Key terms

White-collar crime: defined by Edwin Sutherland as 'crimes committed by persons of high social status and respectability in the course of their occupations'. A typical white-collar crime is a crime committed by a doctor, lawyer or accountant. White-collar crimes could include bribery, corruption and fraud.

Summary questions

7 What do functionalists say about crime, social class and age?

8 What do traditional Marxists say about crime, social class and age?

9 Give three examples of white-collar crimes.

Victims and crime

Learning objective:

■ Examine the victims of crime by gender, ethnicity and age.

The study of victims of crime is known as victimology and is a relatively new approach in criminology. In 1983 the Home Office published the first British Crime Survey (BCS). This is a victim survey which asks individuals if they have been the victim of a crime in the previous year. By 1998 seven surveys had been carried out, and from 2000 it became an annual publication. The BCS is a large-scale social survey completed by over 40,000 adults aged 16 or over. The 2007 BCS showed that nationally about 1 in 4 people (24 per cent) experienced a crime against themselves or their household (Figure 5.2.4). Those most at risk of violent crime were young men aged 16–24 (13.8 per cent), full-time students (9.3 per cent) and the unemployed (9.0 per cent). The risk for people aged 75 and over was just 0.4 per cent.

Fig. 5.2.4 *Do the facts bear out older people's fears? It is young men who are at greatest risk from violent crime*

■ Gender and victimisation

Men are far more likely than women to be victims of violent street crime, but women are far more likely to be victims of rape and domestic violence. According to the Home Office website, domestic violence accounts for 16 per cent of all violent crime: it will affect 1 in 4 women and 1 in 6 men; 72 per cent of victims of domestic violence are women;

Crime and deviance

there is one incident of domestic violence reported to the police every minute; and two women are killed each week by a current or former partner.

■ Ethnicity and victimisation

According to the BCS and other Home Office statistics, minority ethnics are more likely to be victims of most crimes than whites. All minority ethnic groups are more likely to be victims of burglary and vehicle theft than whites, black and Indian ethnic groups are more likely to be robbed, and blacks are far more likely than whites to be assaulted or murdered. Reasons for these differences could include the areas where minority ethnics live, higher rates of unemployment, the number of younger minority ethnics compared to whites, and the effect of gang activity on the black homicide rate.

■ Age and victimisation

One clear problem with the BCS is that it only looks at adults aged 16 and over. There is limited information on how many under 16s are victims of crime. But in 2003 the Home Office published a separate Crime and Justice Survey that included interviews with 10–15 year olds. This is an example of a self-report study which looks at the extent and nature of crimes committed, drug and alcohol use, attitudes to and contact with the criminal justice system, and experiences of victimisation. It found that 35 per cent of 10–15 year olds had been victims of at least one personal crime such as assault, robbery or theft. About 20 per cent had been physically assaulted.

Other surveys have produced different findings though. A 2004 MORI survey of 11–16 year olds found the incidents of assaults at 13 per cent. A 2004 survey by the Howard League for Penal Reform of 500 primary school children, found that 95 per cent had experienced crime. The problem here is clearly one that affects all victim studies, but particularly those involving younger people, and that is what constitutes a crime? A friend pushing you in a moment of anger, is that an assault? Taking someone's PE kit by mistake, is that a theft? The difficulty faced by pupils in filling in a victim survey clearly raises questions about its validity, and therefore its usefulness.

■ Link

See page 299 for more on self-report studies.

Examiner's tip

In any answer about gender, age or ethnicity, it is worth looking at these groups as victims, not just at perpetrators.

■ Summary questions

10 What is the correct name for the study of crime victims?

11 What is the BCS?

12 Why is the BCS so useful to sociologists?

Globalisation

Globalisation and crime

Learning objective:

■ Examine how globalisation has affected drug trafficking, people trafficking, cybercrime and other crimes.

■ Link

See page 266 for more on Charles Murray.

Globalisation refers to the shrinking of the world in a social, cultural and an economic sense. McGrew (1992) defines globalisation as the process whereby events, decisions and activities in one part of the world have significant consequences for people in quite distant parts of the globe: 'Nowadays goods, capital, people, knowledge, images, communications, crime, culture, pollutants, drugs, fashions and belief all readily flow across territorial boundaries.' This is all made possible by the development of cheaper and quicker air travel and by the development of information technology such as the internet. Although some aspects of globalisation may be seen as positive, this chapter explores the connection between globalisation and crime.

■ Ian Taylor: globalisation and crime

One of the key writers in this area is Ian Taylor (1997). He looked at how global capitalism allows multinational corporations to move from country to country in the search for profitability. This has reduced job security and increased unemployment, particularly in the manufacturing sector, which has caused some young working-class men, in particular, to turn to crime. In a similar way to Murray, Taylor believes an underclass has developed in American and British cities, but he thinks underclass criminality is caused by material deprivation and job insecurity, not a dependency culture.

In addition, the increase in part-time and temporary jobs encourages the employment of people who are working illegally, especially illegal immigrants and those working and claiming benefits, and makes it more likely that employers pay low wages and ignore health and safety regulations. Some other areas where globalisation has affected crime are drug trafficking, people trafficking and cybercrime.

■ Drug trafficking

The drug trade was the first illegal sector to maximise profits in a globalised world. Drugs grown in South American countries such as Colombia and Middle Eastern countries like Afghanistan make their way to the UK and US via well-established routes. Globalisation has made drug trafficking far quicker and easier, and detection less likely. The more people and goods that flow in and out of a country, the more chances for drugs to be smuggled in. The potential profits are immense and the human cost devastating. It has been estimated that illegal drug use is responsible for 52,000 American deaths each year.

■ People trafficking

People trafficking is as old as human history, but is made easier and more profitable by globalisation (Figure 5.3.1). In the same way that drugs can be moved around the world, so can people. Adults are trafficked for

Crime and deviance

Fig. 5.3.1 *Globalisation has made people trafficking easier and more profitable*

Take it further

Identity theft

There are a number of methods in which a criminal can obtain an individual's personal details with a mind to committing fraud. Such methods range from the global to the local:

- Going through a person's rubbish
- Stealing identity or payment cards
- Obtaining personal information from others in public i.e. observing transactions at cash machines or in shops
- Computer hacking to find the personal details of victims in databases
- Social networking sites – criminals browse through sites such as MySpace and Facebook for online details which have been posted by users
- Using the internet to research the victims via search engines and public records databases.

prostitution, forced labour and the removal of organs. Children are trafficked for prostitution, illegal adoption, forced marriage and as soldiers. Traffickers use deception, coercion, fraud or abduction.

Cybercrime

Cybercrime is one of the fastest-growing criminal activities in the developed world. It covers a wide range of illegal activities, including financial scams, computer hacking, virus attacks, creating websites that promote racial and religious hatred, stalking by email and identity theft. Cybercrime has been made possible by the increased reliance on computers in homes and businesses, and by the spread of the internet. It has been estimated that a new cybercrime is committed every 10 seconds in the UK, with most cybercrime undetected and unreported. Most cybercrime is in the form of hacking, much of it by teenagers doing it for fun rather than to make a profit. But some hackers have broken into banks' computer systems to steal credit card numbers and account details. Identity theft is when criminals find out someone's personal details and use them to open bank accounts or get credit cards, loans, state benefits and personal documents such as passports.

Summary questions

1. What is meant by the term 'globalisation'?
2. What three types of crime are particularly influenced by globalisation?
3. Why did cybercrime not exist 20 years ago?

Environmental or green crime

Learning objective:

- Examine the environmental crimes committed by individuals, businesses and governments.

Environmental crimes, or green crimes, are crimes that damage the environment. This relatively new area of criminology is becoming increasingly relevant as environmental concerns take centre stage in the 21st century. Green crimes can be committed by individuals, businesses and governments (Figure 5.3.2). Some green crimes committed by individuals are illegal dumping of waste (fly-tipping), littering, picking protected wild flowers and dealing in endangered animals. Green crimes committed by businesses include pollution and fly-tipping. Some green crimes committed by governments include pollution and the transportation and dumping of waste material. Some environmentalists think that activities such as whaling should also be seen as criminal.

Fig. 5.3.2 *Green crimes are committed by people, businesses and governments*

Take it further

In 2005 the Environment Agency brought prosecutions against 317 companies, and nearly half were fined over £10,000 for crimes such as illegal waste disposal and water pollution. According to its website (www.environment-agency.gov. uk), in 2006 there were 910 serious pollution incidents in the UK, the lowest on record. Most were water pollution, followed by land and air pollution.

Use the Environment Agency website as a starting point to investigate this new area in more detail.

Individual green crime

Individual green crime is different to other types of crime in that many of the people involved will not consider themselves criminals. In the past, it wasn't seen as deviant to dump rubbish in lay-bys or to throw rubbish from car windows. It is only relatively recently that the public have become aware of such things, partly by the actions of the Environment Agency, the UK body responsible for protecting the environment, and partly by wider environmental concerns over global warming, etc., which have made people more environmentally aware. More unusual green crimes include the shooting of birds of prey, egg collecting (illegal since 1954), illegal poaching and badger baiting (using dogs to fight badgers). Badger baiting has been illegal since 1835 but still goes on today. An interesting example of the relative nature of crime and deviance is fox-hunting, banned in the UK in 2005. Opponents say it often damaged the environment, whereas supporters say it was a sport that helped protect the countryside.

Crime and deviance

281

■ Government green crime

A key environmental issue for countries with nuclear power stations and weapons is how to safely dispose of the waste. Some environmental charities such as Greenpeace and Friends of the Earth have argued that nuclear power is never going to be an environment-friendly form of power, and that instead of building more nuclear power stations, as the UK government plans to do, they should invest more in green energy such as wind, solar and water. Another area of concern is the danger of nuclear disasters such as the 1986 Chernobyl disaster, when a Russian nuclear power station exploded.

Whaling has taken place for thousands of years, but has led to five of the 13 species of great whales becoming endangered. Some countries that continue whaling, despite international opposition, are Canada, Norway, Iceland and Japan. Japan controversially whales for 'scientific purpose'; critics say that most of the whales end up in Japanese restaurants.

■ Summary questions

4 What is meant by green crime?

5 Give four examples of green crime.

6 Why is green crime a new study area for criminologists?

State crime

Learning objective:

■ Understand the elements of state crime, including war crimes and genocide.

Key terms

State crime: a crime committed by the government, such as a war crime, genocide and torture.

State crime is clearly an area of interest to Marxist sociologists, who generally see the government as controlled, or at least heavily influenced, by the bourgeoisie. But it would be a mistake to think that only Marxists are interested in **state crimes**, and much of the investigative work is done by journalists.

War crimes

War crimes can be committed by individuals, groups and the state. They are punishable offences under international law. War crimes committed by the state include directing attacks against civilians, torture or inhumane treatment of prisoners, taking hostages, using civilians as shields, using child soldiers, and settlement of an occupied territory. A famous series of war crimes trials were held at Nuremberg to prosecute prominent Nazis after the Second World War. Some more recent trials are the trial of former Yugoslavian president Slobodan Milosevic, who died in custody in 2006, and former Iraqi president Saddam Hussein, who was found guilty by an Iraqi court and then hanged.

It is problematic and controversial to decide what is a war crime and who is a war criminal. Some examples include the atomic bombs dropped on Hiroshima and Nagasaki and the firebombing of Dresden during the Second World War. More recently, some commentators have argued that the war in Iraq was an illegal war and that George W. Bush and Tony Blair should be tried for war crimes because of the hundreds of thousands of Iraqis who died as a result of the conflict.

Genocide

The term 'genocide' refers to violent crimes committed against national, ethnic, racial or religious groups. The word was invented by a Polish-Jewish lawyer, Raphael Lemkin, for the Nazi policy to systematically murder Jews in concentration camps during the Second World War. A more recent example of genocide is Rwanda. During just 100 days in 1994 some 937,000 Tutsis and moderate Hutus were killed by Hutus. Although they knew what was going on, the other countries of the world chose not to intervene and the slaughter continued. A more recent example is Darfur, a region of Sudan, where a civil war has been raging since 1983. It has been argued that there is an organised campaign by Janjaweed militants, nomadic Arab shepherds supported and armed by the Sudanese government, to wipe out 80 black African groups. To date, over 2 million people have been killed and 4 million displaced, with many thousands more tortured, injured and raped.

AQA Examiner's tip

Within crime and deviance, it is very important to be topical and refer to recent events. When looking at genocide, for example, refer to recent events, not just the Second World War. It is a good idea to watch the news and relevant TV programmes and to read a quality newspaper.

Summary questions

7 What is a state crime?

8 What is meant by the term 'genocide'?

9 Why are current events in Darfur an example of genocide?

Crime and deviance

Mass media and crime

Learning objective:

- ■ Understand how the mass media links to crime.

The mass media is the main source of information for most people about crime and deviance in society. The mass media tends to stereotype and sensationalise deviant behaviour. It has been estimated that personal violent crime makes up over 60 per cent of the space allocated to crime news in British newspapers such as the *Sun*, but it is less than 20 per cent of crimes reported to the police. Newspapers often show pictures of the elderly as victims of violent attacks, when in reality they are the group least likely to be attacked. Young men aged 16–24 are most at risk of violent assaults.

■ Mass media and deviancy amplification

An influential study of the mass media and its role in deviancy amplification is S. Cohen's 1972 book *Folk Devils and Moral Panics*. This is a study of the Mods and Rockers, two youth subcultures of the 1960s. The Mods listened to pop and soul music and rode scooters. The rockers listened to rock and roll and rode motor bikes. Cohen was not interested in why someone became a Mod or a Rocker, but he was interested in the role of the mass media in deviancy amplification. He focused on disturbances between the Mods and Rockers during a 1964 bank holiday weekend in Clacton (Figure 5.3.3). The media took these very minor disturbances and exaggerated them into violent clashes.

Link

Other sociologists besides Cohen have written about the mass media's role in deviancy amplification. See page 253 for Owen Gill's *Luke Street* and page 263 for Stuart Hall's *Policing the Crisis*.

At subsequent meetings the police, sensitised by the media, made more arrests and targeted anyone that looked like a Mod or Rocker. More lurid media reports followed, along with predictions of future clashes, advertising an exciting event to teenagers who more readily identified themselves as a Mod or Rocker. In other words, the mass media had partly created the very problems it condemned. The folk devils in the title are the Mods and Rockers. The moral panic is the panic generated by the mass media over the dangerous teenage gangs.

Moral panics today

It could be argued that the concepts described by Cohen are outdated. Music and fashion have become more diverse, and young people now rarely identify themselves with one particular style. Secondly, society has become more complex, fragmented and liberal, and it is less clear what constitutes deviant behaviour. Thirdly, politicians are wary of trying to create a moral panic over, say, teenage mums, in case they are seen as old-fashioned bullies. McRobbie and Thornton argue that society and the media have moved on, and that new concepts and ideas, perhaps drawn from postmodernism, are needed to study them.

Fig. 5.3.3 *Mods and Rockers: the media exaggerated the Clacton clash of 1964*

Summary questions

10 What is deviancy amplification?

11 Who were the folk devils in Cohen's book?

12 What is a moral panic?

Crime control

Crime control, prevention and punishment

Learning objective:

- Understand the different methods to try to prevent crime.

This chapter explores the three connected areas of crime control, crime prevention and punishment. It is very topical and relevant as hardly a week goes by without some new government initiative to tackle crime, especially antisocial crime. This area is linked to politics, as politicians decide what measures should be taken to reduce crime, and political parties compete to offer the most effective measures for tackling crime. As the next section shows, these measures vary greatly according to time and location.

A brief history of punishment

The main forms of punishment until the 19th century were brutal by most standards today. They included putting people in the stocks, branding with hot irons and whippings. The death penalty existed in the UK for murder until 1965 and most executions were public hangings, often attended by whole families who wanted to be entertained. Some executions attracted thousands of people. Those about to die often protested their innocence or asked forgiveness from God, and the crowd would respond with pantomime-style boos, hisses or cheers. Although prisons did exist in cities, they mainly contained prisoners awaiting execution, and were very different from the prisons built in great numbers from 1801 onwards.

These new Victorian prisons had their origins in the workhouse, where vagrants, the unemployed, the physically sick and the mentally ill were all interned together and expected to work hard in return for very basic food and shelter. During the 18th century, prisons, asylums for the mentally ill and hospitals gradually became distinct from each other. Traditional forms of punishment increasingly became seen as barbaric, and there emerged the more modern idea of using prisons to separate criminals from the rest of the population, to punish and rehabilitate them. Most of the prisons that exist today were built by the Victorians. Other forms of punishment have developed over time, including probation, fines and community service work orders. More recent punishments such as antisocial behaviour orders (ASBOs) are discussed in the next section.

New Labour and crime

New Labour was elected in 1997. One of its slogans was 'tough on crime, tough on the causes of crime'. The first part refers to catching and punishing criminals, and the second part to dealing with the causes of crime. New Labour politicians argue that since 1997, possible causes of crime such as poverty, unemployment and poor housing have all been reduced, as has the overall crime rate. Politicians from other parties no doubt disagree. What is certainly true is that since New Labour came to power it has introduced a great many laws to be 'tough on crime', particularly criminal behaviour that is deemed antisocial. New Labour has introduced ASBOs, acceptable behaviour contracts (ABCs), parenting contracts, on-the-spot fines and curfew and dispersal orders. It has also introduced community support officers (CSOs) to support the police.

ASBOs

Antisocial behaviour orders (ASBOs) were introduced in 1998. Behaviour is considered antisocial if it causes, or is likely to cause, harassment, alarm or distress. ASBOs are civil orders, usually sought by local councils, and issued by magistrates' courts. If an ASBO is breached, or broken, it becomes a criminal matter which can lead to a fine or even a jail sentence. ASBOs have been given for vandalism, theft, abusive behaviour, harassment, fly-posting, organising illegal raves and begging. By the middle of 2006 the Home Office announced that 7,356 ASBOs had been given out since 1999 in England and Wales.

Criticisms of ASBOs

The introduction of ASBOs has not been without controversy (Figure 5.4.1). It has been argued that they do not tackle the root causes of crime and are used to target the weakest and most vulnerable in society. Young people in particular can be labelled as troublemakers and given ASBOs, when in the past they would merely be cautioned by the police. It has

Fig. 5.4.1 *Do they deserve an ASBO?*

also been argued that they are ineffective as they are often breached. Some teenagers see ASBOs as badges of honour that show just how deviant they are. ASBOs can also be seen as a further attempt to destroy civil liberties and increase the power of the police and courts. There are few restrictions on what a court may impose as the terms of the ASBO, and little restriction on what can be designated as antisocial behaviour. Some fear that criticising government policies could one day be seen as enough to warrant an ASBO.

ABCs

Acceptable behaviour contracts (ABCs) are voluntary contracts. The idea behind them is to force a person to recognise how their behaviour is affecting others and to change it. They are mostly used on teenagers and are tailored to a person. If they are breached, all of the interested parties, typically the police, local council and social workers, must decide on the next step, such as an ASBO.

Parenting contracts and orders

Parenting contracts and orders target the parents of unruly children. Parenting contracts are the first step; they try to encourage the parent to improve their parenting skills and think about their responsibilities, perhaps by attending good parenting classes. Parenting orders are the next step; they can be made by magistrates' courts if the child is involved in criminal behaviour. A parenting order can require a parent to attend classes for up to three months; in extreme cases an entire family can be made to attend a residential course to sort out their problems.

Curfew and dispersal orders

Curfew and dispersal orders have caused perhaps the most controversy. They effectively ban children from public places and allow the police to deal with them if they don't comply. Councils can seek a local child curfew order for up to 90 days at a time. This requires all children under 16 in a designated area to be home before 9 o'clock, unless accompanied by an adult. The separate dispersal power, first introduced in 2004, gives police the power to break up groups of two or more if they are seen as a nuisance. If the youths try to sneak back to an area, they can be arrested and held overnight in a police cell.

These laws give the police a considerable amount of power, and critics argue that they simply result in young adults being targeted and labelled unfairly. The Children's Society, a charity that supports children, has argued that these new laws simply 'demonise young people' and give the impression that children should be locked up indoors like dangerous animals, rather than having the same rights as adults to be outside when they want to. In 2005 a boy aged 15 won a landmark High Court challenge to the legality of child curfew zones in Richmond, London. He claimed that they breached his rights under the European Convention on Human Rights. The High Court ruled that the law did not give the police a power of arrest, and officers could not force someone to come with them.

Crime and deviance

Summary questions

1. What does ASBO stand for?
2. How has the use of ASBOs been criticised?
3. Why are curfew and dispersal orders controversial?

The role of the criminal justice system

- Understand the role of the police, courts and prisons in the UK criminal justice system.

The role of the police and the courts

The role of the police is to enforce the law by protecting the public and catching criminals, and the role of the courts is to determine guilt and impose appropriate sentences. But sociologists' views on the role of the police and courts vary according to their sociological perspective.

For most functionalists, subcultural theorists, urban criminologists and those that hold right-wing perspectives, the role of the police and courts is to catch and punish mainly male working-class criminals. Most crime is committed by this group, so it is inevitable that the main role of the police and courts will be to deal with them and protect the rest of the law-abiding population. For social action theorists the role of the police is to label some groups as more criminal than others, then to target and arrest them. Other equally criminal groups are ignored. From this perspective, the working class only appears to be more criminal. The courts then impose heavier sentences on the working class than the middle class.

The traditional Marxist view argues that business crime and state crime are often ignored, and the role of the police is to target those with less power, especially the working class. Some more contemporary Marxists add minority ethnics to the list of people targeted unfairly by the police and courts. On the rare occasions when the rich and powerful do go to court, they tend to receive very light sentences. Feminists argue that the police and courts do not operate fairly, as they treat men and women differently.

The role of prisons

Being sent to prison is the most common form of punishment in the world. The world prison population is about 9 million. The US has the world's highest prison population rate at about 700 per 100,000. The UK has the highest rate in Europe at approximately 140 per 100,000. There were 18,000 prisoners in the UK in 1900. Today there are 87,000 and rising. Each prisoner costs an estimated £36,000 per year to look after. The UK has 157 prisons, and 19 new ones have been built since 1995. Given that the UK prison population is so large and expensive, it makes sense to ask what its purpose is.

Prisons have generally been seen as having at least four key goals. The importance of each goal varies with time and location.

- **Protect the public** – prisons lock away dangerous, violent, antisocial and generally undesirable people.
- **Punish criminal behaviour** – prisons are often described in the media as too soft, but most are places where few people would want to stay very long. They are increasingly overcrowded, often violent, degrading and boring.
- **Reform criminals** – educational programmes in prisons help prisoners to learn new skills so they can lead an honest life when they are released.
- **Deter people from crime** – the threat of being sent to prison should ensure most people never break the law.

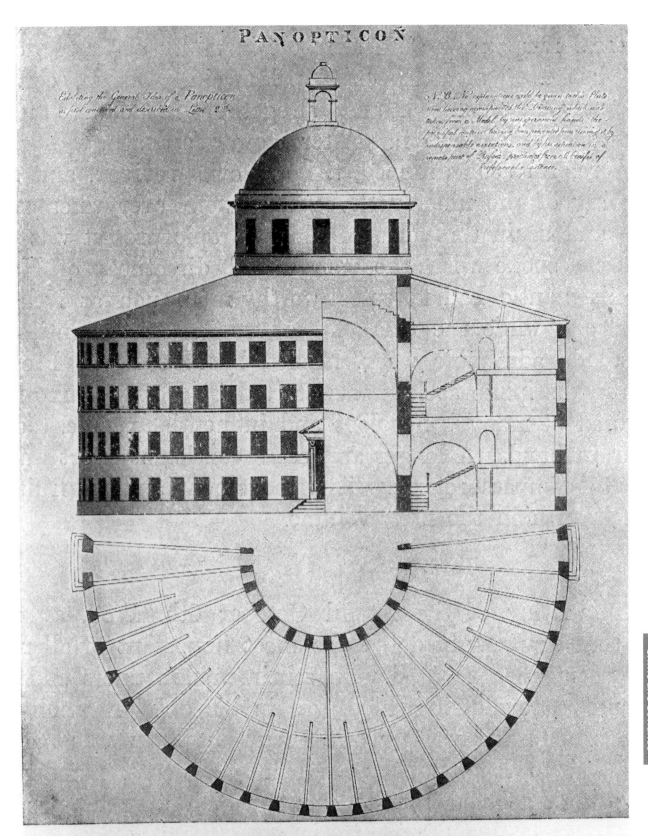

JEREMY BENTHAM'S "PANOPTICON."
(*After the original drawing of 1791.*)

Fig. 5.4.2 *Panopticon: an all-seeing prison designed by Jeremy Bentham*

■ Do prisons work?

It is very difficult to answer this question as it depends on which of the four key goals you focus on. The public are clearly protected from the most dangerous criminals if they are kept in prison for life, but not if they are released early and reoffend. Punishing criminal behaviour will depend on how strict you want prison life and conditions to be. The third goal doesn't seem to be met as about 70 per cent of prisoners reoffend, according to recent research. It is difficult to measure whether prison is an effective crime deterrent, but the size of the UK prison population indicates that perhaps it isn't.

■ Michel Foucault

Michel Foucault (1977) is a French philosopher and sociologist who has written extensively and influentially on the nature of organisations such as prisons and how they link to wider areas such as power, politics and social control. He wrote that the architecture or building of an organisation must be understood in its wider social and political context. The modern prison, according to Foucault, has its origins in a building called the panopticon, proposed by the philosopher Jeremy Bentham in 1785 (Figure 5.4.2). Although the design was never copied exactly, many of its key features were included in prisons built in the 19th century and today. The panopticon was a circular prison with an inspection tower in the centre, and the prison cells built around the outside edge. Each cell had two windows – one facing out and the other facing the inspection tower, so prisoners were visible to guards at all times.

Many modern prisons have a similar design, and Foucault points out that this surveillance pervades all of society: 'Is it surprising that prisons resemble factories, schools, barracks, hospitals, which all resemble prisons?' With the spread of closed-circuit television (CCTV) and the increase in personal data held by government departments, according to Foucault, we are all becoming prisoners. These ideas are also expressed in the novel *Nineteen Eighty-Four* by the British author George Orwell, who wrote in chilling terms of a society where individual freedom no longer exists as Big Brother is always watching. In the UK, many commentators talk about the growth of the 'nanny state', which refers to the increased controls placed over us, and continual advice about things such as smoking, drinking, diet and exercise. Some see the proposed introduction of a UK identity card as a sign that freedoms once taken for granted are slowly but surely being withdrawn.

■ Take it further

The ideas of Foucault are particularly challenging. If you have a broad interest in philosophy, politics and history, as well as sociology, make the effort to investigate them.

■ Summary questions

4 What are the four key goals of prisons?

5 What is the panopticon?

6 Explain the idea 'surveillance society'. How has its growth been criticised?

Sociology of suicide

Suicide and Durkheim

The sociology of suicide is of great interest to sociologists. Firstly, along with mental illness, suicide is a good example of deviant behaviour in society. Secondly, it illustrates the key differences between positivist and anti-positivist, or interpretivist, approaches to the study of society. Thirdly, it demonstrates how an act as seemingly individualistic as committing suicide can be studied not just psychologically, but also sociologically.

According to the official statistics, suicide rates in the UK have been declining since the early 1990s. The UK suicide rate is now about 10 per 100,000. In 2005 there were nearly 5,700 suicides, 1 per cent of all adult deaths. Three-quarters were men, which is typical of suicides in the UK in most years. The highest suicide rate normally applies to men aged 15–44, although young women aged 15–19, according to some studies, are most at risk of attempted suicide. According to the Samaritans, a charity that helps those who are depressed and considering suicide, suicide accounts for one-fifth of all deaths among young people aged 15–24, and is the second most common cause of death among young people after accidental death. The suicide rate among the homeless is about 35 times the suicide rate among the general population, and the suicide rate among young Asian women is about three times the suicide rate among young white women. According to the mental health charity Mind, some risk factors that can lead to suicide are stress, separation, divorce, social isolation, unemployment.

■ Hint

Remember that suicide is a very sensitive subject. Some people may have been directly affected by suicide. It is not a subject to joke about.

■ Durkheim on suicide

Emile Durkheim, a French sociologist, published his famous book *Suicide: A Study in Sociology* in 1897. He chose to study suicide because he wanted to show that sociology, a relatively new subject at the time, could be used to study areas previously seen as the domain of psychology. He also wanted to show that sociology was a respectable and highly academic subject, and one that could be compared to well-established and prestigious subjects like physics and chemistry. Durkheim thought sociology was also a science, and although sociology studied social groups not atoms or chemicals, the scientific principles underlying the subjects were the same.

In many ways Durkheim was a positivist. The idea of positivism was first used by the French sociologist Auguste Comte (1798–1857), and this strongly influenced Durkheim's work on suicide. Positivism is the belief that the social sciences, such as sociology and psychology, are fundamentally the same as the natural sciences of physics, chemistry and biology. Sociologists must approach the study of society in the same way as a natural scientist studies the natural world. The sociologist, like the natural scientist, must be **objective** and ensure that all research is **reliable** and **quantitative**. For his study of suicide, Durkheim used the comparative method, which in this case meant comparing the suicide rates from different European countries.

■ Key terms

Objective: free from bias or subjectivity; based on fact, not emotions.

Reliable: research is seen as reliable if it produces the same results when repeated using exactly the same methods.

Quantitative: pertaining to or concerned with quantity or its measurement; ascertaining or expressing quantity.

Crime and deviance

Durkheim considered suicide statistics to be social facts. He considered the suicide statistics gathered in each country to be a true reflection of how many people had taken their own lives. Durkheim found that the suicide rates within each country were fairly constant over a number of years. In other words, in a league table of suicides, some countries always seemed to be near the top and other countries always seemed to be lower down. Denmark and Germany, for example, were often nearer the top, and Italy, Ireland and Belgium further down. He also found that within each country, some groups seemed more likely than others to commit suicide. Protestants were more likely to commit suicide than Catholics, the unmarried more likely than the married, people without children more likely than people with children, younger people more likely than older people, educated people more likely than uneducated people, and rural dwellers more likely than city dwellers.

From his detailed analysis of suicide statistics, Durkheim felt able to conclude that the suicide rate was determined not by a person's psychological state, but by their relationship to society. Two key areas are particularly important: integration and social control. By integration Durkheim meant how connected, involved and 'bonded' a person was to society. By social control he meant how much freedom a person feels they have, and the regulations and controls placed upon them. Durkheim used these ideas to show that there are four main types of suicide in society, each linked to integration or control.

■ Types of suicide

Egoistic suicide

Egotistic suicide is when a person has too little integration and is characteristic of most suicides today, particularly in Western countries. If you are not connected or bonded to society, you are more likely to kill yourself. This is why younger, unmarried and childless people are more likely to kill themselves, because they have fewer links or roots to integrate them. It is also why the suicide rate for Catholics is lower than for Protestants, because the Catholic religion integrates its members more, through long-established rituals and beliefs. Catholicism has always been more of a communal religion and cannot be practised in isolation. Catholics are expected to attend church regularly and go to confession. Protestantism, on the other hand, is more individualistic, and there is the possibility of believing but not belonging. According to Durkheim, Protestants are also more able to question and challenge their faith, which may lead to uncertainty and an increased chance of suicide. Imagine you are a tree with roots. The more roots you have connected to family, friends, religion, clubs, and commitments, the less likely you are to commit suicide.

Altruistic suicide

Altruistic suicide is when a person has too much integration and sacrifices themselves for the good of the social group. It was more common in the past, although it is still relevant in some Asian and Middle Eastern countries. It is particularly relevant in countries where religion or national identity is strong. One example is sutteeism, where Hindu widows kill themselves at their husband's funeral by throwing themselves on the funeral pyre. Another example is Japanese kamikaze pilots crashing their planes into American warships during the Second World War. A more recent example is suicide bombers who are so well integrated with their religion that death by suicide seems like martyrdom

Fig. 5.5.1 *The aftermath of a suicide bombing*

(Figure 5.5.1). Altruistic suicide occurs when the person thinks of themselves less as an individual and more as part of a greater social group, such as a country or religion.

Anomic suicide

Anomic suicide is when a person has too much freedom and lack of regulation placed on their behaviour; it is another suicide common today in Western countries, although less common than egoistic suicide. Durkheim thought that anomic suicides occurred when society did not regulate or control the individual sufficiently. This may occur, for example, when society is going through a period of rapid social change which causes confusion and uncertainty, a process Durkheim called anomie. A classic example of this was the Wall Street Crash of 1929, when many American investors lost all their savings and some committed suicide. Anomic suicide could also take place on a smaller scale. Durkheim argued that the unexpected death of a husband could leave a widow unable to cope and this could lead her to take her own life.

Fatalistic suicide

Fatalistic suicide is when an individual has too little freedom. It is more relevant to the past, particularly slave societies such as in Greece and Rome, where slaves often committed suicide to escape the hopeless and oppressive situation they faced.

■ Criticisms of Durkheim

The main problem of Durkheim's research on suicide, according to anti-positivists or interpretivists, is that he treats suicide statistics as social facts when they should be seen as social constructs. This is not to say that suicide is an invention – it is very real – but that statistics on suicide do not reflect the truth. They are the truth as interpreted by a number of people, in particular the coroner.

Crime and deviance

The role of the coroner

The coroner is an official appointed to investigate any sudden, unexplained or suspicious death. The police normally call on the coroner, who will be an expert in medicine or the law. On suicide the coroner must be satisfied of two things: that the person killed themselves and that they intended to kill themselves. If, after their investigation, the coroner is satisfied that both these criteria have been met, a suicide verdict will be recorded. Coroners' decisions become the official suicide statistics, and it is here that anti-positivists or interpretivist sociologists challenge Durkheim.

J. D. Douglas

Durkheim accepted suicide statistics as the truth. J. D. Douglas, an interpretivist, sees them as social constructs. Douglas is particularly interested in the roles and interactions taken by all of the concerned parties after a suicide, particularly family members, friends and the coroner. He argues that if a person is well integrated into a social group, family and friends may be reluctant to accept the possibility of suicide and may try to convince the coroner that the death was an accident. They may even remove evidence of a suicide, such as destroying suicide notes. Without the suicide note, coroners are more reluctant to reach a verdict of suicide and are more likely to record the death as an accident or to record an open verdict.

In some situations, other types of evidence may be tampered with, or the body may even be moved to avoid a suicide verdict. Interpretivists like Douglas argue that the reason the suicide rate is so low in Catholic countries is not because fewer people actually kill themselves, but because of the reluctance in a Catholic country to record a verdict of suicide. In other words, it appears that the suicide rate is linked to integration, as Durkheim claimed, but in reality the level of integration simply affects the chances of a death being recorded as a suicide.

Douglas argues that although suicide statistics are social constructs – the result of negotiations between the different parties involved – it is still possible to get closer to more valid suicide statistics by carrying out case studies. This involves a very detailed qualitative analysis of each suicide, interviewing all those who knew the deceased, reading diaries, investigating their physical and mental health and examining in detail the circumstances leading up to the death. An obvious problem is that despite all this effort, the researcher will still be doing what the coroner attempts, and mistakes will still be made. The dead person is the only one that really knew whether their death was suicide, accident or murder. Despite not carrying out detailed research, Douglas still develops a list of suicide types:

- **Transformation of the soul suicide** – suicide is used as a way of getting to heaven or the 'next level'. Thirty-nine members of the religious sect Heaven's Gate took this approach in 1997.
- **Transformation of the self suicide** – suicide is used to get others to think of you differently.
- **Sympathy suicide** – suicide is used as a way of making people feel sorry for you.
- **Revenge suicide** – suicide is used as a form of revenge by making people feel guilty about your death.

■ Link

A number of religious sects, most notably Heaven's Gate, the People's Temple and the Branch Davidians, have ended in suicide. The Heaven's Gate suicides could be seen as transformation of the soul suicides, and the People's Temple and Branch Davidian suicides could be seen as murders.

Crime and deviance

J. Baechler

The French sociologist Jean Baechler (1979) agrees with Douglas that case studies of suicide enables researchers to get closer to valid suicide statistics. From an analysis of the existing material available on suicide, he argues that suicidal behaviour is best seen as an extreme form of 'problem solving' by people who can see no other solution to their situations. Here are three of the main types of suicide according to Baechler:

- **Escapist suicides** are where suicide is used as an escape from problems such as grief or a terminal illness.
- **Aggressive suicides** are where suicide is used as a way of punishing someone; they are the same as revenge suicides.
- **Transfiguration suicides** are where suicide is used as a way of going to the afterlife or joining a loved one who recently died.

J. Maxwell Atkinson

The problem with Douglas and Baechler is that they both argue that, with intensive research, it is possible to get close to the 'real' suicide rate. Atkinson (1978), writing as a phenomenologist, argues that this is a futile quest as the real suicide rate doesn't exist and that no amount of research can find it. In many ways, Atkinson is similar to Douglas as they both look at the role of the coroner. The difference is that Atkinson did, more extensive research which led him to conclude that any attempt to develop suicide types, as Durkheim, Douglas and Baechler did, are all doomed to fail, as all coroners do is categorise death, not reveal the truth. Atkinson carried out detailed interviews with coroners, attended coroners' courts, observed a coroner at work and examined records. He argues that coroners, despite their training and experience, still employ a 'common sense theory' of suicide and that if the 'evidence' fits the theory, the death will be categorised as a suicide. Four types of evidence are particularly important:

- Have suicide notes been left? If they have, the recording of the death as a suicide is more likely. The problem here, as Douglas pointed out, is that they could have been destroyed or invented by a murderer.
- How did the death occur? Death by drugs, hanging, drowning or gassing are normally seen as suicide, but not road deaths. Again, it is just the coroner's opinion that a death was or wasn't a suicide. The problem here is that someone may kill themselves by crashing their car to avoid embarrassment to their families, or to avoid complications when claiming life insurance, and that some of the more obvious ways of being killed are accidents or even murder.
- Where did the death occur? Death of a farmer by gunshot, for example, is more likely to be seen as suicide if it happened inside the farmhouse than if it happened outside.
- What was the mental health of the deceased? A history of mental illness, lack of stable home life, abuse in childhood, unemployment and failed relationships are all factors considered by the coroner to be reasons for suicide. The problem here is clearly that the coroner is making educated guesses at best, and only the dead person can say for certain what their mental health was at the point of death.

Atkinson concludes that coroners are simply using their taken-for-granted stereotypes or assumptions about a 'typical suicide', and that these assumptions then become the official statistics on suicide and are seen as social facts. Sociologists who then base their ideas on these official statistics and see them as social facts, such as Durkheim, are clearly making a big mistake. However, equally foolish are sociologists such as Douglas and Bacchler who, despite criticising Durkheim, still believe that a true measure of the suicide rate is possible if you conduct enough qualitative research. They fall into the same trap, and develop typologies of suicide which only work if you know for sure that someone deliberately killed themselves, but that is impossible, according to Atkinson.

One criticism of Atkinson is that he is very dismissive of coroners and sees their work as little more than 'common sense'. Coroners argue that it is difficult to know for certain whether a death is a suicide, but it is their job to get as close to the truth as possible. Coroners recognise the difficulties, which is why an open verdict is used more often than a suicide verdict. If the ideas of phenomenologists like Atkinson are accepted, then no research is possible as everything is ultimately a social construct, including the ideas of phenomenologists.

Steve Taylor

Steve Taylor (1982) has looked at people hit by tube trains on the London Underground. Over a 12-month period he found 32 deaths with no witnesses and no suicide notes. Of these, 17 were recorded as suicide, 5 as accidental deaths and 10 were given open verdicts. Taylor agrees with Douglas and Atkinson that coroners use 'common sense assumptions' such as a history of mental illness, family problems and unemployment. Taylor then constructs a fourfold typology of suicides in a similar way to Douglas and Baechler. Yet, as Atkinson might observe, there is no point constructing a list of suicide types unless you are 100 per cent sure that someone killed themselves. As you can never have that certainty, don't construct suicide typologies.

AQA Examiner's tip

In any question on the advantages and disadvantages of official statistics as a research method, it is essential to include Durkheim's use of suicide statistics and how it was criticised, plus the information in the next section.

Summary questions

1. What was Durkheim's research method?
2. What are Durkheim's four types of suicide?
3. How does Douglas criticise Durkheim?
4. What is the problem with constructing any suicide typology?

Research methods

Official crime statistics, self-report studies, etc.

Learning objective:

 Examine the different methods used to study crime.

Link

See pages 301–302 for more on the British Crime Survey.

Crime in England and Wales is measured using two different sources – the crimes reported to the police and recorded by the police, and the British Crime Survey. Both of these statistical sources have different strengths and weaknesses.

Police recorded crime

The most recent official Home Office report states that 5.4 million crimes were recorded by the police in 2006, down 2 per cent on the previous year. Violent crime, burglary and offences against vehicles were down, but robbery was up by 3 per cent. The problem with statistics like these is that they depend on two key areas – the reporting of crime to the police and the recording of crime by the police.

Reporting crime

Not all crimes are reported to the police, which clearly has a huge impact on the validity of the crime statistics. Here are some reasons why crimes may be unreported:

- fear of reprisals
- the crime may involve a family member or friend
- the incident may be seen as too trivial to report
- fear or distrust of the police
- embarrassment if it is a sexual crime
- lack of awareness that a crime has been committed.

Recording crime

Not all crimes are recorded by the police, which has a huge impact on the validity of the crime statistics. The police may not record a crime because they do not believe that a crime has been committed. The police use their discretion and issue a warning or advice without making it official. If the police arrested every drunk causing a nuisance on a Saturday night, the police cells would be even fuller than they already are, and the police would never complete all the paperwork that goes with each arrest. The priorities of the chief constable will also make a difference. If they order a crackdown on a particular group, such as joyriders, the police records will show an increase in joyriding over the period of the crackdown, but nothing has changed in reality.

British Crime Survey

The British Crime Survey (BCS) is used by the Home Office to give a more accurate picture of levels of crime in the UK. It is a large-scale questionnaire which asks a representative sample of over 40,000 people aged 16 or over if they have been a victim of crime. The latest survey shows an overall decline in crime since 1995 but that people's fear of

Crime and deviance

crime has risen. It estimated that 11.3 million crimes had been committed, over twice those recorded by the police.

Advantages

■ Victim surveys such as the BCS provide a more valid measure of crime than using police records alone.

■ They allow comparisons to be made between variables such as gender, ethnicity and age to see what type of crime affects what social group.

■ As they are carried out by asking the same questions each year, they should be more valid than relying on police records, which may be affected by changes in how crimes are recorded.

■ The BCS is a social survey, so it gives quantitative data that is representative and reliable. It is a method favoured by positivists.

Disadvantages

■ People may have difficulty remembering exactly whether and how often they have been victims of crime.

■ People may have been a victim of crime and not realise it.

■ People may not take the questionnaire seriously and give false answers.

■ The BCS doesn't cover all crimes. Fraud, drug offences and corporate crimes are not included.

■ The BCS aims to be representative by including respondents from all over the country, but this just provides an average figure of the amount of crime experienced and may disguise the fact that crime is far higher in some areas than others.

■ The 2006 survey showed that violent crime, for example, hadn't increased, but this is just an average for the whole of the UK, and in some inner-city areas it could well have increased.

■ Some people may think they have been a victim of crime when they haven't really. A late-night knock on the door could be seen as an attempted burglary or a misplaced credit card could be seen as theft.

■ As a social survey, the BCS may be criticised by anti-positivists for lack of qualitative data, validity and *verstehen*.

Key terms

Verstehen: the use of empathy in the sociological or historical understanding of human action and behaviour.

Is there more crime now than in the past?

According to the Home Office, crime in England and Wales increased between 1981 and 1995, then fell sharply and is now stable. The Home Office claims there has been an overall fall of 42 per cent since 1995. Politicians from other parties, and many academics, dispute these claims for the reasons discussed above. Several other factors affect the crime rate in society:

■ As police training and equipment improve, more people are arrested, but this doesn't necessarily mean that more crime has been committed. The use of genetic fingerprinting will also lead to higher detection rates.

■ If police numbers are higher, more people will be arrested. If there is a shortage of officers, arrest rates will decrease.

■ If the police target a specific group, such as prostitutes, arrest rates for that group will obviously increase. This does not mean that prostitution has increased.

■ Mobile phone theft is far higher now than in the 1990s (Figure 5.6.1). This may be because street crime has increased, or it may be because there are more mobile phones to steal.

When a crime becomes publicised, such as domestic violence or child abuse, reporting of it increases and more arrests are made. This doesn't mean that the crime is increasing.

How do theories view official crime statistics?

Sociologists have taken two broad approaches to the usefulness of official statistics on crime and deviance. The early sociological theories such as functionalism, subcultural and environmental criminology, and perspectives from the right, tend to see them as social facts. In other words, they accept them as valid – the truth. They then develop theories to explain why young working-class men become criminal, such as strain or subcultural theories. Later perspectives, including social action and Marxist theories, tend to see them as social constructs. In other words, they do not see them as valid, so they use different concepts such as labelling, deviancy amplification and selective law enforcement to explain crime.

Fig. 5.6.1 *Mobile phone theft is far higher now than in the 1990s*

Self-report studies

Self-report studies involve asking people about their own illegal activities. They are usually based on anonymous questionnaires. The feminist sociologist Campbell used self-report studies in her research on delinquent girls. These studies show higher rates of crime and deviance than the official statistics. They also show less difference between males and females, working class and middle class, young and old. Sociologists such as feminists, social action theorists and Marxists argue that these findings confirm their doubts about the validity of official statistics.

Advantages

- They may be more valid than official statistics.
- They can be compared with official statistics to see what groups are over-represented.
- They can uncover 'victimless' crimes such as illegal drug use.
- Self-report studies are social surveys, so they generally have the advantages of social surveys.

Disadvantages

- It is very possible that people do not tell the complete truth when filling in a self-report study. Despite the guarantee of anonymity, some people may understate their deviant activity due to embarrassment and shame. Younger people may exaggerate due to bravado and the desire to appear hard.
- Under-reporting may also occur due to forgetfulness, especially if an older person tries to remember their teenage years.
- Self-report studies are social surveys, so they generally have the disadvantages of social surveys.

Alternative methods to study deviance

Participant observation

One of the most famous studies using covert participant observation was James Patrick's 1973 study *Glasgow Gang Observed*. Patrick, a teacher at an approved school, was invited by a gang member to see for himself what life was like in a Glasgow street gang. Patrick joined in most of the activities of the gang but was forced to leave when other gang members became suspicious about his real motives for being in the gang.

Crime and deviance

Link

See page 255 for more on the RDU.

Erving Goffman (1961) also used this method when he studied life in an American mental institution, or asylum. He worked as the assistant athletics coach, a covert role that allowed him to see at first hand how patients responded to life in a mental institution and how the patients used a number of different strategies to cope. Chambliss used overt participant observation in his study of the RDU. Paul Willis (1977) used overt participant observation in his study of 12 working-class deviant 'lads' who engaged in antisocial behaviour and the development of an anti-school subculture.

Hobbs (1988) used a variety of methods in his study of petty criminals and the police in the East End of London. He conducted overt participant observation of police detectives in a criminal investigation department (CID) office and covert participant observation in pubs, courts and court canteens. He also carried out informal and formal interviews with a detective who became his main informant, and overt participant observation with petty criminals in a pub, who were aware that he was researching them. Hobbs was brought up in the East End of London; he had the right personal characteristics of working-class background, accent and local knowledge to fit in with his research subjects.

Advantages

- This method should allow for the most verstehen, or empathy, of any research method. In the studies discussed above, the researchers were was able to immerse themselves into the lives of those being studied. And as far as possible, they were able to see the world through someone else's eyes.

- If the group don't realise they are being observed, this should be a method that has a high degree of validity. Even if the research is overt, if the researcher spends a long time with the group and gains their trust, the research should have high validity.

- The research takes place in a natural setting not an artificial setting.

- The researcher may discover areas to research that they were unaware of initially.

- The method is time-consuming but inexpensive.

Disadvantages

- There are ethical problems such as lack of informed consent if the research is covert. Patrick was also breaking the law by carrying weapons and acting as a lookout for the police when the gang were engaged in criminal activities. On one occasion he took illegal drugs. Hobbs held information on criminal activities that would have been useful to the police, but he kept it to himself.

- Are the group going to behave normally with the presence of an outsider, even if they accept the new person as one of their own?

- It is difficult to record the findings. Patrick and Hobbs had to rely on memory to record what they had observed. You cannot take notes or use a tape recorder when you are undercover.

- There is a danger of going native or becoming too involved and subjective. Patrick knew at least one of the gang members, so he may have found it difficult to be a neutral participant.

- Small samples may not be representative. Patrick recognised this in his book and made it clear that his study looked at just one gang in one city at one particular time; it was not intended to be a representative piece of research.

Informal interviews

Pat Carlen used informal or semi-structured interviews to study women. Dobash and Dobash (1979), a husband and wife team, also used this method to interview female victims of domestic violence in refuges in Scotland. They used female research assistants to conduct the interviews, as male interviewers would have been inappropriate for ethical and practical reasons.

Advantages

- This method allows people to speak openly and without the restrictions of a social survey. It is unlikely that the women in Carlen's study, for example, would have responded openly and positively to a questionnaire.
- This method allows for some degree of verstehen, or empathy, with those interviewed.
- This method should have high validity as long as the interviewees tell the truth.
- Feminists favour this method as it is seen as more democratic and non-hierarchical than other methods.

Disadvantages

- Small samples may not be representative and may not allow generalised statements to be made. Carlen interviewed only 39 women.
- The age, sex, gender or social class of the interviewer could influence the answers given by the interviewee.
- The interviews and the subsequent analysis of data may be time-consuming. Some of the interviews in the Dobash and Dobash study were up to 12 hours long.

Field experiments

Rosenhan did field experiments to study admissions to psychiatric hospitals.

Advantages

- The research takes place in a natural setting.
- If those being experimented on don't realise it, the research should be valid.
- The experiment may be the only method that can be used to expose the weakness of something. This was true of Rosenhan's research.

Disadvantages

- Experiments normally involve small samples and the samples may not be representative.
- Experiments have ethical issues such as lack of informed consent and potential harm to those taking part.
- The age, sex, gender or social class of the experimenter and the participants could make a difference to the findings.

Social surveys

The British Crime Survey (BCS) is a good example of a social survey or questionnaire. It is administered in the form of a structured interview carried out by interviewers from an independent research agency.

Link

See page 273–275 for more on Pat Carlen's informal or semi-structured interviews to study women in prison.

Link

See pages 258–259 for more on Rosenhan's study of people admitted to psychiatric hospitals.

Crime and deviance

Link

See page 297 for more on the British Crime Survey.

The sample is a nationally representative sample created using randomly selected addresses from the Post Office address file – the sampling frame. It is not compulsory to take part in the sample and all information gathered is confidential. The response rate is over 80 per cent.

Secondary sources

Official statistics on crime and suicide are the main secondary sources used by sociologists. One other secondary method used by Brown and Clare (2005) is personal historical documents in the form of prison autobiographies. They examined a range of autobiographies written by prisoners and published since the mid 19th century. These autobiographies provide an alternative account to the official reports on prison life. This is a method favoured by anti-positivists as it allows for some degree of verstehen and is a qualitative source of rich and emotional data. Positivists say the research lacks representativeness and objectivity.

Summary questions

1 How is crime in England and Wales measured?
2 Give three reasons why someone may not report a crime.
3 What is a self-report study?
4 Are qualitative methods the best way to study crime?

Topic summary

- Crime is behaviour that breaks the formal written laws of a society.
- Deviance is behaviour that goes against the norms of a society.
- Crime and deviance are social constructs that change according to time and location.
- Sociologists hold very different views on which social class, gender, age and ethnic groups commit the most crimes in society.
- Sociologists hold very different views on the usefulness of official crime statistics.
- Functionalist theory argues that a limited amount of crime can be useful. Deviance is caused by inappropriate responses to achieving the American dream.
- Subcultural theory looks at how crime is committed collectively in gangs.
- Environmental theory looks at the relationship between patterns of crime and where people live, work and have their leisure.
- Social action theory looks at how groups with the least power in society become unfairly labelled as deviant by those with the greatest power.
- Traditional Marxists argue that capitalism is itself criminal and that it causes crime.
- New criminology proposes the need for a 'fully social theory of crime and deviance' and focuses particularly on the relationship between ethnicity and crime.
- New Left realists challenge other Marxist views and take an alternative view on ethnicity and crime.
- Perspectives from the right move away from explaining crime to focus on preventing crime.
- Postmodernists challenge all the theories considered so far.
- Social composition looks at the relationship between crime and ethnicity, gender, social class and age.
- Victimology focuses on the victims of crime.
- Globalisation looks at how the shrinking of the world has affected crime.
- Environmental crimes are crimes that damage the environment.
- State crimes are crimes committed by governments; examples are political corruption, war crimes and genocide.
- The mass media can increase crime, a process known as deviancy amplification.
- Throughout history different attempts have been made to reduce crime.
- Sociologists take very different approaches to the role and usefulness of the police, courts and prisons.
- Suicide is a good example of deviant behaviour and illustrates the key differences between positivist and anti-positivist approaches in sociology.
- Crime and deviance research methods can be quantitative or qualitative; their usefulness depends on the theoretical approach of the sociologist.

■ Further resources

Books and articles

Here are some of the most important, influential or interesting books and articles about crime and deviance.

■ J. Atkinson, *Discovering Suicide*, Macmillan, 1978

■ H. Becker, *Outsiders: Studies in The Sociology of Deviance*, Macmillan, 1963

■ P. Carlen, *Women, Crime and Poverty*, Open University Press, 1988

■ W. Chambliss, The Saints and the Roughnecks. *Society*, Vol. 11, 224–231, 1973

■ A. Cohen, *Delinquent Boys, the Culture of the Gang*, Free Press, 1955

■ S. Cohen, *Folk Devils and Moral Panics*, Routledge, 2002; first published 1972

■ O. Gill, *Luke Street*, Macmillan, 1977

■ E. Goffman, *Asylums*, Penguin, 1968

■ S. Hall, *Policing the Crisis*, Macmillan, 1979

■ J. Lea and J. Young, *What Is To Be Done About Law and Order*, Penguin, 1984

■ R. Merton, 'Social structure and anomie'. *American Sociological Review*, Vol. 3, 672–682, 1938

■ J. Patrick, *A Glasgow Gang Observed*, Eyre-Methuen, 1973

■ I. Taylor, P. Walton and J. Young, *The New Criminology*, Routledge & Kegan Paul, 1973

Websites

■ www.homeoffice.gov.uk
Information on crime statistics and victim studies

■ www.crimeinfo.org.uk
A useful summary of crime-related topics and further weblinks

■ www.greenpeace.org.uk
Information on environmental crimes

■ www.sane.org.uk
Information on mental illness

■ www.samaritans.org.uk
Information on mental illness and suicide

■ www.liberty-human-rights.org.uk
Information on civil liberties and human rights

Films

■ *One Flew Over the Cuckoo's Nest* (1975)
About conditions in an American mental institution; it is relevant to social action views on mental illness

■ *Girl, Interrupted* (1999)
Another film about conditions in an American mental institution; it is relevant to social action views on mental illness

■ *A Beautiful Mind* (2001)
About schizophrenia; it is relevant to social action views on mental illness

■ *This Is England* (2006)
About UK gangs

■ *Rogue Trader* (1999)
Relevant to white-collar crime

■ *JFK* (1991)
Relevant to state crime

■ *Crash* (2004)
Relevant to racism in the US

- *City of God* (2002)
  About street gangs in Brazil
- *Donnie Brasco* (1997)
  Relevant to the research method of participant observation
- *The Godfather* (1972)
  About organised crime

AQA Examination-style questions

General Certificate of Education
Advanced Level Examination
Section A from Paper 4

SOCIOLOGY Unit 4
For this paper you must have:
a 12-page answer book
Time allowed 2 hours

Instructions

Use black ink or black ball-point pen.

Write the information required on the front of your answer book. The Examining Body for this paper is AQA. The paper reference is SCLY4.

This paper is divided into **two** Sections.

Choose **one** section and answer **all** parts of the question from that Section.

Do not answer questions from more than one section.

Information

The maximum mark for this paper is 90.

The marks for part questions are shown in brackets.

SAMPLE 1

Section A: Crime and Deviance

You are advised to spend approximately 45 minutes on Question 1
You are advised to spend approximately 30 minutes on Question 2
You are advised to spend approximately 45 minutes on Question 3
Total for this section: 90 marks

1   Read Item A below and answer the question that follows.

> **Item A**
>
> In recent years there has been an increasing focus on the problems of gangs in the British urban environment. Typically such gangs are seen to consist of young men, often from economically disadvantaged or immigrant groups. One disturbing phenomenon is that the ages of the gang members can be as low as 10 or 11. Commentators have become increasingly concerned that in some inner-city areas young children are growing up surrounded by a sub-culture which seems to glorify drugs and violence.

This sub-culture is seen as the major factor in the growth of knife and firearms-related crime among young people in British inner cities. In an attempt to respond the Government has adopted a three-pronged approach. This uses a combination of targeted policing and heavier sentences, and the development of community facilities for young people. The last is supposed to alleviate the criticism most often raised by young people themselves, that 'there is nothing for them to do.' Money has also been poured into educational facilities, in much the same way as the US government did in the 'Head Start' programmes of the 1960s.

Although it has only acquired major media coverage in Britain over the last decade or so, gang membership is not a new phenomenon. Much of the sociological research into deviant and criminal behaviour in America in the 1950s and 1960s focused on gang membership and sub-cultures, again usually amongst the economically deprived.

Source: Written by Hamish Joyce

(a) Examine the effectiveness of recent Government initiatives to tackle levels of violent crime amongst young people in Britain.

(12 marks)

(b) Assess the value of sub-cultural approaches to our understanding of deviant behaviour.

(21 marks)

2 This question requires you to apply your knowledge and understanding of sociological research methods to the study of this particular issue in crime and deviance.

Read Item B below and answer parts (a) and (b) that follow.

Item B

The study of suicide is seen by many sociologists as typical of the ongoing methodological and theoretical debate between those who support a rigorously-structured, large-scale scientific approach to the study of society, and those for whom such an approach cannot deliver the true meanings and understandings given by actors in social situations. As a result such critics prefer a more in-depth, qualitative approach. Typically the former group are lumped together under the positivist label, and the latter group referred to variously as phenomenologists or interpretivists.

Suicide is seen as epitomising this debate because the seminal work 'Le Suicide' by Emile Durkheim in many ways represents the first sustained attempt by a sociologist to justify through statistical research the assertion that all human behaviour is socially derived, and can be both observed and measured scientifically. Durkheim's attempts to establish variables which make someone more or less likely to commit suicide is often contrasted with phenomenologist Atkinson's work, which claims that suicide is death as defined by coroners, who apply a 'common-sense theory' to a given set of circumstances. If the death fits a previously-defined pattern, they classify it as suicide.

Source: Written by Hamish Joyce

(a) Identify and briefly explain three problems of using phenomenological approaches to research suicide rates.

(9 marks)

(b) Using material from Item B and elsewhere, assess the strengths and limitations of positivist research into the study of deviant behaviour.

(15 marks)

3 'Despite its origins in the early industrial society of the nineteenth century, Marxism remains the only sociological perspective to offer a coherent and all-encompassing explanation for social change'. To what extent do sociological arguments and evidence support this view?

(33 marks)

SAMPLE 2

Section A: Crime and Deviance

You are advised to spend approximately 45 minutes on Question 1

You are advised to spend approximately 30 minutes on Question 2

You are advised to spend approximately 45 minutes on Question 3

Total for this section: 90 marks

1   Read Item A below and answer the question that follows.

Item A

For much of the 1970s and early 1980s football hooliganism was regarded as a serious social problem in Britain. Media reports contrasted terraces full of scarf-wearing, chanting yobs with the more peaceful, family-oriented mass spectator sports of the USA, and the allegedly more civilised fans in our European neighbours. Media outrage reached its height at the time of the Heyssel Stadium disaster in 1981, when dozens of Italian fans lost their lives after part of the stadium collapsed as a result of crowd trouble between Liverpool and Italian Supporters.

More recently, regular football hooliganism has largely been eradicated in Britain by redesigning stadia, more sophisticated security and policing, and by the use of banning orders on known hooligans. However, British fans are still notorious for their behaviour at matches overseas, with television pictures of drunkenness and running battles with other fans and police almost seen as almost inevitable every time there is a major European tournament. However many sociological commentators suggest that much of this behaviour is a direct result of the level of media interest, with British fans and their European counterparts acting out roles for mass audience consumption that are ascribed to them by media creation of moral panics.

Source: Written by Hamish Joyce

(a)   Critically examine sociological research on the role of the media on levels of antisocial behaviour (such as football hooliganism) in society (Item A).   *(12 marks)*

(b)   Assess the usefulness of labelling theory to an understanding of deviance.   *(21 marks)*

2   This question requires you to apply your knowledge and understanding of sociological research methods to the study of this particular issue in crime and deviance.

Read Item B below and answer parts (a) and (b) that follow.

Item B

Traditional Marxist approaches to crime tended to see it in terms of the power relationships in society, pointing to laws which were designed to preserve the rights of the bourgeoisie as being responsible for the fact that most crime was committed by the working class. Work published in the 1970s by sociologists such as Chambliss and Pearce also suggested that a considerable amount of so-called white collar crime was hidden by the selective reporting and policing of such activity, and that official statistics therefore presented an ideologically distorted view of the nature and level of crime.

More recent Marxist work, often part of the 'New Criminology', suggests that not only is the majority of crime committed by the working class, but it is also the working class who are most likely to be the victims of crime. A similar conclusion could be reached about the relative prevalence of certain ethnic minority groups in crime statistics. Much of their evidence came from research into perceptions and experiences of crime rather than into convictions, which hitherto formed the basis of most official statistics.

Source: Written by Hamish Joyce

(a)   Identify and briefly explain three reasons why official crime statistics may not give a true picture of the level of crime in Britain.   *(9 marks)*

(b)   Using material from Item B and elsewhere, assess the strengths and limitations of researching perceptions and experiences as a means of measuring the real level of crime in a society.   *(15 marks)*

3   'With the arrival of a post-modernist society the classical sociological structural perspectives have little to offer our understanding of human social action.' How far do sociological evidence and arguments support this view?   *(33 marks)*

END OF THE UNIT 4 SECTION A
SAMPLE QUESTIONS

Stratification and differentiation

Introduction

Stratification describes the formation of layers in a structure. Social stratification refers to the formation of different groups in society where some have greater privileges than others.

Differentiation

Groups that form strata in society often share a common identity that goes beyond simply their name. People who identify themselves as working-class may recognise a common identity that is evident in accents or the areas they live in. If a person from an upper middle-class background chooses a lifestyle that gives them an income that is the same as people from working-class backgrounds, they don't automatically become working-class. Their accent and attitudes will identify them as different. Using income or career as a sole indicator of social class is not always helpful. Some specific differences between people create inequality, and when this is related to the social structure it is known as structured social inequality.

Social inequality

Whereas social stratification refers to relatively fixed and **hierarchical** structures in society, social inequality refers to the differences in life chances that occur. There is unequal distribution of advantages or life chances between people in society and a strong connection between stratification and inequality; the groups in the lower strata will normally be those who experience the most disadvantage.

Some might argue that wealth is the most important factor that determines a person's place in society. Wealth gives people life chances. Of course, money is not the only currency in society. Social status, or prestige, is the extent to which others hold a person in high regard relating to career, heredity or personal qualities. Wealth, **power** and status all influence a person's position in the social structure and the extent to which they have access to positive life chances.

Subcultures

An underclass has emerged from within the traditional British working class; its members have little or no opportunity to improve their situation. They may be the long-term unemployed and people who cannot work because they drink so much alcohol. Alcohol users form a subculture that shares a common identity and a set of norms and values distinct from others in the underclass. Another group of people do not work because they have inherited wealth. They are set apart from the rest of the upper classes by a lifestyle that is not structured around a career or family business. In both these examples, people in the subculture will identify with the strata in society they have emerged from, but they share a common identity within their own subculture.

Social class has undergone a great deal of sociological investigation. Much has been based on an assumption that social class is the primary structure around which society operates. Contemporary sociologists have questioned this assumption. They argue that social class no longer has the relevance it once had, that other formations of groups or subcultures are emerging, and that values besides economic prestige influence social status.

Key terms

Hierarchical: the higher a person's position in a structure, the more prestigious their position in that structure.

Power: the amount of influence a person has to get others to comply with their wishes. It can be political, personal or financial.

Stratification ...

Defining and measuring social class

Learning objective:

- Describe, evaluate and compare the Registrar General's Scale and the new Socio-Economic Classification.

Most people, if asked, would be able to identify three distinct social classes in society: upper, middle and working. Sociologists have also broadly categorised social classes in a similar way but have added a fourth class, the underclass.

- **Upper class** – this group originally consisted of the landowning aristocracy but over the years it has grown to include those who are wealthy from ownership or investment in business. Many people in the upper class inherit wealth from previous generations.

- **Middle class** – anyone who makes their living from non-manual work. This huge group includes a wide range of professions from highly paid professionals, such as judges and consultant physicians to those in public service jobs, such as teachers, nurses and social workers plus secretaries and administrative workers. This class is the largest and most complex and it continues to grow as the number of manual jobs reduces.

- **Working class** – people who earn their living from manual and unskilled work. They have poorer life chances than middle- or upper-class people.

- **Underclass** – people who are long-term unemployed or who rely completely on state benefits for survival. This group has the poorest life chances of all.

The four classes described here give an outline of broad strata in British society. For an accurate definition of social class as accepted by government departments, a much more complex system has to be used. The system of class definition as used by successive governments has been redefined a number of times to make it fit for purpose. Up until 2000 social class was measured using the Registrar General's Scale, or the RG scale (Table 6.1.1).

Table 6.1.1 *RG scale*

Class	Description
1	Professional: lawyers, doctors, directors
2	Intermediate: teachers, nurses, managers
3n	Skilled non-manual: secretaries, IT technicians
3m	Skilled manual: electricians, builders, plumbers
4	Semi-skilled manual: postal workers, factory process workers
5	Unskilled manual: refuse collectors, cleaners

Source: Office of Population Censuses and Surveys (OPCS) 1981

This scale had a number of weaknesses. Figures were based on the employment of the adult male in a household. This meant that if a woman lawyer was married to a male refuse collector, the household would be put in class 5. This was inaccurate and sexist, as it assumed that the highest earner in a household is always an adult male. Other weaknesses include:

- Households where two adults are employed in class 3 and there are no children may be better off financially than a household where there is one income earner in class 1 or 2.
- People who are rich enough not to work are not included.
- Those who have always lived on state benefits are not included.
- Housewives are not included.
- Unemployed people are classed according to their last job.
- There are massive variations between incomes in the class groups: for example, a consultant physician earns much more than a junior doctor.

In 2000 the old RG scale was changed to the National Statistics Socio-Economic Classification (NS-SEC). The new system was developed because major changes to the workforce in Britain made the old system obsolete. These changes included a huge decline in manufacturing industries, a massive increase in service industries and a shift in gender roles that brought the majority of adult women into the workforce. The new classification also addressed some of the problems and anomalies associated with the old system.

NS-SEC (Table 6.1.2) takes account of three different factors:

- **Employment relations** considers whether people are employers, employed or self-employed, whether they are salaried or paid weekly and the size of the organisation.
- **Labour market** considers the size of the person's salary, benefits, prospects and security.
- **Work situation** considers how much authority and influence the person has. For instance, there is the recognition that the managing director of a large organisation has considerable authority and influence over a large number of people as well as a high salary. Some other occupations may have a high salary but less influence, e.g. the owner of a small building firm.

The new classification system is based on a system devised by Goldthorpe for his Oxford mobility studies of 1980 and 1987.

Take it further

Find out more about the change of scale at www.statistics.gov.uk/methods_quality/ns_sec.

Hint

Goldthorpe looked at social class from a neo-Weberian perspective. This perspective recognises that social class is a complex system of layers associated not only with economic power but also with prestige and social and political influence. To get a really good mark for your answer, show that you understand the different perspectives on stratification and how they compare with each another. You can read more about different perspectives on social class later in the topic.

Table 6.1.2 *NS-SEC*

Class	Description
1	Higher managerial and professional: doctors, lawyers, academic professors, company directors
2	Lower managerial and professional: social workers, teachers, police officers, nurses
3	Intermediate: secretaries, paramedics, IT technicians
4	Small employers and self-employed: small shop and restaurant owners, self-employed tradespeople
5	Lower supervisory and technical: shop supervisor, factory overseer
6	Semi-routine: postal delivery worker, sales assistant
7	Routine: waiter, labourer, cleaner,
8	Never worked and long-term unemployed: a person who hasn't worked for more than one year

Source: Office for National Statistics, 2001

How to answer a question on defining and measuring social class

To answer a question about defining and measuring social class, it is important to discuss the change to the classification system and to highlight the differences between the two systems:

- The RG scale was based on skill. NS-SEC is based on employment relations, the labour market and work situation (see above).
- The RG scale had five classes whereas NS-SEC has eight.
- There is no longer a division between manual and non-manual workers.
- The RG scale had no classification for those who have never worked or who live on long-term benefits. NS-SEC recognises their existence and gives them a classification. Note that class 8 does not include those who have never worked because of wealth. It only includes those who have never worked and are disadvantaged. This group may be described as the underclass.
- Some occupations have changed their position on the scale because of market factors. For example, shop assistants are at a lower level and teachers higher because of relative changes in pay and conditions.
- Women are now recognised independently as workers and are not classed according to a spouse's occupation.

Answers that show an ability to evaluate as well as present facts will always gain better marks. To do this you should extend your answer not only to describe differences but also to highlight potential weaknesses:

- Differences in income within one social class are not recognised.
- A person's perception of their own social class may differ from this classification because a person's status is not only about occupation. For instance, the son of a wealthy landowner who trains to be a carpenter may not recognise himself as social class 4 any more than the daughter of a miner who becomes a head teacher may recognise herself as social class 1. The subjective nature of social class and status is not easily classifiable.
- There is still no category for those who are so wealthy that they never need to work. This may be partly due to the difficulty of classifying a diverse group of people. There is a difference between those who inherit old money and move in prestigious social circles and an unemployed person who wins the lottery.

Summary question

1 What are the main differences between the RG scale and NS-SEC?

Theories of social class

Learning objectives:

- Explain functionalist, Marxist, Weberian and postmodern theories of stratification.

- Compare and contrast the explanations.

- Evaluate theoretical explanations by giving at least one strength and one weakness.

AQA Examiner's tip

When revising, make sure you think about how you will give answers that discuss and evaluate the sociological arguments. Prepare to do this by taking notes of the pros and cons of each explanation. Understanding the relationship between different theories helps you think sociologically about theorists' explanations and gives you a much better chance of producing an excellent answer in the exam.

Key terms

Functional prerequisite: something that must be in place for society to function effectively.

Functionalist theory of social class and inequality

The functionalist perspective assumes that society operates as a working whole. Functionalists have described society like the human body in that each part of society, like each part of the body, is needed for the healthy functioning of the whole. When related to social stratification this perspective assumes that each stratum of society has an important function and this explains its development and continued existence. When any structure in society is no longer useful it will simply disappear and be replaced by a structure that meets the functional needs of that society.

Society operates using a system of rewards and negative sanctions based on value consensus. Strata in society are formed and developed through value consensus where generally held views on what is good for society give rise to rewards. Occupations that are highly valued are given higher rewards. According to functionalist thinking, doctors are highly valued members of Western society because of their vital role and because they give up a significant number of years to their training. This explains the relatively high salaries earned by doctors compared to other public servants such as social workers and teachers.

Functionalists claim that different social groups are interdependent and this extends to social stratification. Each of the social classes, according to functionalist thinking, is dependent on the others. Workers depend on managers to provide the structure and organisation for their work. Managers depend on workers to get the job done.

Talcott Parsons argued that inequality is inevitable but claimed that conflict between different groups is kept at a manageable level by the common value system that recognises the appropriateness of unequal levels of rewards. Parsons also recognised the inequality of power and prestige that exists in society and justified it in much the same way as economic inequality. Different levels of power and authority are needed to keep working organisations functional. Some are more able and better qualified to manage the working lives of others and inevitably have higher power and prestige. Parson's argument is that these inequalities are accepted as right and proper by the majority and are essential for the smooth running of society.

Davis and Moore (1967) in their *Principles of Stratification* claimed that stratification is an inevitable outcome of society's **functional prerequisites**. One such prerequisite is the need for effective role allocation and performance:

- All roles must be filled.
- They must be filled by the most able and suitable people.
- The right people for the role must be trained.
- The roles must be performed well.

This argument justifies inequality by stating that there are people who are most capable of fulfilling specific key roles or functions in society and are therefore vitally important. Reward is needed to encourage them to take on the additional education, training and effort required to fulfil these roles.

■ Take it further

If you had to choose between managing without your GP or your refuse collectors for three months, which do you think you would miss the most? Your GP has a vital role in keeping you well but one could argue that the refuse collectors are just as important. The functionalist explanation for social prestige may be rather simplistic. This argument fits with Tumin's idea that it is not necessarily the most important jobs in society that are the most rewarded. Differences in bargaining power rather than functional importance may be the factor that decides the reward an occupation receives.

Critics of functionalism

Tumin (1953), in his critique of Davis and Moore, pointed out that inequality also occurs in the chances individuals have to achieve positions of high social and economic status. Our education system may not be effectively measuring talent and ability, and there is no doubt that a number of other influences affect the selection of people for highly prestigious occupations. These influences include barriers (or gatekeeping) that prevent people of lower social status entering prestigious positions, regardless of ability. Reducing the number of people in high-status occupations gives rise to a high demand for services and people in demand can charge high fees.

■ New Right theories of social stratification

New Right thinking came into existence in Britain in the 1980s and is sometimes called neo-functionalism. It is an explanation of how modern capitalist societies function. New Right ideas suggest that society functions best as a free-market economy and that promoting equality is counterproductive. Motivation is necessary for the market and for individuals to operate most productively, and the free market encourages this. Benefits and other means of spreading wealth more equally through society have the opposite effect by reducing motivation and discouraging effort.

Peter Saunders (1990a), an influential New Right sociological thinker, has made these suggestions:

- Inequality due to stratification is not inevitable but it is beneficial to the market.
- Inequality of reward motivates people to work hard.
- Inequality promotes economic growth by encouraging people to start businesses or train for better jobs.
- Equality of opportunity is vital for a healthy economy, as it encourages growth.
- Market forces are the driving force in a stable economy, and those who can supply services in high demand can earn the highest rewards.
- High reward for services in high demand means that society operates as a meritocracy.
- The middle classes have higher incomes because they are more able, and train and work harder than working-class people.

The last suggestion is the most controversial of New Right ideas but it does not differ significantly from earlier functionalist ideas.

Critics of New Right theory

Gordon Marshall and Adam Swift (1996) respond to New Right ideas as follows:

- There is no real evidence that society is meritocratic as opportunities to do well differ depending on the social class of the individual. The free market does not offer a fair chance for everyone.
- People from working-class backgrounds with the same educational qualifications as those from middle-class backgrounds have less chance of getting top jobs.
- Functionalists and New Right theorists tend to ignore social problems. They choose to believe that a functional society will create its own solutions to these problems through the formation of a healthy economy. Many argue that this is a false belief.

Marxist theory of social stratification

Marx claimed that the struggle or conflict between classes explains the whole structure of society (Figure 6.1.1). On the other hand, functionalists claim that society is based on value consensus. For this reason, Marxist theory is known as conflict theory and functionalism is known as consensus theory.

Marxist theory is a radical alternative to the view of society presented by the functionalists. Rather than seeing the formation of social stratification as a means by which society becomes more functional or better integrated, Marxists claim that social stratification divides society and is used by the rich and powerful to exploit others.

Fig. 6.1.1 *Marx claimed that class conflict explains the structure of society*

Marx stated that in societies where there is social stratification there are basically two classes: a ruling class and a subject class. The power of the ruling class comes from its ownership and therefore control of capital, land and industry, which Marx called the means of production. The subject class, on the other hand, depends on the ruling class for employment in order to live.

In Marxist terms, members of the same class share a similar relationship to the means of production and therefore share common experiences and values. People in the ruling class – Marx called them the bourgeoisie – share a common drive to get the best possible profit from their powerful position of ownership. People in the subject class – Marx called them the proletariat – share a common drive to get higher wages in order to have a better standard of living.

All social structures exist to maintain the status quo – the unequal power relationships in society. Institutions such as education, media, the law and politics all function in a way that maintains the power of the rich and exploits the workers. They also control values in society and therefore shape and control the dominant ideology. Marx claimed that the only solution to the injustice and inequality created by such a system

Take it further

Does Marxist thinking seem far-fetched and perhaps a little paranoid? Consider the tabloid newspapers such as the *Sun*. Do you think these newspapers are designed to represent the interests of the working class? In reality, these papers continually reinforce right-wing thinking. Readers are invited to feel suspicious of other low-income groups, so they become less inclined to work together to improve their lot. Readers are also encouraged to buy more goods and therefore become more dependent on their employers. Workers in debt are not going to object to their working conditions for fear of loss of income.

Take it further

Think about the growing trend towards green living. Groups are forming whose purpose is to explore and encourage ways of living a more eco-friendly lifestyle. Members of these groups may come from a wide range of economic and occupational backgrounds but their shared interest in ecological issues has created a new societal cluster. These groups do not yet appear to have particular social status, but it is possible that over time a social status will emerge as concerns increase about the earth's resources.

Take it further

Can you think of an example of a status group that practised social closure within the past 30 years? Apartheid practised by the dominant white population of South Africa successfully prevented the mixing of different races and kept privileges for the dominant white group. It may surprise you to know that apartheid ended as recently as 1992.

is for the means of production to be collectively owned and the rewards shared equally. He believed that the only way for this to come about was through a workers' revolution.

Erik Olin Wright and neo-Marxism

Traditional Marxism had elements that do not fit with modern society. One obvious problem is that the middle class is not represented in Marx's original model yet it is the largest class group in modern society. Erik Olin Wright (1978) used the term 'petty bourgeoisie' – a corruption of Marx's 'petit bourgeoisie' – to mean a class with some limited influence over the means of production. Middle classes share things in common with ruling and subject classes and may experience a sense of contradiction or dissonance because of the complexity of their position in society. Wright concluded that although modern society is more complex than Marx's society, conflict and exploitation still exist.

Weberian theory of stratification

Marxism and Weberian theory both state that social class is largely based on economic relationships, with people in society competing for wealth. There are echoes of functionalist thinking in Weber's claim that social class is related to market forces so that the more a person's skills and talents are in demand, the higher their position in the market.

Weber differed markedly from Marxism and functionalism in claiming that stratification is neither a simple conflict between two classes nor a meritocracy based on competition, but a very complex set of layers in a hierarchy which values economic power plus social prestige and political power.

Although groups form because of a shared aim to acquire various forms of economic power, there are also groupings who share similar status in society. Status groupings may be concerned with lifestyle issues and economic issues.

Here is Weber's definition of a status group:

- Members share similar social prestige or status.
- Members share similar lifestyles.
- They identify with other members of the group and feel a sense of belonging.
- They may place restrictions on membership.

The last point refers to social closure, where members of the group can prevent others from joining the group.

John Goldthorpe

John Goldthorpe's work was based on a neo-Weberian view of social class, recognising the influence of forces such as market position and status on social class. The Oxford mobility studies (Goldthorpe 1980; Goldthorpe *et al.* 1987) used a seven-class system that was later developed into the current NS-SEC system.

Postmodern theory and social class

Postmodern theory claims that social class is no longer the most important signifier of social position in society. As social mobility increases and people make lifestyle choices that are based on more factors than wealth, the importance of social class has diminished in favour of differences in identity and culture. Postmodern theory argues that people have more personal agency than other theorists suggest, and can shape and form their own identity based on individual perception and choice. Status in the 21st century may be more about values and lifestyle than about wealth and power.

Pakulski and Waters (1996) argue that social class is becoming increasingly insignificant because class groups are not evident any more. Social inequality is based on factors other than social class. They claim that sociology is lagging behind society by continuing to pay too much attention to social class when members of society have ceased to do so. Other dimensions of inequality such as gender and race have a far greater impact.

Although this argument goes some way towards explaining cultural and attitudinal changes in the late 20th century and early 21st century, it has been criticised by a number of theorists. Beverley Skeggs (1997) argues that postmodern sociologists are largely middle-class professionals who underestimate the experience of working-class people and therefore fail to see the importance of class to those whose lived experience is strongly influenced by their class position.

Westergaard (1995) also criticises postmodernist ideas for failing to recognise that differences in social class are still relevant. Life chances and living standards differ significantly between the rich and poor in modern society, therefore social class continues to be a meaningful measure of stratification for a large section of society.

Take it further

One example of the change in attitude to wealth and social status is the increasingly popular lifestyle choice of downsizing. People decide to work in lower-status occupations and move to smaller and more easily managed houses to have a healthier work–life balance. It seems there is a shift away from the individualistic, materialistic life choices of the 1980s to a desire for balance.

Link

See pages 350–351 for more on postmodern arguments.

Summary questions

2 Marxist and Weberian explanations use occupational classifications to describe social classes. How do the two explanations differ?

3 Postmodernists argue that social class is no longer relevant. How might the social class of the sociologists affect their views about the importance of social class?

Nature and significance of social mobility

Social mobility refers to movement between social classes; upward mobility is a rise in class status and downward mobility is a reduction in status. In Britain over the past 50 years there has been evidence of increased social mobility. This is partly the result of a change in working patterns as fewer people are employed in industry and more are employed in white-collar jobs. A decline in industry has been offset by a sharp rise in new technology, so some occupations have disappeared and new ones have emerged. One example of this is the increase in call centres where large numbers of people are employed to answer telephone inquiries. The effect of these changes is that many people have experienced upward social mobility whereas others have experienced downward mobility following a decline in upper management roles. There are three reasons why sociologists are interested in social mobility:

▨ It gives important insight into the way social class is formed and the nature of class identity.

▨ It gives a unique way of analysing the extent to which equality of opportunity for different groups in society truly exists.

▨ It provides information about the life chances of members of society.

▨ Important terms in social mobility

▨ **Closed societies** – where social mobility is rare and people stay in the social class they were born into.

▨ **Open societies** – where social mobility is possible and people can move up or down through social classes, regardless of their family status.

▨ **Ascribed status** – attributed according to family of birth: for example, members of the gentry may have high status through inheritance and marriage.

▨ **Achieved status** – status that is achieved through merit, ambition and hard work.

▨ **Absolute mobility** – a measure of how much mobility there is in any society.

▨ **Relative mobility** – a measure of how much mobility one group has compared with another: for example, do working-class people have as much social mobility as middle-class people?

▨ **Intergenerational mobility** – social mobility between different generations, such as between parents and children.

▨ **Intragenerational mobility** – social mobility in a person's own lifetime, such as moving up through the ranks in a profession or downsizing in later life.

▨ **Social closure** – where access to specific occupations or strata is prevented. This can be achieved by developing criteria for membership that excludes everyone except people from a particular status group.

■ **Meritocratic society** – a society where status is achieved by a person's merit.

Industrial societies

In pre-industrial societies, status and social class were normally ascribed. In general, social class was fixed according to a person's family of birth, race and gender. Upward social mobility was rare and could only be achieved through marriage into a wealthier family or patronage. Fixed social status is maintained through social closure where sections of society can prohibit access through a variety of means. Social closure is still practised in modern society but to a lesser extent than in pre-industrial societies.

In modern industrial society, social class is achieved. This suggests that a person with the right abilities, attitudes and education can achieve high-status positions regardless of their family of birth. A meritocratic society, where status is achieved through merit, will always have a higher level of absolute mobility than a society where status is ascribed, but the nature of relative mobility may vary significantly between different social groups.

Although social mobility can be intergenerational and intragenerational, most sociological research has investigated intergenerational mobility. Sociologists recognise that a rise up the career ladder is relatively common within a person's lifetime, but access to the first rung of the ladder may not always be equal.

Classic studies of social mobility

Glass

The first important study of social mobility in Britain was by David Glass (1954), who compared social class between fathers and sons. Although there was evidence of social mobility, the findings did not reveal equality of opportunity. Glass found that about two-thirds of sons were in a different social class to their fathers, and upward and downward mobility were evenly split. Mobility was usually short-range, with sons in occupations only one or two steps removed from their fathers. Long-range mobility was unusual, with very few moving into or out of the upper classes. High-status occupations tended to use a process of self-recruitment, where candidates for jobs were chosen from the sons of those already in the career structure. This was effectively social closure.

Critique of the Glass study

Glass's work has been criticised. The main focus of the criticism is his sampling techniques as he did not consider the changing nature of work, particularly the significant growth in middle-class occupations. Using samples from mainly working-class and professional participants may have given inaccurate results if most of the social mobility was happening in middle-class occupations. This suggests that Glass underestimated the rate of upward mobility.

The original schedules from Glass's work have been destroyed but we know from his report that he categorised social class using 'arbitrary but convenient boundaries' (Glass 1954: 36). In other words, he devised a system for allocating occupations to social classes that is no longer available. Although there have been criticisms of Glass's work, this is a classic study that laid the ground for future research into social mobility.

■ Link

Goldthorpe's seven-class scheme is discussed in more detail on page 311, because it has been used as the basis for the new NS-SEC system of classification.

Stratification...

Oxford mobility studies

The next significant piece of work on social mobility was the classic Oxford mobility study by Goldthorpe (1980). It was similar to the Glass study in that it compared the social class of fathers and sons but Goldthorpe produced his own seven-class scheme, so the two studies cannot be straightforwardly compared. The seven classes can be fitted into a three-class structure like this:

- Service class = Goldthorpe's classes 1 and 2
- Intermediate class = Goldthorpe's classes 3, 4 and 5
- Working class = Goldthorpe's classes 6 and 7

The Goldthorpe study investigated a range of topics associated with social mobility. Here is a summary of the findings:

- There were higher rates of mobility than in 1949, with 50 per cent of sons in a different class than their fathers.
- More mobility was upward than downward.
- The chances of long-range mobility, from lower class to highest class, were greater than in 1949.
- Some changes were the result of changes to the occupational structure, with more jobs created in the service class.

Life chances

Perhaps life chances improved in the post-war period, but there was still a far greater chance of a middle- or upper-class boy getting a high-status job than a working-class boy. Kellner and Wilby (1980) showed that the data revealed a 1:2:4 rule of 'relative hope': the chances of a working-class boy achieving service-class status are doubled for an intermediate-class boy and quadrupled for a service-class boy. So, if the chances of upward mobility have improved for working-class people, they have improved a whole lot more for those in higher social classes.

Despite evidence of increased social mobility, it is fair to conclude that Britain's social class system was not as open or fair as some might have wished to claim. In 1957 the Conservative prime minister, Harold Macmillan, remarked, 'You've never had it so good!' as post-war austerity and occupational changes gave more people a better standard of living. The findings of the Goldthorpe study show that some had more of the 'good' than others.

Follow-up study

Goldthorpe *et al.* (1987) did a follow-up study that covered a period of recession during the 1970s. The findings of this study showed few differences from the original study; service-class jobs increased, producing a rise in absolute mobility. Relative mobility showed little change, and increased unemployment had a greater impact on working-class people than people in the intermediate or service classes because the chances of unemployment were greater.

Problems with the Oxford mobility studies

- Goldthorpe's studies did not differentiate between elite occupations, i.e. very high-status, high-power occupations and other high-status professional occupations. Evidence suggests that self-recruitment – vacancies filled by sons of other group members – occurred more in the elite groups, hence there was greater social closure than recognised by Goldthorpe.

Hint

Goldthorpe's classic study of social mobility was done in 1972 but not published until 1980. The same study has been called the Oxford study, the Goldthorpe study and the Nuffield study.

Take it further

Go to www.esds.ac.uk/findingData/snDescription.asp?sn=1097 and read the outline of the Oxford mobility study. See an archived version of the original questionnaire at www.data-archive.ac.uk/doc/1097/mrdoc/pdf/a1097uab.pdf. Note the use of language and the layout of the form. How times have changed.

Take it further

Read more about Macmillan at http://news.bbc.co.uk/onthisday/hi/dates/stories/july/20/newsid_3728000/3728225.stm. And http://news.bbc.co.uk/1/hi/business/7213462.stm is a recent analysis of spending by households in Britain.

■ Women were not included in the studies. In response, Goldthorpe *et al*. re-examined the data from the follow-up study and included data on women. They concluded that gender did not significantly alter their results and that social class was the most meaningful factor.

■ Later researchers (Stanworth 1984; Abbott and Payne 1990) have refuted Goldthorpe and Payne, claiming that women are more likely to be downwardly mobile than men and that women who do rise through the occupational strata are much less likely than men to reach the top two levels.

Summary questions

1 Define intergenerational and intragenerational social mobility. Explain why intergenerational mobility is more often researched and analysed.

2 Explain the differences and similarities between the Glass study and the Goldthorpe study. Why is it difficult to compare the results of the two studies?

Take it further

It's easy to lose the meaning by only paying attention to the numbers. Goldthorpe's follow-up study appeared to show that social mobility had changed little, but a closer look shows that working-class people had less chance of moving up the status ladder, more chance of becoming unemployed, and poorer life chances. Evidence suggests that, in both directions, women are more mobile than men. The glass ceiling is likely to make it very difficult for women to enter the highest-status professions, even if their fathers are in the highest class.

Changing patterns of social mobility

Learning objectives:

■ Discuss the impact of changes in social mobility.

■ Describe the significance of changes to occupational structures and distribution of wealth.

Take it further

Go to www.num.org. uk/?p=history&c=num&h=13 and read about the miners' strike and the decline of the coal mining industry.

Take it further

Before the introduction of new legislation governing equal pay for women and men, it was common practice to pay women significantly less than men for the same job. This practice was widely accepted as fair because men were considered the main breadwinners. The Equal Pay Act 1970 made it illegal for women to be paid less than men for doing the same job or a similar job. Read about the Equal Pay Act at www. womenandequalityunit.gov.uk/ legislation/equal_pay_act.htm. In 2006 Cumbria County Council was fined £15 million for breaching the act (http://news.bbc.co.uk/1/hi/ england/cumbria/5085244.stm).

Link

See pages 330–336 for more on gender and stratification.

In the previous section we looked at the classic studies on social mobility and considered their importance. In this section we will consider how changes in working patterns and income distribution have altered the social landscape and influenced social mobility.

From manufacturing to service industries

The 20th century was a time of enormous change to the occupational structure of Britain, with manual jobs decreasing in number as manufacturing industries changed and declined. According to the General Household Survey, the proportion of workers employed in manual jobs fell throughout the century from about 80 per cent to 44 per cent, with a decline from 55 per cent to 44 per cent in the last quarter-century. There was a massive increase in non-manual and professional jobs.

One notable example was the huge decline in the coal mining industry. At its height, it employed 750,000 miners but by 1981 this number had fallen to 218,000 and by 1994 to 8,500 (Roberts 2001). Closures to unprofitable collieries in the early 1980s brought about the miners' strike of 1984–85, as the government proceeded with closures despite enormous opposition from one of the most powerful trade unions in the country. These closures changed the nature of Britain's mining industry forever and diminished the power of the trade union movement.

Not all changes to manufacturing industries were a result of low productivity. Rapid developments in new technology meant that productivity could be maintained or even increased with far fewer workers. At the same time, a sharp growth in service and leisure industries produced an increase in non-manual occupations.

Gender role changes

Changing attitudes to gender roles have led to a growing number of women entering the workforce. The traditional role of stay-at-home wife and mother has steadily declined, with at least 70 per cent of adult women now in paid employment. Most women are employed in lower-status non-manual roles, and only a minority achieve high-status positions. In the last quarter of the 20th century, the number of women in high-level jobs increased from 5 per cent to 15 per cent, showing a trend towards greater equality of opportunity. Legislative changes giving women equal rights in selection and pay have helped support these structural changes.

The traditional roles of male breadwinner and female part-time employee have also changed, and far more couples choose mutual responsibility for income generation, home and childcare. The notion of the male breadwinner is declining as gender roles become more equal.

Changes in wealth distribution

Through the second half of the 20th century, most of the population grew wealthier as wartime austerity receded and the economy improved, but this does not mean there was a reduction in the gap between rich and poor in society. Redistribution of wealth through taxation and benefits is one way that inequalities are addressed in society, but in a meritocratic society there will always be greater rewards for those who achieve positions with the highest status. Taxation falls into two categories. Progressive taxes directly tax the rich to foster more equality, whereas regressive taxes tend to disadvantage lower-income groups. Income tax, particularly where higher income earners are taxed at a higher rate, is a progressive tax and value added tax (VAT) is a regressive tax as it is applied to goods bought, so it disadvantages people with less disposable income.

Official figures are useful in showing how effectively measures such as taxation redistribute wealth across different income groups. In the year 2005/6 official statistics showed that the top **quintile** of the population were four times better off than the bottom quintile.

In Figure 6.2.1 original income is compared with final income for each of five groups in society. Original income is income before taxes and benefits. Benefits in this case include non-cash benefits such as health care and education. It is only in the upper two quintiles that original income is higher than final income. The final bars show average income across all households. The massive difference in income between the top income bracket and all others means that 3 out of 5, or 60 per cent, of households have an income below the national average.

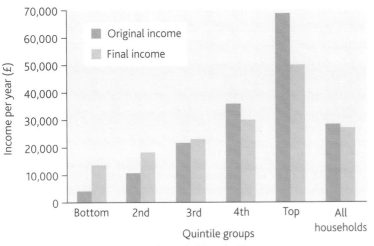

Fig. 6.2.1 *UK: average income per household, 2005/6*

Source: National Statistics Online

The rise of the super-rich under New Labour

Traditionally, Conservative governments have encouraged capitalism and rewarded economic success, whereas Labour governments have supported the working classes and used taxation as a means of creating a more equal division of wealth in society. In recent years, New Labour has appeared to move away from traditional Labour principles by failing to tax the superwealthy and failing to reverse Conservative policies on taxation. New Labour has failed to reinstate higher rates of income tax and has continued to apply regressive taxation, effectively disadvantaging lower-income groups.

One explanation of this apparent reverse of Labour principles is the need for successive governments to protect the interests of capitalism in order to survive in the world's economy and attract investment into Britain. John Scott (1991) points out that Labour governments have not effectively challenged the ruling capitalist class because governments are ultimately dependent on capitalism. The most wealthy members of society now own 99 per cent of the wealth of Britain and, according to Scott, this is unlikely to change.

Key terms

Quintile: a proportion of a data set that has been divided into five equal groups.

Hint

National statistics are only as accurate as the responses given. Many people in society do not disclose the full extent of their income, so they will not respond truthfully to questions in a survey. Much government money has been spent in trying to reduce benefit fraud but it is higher-paid people who have the greatest opportunity to hide income from the Inland Revenue.

Hint

Social science can be frustrating if you think there is a right and a wrong answer. In sociology it's a good thing if you can see the strengths and weaknesses of different arguments. Back up your evaluations with reasoned arguments to show the strengths and weaknesses of each perspective or theory you discuss. Remember that no theory survives without some evidence to support it.

Summary questions

3 Explain how changes to occupational structures have increased levels of social mobility.

4 Give a brief explanation of the existence of the super-rich group in society from a Marxist viewpoint and a New Right viewpoint.

Stratification …

Differentiation: dimensions of inequality

Life chances

- Explain life chances and, using recent statistics, give examples of their impact.

- Understand the relationship between disadvantage and life chances.

The American Declaration of Independence states: 'All men are created equal'. The study of stratification and differentiation may cause you to disagree. The moment we are born, we are affected by our place in the social strata. The lower down we are, it is more likely we will experience the biggest challenges to our future development.

In a society that is meritocratic there are winners and losers. Some will attain prestige and wealth, getting all the requirements to live well and prosper, whereas others will experience the opposite. Their disadvantage mirrors the advantages of those who have prospered. This is the true meaning of inequality.

There is evidence to suggest that a person's social class has an impact on almost every element of life: health, education, social opportunities, skill acquisition, job and promotion prospects, and lifespan.

Life chances are the chances or opportunities a person experiences throughout their lifetime that can improve their lot in life. Poor life chances mean that a person is more likely to have limited or negative experiences compared with a person who has good life chances.

Chances throughout life

A person born into a low social class has a lower chance of survival beyond the first year of life. Infant mortality is falling in developed countries but Figure 6.3.1 shows the impact of social class on a child's chances of survival beyond the first year of life. Moving on a few years, it becomes clear that those from higher social classes are more likely to succeed in our education system. Children with parents in professional occupations are far more likely to attain five or more GCSEs than those in lower-level occupations (Figure 6.3.2).

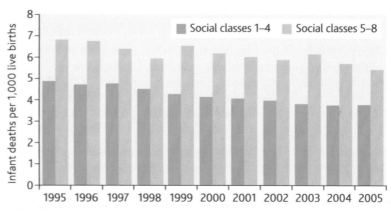

Fig. 6.3.1 *Impact of social class on a child's chances of survival beyond the first year of life. Although falling, infant deaths are 50 per cent more common among people from manual backgrounds than among people from non-manual backgrounds*

Source: www.poverty.org.uk

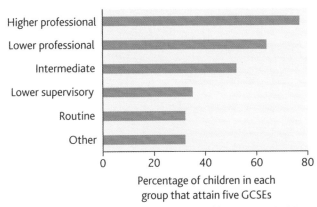

Fig. 6.3.2 *England and Wales: attainment of five or more GCSE grades A* to C by parental NS-SEC*

Source: National Statistics Online

Once a young person from a lower socio-economic background leaves school, they are far more likely to be unemployed, because they have lower qualifications and therefore less access to high-level education and training. Low-level, unskilled jobs offer less security and are often temporary or seasonal. People in unskilled and manual occupations earn less than people in non-manual occupations. Table 6.3.1 compares manual and non-manual incomes, male and female incomes.

Table 6.3.1 *UK: weekly pay composition as a percentage of average gross weekly earnings of employees, April 2002*

	Overtime	Bonuses and commissions	Shift premia	Average gross weekly earnings (£)
Males				
Manual	11.8	11.8	3.0	366.6
Non-manual	2.3	4.6	0.7	608.7
Females				
Manual	5.5	2.4	2.7	250.3
Non-manual	1.5	2.4	0.9	404.0
All employees	**4.1**	**3.6**	**1.2**	**462.6**

Source: New Earnings Survey, *Office for National Statistics*

Those in manual work have significantly lower income than those in non-manual work. Women have lower average weekly incomes than men, demonstrating the effect of multiple disadvantage (see below). A person's health is affected by their social class to the extent that a man in social class 6 and 7 is far more likely to die before age 64 than a man in social class 1 and 2 (Figure 6.3.3).

Poorer general health is caused by a range of factors. A person in an hourly paid job is far less likely to take time off work to go to the doctor or dentist. This is because manual workers tend to be paid only for hours worked, whereas professional people can take time out to go to essential health appointments without loss of income. Even if income is lost, there is less impact on a person with higher income.

Hint

It is not only social class that influences a person's life chances. Some negative influences on life chances are having a black or minority ethic background or being disabled, gay, older or female.

Stratification…

Take it further

In 2003 the Joseph Rowntree Foundation analysed people who were unemployed and identified six characteristics associated with non-employment and subsequent poverty: single parents, especially women, people with poor qualifications and skills, people over 50, people who live in an area of low employment, disabled people and black and minority ethnic (BME) groups, not including Chinese. Read about the study at www.jrf.org.uk/knowledge/findings/socialpolicy/313.asp.

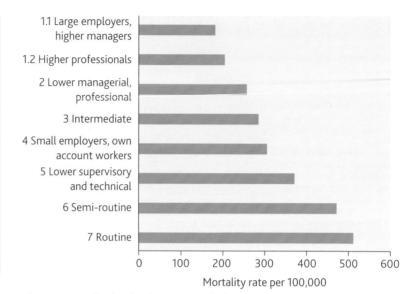

Fig. 6.3.3 *England and Wales: age-standardised mortality rate by NS-SEC for men aged 25–64, 2001–3*

Source: National Statistics Online

Summary questions

1 Define the term 'life chances' and write a brief account of the possible effects of poor life chances on a girl born into a deprived area.

2 Explain the meaning of multiple disadvantage.

Power, influence and choice

Learning objectives:

 Understand the relationship between different forms of power.

 Describe different forms of power and influence.

 Understand that economic power underpins most forms of inequality.

Social class tends to be measured according to occupation and income, but other factors that influence a person's life chances are less directly connected to income. Factors such as personal, professional and economic power will affect the amount of influence a person has over their environment. Similarly, a person who has personal, professional or economic power will have more choice in life than a person who is without power.

Mark and Jim

Read these two stories and try to imagine what the outcome would be for the two boys.

 Mark is picked up by the police one night after he is found weaving down the street singing loudly and waving a bottle of beer. After he sobers up in the cells, he explains to the police officer that he has just heard that he has been granted entry to Oxford University and was out celebrating his success. When asked who to contact, he gives the name of his father, a well-known solicitor.

 Jim is picked up by the police one night after he is found weaving down the street singing loudly and waving a bottle of beer. After he sobers up in the cells, he explains to the police officer that he got his benefit money that day and was out celebrating. The address he gives is on a local housing estate known for its problem with youth gangs.

Chances are that Mark will be sent home with a firm but kindly warning, but Jim will spend the night in the cells and be in court next morning for breach of the peace. What is likely to influence how the boys are treated is not father's income but father's social influence.

Professional and economic power

Think back to the different theories of social class at the start of this topic. Marxist and Weberian approaches refer to issues of power as well as income. Marxist theory refers to the owners of production, the bourgeoisie, having control over the workers, the proletariat, and using their dominant position to exploit them. According to Marx, all structures in society are instruments of the dominant, hence powerful, ruling class.

While recognising the impact of economic power, Weberian theory observes that power and influence do not belong exclusively to the owners of production. Workers with highly marketable skills have power and prestige in society. This explains the growth and nature of the middle classes and the different levels of power and influence, or status, within the middle classes. Weber also identified status situation as an important factor in social position.

W. G. Runciman (1990) developed a different system of social stratification. Recognising the difficulty of using only occupational roles as indicators of social status, he suggested that a person's position in the class structure be based on a number of roles. He agreed that occupational roles were the most important, but he pointed out that the immediate family of a person in a high-status occupation shared the

Stratification...

327

status of that person. Where different members of the family unit or couple have jobs of different statuses, the job with the highest status classifies the couple or family.

Perhaps more interesting was Runciman's view of economic power in social stratification. He suggests that economic power has three elements:

- **Ownership** – this is the classic idea about owning the means of production, first suggested by Marx. If a person owns a means of production or other industry, then they have power.
- **Control** – a person has control if they have the right to control or direct the production or service provision within a trade or industry. Examples are managers and supervisors.
- **Marketability** – this is a person's ability to attract a high price for their labour. It is influenced by skills, qualifications and experience.

Runciman suggested that a person who is in the highest-status position will usually have all three of these elements of economic power. A person who has none of these three elements will be in the lowest-status positions.

Although Runciman's work was originally intended as another way of analysing social stratification and as a tool for research, it is perhaps more interesting and useful as a means of explaining the way that economic and professional power can be achieved.

When thinking about social inequality, this model shows that economic and professional power can be achieved in more than one way, not simply through ownership of the means of production as argued by Marx. More economic power means a better standard of living.

■ Personal power and authority

Power extends beyond the workplace and notions of economic power. Power exists in all social relationships and is best defined as the ability to get others to do what you want them to do. In other words, power is the ability to get your own way. Put simply, in any social relationship there is likely to be an inequality of power, as one person in the relationship will always have more power than the others. The more power a person has, the more they will have the ability to get what they want out of life.

Authority is one form of power that was described by Weber as having three different sources:

- **Charismatic authority** – personal qualities that inspire others to submit themselves to that person.
- **Traditional authority** – power and status positions that are usually inherited, such as the ruling monarch and feudal landlords.
- **Legal authority** – power and status positions, such as judges and the police, that are accepted because laws of the land support their existence.

Weber pointed out that most positions of authority do not fall neatly into any of these categories: for example, the Archbishop of Canterbury has an authority that covers all three positions to some extent. He was chosen because of his personal qualities but his role is traditional and has the legal authority that belongs to a member of the House of Lords.

This analysis of power and authority suggests that the only form of authority not connected to social class is charismatic authority. Charismatic authority exists even in the poorest environments. Some people will have more charismatic authority and therefore more potential access to the resources that are available. Their use of those resources depends on personal choice, so it does not follow that all powerful people use their power to keep the best for themselves.

Choice and inequality

In its most extreme forms, inequality leads to poverty and social exclusion. A person without access to any means to improve their life has few or limited choices. Ill health, low life expectancy and poor skills acquisition can be caused by a range of factors, some of which may be connected to personal choice, but a person who lives in poverty is more likely to experience these things and has very little choice about the outcome. Households with children are more likely to live in poverty. Figure 6.3.4 shows that 19 per cent of children in Britain lived in poverty in the mid 1980s, where poverty is measured as an income less than 60 per cent of the national average.

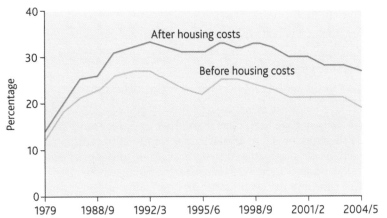

Fig. 6.3.4 *Percentage of children living in households below 60 per cent of median income*
Source: National Statistics Online

Summary question

3 Explain why economic power is the basis for most forms of inequality. Justify your answer.

Stratification

329

Stratification and gender

A woman's work

Learning objectives:

- Understand the relationship between stratification research and gender.

- Explain the connection between domestic responsibility and career development.

Sociologists who analysed stratification during the 20th century had different views on the place of women and the importance of gender difference. In the early studies of stratification there was no issue, because women were simply ignored. The male breadwinner was the only person in the household worth considering to decide the class of the household. These assumptions were made until the 1981 census:

- Men are the main breadwinners.
- Women seldom have lifelong careers, because the vast majority marry and have children.
- Once a woman has had children, she steps off the career ladder.
- If a woman works after she has had children, she will do part-time work because she has domestic duties to perform.
- The man in the household normally has the highest-status occupation.

These notions may have been plausible earlier in the century, when men dominated the workforce, but the latter part of the 20th century showed a massive change in occupational structures. More and more women entered the workforce, there was increasing acceptance of women working full-time and using childcare, and new equality legislation made it illegal for employers to treat women differently on opportunity, pay or conditions. Britain's workforce was becoming increasingly feminised.

Sociologists have been divided over the relationship between stratification and gender because it is not clear whether women are a separate group within each of the classes or whether the gender of the person is not relevant to a study of stratification. Should sociologists be studying people as a group within the classes or should they separate the genders? Is a woman's identity more about her class than her gender? Class identity is certainly important in stratification studies but does it differ between men and women? These questions create a theoretical dilemma for sociologists. Things would undoubtedly have been simpler if women had become truly equal in the workforce. In fact, women remain more likely than men to work part-time, and women's average earnings in full-time work are lower than men's. Evidence suggests that women still carry the main burden of responsibility for domestic duties.

Westergaard and Resler (1976) claimed that it is the class of the family unit that is most relevant to the study of social class; they claimed that evidence showed it was the man's occupation that had the biggest influence on the class of the household. Goldthorpe (1983) agreed that the whole household is the best indicator of class, as everyone in the household shares the same social class, but he argues that it is the member of the family who has the main role in supporting the family that indicates the family's class. This may not always be the man of the house. Yet he did point out that as women normally withdraw from the workforce at certain times in their lives, it is usually the man's occupation that determines the class of the household.

There is a difference between deciding how best to decide what social class a person belongs to and the impact of a person's experience. Sociologists may argue whether men and women should be considered as separate entities in an analysis of class, but men and women undoubtedly have different experiences of life in the workplace and the family unit. Most sociological research about stratification and the workforce has been exclusively on men, then results have been generalised to include women. This assumption implies that the experience of women is the same as the experience of men. Feminist research has shown this assumption is false.

It is clear that women earn less than men and are prevented from entering high-level occupations by the **glass ceiling**. Evidence of the glass ceiling is found in occupational statistics. Both **vertical segregation** and **horizontal segregation** are evident, showing that women have a different experience in the workplace because of their gender.

Figure 6.4.1 shows there are twice as many men than women in higher managerial and professional occupations and two-thirds more women than men in intermediate occupations. Note that there are more women in lower managerial and professional occupations than men. This suggests that women can rise to some level in the professions but the final step – breaking through the glass ceiling – is much harder. Some caring professions such as childcare, nursing and primary teaching are predominantly female, whereas skilled and technical jobs are predominantly male. Men are more likely to be self-employed and own their own businesses. Differences in pay between men and women are reducing but remain significant (Figure 6.4.2). Evidence suggests that women take on a larger share of household responsibilities (Figure 6.4.3).

Spending more time in unpaid work and having less opportunity to achieve high-status and high-income jobs has a negative effect on women's life chances, although women still outlive men by an average of five years.

Key terms

Glass ceiling: an invisible barrier to top jobs in an occupational structure.

Vertical segregation: segregation according to pay and status. High-status and high-paid occupations are more likely to go to men.

Horizontal segregation: where men and women in the same class do different jobs; for example, women do care work and men do computer work.

Take it further

Times have changed. Men are much more likely to share childcare and domestic duties than 20 years ago. The important thing is not who does what around the house but who takes responsibility for the overall running of the home. The difference is subtle but important. Do you ever hear a person say, 'I've done the vacuuming for you.' or 'Could you watch the children on Saturday while I go shopping?'? Think about how the wording of these statements implies that the woman is primarily responsible. Equality comes when responsibility is equally shared.

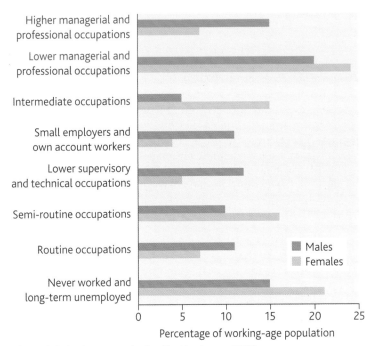

Fig. 6.4.1 *Socio-economic classification by sex, 2005*

Source: www.esrc.ac.uk

Stratification…

331

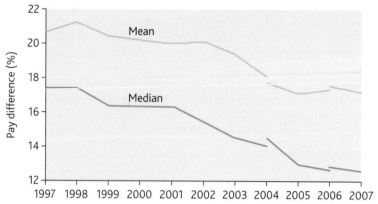

Fig. 6.4.2 *Percentage difference in pay between men and women, 1997–2006*

Source: National Statistics Online

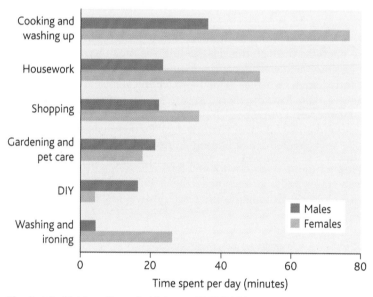

Fig. 6.4.3 *Division of household chores, 2000/2001*

Source: National Statistics Online

Summary question

1 Give a possible explanation for the fact that there are more women than men in the lower management and professional group of occupations.

Theories of gender inequality

Learning objectives:

- Evaluate different theories of gender inequality.

- Understand the impact of gender inequality.

One functionalist explanation of gender differences suggests that the nuclear family is necessary for the socialisation of children and the stability of adults (Parsons 1955). This crucial function of the family makes the female role essential, as it is the woman who bears children. Parsons describes a woman's role as expressive, meaning that she is biologically determined to provide the emotional security and warmth that a family needs. This expressive role is not just for the children, but also to help her husband cope with the stresses of being the breadwinner. According to Parsons, the husband has an instrumental role and needs his wife's warmth and comfort at the end of the day. This explanation of the division of labour between the sexes was based on a biological assumption that there are differences in the make-up of the sexes that account for their different roles. Only women can produce children, but this argument does not explain how women have had the greatest responsibility for all domestic duties.

The functionalist explanation represents a traditional view of a woman's work that has declined in popularity over the years. Nevertheless, inequalities still exist, particularly in the workplace. Women are generally paid less than men and they are more likely to be employed part-time because of their domestic responsibilities. They are more likely than men to do low-status jobs such as care work, and women in professional occupations are less likely to achieve the highest status. Jobs that are traditionally female, such as jobs in primary education, do not have the same status or pay and conditions as professional jobs that are traditionally male, such as surveyors or architects.

Human capital theory

Human capital theory is an economic idea based on functionalist principles. It suggests that women are disadvantaged in the workplace because they are less committed to their careers. This is a direct result of career breaks during childbearing years, either because of the breaks themselves or because of an attitude that puts family and childbearing above career, making a woman less likely to take opportunities for further training or advancement.

This notion has been refuted by a number of sociologists. Sloane (1994) investigated labour markets across the UK and found that although professional qualifications made a big difference to the income of workers, gender was also a significant variable. He found a considerable pay differential that could not be explained by human capital theory. Witz (1993) argues that even when women do not take career breaks, they remain less likely than men to move to the top of the career ladder.

Marxist and feminist sociologists explain gender inequality in terms of women's place in the labour market. They say that economic disadvantage is at the root of gender inequality. The pay gap between men and women has been steadily narrowing since 1971 but the Office for National Statistics found that the median weekly earnings of women doing full-time work in 2007 were £394, 21 per cent less than men at £498.

Stratification ...

■ **Take it further**

Every autumn, newspapers and shop windows carry ads for people to work in the run-up to Christmas. Students and housewives often apply so they can earn money to pay for their own Christmas festivities. They are the reserve army of labour who will no longer be required in January. Marx claimed that capitalist ideology creates these booms. We are urged to buy more than we need through advertising and social pressure, and we must find a way to fund these purchases. The people who benefit from the booms are the owners of production.

■ **Key terms**

Radical feminism: a form of feminism that seeks to abolish patriarchy in society, hence to end exploitation of women by men.

Private patriarchy: male dominance in the home that is usually evidenced by the adult male, e.g. husband or father, having control of other family members, especially the wife.

Public patriarchy: dominance of men in public life, particularly the workplace, that can be used to explain gender inequality.

Patriarchy: a system of society or government in which men hold the power and women are largely excluded from it.

■ **Take it further**

Sexual harassment legislation was updated in 2005, and the kind of behaviour Stanko describes may now be less evident. Certainly women are increasingly better protected against harassment in the workplace, as are men. Remember that men can experience similar harassment, especially in a female-dominated profession.

Working from a Marxist perspective, Braverman (1974) suggests that women are victims of a general and progressive deskilling of the workforce. Women tend to be employed in retail, clerical or service industries and these jobs have become increasingly deskilled. Braverman's emphasis on deskilling may be simplistic as not all women are employed in unskilled jobs. Deskilling does not explain the inequality women experience in the workplace.

■ Reserve army of labour

According to Marx, workers are exploited by the creation of a reserve army of labour. Because capitalist societies swing between times of boom and recession, there will be times when more workers are needed. The ability to take on workers in boom times and to lay them off in recession is important to industry, so a reserve army of labour is required to fill the demand.

Veronica Beechey (1986) argued that women are ideally placed to be this reserve army of labour because their main commitment is often to family life. Marx's view of family life was more radical: he said that the family is part of the dominant ideology as the emotional and social pressures to provide for the family make workers more docile for employers to exploit.

It is often assumed that women enter part-time employment because it is more convenient for their lifestyles, but it can be argued that part-time workers are better for employers because they are cheaper and more flexible. The reserve army of labour has less stability of employment and tends to earn a lower hourly rate than full-time workers. Marxist theory says this is exploitation of the workforce.

■ Feminism

Marxist feminist explanations of inequality in the workplace, such as Beechey (1986), are concerned with women's relationship to the labour market. Other feminists tend to explain inequality by women's relationship to men. According to **radical feminism**, men exert power over women in the workplace. In occupations that are predominantly male, Stanko (1988) says women are sexually harassed and find themselves unable to complain because of the dominant position of men in the organisation.

Sylvia Walby (1986) in *Patriarchy at Work* discussed the difference between **private patriarchy** and **public patriarchy**. She claimed that trade unions were responsible for disadvantaging women in the workforce. She says that using male strength and dominance to exclude women from high-status jobs, or from specific types of traditionally male occupations, is a form of patriarchy that has little to do with capitalism. Walby does not deny the existence or the power of capitalism but stresses that gender relations and male dominance are the main reason for gender inequality in the workplace. Trade unions have traditionally been male-dominated and have tended to act in the interests of men.

A strength of Walby's work on **patriarchy** is that it takes account of different forms of patriarchy, recognising that there are social and cultural differences between women's experiences. However, she has also been criticised for using a structured approach to her research. Feminist theorists often argue that sociological research of women's experiences should be **phenomenological**.

Attitudinal research into gender inequalities

As part of a campaign to get equal pay for women and men, in 1999 the Equal Opportunities Commission funded research into attitudes to the gender pay gap. In 1999 men's income was 21 per cent greater than women's income, which surprised most participants. The survey found that more than half of participants, women and men, believed the pay gap to be unfair but far more women than men were angry or disappointed, and younger people were more shocked than older people.

These results suggest that changes in attitudes to women in the workplace are having an impact; only a very small number of respondents said that pay inequality is acceptable. Perhaps more interestingly, most line managers said that men are the main breadwinners in the family. This attitude kept women's wages low and blocked opportunities for advancement until equal opportunities legislation was introduced in 1970. The attitude remains prevalent, which could explain the slow decline of pay differentials between men and women.

Research into causes of pay inequality

Grimshaw and Rubery (2001) were commissioned by the Equal Opportunities Commission to look at causes of pay inequality between men and women. Here are some of their findings:

- Part-time hourly rates are on average only 60 per cent of full-time rates. More women than men are in part-time employment.
- Women tend to work in care jobs and the public sector. Care work has traditionally been low-paid and public sector salaries have declined compared with private sector salaries.
- Increased use of subcontracting and franchising has brought pay and conditions down in traditionally female occupations: for example, contract cleaners in hospitals earn less and have poorer conditions than permanent cleaners.
- Awarding individual pay and conditions based on merit and performance can mean that unfair practices are hidden.

Grimshaw and Rubery concluded their report by saying that there needs to be a deliberate and conscious effort to address inequality of pay and conditions.

Equality: the way forward?

In 2001 a task force was set up by the Equal Opportunities Commission to find ways to eliminate gender pay inequality. Using action research as a methodology, it set up hearings throughout the UK and invited a wide range of participants from all areas of the workforce. Its initial research found that the effects of unequal pay were poverty, social exclusion, inability to build up an adequate pension fund, and reduction of motivation. Its report (see Link on the next page) highlighted five main barriers to equal pay for women:

- lack of awareness and understanding of the issue

Key terms

Phenomenological: relating to lived experience. Phenomenological research takes account of participants' subjective responses to an experience and is therefore qualitative.

Link

See page 359 for more on action research.

Stratification …

Link

Go to www.equalityhumanrights.com/Documents/EOC/PDF/Research/just_pay_report.pdf and download the report of the Equal Pay Task Force as a PDF.

- ineffective, time-consuming and cumbersome equal pay legislation
- lack of expertise in addressing the problem
- lack of transparency and accountability for implementing equal pay
- social and economic policy measures that have failed to keep pace with women's changing place in the labour market.

Summary question

2 Evaluate the argument that domestic responsibilities prevent women from attaining high-status positions in the workplace.

Discrimination and prejudice

Britain has always been an ethnically diverse population. From the Danes, Vikings and Romans through to Irish and Jewish settlers, and more recent immigration from the colonies in the mid 20th century, there has been a steady flow of immigrants into the British Isles. This means there is no such thing as a pure-bred British person. All of us have diverse ancestry.

Britain: a diverse nation

Humans commonly show mistrust and prejudice towards other races, and Britain has experienced waves of anti-immigrant feeling throughout its history. Perhaps this was understandable in the days when settlers were taking over the land, raping and pillaging as they went, but it has continued to the present day: significant numbers of people express the firm belief that Britain belongs to the British. Prejudice is most commonly felt towards people who are visibly different to the norm in a society. People whose skin colour or cultural dress codes are different to the majority are most at risk from prejudice.

After the Second World War, Britain experienced a labour crisis because it had lost so many young men. The government decided to resolve this labour shortage by encouraging immigration from Commonwealth countries. There was an influx of West Indian, Indian and Pakistani immigrants, and some of the major beneficiaries were the health service, London Transport, hotels and heavy industry. Many of the workers who were encouraged to enter Britain took up jobs that were unpleasant and poorly paid – jobs that British people were unwilling to do.

Many people remained unaware of the government's active part in this post-war migration into Britain, preferring to believe stories of black people coming into the country to steal their jobs. Race riots in the 1950s and 1960s led to the Commonwealth Immigrants Acts of 1962 and 1968, but it became clear that immigration controls specifically controlled the entry of black immigrants; they had no impact on white immigrants from Commonwealth countries.

In recent years, immigration has been increasingly tightly controlled from countries outside the European Union (EU), particularly in response to the increasing number of asylum seekers who want to enter Britain to escape persecution. It is now extremely difficult for an asylum seeker to enter Britain legally as the need for a visa or a British passport puts insurmountable barriers on people whose lives are at risk in other countries (Parekh *et al.* 2000).

Members of the EU have free movement between member states, which means that most immigration to Britain is now from other EU countries, particularly Eastern Europe, where the standard of living is much lower than in the West. Britain continues to be a culturally and racially diverse nation, so it must continue to deal with a range of political, social and economic challenges associated with its diversity. Table 6.5.1 gives a breakdown of the UK population by ethnic group.

Stratification...

Table 6.5.1 *UK population by ethnic group, 2001/2*

	Share of the total population (%)	Share of the minority ethnic population (%)
White	92.4	NA
Mixed	0.8	11.0
Asian or Asian British		
Indian	1.7	21.7
Pakistani	1.3	16.7
Bangladeshi	0.5	6.1
Other Asian	0.4	5.7
Black or Black British		
Black Caribbean	1.0	13.6
Black African	0.9	12.0
Black Other	0.1	1.5
Chinese	0.3	4.2
Other	0.6	7.4
Not stated	0.2	NA
All minority ethnic population	7.6	100.0
All population	100	
Unweighted base = 100%	361,644	25,049

NA = not applicable or not available

Source: Annual Local Area Labour Force Survey 2001–2002, *Office for National Statistics*

Take it further

Are you surprised to see that the total number of minority ethnic people in Britain is less than 8 per cent of the population? Ask some friends and family what percentage of the population of the UK are black and minority ethnic groups. You will probably find that most people think the percentage is much higher. Why? Because we notice difference.

Key terms

Stereotype: a preconceived, standardised and oversimplified impression of the characteristics which typify a person, situation, etc., often shared by all members of a society or certain social groups; an attitude based on such a preconception.

Prejudice: a positive or negative judgement based on stereotyped beliefs.

Discrimination: acting differently towards a person or group because of stereotyped beliefs.

Take it further

Consider these stereotypes. Black people have a good sense of rhythm. Gay men live in tasteful, tidy homes. Indians live in huge houses full of children. Lesbians wear dungarees and boots and don't shave their legs. Travelling people are untrustworthy. Rich people are snobs. Women are bad drivers. Can you think of any others? Many people outside these groups fit the descriptions, and many people in these groups don't fit the descriptions.

Stereotype, prejudice and discrimination

Stereotypes are overgeneralised ideas about particular groups of people and are often the basis of prejudiced attitudes. The **stereotypes** in the 'Take it further' box are probably some of the least harmful. You probably thought of some that are inappropriate to print. Stereotypes offer a way of classifying people and situations to help make quick judgements in a social setting, and to some extent they are useful. Teaching children not to trust strangers is probably important as is knowing the dangers of specific places or settings and the kinds of people who frequent them. Being careful not to carry too much cash or valuables abroad is not the same as saying that all foreigners are thieves.

If a stereotype is a positive or negative judgement about a particular group, then the stereotype is considered prejudicial. A **prejudice** can be positive or negative. We might evaluate someone more positively because they belong to a different group just as easily as we might think more negatively of a person. Either way is prejudice. Discrimination is when a person acts differently towards someone because of an evaluation based on their group or nationality.

The effect of **discrimination** is inequality. People in Britain who are from black and minority ethnic backgrounds are more likely to have lower success in the education system, earn lower incomes or be unemployed and live in poorer housing than the average population. Their life chances are poorer because of the impact of prejudice and discrimination. Interestingly, these effects are not the same across all minority ethnic groups.

Figure 6.5.1 shows that white people in Britain are much less likely to be unemployed than people from minority ethnic groups. The national

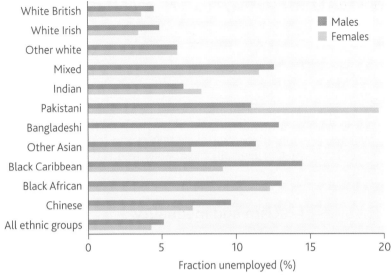

Fig. 6.5.1 *Great Britain: unemployment: by ethnic group and sex, 2004*

Source: National Statistics Online

average unemployment rate is approximately 6 per cent, which means that some groups represented in this graph experience unemployment at two or three times the national average. Note that Pakistani women have the highest rate of unemployment.

It is not possible to prove a direct cause and effect relationship between discrimination and unemployment figures but there is evidence of deep-seated racism in British institutions. The 1981 Scarman Report after the Brixton riots stated that British institutions were not racist but that there were 'unintended consequences … of public policy … that disadvantaged ethnic minorities'. Scarman made recommendations to put right these anomalies. The 1999 Macpherson Report on the investigation of the Stephen Lawrence murder said that the British police were institutionally racist. It found that the recommendations of the Scarman Report had been ignored. In 2000 the Trades Union Congress (TUC) set up a Stephen Lawrence Task Group to investigate **institutional racism** in the workplace and concluded that black and minority ethnic groups were more likely to be unemployed or in low-paid and low-skilled jobs because of institutional racism (Table 6.5.2).

Summary questions

Look at Table 6.5.1 and answer these questions.

1 What are the two largest minority ethnic groups in Britain?

2 What percentage of the whole population do each of these two groups represent?

3 What percentage of the whole population is from black and minority ethnic groups?

4 How did the police respond to the Scarman Report? Does the police response support the claim that they were institutionally racist?

Key terms

Institutional racism: racism that is built into the policies and procedures of an institution or organisation. It is often hidden or covert.

Table 6.5.2 *Percentage of people in employment who were in the higher managerial and professional group, 2001–2*

Other	13.5
Chinese	10.5
Black African	7.9
Black Caribbean	4.9
Other Asian	11.6
Bangladeshi	3.0
Pakistani	4.4
Indian	13.6
Mixed	7.1
White other	15.6
White Irish	10.3
White	8.4

Source: Annual Local Area Labour Force Survey, *Office for National Statistics*

Sociological explanations of ethnicity and inequality

Learning objectives:

- Discuss different theories of racism in relation to inequality.

- Evaluate the argument that a black underclass exists in Britain.

Key terms

Dual labour market theory: the primary labour market has high wages, good working conditions and good job security. The secondary labour market has low wages, poor working conditions and poor job security. Some members of society are more likely to be represented in the secondary labour market, including women and minority ethnic workers.

Many sociologists believe that racism is the reason why black people experience higher rates of unemployment and lower numbers in high-status, high-salary positions. Even when the cause can be attributed to poor educational qualifications, it is likely that racism is the root of the problem, as black children generally have poorer results than white children.

Theories of racism and inequality

Weberian theories of racism are based on the notion of status inequality. Power is in the hands of the white majority, so decisions are made that are in the best interests of that majority. The result is that the interests of minorities are not represented. Rex and Tomlinson (1979) studied black workers in Birmingham. They state that black and minority ethnic groups experience class and status inequality and therefore become poor and powerless. The result is alienation, which may lead to race riots and violence.

Rex and Tomlinson were supporters of the **dual labour market theory**. They found that immigrant workers were over-represented in the secondary labour market, with low wages and poor working conditions. This came about largely because of the influx of workers from the colonies to take up unskilled and badly paid jobs in the 1950s and 1960s. Rex and Tomlinson conclude that these disadvantages have caused a black underclass to form.

Marxist theory bases its explanation on capitalism and the exploitation of workers. One classic theory of racism was proposed by Cox (1970), based on Marxist principles. He refuted earlier ideas that racism was common to the human condition or that it was caused by some kind of abnormal psychology. Cox stated that racism is caused by colonisation, a form of exploitation that has its roots in early capitalism. By colonising other countries, capitalists could benefit from other countries' natural resources and turn their people into cheap labour. Racism is a way of justifying this exploitation: by saying that these workers were in some way inferior to themselves, the capitalists could justify treating them badly.

Many theorists have criticised this notion as too simplistic and prefer to explain racism as being multifaceted:

- justification of British military dominance over colonised countries by making reference to the 'savages' who needed controlling
- the exploitation of migrant workers
- the apparent acceptance of racist attitudes and ideas by some minority ethnic groups
- the economic crisis of the 1970s giving rise to a popular feeling that 'sending the blacks home' might help the situation
- idealising British culture as special and different
- language and images that represented white as good and black as bad (Solomos *et al.* 1982).

Robert Miles (1989), also a Marxist, considers race as just one faction within the working class. Like women, ethnic groups have experienced disadvantage but this is related as much to their class position as their race. He points out that there are minority ethnics in the higher strata of society who are committed to capitalism.

Andrew Pilkington (1999) returned to the question of the racial underclass first proposed by Rex and Tomlinson in 1979. He points out that some minority ethnics, especially Asian men, are well represented in higher-status careers and that overall in the past few years minority ethnic workers have improved their status more quickly than white lower-status workers. He denies the existence of a black underclass as there is much overlap between different ethnic groups in society. It would be a mistake to assume that one can analyse all black and minority ethnic workers and find a common experience. Different ethnic groups have very different experiences: some perform better than white people in education and the workplace.

Bangladeshis and Pakistanis appear to experience the worst kind of disadvantage but even in these communities there are others who are successful in the workplace. Pilkington concludes that racial discrimination still exists but that there is too much diversity among black and minority ethnic communities to say there is a racial underclass.

A multi-ethnic Britain

It is common for the white majority in Britain to assume that black and minority ethnics have more similarities than differences. This is a common mistake and it demonstrates a type of internalised racism. There is no reason to believe that people who are non-white have more in common with one another than with white people. Similarly, it would be unreasonable to think that white people from all parts of the world share a common culture. Among the black and minority ethnic community there are more cultural differences than there are similarities. The experience they have in common is **marginalisation**.

Key terms

Marginalisation: being excluded or discounted because a person is on the outside of the majority group in society.

Summary question

5 Evaluate the claim that there is a black underclass in Britain.

Age

Learning objectives:

- Explain the relationship between age, inequality and life chances.

- Understand why changes in the demographics of age in society can affect social influence.

Take it further

Think about attitudes to elderly people among your own social group. Do you assume that elderly people are incapable of intelligent thought? Now think about attitudes towards young people. Do you think that some older people stereotype young people and have negative attitudes towards them?

In 2006 it became illegal in Britain to discriminate on the grounds of age. Whenever legislation is passed to protect groups from discrimination, it is because that discrimination has been discovered. For instance, legislation to prevent discrimination on the grounds of gender and race was developed because real discrimination existed and was being practised in a range of settings. Remember this when you consider age, because age discrimination has been so entrenched in society that it may have gone unnoticed.

Economic inequality

Young people and elderly people experience economic inequality. Young people have lower incomes, perhaps understandably due to lack of work experience, but they are also more likely to be unemployed. According to the 1999 Labour Force Survey, 12.3 per cent of people aged 15–24 were unemployed in 1999, compared with 4.9 per cent of people over 25. Older people experience economic inequality through poor pension provision and greater difficulty in finding employment if they become unemployed in the last 10 years of their working lives.

The population of the UK is ageing: there are more people aged 55–64 in the population than people aged 16–24, yet evidence suggests that employers have traditionally discriminated against applicants for work on the basis of age. According to a 2005 survey by Cranfield School of Management and the law firm Eversheds, 41 per cent of people reported experiencing some form of age discrimination in the workplace. The National Audit Office has estimated that underemployment of people aged 50 and over has cost the UK economy up to £30 billion per year due to the impact of lower tax take, higher benefit costs and lost working potential.

More recently, now that it's a legal requirement, businesses are recognising that it also makes good business sense to employ people from all age groups. According to the Department of Work and Pensions, Marks and Spencer reported higher productivity after it employed staff with diverse ages and adopted the following policies and procedures:

- review policies and make human resources staff aware of age issues
- remove mandatory retirement ages
- increase the use of flexible retirement and introduce flexible retirement policies
- carry out internal marketing to promote the changes in policies
- encourage stores to carry out various local initiatives to target older workers.

Social attitudes

Although economic inequality is common among younger and older people, there are distinct differences in attitudes to the two age groups. A major piece of research by Age Concern and Kent University (Ray *et al.* 2006) found that 1 in 3 respondents thought that people over 70 were incompetent. Interestingly, participants were as likely to hold these stereotyped attitudes to others in their own age group, but not towards themselves. This indicates a level of internalised prejudice towards elderly people. Participants considered ageism to be less serious than other forms of discrimination and there was evidence that reduced life chances were expected for elderly people and therefore not considered important.

Negative attitudes to young people are more likely to be in response to social problems such as youth crime rather than age alone. A study of public attitudes to youth crime (Hough and Roberts 2004) found that public perception of the extent of the problem is far greater than crime figures show. Some 75 per cent of participants believed that youth crime had increased significantly in the two previous years, but police figures showed a fall of 9 per cent. And 42 per cent of respondents said they believed that half of all crime was committed by young people, when the actual figures are 10–20 per cent. Participants claimed that media representation had given substance to these attitudes. This suggests there is bias in media reporting that may indicate stereotyped attitudes towards youth in relation to crime.

Social influence

To get elected, politicians must promise policies that will benefit most of the population, and public services will need to adjust to the needs of an ageing population. Increased life expectancy and a reduction in the birth rate have shifted Britain's age profile so that older people are now in the majority. When a group that was marginalised is no longer in the minority, their influence changes and they become politically stronger. This shift in influence is called political strength. It is useful to compare it with the experience of disabled people (see the next section).

Summary question

1 Give a reasoned argument to support the suggestion that economic inequality is a greater problem for the young than the elderly.

Disability

Learning objectives:

- Understand the social model of disability in relation to disableism.

- Explain the relationship between life chances and disability.

Elderly people are in the majority, which makes them politically strong, whereas disabled people are politically weak as they are in a minority and are more likely to be in the lower strata of society. Here are a few words that are currently used to discuss disability:

- **Disabled person** – a person affected by disability.
- **Impairment** – the condition that causes a person to be disabled: for example, a person with a hearing impairment may have difficulty hearing.
- **Disability** – restrictions and social conditions that limit or negatively affect the life of a person with an impairment; the interaction between different issues that affect a person's life.

Social exclusion

Sociologists use the term 'disableism' to describe the discrimination experienced by disabled people in society. Disableism means that society puts barriers in the way of people with impairments so they cannot take a full and active part in society. Some obvious examples of disableism are stairs up to entrances that prevent wheelchair users from entering buildings and attitudes which assume that disabled people are unable to speak for themselves or have normal social relationships.

Stigmatising attitudes to disability have caused society to push disabled people to the margins. Tom Shakespeare (1994) claims that these attitudes are implicit in language, culture and socialisation. Disabled people are marginalised by reference to disability as a medical problem, searches for cures, and the engendering of pity.

It has been argued that further discrimination arises because many services for disabled people are provided by charities. Able-bodied people do not expect lifts in high-rise buildings to be provided by charity. It is not left to charities to provide care for the ill, the very young or the very old, but disabled people often have to rely on charities as statutory provision is inadequate or non-existent.

The Disability Discrimination Act 1995 made it illegal to discriminate on the grounds of disability in education, employment, health and services. People working in public services are required to consider the impact of their services on disabled people. It is relatively easy to make changes to services and use of language but attitudes are more difficult to change.

Poverty and disability

Disabled people are more likely to live in poverty than other people in society. This is partially explained by their lower likelihood of employment plus their higher living expenses. Figure 6.6.1 is from a study by the Joseph Rowntree Foundation and uses information from the Department of Work and Pensions. It shows that disabled adults are twice as likely to live in poverty than other adults. Further research by the Joseph Rowntree Foundation also found that people in the lower strata of society are also more likely to become disabled. In other words, there is a complex relationship between poverty and disability.

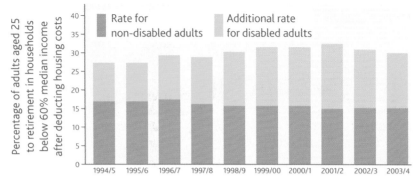

Fig. 6.6.1 *Disabled adults are twice as likely to live in poverty than other adults*
Source: Households Below Average Income, Department of Work and Pensions. Cited in *Monitoring Poverty and Social Exclusion in the UK 2005*, December 2005, Joseph Rowntree Foundation

False assumptions about the nature of disability often lead people to believe that all disabled people are born with an impairment. In fact, a person is much more likely to develop an impairment in adult life and the risks are much greater for people who have the lowest educational qualifications (Figure 6.6.2). People from the lowest social classes experience poorer life chances, including less success in the education system. These findings by the Joseph Rowntree Foundation show that they have a greater likelihood of becoming disabled.

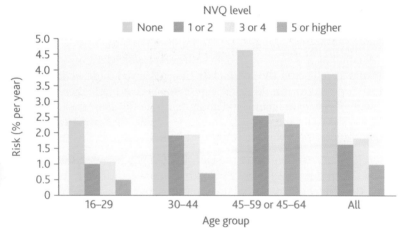

Fig. 6.6.2 *Risk of becoming disabled, by age and educational qualifications*
Source: Social Exclusion and the Onset of Disability, November 2003, Joseph Rowntree Foundation

One explanation for disabled people living in poverty is the increased likelihood of unemployment. Oppenheim and Harker (1996) say this is caused by exclusion from the workforce through stigmatising attitudes. Barnes (1991) found that when applying for work, disabled applicants were six times more likely to be unsuccessful. Although it can be argued that the experience of people with disabilities in applying for and managing their experience of work can be improved by better awareness and appropriate legislation, there is still no doubt that public attitudes marginalise disabled people.

Summary question

2 Sociologists have argued that people with impairments are disabled by societal attitudes. Explain the relationship between life chances and attitudes.

Stratification…

345

Changes in structures of inequality

Changes in class structure

Learning objectives:

- Describe changes to each of the social classes.
- Explain differences in Marxist, Weberian and New Right explanations of these changes.

Changes to the working class

The working class has changed as the occupational structure of Britain has changed. Advances in technology have removed some jobs from the market altogether and increased productivity in other areas. Heavy industry has declined as business increasingly takes advantage of cheaper labour overseas. More people than ever are employed in service industries as increases in living standards have produced a significant rise in the leisure industries. One assumption made about the classification of the working class is that it refers to those doing manual jobs. Not all sociologists have agreed with this notion and some think the working class includes people who have routine non-manual jobs.

This lack of agreement highlights a difficulty with social class as a means of classification. There are no absolute criteria on which to base an individual's class. Some manual workers earn more than some white-collar workers, yet Marshall *et al.* (1988) found that manual workers tended to describe themselves as working-class and non-manual workers as middle-class. Marshall *et al.*'s method of data collection involved asking participants to self-select the social class they perceived themselves to belong to. A problem with this kind of research is that it assumes that all those involved, i.e. participants and analysts, share the same meaning about the variables in the research. It is impossible to be certain that every participant understood 'working-class' and 'middle-class' in the same way.

This type of research highlights the fact that the gap between the working class and the middle class is not as clearly defined as it used to be. The very fact that there may be some uncertainty about what social class individuals perceive themselves to belong to indicates that the differences may be somewhat blurred or indistinct. The formation of a class identity or consciousness is less likely when the class is less distinctive: this has led sociologists to suggest that the working class has become divided and is in danger of disappearing. This notion is further upheld by the fact that a huge reduction in industrialisation in Britain has led to a significant reduction in manual workers.

The formation of an underclass

An important change to structural inequality is the formation of an underclass that consists of the most disadvantaged groups in society. Sociologists have shown different degrees of interest in the underclass: some have concentrated on economic position and some on differences in behaviour. The behaviour of the underclass has been described as departing from the norms of the rest of society. This suggests that the underclass is somehow marginalised from the rest of society and represents a social problem which some see as a threat to society. Charles Murray (1984) described an American underclass that was largely black and unemployed and posed a threat to the economic and social structure of American society.

Taking a somewhat right-wing approach, he claimed in 1989 that Britain was also developing an underclass consisting of single mothers and young people unwilling to work (Murray 1989). He claimed that the welfare state was encouraging the existence of the underclass and that traditional values were declining as the underclass behaved in ways that challenged these principles. This approach ignores the connection between the economy and poverty and suggests that the underclass has caused its own problems. Murray's work has been criticised as poorly evidenced and lacking a cohesive argument. Murray's New Right definition is unpopular with most sociologists.

Giddens (1973) claimed that the underclass consisted of those who were most disadvantaged in society. He described a secondary job market for such people that has low wages and poor job security. These jobs currently tend to be taken by immigrants from Eastern European countries, who find themselves marginalised and disadvantaged on arriving in Britain. Runciman (1990) stated that the underclass consists of people who live on welfare benefits without hope of getting work. This group may include the disabled and those who have limited education or low literacy skills.

Is the underclass a separate class or is it simply the lower levels of the working class? Here some points to bear in mind:

- Long-term unemployed people cannot be placed in the current system of stratification.
- Long-term unemployment or living on benefits creates significant changes to a person's lifestyle.
- A separate social class will have a distinct shared cultural identity. Sociologists disagree about whether the underclass shares an identity or whether it shares its identity with elements of the working class.

Changes to the middle class

Professionals are normally considered to be upper middle-class because of their ability to command higher salaries and social prestige. The lower middle class includes more routine clerical workers and retail workers. Changes to the experience of the middle class include a reduction in status and relative pay and conditions of public service employees. Civil servants were once highly respected professionals but Savage *et al.* (1992) claims that government emphasis on reducing public spending has weakened their position considerably.

Comparing public and private professionals, Savage claimed that the lifestyles of different members of the middle class varied according to their employment sector. Professionals working in the private sector were better paid than public servants and had a distinctly different lifestyle. This suggests a division within the middle class that goes beyond the traditional divide between professionals and routine white-collar workers.

The members of the lower middle class are routine clerical workers, secretaries, shop workers and call-centre staff. According to Marxist theory, this group have become working-class – the proletarianisation thesis – as their jobs have been deskilled by the growth of technology (Braverman 1974). The Weberian view is that lower middle-class workers still have a better market position than their working-class colleagues as their jobs are stepping stones to management. The Weberian view of work considers social prestige and market position such as job security, so it argues that clerical workers are still a distinctly middle-class group (Lockwood 1958).

Stratification …

There is no doubt that the middle classes have grown and changed. Sociologists are not in agreement about whether there is still a distinct middle class or several smaller groups whose social mobility, market position and life chances vary according to their role. Giddens (1973) argues that there is still a distinct middle class whose currency is brain power and skill rather than brawn and strength. Their potential for social mobility is greater through promotion and they are offered a degree of security because of their superior qualifications, skills and knowledge.

■ Changes to the upper class

The Marxist notion of people who own the means of production has inevitably changed as the importance of production has declined and the importance of service and financial industries has grown. According to Westergaard and Resler (1976), the upper class now consists of owners of production plus higher professionals and company directors, most of whom are major investors in the private sector. Westergaard calls them the power elite.

In an alternative to this Marxist idea, Saunders (1990a) suggested there is an economic elite in British society that consists of the people Westergaard describes as the ruling class. Arguing from a New Right perspective, Saunders claims that their influence is not as all-encompassing as the Marxist ruling-class theory suggests. By the end of the 20th century there had been a steep decline in the family ownership of large companies: most were increasingly owned by pension funds and private investment, making it more difficult to identify a ruling class. The upper class still exists in Britain and continues to regenerate itself through public schooling and social networking, but it could be argued that its size and influence have diminished.

■ Summary questions

1 Explain at least one connection between changes in the structure of social classes and the formation of class identity.

2 Explain why the distinction between social classes might be described as less clear.

Theories of change

Learning objective:

- Evaluate major studies of changes in class structures.

Take it further

Jim is a plumber. He owns his own home and enjoys a comfortable lifestyle which includes two holidays a year and membership of the local golf club. Recently his wife has started working full-time to fund private education for their two children. They want their children to do well in life and realise that a good education will give them more opportunities. Is Jim working-class or middle-class?

Changes in the working class

Marx predicted that the petty bourgeoisie and other intermediate groups would disappear and become subsumed into the working class as society became increasingly divided between the bourgeoisie and the proletariat. In reality, it is the middle classes that have grown and developed, and there is evidence of some diminution in the size and influence of the working class and the upper class. One explanation of this change is the theory of embourgeoisement, where many manual workers have entered the middle classes through increased market demand for their skills and a better standard of living.

The idea of embourgeoisement was questioned by a number of sociologists. Findings suggested that an improved standard of living does not necessarily mean that a person becomes middle-class. Goldthorpe *et al.* (1969) compared the experience of manual and white-collar workers in the relatively affluent area of Luton in Bedfordshire. Wages and prospects for manual workers in the area were good and this led to an influx of workers from other areas. Recognising that a person's social class is as much about lifestyle and attitudes about income, Goldthorpe and Lockwood looked at a range of factors. They assumed that if manual workers had become middle-class, their responses would be similar to the white-collar group. Here is what they found:

- **Attitudes towards work** – manual workers thought of work as a way of earning money to support a better lifestyle but white-collar workers expressed a level of job satisfaction. Manual workers did not think in terms of promotion prospects or a career structure but this was important to white-collar workers.
- **Social relationships** – there was no evidence of mixing between the classes; people made friends from among their own class.
- **Outlook on life** – both groups lived a 'privatised' family life, with home as the centre of social existence. This differed from the traditional view of working-class life, where social relationships tended to be more communal, but this could be explained by the fact that many of the workers had moved into the area to take advantage of the potential for good wages.
- **Political views** – higher-paid manual workers did not shift towards more middle-class political allegiance, but neither did they have the strong commitment to the Labour Party and trade unions that was typical of the traditional working class. This was explained as an outcome of a more instrumental attitude to work, which seeks a means to an end, such as good wages. This approach had replaced the emphasis on solidarity of the traditional working classes.

Goldthorpe *et al.* concluded that there was no evidence of embourgeoisement in the manual workers but that a new working class had emerged which was more committed to the capitalist society and therefore viewed work as an instrument to enable a better lifestyle. Their findings also suggested that Marx's prediction of a growing working class that would rise up in revolt against the capitalist owners of production was receding as workers became less collective and adopted a privatised lifestyle.

■ Changes in the middle class

Changes in the middle class were examined by Savage *et al.* (1992) in a major study looking at aspects of social class structure and identity. Savage *et al.* took a neo-Marxist approach which assumed that social class is based on exploitation. They proposed that social classes share a culture of exploitation of others rather than a shared lifestyle. They describe members of the middle class as having one or more assets that make exploitation possible:

- ■ **Property** – this is the basis of capital assets such as a business. Owners of property can exploit others by withholding a fair wage for work done.
- ■ **Organisation** – a person who holds a position of power or authority in large organisations has exploitative power over workers in lower positions.
- ■ **Culture** – cultural assets are gained through education and mixing with other middle-class people. They can be used to achieve better positions in the workplace, such as by gaining additional qualifications in business or economics, or by mixing with higher-status people in cultural activities.

Savage suggests that different assets have greater or lesser importance over time and this explains changes in the middle classes over time. One such change is the weakening of public service positions through the effect of government policies. He claims that the impact of this change is to make a division between public and private sector professionals, with corresponding differences in lifestyle and culture. The ability of public service professionals to exploit others to gain greater rewards has been diminished and their lifestyles reflect a lesser attachment to capitalism. Those in the private sector are more concerned with cultural assets and live a more lavish lifestyle, supported by higher incomes. Savage's work is important because it reflects the constant change that occurs in social groups and explains the divisions that have arisen in the middle class.

■ Are class structures disappearing?

Postmodern theories suggest that changes to the economic structures in society have led to a change in society's values and this has ended social class as a meaningful analysis of society. Pakulski and Waters (1996) claim that new approaches to social life such as a greater interest in ecology and a greater commitment to equality have weakened the class structure to the point that it is no longer significant. Although they recognise that inequality still exists, they point out a greater willingness to address it and the emergence of new groupings of people whose shared identities can be based on a range of different things.

Preferences and differences in culture, religion, ethnicity and gender are rising in importance as social class differences decline, whereas traditional status positions are losing ground in favour of other values and preferences. It may be more culturally and socially significant to be a writer or an artist than a high-ranking civil servant and there may be more social currency in making the decision to downsize than to continually seek bigger and better property and income.

According to Pakulski and Waters, change is happening more rapidly in modern society as people recognise that it is possible to be more autonomous in their values and behaviour. Values have become more diverse, with a greater acceptance of difference and a weakening of traditional values that carried the threat of social sanctions on those who departed from them.

One way in which the old ideas of class and the new postmodern attitudes to society coincide is the commitment to consumerism. Pakulski and Waters claim it is the consumption of goods that depicts a person's lifestyle. The greater consumption and the depiction of good taste in a person's pattern of consumption says more about a person than their social class. They claim that the underclass exists because of its inability to consume goods beyond those that are necessary for survival rather than because of exploitation.

This theory is interesting and offers explanations for some important cultural and social changes in recent years, but it has been criticised for failing to give a consistent and coherent view of social class and for failing to recognise the importance of class alongside other areas of differentiation. There is no doubt that the ability to consume is part of social status but this is also the basis for theories of social class that have been disregarded by Pakulski and Waters.

> **Hint**
>
> Theories such as the postmodern view of social class have been heavily criticised by more traditional sociologists, but it is important to pick out the strengths of the arguments as well as the weaknesses. Think about Pakulski and Waters' views on changes in social values and compare them to New Right theories of social class. The next summary question will help to focus your thinking.

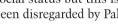 **Summary question**

3 Compare the following explanations of the underclass: Charles Murray's New Right approach, Runciman's Weberian approach and Pakulski and Waters' postmodernist approach.

Stratification...

The study of stratification and differentiation

Applying theory and method

Learning objectives:

- Analyse theory and methods with stratification and differentiation.

- Discuss advantages and disadvantages of different methods.

- Discuss data analysis and why the same data can produce different results.

Link

When you revise this material, add your knowledge from the theory and methods section to the specific points in hint boxes.

AQA Examiner's tip

Paper 4 of the examination contains one question that links the study of stratification with theory and method. You will need a good knowledge of the theory and method chapters in the AS and A2 books plus an ability to think on your feet and apply your knowledge well. Here 'apply knowledge' means work out the strengths and weaknesses of a given method to study stratification and express them clearly, and apply this knowledge further by evaluating a given method to study a specific topic related to inequalities.

Link

Use the content on theory and methods in the AS and the A2 books as your main sources of information. This section gives a brief tour of the methods and relates them to stratification and differentiation.

To give a good answer to questions about stratification and theory and method, you need general knowledge and specific knowledge. Knowledge of sociological approaches and methods underpins the whole subject and is essential for questions in the theory section and other sections, particularly stratification and differentiation. You will find this information in Topic 7. When it comes to specific knowledge, you will need to show that you understand the theoretical background to stratification and differentiation so you can evaluate the theories and comment on research methods.

Evaluating methods of data collection

Data collection can be divided into two categories:

- **Primary data** is data gathered by the researcher first-hand from the participants.
- **Secondary data** is data gathered from official statistics and other records such as historical information, church registers and diaries.

There are advantages and disadvantages in all methods of data collection, and sometimes they are peculiar to the research topic. For instance, the issue of honesty in responses to questionnaires is commonly quoted as a disadvantage. When official statistics on income depend on information from the Inland Revenue it is clear that reliability of information may be a particular problem.

Methods in stratification studies

Surveys

Surveys are often used in studies of stratification and differentiation. Questions might include information about class, country of origin, education, occupation and income that can be compared to gather information about the impact of one variable on another. For instance, a survey could be used to compare occupational outcomes between people from different social class backgrounds. Many surveys are carried out by government-funded organisations to provide information about society. Government data is therefore used routinely by sociologists as secondary data in research studies.

Advantages

- Large-scale studies are relatively inexpensive.
- A range of different variables can be compared.
- Surveys gather information about a broad cross-section of society.

Disadvantages

- Groups that are already disadvantaged by poverty, educational limitations or disability may be least likely to complete large questionnaires.

- Groups or individuals who are alienated from society and those who are disenfranchised through homelessness or other social problems are unlikely to be included.
- Where questionnaires involve information that may be perceived as useful to government departments, there may be some reluctance to give accurate information.

Interviews

Interviews offer an alternative method of gathering data from individuals or groups. Unstructured interviews offer the possibility of gathering data that is qualitative and therefore richer in detail. Personal experience and meaning can be explored, giving a fuller understanding of a group.

Advantages

- Individual experience and meaning can be explored.
- Adequate care can be taken to make certain that participants with particular needs can be included, such as using interpreters when English is not a person's first language (this includes sign language for deaf people).

Disadvantages

- It is a labour-intensive method of gathering and analysing data.
- Participants' responses may be affected by their opinion of the interviewer.

Actor tests

Actor tests, or situation tests, are used to investigate responses to different types of people in a given setting. For instance, actors may be used to discover how much the race or the physical appearance of a person affects the way people respond to them in a job interview. To investigate ageist attitudes, young actors may use a service, get made up as an elderly person, then reuse the service.

Advantages

- There is less chance of emotional distress if the research uses actors.
- There is some control of other variables such as personality and attitude.
- Actors can affect changes to some variables to offer other interesting data, such as race and accent. Would a person with a local accent be treated differently to a person with a foreign accent, regardless of skin colour?

Disadvantages

- Data is usually gathered covertly, which creates ethical problems.
- Participants are deceived if they believe the person is genuine, not an actor.
- The respondent may have been affected by some, perhaps unconscious, recognition of artificiality.

Participant observation

Participant observation is designed to gather the richest data possible by having the researcher become directly involved in the life of the group under study. In the study of social stratification, participant observation may be used to investigate the experience of particular groups.

Stratification…

The researcher could join a group of unemployed people as they take part in local initiatives to get them back to work. These initiatives are often compulsory after a period of unemployment, so some people may not participate willingly. The AS Sociology student book contains general information on the ethical dilemmas of participant observation.

Advantages

■ The researcher gathers authentic data that is not affected by the research process.

■ Other insights and information may be gathered, such as insights into bureaucratic processes that disadvantage or frustrate people.

Disadvantages

■ There is an ethical dilemma about deceiving people with whom the researcher forms a relationship.

■ It is difficult to estimate the hidden effects of background and education, even when they are not disclosed. The researcher may be treated differently to other members of the group they investigate.

■ Types of data

Quantitative and qualitative data

Data is collected in two main forms, quantitative and qualitative. Quantitative data is numerical and can be analysed to provide statistical evidence. Quantitative data is created by many research methods in sociology, such as surveys, official statistics, structured interviews and experiments. In general, quantitative methods are favoured by positivists and criticised by interpretivists. Here are some strengths of quantitative data gathering:

■ Research can be easily repeated, or replicated.

■ Large samples can be used.

■ Data can be easily analysed.

These strengths emphasise reliability of the research process. Here are some weaknesses of quantitative data gathering:

■ Meaning is not explored.

■ Individual experience can be lost when data is statistically analysed.

■ Motives for people's actions are not considered.

These weaknesses emphasise lack of insight into lived experience. In relation to the study of stratification and differentiation, you could argue that quantitative data gives broad insight into the state of the economy and the relative wealth of different groups in society, but it does not give any useful insight into the experience of different groups. Quantitative data can compare the income and occupational status of men and women, but it does not give information about the experience of women who encounter the glass ceiling or need to find childcare.

Qualitative data is descriptive and is gathered by asking people about their experiences and responses. Qualitative data gathering involves using interviews and asks people to describe their experiences and feelings related to that experience. Here are some strengths of qualitative data gathering:

■ Rich data is gathered.

■ Meaning and motive can be explored with the respondent.

■ Individual experience is emphasised.

Weaknesses of qualitative data gathering include:

- Research cannot be replicated.
- Samples tend to be small.
- It is relatively costly for the amount of data gathered.
- Analysis of data is difficult.

Thinking about the strengths and weaknesses of the two methods of data gathering it is clear that they offer virtually polar opposite advantages and disadvantages. For this reason many researchers will use a mixture of the two methods (triangulation) to get the best possible results.

Primary and secondary data

In primary data collection the researcher gathers first-hand information from participants. In secondary data collection the researcher uses existing sources such as official statistics. Primary and secondary data can be quantitative or qualitative. Here are some examples: surveys provide quantitative primary data, unstructured interviews provide qualitative primary data, official statistics provide quantitative secondary data and diaries provide qualitative secondary data. Besides considering the strengths and weaknesses described above, it is important to evaluate how the data was analysed and interpreted.

Sociological studies

Here are some real examples of sociological studies using the different forms of data collection. Note how they were evaluated.

Secondary sources

Saunders (1996) and Savage and Egerton (1997) show that different analyses of the same data can generate contradictory findings. Saunders uses evidence from the National Child Development Study to support claims that Britain is a meritocratic society and that middle-class children have more ability and are more motivated than working-class children. He claims that ability has more impact than class of origin on a person's ultimate social class, and that individual merit is the key factor in determining a person's ultimate status. His findings therefore support his theory that Britain is a meritocracy and the inequalities which exist are appropriate.

Savage and Egerton also used data from the National Child Development Study and compared the results with the Oxford mobility study. Their study differed from the Oxford mobility study in that it gave specific information about social mobility in women. Their findings suggested that upward mobility from the working class had not improved significantly and that a boy from the service class had twice the chance of being employed in that class than a boy from the working class. This did not apply to girls with service-class fathers. Their chances of being employed in the service class were lower than for boys from the same background, but greater than for boys from working-class backgrounds.

Higher rates of upward mobility were found from intermediate classes, and women were more likely to end up in the intermediate classes regardless of their class of origin. Savage and Egerton concluded that ability did have some impact on the chances of a person being upwardly mobile but that boys had other resources, particularly class of origin, to help them gain access to higher-status occupations. Girls appeared to rely more on ability to achieve access to high-ranking occupations.

Hints

- When you evaluate a study, it is important to consider how the researchers collected their data, but it is just as important to consider how they analysed and interpreted their data.

- A potential disadvantage of official statistics is that the data was not gathered specifically for that research study, so it has to be interpreted by the researcher. This may lead to bias.

- Studies that use secondary data may be affected by things they do not take into account.

Stratification …

The main difference between the studies by Saunders and Savage and Egerton is that Savage and Egerton recognise that social class of origin affects a person's chances of educational achievement and their ability to seize opportunities. Cultural capital is as important as ability, and parents from higher-status backgrounds may be able to pass on other cultural advantages to their children. Inequality begins to affect a person's life chances from birth, so it is not possible to make claims about the relative merit of different social classes without taking other factors into account.

Primary sources

Charlesworth (2000) conducted a series of interviews with people living in Rotherham, West Yorkshire. His research was intended to support Bourdieu's (1984) claim that classes develop a distinct habitus – a set of subjective understandings of the world plus choices and tastes. Bourdieu's claim was that the habitus influences the majority of lifestyle choices such as leisure, manner of communication, dress, eating habits and attitudes.

Charlesworth's research attempted to extend Bourdieu's ideas by gathering detailed and meaningful data about life in Rotherham. His findings described a somewhat bleak and depressing picture of life in Rotherham. He associates the lifestyles of the town's inhabitants with struggles against poverty and describes an inability to find a way out of poverty because of barriers to education and occupational success.

Charlesworth was born and brought up in Rotherham and did this research as a student of Cambridge University. In his introduction he describes his alienation from the university and appears to suggest that there was resistance to his work rather than support. His research does not acknowledge that some people are successful in the education system and achieve high-status occupations, even though this is his own experience.

Charlesworth's research has been supported by other theorists, who point out the insightful nature of the work and the richness of the data gathered, but there are some obvious contradictions in his analysis. He claims that solidarity is all that the working class has left and then says that solidarity is breaking down. He paints a very bleak picture of the area without making the observation that Rotherham is untypical of the majority of working-class towns. There is little evidence that his own assumptions have been challenged by approaching this study.

Methods in triangulation

Many sociologists use a mixture of methods to gather the fullest and richest data possible. There are obvious advantages of using a mixture of methods – methods in triangulation – as the weaknesses in one method can be offset by strengths in another. But gathering data in more than one way does not guarantee an elegant piece of research. Here are some points to bear in mind:

■ Gathering full and rich data is only useful if all the data is used.

■ Good analysis of the data is essential. Qualitative data is very difficult to analyse well and important insights can be missed.

■ Some researchers pay more attention to quantitative data: they believe it to be more reliable because of the more scientific nature of the data analysis.

> ### ■ Hint
>
> Interpretivist studies can offer rich descriptive insights into people's experience. When the researcher is emotionally and culturally invested in the research, it is possible that personal experience prevents the researcher from seeing the whole picture.

> ### ■ Link
>
> See page 349 for more on the study by Goldthorpe *et al.* (1969).

Goldthorpe *et al.* (1969) used a mixture of interviews, case studies and surveys to examine the notion that achieving higher salaries and better working conditions resulted in the embourgeoisement of workers. Their methods were very detailed. Their interviews included a number of open questions that led to full discussions. They gathered qualitative and quantitative data, and their field notes contained rich detail on the participants' attitudes to class, society, politics and social structures.

Savage (2005) points out that despite the richness of the data, the final report used only a small amount of this evidence and rarely used actual quotations from participants. Goldthorpe *et al.* presented most of their evidence in quantitative form and did not use the qualitative evidence they had gathered in a descriptive way. This may have been partly due to a perceived requirement to represent sociology as a scientific discipline. The raw data was painstakingly categorised so it could be presented in descriptive statistics rather than in a discursive format.

Action research

Action research is designed to drive or support change in a particular setting. It may involve assessing the impact of a change of policy or practice, or it may give voice to a marginalised group. Sociologists with a particular interest in inequality may use action research to raise awareness or motivate changes in attitudes. The researcher is likely to choose a topic of particular personal interest, which may bring a unique richness to the research but its value may be undermined by subjectivity.

Beverley Skeggs (1997) used a wide range of research methods to study 11 years in the life of a small group of working-class women. Her methods included interviews, secondary sources and participant observation; from the start, she made it clear that her research was politically motivated. Put another way, it was Skeggs' intention to give a voice to the experience of working-class women because she perceived them to be marginalised.

The findings of this research are highly detailed and describe a range of topics such as respectability and desirability. Small details of dress codes and attitudes to sexuality and attractiveness are described alongside topics such as class identity and culture. Skeggs' research has been criticised and praised for the same reason. The sample was small. This meant she could give in-depth data and observations about the participants over a long period of time, but it was impossible to generalise her findings.

Skeggs admits to an element of self-referencing in research, and she is no exception. Skeggs came from a working-class background, but unlike Charlesworth, she acknowledges her personal interest in the topic and addresses personal assumptions and preconceptions.

Summary question

1 Using material from this section and Topic 7, give an account of the advantages and disadvantages of using interviews in studies of social mobility.

■ Hints

- ■ Studies in triangulation offer the possibility of gathering the richest data.
- ■ Treatment of the data may limit its usefulness.
- ■ Qualitative data is particularly challenging to analyse. There are particular problems in attempting to present qualitative findings in a quantitative format.
- ■ Academia may tend to rate quantitative data more highly than qualitative data.

■ Hints

- ■ Small-scale research can be an advantage and a disadvantage.
- ■ Highly detailed work is an advantage and the difficulty of generalising results is a disadvantage.
- ■ Action research tends to be driven by the personal or political interests of the researcher.
- ■ The potential problems with subjectivity can be offset by the researcher's willingness to state their interests.

■ Take it further

To read an interview with Beverley Skeggs, download a PDF (www.britsoc.co.uk/Library/BSA_86Network_A4Version.pdf) from the British Sociological Association.

Topic summary

- The RG scale has been superseded by NS-SEC.

- Functionalist theory claims that differences between classes exist because some roles are more important than others, hence better rewarded than others.

- New Right theories of social class are a modern form of functionalism and emphasise the importance of motivation and the free-market economy.

- Marxist theory claims that there are only two basic classes: the workers and the owners of production.

- Functionalist theory is called consensus theory because of the idea that things work in society through consensus. Marxist theory is known as conflict theory because of the conflict between the two classes.

- Weberian thinking on stratification is more complex: it suggests that hierarchy in society is based on economic power, social prestige and political power.

- Postmodern thinkers claim that social class is no longer important in modern society.

- Social mobility refers to movement between classes that can occur between generations (intergenerational) or in a person's own lifetime (intragenerational).

- Evidence suggests that people who originate from lower social classes are less likely to make it to the top of the class hierarchy.

- Changes in employment structures have changed the pattern of social mobility in the UK.

- Women are more likely than men to have downward social mobility.

- In recent years there has been a rise in the number of super-rich people in Britain.

- Life chances influence every area of life: education, health, lifespan, etc.

- Gender, age, ethnic background, sexuality and disability all affect a person's life chances.

- People with multiple disadvantages belong to more than one inequality group.

- Despite legislation, women are disadvantaged in the workplace.

- Motherhood is one explanation for women's lower status in the workplace.

- Black and minority ethnic groups are disadvantaged in economic and occupational status and life chances.

- New legislation makes it illegal to discriminate by age.

- As older people become a greater fraction of society, they acquire greater social and political influence. Future governments will need to pay attention to their needs.

- New legislation means that organisations and services, including education, will need to provide full access to disabled people and be more inclusive.

- Disabled people are twice as likely as non-disabled people to live in low-income households.

- Postmodern thinkers suggest that social class is no longer the most important determinant of social status and that other status groups are forming.

- To give good exam answers, you need a good general understanding of methods plus specific knowledge of methods to study stratification and differentiation.

Further resources

Website

- www.statistics.gov.uk/methods_quality/ns_sec
  The National Statistics Socio-Economic Classification

Books and articles

- K. Davis and W. E. Moore, Some principles of stratification. In R. Bendix and S. M. Lipset (eds), *Class, Status and Power*, Routledge & Kegan Paul, 1967

- J. H. Goldthorpe, *Social Mobility and Class Structure in Modern Britain*, Clarendon, 1980

- G. Marshall and A. Swift, Merit and mobility: a reply to Peter Saunders. *Sociology*, Vol. 30, no. 2, 375–386, 1996

- J. Pakulski and M. Waters, *The Death of Class*, Sage, 1996

- T. Parsons, *Essays in Sociological Theory*, Free Press, 1964

- P. Saunders, *Social Class and Stratification*, Routledge, 1990

- B. Skeggs, *Formations of Class and Gender*, Sage, 1997

- M. M. Tumin, Some principles of stratification. In R. Bendix and S. M. Lipset (eds), *Class, Status and Power*, Routledge & Kegan Paul, 1967

- E. O. Wright, *Class, Crisis and State*, New Left Books, 1978

AQA Examination-style questions

General Certificate of Education

Advanced Level Examination

Section B from Paper 4

SOCIOLOGY Unit 4

For this paper you must have:

a 12-page answer book

Time allowed 2 hours

Instructions

Use black ink or black ball-point pen.

Write the information required on the front of your answer book. The Examining Body for this paper is AQA. The paper reference is SCLY4.

This paper is divided into **two** Sections.

Choose **one** section and answer **all** parts of the question from that Section.

Do not answer questions from more than one section.

Information

The maximum mark for this paper is 90.

The marks for part questions are shown in brackets.

Stratification…

359

SAMPLE 1

Section B: Stratification and Differentiation

You are advised to spend approximately 45 minutes on Question 4

You are advised to spend approximately 30 minutes on Question 5

You are advised to spend approximately 45 minutes on Question 6

Total for this section: 90 marks

4　　Read Item C below and answer the question that follows.

Item C

Many sociologists and politicians have argued that the increasingly complex, technological nature of the post-industrial Western world mean that the old social distinctions are breaking down. As economic change has accelerated over the last twenty or so years so, social mobility has increased, particularly as the 'old' manual jobs have disappeared. More and more, jobs are now allocated on the basis of 'what you know rather than who you know'. In the eyes of social democratic and liberal thinkers, the vast expansion of educational opportunity is breaking down the old social barriers as never before, assisted by the profound cultural change emanating from the global communications revolution.

However critics of this view point to the continued existence of a political, social and economic elite in most Western societies, whose lives are intertwined and largely closed to outsiders, however wealthy. They point out that most of the senior positions in British society are still held by the sons (and to a much lesser extent, the daughters) of the public-school, Oxbridge elite who have governed Britain since the fall of the landed aristocracy. However wealthy the Wayne Rooneys of this world are, they will remain working class in all other aspects of their lives.

Source: Written by Hamish Joyce

(a)　　Examine some of the arguments for and against the view that increased educational opportunity has led to increased social mobility in Britain in the last thirty years. *(12 marks)*

(b)　　Critically examine the view that social class is as much culturally as economically defined. *(21 marks)*

5　　This question requires you to apply your knowledge and understanding of sociological research methods to the study of this particular issue in stratification and differentiation.

Read Item D below and answer parts (a) and (b) that follow.

Item D

In recent years disability has moved from being something that was not discussed in polite society for fear of causing offence, to a major political and social issue. In part this can be seen as a consequence of the increasingly effective disability rights movement, but it is also because of the economic cost of disability to the state. Currently there is political debate around the large number of people who claim Incapacity Benefit, and politicians are keen to demonstrate they are 'tough on benefit cheats.' It is now widely recognised that for most people being disabled has an adverse economic and social effect on life chances.

Many sociologists have always seen disability (and many other 'medical' conditions) as being socially constructed, rather than physically defined. This is particularly the case with mental illness, with research as far back as Goffman's into Total Institutions still seen as highly relevant today. Similarly, writing in the mid-1970s Interactionist sociologist Fred Davis used lengthy, semi-structured interviews with blind, facially disfigured subjects to see how 'normal' people dealt with the disabled individual's desire to be seen as someone who is different physically, but otherwise a normal person.

Source: Written by Hamish Joyce

(a)　　Identify and briefly explain three problems of using disability as a variable in determining life chances *(9 marks)*

(b)　　Using material from Item D and elsewhere, assess the strengths and limitations of using semi-structured interviews to investigate the effects of disability and other social variables. *(15 marks)*

6　　'Many phenomenological writers argue that the social world is made up of the constructs, interpretations and understandings of individual social actors. Collectively these constitute what we choose to describe as reality.' Critically examine this approach to the study of society. *(33 marks)*

SAMPLE 2

Section B: Stratification and Differentiation

You are advised to spend approximately 45 minutes on Question 4

You are advised to spend approximately 30 minutes on Question 5

You are advised to spend approximately 45 minutes on Question 6

Total for this section: 90 marks

4   Read Item C below and answer the question that follows.

> **Item C**
>
> Feminist sociologists may broadly agree that women occupy generally lower and less influential positions in stratification systems, be these based on gender, class, status, income or any other variable, but they cannot agree as to which variable is the most important one. Marxist feminists not unnaturally regard economic class as the most significant factor in women's oppression, whereas more radical feminists believe that all men oppress all women, irrespective of class. Other writers such as Hacker (1972) have suggested that women's position is comparable to that of a minority group such as black people in America.
>
> Writers such as Eichler (1980) have attempted to bridge the gap between class-based and gender-based theories. Eichler pointed out that much of the exploitation of women occurs outside the work place, and therefore does not 'fit' into conventional Marxist approaches to the distribution of economic and social power. However, critics of feminists would argue that the massive increase in the number of women in work, the success of girls in the education system and, crucially, the growing number of women in top positions in Western societies makes all feminist theory increasingly outdated.
>
> Source: Written by Hamish Joyce, but this owes a little to Haralambos, 4th Edition pp 630-631

     (a)   Examine some of the reasons for changes to the status of women in the occupational structure of Western societies over the last forty years.   *(12 marks)*

     (b)   Assess sociological explanations of the importance of gender in social stratification systems in contemporary Western societies.   *(21 marks)*

This question requires you to apply your knowledge and understanding of sociological research methods to the study of this particular issue in stratification and differentiation.

5   Read Item D below and answer parts (a) and (b) that follow.

> **Item D**
>
> There has never been a total consensus within sociology as to the definition of class, nor is there a shared view as exactly which criteria to use when operationalising social class in research. At various times sociologists have used, economic position, occupational status, skill levels, income and a mix of some or more of these to determine a subject's class, but the debate within sociology as the importance of class as a determinant of social action is reflected in an equally strong debate as to how to measure it.
>
> The problem of operationalising class has been made more difficult in the last forty years by the constant impact of technological change. As a result of this the skill levels required for many jobs that were previously seen as routine manual work have increased dramatically. At the same time office work which used to have relatively high status has in many ways been deskilled by the advent of ICT systems. The vast increase in the number of women working also leads feminist writers to argue that to categorise women on the basis of husbands' occupations is methodologically unsound. Other critics would argue that any classification is by its very nature deterministic, since not only does it impose the researcher's own values on the actions of individuals, but it also fails to take any account of such individuals' perceptions of their social class.
>
> Source: Written by Hamish Joyce

     (a)   Identify and briefly explain three problems of operationalising class, other than those mentioned in the extract.   *(9 marks)*

     (b)   Using material from Item D and elsewhere, assess the strengths and limitations of using classifications of social class as a means of investigating social stratification.   *(15 marks)*

6   'Functionalist sociology is little more than an intellectual justification for the American way of life and a conservative status quo.' How far do sociological evidence and argument support this criticism?   *(33 marks)*

END OF THE UNIT 4 SECTION B SAMPLE QUESTIONS

Introduction

Key terms

Modernity: a stage in the development of society characterised by a belief in science, complex social structure and a complex division of labour.

Postmodernity: according to postmodernists, this is a new period following modernity. It is distinguished by increased choice and diversity, because of the globalisation made possible by information and communication technology.

Sociology came about during a period of social change in the late 18th century and early 19th century. This created **modernity**, a new stage in the development of society characterised by a change from feudalism to capitalism and from myth and magic to reason and science. This broke traditional ways of life, generating important questions that the founding fathers of sociology tried to answer. How does industrial society affect a person's behaviour? How do societies change? What does the future hold? Marx, Durkheim and Weber believed that reason and science could be applied to these questions and modernity could be understood through sociological theory.

These questions generated a vast range of theory and research, explored in previous chapters. Sociological theory can be complex and cause us to ponder questions that never seem to have fixed answers. This topic considers how sociologists try to explain the complex relationship between individual and society. How are people shaped by society? How do people shape society? And how does society hang together? Here is what it covers:

- a range of theories that focus on social structure or individual action: consensus, conflict and microsociological theories
- how some of these theories explain social structure, some social action and some both
- how classical theory explains modernity and how contemporary sociologists suggest that the features of modernity have changed to a state of **postmodernity**, or second age of modernity
- different theories of methodology – positivism, interpretivism and realism – that affect which research method sociologists use and how they explain behaviour
- the role that theory and research can play in the development and evaluation of social policies
- a range of research methods and data that sociologists draw on
- how far sociology can be seen as value-free and scientific.

These areas will help you understand the theory and methods involved in this book and think critically about contemporary society.

Sociology currently faces difficult questions caused by changes in society. Sociologists such as Beck and Sznaider (2006) argue that modernity has undergone global transformation. This undermines many of the concepts developed to understand modern society because they were designed to understand a society that no longer exists. Earlier sociology considered areas such as culture, gender, social class and ethnicity as existing within distinct boundaries. But globalisation breaks down these boundaries. As a result, sociology has moved into a new phase, which Urry (2000a) calls the 'post-societal stage of sociology'. These ideas raise a number of questions:

- Which concepts that were developed to understand modernity are still relevant?
- Which research methods should be used to understand globalisation?
- If we have moved beyond societies, what is the subject matter of sociology?

7.1 Sociological theory, consensus and conflict

Society as a functional unit

Learning objectives:

★ Know the importance of values to social order.

★ Understand a view of society as a functional system.

★ Recognise the advantages and disadvantages of functionalism.

Key terms

Objective: free from bias or subjectivity; based on fact, not emotions.

Social system: a set of socially interconnected parts such as institutions.

Functional prerequisite: something that must be in place for society to function effectively.

Link

Durkheim's theory of suicide is explained in the crime and deviance topic on pages 291–293.

Fig. 7.1.1 *Think of Parsons' theory like a filing cabinet*

★ Emile Durkheim and social facts

Durkheim is acknowledged as one of the founding fathers of sociology. His work influenced the work of Parsons and Merton and can be described as functionalism. Durkheim believed that sociology should be the study of social facts. Social facts such as money, law or language are: **objective** in the sense that they can be measured; external in that they exist before and beyond us; and constraining in that collective values within them place limits on our actions. In short, society has a distinct quality that cannot be reduced to the motives of individuals. Consider a football team that is made up of individuals with their own specific qualities, but who have a different quality when they come together as a team. The team, like society, shapes individual behaviour.

In his theory of suicide, Durkheim took the concept of external constraint and suggested that this involves social integration (connections to groups, such as being involved in the local community) and moral regulation (how values set limits to our behaviour, such as respect for elders). Too much or too little integration or regulation could lead to suicide. Durkheim was therefore arguing that the level of external constraint in society could shape individual behaviour.

Durkheim's concept of social facts established sociology as a distinct subject. It explains how any individual's action, for example, a decision to commit suicide, can be shaped by wider patterns of integration and regulation. His main concern was with how society hangs together through shared values. He referred to shared values as the collective conscience.

★ Parsons and society as a social system

Parsons made significant contribution to sociological theory by considering society as made up of linked elements that meet basic needs. Some see his work as like a large filing cabinet: when you open one draw, it reveals a lot of complex files with further divisions and even more complex files (Figure 7.1.1). Here is a summary of Parsons' ideas:

★ Society is a functional unit.

★ People have the capacity to make decisions.

★ Core values and norms create social integration.

These three themes are expressed in his view that society is made up of a number of interlinked systems. There are three main systems, each with their own concerns (Figure 7.1.2 and Table 7.1.1).

Although society has three systems, the central system is the **social system**. For the social system to function and survive, it must fulfil specific needs called **functional prerequisites** (Table 7.1.2).

Society or the social system is therefore made up of a number of institutions that fulfil basic needs. Parsons suggests that the systems are

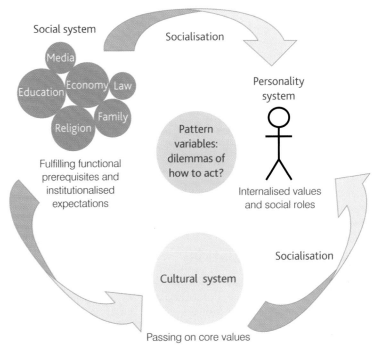

Fig. 7.1.2 *Parsons' three systems*

Table 7.1.1 *Parsons' three systems*

System	Concerned with
Personality system	A person's beliefs, goals and internalised values
Social system	Institutionalised expectations expressed in roles such as teacher/student in education or parent/child in the family
Cultural system	Core values and shared history that make a society distinct

Table 7.1.2 *Functional prerequisites*

Functional prerequisite	Concerned with	Institution
Adaptation	Economic production and manipulation of the environment	Economy
Goal attainment	Legitimate use of power through leadership	Government
Integration	Formal and informal control	Police, family, media, religion, peer groups
Pattern maintenance	Socialisation and reinforcement of core values	Family, media, religion

■ Link

See pages 375–377 for an explanation of social structure and social action. See pages 11, 59, 132 and 208 in the AS Sociology student book for more on the functionalist account of the role of society in culture, the family, education and sickness.

interconnected. The personality system, for example, is connected to the social system through the social role. A social role is a learned expectation of how to behave in a given situation, such as a student who knows to sit quietly in class. Over time, these roles become institutionalised in the social system and passed on through socialisation. However, Parsons is keen to link social structure to social action and suggests that people can choose their own courses of action. **Pattern variables** represent the range of dilemmas people encounter in social action (Table 7.1.3).

■ Key terms

Pattern variables: a range of dilemmas that people face in social action.

Take it further

It is common sense to think that a cause has an effect. A kick affects the movement of a ball. You would expect that individual behaviour (cause) creates an institution (effect). Functionalists reverse the view that there is a cause that creates an effect. Functionalists think that people can only develop within a social structure which already exists (effect). For example, the function of the family to socialise the young (cause) cannot be fulfilled unless an institution exists (effect).

Key terms

Deterministic: an approach that focuses on how a society causes individual behaviour at the expense of explaining individual thought.

Equilibrium: a tendency for a system to be stable and work in harmony.

Ideology: a system of ideas or way of thinking pertaining to a class or individual, especially as a basis of some economic or political theory or system, regarded as justifying actions and especially to be maintained irrespective of events.

Table 7.1.3 *Pattern variables*

Pattern variable	Dilemma	Example
Affectivity versus affective neutrality	Do I become emotionally involved or do I act in a businesslike way?	Parent/child: affective Colleague at work: affective neutrality
Specificity versus diffuseness	Do I act to another in relation to one interest or in terms of a number of common interests?	Shop assistant: specific Marriage partner: diffuse
Universalism versus particularism	Do I act to another in terms of general rules or do I apply specific rules?	Driving instructor: universal Parent: particular

■ Analysis and evaluation

Although Parsons is keen to include choice through pattern variables, the expected social roles effectively determine how we should act. The social system, therefore, provides the solution to the dilemma rather than the individual. Institutionalised role expectations in the social system such as those of a dentist or driving instructor tell us how to behave. The role of examiner, for example, falls on the side of universalism, affective neutrality and performance. Therefore there is no dilemma about how to act. There are a number of further problems with his approach:

■ Even though Parsons tries to include choice through the pattern variables, for Wrong (1967) the theory has an 'oversocialised' view of the individual. Parsons' emphasis on shared values assumes that people automatically conform, without resistance, to internalised norms. He therefore explains how people are shaped by society at the expense of individual drives and motives.

■ The theory can be described as **deterministic**. Giddens (1976) argued that Parsons' theory explains how society reproduces itself through socialisation into roles, but it fails to explain how individuals produce roles. People appear to passively acquire roles and behave in line with cultural expectations. This ignores how people may creatively reinvent and bend roles and norms.

■ Parsons overstressed the extent of consensus and **equilibrium** in society. As a result of this stress on harmony and social integration, he has been described as a conservative thinker. He ignores the inequalities of capitalist society and the divisions between different social groups. For Parsons, powerful groups have legitimate power and therefore there is no need for **ideology**. He therefore has no concepts to explain oppression.

■ Parsons work is based on speculation rather than empirical research. He offers a complex classification system at the expense of unpacking the subtle detail of everyday social interaction.

■ Merton

The work of Merton represents an important variation of functionalism. Merton thought that Parsons missed how people could be motivated by material interests. Merton recognised that people may accept the goals of society, but do not necessarily conform to core values such as 'respect authority'. In his work on deviance, he develops Durkheim's concept of anomie into what is known as strain theory. He suggests that individuals may respond in five different ways to the goals of society and the means to achieve them. For example, someone who accepts materialistic goals of society, but does not have the means to achieve them, may obtain the goals by committing a crime. Merton's view not only avoids the determinism of Parsons' work, but also recognises how disadvantages influence individual behaviour. Educational disadvantage or racial discrimination, for example, may lead to innovation or retreatism.

Merton (1968) put forward arguments against early functionalist theory and offered what can be seen as a softer form of functionalism. He questioned three areas:

- **Functional unity** – not all parts of society are necessarily connected into a functional unit. We cannot assume that society is a smoothly functioning whole.
- **Universal functionalism** – not all institutions have a positive function, some may be dysfunctional.
- **Indispensability** – an institution may exist, but are there any functional alternatives?

Despite these questions, he was keen to identify the functions of various actions. He did this through the concept of manifest and latent functions. A **manifest function** refers to the intended function such as a religious ceremony to bring rain. The **latent function** or unintended consequence of this action is to unite the group, creating order in a time of difficulty. Sociology should therefore proceed by exploring latent functions. This approach encouraged sociologists to ask questions about the degree of order in society. These three arguments force us to ask how useful functional analysis is?

Key problems with a general functionalist approach

Although there are significant differences between Parsons and Merton, there are problems with the general functionalist approach. Functionalists neglect meanings that individuals give to situations. This is developed through the sociology of everyday life considered in the next chapter. Also, functionalism does not give a full account of social conflict. This area is explored by conflict theorists such as Marxists and feminists.

Summary questions

1. What is meant by the term 'social fact'?
2. Identify a general problem with the functionalist approach?
3. In the functionalist approach, why is society seen as a functional unit?

Theory and methods

Link

See pages 244–245 for Merton's five responses, including innovation and retreatism.

Key terms

Manifest function: the apparent function.

Latent function: the unintended function.

 Examiner's tip

In the exam, remember to include the analysis and evaluation of each theory and the general problems of the approach. The general problems are usually the major focus of different approaches.

Ideology, capitalism and domination

- Know the importance of conflict and ideology to social order.

- Understand society as a class-based system.

- Recognise the advantages and disadvantages of Marxism.

Hint

Marx's theory has many different parts to it. The key point is that Marx disliked how capitalism generates alienation and exploitation.

Key terms

Exploitation: where a capitalist takes from workers part of the value created by them.

The work of Karl Marx and later Marxists emphasises conflict as a routine feature of society. Rather than core values integrating society into a functional unit, power and domination hold capitalist society together.

Karl Marx: the inequalities and predicted downfall of capitalism

Like Durkheim, Karl Marx is acknowledged as a founding father of sociology. Marx's ideas have influenced a significant range of subjects. Some central themes in his works are relevant to sociology. Throughout history, people have shaped their environment through their ability to work. The organisation of production in a society profoundly shapes the nature of society. Marx refers to this as the base/superstructure distinction (Figure 7.1.3). The base refers to the economy, whereas the superstructure refers to the social, cultural, political and ideological parts of society. Marx thought that the economic base, or production processes, determines the ideas of society. In a capitalist society, the economic relationship of **exploitation** requires ideologies in the superstructure to cover up inequality. Marx thought these ideologies in society are not neutral or innocent, because they justify inequality and serve the interests of powerful groups.

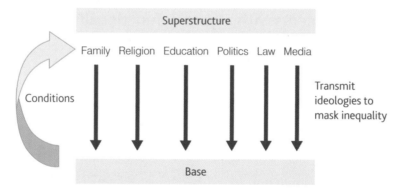

Fig. 7.1.3 *The base/superstructure distinction*

Marx focuses on the inequalities of capitalism. Capitalism is a society that is organised around the creation of wealth, profit and capital. He thought that capitalist society consists of two central social groups (Figure 7.1.4). The first is the bourgeoisie, who dominate the economy, hold power and own large amounts of capital. The second is the proletariat, who sell their ability to work to the bourgeoisie in return for a wage. The unequal relationship between these groups affects not only the experience of people within capitalism, but also the development of society.

The unequal relationship between the groups results in the bourgeoisie dominating the economy. Therefore the proletariat engage in work from which the bourgeoisie obtain a surplus value. For example, imagine a factory where the worker receives £50 for a day's work. The cost of the final product includes not only the cost of labour and materials, but also a surplus value, or profit, which is taken by the bourgeoisie.

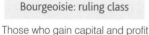

Bourgeoisie: ruling class

Those who gain capital and profit

Conflict

Proletariat: working class

Those who receive a wage and experience exploitation and alienation

Fig. 7.1.4 *The class structure in capitalist society*

Marx believed that wage labour could be manipulated because people could be forced to work for longer periods or could be paid less. Therefore capitalist society, geared towards the creation of wealth, exploits the proletariat. The proletariat also experience alienation. Marx argued that the nature of routine work in capitalist society had psychological consequences on individuals. People become alienated from their natural talents as they engage in routine work that undermines their creativity and individuality.

Marx believed that the exploitation and **alienation** of the proletariat couldn't always be held in check by **ideologies**. Over time the bourgeoisie seek to generate more profit through technological innovations or changes in working conditions. The worsening conditions, or pauperisation, of the workers results in a situation where the proletariat become aware of their class position and that they could be better off. Through political organisation they unite in a state of revolutionary consciousness and liberate the economy. Marx thought revolution was inevitable. He argued for an end to inequality, exploitation and alienation.

For Marx, communist society provided the logical solution to the ills of capitalism and a class-divided society. Marx put forward a theory of social change where society developed through a number of stages: primitive communism; ancient society; feudalism; capitalism; and communism. In each stage the inevitable conflict between opposing groups leads to social change.

Analysis and evaluation

Marx outlined the development of society and predicted an end state which has not occurred. We cannot predict what future discoveries there will be in society. If we could predict them they wouldn't be discoveries. Further, if Marx had discovered the logic behind the development of society, why has his revolution not taken place? Why was a communist manifesto needed if the conflict between groups inevitably created change? Despite big problems with his conception of history and its interpretation, Marx has made a significant contribution to understanding inequality, alienation and the nature of power in society.

Structural Marxism: Althusser

Whereas Marx outlined the possibilities of revolution, Althusser (1971) was keen in his interpretation to explain the stable features of capitalism. His focus was on how capitalist society regenerates itself over time. Althusser thought that there are a number of underlying social structures that determine our actions. Society is a 'social formation' made up of three different structures: economic level; political level; and ideological level.

Each level has relative autonomy. Each level is connected to the other levels but it is not totally dependent on the other levels or totally independent of the other levels. Imagine a three-storey building with a shop on the ground floor, an office on the first floor and a flat on the second floor. One floor does not cause the next, but they are connected. People in the flat may purchase essentials in the shop. The floors therefore have relative autonomy. Althusser argued that contradictions within the different levels could bring about change and disorder.

To stop capitalist society collapsing into disorder, specific 'conditions of existence' must be met. For example, children must be socialised with

Key terms

Alienation: a feeling of separateness, of being alone and apart from others; where a worker is denied their essential human nature.

Ideology: a system of ideas or way of thinking pertaining to a class or individual, especially as a basis of some economic or political theory or system, regarded as justifying actions and especially to be maintained irrespective of events.

Link

See pages 11, 63, 109, 133 and 209 in the AQA AS Sociology student book for more on the Marxist approach to the role of culture in society, the family, wealth and poverty, education and health.

AQA Examiner's tip

Outline and evaluate a range of Marxist theories that developed from Marx.

Key terms

Ideological state apparatus (ISA): a collection of institutions that transmit ideologies to carry on the existing social arrangements.

Hegemony: the ideological control that the ruling-class elite have over the masses.

the appropriate work values of capitalism. The **ideological state apparatus (ISA)** performs this function by transmitting ideologies that perpetuate the existing social arrangements. The ideologies that are passed on through institutions such as education, family and media ensure the continuation of capitalism. In extreme circumstances such as strikes, the 'repressive state apparatus' such as the army and police keep order.

Structural Marxism has been criticised for placing too much emphasis on social structure at the expense of social action. Individuals are seen as puppets of social structure through the concept of ideology. Like Parsons, the theory has been attacked for being abstract and lacking empirical research. The approach prefers the study of unobservable social structures through conceptual models.

Humanist Marxism: Gramsci

Humanist Marxists focus on the dehumanising aspects of capitalism rather than the structure of capitalism, such as the lack of human fulfilment in alienating work. Despite his concept of relative autonomy, Althusser believed that the economic level determined the other levels of analysis in the 'last instance'. Gramsci (1978) was keen to reject the importance of the economy and suggest that politics and ideology were independent of the economy.

The stability of capitalist society was due to **hegemony** or the ideological domination of the working classes. The institutions of society, such as education, pass on ideologies which people consent to, such as the ideology that you have to have a degree to get a good job. You therefore take a student loan to pay for your degree. You then spend many years in alienating work to pay off the loan. This control is effective if people are not forced into it, but believe that they have made a conscious choice. True hegemony, however, is not possible because people have a 'dual consciousness'. One part may be oppressed by the ideologies of the state, but the other consists of a potentially revolutionary consciousness. Gramsci argued that people could change their subservient position in society through collective struggle. Collective action, led by intellectuals, could lead to radical social change. An example of this are the student demonstrations on top-up fees in 2005.

The Frankfurt School

Theorists such as Adorno and Horkheimer (1972) and Marcuse (1964), who went into exile during the Second World War, argued that the early form of capitalism analysed by Marx had disappeared. The main theme connecting the theorists of the Frankfurt School is the domination of human fulfilment. The Frankfurt School were critical of instrumental reason, domination of the mass media and late capitalism. Instrumental reason has become a dominant way of thinking in modern society. Resources such as money and people are seen as tools that we can use to achieve our own ends rather than as sources of genuine fulfilment. Your boss at work sees you as someone that has a useful skill to exploit, not as a person.

The Frankfurt School were also critical of the domination of the mass media, which takes away human potential in modern capitalism. People purchase fast cars and listen to the same repetitive music to make them happy. The mass media therefore generates false needs, and human creativity is thwarted at the expense of fulfilling true needs. A true need is an activity that uses the creative potential of humans and enriches human relationships. Late capitalism creates a weak self-absorbed personality that can be easily manipulated by forces outside the family, such as pop stars and politicians. The Frankfurt School has been criticised for speculation and making overgeneralisations.

Key problems with a general Marxist approach

Marx's ideas have been developed by various theorists, but there are problems with the general Marxist approach. Firstly, it fails to provide a thorough account of social interaction. Sociologists concerned with the sociology of everyday life think that society cannot be reduced to the conflict between the bourgeoisie and the proletariat. Secondly, it assumes a central system of power stemming from the top of society. Marxists fail to recognise how power may be fragmented and rest in the hands of different groups. Finally, Marxist theory focuses on social class at the expense of other marginalised groups, such as women, the elderly or ethnic minority groups. It recognises conflict but ignores important divisions.

Summary questions

4   What does Marx mean by the base/superstructure distinction?

5   What did Marx argue against throughout his life?

6   Explain the differences between structural Marxism, humanist Marxism and the Frankfurt School.

Feminism, patriarchy and identity

Learning objectives:

■ Know the origins and varieties of feminism.

■ Understand the concept of patriarchy.

■ Recognise the advantages and disadvantages of feminism.

Key terms

Patriarchy: a system of society or government in which men hold the power and women are largely excluded from it.

Discourse: a shared set of assumptions and way of thinking about a particular subject.

Link

A definition of postmodernism can be found on page 362.

Feminism aims to explain the subordinate position of women in society. This approach involves the analysis of gender differences through the concept of **patriarchy**.

Origins of feminism

Feminism as a sociological theory is part of a wider cultural feminist movement. This movement campaigned for equal voting rights in the 1920s and the general emancipation of women in the 1960s. There are different waves in the development of feminism:

■ **Wave 1** is concerned with creating equality between men and women. This was based on the ideas in *A Vindication of the Rights of Women* (Wollstonecraft 1792) and was expressed politically through the suffragette movement.

■ **Wave 2** is concerned with the radical transformation of society to overcome patriarchy. Based on radical ideas of anarchism, Marxism and psychoanalysis, it was expressed in the work of authors such as Firestone (1971), who saw patriarchy as imposed on women because of their biology.

■ **Wave 3** is concerned with diverse and local forms of feminism. It draws on postmodernism to reject a universal explanation of women. Second-wave feminism was seen as reflecting the views of white middle-class women. Butler (1999) argues that gender appears fixed, but is a fluid, socially constructed category. We repeatedly perform gender through particular **discourses** that define acceptable actions.

Varieties

Feminism has evolved through theoretical perspectives such as liberalism, Marxism and postmodernism (Table 7.1.4). Feminism questioned traditional sociological theory for its 'male' perspective, placing gender instead at the centre of inquiry (Figure 7.1.5).

Fig. 7.1.5 *The glass ceiling prevents women reaching their potential at work*

Table 7.1.4 *Five approaches to feminism*

Key idea	Analysis and evaluation
Liberal feminism To generate equality between men and women, ending discrimination through the transformation of attitudes and laws. This involved acts such as the Equal Pay Act 1971 and the Sex Discrimination Act 1975 to overcome the pay gap	Seeks gradual change within society at the expense of fully overcoming the cause of oppression: patriarchy. Does oppression persist despite legal and attitudinal changes?
Radical feminism To explain the existence of a system of patriarchy within society where men dominate. For Firestone (1971) there exists a 'biological inequality' within the family where women, because of childbirth, become dependent on men. Male violence, through domestic violence, rape and sexual harassment, is part of a system of oppression. Women are objectified through the media, where they are effectively sexual objects	Gender inequality can only be overcome through the radical transformation of society. The alternatives suggested by radical feminism such as the abolition of the family and separatism, where men and women live in separate communes, are seen as too extreme
Marxist feminism To explore how class-based inequality within capitalism intensifies patriarchy. Property is inherited down the male line. The role of homemaker and carer excludes women from work and encourages women to consume the products of capitalism. Women act as a safety valve for the tensions of alienated men	Do the central concepts of Marxism and the concept of patriarchy effectively combine? The approach may have lost validity given the increasing participation of women in the labour market and the decline of the traditional housewife role
Black feminism To recognise that earlier versions of feminism generalised patriarchy from white middle-class women to all women. They ignored the unique experience of patriarchy for particular ethnic groups	The approach uses histories of particular groups to understand the position of women in contemporary society. The approach integrates racism and class into an explanation of black women's place in society
Postmodern feminism To recognise that there is no fundamental essence of gender and to explain local and diverse forms of gender. To explain how repeated acting makes gender appear fixed, when it is fluid	Does the approach dilute the concept of patriarchy and prevent political change?

Link

See page 61 in the AS Sociology student book for more on these approaches applied to the family.

Unpacking patriarchy

Walby (1990: 20) defines patriarchy as 'a system of social structures and practices in which men dominate, oppress and exploit women'. Rather than identifying a single cause of patriarchy, such as the family, she identifies structures in which patriarchy operates:

- **Housework –** if women are trapped in unpaid, low-status domestic work, it frees men to participate in higher-status paid work.

- **Paid work** – large numbers of women trapped in part-time and low-paid work contributes to a pay gap between men and women.
- **State** – social policies benefit men, such as longer maternity leave: this traps women in the housewife role.
- **Male violence** – systematic violence is accepted in society; the number of reported cases of domestic violence is low.
- **Cultural institutions** – institutions such as religion, media and education represent women 'within a patriarchal male gaze'. This defines roles such as women caring for children.

Although these structures interact in the oppression of women, Walby identifies two forms of patriarchy: private and public. Private patriarchy is domination within the household. Public patriarchy is collective patriarchy where women experience oppression in wider society such as the workplace. She argues that huge progress has been made in private patriarchy, but that public patriarchy still persists.

Understanding gender relations

One approach attempts not only to understand the position of women, but also that of men, masculinity and femininity. Connell (1995) explores how male power perpetuates gender inequality. He argues that there are a number of aspects of society, such as work and personal relationships that form a **gender order**. **Gender regimes** exist within this overall pattern of power relations. They govern smaller settings: for example, boys dominate the classroom or older girls play with young babies in the family. Gender relations are not fixed, but socially constructed. The gender order could therefore be changed through the actions of individuals.

Faludi (1999) argues that there is currently a crisis of masculinity where men are experiencing uncertainty in their gender roles. Changes in working practices and the rise of female independence have fundamentally changed the experiences of men. It is a myth that they dominate.

Analysis and evaluation

Feminism has influenced sociological research and indicates a clear sociological theory. Walby (1990), for example, puts forward concepts such as private/public patriarchy and structures of patriarchy that link people to society. It has been criticised as a sociological theory for its apparent gender bias. If feminism is to make a useful contribution to sociological theory, it must do so through an approach that explores masculinity, femininity and various forms of gender. Butler (2004) explores the 'new politics' of gender that has emerged in recent years, considering transgender, transexuality and intersex.

■ Key terms

Gender order: overall patterns of power relations between men and women found in society.

Gender regime: patterns of gender relations within a small setting such as a school.

■ Link

See pages 32, 40, 81, 98 and 194 in the AS Sociology student book for more on gender and identity, gender and leisure, gender and domestic labour, gender and poverty, and gender and health.

AQA Examiner's tip

If you are answering a theory question on feminism, try to link feminism to other topics you have studied, such as domestic division of labour or feminist methodology. This allows you to say that feminism has made a useful contribution because it highlights the unique experiences of women.

■ Link

See pages 393–394 for more on feminist methodology.

■ Summary questions

7 What is the difference between private patriarchy and public patriarchy?

8 What is meant by the term 'gender order'?

9 What is meant by the term 'gender regime'?

7.2 Sociological theory, structure and action

Defining social structure and social action

Learning objectives:

- Know how to define social structure and social action.
- Understand which theories explain social structure.
- Recognise the significance of Max Weber to the sociology of everyday life.

Key terms

Social structure: pre-existing social arrangements that shape behaviour.

Reification: where a society is seen as a thing that exists and acts independently of individual action.

Sociological theory aims to explore the complex relationship between the individual and society. The theories in Chapter 1 explain how social structure shapes individual behaviour. Other sociologists argue that it is important to look at the actions of individuals.

Defining social structure

The term **social structure** is widely used by sociologists. It refers to the pre-existing social structures within which people live and which continue after their death. A child speaks a language they did not invent, uses it throughout their life and it exists after their death. Social structures are the wider contexts within which people act, such as the education system. Consequently, social structure is associated with a macro level of analysis that considers how elements of a society – institutions, systems, culture, etc. – shape individual behaviour.

The idea of social structure assumes that society consists of reproduced orderly patterns that cause behaviour. Theories that focus on social structure ask how social context, be it a social system, institution or culture, shapes individual behaviour. The concept of social structure remains problematic for many sociologists because it is not something that is directly observable or verifiable. The term therefore leads to **reification**, suggesting that behaviour is determined by social structure rather than the actions of people. Approaches that focus on structure can be criticised for denying the importance of choice and creativity expressed in everyday social interaction. Table 7.2.1 summarises explanations of social structure.

Table 7.2.1 *Explanations of social structure*

Theory	Structure
Durkheim	Social facts as external, objective and constraining
Parsons	A social system made up of institutions that fulfil basic needs. Society is a functional unit
Merton	The goals and means of society
Marx	Capitalist society consists of a base that determines the superstructure. A structure of inequality and power relations between the bourgeoisie and the proletariat
Althusser	Society is a social formation of economic, political and ideological levels. Ideological state apparatus reproduces and legitimises inequality
Frankfurt School	A culture industry produces and satisfies false needs
Walby	Structures of patriarchy oppress women

Theory and methods

■ Take it further

Consider this quotation: 'Sociology is a science concerning itself with the interpretative understanding of social action and thereby with a causal explanation of its course and consequences' (Weber 1968: 4).

■ Link

See page 385 for more on Weber's explanation of the Protestant work ethic and the spirit of capitalism.

■ Defining social action

Like Durkheim and Marx, Weber is seen as a founding father of sociology. His ideas cover topics such as power, the origins of capitalism and the rationalisation of the modern world. Weber argues that we should avoid overgeneralised theories because people are not determined by general laws. Instead, social science should proceed by understanding human action.

Weber proposed that sociologists should construct 'ideal types' and use them in the analyses of unique situations. These are analytical constructs or models that may not exist in reality, but they help sociologists understand social action. Weber outlined four ideal types of action:

- **Traditional action** is action carried out because of custom or habit, such as buying gifts at Christmas.
- **Affective action** is action that is influenced by an emotional state, such as crying at a funeral.
- **Rational value-oriented action** is action that is led by an overriding ideal or value. If a person is committed to a particular religious belief, it is rational within that belief system to pray.
- **Rational goal-oriented action** is a highly rational form of action where people calculate the likely results of behaviour in relation to a goal. A student may consider various costs and benefits of different courses of action before selecting a particular behaviour. They may put more effort into an essay for one teacher because they write the student reports.

Weber believed that rational value-oriented and goal-oriented action are suitable for interpretative analysis. This is because they are both based on reflective action not just automatic behaviours. These ideal types can be applied not only to individual actions, but also to wider groups, as in his famous work on the Protestant work ethic. For example, Weber believed that modern society had a tendency towards rational goal-oriented action and described society as an 'iron cage'. He felt that the rationalisation of society has created a disenchanted world devoid of myth and magic.

■ Research study

George Ritzer (2004) developed Weber's view of rationalisation, describing it as 'the process by which the principles of the fast-food restaurant are coming to dominate more and more sectors of American society as well as the rest of the world'. Ritzer is critical of the process of McDonaldisation and its impact on many areas of our lives. Shopping, education, news and diet, for example, become dehumanised, automated and uniform. There are several dimensions of McDonaldisation, such as an emphasis in the modern world on efficiency, calculability, predictability and control through machines.

Weber's work has been influential in the development of the sociology of everyday life. His approach led to a view called methodological individualism, which focuses on how people actively engage in social interaction. Methodological individualism suggests all explanations can be reduced to the actions of the individual and that structures do not determine our behaviour. For example, does the structure of education with its exam system make a student revise, or do they do it because it is a rational goal-oriented action?

Weber was critical of generalised theories and Marx's claim that he had discovered the laws of development. Marx believed that the contradictions within capitalism, the economic structure, would inevitably lead to communism. Weber believed that it is individuals who shape the development of society. However, it seems contradictory to reject generalised theories, then suggest a general trend of rationalisation in society.

Summary questions

1. What is the meaning of social structure?
2. What is an ideal type?
3. What is methodological individualism?

Self and the sociology of everyday life

Key terms

Self: a reflective process on who we are.

Role: the parts people play or social positions they hold, such as teacher. Roles have particular expectations associated with them.

Role taking: where people place themselves in the position of others and take on their roles to engage in interaction.

Take it further

Consider this quotation from Mead (1934): 'Human society as we know it could not exist without minds and selves.'

Link

See page 21 in the AS Sociology student book for more on the concept of self.

Microsociology concerns itself not with social structure and institutions, but with face-to-face social interaction. This approach developed from Max Weber's types of action. The key idea is that social order is the product of the patterned actions of everyday life.

Symbol, self and society

Mead (1934) thought all individuals have a mind which is actively used to understand others and plan future courses of action. Social interaction involves individuals understanding symbols which have common meaning. If you see someone walking down a street towards a red box carrying a brown envelope, what are they going to do? You realise that they are going to a pillar box to post a letter. Human beings therefore use symbols, based on shared meanings, to understand the world and ultimately engage in social interaction. Mead recognised that people had the capacity to reflect on their own actions. This is because everyone has a **self**. The self consists of two parts, 'I' and 'me':

■ 'I' is the reflective part that plans actions and evaluates our actions.

■ 'Me' is the part of the self that exists for others in interactions such as **roles**.

For people to engage in interaction, they must understand symbols and reflect on their own performance, but they must also take on the role of others. This is where an individual places themselves in the position of another person to understand how to act. A student, for example, takes on board the role of the teacher when they sit quietly in class so that the teacher can speak. Mead thought society is the product of people acting on the basis of shared symbols, reflecting on their own actions and **role taking** in order to engage in everyday social interaction.

Symbolic interactionism

Symbolic interactionism drew on the work of Mead, arguing that interaction and meaning are the basis of society (Figure 7.2.1). Social order is based on the totality of social interactions. Blumer (1969) outlined three assumptions behind symbolic interactionism:

■ People act towards objects based on the meaning that they have for them. Red roses represent a romantic gesture.

■ Meanings are the product of social interaction. A red rose given to your grandma is not a romantic gesture.

■ Meanings are handled through a reflective process where people try to make sense of situations. Should I really give her some flowers?

The dramaturgical analogy

The dramaturgical analogy, associated with Goffman (1969), uses the theatre as an analogy for everyday social life. He argued that actors in social interaction, like in a play, plan their performance to give a particular impression. During his fieldwork in the Shetland Islands, Goffman noticed that the islanders allowed the outsides of their cottages to decay so that they appeared less wealthy to their landlords. As a result, the landlords

Fig. 7.2.1 *For symbolic interactionists, social order is based on shared meanings*

were less likely to increase their rent. Social order therefore rests on social actors using impression management, along with props, to stage a performance. Goffman's theory, developing I and me, provides a descriptive set of ideas to understand everyday life (Table 7.2.2). For example, if you were going on a date, you would plan your performance backstage – your room – then give an onstage performance – maybe in a bar. You act out your script using props such as a type of bag or mobile phone.

Table 7.2.2 *Mead and Goffman: I/me versus backstage/onstage*

Mead	Goffman
I: the part that looks at myself	Backstage: rehearsal, planning, creating
Me: myself as others see me	Onstage: roles, props, acting

Labelling theory

Symbolic interactionism provides the theoretical basis of labelling theory. During social interaction, a person defines situations as real. For example, if someone is suspected of having an affair, many of their actions are defined in those terms. So, quickly putting the telephone down is seen as suspicious rather than simply a wrong number. Labelling theory assumes that 'when a situation is defined as real, it is real in its consequence' (Thomas 1928). The call is seen as real and an argument begins.

This idea has been developed and applied to the sociology of deviance through the work of Becker. He argued that deviant behaviour is behaviour that has been labelled deviant or defined as deviant. The reaction of others to a particular action therefore shapes whether an act is deviant or not. Wearing a specific type of clothing or speaking in a particular way may be seen as deviant in one group, but the norm in another. Labelling theorists such as Becker demonstrate that some labels such as 'mentally ill' or 'underachiever' profoundly affect how individuals see themselves, how others perceive them and how they behave in the future.

Link

See page 199 in the AS Sociology student book for more information on labelling and mental illness, and see page 138 in the AS Sociology student book for more on labelling as a process within the school.

■ Ethnomethodology

Ethnomethodology takes a step towards a more micro perspective than symbolic interactionism. Ethnomethodology is the study of methods that people use for creating social order. It asks what makes interaction and shared meaning possible. Garfinkel (1967) believed that people work together to create meanings and make sense of situations. In his 'breaching experiments' he would ask his students to go home and pretend to be lodgers or ask them to go into a department store and bargain for goods. These experiments disrupted social order and demonstrated the taken-for-granted assumptions that usually make up social life. You don't bargain in a shop.

Society seems to be ordered but confusions and disruptions are common in everyday interaction. In order for interaction to take place, people use repair mechanisms to make sense of situations. If you were to see your head teacher dressed in jeans, you might use the 'et cetera principle' to fill in the rest of the details. You are more likely to assume that they are going on a school trip than that they have put the wrong clothes on. Garfinkel thought society and interaction may appear to be ordered, but it has to be created afresh in every social interaction.

■ Analysis and evaluation

Symbolic interactionism and ethnomethodology move away from studying society as something that stands over and above individuals. They focus on an area of the social world concerned with meanings. Symbolic interactionists focus on a carefully managed performance or the labelling of individuals. Ethnomethodologists take a step back from this and try to explain how interaction is possible. Although both approaches usefully illuminate everyday social action, there are problems with the sociology of everyday life:

- It assumes that human behaviour is generally cooperative, where people actively negotiate smooth interaction or use repair mechanisms to make sense of social situations. It therefore struggles to explain conflict and power. Although it can explain micro interpersonal disruptions, it does not account for macro conflicts such as wider patterns of class, gender, ethnicity, age and regional inequalities.
- The dramaturgical analogy assumes that we are rational actors. It therefore fails to explore irrational emotional action such as explained by Weber in his ideal type of affective action. It also fails to explore the idea of unconsciously motivated action.
- The approach concerns itself with the common-sense aspects of interaction. Although it can explain the patterns of groups, such as the negative labelling of some groups in education, it does not explain the origins of labels and meanings in a wider setting of inequality. Feminists explore why there is a common meaning of a glass ceiling in the workplace for women.
- The approach fears reification and focuses on the individual. This results in a failure to explain the connections between social structure and individual behaviour.

AQA Examiner's tip

Do not list evaluation points when you evaluate theories. Try to include evaluation and analysis in every paragraph of your exam answer.

Summary questions

4 What two parts make up the self?

5 How does microsociology explain social order?

6 Why do symbolic interactionists fear reification?

Structure, agency or both

- Know key terms in the debate: structure, agency and structuration.

- Understand the different positions in the debate.

- Recognise the importance of the debate in relation to a definition of sociology.

Key terms

Agency: ability to act independently of structure.

AQA Examiner's tip

If you are asked to explain a structural or action-based approach, explain the central problem of the perspective before explaining alternative theories.

The debate

The structure/agency, or structure/action debate is an important discussion in sociological theory. It involves two questions (Figure 7.2.2):

- To what extent are people constrained and determined by social structures?

- To what extent do people have **agency**? To what extent are they free to act as they choose?

Different theories answer these questions in very different ways. Some theories focus on social structure, whereas others emphasise social action (Table 7.2.3). What unites them reflects one of the fundamental purposes of sociology – a concern to understand and explore the complex relationship between the individual and society.

Table 7.2.3 *Structure and action: four positions*

Position 1: Structure determines action	Position 2: No such thing as society beyond action
Social system of functional institutions (Parsons)	Act on the basis of meanings (symbolic interactionism)
Economic, political and ideological levels (Althusser)	Methods create a sense of order (ethnomethodology)
Structures of patriarchy (Walby)	Dramaturgical analogy (Goffman)
Criticism: underplays the importance of agency	Criticism: rejects the concept of structure
Position 3: Structure and action are not separate	**Position 4: Structure and agency are linked**
Structuration (Giddens)	Life world and system (Habermas)
Criticism: loses sight of structure	Recognises how systems and action intersect

Fig. 7.2.2 *Do people have agency or are they determined by social structure?*

■ **Key terms**

Structuration theory: a theory that suggests that society is produced and reproduced through the activities of people.

Subjective: biased; based on personal views or feelings.

■ Structuration theory

Giddens (1976, 1984) proposed **structuration theory** as a possible way to overcome the structure/agency debate. His position is based on a number of assumptions:

■ People are knowledgeable about the social world.

■ People are not puppets of external social forces, they have motivations.

■ Sociology is not like natural science: there are no laws of social life.

■ People create and reproduce existing social practices in everyday life.

■ Social structure consists of rules and resources.

Giddens thought that structure and action are not separate, but closely connected. He called this the 'duality of structure'. This means that social structure is not an external force that determines action, but an integral part of action. For example, someone uses language to negotiate a pay rise, at the same time they reproduce the rules and structure of language. Giddens defines structure in a distinct way. He defines structures not as institutions, but as rules and resources:

■ **Rules** exist in different forms, such as keeping personal space in interaction, rules of language, or codes in a workplace such as 'serve your time to get promoted'.

■ **Resources** can be material resources such as wealth or non-material resources such as social status.

In everyday action people draw on rules and resources that are also available to others. The rules and resources enable interaction to take place, and their continual use ensures their continued existence. For example, if you go on a date where you draw on the rule of 'man pays' you recreate a social practice from the past. The structure of rules and resources doesn't exist externally to people, but internally within the very instance in which we draw on rules and resources.

Giddens uses a very different definition of social structure compared to previous sociologists. Instead of seeing structures of patriarchy or capitalism, he sees structure as a set of rules and resources that people draw on. His work therefore redefined one of the key terms of the debate rather than resolving the debate. In redefining structure, he underestimates the externally constraining elements of wider social structures such as a system of patriarchy.

Life world and system

Habermas (1986, 1987a) was part of a second generation of the Frankfurt School. His theory combines three elements: a critical theory of society, a theory of social system and a theory of social interaction. Habermas closely analysed the work of earlier sociologists such as Marx, Durkheim, Weber and Mead to create a general theory of communicative action. This refers to the idea that action is based on the achievement of shared understanding. It involves people convincing each other, through reason, of a particular course of action. One person puts forward their point of view or 'validity claim', which is then questioned by another point of view. A validity claim may be factual or normative or **subjective**. Here are some examples:

■ **Factual** – you should buy a new car because your old one always breaks down.

- **Normative** – you should buy a new car because someone on your income should have a better one.
- **Subjective** – it would feel much safer if you had a new car.

These validity claims exist in what Habermas calls the **life world**. The validity claims are effectively stocks of knowledge or cultural knowledge that enable conversational exchanges to take place. Through living in a particular society we acquire shared assumptions that we use in communicative action.

But Habermas is critical of modern society and argues that over time a system separates itself from the life world, such as government, laws and economic markets. Individual action is then coordinated by rules and regulations, rather than the understanding that was negotiated and established through communicative action. An example is the unquestioning adoption of the husband's surname by the woman in marriage, which links back to inheritance laws. The life world has become dominated and needs to be reclaimed through political action.

The work of Habermas represents an interesting contribution to the structure/agency debate. His concepts of the life world and the system are concerned with how structure and action intersect. His work has been criticised for neglecting the role of emotions and the unconscious in action. The structure/agency debate is a complex debate that reflects an attempt by sociologists to understand the complex relationship between individual and society.

> **Key terms**
>
> **Life world:** the everyday world of action where people try to arrive at common agreement.

> **Hint**
>
> Keep in mind four positions in the debate: (a) structures shape actions, (b) there is no such thing as society beyond action, (c) structure and action are not separate, (d) structure and action intersect.

Summary questions

7 What two questions are involved in the structure/agency debate?

8 What is meant by the duality of structure?

Sociological theory, modernity and postmodernity

Modernity

Learning objectives:

- Know the key features of modernity.

- Understand how classical sociological theory views modernity.

Classical sociological theory tried to come to grips with the radical transformation of society that occurred in the late 18th century and early 19th century. This work rests on a fundamental shift in society to a stage of its development called modernity.

Defining modernity

Sociology as an academic discipline came about during a period of massive social change. This transition from pre-modern society to modern society was associated with the effects of 'twin revolutions' (Lee and Newby 1994):

- **The democratic revolutions** – the French Revolution in 1789 and the American Revolution in 1776 transformed political ideas. These revolutions, drawing from the Enlightenment, emphasised reason over tradition and a democratic system of government. The Enlightenment was a philosophical movement during the 18th century. Enlightenment philosophers believed that reason and science could lead to human progress.

- **The Industrial Revolution** – starting in Britain in the late 18th century, it created a broad set of economic and social changes such as urbanisation, the growth of machine-based production and a new division of labour between capitalists and workers (Figure 7.3.1).

These changes broke with traditional ways of life and generated questions that the founding fathers of sociology tried to answer. Marx, Durkheim and Weber believed that reason and science could be applied to these questions and that modernity could be understood. Table 7.3.1 summarises the key differences between pre-modern society and modern society.

Fig. 7.3.1 *The Industrial Revolution and transition to modernity*

Table 7.3.1 *The key differences between pre-modern society and modern society*

	Pre-modern	Modern
Economy	Feudal system divided by land ownership	Capitalist with a class-based stratification system and machine-based production processes
Belief	Myth and magic	Reason and science could be used to objectively understand the laws of society. Society becomes increasingly secularised and rationalised
Family	Extended family having economic and educative functions	The nuclear family has lost its economic and educative functions to other institutions by a process of **structural differentiation**
Social structure	Simple	Complex
Identity	Ascribed position	Achieved position

■ Durkheim: the division of labour and anomie

Durkheim (1893) distinguished between two types of **social order** based on mechanical or organic solidarity. In primitive or pre-modern societies, social order stems from **mechanical solidarity**. This is where society is based on a common set of beliefs. Durkheim called this the conscience collective. As society develops, the increasing complexity in the **division of labour** leads to the breakdown of mechanical solidarity and therefore moral confusion in society. He used the terms 'anomie' and 'egoism' to describe this situation. But Durkheim felt that a new collective conscience could be established, which he called **organic solidarity**. Occupational associations, such as professional bodies or unions, along with economic ties, would create moral constraint to egoism and anomie. Durkheim was therefore concerned with the extent to which modernity would generate anomie and egoism and how these problems could be overcome.

■ Weber: the 'iron cage of rationality'

Weber believed that modern society had a tendency towards rational goal-oriented action. This type of action is highly organised where people calculate the likely results of behaviour in relation to a goal. For example, a salesperson may give a wealthy client more attention because they will earn them more commission. Weber argued that the process of rationalisation penetrated all areas of modern society and resulted in the 'iron cage of rationality'. He felt that the rationalisation of society created rule-based rational organisations such as government bureaucracy. He even saw formal musical notation as a sign of increasing rationality.

In 1905 Weber outlined the source of rationalisation in *The Protestant Ethic and the Spirit of Capitalism* (Weber 1905). Although this religious activity did not cause capitalism, it had the unintended consequence of generating a culture which emphasised hard work and rational conduct. Weber is critical of rationalisation, seeing modernity as a meaningless 'iron cage'.

■ Key terms

Structural differentiation: a process whereby the functions of one institution become split up between different institutions. Society becomes structurally more complex.

Social order: the consequence of various social processes identified by sociological theory. For example, socialisation into shared norms and values generates social order based on value consensus.

Mechanical solidarity: a clearly defined set of common beliefs found in pre-modern society.

Division of labour: the subdivision of work into different specialised occupational roles.

Organic solidarity: a type of solidarity that could be achieved in modern society, where constraint operates through occupational associations and economic ties.

■ Link

See page 357 for Durkheim's theory of suicide. See pages 291–293 for Weber's explanation of religion and social change. See pages 368–369 for Marx's theory of capitalist society, social change and alienation.

Theory and methods

■ Marx: capitalism, alienation and exploitation

Marx believed that he had discovered the scientific laws of society whereby capitalism would progress, meet its own downfall and make a transition to a final stage of development called communist society. Capitalist society, divided between the bourgeoisie and proletariat, with its exploitative and alienating production processes, would lead inevitably to revolution. Marx was highly critical of modern society and argued throughout his work for an end to inequality, exploitation and alienation. He thought that communist society provided the logical solution to the ills of capitalism and modernity.

■ Analysis

The classical sociologists proposed concepts to understand the social processes in the transition from pre-modern society to modern society: anomie, iron cage and alienation. Beck and Lau (2005) argue that by the 1960s the process of modernisation resulted in society entering a stage of high modernity. This period is characterised by a strong belief in science and a **nation state** of institutions that mutually support one another, such as the nuclear family.

The views of classical sociological theory on the pitfalls of modernity have generated much inquiry in many fields of sociology. However, recent sociologists suggest that society may have moved to a new stage of development, even beyond high modernity. Some argue that there has been a transformation of the basic institutions of modernity, such as the nation state and the nuclear family. Beck and Lau (2005) refer to this as second modernity. Other theorists use the term 'postmodernity' to stress a fundamental break with modernity and the emphasis on discovering the scientific laws of society.

■ Key terms

Nation state: a country with its own distinct geographical boundaries, consisting of a distinct government plus common language, culture and values.

AQA Examiner's tip

If you are discussing the contribution of Marxism or functionalism to an understanding of society, refer back to the founding fathers. To what extent are the concepts of anomie, alienation and iron cage still relevant?

Summary questions

1 Identify the 'twin revolutions' that are associated with the development of modernity.

2 What are the key features of modernity?

3 How does classical sociological theory view modernity?

Globalisation and the cosmopolitan outlook

Learning objectives:

- Know the key features of globalisation and the cosmopolitan outlook.

- Understand the difference between postmodernity, late modernity and the second age of modernity.

Hint

Although there are three key areas in this debate, many of the ideas overlap.

Key terms

Enlightenment: a philosophical movement during the 18th century that believed reason and science could lead to human progress.

Relativism: where there is no fixed truth, because knowledge is the product of a particular historical and cultural context.

Metanarrative: a big story that predicts the future direction of society.

Contemporary sociologists suggest that the defining features of modernity have fundamentally changed. Some argue that there has been a break with modernity to a state of postmodernity, whereas others argue that society has entered a late period of modernity or even the second age of modernity.

Postmodernity

Postmodernism has been used to explore a range of changes in contemporary society since the 1960s, changes which break from the key features of modernity. The term 'postmodernism' was initially used in architecture to refer to an innovative combination of older forms in design (Figure 7.3.2). In sociology, postmodernism questions the **Enlightenment** thinking that influenced the founding fathers of sociology. Lyotard (1984) argued that science was in demise as the two key features of science were actually myths. Firstly, the idea that science could lead to human progress is not credible because of its role in crimes against humanity, such as weapons of mass destruction. Secondly, the perception of science as objective truth is not credible because science is only one of many possible truth claims.

Fig. 7.3.2 *Postmodernist buildings have a degree of irony*

He described this systematic doubt as 'the postmodern condition' which is characterised by 'incredulity towards metanarratives'. This is where there are no guarantees of universal truths, but only multiple truths. This position of **relativism** has a number of implications:

- It rejects the Enlightenment idea that science leads to human progress. Science creates only one of many possible truth claims.

- It rejects **metanarratives** such as those in the theories of sociology's founding fathers. Marx, for example, put forward a theory that he considered to be based on objective scientific laws. He believed in

■ Link

See page 29 in the AS Sociology
student book for more on
postmodernism and identity.

progress, an end to exploitation and the creation of a communist
society based on equality. His theory is described as a metanarrative
and must be approached as just one of many possible big stories.

■ It creates a need to explain the condition of 'pluralism of cultures and
forms of life'. Individuals must construct their own identity in a world
of 'variety, contingency and ambivalence' (Bauman 1992).

■ Late modernity

'Let us first of all dismiss as unworthy of serious intellectual
consideration the idea that no systematic knowledge of human action or
trends of social development is possible' (Giddens 1990: 46–47). Like
Giddens, Habermas (1987b) is critical of postmodernism, suggesting
that general theories and metanarratives can still be constructed and
shaped. Technology may indeed have a positive outcome, creating a
platform for democratic discussion and the reclaiming of the life world.
Many sociologists therefore argue that although modernity has
significantly changed, society is not yet in a stage of postmodernity.
Sociologists such as Giddens, Castells, Beck and Urry explore the
transformation of society in terms of the key process of **globalisation**.
This refers to interconnectedness between nation state societies. Beck
and Sznaider (2006) identify a number of processes that don't fit inside
the boundaries of the nation state:

■ Key terms

Globalisation: increased world
interconnectedness through the
flow of nations, people, ideas,
technology and culture in general.

■ People shop and work internationally.

■ People love and marry internationally.

■ People grow up and are educated internationally.

■ People research internationally via the internet.

■ People live and think transnationally, combining multiple loyalties
and identities.

Giddens (1999) argues that late modernity is characterised by a number of
distinctive features. Firstly, the relationship between space and time has
become reconfigured due to globalisation. Social relationships can take
place over a wider span of time–space. This has created the condition for
disembedding, where social interaction is removed from local contexts. A
business meeting, using electronic communication, can take place across
traditional boundaries of space and time. Secondly, late modern society is
characterised by reflexivity. This is where people actively think about how
to live their lives. The construction of our identity is a 'reflexive project'.
Giddens argues that the separation of time and space, disembedding and
reflexivity explain why living in late modernity is like being aboard a
'careering juggernaut', rather than a well-controlled car. He suggests that
globalisation has created a 'runaway world' (Giddens 1999).

■ The second age of modernity

Beck and Sznaider (2006) argue that at the beginning of the 21st century,
modernity is undergoing a global transformation. This undermines the
concepts developed to understand modernity as they no longer apply to
the 'second age of modernity'. Beck suggests that we should not concern
ourselves with the postmodern condition explored by Lyotard in the
1970s, but focus our attention on understanding the cosmopolitan
condition.

This cosmopolitan condition is created through a process of
cosmopolitanisation. There are several indicators of these transnational
processes:

- increases in the number of local and foreign productions in the cinema, television and radio
- development of immigration and development of labour migration
- development in national and international exchanges through post, telephone and the internet
- development of international travel
- involvement in campaigns like Greenpeace and Amnesty International that cross the boundaries of nation states
- development of international criminality and politically motivated acts of transnational terrorism
- transnational marriages and the births of transnational children
- transnational news coverage.

Beck (1999) argues that the context of cosmopolitanism is a world risk society. This involves a 'network of interdependencies' such as economic crises, terrorist crises and economic crises that connect separate places. The **cosmopolitan outlook** has some implications for sociological research. Beck suggests that sociologists should adopt methodological cosmopolitanism so that research can investigate the transnational phenomena listed above.

Beyond societies

Urry (2000a) argues that the subject matter of sociology has fundamentally changed. Global 'networks' and 'flows' undermine the idea of a nation-state society with distinct social structures. Earlier sociology considered areas such as culture, gender, social class and ethnicity as societally constructed within the boundaries of the nation state. But globalisation has undermined this approach and generated a new phase of sociology. Urry calls this the 'post-societal stage of sociology'. In this stage, sociology must examine the diverse 'mobilities of peoples, objects, images and information' through the central concepts of global networks and flows.

Global networks refer to connections of technology, skills and brands such as McDonald's, Microsoft, Disney or even Greenpeace. Global flows are flows of people, information, money and images. They move chaotically across regional borders. Post-societal sociology should examine horizontal mobilities of people across global networks. This differs significantly from the sociology of vertical social mobility, up or down the class hierarchy, within the boundaries of the nation state.

Analysis and evaluation

The debates surrounding postmodernity and the second age of modernity pose interesting questions. If sociology has moved into a post-societal stage, where the nation state is no longer the organising principle, then research methods and policymaking need to be rethought. Beck and Sznaider (2006) argue that we should do this through **methodological cosmopolitanism**, where we investigate transnational phenomena. However, one of the major problems is to see how this would work for empirical research. For example, how is the negative labelling of a student by a teacher in a classroom linked to a wider cosmopolitan order? Despite this problem it is easy to see how globalisation affects traditional areas of sociology such as the family, belief and crime through reflexivity and the decline in tradition.

■ **Key terms**

Cosmopolitan outlook: an approach that allows sociologists to analyse the interdependencies between social actors across national borders.

Methodological cosmopolitanism: an approach that investigates transnational phenomena in the context of cosmopolitanisation.

■ **Link**

See page 395 for the implications of methodological cosmopolitanism. See page 50 for more on globalisation and global development. See page 100 for more on the mass media, globalisation and popular culture.

■ **Take it further**

Urry suggests that Mann (1993) offers a useful starting point: 'Today, we live in a global society. It is not a unitary society, nor is it an ideological community or a state, but it is a single power network. Shock waves reverberate around it, casting down empires, transporting massive quantities of people, materials and messages, and finally, threatening the ecosystem and atmosphere of the planet.'

AQA **Examiner's tip**

If you answer a question on postmodernity, make it clear that there is a debate over whether we are in a period of postmodernity. Some sociologists think we are in a stage called second modernity.

■ **Summary questions**

4 Outline a feature of the postmodern condition.

5 How does Giddens describe modernity?

6 What does Urry mean by the post-societal stage of sociology?

Theory and methods

Positivism and interpretivism

Learning objectives:

- Know the defining features of positivism and interpretivism.

- Identify the research methods associated with each approach.

- Understand the limitations of each approach.

Key terms

Quantitative data: data that is numerical as opposed to subjective meanings.

Empiricism: the testing of statements using observed facts.

Replication: where research is repeated and similar findings are produced.

Social fact: a social phenomenon that is external, objective and constraining.

Link

See page 291 for more on the positivist approach to suicide.

Positivism and interpretivism are different theories of methodology that affect which research methods sociologists use and how they explain social behaviour.

Positivism

Positivism is a philosophy of science and a theory of methodology which suggests that social behaviour should be researched according to the principles of natural science. Comte, who first used the word 'sociology', argued that sociology should be based on the methodology of the natural sciences. This would result in a 'positive science of society' and would reveal 'invariable laws'. He saw sociology as the 'queen of sciences' and considered it the last and most complex form of science to develop. Early positivists argued that research could lead to the control and improvement of society. Positivism has several defining features.

Firstly, objective facts and theories can be produced on the basis of systematic empirical research. Secondly, causal laws or theories can be discovered that explain the relationship between phenomena. Thirdly, facts are separated from values through researchers adopting a scientific approach. Fourthly, it emphasises research methods such as social surveys that produce **quantitative data**. Positivists believe in **empiricism**. This refers to the testing of statements using factual inquiry based on experience. It involves the use of experiments and statistical techniques to test the relationship between variables. Theories and laws that are tested through **replication** become accepted as scientific knowledge. Objectivity represents the goal of positivism, where research and knowledge are free of bias and prejudice.

Durkheim (1897) tried to establish sociology as a distinct discipline with his famous study *Le Suicide*. Here he adopted a mainly positivist methodology. Durkheim believed that Comte had not successfully established sociology as a scientific discipline. He argued that sociology could be as objective as the natural sciences so long as we study **social facts** as 'things'. This approach involves the detailed inquiry into 'things' just like objects in the natural sciences.

Positivist explanations are often reductionist and deterministic with simplistic conclusions such as poverty causes crime. It has been criticised by proponents of other methodologies:

- **Interpretivism** – positivism focuses on external causes of behaviour, failing to recognise how people engage in meaningful interaction.

- **Realism** – positivism reduces social life to identifiable causes and fails to explain the underlying social processes that may affect behaviour.

- **Critical theory** – the emphasis of positivism on facts from survey research fails to explain why correlations exists between variables. Poverty may correlate with crime, but why?

Theory and methods

■ **Feminism** – positivism uses universal research methods without tailoring the method to understanding the unique experiences of women.

■ **Methodological cosmopolitanism** – positivism locates research within the nation state and fails to recognise the transnational nature of social life.

■ Interpretivism

Interpretivism or interpretative sociology provides an alternative to the positivist scientific tradition. In contrast to positivists, interpretivists argue that society cannot be studied in the same way as objects in natural sciences. Unlike inert objects, people reflect and engage in meaningful interaction. Drawing from Weber's concept of verstehen, or empathetic understanding, sociologists should place themselves in the position of others to understand social behaviour from the viewpoint of the actor. This approach is seen as generating rich and insightful data that reveals the experiences and motives of people. Brown and Clare (2005), for example, analyse themes in prisoners' autobiographies, quoting extracts to illuminate the experience of prisoners past and present. A difficulty with the interpretivist approach is that verstehen explanations are subjective and lack reliability. Different researchers may interpret the same event in different ways. Table 7.4.1 summarises the key differences between positivism and interpretivism.

Table 7.4.1 *The key differences between positivism and interpretivism*

Positivism	Interpretivism
Assumptions on subject matter People are subjects of social forces beyond their control. Society is an external phenomenon that constrains action	People are social actors, having consciousness and subjective motivations. People actively make sense of the social world through the interpretation of meanings. Behaviour is not the result of external constraints, but of interpretations placed upon situations. Society is the product of everyday social interaction
Assumptions on the aims of sociology Sociology should aim to reveal cause and effect relationships to generate laws of human behaviour. These discoveries can lead to the development of society	Sociology should describe, explain and understand the way people make sense of situations. Sociologists should use the concept of verstehen to understand social behaviour from the viewpoint of the social actor
Assumptions on methods Sociologists should study observable phenomena, measuring the relationship between social facts and the correlations between variables. Positivists favour quantitative methods, stressing objectivity and reliability	Sociologists should use qualitative methods because they allow insight into meanings and motives. Methods such as participant observation and unstructured interviews allow researchers to see the world as subjects do. Interpretivists therefore stress validity over reliability

Take it further

Alexander (1996) argues that most sociologists do not accept that the methods of natural science can be applied to social behaviour. However, there is a 'positive persuasion' that dominates much research. Alexander is critical of this persuasion: 'The fear of speculation has technicalised social science and driven it toward false precision and trivial correlational studies. ... The positivist persuasion has crippled the practice of theoretical sociology' (*ibid.*).

AQA Examiner's tip

When you refer to a particular piece of research, try to identify whether it adopts a positivist methodology. You can then use the five criticisms to evaluate the research.

Link

See page 293 for more on the interpretivist approach, which argues that official statistics on suicide are socially constructed and fail to reveal the meanings behind the behaviour.

■ Hint

Use research from the sociology of suicide to help you discuss the extent to which positivism and interpretivism provide useful theories of methodology in sociological research.

■ Conclusion

Although there are differences between positivism and interpretivism, both are based on empiricism. They adopt an inductive methodology where explanation is based on data. For example, interpretivists look at case histories of suicide whereas positivists look at official statistics on suicide before creating their theory. In both approaches 'data orders theory' (Taylor 1990). Alternative approaches to methodology reject this and put forward different solutions to the problem of explaining and researching social behaviour.

Summary questions

1. Briefly explain the difference between positivism and interpretivism.
2. Outline some problems with positivism.
3. What is the similarity between positivism and interpretivism?

Alternative theories of methodology

Positivism and interpretivism are different theories of methodology that affect which research methods sociologists use and how they explain social behaviour. Alternative methodologies make assumptions about the nature of society and how research should be conducted.

Realism

'Conceptualisation is a crucial activity in social science' (Danermark *et al.* 2002: 16). Realism offers a different position to that of positivism and interpretivism. Bhaskar (1978) thought the essential point of **realism** is to explain underlying, often unobservable, structures and mechanisms. Sayar (2000) suggests that realism is a third way between positivism and interpretivism. According to Sayar, realists differ from positivists in that they use abstract concepts that cannot be observed. Realists differ from interpretivists in that they think sociology can be scientific.

Realists think that explanations in the natural sciences and in social science involve revealing underlying and unobservable processes. The purpose of realism is to uncover these hidden structures and mechanisms. Sayar (1984) thought there are two different areas of scientific study: closed systems and open systems. In closed systems, the relevant variables can be controlled, while open systems are systems where the variables cannot be controlled (see page 418 for examples of both types).

It is possible to explain open systems in terms of underlying structures and mechanisms. Much sociology aims to uncover underlying structures and mechanisms: for example, it tries to explain the workings of capitalism in terms of alienation or to explain suicide rates in terms of anomie. Social life, even if it takes place in an open system, can be studied systematically like systems in the natural sciences. Realists propose that the research method must be appropriate to the study. Social science must be critical and must uncover underlying structures and mechanisms.

Taylor (1982, 1990) argues that whereas Durkheim adopted a positivist methodology in his study of suicide, his theoretical approach was realist. The statistics that Durkheim used reflected an underlying pattern of anomie. The concept of anomie cannot be directly observed but reflects a deeper social process. Positivists are critical of this approach and suggest that it is not objective or **value-free**.

Feminist methodology

Feminist methodology offers a critical stance towards positivism and non-feminist research. It aims to avoid gender bias and reveal true experiences of women. Oakley (1981) argued that structured interviews and quantitative research should be replaced with reflexive unstructured interviews. This technique involves avoiding the hierarchical relationship in traditional interviews, focusing instead on greater collaboration in the research process. As a result, feminist research can generate more data on the real experiences of women. A range of research methods have been used by feminists: ethnographies, surveys and statistical studies, experiments, cross-cultural comparisons, oral histories, content analysis and cases studies (Reinharz 1992). Reinharz proposes a number of features of feminist research:

- Feminist research uses a range of methods and gives an ongoing criticism of non-feminist research.
- Feminist research is guided by feminist theory and aims to create social change.
- Feminist research frequently includes the researcher as a person and attempts to develop a special relationship with the people studied.

Feminists think that masculine social science distorts the experiences of women as the researchers are caught up in patriarchal society. They adopt a 'feminist standpoint' where they build up knowledge about women from women's perspectives. This reveals a truer picture of women's everyday experience.

Evaluation

Feminist methodology has been criticised for not being value-free. Because feminists are committed to social change for women, they may misinterpret women's real experience to fit with their political aims. They may impose on women their own value of liberation. Further, in placing their analysis on the oppressed group, they fail to reveal the standpoint of the oppressors. Postmodern feminists reject the idea that research can reveal truth about women. They suggest that there is no unique experience of women. According to postmodern feminists, ideas that are seen as essential truths about particular groups of women are socially constructed through **discourses**.

Social constructionism

Social constructionism suggests that sociologists must question the concepts such as male/female that people use to understand the social world. Drawing from postmodernism, social constructionists are critical of this type of taken-for-granted knowledge. This is because concepts and categories are relative to specific historical and cultural times. Knowledge, therefore, is not the product of objective observation, but is socially constructed through discourse (Burr 1995). Social constructionists propose a method of deconstruction, where they analyse how discourses construct phenomena. In this sense, a discourse refers to shared sets of assumptions about a particular subject.

Social constructionism is demonstrated by Foucault (1967, 1977), who adopted a case study method toward topics such as prisons, medicine and sexuality. He delved into the past, analysing historical documents, to illustrate how discourses shift. For example, medieval societies saw madness as harmless whereas modern societies see madness as part of a medical discourse that requires a cure. The discourse on punishment has shifted from the public punishment of the body to imprisonment and control of the mind. This approach deconstructs what we take for granted.

Evaluation

Social constructionism can be criticised for its relativism. This is where all knowledge is the product of a particular way of seeing the world. Social constructionists believe there can be no truth, because truth varies according to historical and cultural context (Figure 7.4.1).

Fig. 7.4.1 *The changing discourse of punishment*

This makes research problematic. If all knowledge is relative and bound up with a discourse, how can one piece of research be more valid than another?

Methodological cosmopolitanism

Beck and Sznaider (2006) argue that modernity has undergone a global transformation. This shift undermines the concepts developed to understand modern society as they are less relevant to the 'second age of modernity'. Urry (2000a) adopts a similar position, suggesting that global 'networks' and 'flows' undermine the idea of a nation-state society with distinct social structures. Earlier sociology considered areas such as culture and ethnicity as societally constructed within the boundaries of the nation state. The process of globalisation makes these concepts less applicable. Sociology has moved into a new phase, which he calls the 'post-societal stage of sociology'. These ideas pose interesting methodological questions:

- What research methods should be used to understand global networks and global flows?
- How do we adopt a methodology that avoids methodological nationalism where the focus is on the nation state and not the transnational?
- How do we develop a methodology that is not ethnocentric?
- How do we **operationalise** globalisation to research changes within states and our local communities?
- To what extent can processes such as cosmopolitanisation be measured?

Beck and Sznaider (2006) call for a rethinking of the social sciences in terms of methodological cosmopolitanism. Sociologists should adopt this approach so that research can investigate transnational phenomena.

Key terms

Operationalise: to precisely define concepts so they can be measured.

AQA Examiner's tip

Understand the alternative approaches so you can use them to criticise research that adopts a positivist or interpretivist approach.

Conclusion

These alternative approaches offer distinct views on methodology:

- Realism suggests that research should be used alongside concepts such as anomie to reveal underlying structures or mechanisms such as alienation.
- Feminist methodology proposes using methods that capture the unique standpoint of women.
- Social constructionism uses discourse analysis to deconstruct knowledge that is taken for granted.
- Methodological cosmopolitanism poses interesting questions about how research is conducted in the second age of modernity.

Despite these contributions, the approaches raise important questions about whether sociology can be a science or value-free.

Summary questions

4 How do realists differ from positivists and interpretivists?

5 What is the feminist standpoint?

6 Why is the relativism of social constructionism a problem for positivists?

7.5 Social policy and unintended consequences

The role of sociology in social policy

Key terms

Social policy: a government initiative, central or local, that aims to meet the welfare needs of the population.

Social problem: an area of concern in society that causes politicians, the media or the general public to think that something needs to be done.

Link

See pages 65, 154 and 159 in the AS Sociology student book for more on social policy and the family, and social policy and education.

AQA Examiner's tip

If you answer a question on social policy, give examples of social policies from the four units you have studied.

For many sociologists, the purpose of sociology is to engage in making policy proposals based on informed research. These proposals address social problems and contribute to the development of society. Some sociologists are critical of the relationship between sociology and **social policy**.

■ Social policy and social problems

Social policies govern many areas of social life such as education and health. Social policies address **social problems** such as racism and youth offending. Mills (1970) argued that sociology should not be simply the accumulation of facts. Sociology should explain social problems and suggest policy solutions.

■ The role of sociology in social policy

Giddens (2001) identified ways in which sociology relates to social policy. Firstly, sociology can inform policymakers of viewpoints other than their own: for example, it can inform policymakers of cultural differences. Secondly, sociological research helps assess the results of policy initiatives. Thirdly, sociology may generate greater self-understanding. This knowledge may lead to the questioning of government policies and the creation of protest groups with alternative non-governmental initiatives. For example, Amnesty International aims to bring about reform of existing policies. When sociologists do research, they often reveal unintended consequences of social policies. These outcomes may take the form of patterned differences for particular social groups.

The Economic and Social Research Council (ESRC) funded research by Middleton *et al.* (2005) into pilot schemes to test which policies could be introduced to increase participation rates in post-16 education and reduce the number of young people not in education, employment or training. Initial research indicated that the pilot scheme of educational maintenance allowances (EMAs) increased participation rates by almost 6 per cent. This research suggested that paying the money to young adults, rather than their parents, encouraged higher levels of participation after age 16. The EMA policy was therefore set up as a national policy in 2004.

Young people from the first pilots were tracked over several years. The key findings were that the estimated national impact of EMAs on all 16-year-olds was a 3.8 per cent increase in participation. Although quantitative analysis did not detect a significant impact of EMAs on post-16 attainment, EMAs had a stronger impact on participation rates for young men than for young women. This study indicates that EMAs fulfilled the policy objective of increasing participation rates in post-16 education. The unintended consequence was a greater impact on males than females.

Sociological research takes place in settings such as politically aligned research institutes, think tanks and universities. In 2007/8 the Department for Innovation, Universities and Skills (DIUS) gave £181 million to the ESRC. The ESRC has several aims: to carry out research into globalisation, climate change, demographic change, religion and identity, and the determinants (economic, social or cultural) of human well-being; to answer questions relevant to public policy and develop understanding of the problems society faces; and to fund more speculative projects in theory and research methods to develop academic disciplines.

How does low family income translate into poorer outcomes for children? Research by Gregg *et al.* (2007) at the Centre for Social Exclusion used a group of 6,000 children born in and around Bristol in 1991 and 1992. The research considered various categories of development such as school performance, self-esteem and intelligence quotient (IQ). These areas were analysed in relation to parental income and behaviours. Behaviours included depression, the food the children ate, reading to children and physical environment.

The research found that by age 7, children in low-income families were doing worse than their peers on all outcomes. The children had lower performance in school tests, had lower self-esteem and were at greater risk of obesity. Secondly, the greater car ownership of wealthy families increased the risk of child obesity by discouraging physical activity. Thirdly, long hours in childcare for children aged 3 and 4 generated greater behavioural problems for affluent families. The research proposed that policy interventions must recognise that the impact of income operates in different ways. A multifaceted approach is needed in policymaking.

■ Critical views

Much of the research used to inform social policy is based on positivism. It assumes that quantitative methods address social problems. Critical theory, associated with the Frankfurt School, questioned positivism, arguing that research produces data at the expense of sociological interpretation. Positivism assumes that society can be rationally understood and controlled. The Frankfurt School thinks this fails to recognise the impact on policymaking of domination and power. The role of sociology in informing and assessing social policies can be undermined by a number of factors. A government may reject a research proposal if it is too radical or too expensive. A government may also reject a proposal if its timescale goes beyond the remaining life of the government or if the findings are politically embarrassing.

The relationship between sociology and social policy can also be placed in the debate about the second age of modernity and postmodernity. Theorists of postmodernity question categories such as social class and gender, emphasising choice in the construction of identity. How can social policy based on these categories be useful if the categories no longer apply? Theorists of the second age of modernity argue that social policy should be understood in terms of key changes such as globalisation, global risks and the reduced role of national politics (Beck and Lau 2005).

■ Take it further

Sociologists such as Giddens (1998, 2007) have been influential in policymaking. His work on Third Way politics was seen as the manifesto for New Labour. His recent book, *Over to You, Mr Brown*, outlines the current issues that need to be addressed by New Labour after Tony Blair. Giddens' theoretical ideas can therefore be seen as setting the political agenda for policymaking.

■ Summary questions

1　How does sociology relate to social policy?

2　Why are some sociologists critical of the relationship between sociology and social policy?

Sources of data

Learning objectives:

- Know the central research methods used in sociological research.

- Recognise the advantages and disadvantages of the different sources of data.

- Understand that researchers may combine different types of method.

Key terms

Validity: a valid method gives a true picture of what is being studied.

Reliability: a reliable method gives the same results when the research is repeated.

Representative: representative research is typical of the target population.

Sociologists may draw from a range of different research methods when they do research. This section highlights the key issues in using survey methods, ethnographic methods, experiments and secondary sources. It assumes that you have studied the research methods in the AS Sociology student book and the sections on research methods in context. Sociological research is crucial because it aids our understanding, leads to the development of theories and can contribute to effective social policies. Sociological research aims to provide a valid picture of society, particular groups or social behaviour. Research can be evaluated on its **validity** and **reliability** and whether it is **representative**.

Social surveys

The National Survey of Sexual Attitudes and Lifestyles (NSSAL) was funded by the Wellcome Trust and came about due to the rise of HIV in the 1980s and the need to gather data to prevent its future spread. Wellings *et al.* (1994), the NSSAL researchers, were also interested in how the universal capacity for sexual activity is patterned in terms of social variables such as class, ethnicity and age. They organised 18,876 face-to-face interviews up to one hour long. Before the interviews they did a pilot study and a feasibility study that focused on sampling, gaining cooperation and question wording. The potential interviewees received briefing documents and were given the choice to be interviewed by a man or woman. The researchers used the postcode address file and achieved a response rate of 63 per cent. Some of the key findings are a decline in the age of first experience of sexual intercourse, estimates of the homosexual population, and the finding that non-graduate men were three times more likely to have had sex before age 16 than were graduates.

There were several issues in conducting the Wellings *et al.* research. At the time of the study there was a widespread moral panic over the HIV crisis, a debate in government about outlawing the promotion of homosexuality in schools, and government fears that the research was an invasion of privacy and that it would reveal a gap between conservative family values and actual sexual practices. The research funding was therefore halted in 1989 at Cabinet level with media headlines such as 'Thatcher Halts Survey on Sex'. The Conservative government refused to sponsor the research and the Wellcome Trust stepped in with a grant of £900,000.

The pilot survey was used to work out acceptable terminology and levels of embarrassment. The researchers used face-to-face interviews to put people at ease and make any clarifications. The questions progressed from neutral to more sensitive questions, using show cards with potential answers where people could say codes to avoid embarrassment. Items that were highly embarrassing were put in a self-completion questionnaire that included clearly defined terms.

Social surveys like NSSAL or the British Crime Survey (BCS) aim to collect information systematically about a given population (Table 7.6.1). NSSAL demonstrates many of the practical and ethical issues involved in conducting survey research. Research surveys can use a range of methods to understand attitudes or patterns of behaviour; Gregson and Lowe (1994) is a good example (page 402–403).

Table 7.6.1 *Survey methods: strengths and limitations*

Key strengths	Key limitations
Pilot study or feasibility study Sampling techniques can be tested. Questions, interview schedules and procedures can be checked. Training can take place. Early results can be used to obtain funding	Time, cost and extra work
Questionnaires Self-completion questionnaires avoid interviewer effects. Large samples can be used. Standardised questions can be repeated to test reliability. Modern technology allows data to be easily handled. Different types of questions allow different types of data to be collected Questionnaires can use closed questions, open questions, multiple-choice options and scaled options. They can be administered by post, telephone or email	Generally there is a low response rate, especially in postal questionnaires. The validity of a questionnaire rests on the quality of the question wording. Respondents may be forced into artificial categories. Respondents may not be honest. It is not always clear who has answered the questionnaire
Interviews The presence of a researcher enables any issues to be clarified. Structured interviews can be replicated and produce quantitative data. Unstructured interviews enable probing and help to establish rapport with the interviewee. The qualitative data often provides rich insight into behaviour. The interview may be used as part of ethnographic research. The truthfulness of the respondent can be assessed. They achieve higher response rates than questionnaires Interviews can be structured, semi-structured or unstructured. They can be conducted by telephone or face-to-face	Interviewees may wish to please the interviewer, or the personal characteristics of the interviewer may influence the interviewee. The validity of an interview rests on the quality of the question wording. All types of interview are more time-consuming than questionnaires. Unstructured interviews are difficult to replicate and they use small samples. Structured interviews may force people into artificial categories
Longitudinal surveys Longitudinal surveys can be used to obtain quantitative or qualitative data over time and to analyse change without the sample fully changing	A longitudinal survey requires long-term funding. It requires commitment from participants and the research team. For questionnaires, the validity of the research rests on the question wording, and for interviews, the validity of the research rests on the effectiveness of the interviewer

■ **Link**

See page 232 in the AS Sociology student book for more on social surveys.

Ethnography

Table 7.6.2 summarises the strengths and limitations of ethnographic methods. Hobbs (1988) conducted a participant observation of petty criminals and the police (Metropolitan Police CID) in the East End of London. Hobbs was initially brought up in the East End and worked in low-level jobs before moving to the north of England. He worked as a dustman in both areas and 'became aware of both the diverse nature of working-class culture and particularly the uniqueness of the East End'. Hobbs eventually trained as a teacher and returned to the East End, where he gained access to petty criminals and the criminal investigation department (CID). His accent, style and local knowledge allowed him to play an insider role. Much of his research was conducted in a pub, where petty criminals recounted stories and where he observed trading activities. The petty criminals were aware that he was researching them, but his 'willingness to drink beer' allowed him to pass within the group. He gained access to the CID as the pub he used was also used by some CID informants. One of the boys he coached for football had a father who was a detective.

Table 7.6.2 *Ethnographic methods: strengths and limitations*

Key strengths	Key limitations
Observations The researcher observes behaviour in its true setting, so their evidence is likely to be valid. Qualitative data is often interesting to read and reveals meanings and motives behind behaviour. The research is based on verstehen, where behaviour is seen from the viewpoint of the actor. The researcher can pursue new avenues of research as they emerge in the research. It allows researchers to study behaviour that is seldom revealed in survey-based research, such as the behaviour of deviant or criminal groups An observation may be a complete participant (covert), a participant observation (overt) or a non-participant observation	The research often studies small groups so it may not be representative. It is often difficult to corroborate and replicate. The presence of the researcher may alter the behaviour of the group. Objectivity may be undermined as the researcher becomes involved in the group or goes native. It is often time-consuming. Covert research faces distinct limitations on lack of informed consent, breaking cover and engaging in morally reprehensible or illegal activities
Case studies and community studies Case studies are in-depth studies of a particular event such as working life in a factory. Community studies are in-depth studies of a whole community, generating rich insight. In both studies, multiple methods are often used to gain data in the workings of the group.	It may not be possible to generalise the data from one case/community to other case/communities. The presence of the researcher may alter the behaviour of the case/community. In using multiple methods the research may encounter problems with each specific research method.
Life histories It generates an in-depth history of a socially interesting individual. Multiple methods such as interviews, observations and diaries are used to build up a valid picture of their experiences	When using multiple methods, each method may have its own set of problems. There may be interviewer effects and bias in documents. A life history of a marginalised individual may be difficult to generalise

Theory and methods

Link

See page 238 in the AS Sociology student book for more on ethnographic research and participant observation.

This contact became his main informant, giving him formal and informal interviews, documents and introductions to other individuals. His ethnography of the CID involved overt research in a CID office and covert observations in the pub, courts and court canteens. Hobbs used his ethnography to argue that the unique culture of the East End shapes social control in the area. The trading culture of the East End was adopted and accepted by the police. There are several issues with this research. Firstly, it is difficult to check and corroborate stories that were told in the pub where alcohol was involved. Further, people knew that Hobbs was observing them and this could have led to criminals exaggerating their criminality. Secondly, Hobbs engaged in criminal activities and included people in the research that were his friends and family. Finally, he had a less than critical view of the workings of the CID and was clearly on the side of the petty criminals. This raises issues of value freedom. Did he exaggerate the uniqueness of the East End at the expense of making generalisations to similar cultures across the country?

Experiments

Laboratory experiments are widely used in natural science and by psychologists. They are deemed to produce hard scientific data through the refutation of hypotheses and the observed effects of an independent variable on a dependent variable. This type of methodology has limitations in sociology because the laboratory artificially reconstructs social settings. Further, there are significant investigator effects where participants read the experiment and act in various ways that they think are expected. In short, social behaviour does not lend itself to laboratory research because it is very difficult to isolate particular variables and manipulate their effects. For example, it is difficult to manipulate the relationship between poverty and crime in a laboratory setting.

Link

See page 245 in the AS Sociology student book for more on experiments.

In response to these criticisms, there are examples where sociologists have used field experiments. This is where the experiment takes place in a real social setting, revealing the hidden meanings of social interaction. Garfinkel (1967) carried out a form of field experiment in his breaching experiments, where he asked his students to go home and pretend to be lodgers or where he asked them to go into a department store and bargain for goods. This type of research often gains rich insight into social action, but it risks breaking ethical codes by distressing participants and by not gaining informed consent.

Secondary sources and multiple methods

Table 7.6.3 summarises the strengths and limitations of secondary data. Gregson and Lowe (1994) explored the relationship between work-rich dual-career families and the growth of waged domestic labour using multiple methods. They chose Newcastle and Reading as their two case study areas. Their research included three methodologies. Firstly, they analysed advertisements from *The Lady*, a national magazine, and the local newspapers to establish national and local demand. The adverts were coded by the researchers into different regions in the country to give a picture of demand not captured by official statistics. Secondly, they conducted a survey to establish the incidence of waged labour. This involved questionnaires sent to 1,140 couples in Newcastle and 977 in Reading, giving a total response of 542 questionnaires. The sample was

Table 7.6.3 *Secondary data: strengths and limitations*

Key strengths	Key limitations
Official statistics Official statistics are a useful source of existing information. The information is easy to access and widely available. They use large sample sizes so they tend to be representative. They enable comparisons to be made over time. They are held on a wide range of topics Official statistics may come from government surveys, registration data and record-keeping data	Soft statistics such as crime statistics or unemployment data do not give a valid picture, because the data has missing categories or has been massaged for political purposes. Interpretivists argue that statistics are not facts, but the product of a complex process of definitions and decision-making at various levels. Official statistics may not operationalise concepts in the way the researcher wants, or they may not be available for the researcher's specific topic
Documents Documents can provide quantitative or qualitative data. They can be used as the basis of content analysis to give access to data that is not held in official statistics. Gregson and Lowe (1994) used newspapers to build up a picture of an overall national trend. Documents provide first-hand insight into previous events Documents may be personal documents, expressive documents and more formal public documents	Documents may not be credible, authentic or representative. The meanings may be difficult to comprehend (Scott 1990)

obtained by approaching workplaces that were known to employ women in professional and managerial jobs.

Thirdly, 139 semi-structured interviews, obtained through a snowballing sample, were conducted with employers and employees. These methods generated quantitative and qualitative data. The researchers found increasing demand for waged domestic labour, particularly in the affluent areas in the south of England. The local workplace survey found that 40 per cent of middle-class households with young children employed a nanny and 67 per cent employed a cleaner. In terms of the interviews, most cleaners were 51 and older and left school with no qualifications. The nannies were younger, lower middle-class women of medium academic achievement. Both groups received low pay but their different roles meant they experienced different relationships with the families.

Gregson and Lowe concluded that middle-class women have removed themselves from doing some domestic work, whereas lower middle-class and working-class women are more closely associated with this type of work. The rise of successful dual-career families has led to the growth of distinct class divisions between women. However, this research is problematic because the magazine and the newspapers had low circulations and because not all waged domestic labour is advertised. Consequently, the formal content analysis used to generate statistics on overall demand may not be reliable. Further, most of the middle-class families didn't employ nannies, so Gregson and Lowe's conclusions may be exaggerated.

Link

See pages 248 and 250 in the AS Sociology student book for more on secondary data and secondary sources.

AQA Examiner's tip

When discussing sources of data, remember the evaluation criteria in the AS Sociology student book. Is the method of data collection reliable? Is the data valid? Are the people and the social setting representative?

■ Conclusion

The three pieces of research outlined in this chapter – sexual behaviour, petty criminals and waged domestic labour – demonstrate that multiple methods are often used in practice. They also highlight that sociological research is not simply a matter of selecting one research method because it gives you quantitative or qualitative data. Research is a very complex and messy process.

Summary questions

1 What is the difference between validity and reliability?

2 Why is ethnographic research said to produce valid data?

3 Identify a problem with the research methodology in one of the research studies?

Types of data

Learning objectives:

- Know the difference between primary data and secondary data.

- Know the difference between quantitative data and qualitative data.

- Recognise the strengths and limitations of each type of data.

- Understand that researchers may combine different types of data.

Link

See page 33 for an example of the social construction of official statistics. See page 413 for an explanation of positivism and interpretivism. See page 254 in the AS Sociology student book for more on deciding what kind of data to use.

Different research methods allow sociologists to gain an insight into a particular topic, such as the workings of the police, experiences of poverty, patterns of educational achievement or sexual behaviour. The different research methods produce difference types of data. Each type has strengths and limitations. It is common for researchers to use a range of data types in their research.

Quantitative data

Quantitative data is numerical data; it is associated with positivist research. Quantitative data can be obtained from a range of research methods such as surveys, official statistics, structured interviews and experiments. Sociologists use various statistical software packages to analyse causal relationships, calculate the strength of correlations and carry out significance tests. This analysis allows trends and patterns to be identified, and can also compare new data with old data. Quantitative data is favoured by positivists because the methods that produce the data can be repeated so other researchers can assess the reliability of the research. Quantitative research often involves large samples, so the data is more likely to represent the population. Despite these apparent strengths, quantitative data is criticised by interpretivists for failing to give a real insight into the meanings and motives of people. For example, the operationalisation of poverty, unemployment and crime in official statistics may give a distorted picture of a particular phenomenon. It fails to capture the reasons for people's behaviour as well as their distinct experiences.

Qualitative data

Qualitative data is seen as meaningful and is associated with interpretivist research. It is produced by a range of methods such as observations, unstructured interviews and diaries; it is presented in the form of quotes and extracts. The methods that generate this data are often highly involved and require the researcher to build up a rapport with an interviewee or the observed. Qualitative data is seen as more valid because the researcher reveals the meanings and motives behind behaviour without forcing people into the artificial categories of some questionnaires. Qualitative data is criticised because it is generated from small samples and may not be representative. Some of the research methods that produce qualitative data, such as unstructured interviews and participant observation, are difficult to replicate, so it is hard to assess the reliability of the findings. Positivists argue that this type of data is the product of the subjective interpretation of the researcher in selecting what they see as the most significant findings.

Primary data

Primary data is quantitative or qualitative data that has been collected first-hand by the researcher. It is produced by a wide range of methods such as surveys, interviews, questionnaires or ethnographic methods. Primary data is useful to sociologists because it is original and up to date. The researcher has control over the validity and reliability of the data through the selection of an appropriate research method. Primary data may be undermined by several factors. For example, the validity and reliability of the data can be affected by problems in the research design, such as a sample that does not represent the population or a sample that cannot be generalised to another similar setting. Further, the researcher's values may influence how key concepts are operationalised and this could generate bias. It may also be impossible to collect primary data because of practical issues, such as access and costs, or for ethical reasons, such as not being able to obtain informed consent. Then secondary data may offer a more viable solution.

In their research, Finch and Mason (1993) give equal status to quantitative and qualitative data. Their study was funded by the ESRC and revealed the complex nature of support people expect and receive from their extended families. Interestingly, people avoid having to call on their wider kin for support. Finch and Mason used a two-stage research strategy, involving a face-to-face survey of 978 randomly sampled adults and semi-structured interviews with 88 people, some of whom were interviewed more than once. The survey aimed to reveal the values towards family responsibilities, whereas the interviews aimed to understand the normative views in practice.

The survey was based on a representative sample and involved the vignette technique, where a hypothetical scenario is outlined and people are asked to respond. For example, a young couple with a child are struggling to buy or rent a home together. Should their relative offer to have the family in their home? The interviews involved theoretical sampling, where appropriate people are selected who support or challenge the theoretical ideas of the researcher. Finch and Mason selected people who were likely to have experiences of negotiation within the family, such as the newly divorced, the newly remarried and people aged 18–24.

This methodology allowed the researchers to compare expressed beliefs with the reality of family relationships. Some data seemed to contradict other data. For example, the survey suggested that after divorce people saw it as acceptable to offer support to in-laws, but in practice there were few interviewees who could back this up. Instead of accepting one type of data as more accurate than the other, Finch and Mason found one divorced interviewee who was involved in a supportive relationship with her ex-husband's mother. They then identified features of this case that appeared in the survey data, such as history of support and desire to maintain relationships between grandchildren and grandparents after divorce. The data sets were then reanalysed by looking at occasions when similar circumstances had led to different outcomes. The relative importance of these features could then be explored.

■ Secondary data

Secondary data is quantitative or qualitative data that already exists or that has previously been collected. Sociologists may analyse data that they have not generated themselves, such as letters, emails, newspapers, diaries, official statistics and existing sociological research. Secondary data is very useful to sociologists because it can be quick to obtain and is readily available. Sociologists may use this data to analyse past events and make comparisons over time. Although the researcher bypasses the practical and ethical issues of obtaining the data, they may be using data that lacks validity and reliability. Official statistics of crime, for example, may give a useful snapshot of crime that can be used to make comparisons over time, but they may lack validity because of the under-reporting of some crimes. Documents may appear to offer a rich insight into the meanings and motives of people, but the documents may not be credible, authentic or representative and the meanings may be difficult to comprehend (Scott 1990).

Brown and Clare (2005) used prison autobiographies published since the mid 19th century to capture the experience of prison life from the position of the prisoners. They selected a broad range of prisoner writings and analysed the consistent themes and conflicts in the texts. They highlighted themes of deprivation, autonomy, identity and self-esteem, and staff–prisoner relations. This research generates an alternative view of prisons and highlights the unintended consequences of social policies on the experiences of prisoners. Brown and Clare recognise that many of the authors may not be representative of all prisoners and may write for different reasons, such as protesting innocence or to campaign for prison reform. They are also aware of how the autobiographies rely on the accurate recording of memories and how the accounts may be a biased interpretation of events. However, Brown and Clare argue that the accounts reveal a 'consistency and persistence of experience'.

Conclusion

There are many types of data available to sociologists, and each type has its strengths and limitations. It is common for sociologists to use multiple methods or triangulation. This can be done by using a range of methods that produce the same form of data or, like Finch and Mason (1993), by using methods that produce quantitative and qualitative data. Many researchers face difficulties when using a range of methods because it creates inconsistencies between the data sets and it is complex to handle the different data. All data must be approached with caution and given careful consideration to see how it was generated.

Summary questions

4   Identify a limitation with quantitative data.

5   Briefly explain Scott's (1990) criteria for evaluating documents.

6   Identify a problem with using the vignette technique in Finch and Masons' research.

Link

See pages 248 and 250 in the AS Sociology student book for more on secondary data and secondary sources.

AQA Examiner's tip

If you write an essay on types of data, cover several research studies to discuss the strengths and limitations of types of data. Remember that researchers often combine types of data.

Conducting research

Theory and methods

- Know the stages involved in conducting sociological research.

- Understand validity, reliability and representativeness in research.

Sociologists face various issues in their research design. Much sociological research has distinct stages where the validity, reliability and representativeness can be questioned.

Research question and research hypothesis

A researcher will chose a particular topic for a variety of reasons according to their values and interests, current academic debates or issues relating to moral panics generated by the media. Interpretivist research, such as Hobbs' (1988) research on petty criminals and detectives, starts with a research question or hunch. From his own experience, Hobbs 'became aware of both the diverse nature of working-class culture and particularly the uniqueness of the East End'. His research question was very general in terms of exploring how the history of the East End and its unique culture shaped the behaviour and working of the CID.

Survey-based research is often more focused and has a specific statement that can be tested using quantitative data. Gregson and Lowe (1994), for example, had a hunch that the demand for waged domestic labour had increased among dual-working middle-class households. Once the quantitative data is collected, sociologists do statistical calculations to test whether the data is significant and how confidently they can accept their hypothesis. This approach is favoured by positivists because of its greater precision and reliability. Further, the formulation of a precise hypothesis often involves the careful operationalisation of key concepts or variables.

Operationalising concepts

The operationalisation of central concepts is a crucial step in research. Different researchers go to different lengths to operationalise concepts and this is often an interesting area to consider when evaluating their research. Take, for example, a proposed piece of ethnographic research on the informal rules that govern passing behaviour on a street. When we think about how we can observe this, we quickly start to operationalise 'passing behaviour'. For example, we may identify types of passes, such as a friendly pass, an aggressive pass and an embarrassed pass, and begin to identify different factors that may affect the type of pass, such as age, gender, locality or whether the person is carrying an object.

Although operationalisation takes place to different degrees of precision, all research involves the operationalisation of concepts. Hobbs operationalised crime to petty crime and trading behaviour, giving him a distinct group to focus on. Survey-based research often involves more rigorous definition of particular types of behaviour so they can be measured. The Wellings *et al.* (1994) research on sexual behaviour used pilot studies to carefully develop questions so that various sexual behaviours were identified and precisely defined and questioned. Finch and Mason (1993) used the vignette technique to operationalise various aspects of family helping behaviour.

One of the crucial difficulties in sociological research is that some areas are much easier to operationalise than others. If you are interested in the age when people marry, it is very straightforward to operationalise the research in terms of age and marriage. But other areas such as poverty, crime or class are much less clear-cut. If the central concept has been inadequately operationalised, the validity of the research data is called into question. The accuracy of the operationalisation closely links to the validity of the research.

Piloting and feasibility studies

Much sociological research involves the careful **piloting** of research methodologies. It was crucial to pilot the research into sexual behaviour, not only because of its scale, but also because of its subject matter. The questions needed to be very carefully developed if total strangers were to ask people intimate questions about their sexual activity. They needed to find out the extent of sexual information people were willing to reveal, the most commonly used terminology and the levels of embarrassment some questions would cause. Piloting allowed the researchers to develop procedures and make a decision on the feasibility of particular research methods.

The response to the pilot interviews suggested that the research couldn't be conducted over the telephone as there may have been eavesdropping and people could be more readily put at ease in a face-to-face interview. Despite the big advantages of piloting, not all researchers need go to the same lengths to develop their research. Hobbs' observational method allowed him to formulate questions and pursue alternative avenues as his ethnography progressed. Further, some researchers may not have the time or money to carry out detailed pilot studies.

Sampling

Sociologists must select an appropriate sample before they begin to collect data. Sampling is central to research because sociologists do not have the time or money to investigate the whole population. The aim of sampling is to create a sample that represents the **target population** as far as possible. Sociologists make an important distinction between random sampling and non-random sampling.

Random sampling is the random selection of people from a **sampling frame**. A sampling frame is a list of names such as the postcode address file or even a list of names of students in a college. Every person on the list has an equal chance of being selected. Examples of random sampling methods are stratified sampling, where the groups in the sample have the same proportions as in the population, and simple random sampling, where everyone has an equal chance of selection.

Non-random sampling does not use a sampling frame and people do not have an equal chance of being selected. Some non-random sampling methods are quota sampling, where people who fit specific categories are searched for, and snowball sampling, where an initial contact suggests a new contact. Another non-random sampling method is convenience sampling, where a researcher selects a sample of people that are easy to contact, such as a local police department.

Random sampling methods are often used when large samples are involved. The Wellings' sexual behaviour research selected 50,010 items from the postcode address file, but only 60 per cent of these address actually consisted of an eligible resident, because some addresses were too far away or the residents were too old. Within the eligible addresses,

Key terms

Pilot: to develop procedures and check the feasibility of research before doing a larger-scale study.

Target population: the identified population of interest that the sample aims to represent.

Sampling frame: a list of names used to create a random sample; all names have the same chance of being selected.

some people could not take part as they were ill, they refused to participate or they didn't speak English. The Wellings acknowledged that the achieved sample under-represented men and women over 50 and over-represented younger men and women.

The researchers were able to calculate the level of representativeness as they knew the proportions of age, class and gender in the general population. This contrasts with non-random sampling methods where there is little knowledge of the overall target population. Hobbs' research on the CID used snowballing, where a key informant suggested new contacts. Non-random sampling methods run the risk of not being representative of the population because you cannot be sure that your informant and contacts are typical. Consequently, it is difficult to generalise the findings to other settings.

Practical considerations

Before research and during research, sociologists have to consider practical and ethical matters. The research studies outlined here demonstrate that sociologists often use a range of research methods: they do not confine themselves to quantitative research or qualitative research. Here are some practical considerations.

Opportunity constraints

Some areas of social life can be more accessible than others. Hobbs' personal contacts gave him access to petty criminals and the CID. Other areas require more innovative strategies to access groups. The lack of official statistics on waged domestic labour meant that Gregson and Lowe had to use an alternative method to generate data. This involved a content analysis of adverts in a magazine and two newspapers. In other research, despite having a sampling frame, people may simply refuse to be interviewed. But perhaps the people who refuse to be interviewed or refuse to answer questionnaires are more representative of the population.

Characteristics and skills of the researcher

Some researchers have personal characteristics that allow them to use a particular method. Ethnographic research was suitable for Hobbs as his accent, style and local knowledge allowed him to play an insider role. Other researchers would find it difficult to do this research and may be more skilled in other methodologies such as surveys.

Time and financial constraints

Large-scale surveys, such as the sexual attitudes survey, cost a lot in salaries, administration, travel expenses and equipment. The survey on sexual attitudes had its funding withdrawn by the government, but resumed after a grant of £900,000 from the Wellcome Trust. There is considerable pressure on sociologists to conduct research and compete for ESRC funding. The extent of funding can affect sample sizes and the amount of time a sociologist can give to a project. Secondary research such as the analysis of prisoner diaries requires considerably less funding than large-scale surveys.

Ethical considerations

The British Sociological Association has a statement of ethical practice to raise awareness and offer advice on ethical conduct. It outlines: professional integrity, the researcher's relationship and responsibilities to participants, the importance of anonymity and privacy, the relationship between research and the funding body, and when to use covert methods. Ethical considerations can be divided into four areas:

- Avoid emotional harm and distress to participants and damage to their reputations.
- Be honest and open.
- Ensure all participants have the right to privacy and anonymity.
- Avoid involvement in criminal activity and behaviour that is morally reprehensible.

Despite these guidelines, the very nature of trying to understand the complexity of human society and behaviour means that research raises ethical questions. The survey on sexual attitudes tried to minimise embarrassment, but some people may still have been uncomfortable. During his research, Hobbs engaged in criminal activities but this may make his ethnography all the more valid. Practical and ethical considerations influence the choice of method and may emerge during the research process.

Evaluating research

To be published in sociological journals, research must undergo peer review and assessment. Published research is evaluated and discussed by other sociologists as they develop their ideas. Research is also published in books. Some published research includes lots of quantitative data, such as Gregson and Lowe's, whereas other published research quotes heavily from qualitative data, such as the research on prison life. Evaluate all research in three key areas:

- To what extent is the data valid, reliable and representative? Consider the research question, research hypothesis, operationalisation of concepts, data sampling and data collection.
- To what extent did the researcher overcome practical, ethical and theoretical issues in their research?
- To what extent is the research value-free?

Conclusion

Sociological research is often a very complex process that uncovers various issues at different stages of the research process. Many factors affect the conduct of research and undermine the validity and reliability of the findings. Besides methodological problems, sociologists face further problems because of significant contemporary changes such as globalisation and the cosmopolitan outlook. Recent sociologists such as Urry (2000a) argue that globalisation has moved sociology into a new stage called 'post-societal sociology'. Beck and Sznaider (2006) call for a rethinking of the social sciences in terms of methodological cosmopolitanism. They argue that sociologists should adopt this approach so that research can investigate transnational phenomena. Their work poses interesting questions about the most appropriate research methods to investigate transnational phenomena and how far globalisation can be measured.

Link

See page 220 in the AS Sociology student book for more on choosing what to research. See page 229 in the AS Sociology student book for more on ethics in sociological research.

Link

See pages 418–420 for more on bias and the value freedom debate. See page 226 in the AS Sociology student book for evaluation criteria.

AQA **Examiner's tip**

If you write an essay on conducting research, try to clarify issues such as validity, reliability and representativeness with examples from research studies.

Summary questions

7 What is meant by the term 'operationalise'?

8 What is the difference between a random sample and a non-random sample?

9 To what extent can current research methods be used to understand transnational phenomena?

7.7 The science debate

Accepting sociology as a science

Learning objectives:

- Know how to define science.

- Understand different views that accept sociology as a science.

- Recognise limitations of these views.

Key terms

Replication: where research is repeated and similar findings are produced.

The science debate divides sociologists and includes a broad range of ideas. To understand how far sociology can be seen as a science, it is important to define the meaning of 'science'.

Natural sciences

In this debate sociologists refer to the natural sciences, such as biology and chemistry. Natural sciences have several key aims, such as searching for natural laws like the law of gravity and giving causal explanations for regular patterns in the natural world. They aim to base laws and theories on objective facts obtained through the investigation of observable phenomena (Figure 7.7.1). Natural sciences rest on empiricism and objectivity. Empiricism refers to the testing of statements using observed facts. This involves the use of experiments and statistical techniques to test the relationships between variables. Theories and laws that are tested by **replication** become accepted as scientific knowledge. Objectivity is the goal of scientific inquiry, where research and knowledge are free of bias and prejudice.

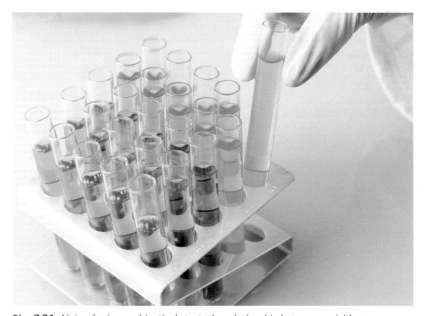

AQA Examiner's tip

Clearly define natural sciences before assessing whether sociology is a science.

Fig. 7.7.1 *Natural science objectively tests the relationship between variables*

Sociology as a science

Sociology is often called social science and includes subjects such as psychology and economics. Some sociologists argue that society can be studied objectively and empirically in the same way as phenomena explained by natural sciences. There are two key areas in this section of the debate: positivism and Popper.

Positivism

Sociology developed at the turn of the 19th century. An agricultural economy was replaced by industrial capitalism, a process of urbanisation had taken place and a new class system had emerged. At an intellectual level, science began to dominate religion as the basis of knowledge. The idea of reason, stemming from the philosophical ideas of the Enlightenment in the form of science, was seen as a means to solve the ills of society. Sociologists such as Marx, who developed the idea of reason, were early positivists. They had a number of key ideas.

Early positivists argued that the study of society could lead to the control and improvement of society. Comte argued that sociology should be based on the methodology of the natural sciences. This would result in a 'positive science of society' and would reveal 'invariable laws'. He referred to sociology as the 'queen of sciences' and saw it as the last and most complex form of science to develop.

Durkheim (1893) believed that Comte had not successfully established sociology as a scientific discipline. He argued that sociology could be as objective as the natural sciences so long as we studied social facts as 'things'. It involves the detailed inquiry into things just like objects in the natural sciences. But this is not easy as social facts are often invisible, so sociologists should proceed by avoiding prejudices and ideologies in constructing concepts like anomie that represent social things. They must study the effects of social facts such as the suicide rate.

Link

See pages 291–293 for Durkheim's explanation of suicide. See page 390 for an explanation of social facts. See pages 390–391 for the key assumptions of positivism.

Popper

Karl Popper (1959) contributed to the philosophy of science through his concept of **falsification**. He believed that a valid science must aim to refute hypotheses. If social sciences were based on falsification, sociology could be accepted as a science. This is when a scientist tries to find evidence to falsify a theory. We can use falsification to test the following statement: All swans are white. If we can find a black swan, we can challenge the statement and say it is not a scientific truth. Popper thought that science can never discover the final truth, but the longer there is no falsification, the truer it is. Sociology could be accepted as scientific if it used the concept of falsification. But to achieve this, it had to propose testable hypotheses. That is why Popper rejects Marxism, because it generates concepts such as false consciousness that cannot be falsified. Popper thought that Marxism was a pseudo-science, or pretend science.

Popper's approach differs significantly from positivism. Positivists use an inductive method where they examine data, create a theory and defend the theory. Theories should come from evidence. Popper thought that a deductive method should be used. In short, you start with a theory then test it against evidence. You should operate with the concept of falsification. Popper has been criticised, because scientists do defend their views by verification not refutation. They seek to maintain **paradigms**, not to destroy them. Further, science also has assumptions that cannot be falsified, such as 'every event has a cause'.

Key terms

Falsification: a view that science should proceed through the refutation of hypotheses.

Paradigm: a mode of viewing the world which underlies the theories and methodology of science in a particular period of history.

Analysis and evaluation

Sociologists do adopt systematic methods, analyse data and apply logical thought to given problems. They apply 'systematic doubt' towards all assertions. However, the view of sociology as a science has faced many criticisms, primarily because the subject matter of sociology is so very different from the subject matter of the natural sciences. Unlike objects, people reflect and act on the basis of meanings. Sociologists are also part of the social world they are analysing. Unlike many objects, society is constantly changing. Consequently, there are crucial problems in accepting sociology as a science. Firstly, in terms of positivism, not all sociologists believe that humans are passive subjects of external forces. This interpretivist view is explained in the next section. Secondly, do Popper and the positivists have an idealised view of science? Finally, scientific advances may not occur through systematic falsification but through scientific revolutions.

Summary questions

1 What are the aims of the natural sciences?
2 What is meant by falsification?
3 Identify one problem in accepting sociology as a science.

Contesting sociology as a science

Learning objectives:

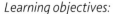 Know how sociology differs from the natural sciences.

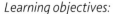 Understand different views that say sociology is not a science.

Link

See page 391 for the key assumptions of interpretivism.

Many sociologists argue that the subject matter of sociology is fundamentally different from the natural sciences and propose that we may have an idealised view of science.

Interpretivism

Interpretivism, or interpretative sociology, provides an alternative to positivism. Interpretivists argue that society cannot be studied in the same way as objects in natural sciences. Unlike inert objects, people engage in meaningful interaction. Drawing from Weber's concept of verstehen, or empathetic understanding, sociologists should place themselves in the position of others to understand social behaviour from the viewpoint of the actor. One of the major difficulties with this approach is that verstehen explanations are subjective. Different researchers may interpret the same event in different ways. That is why sociology is not like the natural sciences.

There are two sides in the debate: those who argue that sociology can follow the natural sciences, and interpretivists who believe this is simply not possible. We look at how sociologists have analysed the nature of science and questioned the idealised view of science.

Thomas Kuhn: the structure of scientific revolutions

Kuhn (1970) provides a detailed analysis of the history of natural science, arguing that science does not change gradually as knowledge is acquired but goes through scientific revolutions where a 'paradigm shift' takes place. He outlined three stages in the evolution of science: pre-science, normal science and revolutionary science. Pre-science has no central paradigm. Normal science is characterised by a period of stability, where scientists solve puzzles within a paradigm. Revolutionary science is characterised by a crisis point within science, where explanations come under scrutiny.

Kuhn argues that normal science operates within a paradigm. This is where a scientific community works with a shared set of techniques and theoretical values. This acts as a 'blinker' to how they perceive the world. For long periods, science operates in the stability of normal science. However, when a contradiction in the old paradigm becomes apparent, one way of thinking is swept away by another (Figure 7.7.2). Examples are the change from Newton's physics to Einstein's physics or the discovery by Copernicus that the earth goes round the sun, not the sun round the earth. Normal science then returns until the next scientific revolution.

Sociology fits into Kuhn's concept of pre-science, with lots of competing perspectives and no dominant perspective. Many sociologists liked Kuhn's idea, arguing that it justified sociology as a young science. Other sociologists argued that if normal science is less unified than Kuhn suggests, with many competing paradigms, then sociology may be more like normal science. Kuhn therefore offers a third position on whether sociology is a science – yes and no.

Copernicus (1473–1543)

Fig. 7.7.2 *Scientific revolutions lead to paradigm shifts*

The social context of science

Kuhn's work suggests that it may not be possible to establish an objective truth. As paradigms shift, the truth shifts. This position has been developed to argue that science is not necessarily the objective pursuit of knowledge. Science, studied within a social context, may lead to harm:

- **Military harm** – government-backed scientific research may be used not only to defend a country, but also to further its power.
- **Medical harm** – the advance of medical science may extend life expectancy and reduce infant mortality, but this is called into question by research on the extent of doctor-caused illness, or iatrogenesis.
- **Political harm** – Darwin's theory of evolution enables a detailed description of the origins of species, but its misuse in the Second World War led to racism and mass extermination.

Scientific knowledge may be influenced by social factors simply because science conducts itself within a social, political and economic context. Can natural or social science ever be truly objective?

Realist view of science

A key idea of positivism involves the investigation of observable phenomena. Realism represents an alternative methodology to this. For realists, explanations in natural science and social science involve revealing underlying and unobservable processes. The purpose of realism is to uncover these hidden structures and mechanisms. Sayar (1984) thought there are two different areas of scientific study: closed systems and open systems. Examples of closed systems are lab experiments where all the relevant variables can be controlled and measured. Open systems are systems where the variables cannot be controlled and where precise predictions cannot be made. Weather systems cannot be precisely predicted and manipulated, and evolution occurs in an open system.

It is possible to use underlying structures and mechanisms to explain open systems where human behaviour occurs. Realists think that science must unearth these underlying mechanisms. Many of these mechanisms are unobservable, such as natural selection, so science must go beneath the surface. Much of sociology aims to uncover underlying structures and mechanisms such as patriarchy. Even if it takes place in open systems, social life can be studied systematically and rigorously, like open systems are studied in the natural sciences.

Analysis and evaluation

There is a debate between those who say sociology is like a science (positivists), those who say it could be a science (Popper), those who say it is not a science (interpretivists) and those who analyse the nature of science and compare it to sociology (Kuhn and the realists). Even positivists recognise that they cannot precisely follow the scientific method. Whether or not sociology is a science depends on the definition of science. If science is the use of systematic methods of empirical research and the logical assessment of theories, then sociology is scientific. The major difference between the two is the fact that sociology involves a 'double hermeneutic' (Giddens 1996), where sociologists are involved in the interpretation of people who are already interpreting the world. The concepts of sociology such as social class or globalisation become part of everyday language and the social world, which is then researched again by sociologists. Social science cannot be neutral, because it influences the very behaviour it tries to explain.

AQA Examiner's tip

Remember that positivism, interpretivism and realism also come up in the value freedom debate. In one paragraph, you could make a brief link with the value freedom debate, but keep your answer focused on the science debate.

Summary questions

4 What is meant by the term 'verstehen'?

5 In Kuhn's stages of science, at what stage is sociology?

6 What is meant by the term 'double hermeneutic'?

7.8 The value freedom debate

Sociology, objectivity and subjectivity

Learning objectives:

■ Know the difference between value relevance and value freedom.

■ Understand views that suggest sociology can be objective.

■ Understand views that suggest sociology is subjective.

■ Key terms

Value freedom: of a methodology or theory, not biased by a researcher's values.

Value relevance: where researchers select topics and construct concepts that closely link to their own values and interests.

■ Link

See page 390 for more on positivism.

Sociologists disagree about whether sociology is, can be or should be value-free. Value freedom is the idea that all bias should be eliminated from research. If a piece of research achieves **value freedom**, then it can be described as objective. But values are complex and can affect what a researcher chooses to study. This is known as **value relevance**. The theoretical perspective adopted by a particular sociologist has values and assumptions that may influence the purpose of the research.

■ Sociology and objectivity

Positivists and Weber differ significantly, but both believe that sociology can be objective.

Positivism

Positivists believe that sociology should study observable phenomena, measuring the relationship between social facts and the correlations between variables. Sociological inquiry should be no different from natural scientific inquiry. Quantitative research methods can be used to obtain objective data about society. The validity and reliability of this data can be checked and the research can be scrutinised by other sociologists. Sociology can therefore be value-free as facts can be separated from values.

Weber

Weber believed that sociology involved the interpretative understanding of social action. Sociologists, however, should avoid making value judgements where action is viewed as being good or bad. This would amount to bias. Weber recognised that value relevance was a key factor influencing which topics sociologists would chose to investigate and how they create their concepts. He therefore argued that sociologists should interpret action from a value-laden perspective. Different researchers could formulate very different concepts because of their pre-existing values of the world. But once a concept is generated, objectivity is possible. If a value-relevant concept does not generate meaningful research that can be verified, then new value-relevant concepts are required. In short, once the topic has been conceptualised, research can be carried out objectively.

Values in the research process

Weber and the positivists propose value neutrality in research, but values can influence many areas of the research process. This makes objectivity very difficult to achieve. Values can enter the research process at different stages:

■ choosing which topic to research

■ obtaining funding

■ choosing a research method

- operationalising key concepts
- selecting appropriate questions
- recording responses
- interpreting findings
- selecting which findings to include in the research report
- deciding where the report will be published or what it will be used for.

These problems have led sociologists to believe that facts cannot be separated from values in research. Sociological research is therefore a subjective process.

Link

See page 228 in the AS Sociology student book for more on values and bias in sociological research.

Sociology and subjectivity

Interpretivists

In contrast to positivists, interpretivists argue that sociology cannot be objective or value-free because the subject matter of sociology is fundamentally different from the subject matter of the natural sciences. People are social actors and have subjective motivations. People make sense of the social world through interpretation of meanings. Behaviour is not the result of external constraints, but of interpretations placed on situations such as, 'Why did he look at me in that way?' Society is the product of everyday social interaction.

Sociologists must therefore use qualitative methods because they allow insight into meanings and motives. Methods such as participant observation and unstructured interviews allow the researcher to see the world as the subjects do. Sociology cannot be value-free as the research places so much emphasis on subjective interpretation. This is because interpretivists express a value position in their choice of topic and how they interpret their findings. Different researchers may interpret the same event in different ways. Interpretivists may generate rich and meaningful findings, but these findings are not replicable.

Becker (1967) believed that is impossible to carry out research that is uncontaminated by personal and political beliefs. All research is influenced by values, so the dilemma in research is to decide whose side we are on. Becker maintains that we can never avoid taking sides because we should always analyse behaviour from the viewpoint of the actor. But it is crucial not to allow our sympathies for particular groups to render sociological research invalid. One way to achieve this is by clearly stating the limitations of the research. Value freedom may not be possible, but we can aim for validity.

Link

See page 391 for more on interpretivist methodology. See page 378 onwards for more on the sociology of everyday life.

Values in theory: political alignment

Much sociological theory is politically aligned, due to the history of the perspective, when the theory was developed and the values of the sociologists behind the theory. Much sociological theory can be placed on a political spectrum from left to right. The political nature of some theories means they cannot be value-free. Marxism and feminism can be described as committed sociology, where sociology cannot be neutral because it must propose ways in which society can become fairer. Feminists, for example, are committed to explaining gender inequality and patriarchy. They carry out critical research that aims to bring about social change.

Because feminists are committed to social change for women, they may misinterpret women's real experience to fit their political aims. They may

Link

See pages 263–265 for more on left realism and right realism. These theories clearly indicate the political alignment of theory. See pages 393–395 for more on feminist methodology.

Link

See pages 13–14 for more on postmodernism. See page 394 for more on social constructionism.

AQA Examiner's tip

If you are answering a question on value freedom, remember to include a range of views on value freedom, not just positivism and interpretivism.

impose on women their value of liberation. Further, in placing their analysis on the oppressed group, they fail to reveal the standpoint of the oppressors. This bias can be seen as preventing value freedom. However, feminists don't claim to be value-free, so it is difficult to criticise the theory for not being value-free.

Social constructionism and subjectivity

Lyotard (1984) argued that the postmodern condition is characterised by 'incredulity towards metanarratives' – there are no guarantees of universal truths, only multiple truths. Social constructionists suggest that sociologists must question the concepts and categories, such as male and female, that people use to understand the social world. They are critical of taken-for-granted knowledge, because concepts and categories are relative to specific historical and cultural times. Knowledge is not the product of objective observation, but is socially constructed through discourse (Burr 1995). They propose a method of deconstruction, where they analyse how discourses construct phenomena.

Although this approach is criticised for its relativism, it indicates that sociology cannot be value-free as it is bound up with a particular discourse and values. If all knowledge is the product of a particular way of seeing the world, there can be no objective truth, because truth varies according to the values of a historical and cultural context. This makes research problematic. If all knowledge is relative and bound up with a discourse, how can one piece of research be more objective than another? Postmodernists don't think it can.

Conclusion

Gomm (2004) argues that sociology cannot avoid values as society is, among other things, made up of values. Sociologists are members of society and they cannot avoid the influence of cultural beliefs on their own work. Gouldner (1962) described this as the 'myth of a value-free sociology'. He argues that separating sociologists from values is impossible because of 'domain assumptions'. Domain assumptions are basic assumptions about social life and the nature of society, similar to Kuhn's (1970) idea of a paradigm. They influence the research method chosen and the types of questions asked. A feminist, for example, takes a feminist standpoint and may use unstructured interviews to capture women's 'real' experiences. If domain assumptions mean that facts cannot be separated from values, sociologists must bring their assumptions and values into the open so that others are aware of possible bias. This is effectively an issue of integrity if research findings are to be used in policymaking and fed back into cultural beliefs.

Summary questions

1 What is the difference between value freedom and value relevance?

2 Outline views that suggest sociology cannot be value-free?

3 What does Gouldner mean by the 'myth of a value-free sociology'?

Theory and methods

Topic summary

- Consensus theories see society as a functional unit.

- Functionalists neglect meanings that individuals give to social situations and don't give a full account of social conflict.

- Conflict theories are based on ideology, capitalism and domination.

- Marxism is criticised for not providing a thorough account of social interaction and for having an oversimplified view of power.

- Conflict theories such as feminism divide into several branches; the key concept of feminism is patriarchy.

- Feminism has influenced a broad range of sociological research in areas such as the family and the workplace.

- Consensus and conflict theories explain how social structure shapes individual behaviour.

- Weber identified four types of action and was influential in the development of the sociology of everyday life.

- Microsociology is concerned with face-to-face social interaction.

- Microsociology is criticised for struggling to explain conflict and failing to explain the connections between individuals and society.

- The structure/action debate is an important debate in sociology.

- Classical sociologists propose concepts to understand the social processes involved in the transition from pre-modern society to modern society: anomie, iron cage and alienation.

- Contemporary sociologists suggest that the defining features of modernity have changed.

- Urry argues that the process of globalisation has generated a 'post-societal stage of sociology'.

- Positivism and interpretivism are different theories of methodology that affect which research methods are used.

- The sociology of suicide can be used to highlight the difference between positivism and interpretivism.

- Alternative theories of methodology make assumptions about society and how research should be conducted.

- Many sociologists think the purpose of sociology is to make policy proposals based on research.

- Some sociologists are critical of the relationship between sociology and social policy.

- Sociologists use a range of methods to do research.

- Sociological research can contribute to effective social policies.

- The different research methods produce difference types of data with their own strengths and limitations.

- It is common for researchers to use a range of different data in their research.

- Sociologists who design research face issues about operationalisation of concepts, data sampling and data collection.

- Much sociological research involves distinct stages where the validity, reliability and representativeness can be questioned.

- The science debate divides sociologists and includes a broad range of ideas.

- Positivists argue that society can be studied objectively and empirically, like natural scientists study natural phenomena.

- Popper thought that if social sciences were based on falsification, sociology could be accepted as a science.

- Many sociologists contest the positivist scientific tradition.

- Sociologists disagree about whether sociology is value-free.

- Gomm argues that sociology cannot avoid values as society is made up of values, among others things.

■ Further resources

Websites

- www.bbc.co.uk/radio4/history/inourtime/greatest_philosopher_karl_marx.shtml
  A BBC summary on Karl Marx

- www.uta.edu/huma/illuminations
  The critical theory website

- www.londonmet.ac.uk/thewomenslibrary
  Hosts a collection on the history of women in the UK

- http://feminist.com

- www.mcdonaldization.com

- www.theory.org.uk/giddens.htm

- www.michel-foucault.com
  A summary of Foucault's work

- www.esrc.ac.uk
  The website of the Economic and Social Research Council

- www.news.bbc.co.uk/1/hi/uk_politics/458626.stm
  A BBC article that explains Third Way politics

- www.bbc.co.uk/radio4/reith1999
  Listen to Giddens' Reith lecture series, 'Runaway World'

- www.womensaid.org.uk
  Women's Aid

- www.amnesty.org
  Amnesty International

- www.politics.guardian.co.uk/thinktanks
  Research institutes and their political alignments

- www.britsoc.co.uk/about/research.htm
  Summarises issues of research methodology and the BSA code of ethical practice

- www.bbc.co.uk/radio4/history/inourtime/greatest_philosopher_karl_popper.shtml
  A BBC summary on Popper with useful links

- www.bbc.co.uk/radio4/history/inourtime/inourtime_20070208.shtml
  A BBC audio discussion on Popper

- www.eeng.dcu.ie/~tkpw
  The Karl Popper webpage

- http://news.bbc.co.uk/1/hi/health/2669813.stm
  See examples of medical science gone wrong

http://qb.soc.surrey.ac.uk/
The Question Bank, an information resource for social research, especially quantitative survey methods

Books

- I. Craib, *Modern Social Theory from Parsons to Habermas*, 2nd edn, Harvester Wheatsheaf, 1992

- F. Devine and S. Heath, *Sociological Research Methods in Context*, Palgrave Macmillan, 1999

- D. Layder, *Understanding Social Theory*, 2nd edn, Sage, 2006

- P. McNeill and S. Chapman, *Research Methods*, 3rd edn, Routledge, 2005

- K. Marx and F. Engels, *The Communist Manifesto,* Penguin, 1848

- M. Slattery, *Key Ideas in Sociology*, Nelson Thornes, 2003

AQA Examination-style questions

Here are examples of the written paper's third question (at the end of either Section A or Section B, whichever is chosen) on theory and methods. All are worth 33 marks.

1   Assess the usefulness of functionalist theory to an understanding of society as a functional unit.

2   Marxism is no longer relevant to an understanding of contemporary society. To what extent do sociological arguments and evidence support this view?

3   Assess the usefulness of feminism and feminist research to an understanding of society.

4   Assess the usefulness of microsociology to our understanding of society.

5   Assess the extent to which the structure/agency debate has been resolved.

6   Assess the extent to which theories of modernity are relevant to understanding contemporary society.

7   Assess the extent to which sociological arguments and evidence support the view that society has entered a stage of postmodernity.

8   Assess the extent to which positivism can be seen as a useful theory of methodology in sociological research.

9   Alternative theories of methodology are far more useful for gaining an understanding of society today than those used by positivists and interpretivists. To what extent do sociological arguments and evidence support this view of sociological research?

10   Sociology is not very useful in informing social policy. To what extent do sociological arguments and evidence support this claim?

11   Assess the view that survey-based research does not produce a valid picture of social behaviour.

12   Assess the view that qualitative data is the most valid and reliable type of data.

13   Assess the practical, ethical and theoretical factors that sociologists face in conducting research.

14   Sociology can be like the natural sciences. To what extent do sociological arguments and evidence support this view?

15   Assess the extent to which sociology can be value-free and objective.

Bibliography

A

Abbott, P. and Payne, G. (1990) *The Social Mobility of Women*, Falmer, Basingstoke

Abbott, P. and Wallace, C. (1990) *An Introduction to Sociology: Feminist Perspectives*, Routledge, London

Abercrombie, N. (1996) *Television and Society*, Polity Press, Cambridge

Abercrombie, N. (1999) *Audience: Theory of Performance and Imagination'*, Sage Publications

Adler, F. (1975) *Sisters in Crime*, McGraw Hill, New York

Adorno, T. W. (1991) *The Culture Industry*, Routledge, London

Adorno, T. W. and Horkheimer, M. (1972) *Dialectic of Enlightenment*, Herder & Herder, New York

Aldridge, A. (2000) *Religion in the Contemporary World*, Polity, Cambridge

Alexander, J. C. (1996) 'Positivism', A. Kuper and J. Kuper (eds), *The Social Science Encyclopedia*, 2nd edn, Routledge, London

Althusser, L. (1969) *For Marx*, Penguin, Harmondsworth

Althusser, L. (1971) 'Ideology and ideological state apparatuses', *Lenin and Philosophy*, New Left Books, London

Altvater, E. (1998) 'Global order and nature'. In R. Kleit (ed.), *Political Ecology: Global and Local*, Routledge, London

Anderson, C. A. (1998) 'The production of media violence and aggression research', *American Behavioral Scientist* Vol. 8, 1266–1279

Anderson, C. A. and Bushman, B. J. (2001) 'The effects of violent video games on social behaviour', *Psychological Science*, Blackwell Synergy, Vol. 295, 2377–2379

Anderson, C. A. and Dill, K. E. (2000) 'The influence of video games on youth', *Journal of Personality and Social Psychology*, Vol. 78, 772–790

Anderson, M. (1997) *Frontiers: Territory and State Formation in the Modern World*, Polity, Cambridge

Andre, C. and Platteau, J. P. (1996) *Land Tenure under Unendurable Stress: Rwanda Caught in the Malthusian Trap*, CRED, Namur

Anheier, H., Kaldor, M. and Glasius, M. (eds) (2001) *Global Civil Society*, Oxford University Press, Oxford

Arendt, H. (1951) *The Origins of Totalitarianism*, Harcourt Brace, London; 1966 edition

Armstrong, K. (1993) *A History of God*, Heinemann, London

Aronson, E. (1999) *The Social Animal*, Wallis Publishers, New York (first published 1972)

Atkinson, J. (1978) *Discovering Suicide*, Macmillan, London

Aydon, C. (2008) *Charles Darwin: His Life and Times*, Robinson, London

B

Bachrach, P. and Baratz, M. (1963) 'Decisions and non-decisions: an analytical framework', in *American Political Science Review* 57

Baechler, J. (1979) *Suicides*, Blackwell, Oxford

Baldwin, J. and Bottoms, A. E. (1976) *The Urban Criminal: A Study in Sheffield*, Tavistock Publications, London

Bale, T. (2005) *European Politics: A Comparative Introduction*, Palgrave, Basingstoke

Bandura, A. (1977) *Social Learning Theory*, 2nd edition, Prentice Hall, Englewood Cliffs, NJ

Barker, E. (1989) *New Religious Movements: A Practical Introduction*, HMSO, London

Barnes, C. (1991) *Disabled People in Britain and Discrimination: A Case for Anti-discrimination Legislation*, Hurst/BCODP, London

Barry, A. (1992) 'Black mythologies', in *Black and White Media Book*, Trentham Books, London

Baudrillard, J. (1983) *Simulations, Semiotexte*, New York

Baudrillard, J. (1991) 'The reality gulf', *Guardian*, 11 January 1991

Bauer, P. T. (1971) *Dissent on Development: Studies and Debates in Development Economics*, Weidenfeld & Nicolson, London

Bauman, Z. (1992) *Intimations of Post-modernity*, Routledge, London

Beck, U. (1992) *Risk Society*, Sage, London

Beck, U. (1999) *World Risk Society*, Polity, Cambridge

Beck, U. (2000) 'The cosmopolitan perspective: sociology of the second age of modernity'. *British Journal of Sociology*, Vol. 51 no. 1, 79–105

Beck, U. (2006) *Cosmopolitan Vision*, Polity, Cambridge

Beck, U. and Lau, C. (2005) 'Second modernity as a research agenda: theoretical and empirical exploration in the "meta-change" of modern society'. *British Journal of Sociology*, Vol. 56 no. 4, 525–557

Beck, U. and Sznaider, N. (2006) 'Unpacking cosmopolitanism for the social sciences: a research agenda'. *British Journal of Sociology*, Vol. 57, no. 1, 1–23

Becker, G. S. (1975) *Human Capital: Theoretical and Empirical Analysis with Special Reference to Education*, University of Chicago Press, London

Becker, H. (1963) *Outsiders: Studies in the Sociology of Deviance*, Macmillan, Basingstoke

Becker, H. (1967) 'Whose side are we on?' *Social Problems*, Vol. 14, no. 3

Becker, D. *et al.* (1987) *Postimperialism: international capitalism and development in the late twentieth century*, Lynne Rienner, Boulder

Beckford, J. A. (1996) 'Postmodernity, high modernity and new modernity: three concepts in search of religion', in Flanagan, K. and Jupp, P. *Postmodernity, Sociology and Religion*, Macmillan, Basingstoke

Beechey, V. (1986) 'Women in employment in contemporary Britain'. In V. Beechey and E. Whitelegg (eds), *Women in Britain Today*, Open University Press, Milton Keynes

Bell, D. (1960) *The End of Ideology? On the Exhaustion of Political Ideas in the 1950s*, Free Press, New York

Bell, D. (1987) 'The world and the United States in 2013'. *Daedalus*, vol. 116, 1–31

Bellah, R. N. (1970) 'Civil Religion in America' in *Beyond Belief: Essays in Religion in a Post-traditional World*, Harper and Row, New York

Bellah, R. N. (1976) 'New religious consciousness and the crisis in modernity', in Glock, C. Y. and Bellah, R. N. (eds) *The New Religious Consciousness*, University of California Press, Berkley, California

Belsky, J. and Rovine, M. (1987) 'Temperament and attachment security in the strange situation: a rapprochement'. *Child Development*, 58, 787–95

Bennett, T. and Holloway, K. (2004) 'Gang membership, drugs and crime in the UK. *The British Journal of Criminology*, 44, 305–323

Berger, P. (1967) *The Sacred Canopy*, Anchor, New York

Beyer, P. (1994) *Religions and Globalisation*, Sage, London

Bhaskar, R. (1978) *A Realist Theory of Science*, 2nd edn, Harvester, Brighton

Billig, M. (1995) *Banal Nationalism*, Sage, London

Bilton, T., Bonnett, K., Jones, P., Skinner, D., Stanworth, M. and Webster, A. (1996) *Introductory Sociology*, Macmillan, London

Bilton, T., Bonnett, K., Jones, P., Lawson, T., Skinner, D., Stanworth, M. and Webster, A. (2002) *Introductory Sociology*, 4th edn, Palgrave Macmillan, Basingstoke

Birch, A. (1964) *Representative and Responsible Government*, Allen & Unwin, London

Bird, J. (1999) *Investigating Religion*, Collins, London

Blackstone, W. (1765) *Commentaries on the Laws and Constitution of England*, Adamant, Boston MA; 2000 edition

Blaikie, A. (1998) *Ageing and Popular Culture*, Cambridge University Press, Cambridge

Blondel, J. (1969) *Voters, Parties and Leaders*, Penguin, Harmondsworth

Blumer, H. (1969) *Symbolic Interactionism: Perspective and Method*, Prentice Hall, Englewood Cliffs NJ

Bodin, J. (1955) *Six Books of the Commonwealth*, Harvard University Press, Cambridge MA; 1962 edition

Boggs, C. (1986) *Social Movements and Political Power: Emerging Forms of Radicalism in the West*, Temple University Press, Philadelphia

Borge, A., Rutter, M., Cote, S. and Tremblay, R. (2004) 'Early childcare and physical aggression: differentiating social selection and social causation'. *Journal of Child Psychology and Psychiatry*, 45:2, 367–76

Boserup, E. (1965) *Conditions of Agricultural Growth: the Economics of Agrarian Change under Population Pressure*, Allen & Unwin, London

Bourdieu, P. (1984) *Distinction: A Social Critique of the Judgement of Taste*, Routledge & Kegan Paul, London

Box, S. (1981) *Deviance, Reality and Society*, Holt, Rinehart and Winston, London

Braithwaite, J. B. (1989) *Crime, Shame and Reintegration*, Cambridge University Press, Cambridge

Braverman, H. (1974) 'Labour and Monopoly Capitalism', *Monthly Review Press*, New York

Brecher, J. *et al.* (2000) *Globalization from Below*, South End Press, Cambridge MA

Brierley, P. (ed.) (2001) *Religious Trends 3*, Christian Research, London

Brierley, P. (ed.) (2008) *Religious Trends 7*, Christian Research, London

Brown, A. and Clare, E. (2005) 'A history of experience: exploring prisoners' accounts of incarceration'. In C. Emsley (ed.), *The Persistent Prison: Problems, Image and Alternatives*, Francis Boutle, London

Bruce, S. (1995) *Religion in Modern Britain*, Oxford University Press, Oxford

Bruce, S. (2002) *God Is Dead: Secularisation in the West*, Blackwell, Oxford

Brundtland, G. H. (1987) *Our Common Future*, Oxford University Press, Oxford

Buchmann, D. and Funk, J. 'Video and computer games in the 1990s', *Children Today* Vol. 24, 13–16

Buckley, K. (2006) *A Theoretical Model of the Effects and Consequences of Playing Video Games*, Oxford University Press, New York

Burr, V. (1995) *An Introduction to Social Constructionism*, Routledge, London

Butler, C. (1995) 'Religion and gender: young Muslim women in Britain', *Sociology Review* 4(3), Philip Allen, Oxford

Butler, D. and Kavanagh, D. (2005) *The British General Election of 2005*, Palgrave, Basingstoke

Butler, D. and Stokes, D. (1969) *Political Change in Britain*, Macmillan, Basingstoke

Butler, J. (1999) *Gender Trouble: Feminism and the Subversion of Identity*, Routledge, London

Butler, J. (2004) *Undoing Gender*, Routledge, London

Butler, M. and Paisley, W. (1980) *Women and the Mass Media*, Human Sciences Press, New York

Butsch, R. (2002) *Ralph, Fred, Archie and Homer*, Sage Publications

C

Callinicos, A. (1989) *Against Postmodernism*, Polity, Cambridge

Callinicos, A. (2003) *An Anti-Capitalist Manifesto*, Polity, Cambridge

Campbell, A. (1984) *The Girls in the Gang*, Blackwell, Oxford

Campbell, R., Norris, P. and Lovenduski, J. (2004) *Gender and Political Participation*, Electoral Commission, London

Carlen, P. (1988) *Women, Crime and Poverty*, Open University Press, Milton Keynes

Chambliss, W. (1973) 'The Saints and The Roughnecks', *Society*, Vol. 11, 224–231

Charlesworth, S. J. (2000) *A Phenomenology of Working Class Experience*, Cambridge University Press, Cambridge

Childs, S. (2005) 'Feminising politics: sex and gender in the election'. In A. Geddes and J. Tonge (eds) *Britain Decides: The UK General Election 2005*, Palgrave, Basingstoke

Chomsky, N. (2001) The Rediff interview with Professor Noam Chomsky. From http://www.robert-fisk.com/chomsky_interview4_nov2001.htm

Clark, R.D. (1989) 'Effect of number of majority defectors on minority influence'. *Group Dynamics: Theory, Research and Practice*. Vol 3(4), 303–12

Clarke, H., Stewart, P. and Whiteley, P. (2001) 'The dynamics of partisanship in Britain: evidence and implications for critical election theory'. In J. Tonge, L. Bennie, D. Denver and L. Harrison (eds), *British Elections and Parties Review 11*, Taylor & Francis, London

Cloward, R. A. and Ohlin, L. E. (1961) *Delinquency and Opportunity*, The Free Press, Glencoe

Cohen, A. K. (1955) *Delinquent Boys*, The Free Press, Glencoe

Cohen, S. (1972) *Folk Devils and Moral Panics*, Paladin, London

Cohen, S. and Young, J. (1973) *The Manufacture of News*, Sage Publications, London

Connell, R. W. (1987) *Gender and Power: Society, the Person and Sexual Politics*, Polity, Cambridge

Connell, R. W. (1995) *Masculinities*, Polity, Cambridge

Cox, O. (1970) 'Caste, Class and Race', *Monthly Review Press*, New York

Crewe, I., Searing, D. and Conover, P. (1996) *Citizenship and Civic Education*, Citizenship Foundation, London

Crook *et al.* (1992) *Postmodernisation: Changes in Advanced Society*, Sage, London

Crouteau, W. and Haynes, W. (2003) *Media Society, Industry: Images and Audiences*, Sage Publications, London

Cumberbatch, G. (2004) *Media, Culture and Society*, Routledge, London

Cumberbatch, G. and Negrine, R. (1992) *Images of Disability on Television*, Routledge, London

D

Dahl, R. (1961) *Who Governs? Democracy and Power in an American City*, Yale University Press, New Haven CT

Dahl, R. (1989) *Democracy and Its Critics*, Yale University Press, New Haven CT

Daly, M. (1985) *Beyond God the Father*, Beacon Press, Boston

Danermark, B. *et al.* (2002) *Explaining Society: An Introduction to Critical Realism in the Social Sciences*, Routledge, London

Davie, G. (1994) *Religion in Britain since 1945*, Blackwell, Oxford

Davis, K. and Moore, W. E. (1967) 'Some principles of stratification'. In R. Bendix and S. M. Lipset (eds), *Class, Status and Power*, Routledge and Kegan Paul, London 1967, first published 1945

Dawkins, R. (2006) *The God Delusion*, Bantam, London

Dobash, R. and Dobash, R. (1979) *Violence Against Wives*, Open Books, London

Downes, D. (1966) *The Delinquent Solution*, Routledge & Kegan Paul, London

Dunleavy, P. and Husbands, C. (1985) *British Democracy at the Crossroads*, Allen & Unwin, London

Durkheim, E. (1952) *Suicide*, Routledge & Kegan Paul, London (first published 1897)

Durkheim E. (1961) *The Elementary Forms of Religious Life*, Collier, New York (first published 1912)

Durkheim, E. (1982) *The Rules of Sociological Method*, Macmillan, London (first published 1893)

Durkheim, E. (1984) *The Division of Labour in Society*, Macmillan, London (first published 1893)

Dyer, R. (2002) *Now You See It: Studies in Lesbian and Gay Kin*, Routledge, London

E

Ehrenreich, B. (1989) 'The Silenced Majority', Media Left, available on http://medialeft.net

Ehrlich, P. R. (1972) *The Population Bomb*, Pan Books, London

El Sadaawi, N. (1980) *The Hidden Face of Eve: Women in the Arab World*, Zed Books, London

Eskeland, G. and Harrison, A. (1997) *Moving to Greener Pastures? Multinationals and the Pollution Haven Hypothesis*, World Bank, Washington

Evans, P. (1997) 'State-Society Synergy: Government and Social Capital in Development', *IAS Research Series* No. 94, University of California, Berkeley CA

F

Faludi, S. (1999) *Stiffed: The Betrayal of the Modern Man*, Chatto & Windus, London

Fesbach and Sanger (1971) *Television and Aggression*, Jersey Press, San Francisco

Festinger, L. A. (1957) *Theory of Cognitive Dissonance*, Row Peterson, Evanston IL

Field, T., Masi, W., Goldstein, D., Perry, S. and Parl, S. (1988) 'Infant daycare facilitates preschool behavior'. *Early Childhood Research Quarterly*, 3, 341–59

Finch, J. and Mason, J. (1993) *Negotiating Family Responsibilities*, Routledge, London

Finer, S. (1967) *Anonymous Empire*, Pall Mall, London

Firestone, S. (1971) *The Dialectic of Sex: The Case for Feminist Revolution*, Cape, London

Flew, T. (2005) *New Media: An Introduction*, Oxford University Press, Melbourne

Foucault, M. (1967) *Madness and Civilisation*, Routledge, London

Foucault, M. (1977) *Discipline and Punish: The Birth of the Prison*, Tavistock, London

Fox, N. (1977) 'Attachment of Kibbutz infants to mother and Matapelet'. *Child Development* 48, 1, 288–339

Fox, N., Kimmerley, N.L. and Schafer, W.D. (1991) 'Attachment to mother/attachment to father: a meta analysis'. *Child Development*, 62, 210–25

Francis, D. (1995) 'When nimble fingers make a fist'. *New Internationalist*, no. 263

Frank, A. G. (1967) *Capitalism and Underdevelopment in Latin America*, Penguin, Harmondsworth

Fraser, N. (1995) 'Politics, Culture and The Public Sphere: towards a Postmodern Conception', in Nicholson, L. J. and Seidman, S. (eds) *Social Postmodernism: Beyond Identity Politics*, Cambridge University Press, Cambridge

Freedman (2002) *Media Violence and its Effect on Aggression*, University of Toronto Press, Toronto, Canada

Freire, P. (1972) *Pedagogy of the Oppressed*, Sheed & Ward, London

Friedman, M. (1962) *Capitalism and Freedom*. University of Chicago Press, Chicago IL

Friedman, T. (1999) *The Lexus and the Olive Tree*, Harper Collins, London

Fukuyama, F. (1989) *The End of History and the Last Man*, Penguin, Harmondsworth

G

Gandhi, M. (1924) *Young India*, Ganesan, Madras

Garfinkel, H. (1967) *Studies in Ethnomethodology*, Prentice Hall, Englewood Cliffs NJ

Garner, R. (2000) *Environmental Politics*, Macmillan, Basingstoke

Gauntlet, D. (2002) *Media, Gender and Identity*, Routledge, London

Gellner, E. (1974) *Legitimation of Belief*, Cambridge University Press, Cambridge

George, S. (1992) *The Debt Boomerang: How Third World Debt Harms Us All*, Pluto, London

Geraghty, R. (1991) *Women and Soap Opera*, Polity Press, UK

Giddens, A. (1973) *The Class Structure of the Advanced Societies*, Hutchinson, London

Giddens, A. (1976) *New Rules of Sociological Method*, Hutchinson, London

Giddens, A. (1977) *Sociology*, Polity, Cambridge

Giddens, A. (1984) *The Constitution of Society*, Polity, Cambridge

Giddens, A. (1990) *The Consequences of Modernity*, Polity, Cambridge

Giddens, A. (1991) *Modernity and Self-Identity: Self and Society in the Late Modern Age*, Polity Press, Cambridge

Giddens, A. (1996) *In Defence of Sociology: Essays, Interpretations and Rejoinders*, Polity, Cambridge

Giddens, A. (1997) *Sociology* 3rd edition, Polity Press, Cambridge

Giddens, A. (1998) *The Third Way: The Renewal of Social Democracy*, Polity, Cambridge

Giddens, A. (1999) *Runaway World: How Globalisation is Reshaping Our Lives*, Profile Books, London

Giddens, A. (2001) *Sociology* 4th edition, Polity Press, Cambridge

Giddens, A. (2007) *Over to You, Mr Brown: How Labour Can Win Again*, Polity, Cambridge

Gill, O. (1977) *Luke Street*, Macmillan, London

Gilroy, P. (1982) 'The myth of black criminality?' *Socialist Register*, Merlin Press, London

Glass, D. V. and Hall, J. R. (1954) Social mobility in Britain: a study of intergenerational changes in status. In D. V. Glass (ed.), *Social Mobility in Britain*, Routledge and Kegan Paul, London

Glendinning, T. and Bruce, S. (2006) 'New ways of believing or belonging: is religion giving way to spirituality?' *British Journal of Sociology*, Vol. 57, no. 3, 399–414

Glock C. Y. and Bellah, R. N. (1976) *The New Religious Consciousness*, University of California Press, Berkeley

Goffman, E. (1961) *Asylums*, Penguin, Harmondsworth

Goffman, E. (1969) *The Presentation of Self in Everyday Life*, Penguin, Harmondsworth

Goldschmied, E. and Jackson, S. (1994) 'People under three – Young children in day-care'. In L. Dryden, R. Forbes, P. Mukherji and L. Pound (2005) *Early Years*. London: Hodder and Stoughton

Goldthorpe, J. H. (1980) *Social Mobility and Class Structure in Modern Britain*, Clarendon, Oxford

Goldthorpe, J. H. (1983) 'Women and class analysis: in defence of the conventional view'. *Sociology*, no. 14

Goldthorpe, J. H., Lockwood, D., Bechhofer, F. and Platt, J. (1969) *The Affluent Worker in the Class Structure*, Cambridge University Press, Cambridge

Goldthorpe, J. H., Llewellyn, C. and Payne, C. (1987) *Social Mobility and Class Structure in Modern Britain*, 2nd edn, Clarendon, Oxford

Gomm, R. (2004) *Social Research Methodology: A Critical Introduction*, Palgrave Macmillan, Basingstoke

Gould, S. J. (1999) *Rock of Ages*, Ballantine Books, New York

Gouldner, A. W. (1962) 'Anti-Minotaur: the myth of a value-free sociology'. *Social Problems*, Vol. 9, no. 3, 199–213

Gouldner, A. W. (1971) *The Coming Crisis of Western Sociology*, Heinemann, London

Gramsci, A. (1971) *Selections from the Prison Notebooks: Notebooks of Antonio Gramsci*, Lawrence & Wishart, London

Gramsci, A. (1978) *Selections from the Political Writings*, Lawrence & Wishart, London

Grant, W. (2000) *Pressure Groups and British Politics*, Palgrave, Basingstoke

Gregg, P. *et al.* (2007) 'Parents' income and kids' outcomes'. CASE Annual Report, LSE, London

Gregson, N. and Lowe, M. (1994) *Servicing the Middle Classes: Class, Gender and Waged Domestic Labour in Contemporary Britain*, Routledge, London

Grimshaw, D. and Rubery, G. (2001) *The Gender Pay Gap: A Research Review*, Equal Opportunities Commission, Manchester

Gross, L. (1993) *Contested Closets: The Politics and Ethics of Outing*, University of Minnesota Press, Minneapolis USA

Guibernau, M. (1999) *Nations Without States: Political Communities in a Global Age*, Polity

GUMG (1976) *Bad News*, Routledge, London

GUMG (1985) *War and Peace News*, Open University Press, Milton Keynes

Guttsman, W. (1963) *The British Political Elite*, Basic Books, New York

H

Habermas, J. (1986) 'The Theory of Communicative Action', Vol. I, *Reason and the Rationalisation of Society*, Polity, Cambridge

Habermas, J. (1987a) 'The Theory of Communicative Action', Vol. II, *The Critique of Functionalist Reason*, Polity, Cambridge

Habermas, J. (1987b) *The Philosophical Discourse of Modernity*, MIT Press, Cambridge MA

Hadaway, C. K., Hackett, D. G. and Miller J. F. (1984) 'The Most Segregated Institution', *Review of Religious Research 23*, 204–219

Hague, R. and Harrop, M. (2004) *Comparative Government and Politics: An Introduction*, Palgrave, Basingstoke

Hall, S. (1989) *Resistance through Rituals*, Routledge, UK

Hall, S. (1998) *Critical Dialogues in Cultural Studies*, Routledge

Hall, S. *et al.* (1978) *Policing the Crisis*, Macmillan, London

Hallsworth, D. (1994) 'Understanding New Social Movements', *Sociology Review* 4:1, Philip Allen, Oxford

Haralambos, M. and Holborn, M. (2004) *Sociology: Themes and Perspectives*, 6th edn, Harper Collins, London

Harff, B. and Gurr, T. R. (2002) *Ethnic Conflict in World Politics*, Westview, Boulder CO

Harrison, M. (1985) 'TV News: Whose Bias?' in *Heritage Policies Journals*, London Polity Press, London

Hay, C. (2002) *Political Analysis: A Critical Introduction*, Palgrave, Basingstoke

Hayek, F. (1944) *The Road to Serfdom*, University of Chicago Press, Chicago IL

Hayek, F. (1964) *The Constitution of Liberty*, University of Chicago Press, Chicago IL

Hayter, T. (1990) *The Creation of World Poverty: An Alternative View to the Brandt Report*, Pluto, London

Heath, A. *et al.* (1985) *How Britain Votes*, Pergamon Press, Oxford

Heelas, P. and Woodhead, L. (2005) *The Spiritual Revolution*, Blackwell, Oxford

Held, D. (ed.) (1993) *Prospects for Democracy*, Polity, Cambridge

Held, D. (1999) *Global Transformations: Politics, Economics and Culture*, Polity, Cambridge

Herberg, W. (1960) *Protestant, Catholic, Jew*, Anchor Books, New York

Heywood, A. (1992) *Political Ideologies*, Macmillan, London

Himmelweit, H. (1958) *TV and the Child*, Oxford University Press, Oxford

Himmelweit, H., Humphries, P., Jaegar, M. and Katz, M. (1981) *How Voters Decide*, Academic Press, New York

Hindle, T. (2003) 'The third age of globalisation: the world in 2004'. *Economist*, 20 May

Hirst, P. and Thompson, G. (1996) *Globalization in Question: The International Economy and the Possibilities of Governance*, Polity, Cambridge

Hobbs, D. (1988) *Doing the Business: Entrepreneurship, the Working Class and Detectives in the East End of London*, Oxford University Press, Oxford

Hobbs, D. and Lister, S. (2000) 'Receiving Shadows: Violence in the Night Time Economy', *British Journal of Sociology*, Vol XX 682–700

Hobsbawm, E. 'Europe – The Elephant Test'. *Observer*, 10 December 2000

Holm, J. and Bowker, J. (eds) (1994) *Women in Religion*, Pinter, London

Hoselitz, B. F. (1965) *Theories of Economic Growth*, Free Press, New York

Hough, M. and Roberts, J. V. (2004) *Youth Crime and Youth Justice: Public Opinion in England and Wales*, Policy Press, Bristol

Hughes, G. (1991) 'Taking crime seriously? A critical analysis of New Left Realism', *Sociology Review* Vol. 1 No.2

Hunter, F. (1963) *Community Power Structure*, Doubleday, London

Hutton, W. (1996) *The State We're In*, Vintage, London

I

Inglehart, R. (1977) *The Silent Revolution*, Princeton University Press, New Jersey

Inglehart, R. (1990) *Culture Shift in Advanced Industrial Society*, Princeton University Press, New Jersey

Inglehart, R. (1997) *Modernization and Postmodernization: Cultural, Economic, and Political Change in 43 Societies*, Princeton University Press, Princeton NJ

J

Jhally, S. and Lewis, J. (1992) *The Cosby Show Audiences and the Myth of the American Dream*, Westview Press, Colorado

Johal, S. (1998) 'Brimful of Brasia', *Sociology Review* 8(1), Philip Allen, Oxford

Jones, M. and Jones, E. (1999) *Mass Media*, Palgrave Macmillan, UK

Jorgensen, N., Bird, J., Heyhoe, A., Russell, B. and Savvas, M. (1997) *Sociology: An Interactive Approach*, Collins, London

K

Karpf, A. (1988) *Doctoring the Media*, Routledge, London

Katz, E. and Lazarsfeld, P. (1955) *Personal Influence*, Free Press, New York

Kautsky, K. (1953) *Foundations of Christianity*, Russell, New York

Kavanagh, D. and Butler, D. (2005) *The British General Election of 2005*, Palgrave, Basingstoke

Kellner, P. (1983) 'Labour's Future'. *New Society*, 2 June 1983

Kellner, P. (1995) *Media and Culture: Cultural Studies, Identity and Politics between the Modern and Postmodern*, Routledge, London

Kellner, P. and Wilby, P. (1980) 'The 1:2:4 rule of class in Britain'. *Sunday Times*, 13 January

Klein, N. (2000) *No Logo*, Harper Collins, London

Knott, K. (1994) 'Women and religion in post-war Britain'. In G. Parsons (ed.) *The Growth of Religious Diversity: Britain from 1945*, Vol. II, Issues, Routledge, London

Koluchova, J. (1991) 'Severely deprived twins after 22 years of observation'. *Studia Pschologica*, 33, 23–8

Korem, D. (1994) *Suburban Gangs: The Affluent Rebels*, International Focus Press, Richardson

Kuhn, T. (1970) *The Structure of Scientific Revolutions*, University of Chicago Press, Chicago IL

Kuhn, T. (1972) 'Scientific Paradigms' in Barnes, B. (ed) *Sociology of Science*, Penguin, Harmondsworth

L

Laidler, K. J. and Hunt, G. (2001) 'Accomplishing femininity among the girls in the gang,' *British Journal of Criminology* Vol. 41(4), pp. 656–678

Lamb, M.E. (1983) 'Fathers: forgotten contributors to child development'. *Human Development*, 18, 245–66

Lasch, R. (1979) *The Culture of Narcism*, Norton, New York

Lazarsfeld, P. (1968) *The People's Choice*, Columbia University Press, New York

Lee, D. and Newby, H. (1994) *The Problem of Sociology*, Routledge, London

Leonard, E. (1982) *Women, Crime and Society*, Longman, New York

Levitt, M. A. (1993) *The influence of a church primary school on children's religious belief and practices: a Cornish study*, University of Exeter

Lockwood, D. (1958) *The Black Coated Worker*, Allen & Unwin, London

Lovenduski, J. (2005) *Whose secretary are you, minister?* Guardian, 7 December 2004

Lowe, P. and Goyder, J. (1983) *Environmental Groups in Politics*, Allen & Unwin, London

Luckmann, T. (1967) *The Invisible Religion*, Macmillan, New York

Lukes, S. (1974) *Power: A Radical View*, Macmillan, London

Lyon, D. (2000) *Jesus in Disneyland: Religion in Postmodern Times*, Polity, Cambridge

Lyotard, J.-F. (1984) *The Postmodern Condition: A Report on Knowledge*, 2nd edn, Manchester University Press, Manchester; first published 1979

Lyotard, J.-F. (1992) 'Abandoning the Metanarratives of Modernity', in Hall, S., McGrew, T. and Held, D. (eds) *Modernity and its Futures*, Polity, Cambridge

M

Maduro, O. (1982) *Religion and Social Conflicts*, Orbis Books, New York

Mair, P., van Biezen, I. (2001) 'Party membership in Europe 1980–2000' in *Party Politics* (7)

Malinowski, B. (1915-1918) *Ethnography of Malinowski: Trobriand Islands*, Kegan Paul, London

Malthus, T. R. (1798) *An Essay on the Principle of Population*, J. Johnson, London

Mann, M. (1993) *The Sources of Social Power*, Vol. 2, Cambridge University Press, Cambridge

Marcuse, H. (1964) *One-Dimensional Man*, Routledge & Kegan Paul, London

Marshall, G. and Swift, A. (1996) 'Merit and mobility: a reply to Peter Saunders'. *Sociology*, Vol. 30, no. 2, 375–386

Marshall, G., Newby, H. *et al.* (1988) *Social Class in Modern Britain*, Hutchinson, London

Martin, D. (1978) *A General Theory of Secularisation*, Blackwell, Oxford

Marx, K. (1844) *The Economic and Philosophical Manuscripts*, International Publishers, New York; 1964 edition

Marx, K. (1867) *Das Kapital*, Lawrence & Wishart, London; 1970 edition

Marx, K. (1957) *On Religion*, Progress Publishers, Moscow

Marx, K. and Engels, F. (1848) *The Communist Manifesto*, Penguin, Harmondsworth; 1967 edition

Marx, K. and Engels, F. (1968) *Selected Works*, Lawrence & Wishart, London

Matza, D. (1964) *Delinquency and Drift*, John Wiley & Sons, New York

Mazzarella, S. and Pecora, N. (2001) 'Grown Up Girls: Popular Culture and the Construction of Identity', *Adolescence* Vol 40, Peter Lang, New York

McChesney, R. (2005) *Rich Media Poor Democracy*, New York Press, New York

McGrew, A. (1992) 'A global society?' In S. Hall, *et al.* (eds), *Modernity and its Futures*, Polity, Cambridge

McKenzie, R. T. (1963) *British Political Parties*, Heinemann, London

McKeown, T. (1988) *Origins of Human Disease*, Basil Blackwell, Oxford

McLuhan, H. M. (1962) *Gutenberg Galaxy: The Making of Typographic Man*, Routledge & Kegan Paul, London

McQuail, D. (1968) *Television in Politics: Its Uses and Influences*, Faber, London

Mead, G. H. (1934) *Mind, Self and Society*, University of Chicago Press, Chicago IL

Melhuish, E.C. (1990) 'Research on day care for young children in the UK'. In E.C. Melhuish, and P. Moss (eds), *Day care for young children: International perspectives*. London, Routledge

Melhuish, E.C. (1991) 'International perspectives on day care for young children'. *Journal of reproductive and infant psychology*, 9, 181–9

Melton, J. G. (1993) 'Another Look at New Religions', *The Annals of the American Academy of Politics and Social Science*, Vol 527, May 1993

Melucci, A. (1989) *Nomads of the Present*, Hutchinson Radius, London

Merton, R. (1938) 'Social structure and anomie', *American Sociology Review* Vol.3 pp. 672–682

Merton, R. K. (1949) *Social Theory and Social Structure*, New York Free Press, New York

Merton, R. K. (1968) *Social Theory and Social Structure*, Free Press, Glencoe NJ

Messner, S. F. and Rosenfeld, R. (1994) *Crime and the American Dream*, Belmont, Wadsworth

Michels, R. (1911) *Political Parties*, Dover, New York

Middleton, S. *et al.* (2005) 'Evaluation of education maintenance allowance pilots: young people aged 16 to 19 years. Final report of the quantitative evaluation'. Brief RB678, Department for Education and Science

Mies, M. and von Werlhof, C. (1988) *Women: The Last Colony*, Zed, London

Milbrath, L. and Goel, M. (1977) *Political Participation: How and Why Do People Get Involved in Politics?* Rand McNally, Boston MA

Miles, R. (1989) *Racism*, Routledge, London

Miliband, R. (1969) *The State in Capitalist Society*, Weidenfeld & Nicolson, London

Miliband, R. (1992) *Capitalist Democracy in Britain*, Oxford University Press, Oxford

Miller, W. B. (1962) 'Lower class culture as a generating milieu of gang delinquency', in Wolfgang, M. E. *et al.* (eds) *The Sociology of Crime and Delinquency*, John Wiley and Son, New York

Mills, C. W. (1956) *The Power Elite*, Oxford University Press, Oxford

Mills, C. W. (1970) *The Sociological Imagination*, Penguin, Harmondsworth

Modood, T., Beishon, S. and Virdee, S. (1994) *Changing Ethnic Identities*, PSI, London

Mooney, J. (1998) 'Moral panics and the new Right: Single mothers and feckless fathers – is this really the key to the crime problem?' in Walton, P. & Young, J. (eds) *The New Criminology Revisited*, Macmillan, Basingstoke

Moore, S., Aiken, D. and Chapman, S. (2006) *Sociology for A2*, Collins, London

Morley, D. (1980) *The Nationwide Audience*, British Film Institute, London

Morris, T. (1957) *The Criminal Area*, Routledge and Kegan Paul, London

Morrison, A. (1999) *Beyond the Third World Web*, University of Oslo, Digital Learning Group

Morrison, P. (1999) *Defining Violence*, University of Luton Press, Luton

Mosca, G. (1939) *The Ruling Class*, McGraw-Hill, New York

Murdock, R. G. (2007) *Media in the Age of Marketization*, Hampton Press UK

Murray, C. (1984) *Losing Ground*, Basic Books, New York

Murray, C. (1989) 'Underclass'. *Sunday Times Magazine*, 26 November

N

Nartey, C. (2006) Workshop wants WTO reforms to favour dev. countries. From http://www.tradeobservatory.org/headlines.cfm?refID=80835

Niebuhr, H. R. (1929) *The Social Sources of Denominationalism*, The World Publishing Company, New York

Nelken, D. (2002) 'White-collar crime' in Maguire, M. *et al.* (eds) *The Oxford Handbook of Criminology, 3rd edition*, Oxford University Press, Oxford

Neuman, W. R. (2003) *The Future of the Mass Audience*, University of Cambridge Press, New York

Nightingale, C. (1993) *On the Edge*, Basic Books, New York

Notestein, F. (1945) 'Population – the long view'. In T. Schultz (ed.), *Food for the World*, University of Chicago Press, Chicago IL

Nugent, N. (2006) *The Government and Politics of the European Union*, Palgrave, Basingstoke

O

Oakley, A. (1981) 'Interviewing women: a contradiction in terms'. In H. Roberts (ed.), *Doing Feminist Research*, Routledge, London

Ohmae, K. (1990) *The Borderless World*, Harper Collins, London

Ohmae, K. (2005) *Next Global Stage: The Challenges and Opportunities in Our Borderless World*, Wharton, Philadelphia PA

Olson, M. (1968) *The Logic of Collective Action: Public Goods and the Theory of Groups*, Schocken Books, New York

Omran, A. (1971) 'The epidemiologic transition: a theory of the epidemiology of population change'. *Milbank Quarterly*, Vol. 49, 509–538

Oppenheim, C. and Harker, L. (1996) *Poverty: The Facts*, 3rd edn, CPAG, London

Orne, M.T. and Holland, C.C. (1968) 'On the ecological validity of laboratory deceptions'. *International Journal of Psychology*, 6, 282–93

O'Sullivan, I. and Jewkes, Y. (1997) *The Media Studies Reader*, Hodder Education, London

P

Pakulski, J. and Waters, M. (1996) *The Death of Class*, Sage, London

Palmer, S. (1992) *Beyond the Cold War*, Cambridge University Press, Cambridge

Parekh, B. *et al.* (2000) *Report of the Commission on the Future of Multi-Ethnic Britain*, Profile Books, London

Pareto, V. (1963) *A Treatise on General Sociology*, Dover, New York

Parry, G. *et al.* (1992) *Political Participation and Democracy in Britain*, Cambridge University Press, Cambridge

Parsons, T. (1951) *The Social System*, Routledge, London

Parsons, T. (1955) 'The American family: its relations to personality and social structure'. In T. Parsons and R. F. Bales (eds), *Family, Socialisation and Interaction Process*, University of Chicago Press

Parsons, T. (1964) *Essays in Sociological Theory*, Free Press, New York

Parsons, T. (1965) 'Religious perspectives in sociology and social psychology', in Lessa, W. A. and Vogt. G. Z. *Reader in Comparative Religon*, Harper and Row, New York

Parsons, T. (1967) *Sociological Theory and Modern Society*, Collier-Macmillan, London

Parsons, T. (1979) *Social System*, Routledge & Kegan Paul, London

Patrick, J. (1973) *A Glasgow Gang Observed*, Eyre-Methuen, London

Peele, G. (2004) *Governing the UK*, Blackwell, Oxford

Philips, C. and Bowling, B. (2002) 'Racism, Ethnicity and Criminal Justice' in Maguire, M. *et al.* (eds) *The Oxford Handbook of Criminology, 3rd edition*, Oxford University Press, Oxford

Philo, G. and Miller, D. (2002) 'Circuits of communication and power: recent developments in media sociology'. In M. Holborn (ed.), *Developments in Sociology 18*, Causeway, Ormskirk

Pilkington, A. (1999) 'Racial disadvantage and ethnic diversity'. In M. Haralambos (ed.)

Polsby, N. (1963) *Community Power and Political Theory*, Yale University Press, New Haven CT

Popper, K. R. (1945) *The Open Society and Its Enemies*, Routledge, London

Popper, K. R. (1959) *The Logic of Scientific Discovery*, Routledge, London

Poulantzas, N. (1975) *Classes in Contemporary Capitalism*, New Left Books, London

Princen, T. and Finger, M. (1994) *Environmental NGOs in World Politics: Linking the Local to the Global*, Routledge, London and New York

Pulzer, P. (1967) *Political Representation and Elections in Britain*, Allen & Unwin, London

Punnett, R. (1971) *British Government and Politics*, Gower, London

Putnam, R. (2000) *Bowling Alone: The Collapse and Revival of American Community*, Simon & Schuster, New York

R

Radway, J. (1984) *Reading the Romance*, University of North Carolina Press

Ramji, H. (2007) 'Dynamics of religion and gender amongst young British Muslims'. *Sociology*, Vol. 41, no. 6, 1171–1189

Ray, S. and Sharp, E. (2006) *Ageism: A Benchmark for Public Attitudes in Britain*, Age Concern

Reinharz, S. (1992) *Feminist Methods in Social Research*, Oxford University Press, Oxford

Rex, J. and Tomlinson, S. (1979) *Colonial Immigrants in a British City*, Routledge & Kegan Paul, London

Ritzer, G. (2004) *The McDonaldization of Society*, Sage, Thousand Oaks CA

Roberts, K. (2001) *Class in Modern Britain*, Palgrave, Basingstoke

Rogers, R. and Hackenberg, R. (1987) 'Extending epidemiologic transition theory: a new stage'. *Social Biology*, Vol. 34, 234–243

Roof, W. C. and McKinney, W. (1987) *American Mainline Religion*, Rutgers University Press, New Brunswick

Rosenhan, D. L. (1973) 'On being sane in insane places', *Science* Vol 179 pp. 250–258

Ross, G., Kagan, J., Zelazo, P., and Kotelchuk, M. (1975) 'Separation protest in infants at home and laboratory'. *Developmental Psychology*, 11, 256–7

Rostow, W. W. (1960) *The Stages of Economic Growth: A Non-Communist Manifesto*, Cambridge University Press, Cambridge

Ruickbie, L. (2004) *Witchcraft Out of the Shadows*, Hale, London

Runciman, W. G. (1990) 'How many classes are there in contemporary British society?' *Sociology*, Vol. 24, 378–396

Rutter, M., Colvert, E., Kreppner., J., Beckett, C., Castle, J., Groothues, C. Hawkins., A., O'Connor, T., Stevens, S. and Sonuga-Barke, E. (2007) 'Early adolescent outcomes for institutionally-deprived and non-deprived adoptees: I: Disinhibited attachment'. *Journal of Child Psychology and Psychiatry*, 48:1 17–30

S

Saggar, S. (2000) *Race and Electoral Politics in Britain*, UCL Press, London

Sampson, A. (2004) *Who Runs This Place? The Anatomy of Britain in the 21st Century*, John Murray, London

Sanders, D. (1995) 'It's the economy, stupid: the economy and support for the Conservative Party, 1979–1994'. *Talking Politics*, vol. 7, no. 3

Santos, J. (2001) 'Globalization and Tradition: Paradoxes of Phillipine Television and Culture', *Media Development* 3, 43–48

Sarlvik, B. and Crewe, I. (1983) *Decade of Dealignment*, Cambridge University Press, Cambridge

Saunders, P. (1990a) *Social Class and Stratification*, Routledge, London

Saunders, P. (1990b) *A Nation of Home Owners*, Unwin Hyman, London

Saunders, P. (1996) *Unequal but Fair? A Study of Class Barriers in Britain*, IEA, London

Savage, M. (2005) 'Working-class identities in the 1960s: revisiting the affluent worker study'. *Sociology*, Vol. 39, 929–946

Savage, M. and Egerton, M. (1997) 'Social mobility, individual ability and the inheritance of class inequality'. *Sociology*, Vol. 31, no. 4

Savage, M., Barlowe, J. *et al.* (1992) *Property, Bureaucracy and Culture: Middle Class Formation in Contemporary Britain*, Routledge, London

Sayar, A. (1984) *Method in Social Science*, Hutchinson, London

Sayar, A. (2000) *Realism and Social Science*, Sage, London

Schaffer, R. (1996) *Social Development*, Oxford: Blackwell

Schindler, P.J., Moely, B.E. and Frank, A.L. (1987) 'Time in day-care and social participation of young children'. *Developmental Psychology*, 23, 255–61

Schleissenger, P. (1978) *Putting Reality Together*, Constable, London

Schultz, T. W. (1971) *Investment in Human Capital: The Role of Education and of Research*, Free Press, New York

Schumacher, E. F. (1973) *Small Is Beautiful: A Study of Economics as if People Mattered*, Blond and Briggs, London

Scott, J. (1990) *A Matter of Record: Documentary Sources in Social Research*, Polity, Cambridge

Scott, J. (1991) *Who Rules Britain?* Polity, Cambridge

Selfe, P. and Starbuck, M. (1998) *Religion*, Hodder & Stoughton, London

Sen, A. K. (1992) *Inequality Re-examined*, Oxford University Press, Oxford

Shakespeare, T. (1994) 'Cultural representations of disabled people: dustbins for disavowal'. *Disability and Society*, Vol. 3, no. 9, 283–301

Shapiro, A. L. (1999) *The Control Revolution: Public Affairs*, the Century Foundation, USA

Shaw, C. R. and McKay, H. D. (1942) *Juvenile Delinquency and Urban Areas*, University of Chicago Press, Chicago

Skeggs, B. (1997) *Formations of Class and Gender*, Sage, London

Sklair, L. (1991) *Sociology of the Global System*, Harvester Wheatsheaf, Brighton

Sklair, L. (1995) *Sociology of the Global System*, Prentice Hall, Hemel Hempstead

Sklair, L. (2003) 'Globalisation, capitalism and power'. In M. Holborn (ed.), *Developments in Sociology 19*, Causeway, Ormskirk

Slapper, G. and Tombs, S. (1999) *Corporate Crime*, Addison Wesley Longman, London

Sloane, P. J. (1994) 'The gender wage differential and discrimination in six SCELI labour markets'. In A. M. Scott (ed.), *Segregation and Social Change*, Oxford University Press, Oxford

Smith, A. (1776) *An Inquiry into the Nature and Causes of the Wealth of Nations*, Whitestone, Dublin

Solomos, J. *et al.* (1982) 'The organic crisis of British capitalism and race: the experience of the seventies', in *Centre for Contemporary Cultural Studies*, 9–39, University of Birmingham

Soros, G. (1998) *The Crisis of Global Capitalism: Open Society Endangered*, Little, Brown & Co., London

Soros, G. (2000) *Open Society: Reforming Global Capitalism*, Little, Brown & Co., London

Stanko, E. A. (1988) 'Keeping women in and out of line: sexual harassment and occupational segregation'. In S. Walby (ed.), *Gender Segregation and Work*, Open University Press, Milton Keynes

Stanworth, P. and Giddens, A. (1974) *Elites and Power in British Society*, Cambridge University Press, Cambridge

Stanworth, M. (1984) 'Women and class analysis: a reply to John Goldthorpe'. *Sociology*, Vol. 18, no. 2

Stark, W. S. and Bainbridge, W. A. (1985) *The Future of Religion*, University of California Press, Berkeley CA

Steele, H. (2001) 'Inter-generational patterns of attachment: recent findings from research'. In L. Dryden, R. Forbes, P. Mukherji and L. Pound (eds) (2005) *Early Years*, Hodder and Stoughton, London

Stewart, J. (1958) *British Pressure Groups*, Oxford University Press, Oxford

Strinati, D. (1993) *An Introduction to Theories of Popular Culture*, Routledge, London

Strinati, D. (1995) *Postmodernism and Popular Culture*, Routledge, New York

Sutherland, E. H. (1960) *White-collar Crime*, Holt, Rinehart & Winston, New York

Sutherland, E. H. and Cressey, D. R. (1974) *Principles of Criminology*, J. B. Lippincott, Philadelphia

T

Tarrow, S. (1998) *Power in Movement: Collective Social Movements and Contentious Politics*, Cambridge University Press, Cambridge

Taylor, I. (1997) 'The political economy of crime' in Maguire, M. *et al* (eds) *The Oxford Handbook of Criminology* 2nd edition, Oxford University Press, Oxford

Taylor, I. *et al.* (1973) *The New Criminology*, Routlege & Kegan Paul, London

Taylor, P., Richardson, J., Yeo, A., Marsh, I., Trobe, K. and Pilkington, A. (1995) *Sociology in Focus*, Causeway, Ormskirk

Taylor, S. (1982) *Durkheim and the Study of Suicide*, Macmillan, London

Taylor, S. (1990) 'Suicide, Durkheim and sociology'. In D. Lester (ed.) *Current Concepts of Suicide*, Charles, Philadelphia PA

Thomas, W. I. (1928) *The Child in America: Behavior Problems and Programs*, Knopf, New York

Thompson, W. (1929) 'Population'. *American Sociological Review*, Vol. 34, no. 6, 959–975

Thrasher, F. M. (1927) *The Gang: A Study of 1313 Gangs in Chicago*, University of Chicago Press, Chicago

Tiano, S. (1994) *Patriarchy on the Line: Labor, Gender, and Ideology in the Mexican Maquila Industry*, Temple University Press, Philadelphia PA

Tomlinson, J. (1999) *Globalisation and Culture*, Polity Press, Cambridge

Troeltsch, E. (1931) *The Social Teachings of the Christian Churches*, University of Chicago Press, Chicago

Tumin, M. M. (1953) 'Some principles of stratification: a conceptual analysis', *American Sociological Review* vol. 18 pp. 387–394

Tumin, M. M. (1967) 'Some principles of stratification'. In R. Bendix and S. M. Lipset (eds), *Class, Status and Power*, Routledge and Kegan Paul, London

Tunstall, J. (1977) *The Media Are American*, Constable, London

Turner, B. (1974) *Weber and Islam*, Routledge and Kegan Paul, London

Turner, B. (1991) *Religion and Social Theory*, 2nd edn, Sage, London

Tylor, E. B. (1871) *Religion in Primitive Cultures*, Peter Smith, Gloucester; 1970 edition

U

Urry, J. (2000a) 'Mobile sociology' in *British Journal of Sociology*, Vol. 51, no. 1, 185–203

Urry, J. (2000b) *Sociology Beyond Societies: Mobilities for the Twenty-first Century*, Routledge, London

V

van Dijk, A. (1991) *Racism and The Press*, Routledge, London

van Zomen, L. (1994) 'The Media in Question', *Sociology*, Vol. 33, no. 2, 451–452, Sage Publications

Vittachi, A. (1992) 'Consuming passions'. *New Internationalist*, September

W

Waddington, P. A. J. *et al.* (2004) 'In proportion – race, and police stop and search', *British Journal of Criminology* 44(6)

Walby, S. (1986) *Patriarchy at Work*, Polity, Cambridge

Walby, S. (1990) *Theorizing Patriarchy*, Blackwell, Oxford

Wallis, R. (1984) *The Elementary Forms of New Religious Life*, Routledge, London

Waters, M. (2000) *Globalization*, Routledge, London

Watson, H. (1994) 'Women and the veil: personal responses to global process', in Ahmen, A. and Donnan, H. (eds) *Islam, Globalization and Modernity*, Routledge, London

Weber, M. (1922) *The Sociology of Religion*, Methuen, London

Weber, M. (1922) *The Theory of Economic and Social Organization*, University of California Press, Berkeley CA; 1957 edition

Weber, M. (1930) *The Protestant Ethic and the Spirit of Capitalism*, Unwin, London (first published 1905)

Weber, M. (1968) *Economy and Society: An Outline of Interpretative Sociology*, Bedminster Press, New York

Wedell, E. (1968) *Broadcasting and Public Policy*, Joseph Books, London

Wellings, K., Field, J., Johnson, A. and Wadsworth, J. (1994) *Sexual Behaviour in Britain: The National Survey of Sexual Attitudes and Lifestyles*, Penguin, Harmondsworth

Westergaard, J. (1995) *Who Gets What? The Hardening of Class Inequality in the Late Twentieth Century*, Polity, Cambridge

Westergaard, J. and Resler, H. (1976) *Class in a Capitalist Society*, Penguin, Harmondsworth

Whale, J. (1977) *The Politics of the Media*, Fontana, London

Williams, H. (2006) *Britain's Power Elites: A Rebirth of the Ruling Class*, Constable & Robinson, London

Williams, R. (1980) *Problems in Materialism and Culture*, Verso, London

Williamson, J. (1990) *Latin American Adjustment: How Much Has Happened*? Institute for International Economics, Washington DC

Willis, P. (1977) *Learning to Labour*, Saxon House, Farnborough

Wilson, B. R. (1966) *Religion in a Secular Society*, C. A. Watts, London

Wilson, B. R. (1982) *Religion in Sociological Perspective*, Oxford University Press, Oxford

Wilson, J. Q. and Kelling, G. (1982) 'Broken windows', *Atlantic Monthly* (March 1982), pp. 29–38

Winship, J. (1987) *Inside Womens' Magazines*, Pandora Press, London

Witz, A. (1993) Women at work'. In D. Richardson and V. Robinson (eds), *Introducing Women's Studies*, Macmillan, London

Wollstonecraft, M. (1792) *A Vindication of the Rights of Women*, Penguin, Harmondsworth

Woodhead, L. (2005) *Christianity: A Very Short Introduction*, Oxford University Press, Oxford

Worrall, J. (2004) 'Why science discredits religion'. In M. Peterson and R. Vanarragon (eds), *Contemporary Debates in the Philosophy of Religion*, Blackwell, Oxford

Worsley, P. (1970) *Introducing Sociology*, Penguin Books Ltd, Harmondsworth

Wright, E. O. (1978) *Class, Crisis and State*, New Left Books, London

Wrong, D. (1967) 'The oversocialised concept of man in modern sociology'. In L. Cosser and B. Rosenberg (eds), *Sociological Theory: A Book of Readings*, Collier-Macmillan, London

Y

Young, J. (1971) 'The role of the police as amplifiers of deviancy, negotiators of reality and translators of fantasy', in Cohen, S. (ed) *Images of Deviance*, Penguin, Harmondsworth

Young, J. and Lea, J. (1984) *What Is To Be Done About Law and Order*? Penguin, Harmondsworth

Yunus, M. (1983) *Group-Based Savings and Credit for the Rural Poor*, Grameen Bank, Dhaka

Z

Zimmerman, P., Becker-Stoll, F., Grossman, K., Scheurer-Englisch, H. and Wartner, U. (2000) 'Longitudinal attachment development from infancy through adolescence'. *Psychologie in Erziehung und Unterricht*, 47 (2), 99–117

Index